Play, Games & Sports

in CULTURAL CONTEXTS

Play, Games and Sports

in CULTURAL CONTEXTS

Edited by

Janet C. Harris, Ph.D.

Assistant Professor, School of Health,
Physical Education, Recreation and
Dance, University of North Carolina at
Greensboro, Greensboro, North Carolina

Roberta J. Park, Ph.D.

Professor, Department of Physical
Education, University of California,
Berkeley, California

Published by
Human Kinetics Books
Champaign, Illinois

Publications Director
Richard D. Howell

Production Director
Margery Brandfon

Proofreader
Dana Finney

Typesetter
Sandra Meier

Text Layout
Lezli Harris

Cover Design and Layout
Laurence W. Harris

Library of Congress Catalog Number: 82-83148

ISBN: 0-931250-36-6
(pbk) 0-87322-266-0

9 8 7 6 5 4 3 2

Human Kinetics Books
A Division of Human Kinetics Publishers, Inc.
Box 5076, Champaign, IL 61825-5076
1-800-DIAL-HKP
1-800-334-3665 (in Illinois)

Contents

PART 2   SPORTS AND RITUALS   175

PART 3   PLAY AND INTERPRETATIONS   311

PART 4   SOCIALIZATION AND ENCULTURATION
THROUGH PLAY, GAMES, AND SPORTS   385

Preface

This book has grown out of our efforts to understand phenomena with which we have dealt in our professional lives on a more or less daily basis, as well as our attempts to answer questions which students and colleagues have asked about play, games, and sports. In particular, we became increasingly concerned with two broad questions: What do play, games, and sports *mean* to the people who engage in such activities? How might beginning students as well as mature scholars come to know something more about the meanings and functions of these cultural phenomena?

The purpose of this volume, then, is to provide undergraduate and graduate students with ready access to some of the better research reports and theoretical discussions which have been guided by such questions. Many of the papers that are included have been highly influential on the work of mature scholars, yet they are not beyond the comprehension of the intelligent undergraduate. The study of play, games, and sports from an anthropological perspective has recently attracted the attention of a growing number of investigators and it is beginning to coalesce into a recognizable scholarly quest. We believe that by reflecting upon the selections included here, the thoughtful reader may encounter a portion of the cutting edge of research and thinking on the cultural phenomena of play, games, and sports. To aid readers who may be unfamiliar with some of the basic concepts and issues that underlie the papers which comprise the volume, a lengthy introductory chapter has been developed.

As physical educators we have long been familiar with the cross-disciplinary approach to scholarly research. Indeed, our academic training exposed us to the merits of looking at questions from a variety of perspectives. Starting from two different subdisciplinary approaches (social psychology and history) to our field, we have independently, at different times in our careers, looked to cultural anthropology for insights about the possible meanings of play, games, and sports in human culture—both present and past. We were encouraged when we discovered that a concern with meaning had become one of the major (some would say *the* major) concerns of anthropology in the 1960s and 1970s. In the aptly titled *Meaning in Anthropology*, Basso and Selby (1976) state:

> So fundamental, in fact, has the concern with meaning become that it now underlies whole conceptions of culture, conceptions which are explicitly grounded in the premise that . . . the full array of signs and concepts men use to communicate to each other and interpret themselves and the world around them . . . should be the central object of description and analysis. (p. 2)

We were even more encouraged when we discovered that several students of culture who deal with symbols, interpretations, and meanings have used examples from games and sports to explicate their analyses (e.g., Geertz, 1972; Turner, 1974, both of which are in this volume). This strengthened our conviction that questions about the kinds of meanings which people *themselves* make out of play, games, and sports have been largely neglected by physical educators, who historically seem to have been more interested in the theories and methodologies of social psychology and sociology than of anthropology. Until quite recently, researchers in the sociocultural area of our field have been far more inclined to approach the "subjects" of their investigations with a set of preformed theories rather than first trying to grasp the meanings of phenomena from the point of view of the individuals they are attempting to understand.

Although our own preference favors the use of anthropological perspectives to study play, games, and sports in contemporary and historical cultures, this does not mean that we view the study of these phenomena from other disciplinary perspectives to be without value—quite the contrary. A scholarly understanding of such complex human cultural phenomena necessitates a multidisciplinary endeavor which must include numerous theoretical and methodological approaches from the social sciences, the behavioral sciences, and the humanities. Indeed, papers written from the perspective of more than one social science appear in this book.

A stroke of good fortune placed us both at the University of California in 1978-79, and it was then that work on this present volume began. Since then we have read exhaustively, argued frequently (with each other and with others who would listen), and found it necessary to re-evaluate many of our previous beliefs. We were extremely fortunate that members of the graduate faculty of the departments of anthropology, sociology, history, and English at the University of California permitted us to sit in on their seminars and gave us the benefits of their expertise. To them we owe a deep intellectual debt. We are also grateful for the very dedicated technical assistance of Baiba Vija Strads. On a broader front, it was also our good fortune that in the early 1970s a group of forward-looking individuals saw the need "to draw together, from different disciplines, scholars capable of promoting the type of research and interaction necessary to better understand the nature, function and place of that phenomenon we label 'play,' within the varied societies of our Global Village" (Salter, 1976, p. v). The Association for the Anthropological Study of Play held its first annual meeting in 1975, and its publications, meetings, and membership have provided a continuing source of information, challenge, and stimulation.

References

BASSO, K.H., & Selby, H.A. (Eds.). *Meaning in anthropology*. Albuquerque: University of New Mexico Press, 1976.

GEERTZ, C. Deep play: Notes on the Balinese cockfight. *Daedalus*, 1972, **101**, 1-37.

SALTER, M. Winds of change. In D.F. Lancy & B.A. Tindall (Eds.), *The anthropological study of play: Problems and prospects*. (Proceedings of the First Annual Meeting of the Association for the Anthropological Study of Play.) Cornwall, NY: Leisure Press, 1976.

TURNER, V. Liminal to liminoid, in play, flow, and ritual: An essay in comparative symbology. In E. Norbeck (Ed.), *Rice University studies: The Anthropological Study of Human Play*, 1974, **60**(3), 53-92.

Janet Harris
Roberta Park

Introduction to the Sociocultural Study of Play, Games, and Sports

This book is about games, sports, and to a lesser extent, play. It is also about culture, interpretations, and meanings. As the reader will quickly discover, the papers that are included are diverse in focus—geographically, historically, and with regard to the topics with which they deal. Some papers are concerned with agrarian, relatively small, non-Western societies; others are concerned with industrialized, large, Western societies. Some papers discuss phenomena that are probably well known and form part of the cultural "context" in which the reader operates on a more or less daily basis; others discuss phenomena that may be entirely new to the reader. The diversity is intentional and is motivated, in part, by a belief which is widely held among anthropologists: By looking at others we not only may learn something of value about them, but we may also learn more about ourselves. Because individuals are deeply enmeshed in their own culture, it is often difficult for them to stand back and analyze it. A certain amount of detachment or "distancing" may be necessary. Familiarity with another culture, then, may help one to be more objective when dealing with one's own culture. Although the papers contained in this volume deal with a broad range of diverse cultures, each raises one or more theoretical issues that may be useful in extending our understanding of the meanings of games, play, and sports in human societies in general.

The volume is composed of a lengthy introductory chapter and five sections of papers. The introduction sets forth definitions of play, games, and sports and provides an overview of the evolution of scholarly interest in these events as sociocultural phenomena. It also introduces a number of basic sociocultural concepts—both theoretical and methodological—utilized by authors of the various papers which comprise the volume, and it establishes the conceptual framework for the five sections into which the papers are organized. The papers in Section 1 focus upon a topic of major importance in sociocultural research—interpretation and meanings—by concentrating upon games and sports as public symbols. This discussion is extended in Section 2 by papers which concentrate upon the idea that sports may at times be part of ritualistic statements about the social order. Section 3 includes recent and influential theoretical studies that are concerned with meanings which play may have for people who play. Because sports and games are sometimes considered to be play, or at least to have playful periods within them, these papers may be useful for helping to expand our scholarly understanding of the play characteristics of these activities. In Section 4, the selections consider ways in which play, games, and sports may help people to learn about their own societies, a process generally referred to as socialization or enculturation. Section 5 includes papers concerned with play, games, and sports of particular cultures which have been adopted and adapted by members of another culture—a process termed acculturation. Other papers in this section deal with play, games, and sports in culturally pluralistic situations where members of different ethnic groups maintain some distinctiveness from one another. A brief epilogue closes the work.

Play, Games, and Sports: Definitions

Games and sports consist of patterns of meaningful, socially defined action, and as such they must be considered to be sociocultural phenomena. Most play is at least partially socially defined, although this phenomenon also seems to have a strong psychobiological component. Because scholars are far from complete in their agreement about the nature of sports, games, and play, some of the major distinctions which have been made among these three need to be noted.

Games are usually considered to be competitive activities that are constituted by rules which define goals and which limit the means that may be used to reach those goals (Suits, 1978). They have often been classified according to the primary means used to reach the goals: skill, strategy, and chance (Roberts, Arth, & Bush, 1959), or competition, chance, mimicry, and vertigo (Caillois, 1958/1961). The category of games is often contrasted with that of *sports*. There has been a tendency to view games as having less codified, more changeable rules, whereas sports are seen as a special type of game involving highly codified rules, large-scale use of the body, use of skills acquired through specialized training, and public display before an audience. A number of scholars (e.g., Loy, 1968; Osterhoudt, 1977; Schmitz, 1972; Weiss, 1969) identify physical prowess, disciplined training, and highly developed specialized skills as major attributes distinguishing sports from games. At the same time, however, activities such as hunting, auto racing, and pleasure boating are also frequently identified as sports, and these activities seem to lack one or more of the characteristics which scholars have tended to associate with sports.

Play is perhaps the broadest of the three terms and seems to have the most diverse meanings. At times the category of play is used to refer to a wide variety of activities engaged in voluntarily, and as such, it may include (but by no means be limited to) games, sports, imitative activities, creative activities, exploration, joking, and make-believe (cf. Bruner, Jolly, & Sylva, 1976; Herron & Sutton-Smith, 1971; Millar, 1968/1974; Stewart, 1979). At other times, play is defined by referring primarily to underlying psychobiological states of the persons involved, with particular attention to stimulus-seeking and arousal (Ellis, 1973). Finally, play sometimes is used to refer to a state of mind, attitude, disposition, or conceptual framework rather than to a structured event or to more overtly observable psychobiological states. This state of mind or interpretive conceptual framework may involve a negation of some of the rules or understandings in ongoing daily life (Bateson, 1955 [chapter 14 in this volume]; Csikszentmihalyi, 1981), a relative lack of commitment to the attainment of extrinsic goals (Harris, 1980), intense enjoyment (Csikszentmihalyi, 1975), and a sense of unstructured total interaction with one's fellow players (Turner, 1972; chapter 15 in this volume). If play is considered to be contingent upon the occurrence of an attitude, then a person could probably play almost anyplace, and an individual might vascillate in and out of a state of playfulness during the course of almost any activity (Harris, 1980). For example, a football player might drift into a state of play for a few moments during a football game and then return to an intense commitment to the activity at hand—winning the game. The same vascillations probably occur among factory workers, students, faculty members, and other individuals from time to time. Amplification of this last definition of play may be found in Section 3.

Evolution of the Sociocultural Study of Play, Games, and Sports

Play and games were topics of interest to scholars in several fields in the late 1800s. The nature of the interest, however, took two different orientations. An article published in the *Pedagogical Seminary* in 1896 aptly summed up the state of research on the subject at the end of the century:

> One class of writers have [sic] simply philosophized about play. They have discussed such questions as the origin of the play instinct, the relative value of free and directed play, and whether games have arisen by evolution or invention. . . . Another group has gone to work to make careful observations of actual facts regarding the plays of children. (Sisson, 1896)

Influenced by contemporary evolutionary theories, Karl Groos (1901) developed a functional definition which postulated that the play instinct served to prepare the child for adult life. Mitchell and Mason (1934) have summarized the impact of Groos' work on play theories utilized by physical educators: "His writings produced a profound effect on the minds of educators by showing to what an enormously wide range play extends, and its value to children not only at the time of participation, but as training for later life" (p. 66). Equally influential upon early physical educators was G. Stanley Hall's "recapitulation" theory, which held that by means of the various stages of play the child repeats the biocultural evolution of the human race. For most early play theorists—and for the physical educators who drew upon such theories—play was a purposeful activity that was physiological, neuromuscular, psychological, and social in nature (Hetherington, 1922; Johnson, 1907; Lee, 1915, 1925; Mergan, 1975; Playground Association of America, 1909).

Problems seen to be associated with urbanization, industrialization, and immigration in the late 1890s also led to an interest in the potential of play as a tool for socialization—for teaching "traditional American values" to an increasingly diverse population. Leaders of the Playground Association of America, founded in 1906, constantly insisted that the Association's work touched on what at the time was often regarded to be in the national interest for "social and civic betterment." The interest of this group was not so much on understanding the voluntary nature of children's play (indeed, most social reformers were anxious to do away with "idle" play), but on how play and games could be used to guide, shape, and mold children to become "good Americans." American physical educators traditionally have been primarily concerned with the physiological, psychological, and sociological correlates of play, games, and sports and, to a considerable extent, with efforts to use these phenomena to develop "character." In his posthumously published *A Philosophy of Play* (1920), Gulick raised such questions as "Why do

Americans play baseball and the English cricket? . . . How are play customs formed? . . . What light does a study of play throw on the nature of the player?'' (p. xi). Yet, in spite of his assertion that one must obtain information from first-hand observation, the book is based upon impressions rather than ethnographic reports.

It has been scholars from other disciplines, most notably anthropology, who have sought to understand the cultural meanings of play, games, and sports. Early ethnographic reports often included descriptions of play and games, frequently under such headings as "religion." In 1879 the noted English anthropologist Sir Edward Tylor discussed the historical and geographic diffusion of games. Culin set forth a theory of the function of games in his *Korean Games, With Notes on the Corresponding Games of China and Japan* (1895). His often-cited *Games of the North American Indians* (1907/1975) described the structures and implements of hundreds of games of chance and dexterity, providing in several instances commentaries on the cultural contexts in which such activities took place. Culin's "Street Games of Boys in Brooklyn" (1891) was based upon data provided by a 10-year-old informant. Newell's *Games and Songs of American Children* (1883/1963) and Gomme's *The Traditional Games of England, Scotland and Wales* (1894-1898/1964) attempted to set forth the formulas of play which children themselves had preserved. These should be considered important pioneer works in the same genre as more recent works, such as the Opies' *Children's Games in Street and Playground* (1969) and the Knapps' *One Potato, Two Potato: The Secret Education of American Children* (1976). Over the decades many anthropologists have included in their ethnographic reports information about the games and sports of the people they have studied. Examples include Firth's (1930; chapter 10 in this volume) investigation of the Tikopian dart contest, Opler's (1944) study of the Jicarilla Apache ceremonial relay race as an aid to understanding cultural exchange among the Jicarilla and certain Pueblo Indian tribes, and Burridge's (1957) description of the game of *taketak* as an exemplar of the Tangu notion of "equivalence." Avedon and Sutton-Smith's *The Study of Games* (1971) contains extensive bibliographic material dealing with ethnographic studies of games as well as reprints of selected works, and Schwartzman's recent, comprehensive *Transformations: The Anthropology of Children's Play* (1978) provides an excellent analysis and synthesis of research and theory pertaining to play and game phenomena. A number of ethnographic studies of sports and games are considered in Guttmann's *From Ritual to Record: The Nature of Modern Sports* (1978), in which the author sets forth his explanation of why sports flourish in many modern societies.

A very few descriptions of the play and games of non-Western peoples appeared in the physical education literature prior to World War II—for example, "Sandwich Island Olympics" (Bauer, 1932), and "Savage Wrestlers of the Black Sudan" (Domville-Fife, 1935). In 1947, Florence Stumpf and Frederick W. Cozens of the Department of Physical Education at the University of California urged physical educators to pay more attention to the systematic sociocultural study of play and games, maintaining that:

> The most cursory examination of the number of fine studies done by ethnologists and anthropologists on the play life, games, amusements, and ceremonial dances of primitive peoples, will convince the most skeptical . . . of the possibilities inherent in such studies with relation to our own field. . . . Surely it is no less the business of the teacher of physical education and the recreation worker than it is of the anthropologist to study human society and culture, to learn the way in which human beings interact in society, to learn the nature and function of social organizations, and means and effects of culture contact and change. (Stumpf & Cozens, 1947a, p. 1)

Short articles on the recreational pursuits of the Maoris (Stumpf & Cozens, 1947b), Fijians (Stumpf & Cozens, 1949), and Samoans (Dunlap, 1951) subsequently appeared in the *Research Quarterly*. Although these studies were based upon sources such as government documents, museum monographs, and traveler's reports—not upon ethnographic fieldwork—the authors did attempt to discuss their data and conclusions within an anthropological framework. Cozens and Stumpf's *Sports in American Life* (1953) must be considered a pioneering contribution to the sociological and cultural study of games, sports, and recreational activities in modern complex societies. Speakers at the 1950/1951 meetings of the American Academy of Physical Education discussed the importance of cultural anthropology and suggested that "findings provided by research in other fields" should be utilized to improve practices in health education, physical education, and recreation (American Academy of Physical Education, Note 1).

One of the most influential works on the subject of play, games, and sports yet to be written appeared near the end of World War II. *Homo Ludens: A Study of the Play Element in Culture* by the eminent Dutch historian Johan Huizinga was first published in German in 1944; an English translation appeared in 1949. *Homo Ludens* (Man the Player) is far more a theoretical than an ethnographic, sociological, or even comparative study of the place of play in human culture. Drawing heavily upon historical sources for his evidence, Huizinga set out to examine to what extent "culture itself bears the character of play" (p. ix). The author was concerned with play as a *cultural* phenomenon, not as a biological/psychological phenomenon, and the reader of *Homo Ludens* will find numerous references to such topics as play and law, playing and knowing, play and war, and play forms in philosophy, as well as discussions of play in relation to sports and contests.

Acknowledging an indebtedness to Huizinga, the French sociologist Roger Caillois drew substantially upon literature from the humanities and the social sciences in developing his *Man, Play and Games* (1958/1961). Caillois declared that traditional studies of games, by focusing on history and equipment, had neglected important questions about meanings of games and their interrelationships with ordinary life (pp. 57-67). So important were games, Caillois declared, that it might be possible to lay "the foundations for a sociology *derived from* games" (p. 67). His work proposed four categories for classifying games—*agon* (competition), *alea* (chance), *mimicry*, *ilinx* (vertigo, disorder)—and stipulated that games could be placed along a continuum from *paidia* (spontaneous, tumultuous exuberance) to *ludus* (disciplined, ordered skills and rules). Whereas Huizinga had been primarily concerned with the creative quality of play and the evolution of culture, Caillois was interested in attempting to determine the correlation between game preferences and other aspects of a culture, suggesting that games may "reinforce established values" or they may "contradict and flout them" (p. 66). This position implies that it is not possible to determine the functions which a game performs unless one analyzes both the game and the rest of the culture, as well as their interrelationships. Until recently, those few physical educators who attempted sociocultural studies of play, games, and sports tended to focus largely, if not exclusively, upon these events themselves and for the most part paid scant attention to the societies in which they took place.

Other scholars have considered play and games in relation to their potential for the promotion of cultural stability or the facilitation of cultural change. In the last two decades, Turner (1969, 1974a, 1974b [see chapter 5 in this volume]) has devoted attention to the play-element in ritual activities and has indicated that playful *liminal* and *liminoid*[1] activities may be sources of cultural change. Such activities, contained within rituals and other expressive elements of culture, invert or flout the social order which is normally accepted in ongoing daily life. Sutton-Smith (1977) has proposed that "games of disorder" and "games of order and disorder" may be expressions of challenge to established social order.

There is general agreement (e.g., Schwartzman, 1978; Townshend, 1980) that Roberts, Arth, and Bush's "Games in Culture," published in 1959 in the *American Anthropologist*, was instrumental in regenerating interest in the scholarly study of games. Using data from the literature and from the Yale Cross-Cultural Survey Files, the authors provided a cross-cultural analysis which suggested that games in three major categories (strategy, chance, and physical skill) are systematically related to other variables in cultures. The findings of this study were subsequently expanded in an often-cited article that explored the relationships between game types and the child-rearing practices of societies (Roberts & Sutton-Smith, 1962). *International Research in Sport and Physical Education* (Jokl & Simon, 1964), edited on behalf of the International Council of Sports and Physical Education of UNESCO, included papers urging physical educators to devote more attention to cultural anthropology. In 1969, Loy and Kenyon's *Sport, Culture, and Society*, although primarily a sociology of sport anthology, included papers written from anthropological perspectives and helped to foster a renewed interest in studying play, games, and sports as social and cultural phenomena.

By the early 1970s, sufficient scholarly interest had developed in the examination of play, games, and sports from anthropological perspectives to encourage the establishment of an organization specifically devoted to the topic. The Association for the Anthropological Study of Play (TAASP) held its first meeting in April 1975. The quarterly *TAASP Newsletter* has provided an avenue for active scholarly exchange, and the varied interests of the current TAASP membership reflect the numerous disciplinary perspectives from which play, games, and sports are currently being investigated.[2]

Culture, Society, and Social System

Definitions

Among the terms most frequently encountered in the sociocultural literature are *culture, society*, and *social system*. A considerable amount of energy has been spent defining each of these concepts and distinguishing among them (e.g., Gamst & Norbeck, 1976; Geertz, 1957; Jaeger & Selznick, 1964/1967; Kluckhohn, 1951/1967; Kroeber & Parsons, 1958). Although some scholars use the concepts "culture" and "society" rather interchangeably, others differentiate between these terms. As Hunter and Whitten (1976) point out, *culture* "is one of the most difficult words in the anthropological vocabulary to define. The difficulty stems from the fact that the concept is used to label various states of awareness occurring at different levels of abstraction" (p. 103). For most anthropologists, "culture is the patterned behavior learned by each individual from the day of birth as he or she is educated (socialized and enculturated) . . . to become, and remain, a member of the particular group into which he or she was born or joined" (p. 103).

Recently, some social scientists (e.g., Agar, 1980a, 1980b; Dolgin, Kemnitzer, & Schneider, 1977; Fine, 1979b; Rabinow & Sullivan, 1979) have tended to stress the idea that culture is constituted by the shared meanings, values, and ideas which develop through social interaction. Ordered patterns of social relationships and social interaction processes are constructed, constituted, or "given life" as people interact with one another. During the interactive process, commonly held meanings are defined. In other words, ordered social interaction depends upon some commonality of understanding of ideas among the people involved. At the same time the development of commonly held concepts or understandings is dependent upon social interaction. According to this viewpoint, it is difficult to separate ideas and values from patterns of social relationships and social interaction processes. Schneider (1976) defines culture as "a system of symbols and meanings" that serves partially to determine social action (p. 197). In recent years, symbols and symbolism have attracted considerable attention among anthropologists, and some have suggested that more recognition must be given to the possible symbolic meanings of games and sports. For example, in his exploration of power relationships and symbolic actions in complex society, Cohen (1974) indicates the importance of studying "the organisation of play of all sorts, sports and leisure-time activities" (p. 3) in addition to other ceremonial, ritual, and artistic occurrences.

For many social scientists, *society* refers to social groupings or collectivities of people. How a society is organized depends to some extent upon its shared beliefs—its culture. Some years ago, Herskovits (1955) offered a succinct and useful distinction between the two terms: "A society is composed of people; the way they behave is their culture" (p. 316).

The concept *social system* has been used somewhat differently by scholars in different disciplines. The literature of sociology reflects a tendency to define social system as the patterns of social relationships and social interaction among people or among groups of people. A group could be very large (as, for example, a nation), relatively small (as, for example, the New York Yankees), or quite small and informal (as, for example, a group of children on a playground). According to this perspective, culture is either considered to be a subsystem comprised of beliefs, meanings, values, and ideas within the overall social system, or culture is seen to be a second system that is parallel to the social system. Other scholars, using different models of society, hold that culture is the more encompassing concept and view the social system as a subsystem within culture. According to this view, the social system consists of the ordered patterns of social relationships and social processes among the persons within the culture. This second viewpoint has tended to be more prominent in anthropological literature.

Ethnographic Cultural Research

Many of the papers included in this book are ethnographic research reports or *ethnographies*. The major goal of these reports is to communicate to outsiders understandings about a culture which are held by members of the culture themselves. Readers whose experience has been with typical survey and experimental research reports in the social and behavioral sciences are likely to find the research reports included in this volume to be quite different from those with which they are familiar. Ethnographers typically spend a relatively long time—from several months to several years—closely involved with the culture which they are studying. During that period of time they use a variety of research methods, and they frequently find it necessary to create methods for particular purposes after having arrived in the culture. This is done to allow the research methods to conform more closely to the culture in an effort to avoid the application of a set of preconceived methods that might lead to alterations in the very cultural phenomena which the researchers have to study. Because of the length of time over which studies take place and the plethora of research methods employed during that time, detailed descriptions of research methods are impractical in most ethnographic research reports. A complete description of research methods for any one ethnographic study would probably fill an entire book. Thus, in ethnographies one typically finds very abbreviated discussions of methods, and these are frequently interwoven with the findings—the cultural descriptions. The cultural descriptions are usually presented in narrative form, with occasional use of diagrams, photographs, and appropriate quotations from members of the culture.

Ethnographic data do not usually lend themselves to extensive quantitative analyses, and thus the use of statistical summary tables which are typical in survey and experimental research reports are noticeably absent from ethnographies. Students who are familiar with historical studies will find a number of similarities between these and ethnographies. One major difference, however, is that historians, whose evidence is often derived largely, but by no means exclusively, from documents, liberally cite their sources. Ethnographers, who usually have spent many months learning about a culture first-hand, often do not cite a specific interview or observation on which they base particular information in their cultural descriptions. Their ethnographies are syntheses of what they have learned from a wide variety of encounters in a particular culture over a long period of time.

A major problem which has confronted students of culture has been that of the *emic* (insider's) and *etic* (outsider's) orientations and understandings.[3] Whose viewpoints does, and should, an ethnographic research report reflect: those of the members of the culture who inform the investigator about their world, or those of the visiting investigator who is trained to think and to write using theoretical concepts from the social sciences (cf. Agar, 1980a, 1980b; Harris, 1981; Pelto & Pelto, 1970/1978; Rabinow, 1977)? This question has received considerable attention in the anthropological literature, and researchers are constantly cautioned about the need to study and to categorize behavior in terms of their informants' conceptualizations of human events, rather than imposing their own structures and categories on the people studied. Actually, there is broad agreement that both perspectives enter into the ethnographic research process and that a research report is a synthesis or combination of these two different viewpoints.

The two broad categories of methods which ethnographers almost always use are *interviewing* and *participant observation*. Although some readers may be familiar with interview techniques used in psychology and sociology, most ethnographic interviews are considerably different from interview techniques in these other disciplines. With the goal of approximating a description of a culture in its own terms, an ethnographer sets out to ask questions that will elicit the language and its meanings used by the members of the culture to describe that culture (Spradley, 1979). Early ethnographic interviews may be extremely unfocused and simply ask a member of the culture to describe in his or her own terms various cultural situations with which he/she is familiar, such as a workplace, eating a meal at home, or playing a particular game or sport. As the interviews continue over the months, the interviewer asks questions which provide more details about the meanings of the argot or "folk concepts" (Spradley, 1979) used by members to characterize their own culture. Even in cases where an ethnographer and the members of the culture speak the same language, numerous specialized terms must often be learned in order to describe the culture from the insider's point of view.

Ethnographic research interviews are usually complemented by periods of participant observation. This second method involves participation on the part of the investigator in ongoing events of the culture as well as observation of what is going on there (Spradley, 1980). Participation and/or observation may be combined in varying amounts at different times or in different situations. These experiences help ethnographers in their quest to understand the meanings of these events from the *emic* (inside) perspective.

Extremely difficult problems may arise when an investigator attempts to study events in his or her own culture. Human beings are so deeply involved in their own culture—their shared traditional ways of interacting with others and making sense of their world—that it is difficult for them to step back and delineate the major cultural patterns or themes (cf. Chinoy, 1954/1977; Linton, 1945). We take a great deal for granted and do not need to think about our own culture very deeply in order to take part in it. If the intent is to broaden our understanding, however, a certain amount of distance from it may be necessary. Until recently, anthropologists have tended to accomplish this distancing by studying cultures other than their own, particularly those of non-Western, nonindustrialized societies.

Of course, not all cultural research is carried out in a culture which is different from that of the investigator. In recent years some anthropologists have turned their attention to more complex, industrialized, urban societies. The Coakley (1980) paper in Section 4 of this volume is an example of a field research project involving play, games, and sports that was carried out in the researcher's own community. It demonstrates quite nicely how beginning students may become involved in fieldwork of a sociocultural nature. Examples of other such undergraduate student field research projects are reported in Spradley and McCurdy's *The Cultural Experience: Ethnography in Complex Societies* (1972). Students who wish to pursue the topic of ethnographic research methods will find the references previously cited in this section to be helpful. Another useful source is Kottak's *A Guide for Student Anthropologists: Researching American Culture* (1982). For those who may be particularly interested in children's sports, games, and play, Schwartzman (1978) provides valuable theoretical and methodological insights, and recent papers by Fine (1980) and Fine and Glassner (1979) contain useful reflections upon the use of participant observation techniques for the study of children in youth baseball settings. Additional general sources which may be useful include Crane and Angrosino (1974), Glaser and Strauss (1967), Ives (1980), Naroll and Cohen (1970/1973), Powdermaker (1966), Wax (1971), and Williams (1967).

Conceptual Framework for the Papers in the Volume

Two broad themes, one theoretical and one methodological, unite the papers in this volume. First, all of the papers deal in some fashion with the nature of the interpretive aspects of play, games, and sports—that is, with ways in which play, games, and sports may provide opportunities for people to make sense of prominent values and social relationships within their society. This theme is developed by the use of such theoretical concepts as ritual, ceremony, symbol, drama, religion, metacommunication, myth, and socialization. Secondly, many of the investigations on which these papers are based were carried out as parts of larger programs of cultural research which were directed toward the attainment of a broader, general understanding of life in particular societies. Therefore, in many cases it is possible to read additional reports by these same authors in which other aspects of the societies they studied are discussed. This should aid readers who may wish to explore further the cultural contexts associated with the games and sports discussed in this volume.

Below are brief discussions of the major ideas which connect the papers in each of the five sections. Many of the papers could appropriately be placed in more than one section, and the reader should be attentive to interrelationships among papers which go beyond the ideas of central concern in any one section.

Section 1. Games, Sports, and Interpretations of Cultures

A *symbol* is an entity that stands for something else with which it has no inherent connection. Many things are (or can become) symbols: objects, actions, words, events, social relationships, and combinations of these and/or other things in the human environment. Human beings shape their reality and communicate meanings to one another largely through their ability to create and manipulate symbols. The use of symbols is of central importance to the process of creating and defining culture. Because the goal of cultural anthropologists is the attainment of a broader understanding of culture, understanding the meaning of symbols has come to occupy a position of central importance. As Foster and Brandes (1980) point out, "although we may vary individually in our evaluation of the *kind* of sense conveyed by particular symbols . . . we cannot but agree that to their users every symbol makes some kind of sense or it would neither come into use nor be perpetuated" (p. 3).

Section 1 deals primarily with considerations of games and sports as shared, public symbols. In some papers the game or sport is considered holistically to be a symbol. Other papers focus more narrowly upon specific or discrete symbolic phenomena associated with games and sports. For example, Geertz (1972; chapter 1 in this volume) discusses in a holistic manner the Balinese cockfight as a "cultural performance" or a "story" that the Balinese tell themselves about themselves (p. 26). At the same time, the Geertz paper also discusses a number of more narrowly defined, specific symbolic meanings which the Balinese associate with fighting cocks. Examination of symbols at this more narrowly focused level is a major concern of chapter 4, the Smith (1973) paper, which presents a discussion of sports heroes as symbols embodying specific meanings for the groups of people who create them.

Several authors have suggested that sports and games reflect the cultures in which they are found (e.g., Boyle, 1963; Lipsky, 1978; Real, 1975). Boyle's *Sport—Mirror of American Life* (1963), one of the earlier works on this topic, offered numerous examples of prevailing American values symbolically reflected in games and sports. The 1978 Lipsky paper (chapter 2 in this volume) highlights the extent to which institutionalized sports in the United States display idealized American values and social relationships (rather than "ordinary" American life), serving the dual purposes of socialization into the culture and escape from the pressures and constraints of ongoing daily life. By means of *reflection*, values and social relationships which are already present may be reinforced and maintained, and individuals may gain a broader understanding of their culture. This reflective process is part of the more encompassing process of *interpretation*, which may lead to an even broader and deeper understanding of the culture by helping to select what is reflected, by assisting with explaining it, and by providing opportunities to criticize it. As Geertz (1972) points out in his discussion of the Balinese cockfight, interpretation involves not only reflection, but also a commentary upon, and perhaps even a critique of, the culture. Loy (1978) has applied Geertz' (1972, 1973) notions of interpretation and symbolism to organized American sports and has suggested that sports go beyond merely reflecting American society by providing a "metasocial interpretation of the moral framework of society" (p. 96).

A recent account of the creation of the first modern Olympics in 1896, MacAloon's *This Great Symbol: Pierre de Coubertin and the Origins of the Modern Olympic Games* (1981), examines how people created and shaped this symbol-laden sports event. Framing his discussion partially with concepts from anthropology and ethnography, MacAloon discusses the multinational milieu out of which the concept of the Games emerged, and he describes the interrelationships between the nature of these nationalistic cultural settings and the nature of the Games which grew out of them. Considering the Olympics to be an international "cultural performance," MacAloon states:

> The Olympic games are first and foremost an immense playground, marketplace, theater, battlefield, church, arena, festival, and Broadway of cultural images, symbols, and meanings. Whatever else they do—including such essentially nonsymbolic things as get people killed or save their lives, line or empty their pockets, ensure their happiness or steal it from them— the Games do because of their capacity to attract, amass, ramify, and distribute vast symbolic energies. (p. 5)

A careful reading of works such as these should make it evident that it is human beings who are doing the reflecting and interpreting. Culture is not "out there" somewhere; culture consists of the knowledge and processes used by people to generate, to share, and to interpret social behavior. *People* create and shape games and sports; *people* assign meanings to events like the Super Bowl, the World Series, championship fights, the Irish Sweepstakes, the Olympic Games, and so on. The process of assigning meanings to sporting events in contemporary, industrialized societies has been discussed recently by several authors. Lipsky (1981) highlights the mounting dramatic tension which is often created by means of journalistic characterizations of opposing teams or particular sports stars prior to important athletic contests. These characterizations are then mingled in the cauldron of the contest:

> The game is . . . the dramatic enactment of a whole series of plots and subplots involving players, teams, and even owners. The game "makes flesh" an entire world that is supported by sagas in the popular magazines, controversies in the daily papers, and inside stories in "behind-the-scenes" biographies. (p. 22)

A New York journalist's personal account of his lifetime fascination with sports (Cohen, 1981) provides numerous examples of these dramatic confrontations. His impressions of the "plots and subplots" (Lipsky, 1981, p. 22) which led up to Super Bowl III between the New York Jets and the Baltimore Colts in the troubled times of 1969 are illustrative:

> My commitment . . . [to the Jets] was unequivocal. The Jets represented New York, the price [betting odds] was against them, and perhaps most important at the time, they had been cast, in Namath's mold, as apostles of dissidence and protest, while the Colts marched under the scimitar of the established order. If the Jets could topple the Colts, one felt—if Broadway Joe, brash and breezy, could outduel the Earl of Morrall, whose very name suggested first royalty and then righteousness—then surely hope might live another day. (p. 184)

Other characterizations which are related more closely to team and individual playing styles or to the physical nature of sporting events may heighten the dramatic tension of athletic contests as well. For example, Cohen (1981) describes a 1958 contest between the New York Giants and the Baltimore Colts as one which pitted "the league's most prolific attack against its stingiest defense" (p. 132). Lipsky (1981) suggests that athletic dramas are often "magnified by the sheer physical risks involved and by the violent intensity of the play" (p. 21).

Reminiscing about a contest afterward may be as important as building it up beforehand for the assignment of popularly constructed meanings. The Edmonds (1973; chapter 6 in this volume) paper provides evidence which suggests that the "plots and subplots" that surrounded the 1938 fight between Joe Louis and Max Schmeling were used both before and after the fight to give meaning to the event. Many American journalists used the pre-World War II animosities between the United States and Nazi Germany as a context for interpreting the contest. Turning to a different international sporting event, MacAloon (1981) discusses the post-performance mythic tales which seem to have been an outgrowth of the extensive public fascination which surrounded the Greek victor of the Olympic Marathon at the 1896 Games in Athens. He summarizes his discussion with the suggestion that,

> in literature—as in newspapers, folklore, proverbs, and gossip—Olympic performances are retold in a way that typically incorporates popular ethnography and accrues mythic, historical, literary, and religious motifs, often of surprising sorts. (p. 239)

This Greek Olympic Marathon winner is only one of many athletes who have been publicly acclaimed as heroes. The public characterizations of heroes may frequently be important in the development of the "plots and subplots" which are sometimes used to give athletic contests meaning. American journalists of the early 1920s seem to have used their portrayals of Jack Dempsey for such purposes (Roberts, 1974). Heroes can be considered to be public symbols embodying some of the idealized values and social relationships that members of a society consider to be important (Klapp, 1949; Smith, 1973; chapter 4 in this volume). Both Smith (1973) and Voigt (1978; chapter 3 in this volume) postulate a close association between an increasingly rational-scientific world view and what seems to be a growing tendency in sports to demythologize the player-hero. Voigt (1978) also suggests, however, that the complex structure of baseball has allowed for the provision of a whole range of American hero-types as well as anti-heroes.

Dramas, religious activities, rituals, mardi gras, games, and similar activities may provide socially acceptable means of displaying judgmental statements about particular aspects of a culture which cannot be made appropriately—or at least easily—during the ordinary course of routine daily activities. In many special expressive activities, it seems to be more acceptable for people to invent, criticize, and experiment with culture. Athough opportunities for interpreting culture do not necessarily lead to social change, the possibility does exist that such activities may serve occasionally as catalysts for transformation. Chapter 5 by Victor Turner (1974b) is pertinent. It discusses the nature of leisure and ritual in pre- and postindustrial societies. Phenomena such as play, games, art, and films, Turner contends, possess "liminal" or "liminoid" (marginal or threshold) characteristics. Through involvement with such phenomena one may find oneself at the edges or margins of conventional culture, where creatively novel combinations of cultural elements may occasionally occur. Such opportunities, Turner holds, may at times open the way to cultural change.

Section 2. Sports and Rituals

Many of the concepts discussed in the previous section—symbols, reflection, interpretation, and cultural performances—are important for understanding the papers in Section 2. The selections in this part of the text differ from those of the previous section in that they deal more specifically with interrelationships between sports and rituals. They share the notion, however, that sports serve interpretive functions within cultures. There is broad agreement that sports and rituals have some things in common. Yet, the extent to which the two phenomena are considered to be similar and the specific characteristics which are compared and contrasted vary from one scholar to another.

Although social scientists disagree somewhat about the nuances of the meaning of the term *ritual*, most are in accord that the concept refers to a category of behavior which is prescribed, predictable, stereotyped, communicative, and shared. Symbolic statements about the social order are frequently expressed in ritual actions which "present in symbol form the underlying order that is supposed to guide the members of the community, in their social activities" (Firth, 1973, p. 167). Although some scholars maintain that rituals must be associated with religious activities, others include formalized, prescribed events of a primarily secular nature within the concept of ritual (e.g., Moore & Myerhoff, 1977). A number of investigators have suggested that games and sports seem to be highly ritualistic (e.g., Arens, 1976; Cheska, 1978; Montague & Morais, 1976; Real, 1975; Stein, 1977; chapter 13 in this volume). The study of rituals in general, then, may help to shed light on the symbolic mechanisms of sports and games, and the study of meanings of rituals in a particular culture may help to illuminate the more specific meanings of the culture's sports and games. Conversely, an expanded understanding of sports and games in a society may help to clarify specific meanings of particular rituals, as well as the more general symbolic mechanisms by which rituals operate. The Harris (1982; chapter 7 in this volume) paper examines some of the similarities and differences between sports and rituals.

Some scholars have suggested that sports and dramas share a number of attributes (e.g., Keenan, 1975; Lahr, 1969; Metheney, 1965; Thomas, Note 2). Stone and Oldenburg (1967) and Stone (1971) examined professional wrestling, and their discussions lead one to conclude that professional wrestling is close to the juncture between these two phenomena. Rappaport (1979, pp. 176-177) maintains that an important characteristic distinguishing rituals from dramas is that in rituals members of the audience actively participate in some manner, whereas in dramas they are more passive spectators. Numerous examples of active participation on the part of sports spectators can be found in the literature. Beyond the commonplace of cheering for one's favorite team, for example, spectators at times have attempted to run onto the field during soccer contests in an effort to influence the game (e.g., Marsh, Rosser, & Harré, 1978; Taylor, 1971). Also, as the Mooney (1890) and Firth (1930) papers point out in chapters 11 and 10 respectively, spectators may be integrally involved in preparations for contests.

Chapter 8 by Max and Mary Gluckman (1977) sets forth an important theoretical issue with the suggestion that sports and rituals should be considered to be different phenomena because sports are much more uncertain than are rituals. The authors also maintain that rituals must involve calling upon the aid of supernatural powers, and that since sports do not involve such requests, they differ from rituals on this count as well. In chapter 9, Salter (1977) offers evidence to the contrary by suggesting that certain North American Indians occasionally engaged in sports activities for the purpose of attempting to influence the weather. Similarly, in chapter 10, Firth (1930) suggests that the Tikopian Islanders of the South Pacific performed dart-throwing contests partially for the purpose of calling upon supernatural powers to ensure good harvests. Mooney's (1890; chapter 11 in this volume) paper on the Cherokee in North Carolina and Firth's (1930) paper on the Tikopians illustrate the elaborateness of the ritual "frames" which have developed in some cultures in connection with sports contests. Elaborate ritual frames can also be associated with highly bureaucratized contemporary sport forms as Stein's (1977; chapter 13 in this volume) paper on University of Nebraska football and Burnett's (1969; chapter 12 in this volume) paper on rituals in American high schools illustrate.

When games and sports are seen to be ritual-like performances in which large numbers of human beings can be actively involved in some manner, it becomes even more evident how very complex the study of such phenomena can be. Moreover, the rapid proliferation of technology has made it possible for television both to expand audience sizes and to manipulate what the audience will view, and this has added another level of complexity. A television broadcast of a sports event is itself a human interpretation of an interpretive event. The televised version of a sporting event may differ substantially from the actual event; hence, television audiences and "live" audiences may actually have two quite different experiences (e.g., Bryant, Comisky, & Zillman, 1977; Comisky, Bryant, & Zillman, 1977). In an interpretive analysis of television programming, Fiske and Hartley (1978) point out that:

> most sport presented on television is now mediated by a full apparatus of commentators, studios full of experts, charts, potted histories and above all discussion. . . . On television, football is invested with other values: games become part of a narrative sequence; physicality is played down; the referee is always right (as the representative of externally defined authority); and

goals—achievement of the competitive 'goal'—are subject to idolatry. Hence there is sport and there is television sport. (pp. 191-192)

By selecting only a limited number of sports for frequent broadcasting, networks may affect the opportunities for and manner in which play, games, and sports function to reflect and interpret culture. It is becoming increasingly apparent that television has a considerable influence upon how some individuals learn about their culture.

Section 3. Play and Interpretation

Games and sports are usually considered to be forms of organized play or, at least, to exhibit at times qualities of playfulness. It is therefore important in an examination of interpretive functions of games and sports to consider interpretive processes which are associated with play. The papers in Section 3 deal with this topic.

The concept of play, it will be recalled, is a broad one and includes many different definitions which have been developed from different scholarly perspectives (cf. Bruner et al., 1976; Herron & Sutton-Smith, 1971; Millar, 1968/1974). These definitions historically have tended to stress one of the following: (a) the *structure* of play activities, including games, sports, and sometimes many other things such as riddling, joking, imitative activities, the arts, and even play-elements of law, war, and philosophy (e.g., Caillois, 1958/1961; Huizinga, 1944/1949; Roberts & Sutton-Smith, 1962); (b) the *psychobiological bases* of play activities, generally focusing upon why people play and/or the consequences of play (e.g., Ellis, 1973; Erikson, 1950; Groos, 1898, 1901; Patrick, 1914; Piaget, 1951/1962); and (c) the *attitudes*, dispositions, or states of mind which are associated with playing and which help to define an experience as play for the people involved (e.g., Bateson, 1955; Csikszentmihalyi, 1975; Turner, 1972). Works from the last three authors comprise Section 3.

Bateson (1955; chapter 14 in this volume) considers play to exist within a metacommunicative frame. *Metacommunication* is a process which is used by people to tell each other how to interpret what is being done or said, or what is about to be done or said. In other words, metacommunication is communication about communication.[4] Play, according to Bateson (1955), is behavior which is accompanied by certain messages that tell others not to take seriously that which is about to occur or is already occurring. Such metacommunicative messages are often sent by nonverbal means such as body movements, muscle contractions, facial expressions, and shifts in rhythm and tone of speech (Bateson, 1966); an example is dogs at play, who seem to know that a nip is not supposed to be considered to be a serious bite. Although he does not discuss sports and games specifically, Bateson would probably contend that people who engage in these activities might at times be playing (not taking the game seriously), and at other times they might be highly serious.

Bateson's idea of a "play frame" can easily be related to Turner's (1969, 1972, 1974b) concepts of "liminal" and "liminoid" activities, mentioned in the discussion of the papers in Section 1, which usually involve marginal behaviors considered to be unacceptable to some extent in ordinary daily life. Like Bateson, Turner suggests that a framing process occurs which communicates to the people involved that ordinarily unacceptable activities are acceptable at certain times. Within the frames proposed by either Bateson or Turner, people may be able to engage in novel activities that may at times be creative sources for cultural change. Turner's conception of this framing process, however, involves more highly elaborated or complex social conventions than does Bateson's model. For Turner, cultural norms define more explicitly when and where ordinarily unacceptable activities are appropriate. For example, in some societies rituals carefully define periods when liminal activities such as thefts, transvestitism, satirical comedies, and public humiliation of others can (or are supposed to) occur and they also define the people who are supposed to engage in them. Similarly, in many industrialized cultures, nonritualistic social norms may define liminoid (liminal-like) periods and/or the people who can appropriately engage in marginal activities. It can be hypothesized that within culturally defined liminal or liminoid periods there may be some normally unacceptable activities which are engaged in because people are *expected* to do them, and there may be other activities that are done within a Batesonian play frame which says to others, "Even these expected liminal activities are not to be taken seriously," or "here are some unexpected liminal activities, but don't take them seriously." There can be levels of understanding within levels, frames within frames.

In addition to the presence of activities that are unacceptable by the standards of ordinary life, Turner (1969, 1972) suggests that the other prominent characteristic of liminal and liminoid periods is a sense of *communitas* among the people involved. During these periods people seem to be relatively free from the usual constraints of the social structure in which they are ordinarily enmeshed. There is temporarily no need to be concerned about status relationships with one another or with one's roles in ongoing daily life. This freedom permits the marginal, ordinarily unacceptable activities of the liminal and liminoid periods to occur, and it also permits a different kind of interaction among the people. Turner (1972) says that "communitas is a fact of everyone's experience" (p. 393) and defines it with the following statement:

> The social has a free or unbound as well as a bonded or bound dimension, the dimension of communitas in which men confront one another not as

role players but as "human totals," integral beings who recognizably share the same humanity. (p. 494)

Whether marginal, frequently creative activities within liminal or liminoid periods go on because it is expected that they be done (as Turner suggests), or whether (in Bateson's sense) the activities which occur mock even the expected liminal or liminoid activities themselves, many scholars would label these events as play. The attitude or state of mind of communitas is important because in some cases it may be a part of players' interpretations of their social interaction within playful activities. To the extent that particular games or sports within a culture might be framed as liminal/liminoid or playful, or to the extent that games and sports contain liminal/liminoid or playful periods embedded within them, the discussions by Turner and Bateson on these marginal situations that occur within cultures are valuable for broadening scholarly understanding of game and sport phenomena. A discussion of games which seem to exhibit these marginal qualities in relation to the cultures of which they are a part may be found in Sutton-Smith's (1977) work on "games of disorder" and "games of order and disorder." The reader is encouraged to digress for a few moments to think about the extent to which contemporary American spectator sports seem characterized by moments of disorder, marginality, or playfulness as defined here.

The concept of *flow* as explicated by Csikszentmihalyi (1975; see chapter 16 by MacAloon & Csikszentmihalyi in this volume) has some commonality with Turner's (1969, 1972) concept of communitas. Both are attitudes or dispositions which seem to accompany playful activities. Both have a holistic quality about them, involving the ability to see the totality of a situation all at one time. Both concepts also denote a "self-lessness." When one is in a state of flow or communitas, one need not pay attention to the plethora of roles and statuses which one normally occupies in society. Flow, however, does not require social interaction—it can occur when one is alone, while communitas involves shared experiences. Flow is likened by Csikszentmihalyi to Maslow's (1964/1970) concept of "peak experiences." It has intense, ecstatic, unforgettable qualities:

> In the flow state, action follows upon action according to an internal logic that seems to need no conscious intervention by the actor. He experiences it as a unified flowing from one moment to the next, in which he is in control of his actions, and in which there is little distinction between self and environment, between stimulus and response, or between past, present, and future. . . .
>
> Games are obvious flow activities, and play is the flow experience *par excellence*. Yet playing a game does not guarantee that one is experiencing flow, just as reciting the pledge of allegiance is no proof of patriotic feelings. Conversely, the flow experience can be found in activities other than

games. One such activity is creativity in general, including art and science. (Csikszentmihalyi, 1975, pp. 36-37)

The term flow was selected to define this state because many of the people whom Csikszentmihalyi interviewed in his studies used this word to describe particular qualities which were part of their experiences.

Flow is most likely to be experienced, according to Csikszentmihalyi (1975), when a person is in a situation where his or her capabilities or skills are about equal to whatever is demanded in the situation in order to function successfully. If a person's capabilities are far in excess of what is demanded, then the individual is likely to experience boredom. This is perhaps one reason why assembly-line workers become bored easily with their jobs; their skills far exceed what is demanded of them by their tasks. On the other hand, if a person's skills are not sufficient to meet the demands of a situation, then the individual is likely to experience anxiety. A rock climber on a sheer cliff with a lack of ability to move either up or down would undoubtedly become extremely anxious and worried. Csikszentmihalyi contends that the experience of flow is an autotelic or intrinsic reward which tends to make an activity something a person wishes to engage in for its own sake. Doing the activity becomes its own reward. Chapter 16 by MacAloon and Csikszentmihalyi (1975) focuses upon the experiences of rock climbers and suggests the possibility that flow may be a source of cultural revitalization or change.

Section 4. Socialization and Enculturation Through Play, Games, and Sports

The terms *socialization* and *enculturation* are often used synonymously to refer to "the basic social process through which an individual becomes integrated into a social group by learning the group's culture and his role in the group" (Theodorson & Theodorson, 1969/1979, p. 396). It is generally believed that socialization/enculturation is a life-long, unending process, and that humans learn the general patterns of their culture by means of formal and informal instruction, imitation, and interpretation. To the extent that play, games, and sports provide opportunities for individuals to examine, interpret, and expand their understanding of their culture, these phenomena should be considered as important socializing/enculturating activities. Because of the immense number of complex sociocultural phenomena existing in all societies, it has been difficult to determine the precise nature of the socializing/enculturating functions of any one particular set. Much of our knowledge about the socializing/enculturating aspects of play, games, and sports is still speculative, derived from logical extensions of our knowledge about their reflective and interpretive properties. Recently, however, Fine

(1979a) employed ethnographic techniques to focus upon the process of moral socialization/enculturation in Little League baseball settings. His data expand our understanding of some of the ways in which coaches' moral values are "communicated [to players] in the course of on-going game-based interaction" (p. 104). The contribution by Schwartzman (1978; chapter 17 in this volume) included in this section reviews much of the work on socialization through play and games, and alerts the reader to the need to pay careful attention to the complexities of cultural contexts in which play and games take place.

Socialization/enculturation involves a host of social learning processes and a large number of different socializing agents. The process of modeling or imitating the behavior of others is considered to be one important mechanism by which socialization/enculturation occurs (Bandura, 1971; Berger & Lambert, 1968). The social models who are imitated can be considered to be important agents of socialization/enculturation. They include parents, peers, and teachers, as well as more distant figures, such as movie and television stars, rock music performers, sports figures, and fictional characters from novels, comic books, movies, and television.

In recent years, some authors have suggested that children may have a more active part in shaping the nature of their games and play activities than is possible when they engage in more highly structured sports events. Thus, the former are hypothesized to be more valuable in socialization/enculturation processes than the latter (e.g., Devereux, 1976; Polgar, 1976; Ralbovsky, 1974). Speaking to this contention, the Coakley (1980; chapter 18 in this volume) paper raises an important, and still little examined, theoretical issue by proposing that play, games, and sports may perform different functions—that different lessons about one's culture may be learned from each. Judgments about the relative values of engaging in play, games, and sports, Coakley suggests, must take into account the possible differences among their socializing/enculturating functions.

Section 5. Acculturation, Cultural Pluralism, Games, and Sports

An examination of the reflective and interpretive properties of games and sports seems to be a useful approach to the study of these phenomena in situations of cultural pluralism and acculturation. *Acculturation* refers to cultural changes that occur when there is contact between cultures—the processes by which members of one culture adopt and adapt such things as social relationships, material objects, and/or values of another culture (Social Science Research Council, 1954). *Cultural pluralism*, on the other hand, refers to the coexistence of several groups with distinct cultural differences within a common political and economic system (Theodorson & Theodorson, 1969/1979). Most of the world's nations are pluralistic; the United States certainly is.

If games and sports provide opportunities for members of a culture to reflect and interpret their society, then what happens when cultures come into close and frequent contact with one another? At times, the readily observable *structure* of a sport or game appears to remain intact in a culture to which it travels, but the *meanings* or understandings associated with the activity by members of the new culture may be quite different from those associated with the sport in the original culture (e.g., Allison & Duda, 1982; Blanchard, 1974; Tindall, 1975; Townshend, Note 3). At other times, however, the overt structure is considerably altered (Heider, 1977; Leach, 1974; Scotch, 1961). Under what circumstances do meanings and/or structures of games and sports change? Under what circumstances do other changes within a culture seem to be associated with the introduction of an outside game or sport? Under what circumstances do the games and sports of a culture fail to be adopted by members of other nearby groups?

To date only a few investigators have undertaken studies dealing centrally with these concerns. Many of these papers are included in Section 5. For example, in chapter 21 Blanchard (1974) analyzes basketball and culture change among the Rimrock Navajo; in chapter 22 Scotch (1961) points out that, in the face of modern science, traditional beliefs in magic were incorporated into the urban Zulu version of the game of soccer; and in chapter 23 Heider (1977) demonstrates how Grand Valley Dani children of highland New Guinea transformed a game which their Javanese school teachers had introduced into an event reflecting Dani, not Javanese, culture. A particularly graphic example of the results of the processes of acculturation involving a sport is shown in the film *Trobriand Cricket* (Leach, 1974). The film gives an account of the ways in which a small island society modified the structure of the English game of cricket, imposed on them originally by foreign missionaries, to make it conform more closely to Trobriand culture. On the other hand, the Fox (1961; chapter 24 in this volume) paper illustrates that the introduction of a foreign game may serve to disturb an existing equilibrium in a society, whereas that society's more traditional games had encouraged social cohesion.

The traditional "melting pot" thesis holds that when members of different ethnic groups come into close and frequent contact with one another, they tend to lose their ethnic distinctions and become one homogeneous society. This belief has been challenged in recent years because cultural pluralism continues to flourish even though cultures throughout the world are coming into more frequent contact with one another. Social scientists are becoming increasingly interested in examining culturally pluralistic societies and cultural pluralism in urban settings. Particular interest has been directed to the concept of the *ethnic group*, generally defined as a group of people who have in common a particular set of cultural traditions (Glazer & Moynihan, 1975; Theodorson & Theodorson, 1969/1979). These traditions may be rooted in such elements of culture as language, religion, social customs, economic organization, or political interaction.

It appears that in pluralistic situations members of different ethnic groups do not always abandon their distinctiveness. In fact, they may work actively to maintain separate ethnic identities by defining and maintaining boundaries which distinguish members of their group from others with whom they come into frequent contact (Barth, 1969). In such situations *boundary markers*, or particular attributes such as styles of communication, manner of dress, religious practices, or types of games, are utilized to maintain the group's distinctiveness. Sports and games may at times be part of the boundary maintenance processes in which members of ethnic groups in close proximity to one another engage. Such a phenomenon is discussed in chapter 20 by Salamone (1979) in his examination of wrestling styles in Northern Nigeria. Although Farrer (1976; chapter 19 in this volume) does not specifically utilize the concept of ethnic boundaries, her analysis of the game of tag as played by Mescalero Apache children illustrates the importance of examining the pluralistic qualities of the cultural context in which games occur. Allison (1979) has more directly sought to encourage scholars to be more concerned with ethnic heterogeneity in situations where there is frequent contact among groups.

Differences among cultures with regard to the ways in which sports are understood may at times become important in international sports events. For example, MacAloon (1981) suggests that although "the 1896 [Olympic] Games had a unity and integrity of rule, purpose, and form" (p. 269) which were greater than those found in other conceptualizations of previous international sports events of that time, people from different nations interpreted certain aspects of the Games somewhat differently. In general, a lack of common understanding seemed to exist about the nature of many of the events:

> Greeks did not quite know whether to take the hurdles as circus comedy or muscular contest; British athletes refused to classify Turner-style gymnastics as sport; no one knew in advance whether the Marathon was an athletic contest or a semireligious ordeal, and few were entirely certain after it. Spectatorial structures of attention, etiquette, and evaluation, no less than athletes' and officials' codes of performance and judgement, were often enough ad hoc. Even persons from national cultures with long histories of amateur athletic games were often brought up short by the novelty of these Olympic games. (pp. 269-270)

It would be several decades before "the Games" would really consolidate as a cross-cultural category of performance, bearing with it, in more or less consensual and predictable form, all the properties that Gregory Bateson, Victor Turner, and Erving Goffman have taught us to recognize in culturally framed performances. In a situation filled with such interpretive ambiguity, it is little wonder that cultural differences influenced the ways in which the 1896 Games were understood.

McIntosh (1979) has recently noted that an increasing number of programs of international sports competition continue to bring together participants who are likely to interpret such abstract concepts as "fair play" in quite different ways. "Do the international federations of sport and above all the International Olympic Committee superimpose their own ideology on the world of sport," McIntosh asks, "and does this supersede the ideologies of societies into which sport at a lower level is seen to socialise its participants?" (p. 158). What the acculturative impact of international sports, which have been largely dominated by Western European value systems, may be on newly developing nations, which often place a considerable premium upon establishing elite national teams, has yet to be determined. Readers interested in finding answers to questions such as these and to others which McIntosh has posed may find that insights suggested by interpretive perspectives upon culture may be of considerable value.

As a substantial number of the papers contained in this volume make considerable use of ethnographic research methodologies with which the reader may not be especially familiar, the reader is encouraged to reread carefully the section of the introduction entitled "Ethnographic Cultural Research." It would also be useful to bear in mind that two broad questions served as the impetus for this volume: (a) What do play, games, and sports *mean* to the people who engage in such activities? (b) How might beginning students as well as mature scholars come to know more about the meanings and functions of these cultural phenomena? The papers which follow should prove useful in helping us to move toward answering these questions.

Notes

1. The concepts "liminal" and "liminoid"—from the Latin *limen* (threshold)—are explicated in chapter 5, Victor Turner's (1974b) comprehensive article. In his analysis, Turner states that his interest in studying "symbolic genres in *large*-scale societies [was aroused] by some implications of the work of Arnold van Gennep . . . in his *Rites de Passage*, first published in French in 1909" (p. 56 in the original; p. 127 in this volume).
2. Readers interested in learning more about this organization and its publications may wish to contact the TAASP Secretary/Treasurer, Professor Janice Beran, Department of Physical Education, Iowa State University, Ames, Iowa.

3. According to P.J. Pelto and G.H. Pelto (1970/1978), the terms "emic" and "etic" seem to have first appeared in Kenneth Pike's *Language in Relation to a Unified Theory of the Structure of Human Behavior* (Vol. 1), University of California: Summer Institute of Linguistics, 1954. "Emic" refers to the "inside" or "native's" point of view of the culture. "Etic" refers to the "outsider's" view, and is often used to label the theoretical approaches with which the anthropologist organizes and categorizes aspects of the culture being studied. There is broad agreement among anthropologists that good ethnographic reports must involve both "emic" and "etic" understandings.

4. Goffman provides extensive discussion of selected metacommunicative messages in his book *Frame Analysis* (1974).

Reference Notes

1. American Academy of Physical Education. *Professional Contributions No. 1.* Papers and reports presented at the annual meeting of the American Academy of Physical Education in Dallas, Texas, April 14-16, 1950, and in Detroit, Michigan, April 13-16, 1951.

2. Thomas, C.E. *Sport, tragedy, and emotional expression.* Paper presented at the National Convention of the American Alliance for Health, Physical Education, and Recreation, New Orleans, March 1979.

3. Townshend, P. *Mankala in Kenya: A case study in the cross-cultural analysis of games.* Paper presented at the Annual Meeting of the Association for the Anthropological Study of Play, Ann Arbor, Michigan, April 1980.

References

AGAR, M. Hermeneutics in anthropology: A review essay. *Ethos*, 1980, 8(3), 253-272. (a)

AGAR, M. *The professional stranger: An informal introduction to ethnography.* New York: Academic Press, 1980. (b)

ALLISON, M.T. On the ethnicity of ethnic minorities in sport. *Quest*, 1979, 31(1), 50-56.

ALLISON, M.T., & Duda, J.L. The nature of sociocultural influences on achievement motivation: The case of the Navajo Indian. In J.W. Loy (Ed.), *The paradoxes of play: Proceedings of the 6th Annual Meeting of the Association for the Anthropological Study of Play.* West Point, NY: Leisure Press, 1982.

ARENS, W. Professional football: An American symbol and ritual. In W. Arens & S.P. Montague (Eds.), *The American dimension: Cultural myths and social realities.* Port Washington, NY: Alfred, 1976.

AVEDON, E.M., & Sutton-Smith, B. *The study of games.* New York: Wiley, 1971.

BANDURA, A. *Psychological modeling: Conflicting theories.* Chicago: Aldine-Atherton, 1971.

BARTH, F. (Ed.). *Ethnic groups and boundaries: The social organization of cultural difference.* Boston: Little, Brown, 1969.

BATESON, G. A theory of play and fantasy. *Psychiatric Research Reports 2 of the American Psychiatric Association,* 1955, 39-51.

BATESON, G. Problems in cetacean and other mammalian communication. In K.S. Norris (Ed.), *Whales, dolphins and porpoises.* Berkeley: University of California Press, 1966.

BAUER, L. Sandwich Island Olympics. *Journal of Health and Physical Education,* 1932, 3(7), 12-15.

BERGER, S., & Lambert, W.W. Stimulus-response theory in contemporary social psychology. In G. Lindzey & E. Aronson (Eds.), *The handbook of social psychology* (Vol. 1). Reading, MA: Addison-Wesley, 1968.

BLANCHARD, K. Basketball and the culture-change process: The Rimrock Navajo case. *Council on Anthropology and Education Quarterly,* 1974, 5(4), 8-13.

BOYLE, R. *Sport: Mirror of American life.* Boston: Little, Brown, 1963.

BRUNER, J.S., Jolly, A., & Sylva, K. (Eds.). *Play—Its role in development and evolution.* New York: Basic Books, 1976.

BRYANT, J., Comisky, P., & Zillman, D. Drama in sports commentary. *Journal of Communication,* 1977, 27(3), 140-149.

BURNETT, J.H. Ceremony, rites, and economy in the student system of an American high school. *Human Organization,* 1969, 28(1), 1-10.

BURRIDGE, K.O.L. A Tangu game. *Man,* 1957, 57(1), 88-89.

CAILLOIS, R. [*Man, play, and games*] (M. Barash, trans.). New York: The Free Press, 1961. (Originally published, 1958.)

CHESKA, A.T. Sports spectacular: The social ritual of power. *Quest,* 1978, 30, 58-71.

CHINOY, E. Society and culture. In P.I. Rose (Ed.), *The study of society: An integrated anthology* (4th ed.). New York: Random House, 1977. (Originally published, 1954.)

COAKLEY, J.J. Play, games, and sport: Developmental implications for young people. *Journal of Sport Behavior,* 1980, 3(3), 99-118.

COHEN, A. *Two-dimensional man: An essay on the anthropology of power and symbolism in complex society.* Berkeley: University of California Press, 1974.

COHEN, S. *The man in the crowd: Confessions of a sports addict.* New York: Random House, 1981.

COMISKY, P., Bryant, J., & Zillman, D. Commentary as a substitute for action. *Journal of Communication,* 1977, 27(3), 150-153.

COZENS, F.W., & Stumpf, F.S. *Sports in American life.* Chicago: University of Chicago Press, 1953.

CRANE, J.G., & Angrosino, M.V. *Field projects in anthropology: A student handbook*. Dallas: Scott, Foresman, 1974.

CSIKSZENTMIHALYI, M. *Beyond boredom and anxiety: The experience of play in work and games*. San Francisco: Jossey-Bass, 1975.

CSIKSZENTMIHALYI, M. Some paradoxes in the definition of play. In A.T. Cheska (Ed.), *Play as context: 1979 proceedings of the Association for the Anthropological Study of Play*. West Point, NY: Leisure Press, 1981.

CULIN, S. Street games of boys in Brooklyn, New York. *Journal of American Folklore*, 1891, **4**(14), 221-237.

CULIN, S. *Korean games with notes on the corresponding games of China and Japan*. Philadelphia: University of Pennsylvania Press, 1895.

CULIN, S. *Games of the North American Indians*. New York: Dover, 1975. (Originally published, 1907.)

DEVEREUX, E.C. Backyard versus Little League baseball: The impoverishment of children's games. In D.M. Landers (Ed.), *Social problems in athletics: Essays in the sociology of sport*. Urbana: University of Illinois Press, 1976.

DOLGIN, J.L., Kemnitzer, D.S., & Schneider, D.M. Introduction: "As people express their lives, so they are. . . ." In J.L. Dolgin, D.S. Kemnitzer, & D.M. Schneider (Eds.), *Symbolic anthropology: A reader in the study of symbols and meanings*. New York: Columbia University Press, 1977.

DOMVILLE-FIFE, C.M. Savage wrestlers of the black Sudan. *Journal of Health and Physical Education*, 1935, **6**(6), 10-11; 55.

DUNLAP, H.L. Games, sports, dancing, and other vigorous recreational activities and their function in Samoan culture. *Research Quarterly*, 1951, **22**(3), 298-311.

EDMONDS, A.O. The second Louis-Schmeling fight: Sport, symbol, and culture. *Journal of Popular Culture*, 1973, **7**, 42-50.

ELLIS, M.J. *Why people play*. Englewood Cliffs, NJ: Prentice-Hall, 1973.

ERIKSON, E.H. *Childhood and society*. New York: W.W. Norton, 1950.

FARRER, C.R. Play and inter-ethnic communication. In D.F. Lancy & B.A. Tindall (Eds.), *The anthropological study of play: Problems and prospects*. Cornwall, NY: Leisure Press, 1976. (Proceedings of the First Annual Meeting of the Association for the Anthropological Study of Play.)

FINE, G.A. Preadolescent socialization through organized athletics: The construction of moral meanings in Little League baseball. In M.L. Krotee (Ed.), *The dimensions of sport sociology*. West Point, NY: Leisure, 1979. (a)

FINE, G.A. Small groups and culture creation: The idioculture of Little League baseball teams. *American Sociological Review*, 1979, **44**, 733-745. (b)

FINE, G.A. Cracking diamonds: Observer role in Little League baseball settings and the acquisition of social competence. In W.B. Shaffir, R.A. Stebbins, & A.

Turowetz (Eds.), *Fieldwork experience: Qualitative approaches to social research*. New York: St. Martin's, 1980.

FINE, G.A., & Glassner, B. Participant observation with children: Promise and problems. *Urban Life*, 1979, **8**, 153-174.

FIRTH, R. A dart match in Tikopia: A study in the sociology of primitive sport. *Oceania*, 1930, **1**, 64-96.

FIRTH, R. *Symbols: Public and private*. Ithaca, NY: Cornell University Press, 1973.

FISKE, J., & Hartley, J. *Reading television*. London: Methuen, 1978.

FOSTER, M.L., & Brandes, S.H. Introduction. In M.L. Foster & S.H. Brandes (Eds.), *Symbol as sense: New approaches to the analysis of meaning*. New York: Academic Press, 1980.

FOX, J.R. Pueblo baseball: A new use for old witchcraft. *Journal of American Folklore*, 1961, 74(291), 9-16.

GAMST, F.C., & Norbeck, E. *Ideas of culture: Sources and uses*. New York: Holt, Rinehart & Winston, 1976.

GEERTZ, C. Ritual and social change: A Javanese example. *American Anthropologist*, 1957, **59**, 32-54.

GEERTZ, C. Deep play: Notes on the Balinese cockfight. *Daedalus*, 1972, **101**(1), 1-37.

GEERTZ, C. *The interpretation of cultures*. New York: Basic Books, 1973.

GLASER, B.G., & Strauss, A.L. *The discovery of grounded theory: Strategies for qualitative research*. Chicago: Aldine, 1967.

GLAZER, N., & Moynihan, D.P. (Eds.). *Ethnicity: Theory and experience*. Cambridge: Harvard University Press, 1975.

GLUCKMAN, M., & Gluckman, M. On drama, and games and athletic contests. In S.F. Moore & B.G. Myerhoff (Eds.), *Secular ritual*. Assen/Amsterdam: Van Gorcum, 1977.

GOFFMAN, E. *Frame analysis: An essay on the organization of experience*. New York: Harper and Row, 1974.

GOMME, A.B. *The traditional games of England, Scotland and Ireland* (2 vols.). New York: Dover Publications, 1964. (Originally published, 1894-1898.)

GROOS, K. [*The play of animals*] (E.L. Baldwin, trans.). New York: Appleton, 1898.

GROOS, K. [*The play of man*] (E.L. Baldwin, trans.). New York: Appleton, 1901.

GULICK, L.H. *A philosophy of play*. New York: Association Press, 1920.

GUTTMANN, A. *From ritual to record: The nature of modern sports*. New York: Columbia University Press, 1978.

HARRIS, J.C. Play: A definition and implied interrelationships with culture and sport. *Journal of Sport Psychology*, 1980, **2**, 46-61.

HARRIS, J.C. Hermeneutics, interpretive cultural research, and the study of sports. *Quest*, 1981, **33**(1), 72-86.

HARRIS, J.C. Sport and ritual: A macroscopic comparison of form. In J.W. Loy (Ed.), *Paradoxes of play: Proceedings of the 6th Annual Meeting of the Association for the Anthropological Study of Play*. West Point, NY: Leisure Press, 1982.

HEIDER, K.G. From Javanese to Dani: The translation of a game. In P. Stevens (Ed.), *Studies in the anthropology of play: Papers in memory of B. Allan Tindall*. West Point, NY: Leisure Press, 1977. (Proceedings from the Second Annual Meeting of the Association for the Anthropological Study of Play.)

HERRON, R.E., & Sutton-Smith, B. *Child's play*. New York: Wiley, 1971.

HERSKOVITS, M.J. *Cultural anthropology*. New York: Knopf, 1955.

HETHERINGTON, C. *School program in physical education*. Yonkers-on-Hudson, NY: World Book, 1922.

HUIZINGA, J. [*Homo ludens: A study of the play-element in culture*] (R.F.C. Hull, trans.). London: Routledge & Kegan Paul, 1949. (Published in German, 1944.)

HUNTER, D.E., & Whitten, P. (Eds.). *Encyclopedia of anthropology*. New York: Harper & Row, 1976.

IVES, E.D. *The tape-recorded interview: A manual for fieldworkers in folklore and oral history*. Knoxville: University of Tennessee Press, 1980.

JAEGER, G., & Selznick, P. A normative theory of culture. In P.I. Rose (Ed.), *The study of society: An integrated anthology*. New York: Random House, 1967. (Originally published, 1964.)

JOHNSON, G.E. *Education by plays and games*. Boston: Ginn & Co., 1907.

JOKL, E., & Simon, E. (Eds.). *International research in sport and physical education*. Springfield, IL: Charles C. Thomas, 1964.

KEENAN, F.W. The athletic contest as a "tragic" form of art. *International Review of Sport Sociology*, 1975, **10**, 39-54.

KLAPP, O.E. Hero worship in America. *American Sociological Review*, 1949, **14**, 53-62.

KLUCKHOHN, C. The study of culture. In P.I. Rose (Ed.), *The study of society: An integrated approach*. New York: Random House, 1967. (Originally published, 1951.)

KNAPP, M., & Knapp, H. *One potato, two potato: The secret education of American children*. New York: W.W. Norton, 1976.

KOTTAK, C.P. (Ed.). *A guide for student anthropologists: Researching American culture*. Ann Arbor: The University of Michigan Press, 1982.

KROEBER, A.L., & Parsons, T. The concepts of culture and of social system. *American Sociological Review*, 1958, **23**(5), 582-583.

LAHR, J. The theatre of sports. *Evergreen*, November 1969, **13**, 38-41; 73-76.

LEACH, J.W. *Trobriand cricket: An ingenious response to colonialism*. Berkeley: University of California Extension Media Center, 1974. (Film)

LEE, J. *Play in education*. New York: Macmillan, 1915.

LEE, J. *The normal course in play*. New York: A.S. Barnes, 1925.

LINTON, R. *The cultural background of personality*. New York: Appleton-Century-Crofts, 1945.

LIPSKY, R. Toward a political theory of American sports symbolism. *American Behavioral Scientist*, 1978, **21**(3), 345-360.

LIPSKY, R. *How we play the game: Why sports dominate American life*. Boston: Beacon, 1981.

LOY, J.W. The nature of sport: A definitional effort. *Quest*, 1968, **10**, 1-15.

LOY, J.W. The cultural system of sports. *Quest*, 1978, **29**, 73-102.

LOY, J.W., & Kenyon, G.S. (Eds.). *Sport, culture, and society: A reader on the sociology of sport*. New York: Macmillan, 1969.

MACALOON, J.J. *This great symbol: Pierre de Coubertin and the origins of the modern Olympic Games*. Chicago: University of Chicago Press, 1981.

MACALOON, J.J., & Csikszentmihalyi, M. Deep play and the flow experience in rock climbing. In M. Csikszentmihalyi, *Beyond boredom and anxiety: The experience of play in work and games*. San Francisco: Jossey-Bass, 1975.

MARSH, P., Rosser, E., & Harré, R. *The rules of disorder*. London: Routledge & Kegan Paul, 1978.

MASLOW, A.H. *Religions, values, and peak-experiences*. New York: Viking, 1970. (Originally published, 1964.)

MCINTOSH, P. *Fair play: Ethics in sport and education*. London: Heinemann, 1979.

MERGAN, B. The discovery of children's play. *American Quarterly*, 1975, **27**(4), 399-420.

METHENEY, E. Symbolic forms of movement: The Olympic Games. In E. Metheney, *Connotations of movement in sport and dance*. Dubuque, IA: W.C. Brown, 1965. (Report of the Fourth Summer Session of the International Olympic Academy, Athens, Greece, 1964.)

MILLAR, S. *The psychology of play*. New York: Jason Aronson, 1974. (Originally published, 1968.)

MITCHELL, E.D., & Mason, B.A. *The theory of play*. New York: A.S. Barnes, 1934.

MONTAGUE, S.P., & Morais, R. Football games and rock concerts: The ritual enactment of American success models. In W. Arens & S.P. Montague (Eds.), *The American dimension: Cultural myths and social realities*. Port Washington NY: Alfred, 1976.

MOONEY, J. The Cherokee ball play. *American Anthropologist*, 1890, 3(2), 105-132.

MOORE, S.F., & Myerhoff, B.G. (Eds.). *Secular ritual*. Assen/Amsterdam: Van Gorcum, 1977.

NAROLL, R., & Cohen, R. (Eds.). *A handbook of method in cultural anthropology*. New York: Columbia University Press, 1973. (Originally published, 1970.)

NEWELL, W.W. *Games and songs of American children, collected and composed*. New York: Dover Publications, 1963. (Originally published, 1883.)

OPIE, I., & Opie, P. *Children's games in street and playground*. Oxford: Clarendon Press, 1969.

OPLER, M.E. The Jicarilla Apache ceremonial relay race. *American Anthropologist*, 1944, **46**, 75-97.

OSTERHOUDT, R.G. The term "sport": Some thoughts on a proper name. *International Journal of Physical Education*, 1977, **14**(2), 11-16.

PATRICK, G.T.W. The psychology of play. *Journal of Genetic Psychology*, 1914, **21**, 469-484.

PELTO, P.J., & Pelto, G.H. *Anthropological research: The structure of inquiry*. Cambridge: Cambridge University Press, 1978. (Originally published, 1970.)

PIAGET, J. [*Play, dreams and imitation in childhood*] (C. Gattegno & F.M. Hodgson, trans.). New York: W.W. Norton, 1962. (Published in English, 1951.)

PLAYGROUND Association of America. *Report of the committee on a normal course in play*, 1909.

POLGAR, S.K. The social context of games: Or when is play not play? *Sociology of Education*, 1976, **49**, 265-271.

POWDERMAKER, H. *Stranger and friend: The way of an anthropologist*. New York: W.W. Norton, 1966.

RABINOW, P. *Reflections on fieldwork in Morocco*. Berkeley: University of California Press, 1977.

RABINOW, P., & Sullivan, W.M. (Eds.). *Interpretive social science: A reader*. Berkeley: University of California Press, 1979.

RALBOVSKY, M. *Destiny's darlings: A world championship Little League team twenty years later*. New York: Hawthorn Books, 1974.

RAPPAPORT, R.A. *Ecology, meaning, and religion*. Richmond, CA: North Atlantic, 1979.

REAL, M.R. Super bowl: Mythic spectacle. *Journal of Communication*, 1975, **25**, 31-43.

ROBERTS, J.M., Arth, M.J., & Bush, R.R. Games in culture. *American Anthropologist*, 1959, **61**(4), 597-605.

ROBERTS, J.M., & Sutton-Smith, B. Child training and game involvement. *Ethnology*, 1962, **1**(2), 166-185.

ROBERTS, R. Jack Dempsey: An American hero in the 1920's. *Journal of Popular Culture*, 1974, **8**, 411-426.

SALAMONE, F.A. Children's games as mechanisms for easing ethnic interaction in ethnically heterogeneous communities: A Nigerian case. *Anthropos*, 1979, **74**, 202-210.

SALTER, M. Meteorological play-forms of the eastern woodlands. In P. Stevens (Ed.), *Studies in the anthropology of play: Papers in memory of B. Allan Tindall.* West Point, NY: Leisure Press, 1977. (Proceedings from the Second Annual Meeting of the Association for the Anthropological Study of Play.)

SCHMITZ, K.L. Sport and play: Suspension of the ordinary. In E.W. Gerber (Ed.), *Sport and the body: A philosophical symposium.* Philadelphia: Lea & Febiger, 1972.

SCHNEIDER, D.M. Notes toward a theory of culture. In K.H. Basso & H.A. Selby (Eds.), *Meaning in anthropology.* Albuquerque: University of New Mexico Press, 1976.

SCHWARTZMAN, H.B. *Transformations: The anthropology of children's play.* New York: Plenum, 1978.

SCOTCH, N.A. Magic, sorcery, and football among the urban Zulu: A case of reinterpretation under acculturation. *Journal of Conflict Resolution*, 1961, **5**(1), 70-74.

SISSON, G. Bibliography of children's plays. *Studies in Education*, 1896, **1**(5), 184-189.

SMITH, G. The sport hero: An endangered species. *Quest*, 1973, **19**, 59-70.

SOCIAL Science Research Council Summer Seminar on Acculturation. Acculturation: An exploratory formulation. *American Anthropologist*, 1954, **56**, 973-1002.

SPRADLEY, J.P. *The ethnographic interview.* New York: Holt, Rinehart & Winston, 1979.

SPRADLEY, J.P. *Participant observation.* New York: Holt, Rinehart & Winston, 1980.

SPRADLEY, J.P., & McCurdy, D.W. *The cultural experience: Ethnography in complex society.* Chicago: Science Research Associates, 1972.

STEIN, M. Cult and sport: The case of Big Red. *Mid-American Review of Sociology*, 1977, **2**(2), 29-42.

STEWART, S. *Nonsense: Aspects of intertextuality in folklore and literature.* Baltimore: The Johns Hopkins University Press, 1979.

STONE, G.P. American sports: Play and display. In E. Dunning (Ed.), *The Sociology of sport.* London: Frank Cass, 1971.

STONE, G.P., & Oldenburg, R.A. In R. Slovenko & J.A. Knight (Eds.), *Motivations in play, games and sports.* Springfield, IL: Charles C. Thomas, 1967.

STUMPF, F., & Cozens, F.W. Hidden possibilities for research in physical education and recreation. *Research Quarterly,* 1947, **18**(2), 104-108. (a)

STUMPF, F., & Cozens, F.W. Some aspects of the role of games, sports, and recreational activities in the culture of modern primitive peoples: I. The New Zealand Maoris. *Research Quarterly,* 1947, **18**(3), 198-218. (b)

STUMPF, F., & Cozens, F.W. Some aspects of the role of games, sports, and recreational activities in the culture of modern primitive peoples: II. The Fijians. *Research Quarterly,* 1949, **20**(1), 2-20.

SUITS, B. *The grasshopper: Games, life and utopia.* Toronto: University of Toronto Press, 1978.

SUTTON-SMITH, B. Games of order and disorder. *The Association for the Anthropological Study of Play Newsletter,* 1977, **4**(2), 19-26.

SUTTON-SMITH, B., Roberts, J.M., & Kozelka, R.M. Game involvement in adults. *Journal of Social Psychology,* 1963, **60**, 15-30.

TAYLOR, I. "Football mad": A speculative sociology of football hooliganism. In E. Dunning (Ed.), *Sport: Readings from a sociological perspective.* Toronto: University of Toronto Press, 1971.

THEODORSON, G.A., & Theodorson, A.G. *A modern dictionary of sociology.* New York: Barnes & Nobel, 1979. (Originally published, 1969.)

TINDALL, A. Ethnography and the hidden curriculum in sport. *Behavioral and Social Science Teacher,* 1975, **2**(2), 5-28.

TOWNSHEND, P. Games of strategy: A new look at correlates and cross-cultural methods. In H.B. Schwartzman (Ed.), *Play and culture: 1978 proceedings of the Association for the Anthropological Study of Play.* West Point, NY: Leisure Press, 1980.

TURNER, V. *The ritual process: Structure and anti-structure.* Chicago: Aldine, 1969.

TURNER, V. Passages, margins, and poverty: Religious symbols of communitas. *Worship,* 1972, **46**(7-8), 390-412; 482-494.

TURNER, V. *Dramas, fields, and metaphors: Symbolic action in human society.* Ithaca: Cornell University Press, 1974. (a)

TURNER V. Liminal to liminoid, in play, flow, and ritual: An essay in comparative symbology. In E. Norbeck (Ed.), *Rice University Studies: The Anthropological Study of Human Play,* 1974, **60**(3), 53-92. (b)

TYLOR, E.B. The history of games. *The Fortnightly Review*, 1879, **25**, 735-747.

VOIGT, D.Q. Myths after baseball: Notes on myths in sports. *Quest*, 1978, **30**, 46-57.

WAX, R.H. *Doing fieldwork: Warnings and advice*. Chicago: University of Chicago Press, 1971.

WEISS, P. *Sport: A philosophic inquiry*. Carbondale: Southern Illinois University Press, 1969.

WILLIAMS, T.R. *Field methods in the study of culture*. New York: Holt, Rinehart & Winston, 1967.

Part 1
Games, Sports, and Interpretations of Cultures

Chapter 1

Deep Play:
Notes on the Balinese Cockfight

CLIFFORD GEERTZ

The Raid

E arly in April of 1958, my wife and I arrived, malarial and diffi-
dent, in a Balinese village we intended, as anthropologists, to
study. A small place, about 500 people, and relatively remote, it was its
own world. We were intruders, professional ones, and the villagers dealt
with us as Balinese seem always to deal with people not part of their life
who yet press themselves upon them: as though we were not there. For
them, and to a degree for ourselves, we were nonpersons, specters, invisible men.

We moved into an extended family compound (that had been arranged
before through the provincial government) belonging to one of the four
major factions in village life. But except for our landlord and the village
chief, whose cousin and brother-in-law he was, everyone ignored us in a

From *Daedalus*, Winter 1972, **101**, 1-37. Copyright 1972 by the American Academy of Arts
and Sciences. Reprinted with permission.

way only a Balinese can do. As we wandered around, uncertain, wistful, eager to please, people seemed to look right through us with a gaze focused several yards behind us on some more actual stone or tree. Almost nobody greeted us; but nobody scowled or said anything unpleasant to us either, which would have been almost as satisfactory. If we ventured to approach someone (something one is powerfully inhibited from doing in such an atmosphere), he moved, negligently but definitively, away. If, seated or leaning against a wall, we had him trapped, he said nothing at all, or mumbled what for the Balinese is the ultimate nonword—"yes." The indifference, of course, was studied; the villagers were watching every move we made and they had an enormous amount of quite accurate information about who we were and what we were going to be doing. But they acted as if we simply did not exist, which, in fact, as this behavior was designed to inform us, we did not, or anyway not yet.

This is, as I say, general in Bali. Everywhere else I have been in Indonesia, and more latterly in Morocco, when I have gone into a new village people have poured out from all sides to take a very close look at me, and, often, an all-too-probing feel as well. In Balinese villages, at least those away from the tourist circuit, nothing happens at all. People go on pounding, chatting, making offerings, staring into space, carrying baskets about while one drifts around feeling vaguely disembodied. And the same thing is true on the individual level. When you first meet a Balinese, he seems virtually not to relate to you at all; he is, in the term Gregory Bateson and Margaret Mead (1942) made famous, "away" (p. 68). Then—in a day, a week, a month (with some people the magic moment never comes)—he decides, for reasons I have never been quite able to fathom, that you *are* real, and then he becomes a warm, gay, sensitive, sympathetic, though, being Balinese, always precisely controlled person. You have crossed, somehow, some moral or metaphysical shadow line. Though you are not exactly taken as a Balinese (one has to be born to that), you are at least regarded as a human being rather than a cloud or a gust of wind. The whole complexion of your relationship dramatically changes to, in the majority of cases, a gentle, almost affectionate one—a low-keyed, rather playful, rather mannered, rather bemused geniality.

My wife and I were still very much in the gust of wind stage, a most frustrating, and even, as you soon begin to doubt whether you are really real after all, unnerving one, when, 10 days or so after our arrival, a large cockfight was held in the public square to raise money for a new school.

Now a few special occasions aside, cockfights are illegal in Bali under the Republic (as, for not altogether unrelated reasons, they were under the Dutch), largely as a result of the pretensions to puritanism radical nationalism tends to bring with it. The elite, which is not itself so very puritan, worries about the poor, ignorant peasant gambling all his money away, about what foreigners will think, about the waste of time better devoted to building up the country. It sees cockfighting as "primitive," "backward," "unprogressive," and generally unbecoming an ambitious nation. And, as with those other embarrassments—opium smoking, begging, or uncovered breasts—it seeks, rather unsystematically, to put a stop to it.

Of course, like drinking during prohibition or, today, smoking marihuana, cockfights, being a part of "The Balinese Way of Life," nonetheless go on happening, and with extraordinary frequency. And, like prohibition or marihuana, from time to time the police (who, in 1958 at least, were almost all not Balinese but Javanese) feel called upon to make a raid, confiscate the cocks and spurs, fine a few people, and even now and then expose some of them in the tropical sun for a day as object lessons which never, somehow, get learned, even though occasionally, quite occasionally, the object dies.

As a result, the fights are usually held in a secluded corner of a village in semisecrecy, a fact which tends to slow the action a little—not very much, but the Balinese do not care to have it slowed at all. In this case, however, perhaps because they were raising money for a school that the government was unable to give them, perhaps because raids had been few recently, perhaps, as I gathered from subsequent discussion, there was a notion that the necessary bribes had been paid, they thought they could take a chance on the central square and draw a larger and more enthusiastic crowd without attracting the attention of the law.

They were wrong. In the midst of the third match, with hundreds of people, including, still transparent, myself and my wife, fused into a single body around the ring, a superorganism in the literal sense, a truck full of policemen armed with machine guns roared up. Amid great screeching cries of "pulisi! pulisi!" from the crowd, the policemen jumped out, and, springing into the center of the ring, began to swing their guns around like gangsters in a motion picture, though not going so far as actually to fire them. The superorganism came instantly apart as its components scattered in all directions. People raced down the road, disappeared head first over walls, scrambled under platforms, folded themselves behind wicker screens, scuttled up coconut trees. Cocks armed with steel spurs sharp enough to cut off a finger or run a hole through a foot were running wildly around. Everything was dust and panic.

On the established anthropological principle, When in Rome, my wife and I decided, only slightly less instantaneously than everyone else, that the thing to do was run too. We ran down the main village street, northward, away from where we were living, for we were on that side of the ring. About half-way down another fugitive ducked suddenly into a compound—his own, it turned out—and we, seeing nothing ahead of us but rice fields, open country, and a very high volcano, followed him. As the three of us came tumbling into the courtyard, his wife, who had apparently been through this sort of thing before, whipped out a table, a tablecloth, three chairs, and three cups of tea, and we all, without any explicit communication whatsoever, sat down, commenced to sip tea, and sought to compose ourselves.

A few moments later, one of the policemen marched importantly into the yard, looking for the village chief. (The chief had not only been at the fight, he had arranged it. When the truck drove up he ran to the river, stripped off his sarong, and plunged in so he could say, when at length they found him sitting there pouring water over his head, that he had been away bathing when the whole affair had occurred and was ignorant of it. They did not believe him and fined him 300 rupiah, which the village raised collectively.) Seeing my wife and I, "White Men," there in the yard, the policeman performed a classic double take. When he found his voice again he asked, approximately, what in the devil did we think we were doing there. Our host of 5 minutes leaped instantly to our defense, producing an impassioned description of who and what we were, so detailed and so accurate that it was my turn, having barely communicated with a living human being save my landlord and the village chief for more than a week, to be astonished. We had a perfect right to be there, he said, looking the Javanese upstart in the eye. We were American professors; the government had cleared us; we were there to study culture; we were going to write a book to tell Americans about Bali. And we had all been there drinking tea and talking about cultural matters all afternoon and did not know anything about any cockfight. Moreover, we had not seen the village chief all day, he must have gone to town. The policeman retreated in rather total disarray. And, after a decent interval, bewildered but relieved to have survived and stayed out of jail, so did we.

The next morning the village was a completely different world for us. Not only were we no longer invisible, we were suddenly the center of all attention, the object of a great outpouring of warmth, interest, and, most especially, amusement. Everyone in the village knew we had fled like everyone else. They asked us about it again and again (I must have told the story, small detail by small detail, 50 times by the end of the day), gently, affectionately, but quite insistently teasing us: "Why didn't you just stand there and tell the police who you were?" "Why didn't you just say you were only watching and not betting?" "Were you really afraid of those little guns?" As always, kinesthetically minded and, even when fleeing for their lives (or, as happened 8 years later, surrendering them), the world's most poised people, they gleefully mimicked, also over and over again, our graceless style of running and what they claimed were our panic-stricken facial expressions. But above all, everyone was extremely pleased and even more surprised that we had not simply "pulled out our papers" (they knew about those too) and asserted our Distinguished Visitor status, but had instead demonstrated our solidarity with what were now our covillagers. (What we had actually demonstrated was our cowardice, but there is fellowship in that too.) Even the Brahmana priest, an old, grave, half-way-to-Heaven type who because of its associations with the underworld would never be involved, even distantly, in a cockfight, and was difficult to approach even to other Balinese, had us called into his courtyard to ask us about what had happened, chuckling happily at the sheer extraordinariness of it all.

In Bali, to be teased is to be accepted. It was the turning point so far as our relationship to the community was concerned, and we were quite literally "in." The whole village opened up to us, probably more than it ever would have otherwise (I might actually never have gotten to that priest, and our accidental host became one of my best informants), and certainly very much faster. Getting caught, or almost caught, in a vice raid is perhaps not a very generalizable recipe for achieving that mysterious necessity of anthropological field work, rapport, but for me it worked very well. It led to a sudden and unusually complete acceptance into a society extremely difficult for outsiders to penetrate. It gave me the kind of immediate, inside-view grasp of an aspect of "peasant mentality" that anthropologists not fortunate enough to flee headlong with their subjects from armed authorities normally do not get. And, perhaps most important of all, for the other things might have come in other ways, it put me very quickly on to a combination emotional explosion, status war, and philosophical drama of central significance to the society whose inner nature I desired to understand. By the time I left I had spent about as much time looking into cockfights as into witchcraft, irrigation, caste, or marriage.

Of Cocks and Men

Bali, mainly because it is Bali, is a well-studied place. Its mythology, art, ritual, social organization, patterns of child rearing, forms of law, even styles of trance, have all been microscopically examined for traces of that elusive substance Jane Belo (1935/1970a) called "The Balinese Temper." But, aside from a few passing remarks, the cockfight has barely been noticed, although as a popular obsession of consuming power it is at least as important a revelation of what being a Balinese "is really like" as these more celebrated phenomena.[1] As much of America surfaces in a ball park, on a golf links, at a race track, or around a poker table, much of Bali surfaces in a cock ring. For it is only apparently cocks that are fighting there. Actually, it is men.

To anyone who has been in Bali any length of time, the deep

psychological identification of Balinese men with their cocks is unmistakable. The double entendre here is deliberate. It works in exactly the same way in Balinese as it does in English, even to producing the same tired jokes, strained puns, and uninventive obscenities. Bateson and Mead (1942, pp. 25-26) have even suggested that, in line with the Balinese conception of the body as a set of separately animated parts, cocks are viewed as detachable, self-operating penises, ambulant genitals with a life of their own.[2] And while I do not have the kind of unconscious material either to confirm or disconfirm this intriguing notion, the fact that they are masculine symbols *par excellence* is about as indubitable, and to the Balinese about as evident, as the fact that water runs downhill.

The language of everyday moralism is shot through, on the male side of it, with roosterish imagery. *Sabung*, the word for cock (and one which appears in inscriptions as early as A.D. 922), is used metaphorically to mean "hero," "warrior," "champion," "man of parts," "political candidate," "bachelor," "dandy," "lady-killer," or "tough guy." A pompous man whose behavior presumes above his station is compared to a tailless cock who struts about as though he had a large, spectacular one. A desperate man who makes a last, irrational effort to extricate himself from an impossible situation is likened to a dying cock who makes one final lunge at his tormentor to drag him along to a common destruction. A stingy man, who promises much, gives little, and begrudges that is compared to a cock which, held by the tail, leaps at another without in fact engaging him. A marriageable young man still shy with the opposite sex or someone in a new job anxious to make a good impression is called "a fighting cock caged for the first time."[3] Court trials, wars, political contests, inheritance disputes, and street arguments are all compared to cockfights.[4] Even the very island itself is perceived from its shape as a small, proud cock, poised, neck extended, back taut, tail raised, in eternal challenge to large, feckless, shapeless Java.[5]

But the intimacy of men with their cocks is more than metaphorical. Balinese men, or anyway a large majority of Balinese men, spend an enormous amount of time with their favorites, grooming them, feeding them, discussing them, trying them out against one another, or just gazing at them with a mixture of rapt admiration and dreamy self-absorption. Whenever you see a group of Balinese men squatting idly in the council shed or along the road in their hips down, shoulders forward, knees up fashion, half or more of them will have a rooster in his hands, holding it between his thighs, bouncing it gently up and down to strengthen its legs, ruffling its feathers with abstract sensuality, pushing it out against a neighbor's rooster to rouse its spirit, withdrawing it toward his loins to calm it again. Now and then, to get a feel for another bird, a man will fiddle this way with someone else's cock for a while, but usually by moving around to squat in place behind it, rather than just having it passed across to him as though it were merely an animal.

In the houseyard, the high-walled enclosures where the people live, fighting cocks are kept in wicker cages, moved frequently about so as to maintain the optimum balance of sun and shade. They are fed a special diet, which varies somewhat according to individual theories but which is mostly maize, sifted for impurities with far more care than it is when mere humans are going to eat it and offered to the animal kernel by kernel. Red pepper is stuffed down their beaks and up their anuses to give them spirit. They are bathed in the same ceremonial preparation of tepid water, medicinal herbs, flowers, and onions in which infants are bathed, and for a prize cock just about as often. Their combs are cropped, their plumage dressed, their spurs trimmed, their legs massaged, and they are inspected for flaws with the squinted concentration of a diamond merchant. A man who has a passion for cocks, an enthusiast in the literal sense of the term, can spend most of his life with them, and even those, the overwhelming majority, whose passion though intense has not entirely run away with them, can and do spend what seems not only to an outsider, but also to themselves, an inordinate amount of time with them. "I am cock crazy," my landlord, a quite ordinary *afficionado* by Balinese standards, used to moan as he went to move another cage, give another bath, or conduct another feeding. "We're all cock crazy."

The madness has some less visible dimensions, however, because although it is true that cocks are symbolic expressions or magnifications of their owner's self, the narcissistic male ego writ out in Aesopian terms, they are also expressions—and rather more immediate ones—of what the Balinese regard as the direct inversion, aesthetically, morally, and metaphysically, of human status: animality.

The Balinese revulsion against any behavior regarded as animal-like can hardly be overstressed. Babies are not allowed to crawl for that reason. Incest, though hardly approved, is a much less horrifying crime than bestiality. (The appropriate punishment for the second is death by drowning, for the first being forced to live like an animal.)[6] Most demons are represented—in sculpture, dance, ritual, myth—in some real or fantastic animal form. The main puberty rite consists in filing the child's teeth so they will not look like animal fangs. Not only defecation but eating is regarded as a disgusting, almost obscene activity, to be conducted hurriedly and privately, because of its association with animality. Even falling down or any form of clumsiness is considered to be bad for these reasons. Aside from cocks and a few domestic animals—oxen, ducks—of no emotional significance, the Balinese are aversive to animals and treat their large number of dogs not merely callously but with a phobic cruelty. In identifying with his cock, the Balinese man is identifying not just with his ideal self, or even his penis, but also, and at the same time, with what he most fears, hates, and ambivalence being what it is, is fascinated by—The Powers of Darkness.

The connection of cocks and cockfighting with such Powers, with the animalistic demons that threaten constantly to invade the small, cleared off space in which the Balinese have so carefully built their lives and devour its inhabitants, is quite explicit. A cockfight, any cockfight, is in the first instance a blood sacrifice offered, with the appropriate chants and oblations, to the demons in order to pacify their ravenous, cannibal hunger. No temple festival should be conducted until one is made. (If it is omitted someone will inevitably fall into a trance and command with the voice of an angered spirit that the oversight be immediately corrected.) Collective responses to natural evils—illness, crop failure, volcanic eruptions—almost always involve them. And that famous holiday in Bali, The Day of Silence *(Njepi)*, when everyone sits silent and immobile all day long in order to avoid contact with a sudden influx of demons chased momentarily out of hell, is preceded the previous day by large-scale cockfights (in this case legal) in almost every village on the island.

In the cockfight, man and beast, good and evil, ego and id, the creative power of aroused masculinity and the destructive power of loosened animality fuse in a bloody drama of hatred, cruelty, violence, and death. It is little wonder that when, as is the invariable rule, the owner of the winning cock takes the carcass of the loser—often torn limb from limb by its enraged owner—home to eat, he does so with a mixture of social embarrassment, moral satisfaction, aesthetic disgust, and cannibal joy. Or that a man who has lost an important fight is sometimes driven to wreck his family shrines and curse the gods, an act of metaphysical (and social) suicide. Or that in seeking earthly analogues for heaven and hell the Balinese compare the former to the mood of a man whose cock has just won, the latter to that of a man whose cock has just lost.

The Fight

Cockfights *(tetadjen; sabungan)* are held in a ring about 50 feet square. Usually they begin toward late afternoon and run 3 or 4 hours until sunset. About 9 or 10 separate matches *(sehet)* comprise a program. Each match is precisely like the others in general pattern: There is no main match, no connection between individual matches, no variation in their format, and each is arranged on a completely ad hoc basis. After a fight has ended and the emotional debris is cleaned away—the bets paid, the curses cursed, the carcasses possessed—seven, eight, perhaps even a dozen men slip negligently into the ring with a cock and seek to find there a logical opponent for it. This process, which rarely takes less than 10 minutes, and often a good deal longer, is conducted in a very subdued, oblique, even dissembling manner. Those not immediately involved give it at best but disguised, sidelong attention; those who, embarrassedly, are, attempt to pretend somehow that the whole thing is not really happening.

A match made, the other hopefuls retire with the same deliberate indifference, and the selected cocks have their spurs *(tadji)* affixed—razor sharp, pointed steel swords, 4 or 5 inches long. This is a delicate job which only a small proportion of men, a half-dozen or so in most villages, know how to do properly. The man who attaches the spurs also provides them, and if the rooster he assists wins its owner awards him the spur-leg of the victim. The spurs are affixed by winding a long length of string around the foot of the spur and the leg of the cock. For reasons I shall come to presently, it is done somewhat differently from case to case, and is an obsessively deliberate affair. The lore about spurs is extensive—they are sharpened only at eclipses and the dark of the moon, should be kept out of the sight of women, and so forth. And they are handled, both in use and out, with the same curious combination of fussiness and sensuality the Balinese direct toward ritual objects generally.

The spurs affixed, the two cocks are placed by their handlers (who may or may not be their owners) facing one another in the center of the ring.[7] A coconut pierced with a small hole is placed in a pail of water, in which it takes about 21 seconds to sink, a period known as a *tjeng* and marked at beginning and end by the beating of a slit gong. During these 21 seconds the handlers *(pengangkeb)* are not permitted to touch their roosters. If, as sometimes happens, the animals have not fought during this time, they are picked up, fluffed, pulled, prodded, and otherwise insulted, and put back in the center of the ring and the process begins again. Sometimes they refuse to fight at all, or one keeps running away, in which case they are imprisoned together under a wicker cage, which usually gets them engaged.

Most of the time, in any case, the cocks fly almost immediately at one another in a wing-beating, head-thrusting, leg-kicking explosion of animal fury so pure, so absolute, and in its own way so beautiful, as to be almost abstract, a Platonic concept of hate. Within moments one or the other drives home a solid blow with his spur. The handler whose cock has delivered the blow immediately picks it up so that it will not get a return blow, for if he does not the match is likely to end in a mutually mortal tie as the two birds wildly hack each other to pieces. This is particularly true if, as often happens, the spur sticks in its victim's body, for then the aggressor is at the mercy of his wounded foe.

With the birds again in the hands of their handlers, the coconut is now sunk three times after which the cock which has landed the blow must be set down to show that he is firm, a fact he demonstrates by wandering idly around the rink for a coconut sink. The coconut is then sunk twice more and the fight must recommence.

During this interval, slightly over 2 minutes, the handler of the wounded cock has been working frantically over it, like a trainer patching a mauled boxer between rounds, putting the whole chicken head in his own mouth and sucking and blowing, fluffs it, stuffs its wounds with various sorts of medicines, and generally tries anything he can think of to arouse the last ounce of spirit which may be hidden somewhere within it. By the time he is forced to put it back down he is usually drenched in chicken blood, but, as in prize fighting, a good handler is worth his weight in gold. Some of them can virtually make the dead walk, at least long enough for the second and final round.

In the climactic battle (if there is one; sometimes the wounded cock simply expires in the handler's hands or immediately as it is placed down again), the cock who landed the first blow usually proceeds to finish off his weakened opponent. But this is far from an inevitable outcome, for if a cock can walk he can fight, and if he can fight, he can kill, and what counts is which cock expires first. If the wounded one can get a stab in and stagger on until the other drops, he is the official winner, even if he himself topples over an instant later.

Surrounding all this melodrama—which the crowd packed tight around the ring follows in near silence, moving their bodies in kinesthetic sympathy with the movement of the animals, cheering their champions on with wordless hand motions, shiftings of the shoulders, turnings of the head, falling back *en masse* as the cock with the murderous spurs careens toward one side of the ring (it is said that spectators sometimes lose eyes and fingers from being too attentive), surging forward again as they glance off toward another—is a vast body of extraordinarily elaborate and precisely detailed rules.

These rules, together with the developed lore of cocks and cockfighting which accompanies them, are written down in palm leaf manuscripts *(lontar; rontal)* passed on from generation to generation as part of the general legal and cultural tradition of the villages. At a fight, the umpire *(saja komong; djuru kembar)*—the man who manages the coconut—is in charge of their application and his authority is absolute. I have never seen an umpire's judgment questioned on any subject, even by the more despondent losers, nor have I ever heard, even in private, a charge of unfairness directed against one, or, for that matter, complaints about umpires in general. Only exceptionally well-trusted, solid, and, given the complexity of the code, knowledgeable citizens perform this job, and in fact men will bring their cocks only to fights presided over by such men. It is also the umpire to whom accusations of cheating, which, though rare in the extreme, occasionally arise, are referred; and it is he who in the not infrequent cases where the cocks expire virtually together decides which (if either, for, though the Balinese do not care for such an outcome, there can be ties) went first. Likened to a judge, a king, a priest, and a policeman, he is all of these, and under his assured direction the animal passion of the fight proceeds within the civic certainty of the law. In the dozens of cockfights I saw in Bali, I never once saw an altercation about rules. Indeed, I never saw an open altercation, other than those between cocks, at all.

This crosswise doubleness of an event which, taken as a fact of nature, is rage untrammeled and, taken as a fact of culture, is form perfected, defines the cockfight as a sociological entity. A cockfight is what, searching for a name for something not vertebrate enough to be called a group and not structureless enough to be called a crowd, Erving Goffman (1961, pp. 9-10) has called a "focused gathering"—a set of persons engrossed in a common flow of activity and relating to one another in terms of that flow. Such gatherings meet and disperse; the participants in them fluctuate; the activity that focuses them is discreet—a particulate process that reoccurs rather than a continuous one that endures. They take their form from the situation that evokes them, the floor on which they are placed, as Goffman puts it; but it is a form, and an articulate one, nonetheless. For the situation, the floor is itself created, in jury deliberations, surgical operations, block meetings, sit-ins, cockfights, by the cultural preoccupations—here, as we shall see, the celebration of status rivalry—which not only specify the focus but, assembling actors and arranging scenery, bring it actually into being.

In classical times (that is to say, prior to the Dutch invasion of 1908), when there were no bureaucrats around to improve popular morality, the staging of a cockfight was an explicitly societal matter. Bringing a cock to an important fight was, for an adult male, a compulsory duty of citizenship; taxation of fights, which were usually held on market day, was a major source of public revenue; patronage of the art was a stated responsibility of princes; and the cock ring, or *wantilan*, stood in the center of the village near those other monuments of Balinese civility—the council house, the origin temple, the marketplace, the signal tower, and the banyan tree. Today, a few special occasions aside, the newer rectitude makes so open a statement of the connection between the excitements of collective life and those of blood sport impossible, but, less directly expressed, the connection itself remains intimate and intact. To expose it, however, it is necessary to turn to the aspect of cockfighting around which all the others pivot, and through which they exercise their force, an aspect I have thus far studiously ignored. I mean, of course, the gambling.

Odds and Even Money

The Balinese never do anything in a simple way that they can contrive to do in a complicated one, and to this generalization cockfight wagering is no exception.

In the first place, there are two sorts of bets, or *toh*.[8] There is the single axial bet in the center between the principals *(toh ketengah)*, and there is the cloud of peripheral ones around the ring between members of the audience *(toh kesasi)*. The first is typically large; the second typically small. The first is collective, involving coalitions of bettors clustering around the owner; the second is individual, man to man. The first is a matter of deliberate, very quiet, almost furtive arrangement by the coalition members and the umpire huddled like conspirators in the center of the ring; the second is a matter of impulsive shouting, public offers, and public acceptances by the excited throng around its edges. And most curiously, and as we shall see most revealingly, *where the first is always, without exception, even money, the second, equally without exception, is never such.* What is a fair coin in the center is a biased one on the side.

The center bet is the offical one, hedged in again with a webwork of rules, and is made between the two cock owners, with the umpire as overseer and public witness.[9] This bet, which, as I say, is always relatively and sometimes very large, is never raised simply by the owner in whose name it is made, but by him together with four or five, sometimes seven or eight, allies—kin, village mates, neighbors, close friends. He may, if he is not especially well-to-do, not even be the major contributor, though if only to show that he is not involved in any chicanery, he must be a significant one.

Of the 57 matches for which I have exact and reliable data on the center bet, the range is from 15 ringgits to 500, with a mean at 85 and with the distribution being rather noticeably trimodal: small fights (15 ringgits either side of 35) accounting for about 45% of the total number; medium ones (20 ringgits either side of 70) for about 25%; and large (75 ringgits either side of 175) for about 20%, with a few very small and very large ones out at the extremes. In a society where the normal daily wage of a manual laborer—a brickmaker, an ordinary farmworker, a market porter—was about three ringgits a day, and considering the fact that fights were held on the average about every 2½ days in the immediate area I studied, this is clearly serious gambling, even if the bets are pooled rather than individual efforts.

The side bets are, however, something else altogether. Rather than the solemn, legalistic pactmaking of the center, wagering takes place rather in the fashion in which the stock exchange used to work when it was out on the curb. There is a fixed and known odds paradigm which runs in a continuous series from ten-to-nine at the short end to two-to-one at the long: 10-9, 9-8, 8-7, 7-6, 6-5, 5-4, 4-3, 3-2, 2-1. The man who wishes to back the *underdog cock* (leaving aside how favorites, *kebut*, and underdogs, *ngai*, are established for the moment) shouts the short-side number indicating the odds he wants *to be given*. That is, if he shouts *gasal*, "five," he wants the underdog at five-to-four (or, for him, four-to-five); if he shouts "four," he wants it at four-to-three (again, he putting up the "three"), if "nine," at nine-to-eight, and so on. A man backing the favorite, and thus considering giving odds if he can get them short enough, indicates the fact by crying out the color-type of that cock— "brown," "speckled," or whatever.[10]

As odds-takers (backers of the underdog) and odds-givers (backers of the favorite) sweep the crowd with their shouts, they begin to focus in on one another as potential betting pairs, often from far across the ring. The taker tries to shout the giver into longer odds, the giver to shout the taker into shorter ones.[11] The taker, who is the wooer in this situation, will signal how large a bet he wishes to make at the odds he is shouting by holding a number of fingers up in front of his face and vigorously waving them. If the giver, the wooed, replies in kind, the bet is made; if he does not, they unlock gazes and the search goes on.

The side betting, which takes place after the center bet has been made and its size announced, consists then in a rising crescendo of shouts as backers of the underdog offer their propositions to anyone who will accept them, while those who are backing the favorite but do not like the price being offered, shout equally frenetically the color of the cock to show they too are desperate to bet but want shorter odds.

Almost always odds-calling, which tends to be very consensual in that at any one time almost all callers are calling the same thing, starts off toward the long end of the range—five-to-four or four-to-three—and then moves, also consensually, toward the short end with greater or lesser speed and to a greater or lesser degree. Men crying "five" and finding themselves answered only with cries of "brown" start crying "six," either drawing the other callers fairly quickly with them or retiring from the scene as their too-generous offers are snapped up. If the change is made and partners are still scarce, the procedure is repeated in a move to "seven," and so on, only rarely, and in the very largest fights, reaching the ultimate "nine" or "ten" levels. Occasionally, if the cocks are clearly mismatched, there may be no upward movement at all, or even a movement down the scale to four-to-three, three-to-two, very, very rarely two-to-one, a shift which is accompanied by a declining number of bets as a shift upward is accompanied by an increasing number. But the general pattern is for the betting to move a shorter or longer distance up the scale toward the, for sidebets, nonexistent pole of even money, with the overwhelming majority of bets falling in the four-to-three to eight-to-seven range.[12]

As the moment for the release of the cocks by the handlers approaches, the screaming, at least in a match where the center bet is large, reaches almost frenzied proportions as the remaining unfulfilled bettors try desperately to find a last minute partner at a price they can live with. (Where the center bet is small, the opposite tends to occur: betting dies off, trailing into silence, as odds lengthen and people lose interest.) In a large-bet, well-made match—the kind of match the Balinese regard as "real cockfighting"—the mob scene quality, the sense that sheer chaos is about to break loose, with all those waving, shouting, pushing, clambering men is quite strong, an effect which is only heightened by the intense stillness that falls with instant suddenness, rather as if someone had turned off the current, when the slit gong sounds, the cocks are put down, and the battle begins.

When it ends, anywhere from 15 seconds to 5 minutes later, *all bets are immediately paid*. There are absolutely no IOUs, at least to a betting opponent. One may, of course, borrow from a friend before offering or accepting a wager, but to offer or accept it you must have the money already in hand and, if you lose, you must pay it on the spot, before the next match begins. This is an iron rule, and as I have never heard of a disputed umpire's decision (though doubtless there must sometimes be some), I have also never heard of a welshed bet, perhaps because in a worked-up cockfight crowd the consequences might be, as they are reported to be sometimes for cheaters, drastic and immediate.

It is, in any case, this formal assymetry between balanced center bets and unbalanced side ones that poses the critical analytical problem for a theory which sees cockfight wagering as the link connecting the fight to the wider world of Balinese culture. It also suggests the way to go about solving it and demonstrating the link.

The first point that needs to be made in this connection is that the higher the center bet, the more likely the match will in actual fact be an even one. Simple considerations of rationality suggest that. If you are betting 15 ringgits on a cock, you might be willing to go along with even money even if you feel your animal somewhat the less promising. But if you are betting 500 you are very, very likely to be loathe to do so. Thus, in large-bet fights, which of course involve the better animals, tremendous care is taken to see that the cocks are about as evenly matched as to size, general condition, pugnacity, and so on as is humanly possible. The different ways of adjusting the spurs of the animals are often employed to secure this. If one cock seems stronger, an agreement will be made to position his spur at a slightly less advantageous angle—a kind of handicapping, at which spur affixers are, so it is said, extremely skilled. More care will be taken, too, to employ skillful handlers and to match them exactly as to abilities.

In short, in a large-bet fight the pressure to make the match a genuinely 50-50 proposition is enormous, and is consciously felt as such. For medium fights the pressure is somewhat less, and for small ones less yet, though there is always an effort to make things at least approximately equal, for even at 15 ringgits (5 days work) no one wants to make an even money bet in a clearly unfavorable situation. And, again, what statistics I have tend to bear this out. In my 57 matches, the favorite won 33 times over-all, the underdog 24, a 1.4 to 1 ratio. But if one splits the figures at 60 ringgits center bets, the ratios turn out to be 1.1 to 1 (12 favorites, 11 underdogs) for those above this line, and 1.6 to 1 (21 and 13) for those below it. Or, if you take the extremes, for very large fights, those with center bets over a hundred ringgits the ratio is 1 to 1 (7 and 7); for very small fights, those under 40 ringgits, it is 1.9 to 1 (19 and 10).[13]

Now, from this proposition—that the higher the center bet the more exactly a 50-50 proposition the cockfight is—two things more or less immediately follow: (a) the higher the center bet, the greater is the pull on the side betting toward the short-odds end of the wagering spectrum and vice versa; (b) the higher the center bet, the greater the volume of side betting and vice versa.

The logic is similar in both cases. The closer the fight is in fact to even money, the less attractive the long end of the odds will appear and, therefore, the shorter it must be if there are to be takers. That this is the case is apparent from mere inspection, from the Balinese's own analysis of the matter, and from what more systematic observations I was able to collect. Given the difficulty of making precise and complete recordings of side betting, this argument is hard to cast in numerical form, but in all my cases the odds-giver, odds-taker consensual point, a quite pronounced minimax saddle where the bulk (at a guess, two-thirds to three-quarters in most cases) of the bets are actually made, was three or four points further along the scale toward the shorter end for the large-center-bet fights than for the small ones, with medium ones generally in between. In detail, the fit is not, of course, exact, but the general pattern is quite consistent: The power of the center bet to pull the side bets toward its own even-money pattern is directly proportional to its size, because its size is directly proportional to the degree to which the cocks are in fact evenly matched. As for the volume question, total wagering is greater in large-center-bet fights because such fights are considered more "interesting," not only in the sense that they are less predictable, but, more crucially, that more is at stake in them—in terms of money, in terms of the quality of the cocks, and consequently, as we shall see, in terms of social prestige.[14]

The paradox of fair coin in the middle, biased coin on the outside is thus a merely apparent one. The two betting systems, though formally incongruent, are not really contradictory to one another, but part of a single larger system in which the center bet is, so to speak, the "center of gravity," drawing, the larger it is the more so, the outside bets toward the short-odds end of the scale. The center bet thus "makes the game," or perhaps better, defines it, signals what, following a notion of Jeremy Bentham's, I am going to call its "depth."

The Balinese attempt to create an interesting, if you will, "deep," match by making the center bet as large as possible so that the cocks matched will be as equal and as fine as possible, and the outcome, thus, as unpredictable as possible. They do not always succeed. Nearly half the matches are relatively trivial, relatively uninteresting—in my borrowed terminology, "shallow"—affairs. But that fact no more argues against my interpretation than the fact that most painters, poets, and play-wrights are mediocre aruges against the view that artistic effort is directed toward profundity and, with a certain frequency, approximates it. The image of artistic technique is indeed exact: The center bet is a means, a device, for creating "interesting," "deep" matches, *not* the reason, or at least not the main reason, *why* they are interesting, the source of their fascination, the substance of their depth. The question why such matches are interesting—indeed, for the Balinese, exquisitely absorbing—takes us out of the realm of formal concerns into more broadly sociological and social-psychological ones, and to a less purely economic idea of what "depth" in gaming amounts to.[15]

Playing with Fire

Bentham's (1931) concept of "deep play" is found in his *The Theory of Legislation*.[16] By it he means play in which the stakes are so high that it is, from his utilitarian standpoint, irrational for men to engage in it at all. If a man whose fortune is a thousand pounds (or ringgits) wages 500 of it on an even bet, the marginal utility of the pound he stands to win is clearly less than the marginal disutility of the one he stands to lose. In genuine deep play, this is the case for both parties. They are both in over their heads. Having come together in search of pleasure they have entered into a relationship which will bring the participants, considered collectively, net pain rather than net pleasure. Bentham's conclusion was, therefore, that deep play was immoral from first principles and, a typical step for him, should be prevented legally.

But more interesting than the ethical problem, at least for our concerns here, is that despite the logical force of Bentham's analysis men do engage in such play, both passionately and often, and even in the face of law's revenge. For Bentham and those who think as he does (nowdays mainly lawyers, economists, and a few psychiatrists), the explanation is, as I have said, that such men are irrational—addicts, fetishists, children, fools, savages, who need only to be protected against themselves. But for the Balinese, though naturally they do not formulate it in so many words, the explanation lies in the fact that in such play money is less a measure of utility, had or expected, than it is a symbol of moral import, perceived or imposed.

It is, in fact, in shallow games, ones in which smaller amounts of money are involved, that increments and decrements of cash are more nearly synonyms for utility and disutility, in the ordinary, unexpanded sense—for pleasure and pain, happiness and unhappiness. In deep ones, where the amounts of money are great, much more is at stake than material gain: namely, esteem, honor, dignity, respect—in a word, though in Bali a profoundly freighted word, status.[17] It is at stake symbolically, for (a few cases of ruined addict gamblers aside) no one's status is actually altered by the outcome of a cockfight; it is only, and that momentarily, affirmed or insulted. But for the Balinese, for whom nothing is more pleasurable than an affront obliquely delivered or more painful than one obliquely received—particularly when mutual acquaintances, undeceived by surfaces, are watching—such appraisive drama is deep indeed.

This, I must stress immediately, is *not* to say that the money does not matter, or that the Balinese is no more concerned about losing 500 ringgits than 15. Such a conclusion would be absurd. It is because money *does*, in this hardly unmaterialistic society, matter and matter very much that the more of it one risks the more of a lot of other things, such as one's pride, one's poise, one's dispassion, one's masculinity, one also risks, again only momentarily but again very publicly as well. In deep cockfights an owner and his collaborators, and, as we shall see, to a lesser but still quite real extent also their backers on the outside, put their money where their status is.

It is in large part *because* the marginal disutility of loss is so great at the higher levels of betting that to engage in such betting is to lay one's public self, allusively and metaphorically, through the medium of one's cock, on the line. And though to a Benthamite this might seem merely to increase the irrationality of the enterprise that much further, to the Balinese what it mainly increases is the meaningfulness of it all. And as (to follow Weber rather than Bentham) the imposition of meaning on life is the major end and primary condition of human existence, that access of significance more than compensates for the economic costs involved.[18] Actually, given the even-money quality of the larger matches, important changes in material fortune among those who regularly participate in them seem virtually nonexistent, because matters more or less even out over the long run. It is, actually, in the smaller, shallow fights, where one finds the handful of more pure, addict-type gamblers involved—those who *are* in it mainly for the money—that "real" changes in social position, largely downward, are affected. Men of this sort, plungers, are highly dispraised by "true cockfighters" as fools who do not understand what the sport is all about, vulgarians who simply miss the point of it all. They are, these addicts, regarded as fair game for the genuine enthusiasts, those who do understand, to take a little money away from, something that is easy enough to do by luring them, through the force of their greed, into irrational bets on mismatched cocks. Most of them do indeed manage to ruin themselves in a remarkably short time, but there always seems to be one or two of them around, pawning their land and selling their clothes in order to bet, at any particular time.[19]

This graduated correlation of "status gambling" with deeper fights and, inversely, "money gambling" with shallower ones is in fact quite general. Bettors themselves form a sociomoral hierarchy in these terms. As noted earlier, at most cockfights there are, around the very edges of the cockfight area, a large number of mindless, sheer-chance type gambling games (roulette, dice throw, coin-spin, pea-under-the-shell) operated by concessionaires. Only women, children, adolescents, and various other sorts of people who do not (or not yet) fight cocks—the extremely poor, the socially despised, the personally idiosyncratic—play at these games, at, of course, penny ante levels. Cockfighting men would be ashamed to go anywhere near them. Slightly above these people in standing are those who, though they do not themselves fight cocks, bet on the smaller matches around the edges. Next, there are those who fight cocks in small, or occasionally medium matches, but have not the status to join in the large ones, though they may bet from time to time on the side in those. And finally, there are those, the really substantial members of the community, the solid citizenry around whom local life revolves, who fight in the larger fights and bet on them around the side. The focusing element in these focused gatherings, these men generally dominate and define the sport as they dominate and define society. When a Balinese male talks, in that almost venerative way, about "the true cockfighter," the *bebatoh* ("bettor") or *djuru kurung* ("cage keeper"), it is this sort of person, not those who bring the mentality of the pea-and-shell game into the quite different, inappropriate context of the cockfight, the driven gambler (*potét*, a word which has the secondary meaning of thief or reprobate), and the wistful hanger-on, that they mean. For such a man, what is really going on in a match is something rather closer to an *affaire d'honneur* (though, with the Balinese talent for practical fantasy, the blood that is spilled is only figuratively human) than to the stupid, mechanical crank of a slot machine.

What makes Balinese cockfighting deep is thus not money in itself, but what, the more of it that is involved the more so, money causes to happen: the migration of the Balinese status hierarchy into the body of the cockfight. Psychologically an Aesopian representation of the ideal/demonic, rather narcissistic, male self, sociologically it is an equally Aesopian representation of the complex fields of tension set up by the controlled, muted, ceremonial, but for all that deeply felt, interaction of those selves in the context of everyday life. The cocks may be surrogates for their owners' personalities, animal mirrors of psychic form, but the cockfight is—or more exactly, deliberately is made to be—a simulation of the social matrix, the involved system of crosscutting, overlapping, highly corporate groups—villages, kingroups, irrigation societies, temple congregations, "castes"—in which its devotees live.[20] And as prestige, the necessity to affirm it, defend it, celebrate it, justify it, and just plain bask in it (but not, given the strongly ascriptive character of Balinese stratification, to seek it), is perhaps the central driving force in the society, so also—ambulant penises, blood sacrifices, and monetary exchanges aside—is it of the cockfight. This apparent amusement and seeming sport is, to take another phrase from Erving Goffman, "a status blood-bath" (1961, p. 78).

The easiest way to make this clear, and at least to some degree to demonstrate it, is to invoke the village whose cockfighting activities I observed the closest—the one in which the raid occurred and from which my statistical data are taken.

As all Balinese villages, this one—Tihingan, in the Klungkung region of southeast Bali—is intricately organized, a labyrinth of alliances and oppositions. But, unlike many, two sorts of corporate groups, which are also status groups, particularly stand out, and we may concentrate on them, in a part-for-whole way, without undue distortion.

First, the village is dominated by four large, patrilineal, partly endogamous descent groups which are constantly vying with one another and form the major factions in the village. Sometimes they group two and two, or rather the two larger ones versus the two smaller ones plus all the unaffiliated people; sometimes they operate independently. There are also subfactions within them, subfactions within the subfactions, and so on to rather fine levels of distinction. And second, there is the village itself, almost entirely endogamous, which is opposed to all the other villages round about in its cockfight circuit (which, as explained, is the market region), but which also forms alliances with certain of these neighbors against certain others in various supravillage political and social contexts. The exact situation is thus, as everywhere in Bali, quite distinctive; but the general pattern of a tiered hierarchy of status rivalries between highly corporate but various based groupings (and, thus, between the members of them) is entirely general.

Consider, then, as support of the general thesis that the cockfight, and especially the deep cockfight, is fundamentally a dramatization of status concerns, the following facts, which to avoid extended ethnographic description I will simply pronounce to be facts—though the concrete evidence-examples, statements, and numbers that could be brought to bear in support of them is both extensive and unmistakable:

1. A man virtually never bets against a cock owned by a member of his own kingroup. Usually he will feel obliged to bet for it, the more so the closer the kin tie and the deeper the fight. If he is certain in his mind that it will not win, he may just not bet at all, particularly if it is only a second cousin's bird or if the fight is a shallow one. But as a rule he will feel he must support it and, in deep games, nearly always does. Thus the great majority of the people calling "five" or "speckled" so demonstratively are expressing their allegiance to their kinsman, not their evaluation of his bird, their understanding of probability theory, or even their hopes of unearned income.

2. This principle is extended logically. If your kingroup is not involved you will support an allied kingroup against an unallied one in the same way, and so on through the very involved networks of alliances which, as I say, make up this, as any other, Balinese village.

3. So, too, for the village as a whole. If an outsider cock is fighting any cock from your village you will tend to support the local one. If, what is a rarer circumstance but occurs every now and then, a cock from outside your cockfight circuit is fighting one inside it you will also tend to support the "home bird."

4. Cocks which come from any distance are almost always favorites, for the theory is the man would not have dared to bring it if it was not a good cock, the more so the further he has come. His followers are, of course, obliged to support him, and when the more grand-scale legal cockfights are held (on holidays, and so on) the people of the village take what they regard to be the best cocks in the village, regardless of ownership, and go off to support them, although they will almost certainly have to give odds on them and to make large bets to show that they are not a cheapskate village. Actually, such "away games," though infrequent, tend to mend the ruptures between village members that the constantly occurring "home games," where village factions are opposed rather than united, exacerbate.

5. Almost all matches are sociologically relevant. You seldom get two outsider cocks fighting, or two cocks with no particular group backing, or with group backing which is mutually unrelated in any clear way. When you do get them, the game is very shallow, betting very slow, and the whole thing very dull, with no one save the immediate principals and an addict gambler or two at all interested.

6. By the same token, you rarely get two cocks from the same group, even more rarely from the same subfaction, and virtually never from the same sub-subfaction (which would be in most cases one extended family) fighting. Similarly, in outside village fights two members of the village will rarely fight against one another, even though, as bitter rivals, they would do so with enthusiasm on their home grounds.

7. On the individual level, people involved in an institutionalized

hostility relationship, called *puik*, in which they do not speak or otherwise have anything to do with each other (the causes of this formal breaking of relations are many: wife-capture, inheritance arguments, political differences) will bet very heavily, sometimes almost maniacally, against one another in what is a frank and direct attack on the very masculinity, the ultimate ground of his status, of the opponent.

8. The center bet coalition is, in all but the shallowest games, *always* made up by structural allies—no "outside money" is involved. What is "outside" depends upon the context, of course, but given it, no outside money is mixed in with the main bet; if the principals cannot raise it, it is not made. The center bet, again especially in deeper games, is thus the most direct and open expression of social opposition, which is one of the reasons why both it and match making are surrounded by such an air of unease, furtiveness, embarrassment, and so on.

9. The rule about borrowing money—that you may borrow *for* a bet but not *in* one—stems (and the Balinese are quite conscious of this) from similar considerations: You are never at the *economic* mercy of your enemy that way. Gambling debts, which can get quite large on a rather short-term basis, are always to friends, never to enemies, structurally speaking.

10. When two cocks are structurally irrelevant or neutral so far as *you* are concerned (though, as mentioned, they almost never are to each other) you do not even ask a relative or a friend whom he is betting on, because if you know how he is betting and he knows you know, and you go the other way, it will lead to strain. This rule is explicit and rigid; fairly elaborate, even rather artificial precautions are taken to avoid breaking it. At the very least you must pretend not to notice what he is doing, and he what you are doing.

11. There is a special word for betting against the grain, which is also the word for "pardon me" *(mpura)*. It is considered a bad thing to do, though if the center bet is small it is sometimes all right as long as you do not do it too often. But the larger the bet and the more frequently you do it, the more the "pardon me" tack will lead to social disruption.

12. In fact, the institutionalized hostility relation, *puik*, is often formally initiated (though its causes always lie elsewhere) by such a "pardon me" bet in a deep fight, putting the symbolic fat in the fire. Similarly, the end of such a relationship and resumption of normal social intercourse is often signalized (but, again, not actually brought about) by one or the other of the enemies supporting the other's bird.

13. In sticky, cross-loyalty situations, of which in this extraordinarily complex social system there are of course many, where a man is caught between two more or less equally balanced loyalties, he tends to wander off for a cup of coffee or something to avoid having to bet, a form of behavior reminiscent of that of American voters in similar situations

(Berelson, Lazersfeld, & McPhee, 1954).

14. The people involved in the center bet are, especially in deep fights, virtually always leading members of their group—kinship, village, or whatever. Further, those who bet on the side (including these people) are, as I have already remarked, the more established members of the village—the solid citizens. Cockfighting is for those who are involved in the everyday politics of prestige as well, not for youth, women, subordinates, and so forth.

15. So far as money is concerned, the explicitly expressed attitude toward it is that it is a secondary matter. It is not, as I have said, of no importance; Balinese are no happier to lose several weeks' income than anyone else. But they mainly look on the monetary aspects of the cockfight as self-balancing, a matter of just moving money around, circulating it among a fairly well-defined group of serious cockfighters. The really important wins and losses are seen mostly in other terms, and the general attitude toward wagering is not any hope of cleaning up, of making a killing (addict gamblers again excepted), but that of the horseplayer's prayer: "Oh, God, please let me break even." In prestige terms, however, you do not want to break even, but, in a momentary, punctuate sort of way, win utterly. The talk (which goes on all the time) is about fights against such-and-such a cock of So-and-So which your cock demolished, not on how much you won, a fact people, even for large bets, rarely remember for any length of time, though they will remember the day they did in Pan Loh's finest cock for years.

16. You must bet on cocks of your own group aside from mere loyalty considerations, for if you do not people generally will say, "What! Is he too proud for the likes of us? Does he have to go to Java or Den Pasar [the capital town] to bet, he is such an important man?" Thus there is a general pressure to bet not only to show that you are important locally, but that you are not so important that you look down on everyone else as unfit even to be rivals. Similarly, home team people must bet against outside cocks or the outsiders will accuse it—a serious charge—of just collecting entry fees and not really being interested in cockfighting, as well as again being arrogant and insulting.

17. Finally, the Balinese peasants themselves are quite aware of all this and can and, at least to an ethnographer, do state most of it in approximately the same terms as I have. Fighting cocks, almost every Balinese I have ever discussed the subject with has said, is like playing with fire only not getting burned. You activate village and kingroup rivalries and hostilities, but in "play" form, coming dangerously and entrancingly close to the expression of open and direct interpersonal and intergroup aggression (something which, again, almost never happens in the normal course of ordinary life), but not quite, because, after all, it is "only a cockfight."

More observations of this sort could be advanced, but perhaps the general point is, if not made, at least well-delineated, and the whole argument thus far can be usefully summarized in a formal paradigm:

THE MORE A MATCH IS . . .

1. Between near status equals (and/or personal enemies)
2. Between high status individuals

THE DEEPER THE MATCH.

THE DEEPER THE MATCH . . .

1. The closer the identification of cock and man (or: more properly, the deeper the match the more the man will advance his best, most closely-identified-with cock).
2. The finer the cocks involved and the more exactly they will be matched.
3. The greater the emotion that will be involved and the more the general absorption in the match.
4. The higher the individual bets center and outside, the shorter the outside bet odds will tend to be, and the more betting there will be over-all.
5. The less an "economic" and the more a "status" view of gaming will be involved, and the "solider" the citizens who will be gaming.[21]

Inverse arguments hold for the shallower the fight, culminating, in a reversed-signs sense, in the coin-spinning and dice-throwing amusements. For deep fights there are no absolute upper limits, though there are of course practical ones, and there are a great many legend-like tales of great Duel-in-the-Sun combats between lords and princes in classical times (for cockfighting has always been as much an elite concern as a popular one), far deeper than anything anyone, even aristocrats, could produce today anywhere in Bali.

Indeed, one of the great culture heroes of Bali is a prince, called after his passion for the sport, "The Cockfighter," who happened to be away at a very deep cockfight with a neighboring prince when the whole of his family—father, brothers, wives, sisters—were assassinated by commoner usurpers. Thus spared, he returned to dispatch the upstarts, regain the throne, reconstitute the Balinese high tradition, and build its most powerful, glorious, and prosperous state. Along with everything else that the Balinese see in fighting cocks—themselves, their social order, abstract hatred, masculinity, demonic power—they also see the archetype of status virtue, the arrogant, resolute, honor-mad player with real fire, the ksatria prince.[22]

Feathers, Blood, Crowds, and Money

"Poetry makes nothing happen," Auden says in his elegy of Yeats, "it survives in the valley of its saying . . . a way of happening, a mouth." The cockfight too, in this colloquial sense, makes nothing happen. Men go on allegorically humiliating one another and being allegorically humiliated by one another, day after day, glorying quietly in the experience if they have triumphed, crushed only slightly more openly by it if they have not. *But no one's status really changes.* You cannot ascend the status ladder by winning cockfights; you cannot, as an individual, really ascend it at all. Nor can you descend it that way.[23] All you can do is enjoy and savor, or suffer and withstand, the concocted sensation of drastic and momentary movement along an aesthetic semblance of that ladder, a kind of behind-the-mirror status jump which has the look of mobility without its actuality.

As any art form—for that, finally, is what we are dealing with—the cockfight renders ordinary, everyday experience comprehensible by presenting it in terms of acts and objects which have had their practical consequences removed and been reduced (or, if you prefer, raised) to the level of sheer appearances, where their meaning can be more powerfully articulated and more exactly perceived. The cockfight is "really real" only to the cocks—it does not kill anyone, castrate anyone, reduce anyone to animal status, alter the hierarchical relations among people, nor refashion the hierarchy; it does not even redistribute income in any significant way. What it does is what, for other peoples with other temperaments and other conventions, *Lear* and *Crime and Punishment* do; it catches up these themes—death, masculinity, rage, pride, loss, beneficence, chance—and, ordering them into an encompassing structure, presents them in such a way as to throw into relief a particular view of their essential nature. It puts a construction on them, makes them, to those historically positioned to appreciate the construction, meaningful—visible, tangible, graspable—"real," in an ideational sense. An image, fiction, a model, a metaphor, the cockfight is a means of expression; its function is neither to assuage social passions nor to heighten them (though, in its play-with-fire way, it does a bit of both), but, in a medium of feathers, blood, crowds, and money, to display them.

The question of how it is that we perceive qualities in things—paintings, books, melodies, plays—that we do not feel we can assert literally to be there has come, in recent years, into the very center of aesthetic theory.[24] Neither the sentiments of the artist, which remain his, nor those of the audience, which remain theirs, can account for the agitation of one painting or the serenity of another. We attribute grandeur, wit, despair, exuberance to strings of sounds; lightness, energy, violence, fluidity to blocks of stone. Novels are said to have strength, buildings eloquence, plays momentum, ballets repose. In this realm of eccentric predicates, to say that the cockfight, in its perfected cases at least, is "disquietful" does not seem at all unnatural, merely, as I have just denied it practical consequence, somewhat puzzling.

The disquietfulness arises, "somehow," out of a conjunction of three attributes of the fight: its immediate dramatic shape; its metaphoric content; and its social context. A cultural figure against a social ground, the fight is at once a convulsive surge of animal hatred, a mock war of symbolical selves, and a formal simulation of status tensions, and its aesthetic power derives from its capacity to force together these diverse realities. The reason it is disquietful is not that it has material effects (it has some, but they are minor); the reason that it is disquietful is that, joining pride to selfhood, selfhood to cocks, and cocks to destruction, it brings to imaginative realization a dimension of Balinese experience normally well-obscured from view. The transfer of a sense of gravity into what is in itself a rather blank and unvarious spectacle, a commotion of beating wings and throbbing legs, is effected by interpreting it as expressive of something unsettling in the way its authors and audience live, or, even more ominously, what they are.

As a dramatic shape, the fight displays a characteristic that does not seem so remarkable until one realizes that it does not have to be there: a radically atomistical structure.[25] Each match is a world unto itself, a particulate burst of form. There is the match making, there is the betting, there is the fight, there is the result—utter triumph and utter defeat—and there is the hurried, embarrassed passing of money. The loser is not consoled. People drift away from him, look through him, leave him to assimilate his momentary descent into nonbeing, reset his face, and return, scarless and intact, to the fray. Nor are winners congratulated, or events rehashed; once a match is ended the crowd's attention turns totally to the next, with no looking back. A shadow of the experience no doubt remains with the principals, perhaps even with some of the witnesses, of a deep fight, as it remains with us when we leave the theater after seeing a powerful play well-performed; but it quite soon fades to become at most a schematic memory—a diffuse glow or an abstract shudder—and usually not even that. Any expressive form lives only in its own present—the one it itself creates. But, here, that present is severed into a string of flashes, some more bright than others, but all of them disconnected, aesthetic quanta. Whatever the cockfight says, it says in spurts.

But, as I have argued lengthily elsewhere, the Balinese live in spurts.[26] Their life, as they arrange it and perceive it, is less a flow, a directional movement out of the past, through the present, toward the future than an on-off pulsation of meaning and vacuity, an arhythmic alternation of short periods when "something" (that is, something significant) is happening and equally short ones where "nothing" (that is, nothing much) is—between what they themselves call "full" and "empty" times, or, in another idiom, "junctures" and "holes." In focusing activity down to a burning-glass dot, the cockfight is merely being Balinese in the same way in which everything from the monadic encounters of everyday life, through the clanging pointillism of *gamelan* music, to the visiting-day-of-the-gods temple celebrations are. It is not an imitation of the punctuateness of Balinese social life, nor a depiction of it, nor even an expression of it; it is an example of it, carefully prepared.[27]

If one dimension of the cockfight's structure, its lack of temporal directionality, makes it seem a typical segment of the general social life, however, the other, its flat-out, head-to-head (or spur-to-spur) aggressiveness, makes it seem a contradiction, a reversal, even a subversion of it. In the normal course of things, the Balinese are shy to the point of obsessiveness of open conflict. Oblique, cautious, subdued, controlled, masters of indirection and dissimulation—what they call *alus*, "polished," "smooth,"—they rarely face what they can turn away from, rarely resist what they can evade. But here they portray themselves as wild and murderous, manic explosions of instinctual cruelty. A powerful rendering of life as the Balinese most deeply do not want it (to adapt a phrase Frye [1964, p. 99] has used of Gloucester's blinding) is set in the context of a sample of it as they in fact have it. And, because the context suggests that the rendering, if less than a straightforward description is nonetheless more than an idle fancy, it is here that the disquietfulness—the disquietfulness of the *fight*, not (or, anyway, not necessarily) its patrons, who seem in fact rather thoroughly to enjoy it—emerges. The slaughter in the cock ring is not a depiction of how things literally are among men, but, what is almost worse, of how, from a particular angle, they imaginatively are.[28]

The angle, of course, is stratificatory. What, as we have already seen, the cockfight talks most forcibly about is status relationships, and what it says about them is that they are matters of life and death. That prestige is a profoundly serious business is apparent everywhere one looks in Bali—in the village, the family, the economy, the state. A peculiar fusion of Polynesian title ranks and Hindu castes, the hierarchy of pride is the moral backbone of the society. But only in the cockfight are the sentiments upon which that hierarchy rests revealed in their natural colors. Enveloped elsewhere in a haze of etiquette, a thick cloud of euphemism and ceremony, gesture and allusion, they are here expressed in only the thinnest disguise of an animal mask, a mask which in fact demonstrates them far more effectively than it conceals them. Jealousy is as much a part of Bali as poise, envy as grace, brutality as charm; but without the cockfight the Balinese would have a much less certain understanding of them, which is, presumably, why they value it so highly.

Any expressive form works (when it works) by disarranging semantic contexts in such a way that properties conventionally ascribed to certain things are unconventionally ascribed to others, which are then seen actually to possess them. To call the wind a cripple, as Stevens does, to fix tone and manipulate timbre, as Schoenberg does, or, closer to our case, to picture an art critic as a dissolute bear, as Hogarth does, is to cross conceptual wires; the established conjunctions between objects and their qualities are altered and phenomena—fall weather, melodic shape, or cultural journalism—are clothed in signifiers which normally point to other referents.[29] Similarly, to connect—and connect, and connect—the collision of roosters with the devisiveness of status is to invite a transfer of perceptions from the former to the latter, a transfer which is at once a description and a judgment. (Logically, the transfer could, of course, as well go the other way; but, like most of the rest of us, the Balinese are a great deal more interested in understanding men than they are in understanding cocks.)

Saying Something of Something

To put the matter this way is to engage in a bit of metaphorical refocusing of one's own, for it shifts the analysis of cultural forms from an endeavor in general parallel to dissecting an organism, diagnosing a symptom, deciphering a code, or ordering a system—the dominant analogies in contemporary anthropology—to one in general parallel with penetrating a literary text. If one takes the cockfight, or any other collectively sustained symbolic structure, as a means of "saying something of something" (to invoke a famous Aristotelian tag), then one is faced with a problem not in social mechanics but social semantics.[30] For the anthropologist, whose concern is with formulating sociological principles, not with promoting or appreciating cockfights, the question is, what does one learn about such principles from examining culture as an assemblage of texts?

Such an extension of the notion of a text beyond written material, and even beyond verbal, is, though metaphorical, not, of course, all that novel. The *interpretatio naturae* tradition of the middle ages, which, culminating in Spinoza, attempted to read nature as Scripture, the Nietzschean effort to treat value systems as glosses on the will to power (or the Marxian one to treat them as glosses on property relations), and the Freudian replacement of the enigmatic text of the manifest dream with the plain one of the latent, all offer precedents, if not equally recommendable ones (Ricoeur, 1970). But the idea remains theoretically undeveloped; and the more profound corollary, so far as anthropology is concerned, that cultural forms can be treated as texts, as imaginative works built out of social materials, has yet to be systematically exploited.[31]

In the case at hand, to treat the cockfight as a text is to bring out a feature of it (in my opinion, the central feature of it) that treating it as a rite or a pastime, the two most obvious alternatives, would tend to obscure: its use of emotion for cognitive ends. What the cockfight says it says in a vocabulary of sentiment—the thrill of risk, the despair of loss, the pleasure of triumph. Yet what it says is not merely that risk is exciting, loss depressing, or triumph gratifying, banal tautologies of affect, but that it is of these emotions, thus exampled, that society is built and individuals put together. Attending cockfights and participating in them is, for the Balinese, a kind of sentimental education. What he learns there is what his culture's ethos and his private sensibility (or, anyway, certain aspects of them) look like when spelled out externally in a collective text; that the two are near enough alike to be articulated in the symbolics of a single such text; and—the disquieting part—that the text in which this revelation is accomplished consists of a chicken hacking another mindlessly to bits.

Every people, the proverb has it, loves its own form of violence. The cockfight is the Balinese reflection on theirs: on its look, its uses, its force, its fascination. Drawing on almost every level of Balinese experience, it brings together themes—animal savagery, male narcissism, opponent gambling, status rivalry, mass excitement, blood sacrifice— whose main connection is their involvement with rage and the fear of rage, and, binding them into a set of rules which at once contains them and allows them play, builds a symbolic structure in which, over and over again, the reality of their inner affiliation can be intelligibly felt. If, to quote Northrop Frye (1964) again, we go to see *Macbeth* to learn what a man feels like after he has gained a kingdom and lost his soul, Balinese go to cockfights to find out what a man usually composed, aloof, almost obsessively self-absorbed, a kind of moral autocosm, feels like when, attacked, tormented, challenged, insulted, and driven in result to the extremes of fury, he has totally triumphed or been brought totally low. The whole passage, as it takes us back to Aristotle (though to the *Poetics* rather than the *Hermeneutics*), is worth quotation:

> But the poet [as opposed to the historian], Aristotle says, never makes any real statements at all, certainly no particular or specific ones. The poet's job is not to tell you what happened, but what happens: not what did take place, but the kind of thing that always does take place. He gives you the typical, recurring, or what Aristotle calls universal event. You wouldn't go to *Macbeth* to learn about the history of Scotland—you go to it to learn what a man feels like after he's gained a kingdom and lost his soul. When you meet such a character as Micawber in Dickens, you don't feel that there must have been a man Dickens knew who was exactly like this: you

feel that there's a bit of Micawber in almost everybody you know, including yourself. Our impressions of human life are picked up one by one, and remain for most of us loose and disorganized. But we constantly find things in literature that suddenly co-ordinate and bring into focus a great many such impressions, and this is part of what Aristotle means by the typical or universal human event. (pp. 63-64)

It is this kind of bringing of assorted experiences of everyday life to focus that the cockfight, set aside from that life as "only a game" and reconnected to it as "more than a game," accomplishes, and so creates what, better than typical or universal, could be called a paradigmatic human event—that is, one that tells us less what happens than the kind of thing that would happen if, as is not the case, life were art and could be as freely shaped by styles of feeling as *Macbeth* and *David Copperfield* are.

Enacted and reenacted, so far without end, the cockfight enables the Balinese, as, read and reread, *Macbeth* enables us, to see a dimension of his own subjectivity. As he watches fight after fight, with the active watching of an owner and a bettor (for cockfighting has no more interest as a pure spectator sport than croquet or dog racing do), he grows familiar with it and what it has to say to him, much as the attentive listener to string quartets or the absorbed viewer of still lifes grows slowly more familiar with them in a way which opens his subjectivity to himself.[32]

Yet, because—in another of those paradoxes, along with painted feelings and unconsequenced acts, which haunt aesthetics—that subjectivity does not properly exist until it is thus organized, art forms generate and regenerate the very subjectivity they pretend only to display. Quartets, still lifes, and cockfights are not merely reflections of a preexisting sensibility analogically represented; they are positive agents in the creation and maintenance of such a sensibility. If we see ourselves as a pack of Micawbers it is from reading too much Dickens (if we see ourselves as unillusioned realists, it is from reading too little); and similarly for Balinese, cocks, and cockfights. It is in such a way, coloring experience with the light they cast it in, rather than through whatever material effects they may have, that the arts play their role, as arts, in social life.[33]

In the cockfight, then, the Balinese forms and discovers his temperament and his society's temper at the same time. Or, more exactly, he forms and discovers a particular face of them. Not only are there a great many other cultural texts providing commentaries on status hierarchy and self-regard in Bali, but there are a great many other critical sectors of Balinese life besides the stratificatory and the agonistic that receive such commentary. The ceremony consecrating a Brahmana priest, a matter of breath control, postural immobility, and vacant concentration upon the depths of being, displays a radically different, but to the Balinese equally real, property of social hierarchy—its reach toward the numinous transcendent. Set not in the matrix of the kinetic emotionality of animals, but in that of the static passionlessness of divine mentality, it expresses tranquility not disquiet. The mass festivals at the village temples, which mobilize the whole local population in elaborate hostings of visiting gods—songs, dances, compliments, gifts—assert the spiritual unity of village mates against their status inequality and project a mood of amity and trust.[34] The cockfight is not the master key to Balinese life, any more than bullfighting is to Spanish. What it says about that life is not unqualified nor even unchallenged by what other equally eloquent cultural statements say about it. But there is nothing more surprising in this than in the fact that Racine and Molière were contemporaries, or that the same people who arrange chrysanthemums cast swords.[35]

The culture of a people is an ensemble of texts, themselves ensembles, which the anthropologist strains to read over the shoulders of those to whom they properly belong. There are enormous difficulties in such an enterprise, methodological pitfalls to make a Freudian quake, and some moral perplexities as well. Nor is it the only way that symbolic forms can be sociologically handled. Functionalism lives, and so does psychologism. But to regard such forms as "saying something of something," and saying it to somebody, is at least to open up the possibility of an analysis which attends to their substance rather than to reductive formulas professing to account for them.

As in more familiar exercises in close reading, one can start anywhere in a culture's repertoire of forms and end up anywhere else. One can stay, as I have here, within a single, more or less bounded form and circle steadily within it. One can move between forms in search of broader unities or informing contrasts. One can even compare forms from different cultures to define their character in reciprocal relief. But whatever the level at which one operates, and however intricately, the guiding principle is the same: Societies, like lives, contain their own interpretations. One has only to learn how to gain access to them.

Notes

1. The best discussion of cockfighting is again Bateson and Mead (1942, pp. 24-25; 140) but it, too, is general and abbreviated.
2. The cockfight is unusual within Balinese culture in being a single-sex public activity from which the other sex is totally and expressly excluded. Sexual differentiation is culturally extremely played down in Bali and most activities, formal and informal, involve the participation of men and women on equal ground, commonly as linked couples. From religion, to politics, to economics, to kinship, to dress, Bali is a rather "uni-sex" society, a fact both its customs and its symbolism clearly express. Even in contexts where women

do not in fact play much of a role—music, painting, certain agricultural activities—their absence, which is only relative in any case, is more a mere matter of fact than socially enforced. To this general pattern, the cockfight, entirely of, by, and for men (women—at least *Balinese* women—do not even watch), is the most striking exception.

3. Christiaan Hooykaas, *The lay of the Jaya Prana* (1958, p. 39). The lay has a stanza (no. 17) with the reluctant bridegroom use. Jaya Prana, the subject of a Balinese Uriah myth, responds to the lord who has offered him the loveliest of 600 servant girls: "Godly King, my Lord and Master/I beg you, give me leave to go/such things are not yet in my mind;/like a fighting cock encaged/indeed I am on my mettle/I am alone/as yet the flame has not been fanned."

4. For these, see V.E. Korn (1932), index under *toh.*

5. There is indeed a legend to the effect that the separation of Java and Bali is due to the action of a powerful Javanese religious figure who wished to protect himself against a Balinese culture hero (the ancestor of two Ksatria castes) who was a passionate cockfighting gambler. See Christiaan Hooykaas (1964, p. 184).

6. An incestuous couple is forced to wear pig yokes over their necks and crawl to a pig trough and eat with their mouths there. On this, see Jane Belo (1970b, p. 49); on the abhorence of animality generally, Bateson and Mead (1942, p. 22).

7. Except for unimportant, small-bet fights (on the question of fight "importance," see below) spur affixing is usually done by someone other than the owner. Whether the owner handles his own cock or not more or less depends on how skilled he is at it, a consideration whose importance is again relative to the importance of the fight. When spur affixers and cock handlers are someone other than the owner, they are almost always a quite close relative—a brother or cousin—or a very intimate friend of his. They are thus almost extensions of his personality, as the fact that all three will refer to the cock as "mine," say "I" fought So-and-So, and so on, demonstrates. Also, owner-handler-affixer triads tend to be fairly fixed, though individuals may participate in several and often exchange roles within a given one.

8. This word, which literally means an indelible stain or mark, as in a birthmark or a vein in a stone, is used as well for a deposit in a court case, for a pawn, for security offered in a loan, for a stand-in for someone else in a legal or ceremonial context, for an earnest advanced in a business deal, for a sign placed in a field to indicate its ownership is in dispute, and for the status of an unfaithful wife from whose lover her husband must gain satisfaction or surrender her to him. See Korn (1932); Pigeaud (1938); H.H. Juynboll (1923).

9. The center bet must be advanced in cash by both parties prior to the actual fight. The umpire holds the stakes until the decision is rendered and then awards them to the winner, avoiding, among other things, the intense embarrassment both winner and loser would feel if the latter had to pay off personally following his defeat. About 10 percent of the winner's receipts are subtracted for the umpire's share and that of the fight sponsors.

10. Actually, the typing of cocks, which is extremely elaborate (I have collected more than 20 classes, certainly not a complete list), is not based on color alone, but on a series of independent, interacting, dimensions, which include, beside color, size, bone thickness, plumage, and temperament. (But *not*

pedigree. The Balinese do not breed cocks to any significant extent, nor, so far as I have been able to discover, have they ever done so. The *asil*, or jungle cock, which is the basic fighting strain everywhere the sport is found, is native to southern Asia, and one can buy a good example in the chicken section of almost any Balinese market for anywhere from four or five ringgits up to 50 or more.) The color element is merely the one normally used as the type name, except when the two cocks of different types—as on principle they must be—have the same color, in which case a secondary indication from one of the other dimensions ("large speckled" v. "small speckled," etc.) is added. The types are coordinated with various cosmological ideas which help shape the making of matches, so that, for example, you fight a small, headstrong, speckled brown-on-white cock with flat-lying feathers and thin legs from the east side of the ring on a certain day of the complex Balinese calendar, and a large, cautious, all-black cock with tufted feathers and stubby legs from the north side on another day, and so on. All this is again recorded in palm-leaf manuscripts and endlessly discussed by the Balinese (who do not all have identical systems), and full-scale componential-cum-symbolic analysis of cock classifications would be extremely valuable both as an adjunct to the description of the cockfight and in itself. But my data on the subject, though extensive and varied, do not seem to be complete and systematic enough to attempt such an analysis here. For Balinese cosmological ideas more generally see Belo (1970c) and J.L. Swellengrebel (1960); for calendrical ones, see Geertz (1966, pp. 45-53).

11. For purposes of ethnographic completeness, it should be noted that it is possible for the man backing the favorite—the odds-giver—to make a bet in which he wins if his cock wins or there is a tie, a slight shortening of the odds (I do not have enough cases to be exact, but ties seem to occur about once every 15 or 20 matches). He indicates his wish to do this by shouting *sapih* ("tie") rather than the cock-type, but such bets are in fact infrequent.

12. The precise dynamics of the movement of the betting is one of the most intriguing, most complicated, and, given the hectic conditions under which it occurs, most difficult to study, aspects of the fight. Motion picture recording plus multiple observers would probably be necessary to deal with it effectively. Even impressionistically—the only approach open to a lone ethnographer caught in the middle of all this—it is clear that certain men lead both in determining the favorite (that is, making the opening cock-type calls which always initiate the process) and in directing the movement of the odds, these "opinion leaders" being the more accomplished cockfighters-cum-solid-citizens to be discussed below. If these men begin to change their calls, others follow; if they begin to make bets, so do others and—though there is always a large number of frustrated bettors crying for shorter or longer odds to the end—the movement more or less ceases. But a detailed understanding of the whole process awaits what, alas, it is not very likely ever to get: a decision theorist armed with precise observations of individual behavior.

13. Assuming only binomial variability, the departure from a 50-50 expectation in the 60 ringgits and below case is 1.38 standard deviations, or (in a one direction test) an 8 in 100 possibility by chance alone; for the below 40 ringgits case it is 1.65 standard deviations, or about 5 in 100. The fact that these departures

though real are not extreme merely indicates, again, that even in the smaller fights the tendency to match cocks at least reasonably evenly persists. It is a matter of relative relaxation of the pressures toward equalization, not their elimination. The tendency for high-bet contests to be coin-flip propositions is, of course, even more striking, and suggests the Balinese know quite well what they are about.

14. The reduction in wagering in smaller fights (which, of course, feeds on itself; one of the reasons people find small fights uninteresting is that there is less wagering in them, and contrariwise for large ones) takes place in three mutually reinforcing ways. First, there is a simple withdrawal of interest as people wander off to have a cup of coffee or chat with a friend. Second, the Balinese do not mathematically reduce odds, but bet directly in terms of stated odds as such. Thus, for a nine-to-eight bet, one man wagers nine ringgits, the other eight; for five-to-four, one wagers five, the other four. For any given currency unit, like the ringgit, therefore, 6.3 times as much money is involved in a ten-to-nine bet as in a two-to-one bet, for example, and, as noted, in small fights betting settles toward the longer end. Finally, the bets which are made tend to be one- rather than two-, three-, or in some of the very largest fights, four- or five-finger ones. (The fingers indicate the *multiples* of the stated bet odds at issue, not absolute figures. Two fingers in a six-to-five situation means a man wants to wager ten ringgits on the underdog against twelve, three in an eight-to-seven situation, twenty-one against twenty-four, and so on.)

15. Besides wagering there are other economic aspects of the cockfight, especially its very close connection with the local market system which, though secondary both to its motivation and to its function, are not without importance. Cockfights are open events to which anyone who wishes may come, sometimes from quite distant areas, but well over 90%, probably over 95, are very local affairs, and the locality concerned is defined not by the village, nor even by the administrative district, but by the rural market system. Bali has a 3-day market week with the familiar "solar-system" type rotation. Though the markets themselves have never been very highly developed, small morning affairs in a village square, it is the micro-region such rotation rather generally marks out—10 or 20 square miles, 7 or 8 neighboring villages (which in contemporary Bali is usually going to mean anywhere from five to ten or eleven thousand people) from which the core of any cockfight audience, indeed virtually all of it, will come. Most of the fights are in fact organized and sponsored by small combines of petty rural merchants under the general premise, very strongly held by them and indeed by all Balinese, that cockfights are good for trade because "they get money out of the house, they make it circulate." Stalls selling various sorts of things as well as assorted sheer-chance gambling games (see below) are set up around the edge of the area so that this even takes on the quality of a small fair. This connection of cockfighting with markets and market sellers is very old, as, among other things, their conjunction in inscriptions (Goris, 1954) indicates. Trade has followed the cock for centuries in rural Bali and the sport has been one of the main agencies of the island's monetization.

16. The phrase is found in the Hildreth translation, International Library of

Psychology, 1931, note to p. 106; see L.L. Fuller (1964, pp. 6ff).

17. Of course, even in Bentham, utility is not normally confined as a concept to monetary losses and gains, and my argument here might be more carefully put in terms of a denial that for the Balinese, as for any people, utility (pleasure, happiness . . .) is merely identifiable with wealth. But such terminological problems are in any case secondary to the essential point: The cockfight is not roulette.

18. Max Weber (1963). There is nothing specifically Balinese, of course, about deepening significance with money, as Whyte's (1955) description of corner boys in a working-class district of Boston demonstrates: "Gambling plays an important role in the lives of Cornerville people. Whatever game the corner boys play, they nearly always bet on the outcome. When there is nothing at stake, the game is not considered a real contest. This does not mean that the financial element is all-important. I have frequently heard men say that the honor of winning was much more important than the money at stake. The corner boys consider playing for money the real test of skill and, unless a man performs well when money is at stake, he is not considered a good competitor" (p. 140).

19. The extremes to which this madness is conceived on occasion to go—and the fact that it is considered madness—is demonstrated by the Balinese folktale *I Tuhung Kuning*. A gambler becomes so deranged by his passion that, leaving on a trip, he orders his pregnant wife to take care of the prospective newborn if it is a boy but to feed it as meat to his fighting cocks if it is a girl. The mother gives birth to a girl, but rather than giving the child to the cocks she gives them a large rat and conceals the girl with her own mother. When the husband returns the cocks, crowing a jingle, inform him of the deception and, furious, he sets out to kill the child. A goddess descends from heaven and takes the girl up to the skies with her. The cocks die from the food given them, the owner's sanity is restored, the goddess brings the girl back to the father who reunites him with his wife. The story is given as "Geel Komkommertje" in Boomkamp (1956, pp. 19-25).

20. For a fuller description of Balinese rural social structure, see Clifford Geertz (1959; 1967b, pp. 210-243); and, though it is a bit off the norm as Balinese villages go, V.E. Korn (1933).

21. As this is a formal paradigm, it is intended to display the logical, not the causal, structure of cockfighting. Just which of these considerations leads to which, in what order, and by what mechanisms, is another matter—one I have attempted to shed some light on in the general discussion.

22. In another of Hooykaas-van Leeuwen Boomkamp's (1956) folk tales ("De Gast," pp. 172-180), a low caste *Sudra*, a generous, pious, and carefree man who is also an accomplished cock fighter, loses, despite his accomplishment, fight after fight until he is not only out of money but down to his last cock. He does not despair, however—"I bet," he says, "upon the Unseen World."

His wife, a good and hard-working woman, knowing how much he enjoys cockfighting, gives him her last "rainy day" money to go and bet. But, filled with misgivings due to his run of ill luck, he leaves his own cock at home and bets merely on the side. He soon loses all but a coin or two and repairs to a food stand for a snack, where he meets a decrepit, odorous, and generally unappetizing old beggar leaning on a staff. The old man asks for food, and the hero spends his last coins to buy him some. The old man then asks to pass the night with the hero, which the hero gladly invites him to do. As there is no food in the house, however, the hero tells his wife to kill the last cock for dinner. When the old man discovers this fact, he tells the hero he has three cocks in his own mountain hut and says the hero may have one of them for fighting. He also asks for the hero's son to accompany him as a servant, and, after the son agrees, this is done.

The old man turns out to be Siva and, thus, to live in a great palace in the sky, though the hero does not know this. In time, the hero decides to visit his son and collect the promised cock. Lifted up into Siva's presence, he is given the choice of three cocks. The first crows: "I have beaten fifteen opponents." The second crows, "I have beaten twenty-five opponents." The third crows, "I have beaten the King." "That one, the third, is my choice," says the hero, and returns with it to earth.

When he arrives at the cockfight, he is asked for an entry fee and replies, "I have no money; I will pay after my cock has won." As he is known never to win, he is let in because the king, who is there fighting, dislikes him and hopes to enslave him when he loses and cannot pay off. In order to insure that this happens, the king matches his finest cock against the hero's. When the cocks are placed down, the hero's flees, and the crowd, led by the arrogant king, hoots in laughter. The hero's cock then flies at the king himself, killing him with a spur stab in the throat. The hero flees. His house is encircled by the king's men. The cock changes into a Garuda, the great mythic bird of Indic legend, and carries the hero and his wife to safety in the heavens.

When the people see this, they make the hero king and his wife queen and they return as such to earth. Later their son, released by Siva, also returns and the hero-king announces his intention to enter a hermitage. ("I will fight no more cockfights. I have bet on the Unseen and won.") He enters the hermitage and his son becomes king.

23. Addict gamblers are really less declassed (for their status is, as everyone else's, inherited) than merely impoverished and personally disgraced. The most prominent addict gambler in my cockfight circuit was actually a very high caste *satria* who sold off most of his considerable lands to support his habit. Though everyone privately regarded him as a fool and worse (some, more charitable, regarded him as sick), he was publicly treated with the elaborate deference and politeness due his rank. On the independence of personal reputation and public status in Bali, see Geertz (1966, pp. 28-35).

24. For four, somewhat variant, treatments, see Susanne Langer (1953); Richard Wollheim (1968); Nelson Goodman (1968); Maurice Merleau-Ponty (1964, pp. 159-190.)

25. British cockfights (the sport was banned there in 1840) indeed seem to have lacked it, and to have generated, therefore, a quite different family of shapes. Most British fights were "mains," in which a preagreed number of cocks were aligned into two teams and fought serially. Score was kept and wagering took place both on the individual matches and on the main as a whole. There were also "battle Royales," both in England and on the Continent, in which a large number of cocks were let loose at once with the one left standing at the

end the victor. And in Wales, the so-called "Welsh main" followed an elimination pattern, along the lines of a present-day tennis tournament, winners proceeding to the next round. As a genre, the cockfight has perhaps less compositional flexibility than, say, Latin comedy, but it is not entirely without any. On cockfighting more generally, see Arch Ruport (1949); G.R. Scott (1957); and Lawrence Fitz-Barnard (1921).

26. Geertz (1966, esp. pp. 42ff). I am, however, not the first person to have argued it: see G. Bateson (1970a, 1970b).

27. For the necessity of distinguishing among "description," "representation," "exemplification," and "expression" (and the irrelevance of "imitation" to all of them) as modes of symbolic reference, see Goodman (1968, pp. 6-10; 45-91; 225-241).

28. There are two other Balinese values and disvalues which, connected with punctuate temporality on the one hand and unbridled aggressiveness on the other, reinforce the sense that the cockfight is at once continuous with ordinary social life and a direct negation of it: what the Balinese call *ramé*, and what they call *paling*. *Ramé* means crowded, noisy, and active, and is a highly sought after social state: crowded markets, mass festivals, busy streets are all *ramé*, as, of course, is, in the extreme, a cockfight. *Ramé* is what happens in the "full" times (its opposite, *sepi*, "quiet," is what happens in the "empty" ones). *Paling* is social vertigo, the dizzy, disoriented, lost, turned around feeling one gets when one's place in the coordinates of social space is not clear, and it is a tremendously disfavored, immensely anxiety-producing state. Balinese regard the exact maintenance of spatial orientation ("not to know where north is" is to be crazy), balance, decorum, status relationships, and so forth, as fundamental to ordered life *(krama)* and *paling*, the sort of whirling confusion of position the scrambling cocks exemplify as its profoundest enemy and contradiction. On *ramé*, see Bateson and Mead (1942, pp. 3, 64); on *paling*, Bateson and Mead (1942, p. 11); and Belo (1935/1970c, pp. 90ff).

29. The Stevens reference is to his "The Motive for Metaphor," ("You like it under the trees in autumn,/Because everything is half dead./The wind moves like a cripple among the leaves/And repeats words without meaning"); the Schoenberg reference is to the third of his *Five Orchestral Pieces* (Opus 16), and is borrowed from H.H. Drager (1961, p. 174). On Hogarth, and on this whole problem—there called "multiple matrix matching"—see E.H. Gombrich (1969, pp. 149-170). The more usual term for this sort of semantic alchemy is "metaphorical transfer," and good technical discussions of it can be found in M. Black (1962, pp. 25ff); Goodman (1968, pp. 44ff); and W. Percy (1958).

30. The tag is from the second book of the *Organon, On Interpretation*. For a discussion of it, and for the whole argument for freeing "the notion of text . . . from the notion of scripture or writing," and constructing, thus, a general hermeneutics, see Paul Ricoeur (1970, pp. 20ff).

31. Lévi-Strauss's "structuralism" might seem an exception. But it is only an apparent one, for, rather than taking myths, totem rites, marriage rules, or whatever as texts to interpret, Lévi-Strauss takes them as ciphers to solve, which is very much not the same thing. He does not seek to understand symbolic forms in terms of how they function in concrete situations to organize

perceptions (meanings, emotions, concepts, attitudes); he seeks to understand them entirely in terms of their internal structure, *indépendent de tout sujet, de tout objet, et de toute contexte*. For my own view of this approach—that is suggestive and indefensible—see Clifford Geertz (1967a).

32. The use of the, to Europeans, "natural" visual idiom for perception—"see," "watches," and so forth—is more than usually misleading here, for the fact that, as mentioned earlier, Balinese follow the progress of the fight as much (perhaps, as fighting cocks are actually rather hard to see except as blurs of motion, more) with their bodies as with their eyes, moving their limbs, heads, and trunks in gestural mimicry of the cocks' maneuvers, means that much of the individual's experience of the fight is kinesthetic rather than visual. If ever there was an example of Kenneth Burke's (1957) definition of a symbolic act as "the dancing of an attitude" (p. 9) the cockfight is it. On the enormous role of kinesthetic perception in Balinese life, Bateson and Meade (1942, pp. 84-88); on the active nature of aesthetic perception in general, Goodman (1968, pp. 241-244).

33. All this coupling of the occidental great with the oriental lowly will doubtless disturb certain sorts of aestheticians as the earlier efforts of anthropologists to speak of Christianity and totemism in the same breath disturbed certain sorts of theologians. But as ontological questions are (or should be) bracketed in the sociology of religion, judgmental ones are (or should be) bracketed in the sociology of art. In any case, the attempt to deprovincialize the concept of art is but part of the general anthropological conspiracy to deprovincialize all important social concepts—marriage, religion, law, rationality—and though this is a threat to aesthetic theories which regard certain works of art as beyond the reach of sociological analysis, it is no threat to the conviction, for which Robert Graves claims to have been reprimanded at his Cambridge tripos, that some poems are better than others.

34. For the consecration ceremony, see V.E. Korn (1960); for (somewhat exaggerated) village communion, Roelof Goris (1960, pp. 79-100).

35. That what the cockfight has to say about Bali is not altogether without perception and the disquiet it expresses about the general pattern of Balinese life is not wholly without reason is attested by the fact that in 2 weeks of December 1965, during the upheavals following the unsuccessful coup in Djakarta, between 40,000 and 80,000 Balinese (in a population of about 2 million) were killed, largely by one another—the worst outburst in the country (John Hughes [1967, pp. 173-183]. Hughes's figures are, of course, rather casual estimates, but they are not the most extreme.) This is not to say, of course, that the killings were caused by the cockfight, could have been predicted on the basis of it, or were some sort of enlarged version of it with real people in the place of the cocks—all of which is nonsense. It is merely to say that if one looks at Bali not just through the medium of its dances, its shadowplays, its sculpture, and its girls, but—as the Balinese themselves do—also through the medium of its cockfight, the fact that the massacre occurred seems, if no less appalling, less like a contradiction to the laws of nature. As more than one real Gloucester has discovered, sometimes people actually get life precisely as they most deeply do not want it.

References

BATESON, G. Bali, the value system of a steady state. In J. Belo (Ed.), *Traditional Balinese culture*. New York: Columbia University Press, 1970. (Originally published, 1935.) (a)

BATESON, G. An old temple and a new myth. In J. Belo (Ed.), *Traditional Balinese culture*. New York: Columbia University Press, 1970. (Originally published, 1935.) (b)

BATESON, G., & Mead, M. *Balinese character: A photographic analysis*. New York: New York Academy of Sciences, 1942.

BELO, J. The Balinese temper. In J. Belo (Ed.), *Traditional Balinese culture*. New York: Columbia University Press, 1970. (Originally published 1935.) (a)

BELO, J. Customs pertaining to twins in Bali. In J. Belo (Ed.), *Traditional Balinese culture*. New York: Columbia University Press, 1970. (Originally published, 1935.) (b)

BELO, J. (Ed.) *Traditional Balinese culture*. New York: Columbia University, Press, 1970. (Originally published, 1935.) (c)

BENTHAM, J. *[The theory of legislation.]* (R. Hildreth, trans.) New York: Harcourt, Brace, 1931.

BERELSON, B.R., Lazersfeld, P.F., & McPhee, W.N. *Voting: A study of opinion formation in a presidential campaign*. Chicago: University of Chicago Press, 1954.

BLACK, M. *Models and metaphors*. Ithaca: Cornell University Press, 1962.

BOOMKAMP, J.H. J. *Sprookjes en verhalen van Bali*. 'S-Gravenhage: van Hoeve, 1956.

BURKE, K. *The philosophy of literary form* (rev. ed.). New York: Vintage Books, 1957.

DRAGER, H.H. The concept of 'Tonal Body'. In S. Langer (Ed.), *Reflections on art*. New York: Oxford University Press, 1961.

FITZ-BARNARD, L. *Fighting sports*. London: Odhams Press, 1921.

FRYE, N. *The educated imagination*. Bloomington: University of Indiana Press, 1964.

FULLER, L.L. *The morality of law*. New Haven: Yale University Press, 1964.

GEERTZ, C. Form and variation in Balinese village structure. *American Anthropologist*, 1959, **61**, 94-108.

GEERTZ, C. *Person, time, and conduct in Bali: An essay in cultural analysis*. New Haven: Southeast Asia Studies, Yale University, 1966.

GEERTZ, C. The cerebral savage: On the work of Lévi-Strauss. *Encounter*, 1967, **48**, 25-32. (a)

GEERTZ, C. Tihingan, a Balinese village. In R.M. Koentjaraningrat, *Villages in Indonesia*. Ithaca: Cornell University Press, 1967. (b)

GOFFMAN, E. *Encounters: Two studies in the sociology of interaction*. Indianapolis: Bobbs-Merrill, 1961.

GOMBRICH, E.H. The uses of art for the study of symbols. In J. Hogg (Ed.), *Psychology and the visual arts*. Baltimore: Penguin, 1969.

GOODMAN, N. *Languages of art*. Indianapolis: Bobbs-Merrill, 1968.

GORIS, R. *Prasasti Bali* (2 vols.). Bandung: N.V. Masa Baru, 1954.

GORIS, R. The religious character of the Balinese village. In J.L. Swellengrebel (Ed.), *Bali: Studies in life, thought and ritual*. The Hague: W. van Hoeve, 1960.

HOOYKAAS, C. *The lay of the Jaya Prana*. London: Luzac, 1958.

HOOYKAAS, C. *Agama tirtha*. Amsterdam: Noord-Hollandsche, 1964.

HUGHES, J. *Indonesian upheaval*. New York: McKay, 1967.

JUYNBOLL, H.H. *Oudjavaansche-Nederlandsche woordenlijst*. Leiden: Brill, 1923.

KORN, V.E. *Het Adatrecht van Bali* (2nd ed.). 'S-Gravenhage: G. Naeff, 1932.

KORN, V.E. *De Dorpsrepubliek tnganan Pagringsingan*. Santpoort, Netherlands: C.A. Mees, 1933.

KORN, V.E. The consecration of the priest. In J.L. Swellengrebel (Ed.), *Bali: Studies in life, thought and ritual*. The Hague: W. van Hoeve, 1960.

LANGER, S. *Feeling and form*. New York: Scribners, 1953.

MERLEAU-PONTY, M. The eye and the mind. In M. Merleau-Ponty (Ed.), *The primacy of perception*. Evanston: Northwestern University Press, 1964.

PERCY, W. Metaphor as mistake. *Sewanee Review*, 1958, **66**, 78-99.

PIGEAUD, T. *Javaans-Nederlands Handwoordenboek*. Groningen: Wolters, 1938.

RICOEUR, P. *Freud and philosophy*. New Haven: Yale University Press, 1970.

RUPORT, A. *The art of cockfighting*. New York: Devin-Adair, 1949.

SCOTT, G.R. *History of cockfighting*. London: C. Skilton, 1957.

SWELLENGREBEL, J.L. (Ed.). *Bali: Studies in life, thought, and ritual*. The Hague: W. van Hoeve, 1960.

WEBER, M. *The sociology of religion*. Boston: Beacon Press, 1963.

WHYTE, W.F. *Street corner society* (2nd ed.). Chicago: University of Chicago Press, 1955.

WOLLHEIM, R. *Art and its objects*. New York: Harper & Row, 1968.

Chapter 2
Toward a Political Theory of American Sports Symbolism

RICHARD LIPSKY

T he last decade and a half has witnessed the proliferation of social
and political protest within and around the world of American
sports. This activity has been characterized by vituperative labor-
management disputes, litigation, boycotts, and scattered incidents of
mass violence. As a result, there has been an increased interest in the
political economy of sport. The intent of this essay is to develop a
theoretical perspective that will begin to clarify the relationships between
sports and the larger political and social systems. Meaningful empirical
investigations of the political economy or sociology of sport will be
greatly aided and accelerated by theory-building. Indeed, theory is essential if we are to avoid the endless proliferation of monographs and barren
accumulations of data that often fail to underscore wider significances.

The attempt to develop a political theory of American sports faces

This paper could not have been written without the collective support of Marshall Berman,
Kenneth Sherrill, and Henry Morton.

From *American Behavioral Scientist*, January/February 1978, **21**(3), 345-360. Copyright
1978 by Sage Publications, Inc. Reprinted with permission.

many obstacles. Sports and political economy in America have traditionally been seen as discrete institutional realms. Sportsworld itself has
encouraged the belief that sports are "fun and games," and has
vigorously fought any attempt at "outside" regulation. As sports
historian John Betts (1974, p. 376) has pointed out, "Except in the sup-
pression of gambling or illegal amusements and in the maintenance of
the Puritan sabbath, Americans traditionally looked upon sport as
private in nature, to be regulated by private governing bodies." The
sports-political economy separation received judicial sanction in 1922
when the Supreme Court ruled that baseball was not a business (Robinson, 1969).[1] This ruling enabled professional sports to operate for many
years as a legal monopoly that denied athletes the rights that workers in
other fields were receiving.

The separation of sports and politics has had ethical overtones as well.
Sports, in contradiction to politics, has been seen as a moral realm where
character is built and virtue pursued. The traditional lionizing of the
sports hero contrasts sharply with many of the negative stereotypes that
the public holds of politicians. This popular contrast is the source of the
fierce vigilance that gatekeepers of sportsworld exhibit over the slightest
appearance of corruption. An inability to police their own realm would
inevitably lead, it is feared, to a political interference that would destroy
the moral and jurisdictional autonomy of sports.[2] Robert Lipsyte's
(1976, p. 40) sharp prose captures the moral contrasts most vividly:

> All their lives they have been told that politics was dirty, that baseball was
> beautiful; that politicians were connivers; that ballplayers had the hearts of
> children; that [the] smoke-filled caucus room was the hellish furnace of
> democracy and that a sunny ballpark was its shrine and reward.

The separating out of athletics from all that is serious in American life
has been one of the most persistent obstacles to meaningful analysis of
the political, economic, and social implications of sports. It is one thing
to analyze societies that set up ministries of physical culture whose aims
unblushingly reflect those of the ruling political party (Morton, 1963). It
is quite a different task to analyze sports in a society where the appearance of political or ideological purpose is minimized or carefully
disguised.

The appearance of sports as "above" politics or pure play was severely
challenged during the upheavals of the 1960s. The assorted protest
movements all appeared to have their own "sports sections." The New
Left hit out at what they perceived to be the "fascist" (Hoch, 1971) and
"anti-life" (Oliver, 1971; Scott, 1971) aspects of sports; the black power
movement indicated the "racist" nature of American sports (Edwards,
1969); while the woman's movement began to see in sports the epitome
of sexism in American life (Lipsyte, 1976). The attack on the sports

establishment ideologically replicated the attacks on other American institutions.

The radical polemics on what had previously been seen as a moral realm provoked an equally emotional defense of sports as integral to the "American way of life" (Rafferty, 1971). This polarization served to underscore the fact that sacred space had been violated and helped to tentatively illuminate some of the ways in which sports had been put to ideological use in the past. The need for athletic elites and their political and journalistic allies to defend the premises of sportsworld, premises that had previously been seen as axiomatic, helped to sharpen the extent to which these premises could be seen as interrelated to the larger political, economic, and social systems.

The conflict of the 1960s also legitimized the serious study of sports. It was now a significant social fact. As Lipsyte (1976, p. xiv) remarks:

> Sports-World, once determinedly anti-intellectual, has become a hotbed of psychologists, physicians and sociologists, questioning premises as well as specific techniques.

Yet what is remarkable amidst all the political protest and counter-protest is the absence of any dispassionate attempt to clarify the political function of sports in American society.[3]

II

Henry Morton's seminal work, *Soviet Sport,* provides a useful point of departure for developing a political theory of sport. Morton suggests that the analysis of a nation at play "reveals the stuff of this social fabric and value system, and tells us much about other facets of political and economic life, particularly in modern industrial society" (Morton, 1963, p. 13). Morton indicates the possible ways in which sports can be used as a level of social control, how the intrinsic enthusiasm of the game can be used as a "transmission belt" for socially important beliefs.

An equally important component of Morton's analysis is his description of the intrinsic appeals of mass sports. He indicates that "sport as a medium has inherent qualities which engender mass enthusiasm while permitting emotional release" (Morton, 1963, p. 25). He goes on to explain that "Sports is a drama. Its great attraction lies in the vicarious experience it imparts to the spectator. It is truly heroic—at once glorious and tragic. Sports telescopes the human struggle for power, offering a spectacle that plays upon the emotions" (Morton, 1963, p. 26). What is curious in this analysis, however, is that Morton finds the intrinsic appeal of sport to be essentially apolitical.

It is my contention that it is more fruitful to analyze the connections between content and the dramatic form of mass sports. The dramatic spectacle (art for art's sake) is most profitably seen within the larger political and social context. Sports can be seen to function—by analogical extension—as a socializer of dominant values. This function of sports is, of course, greatly aided by its aesthetic appeal. At times, however, the drama of sports itself, its ability to separate us from the difficulty of everyday life, is an important vehicle for political and social integration. How this dialectic between form and content operates remains to be explained.

Perhaps we can begin to explain this dialectic through a critical analysis of some of the literature that has addressed itself to the meaning of sports in the American context. This literature runs the gamut from Hoch's (1971) *Rip Off the Big Game*, a self-styled Marxist-Leninist interpretation of American sports, through Edwards' (1973) *The Sociology of Sport*, an avowedly scientific treatise, to 16-year-old Leider's (1976) idealistic essay on the role of football in American life. Despite the apparent diversity of these approaches, there is a common unifying thread: Sport, to use Boyle's (1963) term, is a "Mirror of American life."

When sports is seen as a mirror of American life, however, problems of interpretation arise. None of the people who use the mirror metaphor adequately explain the way sports functions as a mirror. Is sports a passive reflection of the values inherent in American society? At times, this would appear to be the case. Hence, if American society is fascist (Hoch, 1971), sports reflects fascist values. If American society is seen as being dominated by the "business creed" of competition, so is sports (Edwards, 1973). If American values are those of community, cooperation, and brotherhood, it is no accident that sports is "a mirror of ourselves" (Leider, 1976).

Clearly, when radicals like Hoch and Scott, conservatives like Agnew and Rafferty, and a young idealist like Leider all agree on the same *mode* of interpretation, we are faced with some interesting theoretical questions. Sports, as an aesthetic realm, seems to encompass a rich symbolism that functions as a Rorschach for radically different perspectives.

The interpretation of American sports as a mirror of American life exists alongside another interpretation. Many professional observers have emphasized the manner in which sports has served as a safety valve for the pressures of a growing urban society and as an escape from the demands of industrialization (Betts, 1974; Paxon, 1917/1970; Dulles, 1965; Beisser, 1967). Lipsyte (1976, p. xi) again colorfully illuminates this view:

> Sports World is a sweaty Oz, you'll never find in a geography book . . . an ultimate sanctuary, a university for the body, a community for the spirit, a place to hide that glows with that time of innocence when we believed that rules and boundaries were honored.

Clearly, we must continue to investigate how sports can function simultaneously as a mirror of American society (with a myriad of reflections) and as an escape from that same society.[4]

Edwards' research is an important historical documentation of the way in which sports in America has served as a socializer of dominant cultural values. He carefully combed old copies of the *Athletic Journal* and analyzed statements by coaches and athletes. He illustrated the extent to which American sports has developed its own belief system or sports creed. He then pointed out the similarity of this ideology with the business creed of American capitalism. Edwards sees sports as a cultural blueprint: "Such cultural blueprints typically involve some definitions of the 'good' citizen and thus set boundaries on acceptable goals and behavior" (Edwards, 1973, p. 89).

Edwards (1973, p. 89) shows how the morality of sportsworld, congruent with the normative needs of a growing industrial society for hardworking and cooperative citizens, is transposed in the sports drama:

> By infusing exceptional, but "intrinsically" neutral physical activities with socially significant values, societies reinforce prevalent value sentiments regarding acceptable perspectives and behavior. They thus establish avenues of communicating to the populace those values focusing on solutions to critical problems, most notably those involving needs for societal integration and goal attainment.

Thus, it is no accident that the ideology or occupational psychosis of capitalism is metaphorically revealed in the sports, art, and popular culture of industrial society. As Kenneth Burke (1970, p. 41) indicates, "The psychotic force of the competitive ideology, so intense in the initial phase of American industrialization," is probably best revealed in the professionalization of sports . . . [and] in the flourishing of success literature during the late lamented New Era."

Sports, as a social drama, does not naively reflect the cultural assumptions of the larger society. It is an analogical world that dramatizes the dominant values in an arena that excludes much of what is problematic in real life. In general, audiences are subtly encouraged, through the vivid and dramatic portrayals, to accept the underlying ethos and to transpose it to other institutional areas. Sportsworld can be seen as an aesthetic and proverbial world. The sports aesthetic can be seen as facilitating the internalization of the "proper" attitudes towards mobility, success, and competition. In this way, sports is the *symbolic* expression of the values of the larger political and social milieu.

Sportsworld has not only symbolized the business ethos. Its integrative functions encompass other important value premises of American society. The growth of industrialization in America was concomitant with the movement toward democratization and the incorporation of the immigrant (Betts, 1974; Novak, 1976). Sports has played an important role in helping inculcate the belief that America is an egalitarian society, while at the same time giving immigrants symbolic assurance that they too have a place in this society. That this function of sports has mythical characteristics that do not exactly correspond to the reality of American society does not detract from integrative effects of its dissemination.

Sports in the years of its infancy was viewed by many educators and observers as potentially a great promoter of the democratic spirit. As Betts (1974) points out, fair play and sportsmanship were identified with the American ideal. In other words, in America we compete and struggle, but we do so within the clearly demarcated limits provided by democratic rules, sportsmanship, and fair play.

The heuristic value of sports for democratic life was most forcefully expressed by Mallery (as quoted in Betts, 1974, p. 187) in "The Social Significance of Play." His views are representative of that era:

> It seems a far cry from the ideal of fair play in boys' games to the ideal of fair play in the political life of our democracy yet it can be demonstrated that the ideals of fair play and team play are important in forming the character of a community . . . Team games of the playground require the submission of the individual will to the welfare of the team. Rigid rules inculcate fair play . . . New standards are set up; standards of self-control, of helping the other fellow, of fighting shoulder to shoulder for the honor of the team . . . the standards, when translated into the language of political life, we call Self-government, Respect for the Law, Social Service and Good Citizenship.

The feeling that the sporting code represented the democratic concept of law and society was most vigorously promoted by Luther Gulick, a founder of the "Y" movement. Gulick saw play as a preparation for democracy. This feeling was not, however, limited to the natural promoters and beneficiaries of the athletic ideal. Respected academicians like G. Stanley Hall also recognized the social value of sport. Perhaps the most striking manifestation, though, is in Mead's discussion of socialization, equality, and democracy. Mead (1934, p. 134) constantly used the sports metaphor to indicate how the individual self develops a social foundation by recognizing and interacting with others as equals:

> The organized community or social group which gives to the individual his unity of self may be called "the generalized other." The attitude of the generalized other is the attitude of the whole community. Thus, for example, in the case of such a social group as a ball team, the team is the generalized other in so far as it enters as an organized process or social activity—into the experience of any one of the individual members of it.

As Duncan (1968) points out in his commentary on Mead, sports enables the individual to develop a respect for democratic rules and an awareness of the necessity for a cooperative division of labor in an industrial society.

This aesthetic symbolization of the democratic ideal played a significant role in the process of the Americanization of the immigrants. As John Betts (1974, p. 187) points out:

> The code of fair play and sportsmanship was widely praised as promoting good citizenship and deeper understanding of our democratic institutions. Although the repetition of such ideas was most frequently found on the sports page, an ever increasing realization of sport's significance worked its way into the inner fabric of the American mind.

This inner and outer awareness led people to see the ethics and philosophy of sports as analagous to the ideological infrastructure of Americanism.

The identification of sports with American values had a further impact on the assimilation of the immigrant. Sports offered him a road to respectable status. Immigrant successes on the diamond, field, and court helped to facilitate the feeling of acceptability. The sports success of one's ethnic brethren symbolized the possibilities for acceptance and mobility in America. As Walter Camp said (as quoted in Betts, 1974, p. 187), "Americanization is more possible for those who come to our shores through the medium of American sports than in almost any other way." Immigrant involvement in sports encouraged the development of a diffuse attachment to the American way while at the same time fostering toleration by lessening nativist pressures.[5]

III

Sports has acted historically as an important socializer of dominant values. It has done so in a symbolic-aesthetic and analogical sense. The development of sportsworld as a symbolic-aesthetic realm has important implications for understanding the complex and often paradoxical function of sports in the American polity. As we have seen, many analysts have shown quite cogently how sports can be viewed as a practice arena for life in American society. Each of these analysts sees self-discipline, competition, team spirit, and "character" as essential components of American ideology. The problem of seeing sports in this way is that it leaves the observer with the difficulty of understanding sports' appeal once the values of competitive capitalism begin to wane. The question of historical change is raised along with that of the flexibility of sports' adaptation to this change.

It is quite possible that sports, like any other institution or ideology, developed out of certain political, economic, and social conditions, and yet proceeded to achieve a certain degree of autonomy from those conditions, responding to them and yet, at the same time, exerting a reciprocal effect on them. The intrinsic appeal of sports as a symbolic lifeworld apart from the pressures of everyday reality can be seen to acquire increasing significance for social and political integration with the evolution of American industrialization.

In trying to grasp sports as a cultural component of the American political and social totality, we must be alive to the dialectic of socialization and "escape." We can do this by viewing the sportsworld as a semiautonomous symbolic universe of meaning that exists within certain objective political and social conditions. In this sense, the early development of sports in America can be seen as both a reflection of and a compensation for the growth of industrialization. The early sports heroes, collectively portrayed by Gilbert Patten in his Frank Merriwell stories (Boyle, 1963), can be seen as character models for the young strivers for success in industrial America. Merriwell, more Horatio Alger than Alger ever was, can be seen as a fictional "idol of production" whose abilities exemplified what one could achieve in *life* if only one persevered.

Yet, it is also clear that the national pastime at the turn of the century provided an idyllic pastoral retreat from the pressure of urbanization and industrialization. As Umphlett (1975, p. 23) has shown:

> At the same time that the restrictions of city life gave rise to the desire to release inner tensions in some sporting endeavor, there was the impulse to the primitive but ideologized world of nature as symbolized by the sanctified space of the playing area.

The aesthetic nature of sportsworld facilitates its perception as a discrete, "apart" world while at the same time making it easier for spectators to engage themselves with the symbolic values that are being enacted.

In the early period of its growth, we can see how the sports drama inculcated the important values of competitive capitalism. In this sense, when sociologists criticize the idealistic, philosophically abstract, treatment of sports and games, they are very persuasive. Yet, when sports is viewed as an "ideal realm" (Huizinga, 1944/1955; Weiss, 1969) or when organized games are seen as arenas of freedom from reality as play communities, there is much to be learned because these types of analyses can help us understand how sports can become a seemingly contradictory symbolic reality.[6]

As American society shifts from an emphasis on hard work and production to an emphasis on leisure and consumption, we can detect a shift in the dialectical function of sports as well. Lowenthal's (1961) work on popular culture helps illuminate the forces at work in shifting from "idols of production" to "idols of consumption." Instead of Carnegie or Mellon as exemplars we find Babe Ruth; Walt Frazier, and Joe Namath. The shift signals the decline of self-denial and the rise of self-gratification as would befit a society of spenders and consumers.

With the decline of "ruthless competition" and the rise of organization, cooperation, and gregariousness, the sports ethos begins to take on the appearance of a contradictory world, a world where *values* are still adhered to. Sports increasingly becomes not so much a microcosm as a *cosmos* with its own semiautonomous standards. Offen (1974) points this out:

> There is a theory, quite prevalent among analysts . . . that sports is a microcosm of life. It isn't. Sports is life to the nth degree. It is life *in extremis;* every season you are born and you die . . . Sports is a world speeded up and a world of absolutes. There is good and bad, black and white, right and wrong. It's not gray and tentative like the real world. It is hyperlife under glass.

It is this opposite nature of much of sportsworld that must be emphasized. As industrialization and production evolves into post-industrialization and consumption, many political and social theorists have observed an enervation of the traditional social bonds that hold American society together. A widespread alienation from work is observed (Aronowitz, 1973; Terkel, 1972), and people's individual identities are seen as problematic with the decline of nationalism and religiosity (Klapp, 1969; Erikson, 1967). People are seen to long for close individual and communal ties to overcome the perceived impersonality and lack of warmth of bureaucratized and rationalized American society (Klapp, 1969; Nisbet, 1969). In this situation, sportsworld can be seen as a place to escape mechanization while partaking in a set of common experiences.[7]

Sportsworld can thus be analyzed as a cultic movement with its own assumptions. As Reston (1969) has written, "The world of sports has everything the world of politics lacks and *longs for.* . . . They have more pageantry and even more dignity than most occasions in American life; more team work, more unity, and more certainty at the end than most things." Sportsworld has become the realm par excellence that provides the aesthetic form and putative ethical content that contrasts so sharply, in the consciousness of many Americans, with a political and social world seen as deficient in either grace or ideals.

Sportsworld not only creates a seemingly ethical realm, it also creates a communicative bond reminiscent of the powerful Greek festivals. The individual's need for transcendent bonds that unite him to others is supplied by rituals, rallies, communions, and rhetorical exhortations that overlay the rational structure of authority in a political system. Stone (1970, p. 405) emphasizes this idea:

> The solidarity of the larger society rests in part upon the maintenance of a community of experience, people must share both knowledge about and acquaintance with similar salient events.

With the increased bureaucratization and depersonalization of American society, sports increasingly functions as the more "personal," more "concrete," and more "intense" province of meaning (Hoggart, 1970; Coover, 1968; Exley, 1968).[8] This is especially true with the decline of political ideology and the waning of patriotic fervor. Hence, sportsworld attains a high degree of subjective reality. The psychiatrist, Beisser (1967, p. 129), underscores this point:

> Everyone needs to feel he has ties with others. With the dispersal of the traditional extended family, the clan and the tribe, this need to be identified with a group of some kind has become more intense. The sports fan has a readily identifiable group to satisfy this need, at least in part. He has a meeting place, where he is needed to support the team. He can gather with others, don his Dodger cap or some other identification badge, to yell at the top of his lungs for his teams. . . . In effect, by doing all this, he becomes a member of a larger, stronger, family group, or collective entity comparable in some sense to the tribe or clan.

Sportsworld, as Leider's (1976) idealistic essay has eloquently captured, is an ideal place where "we think of ourselves as." In this sense (Novak, 1976, p. 216), it can be perceived as a utopian realm:

> Sports are deeper than politics—deeper than any single political system and deeper in the human heart than political authority. Sports lie at the very root of liberty . . . in the free play of intelligence and imagination. . . . (In heaven, it is rumored, the angels play in the presence of great love and light. Sports yield our metaphors for paradise.) . . . Utopian, paradise, the passing away of proletarianism, the ultimate vision and every culture known to history consists in every lasting play. Which is to say that sports already are in end time. . . . Sports constitute the one place in life where the revolution is *here*.

IV

Sportsworld inculcates values while providing an aesthetic utopian refuge from the demands of American industrial society. The utopianism of sports, however, is integrated within the mechanized and technical environment. Its existence as an opposite realm functions to absorb many of the pressures of rationalization while generating tolerance for the overall political system.[9] Mueller (1970), building on the work of Habermas (1971), sees the growth of sheer technological domination as one important aspect of legitimation in American society. In this analysis, the technical efficiency of the American system, its ability to provide the goods, is seen as a "paraideology." Paraideologies further integration while being divorced from any political or normative rationale of authority.

In this context, it is perhaps legitimate to see sports as part of the paraideology of technology and consumption (Ellul, 1964, p. 382; Mannheim, 1940, p. 313). It creates a common set of symbols that are specifically American while not directly related to the system of political authority. It provides meaning and purpose for millions who would perhaps find life barren otherwise (thereby promoting a diffuse rain or shine attachment that is so dear to the functionalist).[10]

In this evolving dialectic between sports as a socializer and sports as an escape, we can see how the escape component becomes more integral to political and social integration. Yet the socializing function does not become moribund. Sports, as a moral realm, remains to many the unique repository of all that is American and good. In addition, as America becomes a more organized and complex society, the values of teamwork and cooperation, so prevalent in the sports ideology, are important influences. They serve as a useful moral counterpoint to the rebellious appeal of the left to "do your own thing."

The growth of sports as a symbolic mass movement has generated a growing interest in the political, social, and economic aspects of the phenomenon. The increased interest, when coupled with the attacks, counterattacks, and social science investigations, has undermined the discrete status of sportsworld as a world apart. This process of rationalization has opened the door further to the examination of the larger relationships between sports and the major institutional areas of our society. This paper has just begun to explore some of these relationships.

Notes

1. The separation of sports from the mundane and often corrupt world of politics and business is one historical source of its great appeal (Petrie, 1975). The growth of sports as beyond the everyday must be understood in order to come to grips with the contemporary implosion of political and economic concerns within the world of sports.
2. This can be seen in the story of Judge Landis, baseball's first powerful commissioner, commonly referred to as "Czar" (Betts, 1974, p. 288; Voigt, 1976, p. 70).

3. This paper seeks to begin the task of developing a political theory of American sports symbolism. Limitations of space prevent a more detailed examination.

4. An expanded version of my "Reflections on a Mirror" (Note 1) will appear in an anthology edited by Gunther Luschen and published by Addison-Wesley. This paper is congruent with some of the themes discussed here but the analysis is more detailed.

5. Sports also was seen by sympathetic elites to be an antidote to the "pathology" of the city (gangs, drugs, and perversion). The attack on this pathology was often linked to attacks on the immorality of entire immigrant groups. In this respect, the immigrant's adoption of sports sanitized him while reinforcing the image of sport's curative-cleansing value.

6. Weiss and Huizinga analyze the autonomy of sports as a play area. Their work in studying the ideal *form* of sports complements the sociological emphasis on being realistic in examining the direct political and economic implications of sports.

7. In this context, the many similarities between the new left romanticism of the 1960s and the neo-conservative nostalgia for community is instructive.

8. The fiction of Coover and Exley, like the novels of Franz Kafka, does much to capture the symbolism of sports and the potential intensity of fan involvement.

9. Almond and Verba (1963) have pointed to the integrative possibilities of "extra-political" spheres in their ability to create a "diffuse" sense of attachment.

10. Both Ellul and Mannheim, the former damning and the latter praising, have underscored the integrative powers of mass sports in an advanced technological society. In Mannheim's analysis it is part of the rational control of "joy."

Reference Note

1. Lipsky, R. *Reflections on a mirror: The political implications of American sports symbolism.* Paper presented at the Political Science Conference, City University of New York, November 1976.

References

ALMOND, G., & Verba, S. *The civic culture.* Princeton: Princeton University Press, 1963.

ARONOWITZ, S. *False promises: The shaping of American working class consciousness.* New York: McGraw-Hill, 1973.

BEISSER, A. *The madness in sports.* New York: Appleton-Century-Crofts, 1967.

BETTS, J. *America's sporting heritage, 1850-1950.* Reading, MA: Addison-Wesley, 1974.

BOYLE, R. *Sport: Mirror of American life*. Boston: Little, Brown, 1963.

BURKE, K. *Permanence and change*. Indianapolis: Bobbs-Merrill, 1970.

COOVER, R. *The Universal Baseball Association, J. Henry Waugh, prop*. New York: Random House, 1968.

DULLES, F.R. *America learns to play*. New York: Appleton-Century-Crofts, 1965.

DUNCAN, H. *Communication and social order*. New York: Oxford University Press, 1968.

EDWARDS, H. *The revolt of the Black athlete*. New York: Free Press, 1969.

EDWARDS, H. *The sociology of sport*. Homewood, IL: Dorsey Press, 1973.

ELLUL, J. *The tehnological society*. New York: Vintage, 1964.

ERIKSON, E. *Childhood and society*. New York: W.W. Norton, 1967.

EXLEY, F. *A fan's notes*. New York: Random House, 1968.

HABERMAS, J. *Toward a rational society*. Boston: Beacon Press, 1971.

HOCH, P. *Rip off the big game*. Garden City, NY: Doubleday, 1971.

HOGGART, R. *The uses of literacy*. New York: Oxford University Press, 1970.

HUIZINGA, J. *Homo ludens: A study of the play element in culture*. Boston: Beacon Press, 1955. (Originally published, 1944.)

KLAPP, O. *The collective search for identity*. New York: Holt, Rinehart & Winston, 1969.

LEIDER, A. The National Football League and American life. *The New York Times*, January 18, 1976, Section 5.

LIPSYTE, R. *Sports world: An American dream land*. New York: Quadrangle, 1976.

LOWENTHAL, L. *Literature, popular culture and society*. Englewood Cliffs, NJ: Prentice-Hall, 1961.

MANNHEIM, K. *Man and society in an age of reconstruction*. New York: Harvest Books, 1940.

MEAD, G.H. *Mind, self and society*. Chicago: University of Chicago Press, 1934.

MEGGYSEY, D. *Out of their league*. Berkeley: Ramparts Press, 1970.

MORTON, H. *Soviet sport*. New York: Colliers, 1963.

MUELLER, K. *The politics of communication*. New York: Oxford University Press, 1970.

NISBET, R. *The quest for community*. New York: Oxford University Press, 1969.

NOVAK, M. *The joy of sports*. New York: Basic Books, 1976.

OFFEN, N. *God save the players*. Chicago: Playboy Press, 1974.

OLIVER, C. *High for the game*. New York: William Morrow, 1971.

PAXON, F. The rise of sport. In G. Sage (Ed.), *Sport and society*. Reading, MA: Addison-Wesley, 1970. (Originally published, 1917.)

PETRIE, B. Sport and politics. In D. Ball & J. Loy (Eds.), *Sport and social order*. Reading, MA: Addison-Wesley, 1975.

RAFFERTY, M. Intercollegiate athletics: The gathering storm. In J. Scott (Ed.), *The athletic revolution*. New York: Free Press, 1971.

RESTON, J. Sports and politics in America. *The New York Times*, September 12, 1969.

ROBINSON, W.C. Professional sports and the anti-trust laws. In G. Kenyon & J. Loy (Eds.), *Sport, culture and society*. New York: Macmillan, 1969.

SCOTT, J. (Ed.), *The athletic revolution*. New York: Free Press, 1971.

STONE, G. Some meanings of American sport. In G. Sage (Ed.), *Sport and society*. Reading, MA: Addison-Wesley, 1970.

TERKEL, S. *Working*. New York: Avon Books, 1972.

UMPHLETT, W. *The sporting myth and the American experience*. Lewisburg, PA: Bucknell University Press, 1975.

VOIGT, D.Q. *America through baseball*. Chicago: Nelson-Hall, 1976.

WEISS, P. *Sport: A philosophical inquiry*. Carbondale: Southern Illinois University Press, 1969.

Chapter 3
Myths After Baseball: Notes on Myths in Sports

DAVID Q. VOIGT

I. Myths and Man: A Frame of Reference

A myth is not a lie. This proposition should be writ large by scholars because to treat a myth as a lie is to run a risk of misunderstanding the very behavior patterns one seeks to elucidate. Since sports historians draw heavily on journalistic accounts of sports which are seedbeds of this fallacy, sports historians must guard against rhetorical moralizing. Let them heed these words of a life long student of myths: "To say myth equals falsehood . . . *ergo* myth must be combated, disregards the rich storehouses of myth accumulated in many cultures." Such treasuries of myths represent historical acts of faith by people trying to read meaning into the problems of the human condition. To treat them as lies in the light of transitory, present-day standards, is to break faith with the past (Patai, 1972, pp. 28-32).

From *Quest*, Summer 1978, **30**, 46-57. Copyright 1978 by Quest Board. Reprinted with permission.

A myth is a dramatic story that justifes a popular institution or custom, that seeks to explain a given practice or value (Hoult, 1969), that articulates a people's wishful thinking (Benedict, 1959), that justifies present behavior in terms of what supposedly happened in the past (Honigmann, 1963, pp. 189-196). These statements concerning the vital functions of myths remind us that mythmaking is a basic human act and need. Myths are part of a society's folklore and modern myths are the "true" stories of today insofar as people are given to know "truth." The analysis of myths in their sociocultural context provides a penetrating picture of a society's way of life.

> After all, what people choose to talk about is always important for our understanding of them, and the narratives they choose to transmit from generation to generation . . . can hardly be considered unimportant in a fully rounded study of their culture. . . . For people *act* on the basis of what they believe to be true, not on what they think is mere fiction. (Hallowell, 1954)

Human beings cannot live without myths. Because people live in word worlds, myth is present in every word of every language; indeed, the original meaning of myth is "word" (McLuhan, 1960, pp. 288-289). That there is order in a people's myth system stems from the fact that myths follow a people's world view. A world view is a people's way of knowing. It rationalizes reality, explains the relations of man and nature, and organizes the ideas, knowledge, and values that form a basis for a social system. As long as a world view "works" it remains unchallenged and is supported by characteristic myths. But world views change, bringing with them changes in lifeways (Honigmann, 1963, pp. 189-196). Hence, a major function of myth is to explain inevitable social change. Thus, myths often appear as liminal phenomena, telling of a time and place that is "betwixt and between." This function of myth explains how things became what they presently are, as illustrated by myths explaining life crises like birth, mating, disease, death and economic and social changes (Turner, 1968).

To understand modern American myths is to understand the predominant American world view of today. For the past century, rational science has been a dominant American world view. This outlook emphasizes knowledge and control of natural forces. In searching for explanatory principles we extol observation, quantification, calibration, and problem-solving. The "scientist" is our culture hero; his type abounds in most of our social institutions. Scientific knowledge has reshaped our institutions: industry, economics, medicine, politics, communications, sports. With science come new myths, and a major mythmaker is the scientific historian who evokes new myths by his interpretation of "facts" (Honigmann, 1963, pp. 189-196).

It was not always thus. History shows a long exposure to religious world views, including the Christian heritage which rationalized reality in terms of supernatural intervention. Earlier there were magical world views which, like science, saw reality as shaped by forces which man might control by using proper techniques of observation, imitation, and contagion. Like science, with its myths, religion and magic carry their own unique myths. Today science may dominate, but elements of religion and magic still linger to influence behaviors. Indeed, the myths that guide modern Americans are likely to be complex blendings of science, religion, and magic.

Although the scientific world view functions to critique ancient religious and magical myths, science continually creates myths of its own. In McLuhan's view, advertising, TV, and Hollywood dream factories all add to our storehouse of myths. The instantaneous character of today's information dispersal constantly dazzles us with new myths and dramatizes McLuhan's brilliant assertion that the media offer both message and massage. The proliferation of print media enhanced our faith in individualism; new electronic media tend to tribalize (McLuhan, 1960, pp. 268-289). In 1848 Karl Marx predicted that modern myths would exalt industrialism, commerce, technology, parliamentary democracy, and socialism (Levin, 1960, pp. 103-114). Raphael Patai adds a host of others as part of our scientific-industrial heritage. These include utopian myths of a coming triumph for organized labor, modern redeemer myths, myths of gods that failed and died, hero myths, myths of oral gratification, Madison Avenue myths, and new sex myths. What we lack is a dominant "charter myth" for democracy; what we now have is a listing of mythologems, a bewildering array of piecemeal mythical features (Patai, 1972, pp. 90ff). The impact of so many disparate myths, acting at cross purposes with themselves and with surviving magical and religious myths is confusing to the average man. In such a cultural climate, myths lend little guidance. Hopefully, the serious study of modern myths, including those in sports, might breathe some order and point toward a clarified myth curriculum.

II. Myths after Baseball: Reflections of American Society

Our commitment to a rational-scientific world view prompts us to look to natural forces and events to explain the origins of behaviors. American baseball mirrors this quest for scientific understanding. Indeed, a scientist recently declared that our planet is shaped like a much batted baseball, with bulges and depressions running "in twin bonds like the interlocking pieces of horsehide stitched over a baseball" (*New York Times*, 1970). Given the current production of cowhide covered baseballs, and possible plastic covered ones to come, this statement is already dated! Our dominating world view holds man to be the measurer and fabricator of all things, including our course of evolution. Since we view civilization as man's own show, much scientific mythology exalts those creative individuals who unlock nature's secrets and those inventors who devise the technology used to overcome nature. The technological side of our scientific mythology has us worshipping the material abundance produced by technology. The twin engines of science and industry foster a mania for measuring, calibrating, and quantifying countless aspects of human behavior (Mandell, Note 1). Our faith in scientific and technological discovery and invention has made folk heroes of geniuses like Einstein, Ford, and Salk. Our urge to put science to work in industrial production has us making all kinds of sciences and subsciences to fit our institutions. Our zeal for compiling and storing scientific knowledge knows no bounds; today who can deny that banks and office buildings represent temples to science, their plentiful existence testifying to this dominant world view!

The history of American sports mirrors our faith in rational science and offers glimpses into sports' dynamic mythology. The oft-told and oft-discredited myth of baseball's invention by Abner Doubleday is an obvious example. The Doubleday creation myth belongs in that class of myths which exalt scientific pioneers. Embedded in this class of myths is a driving faith in human ingenuity and creative individualism, an idea so strong as to dominate modern psychological theory and to impose its cultural imperative on all Americans. What the myth says is study and learn so that mayhap you can join the ranks of culture creators. The persistence of the myth of young Doubleday, a West Point student inventing the game of baseball in all its symmetry, derives from our acceptance of larger myths of creative individuals. Its lingering presence in baseball folklore angers and baffles historians who are wont to blame uncritical journalists and gullible fans for its persistence. Yet the myth survives learned assaults. This might be partly explained in the function of myths to amuse and to entertain. Another explanation might be that it is useful for squaring American baseball with science. After all, to abandon the Doubleday myth might mean accepting as fact that the game evolved in haphazard, piecemeal, trial-and-error fashion. Perhaps sports historians might be better off accepting the myth as a tall tale which performs a necessary function of reinforcing popular faith in scientific creativity at a time when such faith is sorely strained.

On the other hand, baseball has had legitimate innovators whose inventive and promotional genius strengthened the game and fostered its growth. Personalities like the late Harry Wright and Branch Rickey might be propagated into more realistic mythical heroes. As creators their lives in baseball serve as "a better mythical fit" than Doubleday's.

Harry Wright's long managerial career during the late 19th century brought accepted techniques for training players, for club management and promotion, and for popularizing the major league spectacle. Wright truly deserves the accolade of "father of the professional game." What Wright did in the last century, Rickey did in the present one. During half a century as player, manager, and general manager, Rickey's innovations in recruiting, teaching and training players led to a dazzling number of championship successes. Today Rickey's disciples abound in major league baseball, and their presence as managers, scouts, general managers, and club presidents testifies to his impact on the game's development.

Technology's link to science is vividly mirrored in baseball promotion. It is evidenced in the three great stadium building booms from 1880 to the present. Its most recent manifestations are the air-conditioned, domed stadiums at Houston, Seattle, and New Orleans. Modern player uniforms, pitching machines, cowhide balls, gloves, shoes, bats, bullpen carts, electronic scoreboards, stadium lights, and a host of assorted tools and artifacts testify to the American faith in the good life coming through technology. In the scientifically induced zeal for measuring and quantifying data about a game American baseball yields to no rival sport. Indeed, no other sport is so "scientific" in its gathering, disseminating, and reverencing of statistical information. Surely, baseball's are the most statistically agile fans, and their appetite is fed by annual records of all aspects of the game regularly supplied by statistical bureaus like the Elias Sports Bureau and the *Macmillan Encyclopedia of Baseball*, which enshrines such data for posterity.

Baseball's reverence of statistics mirrors the larger social tendency to reify statistics and to glorify statisticians. Embedded in this passion is yet another of our scientific myths. Call it a widely accepted act of faith in the ability of quantitative data to elucidate and to explain virtually any form of behavior. The fallacy in such a myth is that too often data explain little. Not infrequently have baseball statisticians manipulated data to assume a phony order in the game's history. Certainly statisticians err in comparing exploits of players from different eras. They err by overemphasizing today's standards and by ignoring stylistic characteristics of past eras. The notion that one can homogenize behaviors from vastly different eras is a myth of consistency that permeates our society. One astute observer saw statistics as interesting, but cautioned that they do not count enough. Often they tell little. Baseball games are not randomly uniform; rather each is unique (*The Sporting News*, 1973).

Little more than three centuries have elapsed since the scientific world view came to dominate Western thought, but once it did it profoundly altered our thinking about social relationships (Whitehead, 1948). Under rational-science the nation state took on awesome importance and the world of work was reshaped by industrialism, capitalism, and unionism (Bendix, 1960). Social relationships were also reshaped. New myths followed the world view of rational-science. An important organizational response to the scientific world view has been the growing influence of the nation state. The political sociologist Seymour Lipset stated that after Appomatox America became "the first new nation." What he meant was that American science and industry, having proved decisive in the victory, were welding the country into a modern functioning industrial state (Lipset, 1967, pp. 21ff). What made for a *united* United States after 1865 were new communities, new transportation links, and new bonds of industrial production, distribution, and consumption. The new American nation sought to express its nationalist sentiments. This expression took many forms (i.e., linguistic, literary, and sporting).

In 1865 American baseball rode a popular crest of sporting approval. By 1870 the game was often proclaimed as America's "national game," a claim that grew increasingly strident over the years. Thus, a modern myth was born—the myth of baseball as the national game. Used by promoters like Henry Chadwick, Harry Wright, and Albert G. Spalding, the myth proved to be highly profitable. Certainly it boosted the game's public image to have Presidents open most of the 20th century seasons by throwing out the first ball, or to have politicos couple baseball with other symbols of American unity. On three occasions Spalding harnessed the myth in forlorn efforts to export baseball abroad. Like the myth of America's manifest destiny which promised a millenium to those countries which emulated our national experience, this horsehide version of our destiny proved dangerously disillusioning. The lesson learned from the failure of those missions was that other nations had their own sporting preferences. We would learn that internationally soccer is much preferred to baseball, and that when baseball was planted in other lands, it was not the American form of the game, but a uniquely native one.

As for the myth that baseball is America's national game, baseball leaders would do well to seek a better fitting myth. After all, one of the strengths of American democracy is its cultural pluralism. Were America to have a truly national game presupposes the existence of a monolithic lifestyle which would be anathema to liberty. So long as liberty remains a handmaiden of democracy, there can be no national sport, no national religion, no nationally favored subculture. It seems evident that today's quest for a charter myth for our democracy cannot abide the myth of baseball being the national game (Voigt, 1976, pp. 79-105).

In becoming "the first new nation" in the technological sense, America employed the capitalistic myth as a rationale for binding the states together. As prophesied by Adam Smith in 1776, the capitalistic myth described the workings of a free economy, powered by popular appetites for profit with growth guaranteed by the self-seeking ingenuity of entrepreneurs. As the myth took hold, the entrepreneur industrialists and merchants became culture heroes whose machinations were not to be blocked by government interference.

Throughout its history major league baseball has mirrored the strengths and weaknesses of this myth. A dominant myth of baseball proclaims the right of an owner to "own" not only an urban region as his franchise, but also the players. Invoking this myth in 1876, a new breed of owners overthrew a player-controlled major league which they branded as corrupt and profitless. Later, officially sanctioned histories even denied major league status to that fallen league. By 1890 the owners successfully imposed a reserve clause binding a player to a club for life, established an owner's right to sell or trade players for profit, and placed ceilings on player salaries. Secure in their power and backed by the capitalist myth, owners of the 'nineties styled themselves as "magnates" after the fashion of celebrated captains of American industries (Voigt, 1976, pp. 4-6; 42-46). Today the limitations of the capitalistic ethic are obvious. Although major league baseball has expanded dramatically and profited immensely from TV and other innovations, the limits to growth seem apparent. Rising costs of stadiums have necessitated using public funds, bringing more governmental regulation. Governmental regulation has also been invoked to ensure "free competition" by protecting rights of players. Such assaults reveal the limits to the capitalistic myth. Today the right of an owner to move his franchise is subject to legal and political challenge. Likewise the reserving and selling of players is challenged. Indeed, the right of today's owner to own his territory and players is by no means certain. If free enterprise capitalism is challenged in baseball, it is also under fire in other economic areas. As the capitalistic myth empowered the entrepreneur, so the myth of the general strike held out hope for oppressed workers. In Patai's (1972) opinion the myth is a modification of older utopian myths promising better lives for all men (pp. 90ff). Although the myth has never dominated in America, American workers increasingly embrace the ethic of unionism. Such a myth urges workers to organize in order to claim a fair share of life's comforts.

In 1890 ballplayers mounted an unsuccessful all-out strike against owner oppression. For 70 years players lacked viable union protection. Like teachers, government workers, or white collar workers, players were expected to disdain unions in favor of a "professional approach." Meanwhile the reserve clause stood as a barrier to equity in contract bargaining. In the 1960s came the Major League Players Association under the skilled leadership of veteran unionist Marvin Miller (Parrott, 1976, p. 265). Using existing labor laws on behalf of the players, Miller forced owners to deal with his association. In a series of agreements players scored gains in pensions, salaries, and fringe benefits. In 1976 a new contract drastically limited the reserve clause by allowing veteran players to sell their services in open bidding under the re-entry draft system. A tough negotiator, Miller has rejected arbitrary disciplining of players either by owners or by the Commissioner. We see baseball mirroring the spread of unionism in America. As a device for gaining access to power, unionism extends beyond industry to aid blacks, women, senior citizens, and a host of other groups. Clearly, the myth thrives as a powerful antidote to the excesses of the capitalistic myth.

Two other myths of our industrial-scientific society merit consideration. They are the myths of racial and sexual inequality, each proclaiming that inherited biological weaknesses justify discriminatory treatment. As popularly expressed both hold blacks and women to be socially inferior. Of the two, racist mythology is the more recently formulated. Under the pseudo science of "social Darwinism" blacks and other ethnic groups have been ranked lower on the evolutionary scale and, hence, judged fit to be segregated. If anyone doubts the capacity of science to spawn myths, let them look to this one. Certainly the myth of black and ethnic inferiority is tooted in American baseball. Major league baseball has been one of the most segregated of American institutions. Despite the acclaimed admission of Jackie Robinson to the majors in 1947, official policy has been that of grudgingly slow acceptance. Even now black and Latin-American players must be better than average performers to gain admission. Furthermore, exploits of stars like Hank Aaron or Rod Carew are less acclaimed and earn less endorsement income than those of whites. The notion of a "tipping point" still persists in the minds of some owners who maintain *sub rosa* quota systems. On the other hand, the complexity of the ethnic myth becomes more evident when blacks and Latin-Americans are said to be better endowed athletically than whites, as evidenced for example by a black newspaper's lament that the Phillies lost the 1977 playoffs by not playing enough blacks. Although myths of race superiority or inferiority are scientifically unfounded, they are widely accepted in the land and any hope of attaining the charter myth of democracy requires a wholesale unlearning of such divisive mythology (*New York Times*, 1976).

Much older than racist myths are the sexist myths. In the opinion of the anthropologist H.R. Hays, "the myth of feminine evil," of women as the dangerous sex, is one of the oldest and most universal of all myths. Hays found widespread a belief that, owing to biological differences, women act and think differently from men. There is an attraction and repulsion process between the sexes, with repulsion based on some mythical notion of feminine evil which includes a belief in women's ability to rob men of their physical prowess by draining them sexually and psychologically (Hays, 1964). So widespread is this fear that social restrictions like fixed roles, dress, and decorum have continually been imposed on women, lending credibility to claims by present day liberationists that women's bodies are indeed defined and controlled by myth-bound men (Frankfort, 1972). American baseball mirrors the changing versions of this myth and supports Gordon Rattray Taylor's thesis that over the past century American sex relationships have shifted from patrist (male controlled) to matrist (equalitarian) norms. Baseball's emergence as a man's game reflects older patrist notions calling for the segregation of the sexes and using assumed biological inferiority to bar women from participating in the game. Even today baseball men often assume that indulgence in sexual intercourse saps the strengths of players. At least *a fortiori* criticisms by scientists have exposed the groundlessness of such claims. Players today are generally freer to marry and to indulge in sex. Moreover, women are gaining rights to play in professional leagues and to hold responsible jobs in major league baseball. To be sure, the big league game is still a male preserve, but at least the notion is taking hold that women can hold other jobs than that of sexually seductive usherettes. But baseball has not yet shown up in the vanguard of social change (Voigt, Note 2).

III. Myths after Doubleday:
Some Mini-Myths of Baseball Today

The human tendency to formulate and then modify myths is highlighted in the study of American baseball. In searching the history of the major league game one regularly encounters a bewildering profusion of myths—often contradictory and clashing, culturally supporting and destroying. One learns by their study much about myth-makers and myth-believers. This section probes selected areas of baseball history including fans, Commissioners, players, managers, and the game's image makers. While arbitrary in selection and brief in analysis, it may stimulate further inquiry. As liminal phenomena myths function to explain change and to show how those who are rocked by change try to explain how things became what they are now. Myths always provide temporary explanations of changing behaviors.

In truth very little is known about baseball fans. That they are numerous is clear enough; that they are a highly varied lot is less understood. Hence, widely proclaimed myths by nostalgic-minded sportswriters about the "true" fans are suspect. Some argue that "true" fans are to be found only in the cheap seats or bleachers. Such fans are thought to be more knowledgeable, rebellious, and littering (Furlong, 1966; *New York Post*, 1967; *New York Times*, 1973). An echo of a larger Marxist myth of the goodness of the proletariate, another version of this myth proclaims spring training fans to be the true ones. Such fans crowd the Florida training parks in the spring, and because exhibition games are often played on sunlit, grassy fields with fans and players in close proximity, purveyors of the myth conclude that this is baseball as it was meant to be (*New York Times*, 1977). As social nostalgia such a myth is harmless enough. More menacing is a recently concocted myth which holds that fans are more angry, threatening, and riotous than those of yesteryear. Seeking to validate this claim, one writer blamed TV, night ball, mercenary players, and even "monsterized" players for inciting fans to riot. The latter characterization assumes that fans are provoked by the larger sizes of today's players (Poe, 1975). Such a claim carries little sense of history. As for monstrous sizes and greater mercenary impulses, who can gainsay that players of yesteryear lacked both? As for TV and night ball, these are recent innovations and their link to riotous behavior is certainly not proved. Recent decisions to schedule World Series games at night evoked criticisms from writers who argued that "true fans" at the park were being sacrificed for the convenience of TV audiences. Yet in 1976 the Series games were witnessed by as many as 61 million TV fans whose very number argues for their rights as fans. Indeed, the notion that TV fans today carry baseball merits serious consideration (*The Sporting News*, 1976).

Acting on the myth that baseball fans are an undifferentiated mass audience recently prompted Ralph Nader to subsidize an organization called *Fight to Advance the Nation's Sports* (F.A.N.S.) to act as a consumer action group. F.A.N.S. seeks to represent the views of an estimated 100 million sports fans against leagues, player associations, the media, the owners, Congress, the courts, and any "appropriate forums." But F.A.N.S.' weakness lies in its assumption that all fans have the same interests and desires. Its success, or more likely its failure, could well rest on the fallacious assumption that sporting fans are an undifferentiated mass audience (*Leftfield*, 1977).

Meanwhile the search for answers to the question of how to maintain decorum at games and to shield the game from corruption calls to mind one of the oldest of baseball's mini-myths. This is the Judge K.M. Landis myth—the myth of the game's redeemer. This tale holds that baseball's Black Sox scandal—the game's first major sin (another myth)—prompted a crisis in public confidence. To restore popular faith, Judge Landis, charged with redeeming the game, became High Commissioner in 1921. By punishing guilty players, hounding gamblers, and curbing the excesses of owners and players, the Judge supposedly saved the game. Henceforth major league baseball retained a Commissioner charged with dealing with "any act detrimental to baseball." This myth assumes that the Commissioner is ever able to intervene on behalf of truth and justice (Daley, 1964). The Landis myth needs to be corrected by historical fact. Judge Landis was a human being with a set of malicious prejudices that led him to deny players their civil rights. The owners (the real powers) kept Landis in check and overrode some of his prejudices (i.e., his opposition to farm systems). Yet in his lifetime Landis' public image was rectitude so powerful that any successor must despair in his feeble mortality. Thus it came to pass that the Commissioner's role in baseball steadily weakened (Voigt, 1973, pp. 437-439; Veeck, 1965). After Happy Chandler's ouster came Ford Frick's long tenure, made possible by his toadying to the wishes of powerful owners like Walter O'Malley. After Frick came William Eckert. Dubbed "the unknown soldier" and quickly shunted out, Eckert was replaced by the incumbent, Bowie Kuhn. Although Kuhn vowed to rekindle the myth of the powerful Commissioner, it was an empty vow based on a bad sense of history. Reality shows that since the inception of the Commissioner system, some clique of interest held power over the game and the Commissioner. The record also shows that all Commissioners have placed owner interests over player interests. It is this realization by today's players which has done most to reduce the Commissioner's image (Povich, 1969). The incumbent Kuhn often finds himself caught between owners and organized players. At such times he suffers much *lese majesty*, having been called "the nation's idiot" by owner Charles Finley, and having his role pronounced obsolete by Marvin Miller (Veeck, 1972; Clark, 1972). Indeed, Miller's stature in baseball so far exceeds Kuhn's that Miller has been dubbed the players' commissioner. The title is earned since Miller has been their earthly redeemer.

Myths of the power wielders in baseball now seem to exclude team managers like Harry Wright, John McGraw, Connie Mack, and Joe McCarthy. Such managers were regarded as strategical and tactical geniuses. Because of them the mini-myth said that a manager's skill, dedication, ruthlessness, or charisma is a potent factor in any team's success; support for this myth has been provided by modern managers like the late Casey Stengel, Leo Durocher, Walter Alston, Earl Weaver, and Billy Martin. But recent baseball history suggests the collapse of the managerial myth. A new myth sees the manager's influence as mostly negative; when a team falters the injunction is "fire the manager!" Today's manager appears as the fall guy whose release serves to deflect public criticism from others. The myth of the manager as pilot is currently a shambles. Emasculated, defunctionalized, often bereft of player respect, modern managers are an anxiety-ridden lot who know their days are numbered. In the years 1946-1966 the average tenure for a big league manager was 3 years (Brosnan, 1966). Yet, as evidenced in Billy Martin's 1977 battle with his owner-boss George Steinbrenner, the myth lingers. On the other hand, as owner Phil Wrigley of the Cubs learned when his mid-1960s experiment of using rotating coaches to run games ended amidst national gales of ridicule, you cannot dispense with a manager. Managers yet must be, but their role is diminished.

As changing myths bring status deprivation to managers, so changing myths redefine player-heroes. Prior to 1950 player-hero biographies were tall tales of splendid performers who won fame through hard work, clean living, and battling obstacles. Suffice it to say that such tales are bowdlerized to serve as moralizing myths. But with Jim Brosnan's writings of the late 1950s, Jim Bouton's *Ball Four* and a host of other works a demythologizing trend began to depict heroes as real people with all of the vices of mortals. Indeed the lives of recent players like Reggie Jackson, Joe Pepitone, and Bo Belinsky flaunt behavioral excesses and raise up the new myth of the "swinger-star." This new myth even subjects ancient heroes like the late Babe Ruth to reconsideration. This seems to be a reflection of the widespread cynicism toward heroes which is rife in America today.

Baseball mirrors the large variety of hero postures to be found in America. Using Coffin's (1971) categories one can find prowess heroes like Ruth, tricksters like Ty Cobb, ethical heroes like Landis, Yankee trader types like Rickey, carnival hustlers like Veeck, fool types like Dizzy Dean or Finley, black militants like Robinson, black "Uncle Toms" like Satch Paige. Today's trend is different heroes for differing tastes. Moreover, there is a situational character to today's heroes which renders them readily disposable. By undermining the fans' sense of history, TV accounts for the transitory quality of hero worship. Yet, by precipitating enormous salaries, TV has promoted a new hero—the millionaire ballplayer.

Television's erosion of fans' sense of history may be also responsible for the myth which says that modern baseball heroics are not what they used to be. The myth of relative performance cracks when exposed to the facts, however. Many great records of the past have been surpassed. Lou Brock has bettered Cobb's base stealing totals; Hank Aaron broke Ruth's lifetime home run record; Roger Maris' 61 homers in '61 broke Ruth's seasonal record; Dale Long's eight homers in eight consecutive games in 1956 set a new record; Rod Carew's string of batting titles ranks him close to Cobb and Hornsby for consistency; modern defensive play excels that of the best of oldtime combinations. In double plays, for example, a hoary myth spawned by a F.P. Adams jingle sent Tinker, Evers, and Chance to the hall of fame when actually they once turned as few as 17 during a season! In 1962 if any club's seasonal combination failed to turn 80 double plays, it was regarded expendable. Yet the Tinker, Evers, Chance myth lingers, telling fans that the old days were the glory days. Great infielders with better credentials than the ancient Cub trio have yet to be voted in.

Sports historians must stand ready to evaluate many tall tales of baseball. Some of these sing of a nostalgic past, extolling the rural origins of baseball, the superiority of past heroes, and the moral superiority of baseball over other sports. Like a good batter, the historian of myths needs to keep both eyes on the ball, ever recognizing that myths are human behaviors. Far from being lies, such tales try to justify older behaviors, morals, customs, and institutions. Their lingering presence testifies to public bewilderment in the face of change and to regret over the passing of older beliefs. It is proposed that historians take up the task of criticizing sports myths; but in our zeal to create better fitting myths, let us recall Whitehead's dictum that, "Where attainable knowledge could have changed the issue, ignorance has the guilt of vice."

Reference Notes

1. Mandell, R. *The idea of a sports record.* John Betts Address. North American Society for Sport History Convention, Boston, May 1975.
2. Voigt, D.Q. *Sex in baseball: Reflections on a changing taboo.* Paper presented at the North American Society for Sport History Convention, Eugene, OR, June 1976.

References

BENDIX, R. *Max Weber: An intellectual portrait.* New York: Doubleday, 1960.

BENEDICT, R. Myth. *Encyclopedia of the Social Sciences,* 1959.

BROSNAN, J. The I's, we's and they's of baseball. *New York Times Magazine,* July 3, 1966.

CLARK, T. *Champagne and baloney: The rise and fall of Finley's A's.* New York: Harper & Row, 1976.

COFFIN, T. *The old ball game: Baseball in folklore and fiction.* New York: Harper & Row, 1971.

DALEY, A. Some inescapable facts. *New York Times,* November 11, 1964.

FRANKFORT, E. *Vaginal politics.* New York: Quadrangle, 1972.

FURLONG, W.B. Out in the bleachers where the action is. *Harper's,* July 1966.

HALLOWELL, A.I. Myth, culture and personality (1947). Quoted in W.R. Bascom, Four functions of folklore. *Journal of American Folklore,* 1954, 67(266), 333-349.

HAYS, H.R. *The dangerous sex: The myth of feminine evil.* New York: Putnam, 1964.

HONIGMANN, J. *Understanding culture.* New York: Harper & Row, 1963.

HOULT, T.F. *Dictionary of modern sociology.* New Jersey: Littlefield, Adams & Co., 1969.

LEFTFIELD, November 1977 (monthly publication F.A.N.S.).

LEVIN, H. Some meaning of myth. In H.A. Murray (Ed.), *Myth and myth-making*. New York: George Braziller, 1960.

LIPSET, S.M. *The first new nation*. New York: Doubleday-Anchor Books, 1967.

MCLUHAN, M. Myth and mass media. In H.A. Murray (Ed.), *Myth and myth-making*. New York: George Braziller, 1960.

NEW YORK POST, August 1, 1967.

NEW YORK TIMES, November 29,1970.

NEW YORK TIMES, July 15, 1973.

NEW YORK TIMES, March 2, 1976.

NEW YORK TIMES, January 30, 1977.

PARROTT, H. *The lords of baseball*. New York: Praeger, 1976.

PATAI, R. *Myths and modern man*. New York: Prentice-Hall, 1972.

POE, R. The angry fan. *Harper's*, November 1975.

POVICH, S. *All these mornings*. New York: Prentice Hall, 1969.

SPORTING NEWS, June 2, 1973.

SPORTING NEWS, November 6, 1976.

TURNER, V.W. Myth and symbol. *International Encyclopedia of the Social Sciences* (Vol. 10), 1968.

VEECK, B., Jr. *The hustler's handbook*. New York: Putnam, 1965.

VEECK, B., Jr. *Thirty tons a day*. New York: Viking, 1972.

VOIGT, D.Q. Kenesaw Mountain Landis. *Dictionary of American Biography* (Supplement 3), 1973.

VOIGT, D.Q. *America through baseball*. Chicago: Nelson-Hall, 1976.

WHITEHEAD, A.N. *Science and the modern world*. New York: New American Library, 1948.

Chapter 4

The Sport Hero:
An Endangered Species

GARRY SMITH

What Are Heroes?

In antiquity a hero was a mythical or legendary person who was strong, noble, and brave. Often the hero was thought to be favored by the gods, and in some cases the hero himself was deified. The mythical hero served a valuable function as a medium through which culture was transmitted from generation to generation. Usually, stories about the hero were related to an historical event and attempted to explain some of the basic beliefs, values, and traditions of the society.

A story involving a mythical hero frequently had a basis in fact, but as the story was told and re-told the heroic aspects of the person were magnified. Carlyle (1840) was aware of this penchant for hyperbole where heroes were concerned when he noted: "If a man was great while living he becomes ten-fold greater when dead (p. 26)."

From *Quest*, January 1973, **19**, 59-70. Copyright 1973 by the Quest Board. Reprinted with permission.

Carlyle's major premise was that "society is founded on hero worship" (p. 12), and he believed the hero was "like lightning out of heaven; the rest of men waited for him like fuel, then they too would flame" (p. 77). In this context the hero is regarded as an innovator and a catalyst. The hero is distinct from the ordinary man in that he is more sincere, has greater vision and insight, and has "fully met his obligation of self-development" (Lehman, 1928, p. 26).

To illustrate his theory, Carlyle employed six categories of heroes: the hero as divinity, the hero as prophet, the hero as poet, the hero as priest, the hero as a man of letters, and the hero as king. In this sense the hero truly was a great man as opposed to a merely famous man. Carlyle's heroes were: "the modellers, patterns, and in a wide sense creators, of whatsoever the general mass of men contrived to do or to attain" (Lehman, 1928, p. 56).

Contemporary scholars who have studied the hero have added to Carlyle's great man theory. Lerner (1957) speaks of two kinds of heroes; the history book hero and the vernacular or archetypal hero. The history book hero is roughly the equivalent of Carlyle's idea of the hero as someone who epitomizes the best in cultural and moral values. The vernacular or archetypal hero is more contemporary, and usually is a larger-than-life figure through which people can escape. The vernacular hero has fewer traditional heroic qualities than the history book hero and his fame is much more ephemeral.

Hook (1957) also has a useful way of distinguishing between hero types. He compares the "event-making" to the "eventful" man. In essence, the event-making man is someone who has an effect on significant developments, but who is merely in the right place at the right time. The eventful man is one whose actions are based on his outstanding capabilities rather than on the accident of time or position.

The most penetrating study of heroes is that by Klapp (1962, 1969) in his two books: *Heroes, Villains and Fools* and *Collective Search for Identity*. Klapp divides heroes into five main categories each with several subcategories. The skeleton of this classification system is presented in Table 1.

Klapp's classification scheme is comprehensive, perhaps too much so. Can the great lover, the charmer, and the jester really be heroic in the accepted sense of the word? A second taxonometric problem involves the possibility of a single individual fitting into more than one category. For example, Klapp consigns athletes to the subcategory "heroes of play." It may be equally fruitful to view some athletic heroes as the strong man, showman, martyr, or as a member of several categories at the same time.

Table 1

Categories of Heroes

Category	Theme
Winners (a) strong man (b) the brain (c) the smart operator (d) the great lover	Getting what you want, beating everyone, being a champ.
Splendid Performers (a) showmen (b) heroes of play (c) playboy	Shining before an audience, making a hit.
Heroes of Social Acceptability (a) the pin-up (b) the charmer (c) the good fellow (d) conforming heroes	Being liked, attractive, good, or otherwise personally acceptable to groups and epitomizing the pleasures of belonging.
Independent Spirits (a) bohemian (b) jester (c) angry commentator	Standing alone, making one's way by oneself.
Group Servants (a) defenders (b) martyrs (c) benefactors	Helping people, cooperation, self-sacrifice, group service and solidarity

The Functions of Heroes

The hero is a primary social model used by society to help maintain the social structure. Fishwick (1954) concurs with this viewpoint, although he may overstate the case when he says, "just as a pier holds up the bridge, so does the hero support society" (p. 226). Supposedly, societal models will best represent the major norms, values, and beliefs of the society. When societal models are successful, there should be a close relationship between the models and the rest of the society. A society usually will support its models and it will "recruit, train, and control members of the society in accordance with these models" (Klapp, 1962, p. 18).

The hero as a social model should be consistent in his behavior, and should be considerably better in a positive sense than most of the other members of the society. One of the hero's main functions is to raise the aspiration levels of the people in the society. Klapp (1962) argues that the hero lifts people above where they would be without the model. The essential feature of the hero from the societal vantage point is that the hero should behave in such a way as to perpetuate collective values, affirm social norms, and contribute to the solidarity of the society.

Why People Worship Heroes

Klapp (1969) defines hero worship as "a yearning relationship in which a person, in a sense, gets away from himself by wishing or imagining himself to be like someone whom he admires" (p. 211). Fishwick (1954) feels that hero worship is inherent in human nature. If his assessment is correct, then everyone has the need to worship heroes as a form of escape. According to Fishwick the hero "helps us to transcend our drab back yards, apartment terraces, and tenements, and to regain a sense of the world's bigness" (p. 226). This need to escape via the hero has been described variously by Klapp (1962) as: an identity voyage, psychic mobility, and dream realization. These terms are nearly synonymous and refer to the capacity of an individual to live vicariously through his hero. Assumably by worshipping a hero, the individual adds meaning and fulfillment to what otherwise would be a boring, stultifying existence.

Klapp (1969) suggests that there are three main directions hero worship can take: reinforcement, seduction and transcendence. Reinforcement keeps the individual within the social structure and directs him toward socially approved goals. Seduction keeps the individual within societal bounds, but tempts him to break rules. Transcendence takes the individual outside of the societal structure, and provides him with a new identity, new experiences, and new norms.

A hero that reinforces would be someone who embodies the major social values (John F. Kennedy, for example). The seductive hero would be someone like the fictional James Bond. He lives largely within the social structure, but he tempts us to gamble, to be violent, and to be immoral. The transcendent hero leads us out of this society and forms a new society (Timothy Leary or Charles Manson would be candidates for transcendent heroes).

A person's identity voyage through a hero can be helpful as in a budding athlete learning and imitating the professional's particular skills. Hero worship also may serve a compensatory role in that the adulation may not provide tangible benefit for the person, but he feels good about the experience. Hero worship may serve as an important mechanism in adolescents for whom parents no longer serve as primary models. The heroes chosen by the adolescent may have a significant, positive influence on decisions about careers and life styles. Alternately, the individual may choose a negative model or the individual may become locked into a fantasy world of vicarious heroism and eventually have difficulty coping with reality. The hero worshipper who aspires too unreservedly to follow in his hero's footsteps can suffer psychological trauma if he is thwarted.

The Cult of the Hero

A cultic response to a hero refers to mass hero worship. Mass communication facilities have allowed images to be projected to large numbers of people simultaneously. This in turn has enabled the masses to use media celebrities for their identity voyages. Mass hero worship gives a feeling of fellowship and belonging to the individual worshipper. Mass hero worship seems to sanction the act, with so many people doing it, it must be all right.

A cult is formed when people become devoted to a particular ideal or value and engage in ritual to achieve it. The activity becomes truly cultic when it is the central focus of people's lives. A cult thus differs from a fad in the degree of seriousness and commitment involved. For many, the hero cult is a search for a life style, it fills a spiritual void. Correspondingly, Klapp (1969) feels that cultism is a response to the strain imposed by such factors as emotional impoverishment, banality, and stylelessness. Essentially, then, a cultic reaction to a hero gives meaning and fulfillment to empty lives through the celebration of shared ritual.

How Hero Worship Develops

A child's social learning takes place primarily through social models. The child's first model usually is one of his parents. As he grows older, he is more influenced by models from his peer group and by the multiplicity of models proffered by the mass media. Before the child acquires an identity he will have been confronted with a vast array of model types.

Bandura's (1969) studies on social learning provide a key to understanding how hero worship develops. A person will identify with a model if that model is rewarded in front of observers. The reward has essentially the same effect on the observer as on the model. Heroes are rewarded repeatedly through applause, mass media coverage, and special awards. This has the effect of reinforcing the identification process between fan and hero.

Although a reward may improve the model, punishment may or may not devalue it. If a hero is punished, his followers have one of two choices: (a) drop the hero or (b) vent their anger on the authority who imposes the sanction. When Denny McLain was suspended from the American League for 4 months in 1970, he lost a great deal of his lustre. On the other hand, Maurice Richard's fans reacted to his suspension in 1955 by pelting Commissioner Clarence Campbell with eggs and by rioting and looting in the streets.

Bandura (1969) has further suggested that modeling is more likely to occur if observers feel they have something in common with the model. A person is more likely to be used as a model if, in addition to being socially powerful, highly competent, a purported expert, a celebrity, and a symbol of socioeconomic success, he is of the same sex, ethnic group, and age as the observer.

The Sports Hero

The sports hero has long been an object of adulation. There were encomiums for early Olympic winners, Roman gladiators were given special privileges, and Sir Lancelot usually rode off with the fairest maiden. The sports hero has been popular because people can readily identify with him. It is natural to appreciate the best in any endeavor and the sporting hero is a relatively unrefined model. Athletic hero worship has been accepted and even encouraged because sport represents major cultural values.

As a child grows up he sees his older male models attending sporting events, watching games on television and reading about sports in magazines and newspapers. With so much attention devoted to sport, the child soon learns that sport is important and worthwhile. This idea is further reinforced in school, as certain times are set aside for sports competition, and sport often becomes the focal point for student activity. The better athletes in the school are glorified and receive many rewards as a result of this status. Although only a few students actually can garner the rewards of heroic status, the rest receive vicarious pleasure through watching their athletic counterparts perform.

Coleman (1961) has observed that in the American high school, the athlete is at the top of the status hierarchy.[1] There are numerous case studies which support Coleman's findings, indeed the attention given some high school athletes borders on subservience and obsequiousness. A variety of contemporary accounts (Johnson, 1971; Linderman, 1971; Ricke, 1971) demonstrate how high school athletes can control a community.

Schafer (Note 1) sees the dominance of the high school athlete as an insidious way of inculcating the societal values of competition and goal-orientation.

> With their stress above all on winning as a team and becoming a champion
> as an individual athlete (thereby becoming a hero in the eyes of one's peers

and community), school sports are a significant means by which an instrumental or goal orientation is developed in youth—not only in participants, but in student fans who idolize them as well. (p. 6)

The end product of this socialization process is a person who believes
that sport is significant and worthwhile, and this belief in the importance
of sport frequently is demonstrated by worshipping athletic heroes.

Manifestations of Sports Hero Worship

There is much evidence to indicate that people worship sports heroes,
either collectively (as in teams) or as individuals. Fans clamor for auto-
graphs and engage in fist-fights over a baseball that has gone into the
stands (Wecter, 1963). Attendance at most sporting events is up and
sport on television is very close to the saturation level.

Bubble gum cards[2] of sports heroes are still popular with children, and
magazines containing profiles of sports heroes abound. Newspapers
publish obscure sports statistics and books on sporting teams and individuals have made a dent on the best seller charts.[3]

Athletic stars receive mountains of fan mail, are feted publicly at
benefits and make television appearances on talk shows and in advertisements. The movies even are soliciting sports heroes in an effort to
shore up the sagging box office. Joe Namath and Jim Brown are two of
the most famous athletes who have succumbed to the lure of Hollywood.

Halls of Fame, where former athletes are immortalized, are numerous
as are various fan clubs for teams and players (Kirshenbaum, 1971).
These fan clubs hold regular meetings, publish monthly news letters and
on occasion travel en masse to a game to view and meet the object of
their desires.

The Changing Role of the Sports Hero

One of the most famous athletic heroes in North American history is a
fictional character. His name was Frank Merriwell and he was featured
in a series of dime store novels which appeared in print between 1896 and
1914. Frank was a master of all the sports he played (and indeed he
played most of them). Typical of his athletic prowess was his "double
shoot" pitch which curved in both directions to strike out a batter in the
clutch.

Frank Merriwell in the words of his creator, Gilbert Patten, stood for
truth, faith, justice, the triumph of right, mother, home, friendship, loyalty, patriotism, the love of *alma mater*, duty, sacrifice, retribution, and
strength of soul as well as body. (Boyle, 1963, p. 242)

Frank Merriwell undoubtedly influenced many youngsters' lives. There has never been anyone to really take his place. His disappearance is lamented by many for the reason that his stories taught a sense of values that are missing today. In recent years there have been efforts to revive Frank Merriwell. In some cases through the medium of republication, and in others through the founding of Frank Merriwell clubs, who meet in the name of fair play and sportsmanship and whose motto is "no toadies or bullies allowed."

Frank Merriwell represented the all-around athlete, his counterpart in society was the pioneer, the person who had to be adept in a variety of skills to survive. When Merriwell was at the peak of his popularity there was an emphasis on athletic heroes with strength. People like John L. Sullivan, James J. Corbett, and Louis Cyr were idolized. At the turn of the century strength was still a valuable commodity in North American society.

Gurko (1953), aware that early heroes were noted for their strength, is critical of this superficial role model.

> The idealized American male has leaned strongly in the direction of brawn and egotism. . . . The accent has been on muscle over mind, instinct instead of brain, impulsiveness at the expense of reflectiveness, producing a series of exaggeratedly one-sided, immature personalities. (p. 168)

The rise of technology placed an emphasis on new skills. The importance of physical strength was waning as characteristics such as persistence, finesse, and guile became the required assets to rise in the new society. The athletic heroes of the 1920s and 30s seem to reflect this shift in societal values as Jesse Owens, Red Grange, Babe Ruth, and Johnny Weismueller became the new idols.

The war years were accompanied by a diminution in athletic interest. The few sport heroes who did exist were those who had a military connection. Ted Williams, the ex-marine fighter pilot, was the most popular baseball player and Blanchard and Davis of Army were the two most heralded college football players. Maurice Richard was a Canadian sports hero in the 1940s, but he was heavily criticized for his decision not to join the army.

In the 1950s and 60s, football emerged as the most popular sport. It was a sport for the times; the highly complex organization, specialization, and division of labor in the game coincided exactly with the key characteristics of a highly industrialized society. The sports heroes were the equivalent of business executives; Bart Starr and Johnny Unitas were typical of this breed. Coaches like Vince Lombardi achieved hero status, and teams which were reminiscent of staid, conservative, efficient business corporations were glamorized. The New York Yankees, Green Bay Packers, Montreal Canadians, and Boston Celtics were heroic because of their efficient domination over competitors in the same market-place.

The late 1960s and early 70s have given rise to a counter culture, the chief values of which are an aversion to war, and a distaste for the corporate state and all that it represents. Advocates of the counter culture espouse coming together, sharing, a return to nature, and a variety of antithetical values. Instead of competing, they want to cooperate, instead of fighting they want to make love, and instead of conforming they want to express their individuality. In accord with this philosophy, athletic heroes are beginning to make public their anti-war views and are speaking out against violence, racism, and dehumanization in sport. Athletes also are letting their personalities show through their white shoes, mod clothes, and long hair.

The point to be made is that the sports hero is an accurate barometer of the times. Approximately every 20 years over the past century the type of sports hero in vogue has changed and these changes have roughly paralleled changes in societal values.

Categories of Sports Heroes

In Klapp's (1962) typology of heroes, athletes are listed under the category entitled "heroes of play." Klapp treats the athletic hero quite superficially in that he presents him as being only a unidimensional model. For Klapp, the athletic hero simply is one who performs well in front of an audience. This description really does not differentiate between athletes and entertainers, nor does it take into account the variety of ways in which an athletic hero establishes rapport with his audience. There are many subtleties and nuances in an adequate social model of the athletic hero, and a much more refined system of classification is necessary.

To be a sports hero the athlete must have a high level of physical ability. Sometimes this ability in itself is enough to make the athlete a hero. In other instances the athlete must have particular attributes in addition to his physical skill before he acquires the title of hero. Deford (1969) alludes to this point when he states that "Talent is only the first part of being a superstar. Beyond that, to deserve the title a player must establish a notoriety and an impact that can be turned into box office" (p. 33).

At the basic level many athletes have been decent, honorable, unassuming individuals. They have served as acceptable role models, especially for children and adolescents, the people most prone to emulate their behavior. This type of hero fits into Klapp's (1969) reinforcement category, in that they usually are quiet, respectable, family men who personify middle class values. Athletic heroes of this ilk emerge because of outstanding performances over a number of years. These athletes possess awesome skill, they are dedicated and they reliably produce a quality effort game by game, season by season. The type of athlete who fits this category would be Gordie Howe, Bart Starr, Stan Musial, and Billy Casper.

Another way for the athletic hero to emerge is to be the man of the hour. This refers either to an athlete who makes an outstanding play in the last seconds to win an important game, or to an athlete who makes a spectacular performance over a relatively short time span. An example of the former would be Bobby Thompson hitting a game-winning home run with two out in the bottom of the ninth to win a play-off game for the New York Giants in 1951. Examples of the latter instance would be Don Schollander winning four gold medals in the 1964 Olympics, or Ken Dryden almost single-handedly winning a Stanley Cup for Montreal in 1971.

The underdog is another type of athletic hero. This label applies to players who perform at a high level despite some particular disadvantage. The underdog according to Sagarin (1970) is one who is "not favored or expected to win, by virtue of size, strength, experience or even birth" (p. 430). Sports history is replete with examples of heroes who have overcome severe odds. Golfer Ben Hogan recovered from a near fatal automobile accident to come back within a year to win the United States Open. Jackie Robinson became one of the best players in baseball despite the degradation he suffered as the first black player in the major leagues.

Some athletes became heroes because of their individual flair or charisma. Arnold Palmer was chosen an athlete of the decade in 1970 primarily because of the tenacity and aggressiveness he showed when fighting to come from behind. Joe DiMaggio played the outfield effortlessly with a special kind of classic grace. Willie Mays has an inimitable style, fans like his exuberance, his casual basket catches, and the way his hat flies off when he runs. Mays has so much panache that fans have even said he looks good striking out. Perhaps the best example of a unique style in contemporary sport is Bobby Orr. Dowling (1971) claims that Orr's style as a defenseman is revolutionary, it has permanently changed the game.

The aforementioned athletic hero types are in line with Klapp's socially approved, reinforcing hero. There has been a trend in recent years, however, for athletic heroes to fit more comfortably into the seductive category. Some modern sports heroes are brash and arrogant, they are people who have supreme confidence in their ability and often can back it up. Muhammed Ali's inane though accurate poems telling when his opponent would fall and Joe Namath guaranteeing a Super Bowl victory are examples of this type of sports hero. Deford (1969) aptly describes this new trend in athletic heroes.

All of the most recently ordained Impact Champions have required off-the-field controversy to complement their athletic exploits. Muhammed Ali and Namath had the facility of being heard at an extraordinary distance. (p. 34)

In many cases these athletes are not taken to the public's heart. Admired for their ability, they also are despised because they are too haughty and overbearing. Although seductive heroes don't inspire universal love, they often remain heroes because of their box office magnetism.

The anti-hero is popular in books and movies and in sport as well.

The day of the establishment player is rapidly passing away in favor of sports performers who now live it up more, talk more, think more and raise more hell with management than their predecessors ever considered attempting in the benign old days of boss-dominated sports. (Batten, 1971, p. 2)

The anti-hero is someone who eschews traditional heroic qualities, yet is heroic either in spite of or because of this. The anti-hero is particularly popular with the youth because of their predilection for rankling the silent majority. Joe Namath and Derek Sanderson are the prototypes of the anti-hero in sport. Both are bachelor swingers who frequent night clubs, sport long hair and mustaches, wear mod clothes, and flaunt team rules. Both have penchant for the limelight and the more they irk the older generation, the more they are lionized by the young. Neither of these two athletes portrays the public virtues of the traditional hero: honesty, dedication, and strength of character. Namath is famous for his answer to the stock question inquiring about what he did the night before the big game, "I took a broad and a bottle of scotch to bed" (Batten, 1971, p. 2).[4]

Anti-hero athletes have the seductive quality that Klapp (1969) underscored, a quality which may induce young fans to bend the rules and resist the established order. Since Namath appeared with a Fu Manchu beard and white playing shoes this equipment has become de rigueur for many football players. This is not to say that such influences necessarily are bad, only that seductive heroes inevitably invite changes in established patterns of behavior.

It would be rare for an athlete to fit Klapp's (1969) transcendent category. An athletic hero normally does not have the power to take his followers outside the bounds of the social structure to produce a person with a new identity. Athletics represent stability and conservatism, the antithesis of what the transcendent hero stands for.

The Demise of the Sports Hero

"Where have you gone Joe DiMaggio, a nation turns its lonely eyes to you."[5] This lament from a recent popular song seems to say it all about the disappearance of the traditional hero. What we seem to have left is a collection of incomplete or tarnished quasi-heroes. We still have the need to worship heroes, but the models that are available are becoming less and less exemplary. Klapp (1969) has noticed this trend and has reappraised his definition of a celebrity hero. "A celebrity hero is not someone who is especially good, but only someone who realizes dreams for people that they cannot do for themselves" (p. 214).

Hook (1957) claims that there is little opportunity for genuine heroism in a democratic society. The hallmark of heroism is singularity, and in a democracy it is difficult for one individual to have a significant effect on matters. In this connection, the editors of *Time* (1966) noted that heroes now are emerging as composite figures rather than as individuals. The astronauts are used to illustrate this point, very few people remember all of them individually, but they do have the status of a collective hero. Deford (1969) bemoans the fact that this lack of interest in the individual hero has carried over into sport.

> Sport offers too much tribute to the peripheral contributions of the supernumeraries at the expense of the great stars who really make it. Writers and commentators (must they be "color men?") wallow in mechanical expertise. It is always shrewd planning, gears meshing, wonderful organization. Perhaps it only reflects our anonymous lives, but it is forever the battle plan that is celebrated not the classic individual achievement. (p. 34)

One hundred years ago when there was a paucity of mass communication, myth making was easy, for it was difficult to refute stories about athletic heroes. When mass communications started to cover sporting events they continued to preserve the sanctity of the athletic hero. Comments either written or spoken about athletes seldom were objective, they served only to patronize and glorify the athlete. Often the mass media created heroes out of athletes who were less than deserving. Babe Ruth, for example, was one of the most celebrated sports heroes of all time, but as Schecter (1970) observes, "Ruth had an undisciplined appetite for food, whiskey and women" (p. 119). Schecter goes on to say that "little of this was available to the contemporary public. The Babe was thoroughly protected by the news media" (p. 119). Hook (1957) concurs with the latter judgment when he notes the pervasive control of mass media over the process of hero making.

Today, more than ever before belief in "the hero" is a synthetic product.

Whoever controls the microphones and printing presses can make or un-
make beliefs overnight. (p. 10)

Sport Magazine (1970) in an introspective editorial actually apologized
for its lack of objectivity in covering athletic heroes.

It is true that for many years "Sport" along with the rest of the world
treated the big-name athlete in a Frank Merriwell fashion. We were all content to dote on his statistics, on what he ate for breakfast, on his serene
home life, on his virtues as a man. And we overlaid the portrait with a
heavy helping of pancake makeup, lest any blemishes peek through. (p. 84)

This uncritical attitude on the part of the mass media has changed
somewhat in recent years. Irreverent books such as: Schecter's *The
Jocks* (1970), Meggyesy's *Out of Their League* (1970), Bouton's *Ball
Four* (1971), Conacher's *Hockey in Canada: The Way It Is* (1970) and
Barnes' *The Plastic Orgasm* (1971) have ripped the halos from modern
sports heroes. This type of book is an antidote to cloying trade books like
Robertson's *Rusty Staub of the Expos* (1971). Jennings (1971), when
reviewing the latter, found that after wading through paeans of repeti-
tious praise he "expected an announcement of mass canonization with
every page" (p. 14).

In the electronic media the move away from sugar coating has been
slower, but at least one United States network has attempted a small
gesture in that direction. The American Broadcasting Company employs
the acerbic Howard Cosell as a color man on their Monday night football
telecasts. Cosell's central claim to fame is that he tells it like it is (Lisker,
1971). It seems that the mass media which once pandered to athletic
heroes now is contributing to their decanonization, if not their decline.

Another reason for the loss of interest in sports heroes is that there are
just too many sports and too many teams for people to follow. The
overall growth of sport has had a benumbing effect on fans. Who can
keep the perpetually expanding and reorganizing leagues straight, let
alone the athletes and the tidal wave of related statistics? A further consequence of sport expansion is that there are too many good performers.
It is difficult to distinguish between the great player, the record holder,
and the good player. Perhaps Deford's (1969) term "impact champion"
is useful here, the only true heroes being those athletes whose mere
presence makes a sizable increase in the box office take.

Athletic heroes are losing their credibility and thus their utility for
many fans. More and more it is player holdouts and potential strikes that
fill the sports pages. Fans seek sports heroes to escape, not to be bur-
dened with the economic problems of the professional athlete. It
becomes difficult to sympathize or even identify with the six figure
athlete if you are an $8,000-a-year man yourself.

The athlete also loses credibility when he is seen in less than flattering advertisements. Joe Namath getting $10,000 to shave his beard for a TV commercial is seen as a rip-off by many fans. Famous athletes seen crying for their Maypo and lathering up with Rise are degraded by the banal dialogue placed in their mouths. Ross (1971) declared recently that the testimonial was not a particularly effective method of selling. If the sport testimonial doesn't do much for the product, it may achieve even less for the hero athlete who is doing the shilling.

The public is becoming increasingly wary of being used by their sports heroes. Athletes who have lately tried to use their names as spring boards into politics and business have been rebuffed. In recent Canadian and American elections only those former athletes who were eminently qualified were elected (Ryan, 1970). In business many well-known athletes have found that their name was not enough. Last year a number of athletes with floundering businesses were forced to file for bankruptcy.

The decline of the athletic hero may also be linked to the fact that many of them represent counter culture values. The counter culture is only a subculture and the majority simply do not relate to this system of values (Agnew & Johnson, 1971).

Summary

The hero is an ancient and honorable role of great cultural utility. Heroes are created in many guises and perform many functions. As a special object of adulation, the sports hero is both the instrument of and the mirror for a variety of social processes. Consequently, changes in cultural value systems evoke parallel changes in the archetype elected to heroic status in sport. It is not unexpected, therefore, to find that the relationship between sports heroes and their audience has altered in the fast pace of recent years. Whether the traditional sport hero simply is undergoing a metamorphosis, to later emerge in a new and vital cultural role, or indeed has reached the end of his usefulness and is doomed to extinction, only the unwinding of the century can reveal.

Notes

1. Friesen (1968) claims that this is not the case in Canada, where academics outrank athletics in the high school value system.
2. A quote by J.M. Schwartz (Note 2) is relevant here: "Baseball cards don't just sell bubblegum. They are a small cog in an elaborate socialization system which aids in the process of molding youngsters to fit the American way of life."

3. For example *Paper Lion* and *Bogey Man* by George Plimpton, *Instant Replay* by Jerry Kramer and *Ball Four* by Jim Bouton.
4. Bill Russell (1970) trenchantly summarizes the establishment's point of view when speaking of Joe Namath. Russell says that he likes Namath personally, but that he doesn't admire or respect him because Namath stands for nothing except having a good time.
5. From the song "Mrs. Robinson" by P. Simon and A. Garfunkel.

Reference Notes

1. Schafer, W. *Sport socialization and the school.* Paper presented at the Third International Symposium on the Sociology of Sport. Waterloo, Ontario, August 22-28, 1971.
2. Schwartz, J.M. *Causes and effects of spectator sports.* Paper presented at the Third International Symposium on the Sociology of Sport. Waterloo, Ontario, August 22-28, 1971.

References

AGNEW, S., & Johnson, W. Not infected with the conceit of infallibility. *Sports Illustrated*, June 21, 1971, pp. 61-75.

BANDURA, A. Social-learning theory of identificatory processes. In D.A. Goslin, *Handbook of socialization theory and research.* Chicago: Rand McNally, 1969.

BARNES, L. *The plastic orgasm.* Toronto: McLelland & Stewart, 1971.

BATTEN, J. Whatever happened to the clean-living athletes who were a credit to the game? *Canadian Magazine*, March 13, 1971, pp. 2-6.

BOUTON, J. *Ball four.* New York: Dell, 1971.

BOYLE, R.H. *Sport: Mirror of American life.* Boston: Little & Brown, 1963.

CARLYLE, T. *On heroes and hero worship.* London: Oxford University Press, 1840.

COLEMAN, J. *The adolescent society.* New York: Free Press, 1961.

CONACHER, B. *Hockey in Canada: The way it is.* Toronto: Gateway Press, 1970.

DEFORD, F. What price heroes? *Sports Illustrated*, June 9, 1969, pp. 33-40.

DOWLING, T. The Orr effect. *Atlantic*, April, 1971, **227**(4), 62-68.

FISHWICK, M. *American heroes: Myth and reality.* Washington, DC: Public Affairs Press, 1954.

FRANK Merriwell is dead. (In time out with the editors.) *Sport*, April 1970, p. 84.

FRIESEN, D. Academic-athletic-popularity syndrome in Canadian high school society (1967). *Adolescence*, 1968, 3(9), 39-52.

GURKO, L. *Heroes, highbrows and the popular mind.* Indianapolis: Charter Books, 1953.

HOOK, S. *The hero in history: A study in limitation and possibility.* Boston: Beacon Press, 1957.

JENNINGS, C. Semi-canonization of a sports hero. *Toronto Globe and Mail Magazine*, September 4, 1971, p. 14.

JOHNSON, W. The greatest athlete in Yates Center, Kansas. *Sports Illustrated*, August 9, 1971, pp. 27-31.

KIRSHENBAUM, J. Bats and busts, size-15 sneakers and a dead bird. *Sports Illustrated*, June 28, 1971, pp. 63-74.

KLAPP, O.E. *Heroes, villains and fools.* Englewood Cliffs: Prentice-Hall, 1962.

KLAPP, O.E. *Collective search for identity.* New York: Holt Rinehart & Winston, 1969.

LEHMAN, B.H. *Carlyle's theory of the hero.* Durham, NC: Duke University Press, 1928.

LERNER, M. *America as a civilization* (Vol. 2). New York: Simon & Schuster, 1957.

LINDERMAN, L. The Tom McMillen affair. *Playboy*, November 1971, p. 148.

LISKER, J. Cosell explains his success: A man has to take a stand. *Detroit Free Press*, May 2, 1971, Sec. D, p. 6.

MEGGYESY, D. *Out of their league.* Berkeley: Ramparts Press, 1970.

ON the difficulty of being a contemporary hero. *Time Magazine*, June 24, 1966, p. 24.

RICKE, T. A town where boys are kings and the court business is basketball. *Detroit Free Press Magazine*, March 14, 1971, pp. 6-11.

ROSS, N. Hitch your product to a star. *Washington Post*, August 31, 1971, pp. 1-2.

RUSSELL, W.F. Success is a journey. *Sports Illustrated*, June 8, 1970, pp. 81-93.

RYAN, P. The making of a quarterback 1970. *Sports Illustrated*, December 7, 1970, p. 83.

SAGARIN, E. Who roots for the underdog? *Journal of Popular Culture*, 1970, 4(2), 425-431.

SCHECTER, L. *The jocks.* New York: Paperback Library, 1970.

SCOTT, J. *Sauer power.* Monthly column from the Institute for the Study of Sport in Society, October, 1971.

WECTER, D. *The hero in America.* Ann Arbor: University of Michigan Press, 1963.

Chapter 5
Liminal to Liminoid, in Play, Flow, and Ritual: An Essay in Comparative Symbology

VICTOR TURNER

First I will describe what I mean by "comparative symbology" and how, in a broad way, it differs from such disciplines as "semiotics" (or "semiology") and "symbolic anthropology," which are also concerned with the study of such terms as symbols, signs, signals, significations, icons, signifiers, signifieds, sign-vehicles, and so on. Here, I want to discuss some of the types of sociocultural processes and settings in which new symbols, verbal and nonverbal, tend to be generated. This will lead me into a comparison of "liminal" and "liminoid" phenomena, terms which I will consider shortly.

According to Josiah Webster's lexicographical progeny, the people who produced the second College edition of Webster's New World Dictionary, "symbology" is "the study or interpretation of symbols"; it is also "representation or expression by means of symbols." The term "comparative" merely means that this branch of study involves comparison as a method, as does, for example, comparative linguistics.

From *Rice University Studies*, Summer 1974, **60**(3), 53-92. Copyright 1974 by Rice University. Reprinted with permission.

Comparative symbology is narrower than "semiotics" or "semiology" (to use Saussure's and Roland Barthes's terms), and wider than "symbolic anthropology" in range and scope of data and problems. "Semiotics" is "a general theory of signs and symbols, especially, the analysis of the nature and relationship of signs in language, usually including three branches, syntactics, semantics, and pragmatics."

1. Syntactics: The formal relationships of signs and symbols to one another apart from their users or external reference; the organization and relationship of groups, phrases, clauses, sentences, and sentence structure.

2. Semantics: The relationship of signs and symbols to the things to which they refer, that is, their referential meaning.

3. Pragmatics: The relations of signs and symbols with their users.

In my own analyses of ritual symbols, "syntactics" is roughly similar to what I call "positional meaning"; "semantics" is similar to "exegetical meaning"; and "pragmatics" is similar to "operational meaning." Semiology seems to have rather wider aspirations than semiotics, since it is defined as "the science of signs in general" whereas semiotics restricts itself to signs in language, though Roland Barthes is now taking the position that "linguistics is not a part of the general science of signs . . . it is semiology which is a part of linguistics" (Barthes, 1967, p. 11).

Comparative symbology is not directly concerned with the *technical* aspects of linguistics, and has much to do with many kinds of nonverbal symbols in ritual and art, though admittedly all cultural languages have important linguistic components, relays, or "signifieds." Nevertheless, it *is* involved in the relationships between symbols and the concepts, feelings, values, notions, etc., associated with them by users, interpreters, or exegetes: in short it has *semantic* dimensions, it pertains to meaning in language and context. Its data are mainly drawn from *cultural genres* or *subsystems* of expressive culture. These include both oral and literate genres, and one may reckon among them *activities* combining verbal and nonverbal symbolic actions, such as ritual and drama, as well as *narrative* genres, such as myth, epic, ballad, the novel, and ideological systems. They would also include nonverbal forms, such as miming, sculpture, painting, music, ballet, and architecture—and many more.

But comparative symbology does more than merely investigate cultural genres in abstraction from human social activity. It would become semiology if it did, whose corpus of data "must eliminate diachronic elements to the utmost" and coincide with a "state of the system, a cross-section of history" (Barthes, p. 98). When considering ritual data collected during my fieldwork among the Ndembu people of northwestern Zambia, I wrote that

I could not analyse [these] ritual symbols without studying them in a time series in relation to other "events" [regarding the symbol, too, as an "event" rather than a "thing"], for symbols are essentially involved in social process [and, I would now add, in psychological process, too]. I came to see performances of ritual as distinct phases in the social processes whereby groups became adjusted to internal changes [whether brought about by personal or factional dissensions and conflicts of norms or by technical or organizational innovations], and adapted to their external environment [social and cultural, as well as physical and biotic]. From this standpoint the ritual symbol becomes a factor in social action, a positive force in an activity field. Symbols, too, are crucially involved in situations of societal change—the symbol becomes associated with human interests, purposes, ends and means, aspirations and ideals, individual and collective, whether these are explicitly formulated or have to be inferred from the observed behavior. For these reasons, the structure and properties of a ritual symbol become those of a dynamic entity, at least within its appropriate context of action. (Turner, 1967, p. 20)

We shall take a closer look at some of these "properties" later. But I want to stress here that because *from the very outset* I formulate symbols as social and cultural dynamic systems, shedding and gathering meaning over time and altering in form, I cannot regard them merely as "terms" in atemporal logical or protological cognitive systems. Undoubtedly, in the specialized genres of complex societies such as philosophical, theological, and formal logical systems, symbols, and the signs derived from their decomposition, do acquire this "algebraic" or logical quality, and can be treated effectively in relations of "binary opposition," as "mediators," and the rest, denatured by the primacy of specialist cognitve activity. But "les symboles sauvages," as they appear not only in traditional, "tribal" cultures but also in the "cultural refreshment" genres (poetry, drama, and painting) of postindustrial society, have the character of dynamic semantic systems. They gain and lose meanings—and meaning in a social context always has emotional and volitional dimensions—as they "travel through" a *single* rite or work of art, let alone through centuries of performance, and they are aimed at producing effects on the psychological states and behavior of those exposed to them or obliged to use them for their communication with other human beings. I have always tried to link my work in processual analysis (for example, studies of the ongoing process of village politics in *Schism and Continuity*, 1957) with my work in the analysis of ritual performances.

This is perhaps why I have often focused on the study of *individual* symbols, on their semantic fields and processual fate as they move through the scenario of a specific ritual performance and reappear in other kinds of ritual, or even transfer from one genre to another, for example, from ritual to a myth-cycle, to an epic, to a fairy tale, to citation as a maxim in a case at law. Such a focus leaves the semantic future of each symbol, as it were, open-ended. In contrast, formal analysis of a total set of symbols assumed *a priori* to be a system or a *gestalt*, treated as closed, atemporal, and synchronic, a "corpus," or finite collection of materials, tends to emphasize a given symbol's formal properties and relations and to select from its wealth of meaning only that specific designation which makes it an appropriate term in some binary opposition, itself a relational building block of a bounded cognitive system. Binariness and arbitrariness tend to go together, and both are in the atemporal world of "signifiers." Such a treatment, while often seductively elegant, a *frisson* for our cognitive faculties, removes the total set of symbols from the complex, continuously changing social life, murky or glinting with desire and feeling, which is its distinctive milieu and context, and imparts to it a dualistic *rigor mortis*. Symbols, both as sensorily perceptible vehicles *(signifiants)* and as sets of "meanings" *(signifiés)*, are essentially involved in multiple variability. Living, conscious, emotional, and volitional creatures employ them not only to give order to the universe they inhabit, but creatively to make use also of disorder, *both* by overcoming or reducing it in particular cases and by its means questioning former axiomatic principles that have become a fetter on the understanding and manipulation of contemporary things. For example, Rabelais's disorderly, scatological heaps of symbolic forms standing for the disorderly deeds and attributes of Gargantua and Pantagruel challenged the neatness of scholastic theological and philosophical systems—the result, paradoxically, was to blast away logically watertight obscurantism. When symbols are rigidified into logical operators and subordinated to implicit syntax-like rules, by some of our modern investigators, those of us who take them too seriously become blind to the creative or innovative potential of symbols as factors in human action. Symbols may "instigate" such action and in situationally varying combinations channel its direction by saturating goals and means with affect and desire. Comparative symbology does attempt to preserve this ludic capacity, to catch symbols in their movement, so to speak, and to "play" with their possibilities of form and meaning. It does this by contextualizing symbols in the concrete, historical fields of their use by "men alive" as they act, react, transact, and interact socially. Even when the symbolic is the *inverse* of the pragmatic reality, it remains intimately in touch with it, affects and is affected by it, provides the positive figure with its negative ground, thereby delimiting each, and winning for "cosmos" a new territory.

Narrower in scope than semiotics, comparative symbology is wider than symbolic anthropology, for it proposes to take into account not only "ethnographic" materials, but also the symbolic genres of the so-called "advanced" civilizations, the complex, large-scale industrial societies. Undoubtedly, this broader perspective forces it to come to terms with the methods, theories, and findings of specialists and experts in many disciplines which most anthropologists know all too little about, such as history, literature, musicology, art history, theology, the history of religions, philosophy, and so on. Nevertheless, in making these attempts to study symbolic action in complex cultures, anthropologists, who now study symbols mainly in "tribal" or simple agrarian myth, ritual, and art, would be doing no more than returning to an honorable tradition of their predecessors. Durkheim and the *Année Sociologique* school, Kroeber, Redfield, and their successors, and Professor Singer, have examined cultural subsystems in *"oikoumenes"* (literally "inhabited worlds," used by Kroeber to indicate civilizational complexes, such as Christendom, Islam, Indic, and Chinese civilization, and the like) and Great Traditions.

In my own case, I was pressed towards the study of symbolic genres in large-scale societies by some implications of the work of Arnold van Gennep (1909/1960) (which drew principally on the data of small-scale societies) in his *Rites de Passage*, first published in French in 1909. Although van Gennep himself seems to have intended that his term "rite of passage" should be used for rituals accompanying the change in social status of an individual or a cohort of individuals, and for those associated with seasonal changes for an entire society, his book concentrates on the former type; and the term has come to be used almost exclusively in connection with these "life-crisis" rituals. I have tried to revert to van Gennep's earlier usage in regarding almost *all* types of rites as having the processual form of "passage." What does this term mean?

Van Gennep distinguishes three phases in a rite of passage: *separation, transition,* and *incorporation.* The first phase is *separation,* the phase which clearly demarcates sacred space and time from profane or secular space and time (it is more than just a matter of entering a temple—there must be in addition a rite which changes the quality of *time* also, or constructs a cultural realm which is defined as "out of time," that is, beyond or outside the time which measures secular processes and routines). It includes symbolic behavior—especially symbols of reversal or inversion of secular things, relationships, and processes—which represents the detachment of the ritual subjects (novices, candidates, neophytes, or "initiands") from their previous social statuses. In the case of members of a society, it involves collectively moving from all that is socially and culturally involved in an agricultural season, or from a period of peace as against one of war, from plague to community health, from a previous sociocultural state or condition, to a new state or condition, a new turn of the seasonal wheel. During the intervening phase of *transition,* called by van Gennep "margin" or "limen" (meaning "threshold" in Latin), the ritual subjects pass through a period and area of ambiguity, a sort of social limbo which has few (though sometimes these are most crucial) of the attributes of either the preceding or subsequent profane social statuses or cultural states. We will look at this liminal phase much more closely later. The third phase, called by van Gennep "re-aggregation" or "incorporation," includes symbolic phenomena and actions which represent the return of the subjects to their new, relatively stable, well-defined position in the total society. For those undergoing life-cycle ritual this usually represents an enhanced status, a stage further along life's culturally prefabricated road. For those taking part in a calendrical or seasonal ritual, no change in status may be involved, but they have been ritually prepared for a whole series of changes in the nature of the cultural and ecological activities to be undertaken and of the relationships they will then have with others—all these holding good for a specific quadrant of the annual productive cycle. Many passage rites are irreversible (for the individual subjects) one-shot-only affairs, while calendrical rites are repeated every year by everyone; though, of course, one may attend the passage rites of one's kin or friends innumerable times, until one knows their form better than the initiands themselves—like the old ladies who "never miss a wedding" as compared with the nervous couple at their first marriage. I have argued that initiatory passage rites tend to "put people down" while some seasonal rites tend to "set people up"; that is, initiations humble people before permanently elevating them, while some seasonal rites (whose residues are carnivals and festivals) elevate those of low status transiently before returning them to their permanent humbleness. Van Gennep argued that the three phases of his schema varied in length and degree of elaboration in different kinds of passage: for example, "rites of separation are prominent in funeral ceremonies, rites of incorporation at marriages. *Transition* rites may play an important part, for instance, in pregnancy, betrothal, and initiation." The situation is further complicated by regional and ethnic differences which cut across typological ones. Nevertheless, it is rare to find no trace of the three-part schema in "tribal" rituals.

The passage from one social status to another is often accompanied by a parallel passage in space, a geographical movement from one place to another. This may take the form of a mere opening of doors or the literal crossing of a threshold which separates two distinct areas, one associated with the subject's preritual or preliminal status, and the other with his postritual or postliminal status. (The draft inductee's "two steps forward" may serve as a modern instance of a ritualized move into liminality.) On the other hand, the spatial passage may involve a long, exacting pilgrimage and the crossing of many national frontiers before the subject reaches his goal, the sacred shrine, where paraliturgical action may replicate in microcosm the three-part schema at the shrine itself. Sometimes this spatial symbolism may be the precursor of a real and permanent change of residence or geographical sphere of action. For example, a Nyakusa or Ndembu girl, after her puberty rites, leaves her natal village to dwell in her husband's; in certain hunting societies young boys live with their mothers until the time of their initiation rites into adulthood, after which they begin to live with the other hunters of the tribe. Perhaps something of this thinking persists in our own society, when, in large bureaucratic organizations on the national scale, such as the federal government, a major industrial corporation, or the university system, etc., promotion in status and salary usually involves movement in space from one city to another. This process is described by William Watson (1965) in *Closed Systems and Open Minds* as "spiralism." The "liminoid" phase between leaving one post and taking up another would repay study in terms of comparative symbology, both in regard to the subject (his dreams, fantasies, favorite reading and entertainment) and to those whom he is leaving and joining (their myths about him, treatment of him, and so on). But there will be more of this and of the distinction between "liminal" and "liminoid" later.

According to van Gennep, an extended liminal phase in the initiation rites of tribal societies is frequently marked by the physical separation of the ritual subjects from the rest of society. Thus in certain Australian, Melanesian, and African tribes, a boy undergoing initiation must spend a long period of time living in the bush, cut off from the normal social interactions within the village and household. Ritual symbols of this phase, though some represent inversion of normal reality, characteristically fall into two types: those of effacement and those of ambiguity or paradox. Hence, in many societies the liminal initiands are often considered to be dark, invisible, like a planet in eclipse or the moon between phases; they are stripped of names and clothing, smeared with the common earth, rendered indistinguishable from animals. They are also associated with life and death, male and female, food and excrement, simultaneously, since they are at once dying from or dead to their former status and life, and being born and growing into new ones. Sharp symbolic inversion of social attributes may characterize separation; blurring and merging of distinctions may characterize liminality.

Thus, the ritual subjects in these rites undergo a "leveling" process, in which signs of their preliminal status are destroyed and signs of their liminal nonstatus are applied. I have mentioned certain indicators of their liminality (absence of clothing and names): other signs include not eating or not eating specified foods, disregard of personal appearance, the wearing of uniform clothing, sometimes irrespective of sex. In mid-transition the initiands are pushed as far toward uniformity, structural invisibility, and anonymity as possible.

By way of compensation, the initiands acquire a special kind of freedom, a "sacred power" of the meek, weak, and humble. As van Gennep elaborates:

During the entire novitiate, the usual economic and legal ties are modified, sometimes broken altogether. The novices are outside society, and society has no power over them, especially since they are actually [in terms of indigenous beliefs] sacred and holy, and therefore untouchable and dangerous, just as gods would be. Thus, although taboos, as negative rites, erect a barrier between the novices and society, the society is helpless against the novices' undertakings. That is the explanation—the simplest in the world—for a fact that has been noted among a great many peoples and that has remained incomprehensible to observers. During the novitiate, the young people can steal and pillage at will or feed and adorn themselves at the expense of the community. (1909/1960, p. 114)

If only students in our culture were granted similar immunities concordant with their intellectually liminal situation!

The novices are, in fact, temporarily undefined, beyond the normative social structure. This weakens them, since they have no rights over others. But it also liberates them from structural obligations. It places them too in a close connection with asocial powers of life and death. Hence the frequent comparison of novices on the one hand with ghosts, gods, or ancestors, and on the other with animals or birds. They are dead to the social world, but alive to the asocial world. Many societies make a dichotomy, explicit or implicit, between sacred and profane, cosmos and chaos, order and disorder. In liminality, profane social relations may be discontinued, former rights and obligations are suspended, the social order may seem to have been turned upside down. By way of compensation, cosmological systems (as objects of serious study) may become of central importance for the novices. They are confronted by the elders, in rite, myth, song, instruction in a secret language, and various nonverbal symbolic genres (such as dancing, painting, clay-molding, wood-carving, masking, and the like), with symbolic patterns and structures which amount to teachings about the structure of the cosmos and their culture as a part and product of it, insofar as these are defined and comprehended, whether implicitly or explicitly. Liminality is a complex series of episodes in sacred space-time, and may also include subversive and ludic events. The factors of culture are isolated, insofar as it is possible to do this with multivocal symbols (that is, with the aid of symbol-vehicles—sensorily perceptible forms) that are each susceptible not of a single but of many meanings. Then they may be recombined in numerous, often grotesque ways, grotesque because they are arrayed in terms of possible rather than experienced combinations—thus a monster disguise may combine human, animal, and vegetable features in an "unnatural" way, while the same features may be differently, but equally "unnaturally" combined in a painting or described in a tale. In other words, in liminality people "play" with the elements of the familiar and defamiliarize them. Novelty emerges from unprecedented combinations of familiar elements. In the 1972 American Anthropological Association Meetings in Toronto, Brian Sutton-Smith borrowed a term which I have applied to liminality (and other social phenomena and events), "anti-structure" (meaning dissolution of normative social structure, with its role-sets, statuses, jural rights and duties, and so on). He related it to a series of experimental studies he has been making of children's (and some adult) games both in tribal and industrial societies. Much of what he says, *mutatis mutandis*, can be transferred to the study of liminality in tribal ritual. He writes:

> The normative structure represents the working equilibrium, the anti-structure represents the latent system of potential alternatives from which novelty will arise when contingencies in the normative system require it. We might more correctly call this second system the *proto-structural* system [he says] because it is the precursor of innovative normative forms. It is the source of new culture. (Sutton-Smith, Note 1, pp. 18-19)

Sutton-Smith (Note 1), who recently has been examining the continuum *order-disorder* in games (such as the children's ring-a-ring-a-roses), goes on to say that

> we may be disorderly in games [and, I would add, in the liminality of rituals, as well as in such "liminoid" phenomena as charivaris, fiestas, Halloween masking and mumming, etc.] either because we have an over-dose of order, and want to let off steam [the "conservative" view of ritual disorder, such as ritual reversals, Saturnalia, and the like], or because we have something to *learn* through being disorderly. (p. 17)

What interests me most about Sutton-Smith's formulations is that he sees liminal and liminoid situations as the settings in which new symbols, models, and paradigms arise—as the seedbeds of cultural creativity in fact. These new symbols and constructions then feed back into the "central" economic and politico-legal domains and arenas, supplying them with goals, aspirations, incentives, structural models, and *raisons d'être*.

Some have argued that liminality, more specifically "liminal" phenomena such as myth and ritual in tribal society, is best characterized by the establishment of "implicit syntax-like rules" or by "internal structures of logical relations of opposition and mediation between the discrete symbolic elements" of the myth or ritual. Claude Lévi-Strauss would perhaps take this view. But to my mind it is the analysis of culture into factors and their free or "ludic" recombination in any and every possible pattern, however weird, that is of the essence of liminality, liminality *par excellence*. This may be seen if one studies liminal phases of major rituals cross-culturally and cross-temporally. When implicit rules begin to appear which limit the possible combination of factors to certain conventional patterns, designs, or figurations, then, I think, we are seeing the intrusion of normative social structure into what is potentially and in principle a free and experimental region of culture, a region where not only new elements but also new combinatory rules may be introduced—far more readily than in the case of language. This capacity for variation and experiment becomes more clearly dominant in societies in which *leisure* is sharply demarcated from *work*, and especially in all societies which have been shaped by the Industrial Revolution. Various Lévi-Straussian models, such as the one dealing with metaphorical and oppositional logical relations and the transformation to humanity, from nature to culture, and the geometric model which utilizes two sets of oppositions in the construction of a "culinary triangle," raw/cooked: raw/rotten, seem to me to be applicable mainly to tribal or early agrarian societies where work and life tend to be governed by seasonal and ecological rhythms. The models apply in situations where the rules underlying the generation of cultural patterns tend to seek out the binary "Yin-Yang," forms suggested by simple "natural" oppositions, such as hot/cold, wet/dry, cultivated/wild, male/female, summer/winter, plenty/scarcity, and the like. The main social and cultural structures tend to become modeled on these cosmological principles, which determine even the layout of cities and villages, the design of houses, and the shape and spatial placement of different types of cultivated land. It is not surprising that liminality itself cannot escape the grip of these strong structuring principles. Only certain types of *children's* games and play are allowed some degree of freedom because these are defined as structurally "irrelevant," not "mattering." When children are initiated into the early grades of adulthood, however, variabilities and labilities of social behavior are drastically curtailed and controlled. Law, morality, ritual, even much of economic life, fall under the structuring influence of cosmological principles. The cosmos becomes a complex weave of "correspondences" based on analogy, metaphor, and metonymy. For example, the Dogon of West Africa, according to Marcel Griaule, Genevieve Calame-Griaule, and Germaine Dieterlen, establish a correspondence between the different categories of minerals and the organs of the body. The various soils are conceived of as the organs of "the interior of the stomach," rocks are regarded as the "bones" of the skeleton, and various hues of red clay are likened to "the blood" (see my discussion of Dogon cosmology, 1974, p. 156-165). Similarly, in medieval China, different ways of painting trees and clouds are related to different cosmological principles.

Thus the symbols found in *rites de passage* in these societies, though subject to permutations and transformations of their relationships, are only involved in these *within* relatively stable, cyclical, and repetitive systems. It is to these kinds of systems that the term "liminality" properly belongs. When used of processes, phenomena, and persons in large-scale complex societies, its use must in the main be metaphorical. That is, the word "liminality," used *primarily* of a phase in the processual structure of a *rite de passage*, is applied to other aspects of culture—here in societies of far greater scale and complexity. This brings me to a watershed division in comparative symbology. Failure to distinguish between symbolic systems and genres belonging to cultures which have developed before and after the Industrial Revolution can lead to much confusion both in theoretical treatment and in operational methodology.

Let me try to spell this out. Despite immense diversities within each camp, there still remains a fundamental distinction at the level of expressive culture between all societies before and all societies subsequent to the Industrial Revolution, including the industrializing Third World societies, which, though dominantly agrarian, nevertheless represent the granaries or playground of metropolitan industrial societies.

Key concepts here are *work, play*, and *leisure*. Placing a different explanatory stress on each or any combination of these can influence how we think about symbolic manipulation sets, symbolic genres, in the types of societies we will consider. Each of these concepts is multivocal or multivalent, each has many designations. According to the Oxford English Dictionary, "work" means:

> (1) expenditure of energy, striving, application of effort to some purpose [this fits fairly well with Webster's primary sense: "physical or mental effort exerted to do or to make something; purposeful activity; labor; toil"]; (2) task to be undertaken, materials to be used in task; (3) thing done, achievement, thing made, book or piece of literary or musical composition [note this application of "work" to the genres of the leisure domain], *meritorious act* as opposed to faith or grace; (4) doings or experiences of *specified* kind, e.g., sharp, bloody, thirsty, wild, dry, etc., *work* [work often has this focused, singular capacity]; (5) *employment*, especially the opportunity of earning money by labour, laborious occupation; (6) ordinary, practical (as in *workaday*), etc. [where it has resonances with secular, profane, pragmatic, and so on].

Now in "tribal," "preliterate," "simpler," "small-scale" societies, the types studied by anthropologists, ritual, and to some extent, myth, are regarded as "work" precisely in this sense, what the Tikopia call "the *work* of the Gods." Ancient Hindu society also posits a "divine work." In the third chapter of the *Bhagavadgita* (v. 14-15) we find a connection made between sacrifice and work: "From food do all contingent beings derive, and food derives from rain; rain derives from sacrifice and sacrifice from *work*. From Brahman work arises." Nikhilananda (1952, p. 110) comments that "work" (action) here refers to the sacrifice prescribed in the Vedas, which prescribes for "householders" sacrifice or work. The Ndembu call that which a ritual specialist does *kuzata*, "work," and the same general term is applied to what a hunter, a cultivator, a headman, and, today, a manual laborer, do. Even in fairly complex agrarian societies associated with "city-state" or "feudal" polities, well within the scope of historical documentation, we find terms like *liturgy* which in pre-Christian Greece early became established as "public service to the gods." *Liturgy* is derived from the Greek *leos* or *laos*, "the people," and *ergon*, "work" (cognate with Old English *weorc*, German *werk*, from the Indo-European base, *werĝ-*, "to do, act." The Greek *organon*, "tool, instrument" derives from the same base—originally *worganon*). The work of men is thus the work of the Gods, a conclusion which would have delighted Durkheim, though it could be construed as implying a fundamental distinction between gods and men, since men cooperated in ritual the better to enter into reciprocal, exchange relations with the gods or with God—it was not simply that "the voice of the congregation was the voice of God." A difference was construed between creator and created. Whatever may have been the empirical case, what we are seeing here is a universe of work, an *ergon-* or *organic* universe, in which the main distinction is between sacred and profane *work*, not between work and leisure. For example, Samuel Beal comments in his *Travels of Fah-Hian and Sung-Yun, Buddhist Pilgrims from China to India (400 A.D. and 518 A.D.)* (1869/1964, p. 5) on Chi Fah-Hian's use of the term *Shaman*, as follows: "The Chinese word Shaman represents phonetically the Sanscrit 'Sramana,' or the Pali 'Samana.' The Chinese word is defined to mean 'diligent and laborious'. . . . The Sanscrit root is 'sram,' to be fatigued." (He was referring to the people of Shen-Shen, in the desert of Makhai, part of the Gobi desert region.) It is, furthermore, a universe of work in which whole communities participate, as of obligation, not optation. The *whole* community goes through the *entire* ritual round, whether in terms of total or representative participation. Thus, some rites, such as those of sowing, first fruits, or harvest, may involve everyone, man, woman, and child, others may be focused on specific groups, categories, associations, etc., such as men *or* women, old *or* young, one clan *or* another, one association or secret society *or* another. Yet the whole ritual round adds up to the total participation of the whole community. Sooner or later, no one is exempt from ritual duty, just as no one is exempt from economic, legal, or political duty. Communal participation, obligation, the passage of the whole society through crises, collective and individual, directly or by proxy, are the hallmarks of "the work of the gods" and sacred human work. Without it profane human work would be, for the community, impossible to conceive, though, no doubt, as history has cruelly demonstrated to those conquered by industrial societies, possible to live, or, at least, exist through.

Yet it can be argued that this "work" is not work, as we in industrial societies know it, but has in both its dimensions, sacred and profane, an element of "play." Insofar as the community and its individual members regard themselves as the masters or "owners" of ritual and liturgy, or as representatives of the ancestors and gods who ultimately "own" them, they have authority to introduce, under certain culturally determined conditions, elements of novelty from time to time into the socially inherited deposit of ritual customs. Liminality, the seclusion period, is a phase peculiarly conducive to such "ludic" invention. Perhaps it would be better to regard the distinction between "work" and "play," or better between "work" and "leisure" (which includes but exceeds play *sui generis*), as itself an artifact of the Industrial Revolution, and to see such symbolic-expressive genres as ritual and myth as being at once "work" and "play" or at least as cultural activities in which work and play are intricately intercalated. Yet it often happens that the historically *later* can throw light on the *earlier*, especially when there is a demonstrable sociogenetic connection between them. For there are undoubtedly "ludic" aspects in "tribal," etc., culture, especially in the liminal periods of protracted initiation or calendrically based rituals. Such would include joking relationships, sacred games, such as the ball games of the ancient Maya and modern Cherokee, riddles, mock-ordeals, holy fooling and clowning, Trickster tales told in liminal times and places (in or out of ritual contexts), and a host of other types.

The point is, though, that these "play" or "ludic" aspects of tribal and agrarian ritual and myth are, as Durkheim says, "de la vie sérieuse," that is, they are intrinsically connected with the "work" of the collectivity in performing symbolic actions and manipulating symbolic objects so as to promote and increase fertility of men, crops, and animals, domestic and wild, to cure illness, to avert plague, to obtain success in raiding, to turn boys into men and girls into women, to make chiefs out of commoners, to transform ordinary people into shamans and shamanins, to "cool" those "hot" from the warpath, to ensure the proper succession of seasons and the hunting and agricultural responses of human beings to them, and so forth. Thus the play is in earnest, and has to be within bounds. For example, in the Ndembu Twin Ritual, *Wubwang'u*, described in *The Ritual Process*, in one episode women and men abuse one another verbally in a highly sexual and jacose way. Much personal inventiveness goes into the invective, though much is also stylized. Nevertheless, this ludic behavior is pressed into the service of the ultimate aim of the ritual—to produce healthy offspring, but not *too many* healthy offspring at once. Abundance is good, but reckless abundance is a foolish joke. "Enough's enough, but this is ridiculous!" Hence cross-sexual joking both maintains reasonable fertility and restrains unreasonable fecundity. Joking is fun, but it is also a social sanction. Even joking must observe the "golden mean," which is an ethical feature of "cyclical, repetitive societies," not as yet unbalanced by innovative ideas and technical changes.

Technical innovations are the products of ideas, the products of what I will call the "liminoid" (the "-oid" here, as in aster*oid*, star*like*, ov*oid*, egg-*shaped*, etc., derives from Greek *-eidos*, a form, shape, and means "like, resembling"; "liminoid" *resembles* without being identical with "liminal") and what Marx assigned to a domain he called "the *super*-structural"—I would prefer to talk about the "anti-," "meta-," or "*proto*structural." "Superstructural," for Marx, has the connotation of a distorted mirroring of the "structural," which is, in his terms, the con-stellation of productive relations, both in cohesion and conflict. On the contrary, I would see the "liminoid" as an independent and critical source—like Marx's own liminoid "works." Here we will observe how "liminoid" actions of industrial leisure genres can repossess the character of "work" though originating in a "free-time" arbitrarily separated by managerial fiat from the time of "labor"—and how the liminoid can be an independent domain of creative activity, not simply a distorted mirror-image, mask, or cloak for structural activity in the "centers" or "mainstreams" of "productive social labor." This is to identify liminoid productions with apologia for the political status quo. "Anti-structure," in fact, can generate and store a plurality of alter-native models for living, from utopias to programs, which are capable of influencing the behavior of those in mainstream social and political roles (whether authoritative or dependent, in control or rebelling against it) in the direction of radical change. As scientists we are interested in demar-cating a domain, not in taking sides with one or other of the groups or categories which operate within it. Experimental and theoretical science itself is "liminoid"—it takes place in "neutral spaces" or privileged areas (laboratories and studies) set aside from the mainstream of produc-tive events. Universities, institutes, colleges, etc., are "liminoid" settings for all kinds of freewheeling, experimental cognitive behavior as well as forms of symbolic action, resembling some found in tribal society ("rushing" and "pledging" ceremonies, for example!).

But let us look more closely at this notion of the "liminoid," and try to distinguish it from the "liminal." To do this properly, we have to ex-amine the notion of "play." Etymology does not tell us too much about its meaning. We learn that the word "play" is derived from OE *plegan*, "to exercise oneself, move briskly," and that the Middle Dutch *pleyen*, "to dance," is a cognate term. Walter Skeat, in his *Concise Etymological Dictionary of the English Language* (p. 355) suggests that the Anglo-Saxon *plega*, "a game, sport," is also (commonly) "a fight, a battle." He considers, too, that the Anglo-Saxon terms are borrowed from the Latin *plaga*, "a stroke." Even if the idea of a "danced-out or ritualized fight" gets into subsequent denotations of "play," this multi-vocal concept has its own historical destiny.

For *Webster's Dictionary, play* is:

(1) action, motion, or activity, esp. when free, rapid, or light (e.g., the *play* of muscles) [here, as so often, "play" is conceived of as "light" as against the "heaviness" of "work," "free" as against work's "necessary" or "obligatory" character, "rapid" as against the careful, reflected-upon style of work routines]; (2) freedom or scope for motion or action; (3) activity engaged in for amusement or recreation [here, again, we are verging on the notion of activities disengaged from necessity or obligation]; (4) fun, joking (to do a thing in *play*) [emphasizing the *non*-serious character of certain types of modern play]; (5) (a) the playing of a game, (b) the way or technique of playing a game [here reintroducing the notion that play might be work, might be serious within its non-serious dimension, and raising the problem of what are the conditions under which "fun" becomes "technique" and rule-governed]; (6) (a) a maneuver, move, or act in a game (e.g., the "wishbone" or "T" offensive formation in American football or a specific brilliant move by a team or individual), (b) a turn at playing (e.g., "there's one play left in the game"); (7) the act of gambling [and here we may think of the "gambling" character of divination in tribal and even in feudal society, and, of course, the very word "gamble" is derived from OE *gamenian*, "to play" akin to the German dialect term *gammeln*, "to sport, make merry"]; (8) a dramatic composition or performance; drama, "the play's the thing" [clearly this term preserves something of the earlier sense of "fight, battle" as well as those of "recreation," "technique," and "turns (i.e., acts, scenes, etc.) at playing"]; (9) sexual activity, dalliance.

Here again we can see a shift from the meaning of sex as procreative "work," (a persistent meaning in tribal and feudal societies) to the division of sexual activity into "play" or "foreplay," and the "serious" business or "work" of begetting progeny. Postindustrial birth control techniques make this division practically realizable, and themselves exemplify the division between work and play brought about by modern systems of production and thought, both "objectively," in the domain of culture, and "subjectively" in the individual conscience and consciousness. The distinction between "subjective" and "objective" is itself an artifact of the sundering of work and play. For "work" is held to be the realm of the rational adaptation of means to ends, of "objectivity," while "play" is thought of as divorced from this essentially "objective" realm, and, insofar as it is its inverse, being "subjective," free from external constraints, where any and every combination of variables can be "played" with. Indeed, Jean Piaget, who has done most to study the developmental psychology of play, regards it as "a kind of free assimilation, without accommodation to spatial conditions or to the significance of the objects" (1962, p. 86).

In the liminal phases and states of tribal and agrarian cultures—in ritual, myth, and legal processes—work and play are hardly distinguishable in many cases. Thus, in Vedic India, according to Alain Danielou (1964, p. 144), the "gods [*sura* and *deva*, who are objects of serious sacrificial ritual] play. The rise, duration and destruction of the world is their game." Ritual is both earnest and playful. As Milton Singer has pointed out (1972, p. 160), the "Krishna dance" in an urban *bhajana* program (group hymn singing) is called *lila*, "sports," in which the participants "play" at being the "Gopis" or milkmaids who "sport" in a variety of ways with Krishna, Vishnu incarnate, reliving the myth. But the *Gopi*'s erotic love-play with Krishna has mystical implications, like the *Song of Solomon*—it is at once serious and playful, God's "sport" with the human soul.

Now let us consider the clear division between *work* and *leisure* which modern industry has produced, and how this has affected all symbolic genres, from ritual to games and literature. Joffre Dumazedier, of the Centre d'Etudes Sociologiques (Paris), is not the only authority who holds that leisure "has certain traits that are characteristic only of the civilization born from the industrial revolution" (1968, pp. 248-253; see also 1962). But he puts the case very pithily and I am beholden to his argument. Dumazedier dismisses the view that leisure has existed in all societies at all times. In archaic and tribal societies, he maintains, "work and play alike formed part of the ritual by which men sought communion with the ancestral spirits. Religious festivals embodied both work and play" (1968, p. 248). Yet religious specialists such as shamans and medicine-men did not constitute a "leisure-class" in Veblen's sense, since they performed religious or magical functions for the whole community (and, as we have seen, shamanism is a "diligent and laborious" profession). Similarly, in the agricultural societies of recorded history,

> the working year followed a timetable written in the very passage of the days and seasons: in good weather work was hard, in bad weather it slackened off. Work of this kind had a natural rhythm to it, punctuated by rests, songs, games, and ceremonies; it was synonymous with the daily round, and in some regions began at sunrise, to finish only at sunset . . . the cycle of the year was also marked by a whole series of sabbaths and feast days. The sabbath belonged to religion; feast days, however, were often occasions for a great investment of energy (not to mention food) and constituted the obverse or opposite of everyday life [often characterized by symbolic inversion and status reversal]. But the ceremonial [or ritual] aspect of these celebrations could not be disregarded; they stemmed from religion [defined as sacred *work*], not leisure [as we think of it today]. . . . They were imposed by religious requirements . . . [and] the major European civilizations knew more than 150 workless days a year. (p. 249)

Sebastian de Grazia has recently argued (1962) that the origins of leisure can be traced to the way of life enjoyed by certain aristocratic classes in the course of Western civilization. Dumazedier disagrees, pointing out that the idle state of Greek philosophers and 16th century gentry cannot be defined *in relation to* work, but rather *replaces work altogether*. Work is done by slaves, peasants, or servants. True leisure exists only when it complements or rewards work. This is not to say that many of the refinements of human culture did not come from this aristocratic idleness. Dumazedier thinks that it is significant that the Greek word for having nothing to do *(schole)* also meant "school." "The courtiers of Europe, after the end of the Middle Ages, both invented and extolled the ideal of the humanist and the gentleman" (1968, p. 249).

"Leisure," then, presupposes "work": it is a nonwork, even an anti-work phase in the life of a person who also works. If we were to indulge in terminological neophily, we might call it *anergic* as against *ergic*! Leisure arises, says Dumazedier, under two conditions. First, society ceases to govern its activities by means of common ritual obligations: Some activities, including work and leisure, become, at least in theory, *subject to individual choice*. Secondly, the work by which a person earns his or her living is "set apart from his other activities: its limits are no longer *natural* [my italics] but arbitrary—indeed, it is organized in so definite a fashion that it can easily be separated, both in theory and in practice, from his free time" (1968, p. 249). It is only in the social life of industrial and postindustrial civilizations that we find these necessary conditions. Other social theorists, both radical and conservative, have pointed out that leisure is the product of industrialized, rationalized, bureaucratized, large-scale socioeconomic systems with arbitrary rather than natural delimitation of "work" from "free time" or "time out." Work is now organized by industry so as to be separated from "free time," which includes, in addition to leisure, attendance to such personal needs as eating, sleeping, and caring for one's health and appearance, as well as familial, social, civic, political, and religious obligations (which would have fallen within the domain of the work-play continuum in tribal society). Leisure is predominantly an urban phenomenon, so that when the concept of leisure begins to penetrate rural societies, it is because agricultural labor is tending towards an industrial, "rationalized" mode of organization, and because rural life is becoming permeated by the urban values of industrialization. This holds good for the "Third World" today as well as for the rural hinterlands of long-established industrial societies.

Leisure-time is associated with two types of freedom, "freedom-from" and "freedom-to," to advert to Isiah Berlin's famous distinction. (1) It represents *freedom from* a whole heap of institutional obligations prescribed by the basic forms of social, particularly technological and bureaucratic, organization. (2) For each individual, it means *freedom from* the forced, chronologically regulated rhythms of factory and office and a chance to recuperate and enjoy natural, biological rhythms again.

Leisure is also (1) *freedom to* enter, even to generate new symbolic worlds of entertainment, sports, games, diversions of all kinds. It is, furthermore, (2) *freedom to* transcend social structural limitations, freedom to *play*—with ideas, with fantasies, with words (from Rabelais to Joyce and Samuel Beckett), with paint (from the Impressionists to Action Painting and Art Nouveau), and with social relationships—in friendship, sensitivity training, psychodramas, and in other ways. Here far more than in tribal or agrarian rites and ceremonies, the ludic and the experimental are stressed. In complex, organic-solidary societies, there are obviously many more options; games of skill, strength, and chance can serve as models for future behavior or models of past work experience—now viewed as release from work's necessities and as something one chooses to do. Sports such as football, games such as chess, recreations such as mountaineering can be hard and exacting and governed by rules and routines even more stringent than those of the work situation, but, since they are optional, they are part of an individual's freedom, of his growing self-mastery, even self-transcendence. Hence they are imbued more thoroughly with pleasure than those many types of industrial work in which men are alienated from the fruits and results of their labor. Leisure is potentially capable of releasing creative powers, individual or communal, either to criticize or buttress the dominant social structural values.

It is certain that no one is committed to a true leisure activity by material need or by moral or legal obligations, as is the case with the activities of getting an education, earning a living, or participating in civic or religious ceremonies. Even when there is effort, as in competitive sport, that effort—and the discipline of training—is chosen voluntarily, in the expectation of an enjoyment that is disinterested, is unmotivated by gain, and has no utilitarian or ideological purpose.

But if this is ideally the spirit of leisure, the cultural reality of leisure is obviously influenced by the domain of work from which it has been split by the wedge of industrial organization. Work and leisure interact, each individual participates in both realms, and the modes of work organization affect the styles of leisure pursuits. Let us consider the case of those mainly Northern European and North American societies whose preliminary industrialization was accompanied and infused with the spirit of what Max Weber has called "the Protestant Ethic." This ethical milieu, or set of values and beliefs, which Weber thought was an auspicious condition for the growth of modern, rational capitalism, in my view produced effects in the *leisure* domain quite as far-reaching as in that of work. As everyone now knows, Weber argued that John Calvin and other Protestant reformers taught that salvation is a pure gift from God and cannot be earned or merited by a being so thoroughly depraved in his nature since the Fall of Adam as man. In its extreme form, Predestination, this meant that no one could be certain of being saved, or indeed of being damned. This threatened seriously to undermine individual morale, and a get-out clause evolved at the level of popular culture, though it could not be made theologically watertight. This was that he who is in God's grace and (invisibly) among the elect by God's foreordaining does actually manifest in his behavior systematic self-control and obedience to the will of God. By these outward signs it may be known to others and he can reassure himself that he is among the elect, and will not suffer eternal damnation with the reprobate. But the Calvinist is never finally certain that he will be saved and thus dedicates himself to an incessant examination of the conditions of his inward soul and outward life for evident indications of the work of salvific grace. In a sense, what was in cultural history previously the social "work of the Gods," the calendrical, liturgical round, or, rather, its penances and ordeals, not its festive rewards, became "internalized" as the systematic, nonludic "work" of the individual's conscience.

Calvinist emphasis was also on the notion of one's calling in life, one's vocation. As against the Catholic notion of "vocation" as the call to a religious life, by vows of chastity, obedience, and poverty, the Calvinist held that it was precisely a person's worldly occupation that must be regarded as the sphere in which he was to serve God through his dedication to his work. Work and leisure were made separate spheres, and "work" became sacred *de facto*, as the arena in which one's salvation might be objectively demonstrated. Thus, the man of property was to act as a steward of worldly goods, like Joseph in Egypt. He was to use them not for sinful luxury, but to better the moral condition of himself, his family, and his employees. "Betterment" implied self-discipline, self-examination, hard work, dedication to one's duty and calling, and an insistence that those under one's authority should do the same. Wherever the Calvinist aspiration to theocracy became influential, as in Geneva or in the transient dominance of English Puritanism, legislation was introduced to force men to better their spiritual state through thrift and hard work. For example, English Puritanism affected not only religious worship by its attack on "ritualism," but also reduced "ceremonial" ("secular" ritual) to a minimum in many other fields of activity, including drama, which it stigmatized as "mummery." The Act making stage performances illegal cut 20-odd years from the performance of Jonson's plays. Among the targets of such legislation were, significantly, genres of leisure entertainment which had developed in aristocratic or mercantilist circles in the proto-industrializing period, such as theatrical productions, masques, pageants, muscial performances, and, of course, the popular genres of carnivals, festivals, charivaris, ballad singing, and miracle plays. These represented the "ludic" face of the work-play continuum that had formerly caught up the whole of society into a single process moving through sacred and profane, solemn and festive, phases in the seasonal round. The Calvinists wanted "no more cakes and ale"— or other festival foods that belonged to the work and play of the gods. They wanted ascetic dedication to the mainline economic enterprise, the sanctification of what was formerly mostly profane, or, at least, *subordinated to* and ancillary to the sacred cosmological paradigms. Weber argues that when the religious motivations of Calvinism were lost after a few generations of worldly success, the focus on self-examination, self-discipline, and hard work in one's calling even when secularized continued to promote the ascetic dedication to systematic profits, reinvestment of earnings, and thrift, which were the hallmarks of nascent capitalism.

Something of this systematic, vocational character of the Protestant ethic came to tinge even the entertainment genres of industrial leisure. To coin a term, even leisure became "ergic," "of the nature of work," rather than "ludic," "of the nature of play." Thus, we have a *serious* division of *labor* in the *entertainment* business: acting, dancing, singing, art, writing, composing, and so on, become professionalized "vocations." Educational institutions prepare actors, dancers, singers, painters, and authors for their "careers." At a higher level, there grew up in the late 18th and especially in the 19th centuries the notion of "art" itself, in its various modalities, as a quasi-religious vocation, with its own asceticism and total dedication, from William Blake, through Kierkegaard, Baudelaire, Lermontov, and Rimbaud, to Cézanne, Proust, Rilke, and Joyce, not to mention Beethoven, Mahler, Sibelius, and so forth.

Another aspect of this influence of the Protestant ethic on leisure is in the realm of play itself. As Edward Norbeck (1971) has recently said:

> America's forefathers believed strongly in the set of values known as the Protestant ethic. Devotion to work was a Christian virtue; and play, the enemy of work, was reluctantly and charily permitted only to children. Even now, these values are far from extinct in our nation, and the old admonition that play is the devil's handiwork continues to live in secular thought. Although play has now become almost respectable, it is still something in which we "indulge" (as in sexual acts), a form of moral laxness. (pp. 48-53)

Organized sport ("pedagogic" play) better fits the Puritan tradition than unorganized children's play ("pediarchic" play) or mere dalliance, which is time wasted.

Nevertheless, modern industrial or postindustrial societies have shed many of these anti-leisure attitudes. Technological development, political and industrial organization by workers, action by liberal employers, revolutions in many parts of the world, have had the cumulative effect of bringing more leisure into the "free-time" of industrial cultures. In this leisure symbolic genres, both of the entertainment and instructive sorts, have proliferated. In my book *The Ritual Process*, I have spoken of some of these as "liminal" phenomena. In view of what I have just said, is liminality an adequate label for this set of symbolic activities and forms? Clearly, there are some respects in which these "anergic" genres share characteristics with the "ludergic" rituals and myths (if we contrast the Hindu and Judaic ritual style) of archaic, tribal, and early agrarian cultures. Leisure can be conceived of as a betwixt-and-between, a neither-this-nor-that domain between two spells of work or between occupational and familial and civic activity. Leisure is etymologically derived from Old French *leisir*, which itself derives from Latin *licere*, "to be permitted." Interestingly enough, it ultimately comes from the Indo-European base *leik-, "to offer for sale, bargain," referring to the "liminal" sphere of the market, with its implications of choice, variation, contract—a sphere that has connections, in archaic and tribal religions, with Trickster deities such as Elegba, Eshu, and Hermes. Exchange is more "liminal" than production. Just as when tribesmen make masks, disguise themselves as monsters, heap up disparate ritual symbols, invert or parody profane reality in myths and folktales, so do the genres of industrial leisure, the theater, poetry, novel, ballet, film, sport, rock music, classical music, art, pop art, and so on, *play* with the factors of culture, sometimes assembling them in random, grotesque, improbable, surprising, shocking, usually experimental combinations. But they do this in a much more complicated way than in the liminality of tribal initiations. They multiply specialized genres of artistic and popular entertainments, mass culture, pop culture, folk culture, high culture, counterculture, underground culture, etc., as against the relatively limited symbolic genres of "tribal" society, and within each they allow lavish scope to authors, poets, dramatists, painters, sculptors, composers, musicians, actors, comedians, folksingers, rock musicians, "makers" generally, to generate not only weird forms, but also, and not infrequently, models, direct and parabolic or aesopian, that are highly critical of the status quo as a whole or in part. Of course, given *diversity* as a *principle*, many artists, in many genres, also buttress, reinforce, and justify the prevailing social and cultural mores and political orders. Those that do so, do so in ways that tend more closely than the *critical* productions to parallel tribal myths and rituals—they are "liminal" or "pseudo-" or "post-" "liminal," rather than "liminoid." Satire is a conservative genre because it is *pseudo-liminal*. Satire exposes, attacks, or derides what it considers to be vices, follies, stupidities, or abuses, but its criteria of judgment are usually the normative structural frame of values. Hence satirical works, like those of Swift, Castlereagh, or Evelyn Waugh, often have a "ritual of reversal" form, indicating that disorder is no permanent substitution for order. A mirror inverts but also reflects an object. It does not break it down into constituents in order to remold it, far less does it annihilate and replace that object. But art and literature often do. The *liminal* phases of tribal society invert but do not usually subvert the status quo, the structural form, of society; reversal underlines that chaos is the alternative to cosmos, so they had better stick to cosmos, that is, the traditional order of culture—though they can for a brief while have a heck of a good time being chaotic, in some saturnalian or lupercalian revelry, some charivari, or institutionalized orgy. But supposedly "entertainment" genres of industrial society are often *subversive*, lampooning, burlesquing, or subtly putting down the central values of the basic, work-sphere society, or at least of selected sectors of that society. Some of these genres, such as the "legitimate" or "classical" theater, are historically continuous with ritual, and possess something of the sacred seriousness, even the *"rites de passage"* structure of their antecedents. Nevertheless, crucial differences separate the structure, function, style, scope, and symbology of the liminal in "tribal and agrarian ritual and myth" from what we may perhaps call the "liminoid," or leisure genres, of symbolic forms and action in complex, industrial societies.

The term *limen* itself, the Latin for "threshold," selected by van Gennep to apply to "transition between," appears to be negative in connotation, since it is no longer the positive past condition nor yet the positive articulated future condition. It seems, too, to be passive since it is dependent on the articulated, positive conditions it mediates. Yet on probing, one finds in liminality both positive and active qualities, especially where that "threshold" is protracted and becomes a "tunnel," when the "liminal" becomes the "cunicular"; this is particularly the case in initiation rituals, with their long periods of seclusion and training of novices rich in the deployment of symbolic forms and esoteric teachings. "Meaning" in culture tends to be *generated* at the interfaces between established cultural subsystems, though meanings are then institutionalized and consolidated at the centers of such systems. Liminality is a temporal interface whose properties partially invert those of the already consolidated order which constitutes any specific cultural "cosmos." It may be useful heuristically to consider in relation to liminality in ritual/myth Durkheim's overall characterization of "mechanical solidarity," which he regarded as that type of cohesion plus cooperative, collective action directed towards the achievement of group goals which best applies to small, nonliterate societies with a simple division of labor and very little tolerance of individuality. He based this type of solidarity on a *homogeneity* of values and behavior, strong social constraint, and loyalty to tradition and kinship. The rules for togetherness are known and shared. Now what frequently typifies the liminality of initiation ritual in societies with mechanical solidarity is precisely the opposite of this: ordeals, myths, maskings, mumming, the presentation of sacred icons to novices, secret languages, food and behavioral taboos, create a weird domain in the seclusion camp in which ordinary regularities of kinship, the residential setting, tribal law and custom are set aside. The bizarre becomes the normal, and through the loosening of connections between elements customarily bound together in certain combinations, their scrambling and recombining in monstrous, fantastic, and unnatural shapes, the novices are induced to think (and think hard) about cultural experiences they had hitherto taken for granted. The novices are taught that they did not know what they thought they knew. Beneath the surface structure of custom was a deep structure, whose rules they had to learn, through paradox and shock. In some ways social constraints become stronger, even unnaturally and irrationally stronger, as when the novices are compelled by their elders to undertake what in their minds are unnecessary tasks by arbitrary fiat, and are punished severely if they fail to obey promptly—and, what is worse, even if they succeed. But in other ways, as in the case cited earlier from van Gennep's *Rites de Passage* (1909/1960), the novices also are conceded unprecedented freedoms: they make raids and swoops on villages and gardens, seize women, vituperate older people. Innumerable are the forms of topsy-turvydom, parody, abrogation of the normative system, exaggeration of rule into caricature or satirizing of rule. The novices are at once put outside and inside the circle of the previously known. But one thing must be kept in mind: *All* these acts and symbols are of *obligation*. Even the *breaking* of rules *has* to be done during initiation. This is one of the distinctive ways in which the liminal is marked off from the liminoid. In the 1972 American Anthropological Association Meetings in Toronto, several examples were cited—among them, carnival in St. Vincent in the West Indies, and the La Have Islands, Nova Scotia (Abrahams & Bauman, Note 2)—from modern societies on the fringe of industrial civilizations which bore some resemblance to liminal inversions in tribal societies. But what was striking to me was how even in these "outback" regions *optionality* dominated the whole process. For example, when the masked mummers of La Have, usually older boys and young married men, known as "belsnicklers," emerge on Christmas Eve to entertain, tease, and fool adults, and to frighten children, they knock at house doors and windows, asking to be "allowed" entrance. Some householders actually refuse to let them in. Now I cannot imagine a situation in which Ndembu, Luvale, Chokwe, or Luchazi masked dancers (people I have known and observed), who emerge after the performance of a certain ritual, marking the end of one half of the seclusion period and the beginning of another, to dance in villages and threaten women and children, would be refused entry. Nor do they ask permission to enter; they storm in! Belsnicklers have to "ask for" treats from householders. *Makishi* (maskers) among Ndembu, Chokwe, etc., demand food and gifts as of right. Optation pervades the liminoid phenomenon, obligation the liminal. One is all play and choice, an entertainment, the other is a matter of deep seriousness, even dread, it is demanding, compulsory (though, indeed, fear provokes nervous laughter from the women, who, if they are touched by the *makishi*, are believed to contract leprosy, become sterile, or go mad!). Again, in St. Vincent, only *certain types* of personalities are attracted to the Carnival as performers, those whom Roger Abrahams describes as "the rude and sporty segment of the community," who are "rude and sporty" *whenever* they have an opportunity to be so, all the year round—hence they can most aptly personify "disorder" versus "order" at the Carnival. Here, again, optation is evidently dominant—for people do not *have to* act invertedly, as in tribal rituals; some people, but not *all* people, *choose* to act invertedly at Carnival. And Carnival is unlike a tribal ritual in that it can be attended *or* avoided, performed or merely watched, at *will*. It is a genre of leisure enjoyment, not an obligatory ritual, it is play-separated-from-work not play-and-work ludergy as a binary system of man's "serious" communal endeavor. Abrahams, in his joint paper with Bauman (Note 2), makes a further valid point which firmly places Vincentian carnivals in the modern-leisure-genre category. He stresses that it is overwhelmingly the "bad, unruly (*macho*-type) men" who choose to perform carnival inversions indicative of disorder in the universe and society, people who are disorderly by temperament and choice in many extracarnival situations. To the contrary, in tribal ritual, even the normally orderly, meek, and "law-abiding" people would be *obliged* to be disorderly in key rituals, regardless of their temperament and character. The sphere of the optional is in such societies much reduced. Even in liminality, where the bizarre behavior so often remarked upon by anthropologists occurs, the *sacra*, masks, etc., emerge to view under the guise at least of "collective representations." If there ever were individual creators and artists, they have been subdued by the general "liminal" emphasis on anonymity and normative *communitas*, just as the novices and their novice-masters have been. But in the liminoid genres of industrial art, literature, and even science (more truly homologous with tribal liminal thinking than modern art is), great public stress is laid on the individual innovator, the unique person who dares and opts to create. In this lack of stress on individuality, tribal liminality may be seen not as the inverse of tribal normativeness, but as its projection into ritual situations. However, this has to be modified when one looks at actual initiation rituals "on the ground." I found that, among the Ndembu, despite the novices' being stripped of names, profane rank, and clothes, each emerged as a distinct individual; and there was an element of competitive personal distinctiveness in the fact that the best four novices in the terms of performance during seclusion (in hunting, endurance of ordeal, smartness in answering riddles, cooperativeness, etc.) were given titles in the rites marking their reaggregation to profane society. For me, this indicated that in liminality is secreted the seed of the liminoid, waiting only for major changes in the sociocultural context to set it agrowing into the branched "candelabra" of manifold liminoid cultural genres. If one *has to*, like Jack Horner, pull out a dialectical plum from each and every type of social formation, I would counsel that those who propose to study one of the world's fast disappearing "tribal" societies should look at the liminal phases of their rituals in order most precisely to locate the incipient contradiction between communal-anonymous and private-distinctive modes of conceiving principles of sociocultural growth.

I have used the term "anti-structure," mainly with reference to tribal and agrarian societies, to describe both liminality and what I have called "communitas." I meant by it not a structural reversal, a mirror-imaging of "profane" workaday socioeconomic structure, or a fantasy-rejection of structural "necessities," but the liberation of human capacities of cognition, affect, volition, creativity, etc., from the normative constraints incumbent upon occupying a sequence of social statuses, enacting a multiplicity of social roles, and being acutely conscious of membership in some corporate group such as a family, lineage, clan, tribe, or nation, or of affiliation with some pervasive social category such as a class, caste, sex- or age-division. Sociocultural systems drive so steadily towards consistency that human individuals only get off these normative hooks in rare situations in small-scale societies, and not very frequently in large-scale ones. Nevertheless, the exigencies of structuration itself, the process of containing new growth in orderly patterns or schemata, has an Achilles heel. This is the fact that when persons, groups, sets of ideas, etc., move from one level or style of organization or regulation of the interdependence of their parts or elements to another level, there has to be an interfacial region or, to change the metaphor, an interval, however brief, of *"margin"* or *"limen,"* when the past is momentarily negated, suspended, or abrogated, and the future has not yet begun. There is an instant of pure potentiality when everything trembles in the balance, like the moment when the trembling quarterback with all the "options" sees the very solid future moving menacingly toward him! In tribal societies, due to the general overriding homogeneity of values, behavior, and social structural rules, this instant can be fairly easily contained or dominated by social structure, held in check from innovative excess, "hedged about," as anthropologists delight to say, by "taboos," "checks and balances," and so on. Thus, the tribal liminal, however exotic in appearance, can never be much more than a subversive flicker. It is put into the service of normativeness almost as soon as it appears. Yet I see it as a kind of institutional capsule or pocket which contains the germ of future social developments, of societal change, in a way that the central tendencies of a social system can never quite succeed in being, the spheres where law and custom, and the modes of social control ancillary to these, prevail. Innovation can take place in such spheres, but most frequently it occurs in interfaces and limina, then becomes *legitimated* in central sectors. For me, such relatively "late" social processes, historically speaking, as "revolution," "insurrection," and even "romanticism" in art, characterized by freedom in form and spirit, by emphasis on feeling and originality, represent an inversion of the relation between the normative and the liminal in "tribal" and other essentially conservative societies. For in these modern processes movements, the seeds of cultural transformation, discontent with the way things culturally are, and social criticism (always implicit in the preindustrially liminal), have become situationally central, no longer a matter of the interface between "fixed structures" but a matter of the holistically developmental. Thus, revolutions, whether successful or not, become the *limina*, with all their initiatory overtones, between major distinctive structural forms or orderings of society. It may be that this is to use "liminal" in a metaphorical sense, not in the "primary" or "literal" sense advocated by van Gennep, but this usage may help us to think about global human society, to which all specific historical social formations may well be converging. Revolutions, whether violent or nonviolent, may be the totalizing liminal phases for which the limina of tribal *rites de passage* were merely foreshadowings or premonitions.

This may possibly be the point where we should feed in the other major variable of the "anti-structural," *communitas*. (I will discuss the merits and demerits of talking about "anti-structure," "metastructure," and "protostructure" later.) There is in tribal societies probably a closer relationship between communitas and liminality than between communitas and normative structure, though the modality of human interrelatedness which is communitas can "play" across structural systems in a way too difficult for us at present to predict its motions. This is the experiential basis, I believe, of the Christian notion of "actual grace." Thus, in the workshop, village, office, lecture-room, theater, almost anywhere, people can be subverted from their duties and rights into an atmosphere of *communitas*. What then *is* communitas? Has it any reality base, or is it a persistent fantasy of mankind, a sort of collective return to the womb? I have described (Turner, 1969) this way by which persons see, understand, and act toward one another as essentially "an unmediated relationship between historical, idiosyncratic, concrete individuals." This is *not* the same as Georges Gurvitch's notion of "communion" which he describes as "when minds open out as widely as possible and the least accessible depths of the 'I' are integrated in this fusion (which presupposes states of collective ecstasy)" (Gurvitch, 1941). For me communitas preserves individual distinctiveness — it is neither regression to infancy, nor is it emotional, nor is it "merging" in fantasy. In people's social structural relationships they are by various abstract processes generalized and segmentalized into roles, statuses, classes, cultural sexes, conventional age-divisions, ethnic affiliations, and so on. In different types of social situations they have been conditioned to play specific social roles. It does not matter how well or badly, as long as they "make like" they are obedient to the norm-sets that control different compartments of the complex model known as the "social structure." So far this has been almost the entire subject matter of the social sciences: people playing roles and maintaining or achieving status. Admittedly this does cover a very great deal of what human beings are up to and what quantitatively takes up a great deal of their available time, both in work and leisure. And, to some extent, the authentic human essence gets involved here, for every role-definition takes into account some basic human attribute or capacity, and willy-nilly, human beings *play* their roles in human ways. But *full* human capacity is locked out of these somewhat narrow, stuffy rooms. Even though when we say a person plays his role well, we often mean that he plays it with flexibility and imagination, Martin Buber's notions of *I-and-Thou* relationship and the *Essential We* formed by people moving toward a freely chosen common goal are intuitive perceptions of a nontransactional order or quality of human relationship, in the sense that people do not necessarily initiate action towards one another in the expectation of a reaction that satisfies their interests. Anthropologists, inadvertently, have escaped many of these "hang-ups," for they deal with "man alive," in his altruistic as well as egoistic strivings, in the microprocesses of social life. Some sociologists, on the other hand, find security in ethnocentric questionnaires, which, by the nature of the case, distance observer from informant, and render inauthentic their subsequently guarded interaction. In tribal societies and other preindustrial social formations, liminality provides a propitious setting for the development of these direct, immediate, and total confrontations of human identities. In industrial societies, it is within leisure, sometimes aided by the projections of art, that this way of experiencing one's fellows can be portrayed, grasped, and sometimes realized. Liminality is, of course, an ambiguous state, for social structure, while it inhibits full social satisfaction, gives a measure of finiteness and security; liminality may be for many the acme of insecurity, the breakthrough of chaos into cosmos, of disorder into order, rather than the milieu of creative interhuman or transhuman satisfactions and achievements. Liminality may be the scene of disease, despair, death, suicide, the breakdown without compensatory replacement of normative, well-defined social ties and bonds. It may be *anomie*, alienation, *angst*, the three fatal "alpha" sisters of many modern myths. In tribal and similar societies it may be the interstitial domain of domestic witchcraft, the hostile dead, and the vengeful spirits of strangers; in the leisure genres of complex societies, it may be represented by the "extreme situations" beloved of existentialist writers: torture, murder, war, the verge of suicide, hospital tragedies, the point of execution, etc. Liminality is both more creative and more destructive than the structural norm. In either case it raises basic problems for social structural man, invites him to speculation and criticism. But where it is socially positive it presents, directly or by implication, a model of human society as a homogeneous, unstructured communitas, whose boundaries are ideally coterminous with those of the human species. When even two people believe that they experience unity, all people are felt to be one by those two, even if only for a flash. Feeling generalizes more readily than thought, it would seem! The great difficulty is to keep this intuition alive—regular drugging will not do it, repeated sexual union will not do it, constant immersion in great literature will not do it: Initiation seclusion must sooner or later come to an end. We thus encounter the paradox that the *experience* of communitas becomes the *memory* of communitas, with the result that communitas itself in striving to replicate itself historically develops a social structure, in which initially free and innovative relationships between individuals are converted into norm-governed relationships between social *personae*. I am aware that I am stating another paradox: that the more spontaneously "equal" people become, the more distinctively "themselves" they become; the more the *same* they become socially, the less they find themselves to be individually. Yet when this *communitas* or *comitas* is institutionalized, the new-found idiosyncratic is legislated into yet another set of universalistic roles and statuses, whose incumbents must subordinate individuality to a rule.

I argued in *The Ritual Process* (Turner, 1969) that the spontaneity and immediacy of communitas—as opposed to the jural-political character of (social) structure—can seldom be sustained for long. Communitas itself soon develops a (protective social) structure, in which free relationships between individuals become converted into norm-governed relationships between social personae. The so-called "normal" may be more of a game, played in masks (personae), with a script, than certain ways of behaving "without a mask," that are culturally defined as "abnormal," "aberrant," "eccentric," or "way-out." Yet *communitas* does not represent the erasure of structural norms from the consciousness of those participating in it; rather its own style, in a given community, might be said to depend upon the way in which it symbolizes the abrogation, negation, or inversion of the normative structure in which its participants are quotidianly involved. Indeed, its own readiness to convert into normative structure indicates its vulnerability to the structural environment.

Looking at the historical fate of *communitas*, I identified three distinct and not necessarily sequential forms of it, which I called *spontaneous, ideological*, and *normative*. Each has certain relationships with liminal and liminoid phenomena.

1. *Spontaneous* communitas is "a direct, immediate and total confrontation of human identities," a deep rather than intense style of personal interaction. "It has something 'magical' about it. Subjectively there is in it a feeling of endless power." Is there any of us who has not known this moment when compatible people—friends, congeners—obtain a flash of lucid mutual understanding on the existential level, when they feel that all problems (not just their problems), whether emotional or cognitive, could be resolved, if only the group which is felt (in the first person) as "essentially us" could sustain its intersubjective illumination. This illumination may succumb to the dry light of next day's disjunction, the application of singular and personal reason to the "glory" of communal understanding. But when the mood, style, or "fit" of spontaneous communitas is upon us, we place a high value on personal honesty, openness, and lack of pretensions or pretentiousness. We feel that it is important to relate directly to another person as he presents himself in the here-and-now, to understand him in a sympathetic (not an empathetic—which implies some withholding, some nongiving of the self) way, free from the culturally defined encumbrances of his role, status, reputation, class, caste, sex, or other structural niche. Individuals who interact with one another in the mode of spontaneous communitas become totally absorbed into a single, synchronized, fluid event. Their "gut-" understanding of synchronicity in these situations opens them to the understanding of such cultural forms—derived typically today from the literate transmission of world culture, directly or in translation—as eucharistic union and the I-Ching. The latter stresses the mutual mystical participation (to cite Lévy-Bruhl) of all contemporary events, if one only had a mechanism to lay hold of the "meaning" underlying their "coincidence."

2. What I have called *"ideological communitas"* is a set of theoretical. concepts which attempt to describe the interactions of spontaneous communitas. Here the retrospective look, "memory," has already distanced the individual subject from the communal or dyadic experience. Here the experiencer has already come to look to language and culture to mediate the former immediacies, an instance of what Mihali Csikszentmihalyi (in press) has recently called a "flow-break," that is, an interruption of that experience of merging action and awareness (and centering of attention) which characterizes the supreme "pay-off" in ritual, art, sport, games, and even gambling. "Flow" may induce communitas, and communitas

"flow," but some "flows" are solitary and some modes of communitas separate awareness from action—especially in religious communitas. Here it is not teamwork in flow that is quintessential, but *"being"* together, with being the operative word, not doing. Csikszentmihalyi has already begun to ransack the inherited cultural past for models or for cultural elements drawn from the debris of past models from which he can construct a new model which will, however falteringly, replicate in words his concrete experience of spontaneous communitas. Some of these sets of theoretical concepts can be expanded and concretized into a "utopian" model of society, in which all human activities would be carried out on the level of spontaneous communtas. I hasten to add that not all or even the majority of "utopian" models are those of "ideological communitas." Utopia means "no place" in Greek: The manufacture of utopias is an untrammelled "ludic" activity of the leisure of the modern world, and such manufacture, like industrial manufacture, tends to posit ideal politico-administrative *structures* as prime desiderata—including highly hierarchical ones—rather than what the world or a land or island would look like if everyone sought to live in communitas with his and her neighbor. There are many hierarchical utopias, conservative utopias, fascistic utopias. Nevertheless, the communitas "utopia" is found in variant forms as a central ingredient, connected with the notion of "salvation," in many of the world's literate, "historical" religions. "Thy Kingdom" (which being *caritas, agape*, "love," is an anti-kingdom, a communitas) "come."

3. *Normative communitas*, finally, is, once more, a "perduring social system," a subculture or group which attempts to foster and maintain relationships of spontaneous communitas on a more or less permanent basis. To do this it has to denature itself, for spontaneous communitas is more a matter of "grace" than "law," to use theological language. Its spirit "bloweth where it listeth"—it cannot be legislated for or normated, since it is the *exception*, not the *law*, the miracle not the regularity, primordial freedom not *anangke*, the causal chain of necessity. But, nevertheless, there is something about the origin of a group based even on normative communitas which distinguishes it from groups which arise on the foundation of some "natural" or technical "necessity," real or imagined, such as a system of productive relations or a group of putatively biologically connected persons, a family, kindred, or lineage. Something of "freedom," "liberation," or "love" (to use terms common in theological or political-philosophical Western vocabularies) adheres to normative communitas, even although quite often the strictest regimes devolve from what are apparently the most spontaneous experiences of communitas. This rigor comes about from the fact that communitas groups feel themselves initially to be utterly vulnerable to the institutionalized groups surrounding them. They develop protective institu-

tional armor, armor which becomes the harder as the pressures to destroy the primary group's autonomy proportionally increase. They "become what they behold." On the other hand, if they did not "behold" their enemies, they would succumb to them. This dilemma is presumably not resoluble by a growing, changing, innovative species which invents new tools of thinking as well as of industry and explores new emotional styles as it proceeds through time. The opposition of the old may be as important for change as the innovativeness of the new, inasmuch as together they constitute a problem.

Groups based on *normative* communitas commonly arise during a period of religious revival. When normative communitas is demonstrably a group's dominant social mode one can witness the process of transformation of a charismatic and personal movement into an ongoing, relatively repetitive social system. The inherent contradictions between spontaneous communitas and a markedly structured system are so great, however, that any venture which attempts to combine these modalities will constantly be threatened by structural cleavage or by the suffocation of communitas. The typical compromise here—and I refer the reader to *The Ritual Process* (1969), chapter 4, for illustrative case histories—tends to be a splitting of the membership into opposed factions, a solution which endures only as long as a balance of power is maintained between them. Usually the group which first organizes, then structures itself most methodically, prevails politically or parapolitically, though the key communitas values shared by both groups but put into abeyance by the politically successful one may later become resurgent in the latter. Thus the Conventual Franciscans succeeded in getting the Spiritual Franciscans condemned for their *usus pauper*, or extreme view of poverty, but the Capuchin Reform, beginning about three centuries later in 1525, restored many of the primitive ideals of Franciscan poverty and simplicity, which were practiced before the split into Conventuals and Spirituals in the 13th century. In symbological terms we have to distinguish between symbols of politico-jural systems and those making up religious systems. *Usus pauper* was a political symbol marking the factional cleavage between the two wings of Franciscanism, while "My Lady Poverty"—itself perhaps a Franciscan variant on the themes of "Our Lady Mary" or of "Our Holy Mother the Church" was a cultural symbol, transcending political structural divisions. Communitas tends to generate metaphors and symbols which later fractionate into sets and arrays of cultural values; it is in the realms of physical life-support (economics) and social control (law, politics) that symbols acquire their "social-structural" character. But, of course, the cultural and social-structural realms interpenetrate and overlap as concrete individuals pursue their interests, seek to attain their ideals, love, hate, subdue, and obey one another, in the flux of history. I will not advance at this point the view that the "extended-case method," with the social drama as one of its techniques, offers a useful way of studying symbols and their meanings as events within the total flow of social events, for I am still concerned with the problem of the relationships between symbols, the liminal, the liminoid, communitas, and social structure.

Communitas exists in a kind of "figure-ground" relationship with social structure. The boundaries of each of these—insofar as they constitute explicit or implicit models for human interaction—are defined by contact or comparison with the other. In the same way, the liminal phase of an initiation rite is defined by the surrounding social statuses (many of which it abrogates, inverts, or invalidates), and the "sacred" is defined by its relation to the "profane"—even in a single culture there is much relativity here, for if A is "sacred" to B, he may be simultaneously "profane" to C, and "less sacred" to D. Situational selection prevails here, as in many other aspects of sociocultural process. Communitas, in the present context of its use, then, may be said to exist more in contrast than in active opposition to social structure, as an alternative and more "liberated" way of being socially human, a way both of being detached from social structure (and hence potentially of periodically *evaluating* its performance) and also of a "distanced" or "marginal" person's being more attached to *other* disengaged persons (and hence, sometimes of evaluating a social structure's historical performance in common with them). Here we may have a loving union of the structurally damned pronouncing judgment on normative structure and providing alternative models for structure.

The boundaries of the astructural model of human interconnectedness described by ideological communitas are "ideally coterminous with those of the human species" (and sometimes extend even beyond that to a generic "reverence for life"). Therefore, those who are experiencing, or have recently experienced communitas often attempt to convert a social structural interaction or a set of such interactions (involving the primacy of institutionalized status-role behavior over "freewheeling" behavior) into a direct, immediate, and total confrontation of human identities, that is, into spontaneous communitas. Communitas tends to be inclusive (some might call it "generous"), social structure tends to be exclusive, even snobbish, relishing the distinction between we/they or in-group/out-group, higher/lower, betters/menials. This drive to inclusivity makes for proselytization. One wants to make the Others, We. One famous case in the Western tradition is Pentecost, when people of different linguistic and ethnic groups claimed, under the inspiration of the Holy Ghost, to understand one another completely sub- or translinguistically. After that the Pentecostal throng went forth to missionize the world. The glossolalia of some modern Pentecostals appears to be connected with the notion that whereas articulate speech divides people of different linguistic groups and even expedites "sin," among those of the same speech community, nonsense (archaic) speech facilitates mutual love and virtue. But these conversion attempts by communitarian individuals may be interpreted not only by the power elites of social structure, but *also* by the rank and file who feel safe in their obedience to norm, as a *direct threat* to their *own* authority or safety, and perhaps especially to their institution-based social identities. Thus the expansive tendencies of communitas may touch off a repressive campaign by the structurally entrenched elements of society, which leads in turn to more active, even militant opposition by the communitarians (cf. here the historical process set in train by many millenarian or revitalistic movements); and so on, in an ever spiraling struggle between the forces of structure and the powers of communitas. The struggle is rather like what Frye and David Erdman—drawing on Blake's symbols—have called the Orc-Urizen cycle. "Orc" here represents revolutionary energy and "Urizen" the "law-maker and the avenging conscience" (S. Foster Damon); the cycle itself is a partial anticipation of Pareto's "circulation of elites," the "lion"-like revolutionary elites being succeeded by the "fox"-like strategists and tacticians of power maintenance.

In spite of—and, to a considerable extent, because of—this conflict, communitas serves important functions for the larger, structured, centristic society. In *The Ritual Process* I noted that

> Liminality, marginality, and structural inferiority are conditions in which are frequently generated myths, symbols, rituals, philosophical systems, and works of art. These cultural forms provide men with a set of templates, models, or paradigms which are, at one level, periodical reclassifications of reality (or, at least, of social experience) and man's relationship to society, nature, and culture. But they are more than (mere cognitive) classifications, since they incite men to action as well as thought. (1969, pp. 128-129)

When I wrote this, I had not yet made the distinction between ergic-ludic ritual liminality and anergic-ludic liminoid genres of action and literature. In tribal societies, liminality is often functional, in the sense of being a special duty or performance *required* in the course of work or activity; its very reversals and inversions tend to compensate for rigidities or unfairnesses of normative structure. But in industrial society, the *rite de passage* form, built into the calendar and/or modeled on organic processes of maturation and decay, no longer suffices for total societies. Leisure provides the opportunity for a multiplicity of optional, liminoid genres of literature, drama, and sport, which are not conceived of as "antistructure" to normative structure where "antistructure is an auxiliary function of the larger structure" (Sutton-Smith, Note 1, p. 17). Rather are they to be seen as Sutton-Smith envisages "play," as "experimentation with variable repertoires," consistent with the manifold variation made possible by developed technology and an advanced stage of the division of labor (Note 1, p. 18). The liminoid genres, to adapt Sutton-Smith (he was referring to "anti-structure," a term he borrowed from me, but he claimed that I used it in a system-maintenance sense only),

> not only make tolerable the system as it exists, they keep its members in a more flexible state with respect to that system, and, therefore, with respect to possible change. Each system [Sutton-Smith goes on] has structural and anti-structural adaptive functions. The normative structure represents the working equilibrium, the anti-structure represents the latent system of potential alternatives from which novelty will arise when contingencies in the normative system require it. . . . We might more correctly call this second system the *proto-structural* system because it is the precursor of innovative normative forms. It is the source of new culture. (Note 1, pp. 18-19)

In the so-called "high culture" of complex societies, the liminoid is not only removed from a *rite de passage* context, it is also "individualized." The solitary artist *creates* the liminoid phenomena, the collectivity *experiences* collective liminal symbols. This does not mean that the maker of liminoid symbols, ideas, images, and so on, does so *ex nihilo*; it only means that he is privileged to make free with his social heritage in a way impossible to members of cultures in which the liminal is to a large extent the sacrosanct.

When we compare liminal with liminoid processes and phenomena, then, we find crucial differences as well as similarities. Let me try to set some of these out. In a crude, preliminary way they provide some delimitation of the field of comparative symbology.

1. *Liminal phenomena* tend to predominate in tribal and early agrarian societies possessing what Durkheim has called "mechanical solidarity," and dominated by what Henry Maine has called "status." *Liminoid phenomena* flourish in societies with "organic solidarity," bonded reciprocally by "contractual" relations, and generated by and following the industrial revolution. They perhaps begin to appear on the scene in city-states on their way to becoming empires (of the Graeco-Roman type) and in feudal societies (including not only the European subtypes found between the 10th and 14th centuries in France, England, Flanders, and Germany, but also the far less "pluralistic" Japanese, Chinese, and Russian types of feudalism, or quasi-feudalism). But they first begin clearly to develop in Western Europe in nascent capitalist societies, with the beginnings of industrialization and mechanization, the transformation of labor into a commodity, and the appearance of real social classes. The heyday of this type of nascent industrial society was in the 17th and 18th centuries—climaxing in the "age of enlightenment." It

had begun to appear in Western Europe in the second half of the 16th century, particularly in England, where, a little later, Francis Bacon published his *Novum Organum* in 1620, a work which definitely linked scientific with technical knowledge. Liminoid phenomena continued to characterize the democratic-liberal societies which dominated Europe and America in the 19th and early 20th centuries. These societies were characterized by universal suffrage, the predominance of legislative over executive power, parliamentarianism, a plurality of political parties, freedom of workers and employers to organize, freedom of joint stock companies, trusts, and cartels to organize, and the separation of church and state. Liminoid phenomena are still highly visible in the post-World War Two managerial societies of organized capitalism of the modern United States, Western Germany, France, Britain, Italy, Japan, and other countries of the Western bloc. Here the economy no longer is left even ostensibly to "free competition," but is planned both by the state itself—usually in the interests of the reigning industrial and financial upper middle classes—and by private trusts and cartels (national and international), often with the support of the state, which puts its considerable bureaucratic administrative machinery in their service. Nor are liminoid phenomena absent from the systems of centralized state collectivism exemplified by Russia and China, following their revolutions, and by the "people's democracies" of Eastern Europe (with the exception of Yugoslavia, which has been moving in the direction of decentralized collectivism). Here the new culture tries to synthesize, as far as possible, humanism and technology—not the easiest of tasks—substituting for natural rhythms the logic of technological processes, while attempting to divest these of their socially exploitative character and proposing them to be generated and sustained by the "popular genius." This, however, with collectivism, tends to reduce the potentially limitless freedom of liminoid genres to the production of forms congenial to the goal of integrating humanism (in the sense of a modern, nontheistic, rationalistic viewpoint that holds that man is capable of self-fulfillment, ethical conduct, etc., without recourse to supernaturalism) and technology.

2. *Liminal phenomena* tend to be collective, concerned with calendrical, biological, social-structural rhythms or with crises in social processes, whether these result from internal adjustments or external adaptations or remedial measures. Thus, they appear at what may be called "natural breaks," natural disjunctions in the flow of natural and social processes. They are thus enforced by sociocultural "necessity," but they contain *in nuce* "freedom" and the potentiality for the formation of new ideas, symbols, models, beliefs. *Liminoid phenomena may* be collective (and when they are so are often directly derived from liminal antecedents), but are more characteristically individual products, though they often have collective or "mass" effects. They are not cyclical, but con-

tinuously generated, though in the times and places apart from work settings assigned to "leisure" activities.

3. *Liminal phenomena* are centrally integrated into the total social process, forming with all its other aspects a complete whole, and representing its necessary negativity and subjunctivity. *Liminoid phenomena* develop apart from the central economic and political processes, along the margins, in the interfaces and interstices of central and servicing institutions—they are plural, fragmentary, and experimental in character.

4. *Liminal phenomena* tend to confront investigators rather after the manner of Durkheim's "collective representations," symbols having a common intellectual and emotional meaning for all the members of a given group. They reflect, on probing, the history of the group, i.e., its collective experience, over time. They differ from preliminal or post-liminal collective representations in that they are often reversals, inversions, disguises, negations, antitheses of quotidian, "positive," or "profane" collective representations. But they share their mass, collective character.

Liminoid phenomena tend to be more idiosyncratic or quirky, to be generated by specific named individuals and in particular groups— "schools," circles, and coteries. They have to compete with one another for general recognition and are thought of at first as ludic offerings placed for sale on the "free" market—this is at least true of liminoid phenomena in nascent capitalistic and democratic-liberal societies. Their symbols are closer to the personal-psychological than to the "objective-social" typological pole.

5. *Liminal phenomena* tend to be ultimately eufunctional even when seemingly "inversive" for the working of the social structure, ways of making it work without too much friction.

Liminoid phenomena, on the other hand, are often parts of social critiques or even revolutionary manifestoes—books, plays, paintings, films, etc., exposing the injustices, inefficiencies, and immoralities of the mainstream economic and political structures and organizations.

In complex modern societies both types coexist in a sort of cultural pluralism. But the liminal—found in the activities of churches, sects, and movements, in the initiation rites of clubs, fraternities, masonic orders, and other secret societies, etc.—is no longer society-wide. Nor are liminoid phenomena, which tend to be the leisure genres of art, sport, pastimes, games, etc., practiced by and for particular groups, categories, segments, and sectors of large-scale industrial societies of all types. But for most people the liminoid is still felt to be freer than the liminal, a matter of choice not obligation. The liminoid is more like a commodity—indeed, often *is* a commodity, which one selects and pays for—than the liminal, which elicits loyalty and is bound up with one's membership or desired membership in some highly corporate group. One *works at* the liminal, one *plays with* the liminoid. There may be much moral pressure to go to church or synagogue, whereas one queues up at the boxoffice to see a play by Beckett, a performance by Mort Sahl, a Superbowl Game, a symphony concert, or an art exhibition. And if one plays golf, goes yachting, or climbs mountains, one often needs to buy expensive equipment or pay for club membership. Of course, there are also all kinds of "free" liminoid performances and entertainments—Mardi Gras, charivari, home entertainments of various kinds—but these already have something of the stamp of the liminal upon them, and quite often they are the cultural debris of some unforgotten liminal ritual. There are permanent "liminoid" settings and spaces, too—bars, pubs, some cafés, social clubs, etc. But when clubs become exclusivist they tend to generate rites of passage, with the liminal a condition of entrance into the "liminoid" realm.

I am frankly in an exploratory phase just now. I hope to make more precise these crude, almost medieval maps I have been unrolling of the obscure liminal and liminoid regions which lie around our comfortable village of the sociologically known, proven, tried, and tested. Discussing both "liminal" and "liminoid" requires studying symbols in social action, in praxis, not entirely at a safe remove from the full human condition. It means studying all domains of expressive culture, not the high culture alone nor the popular culture alone, the literate or the nonliterate, the Great or the Little Tradition, the urban or the rural. Comparative symbology must learn how to "embrace multitudes" and generate sound intellectual progeny from that embrace. It must study *total* social phenomena.

I would like to conclude by considering some of the relationships between *communitas*, "flow," the liminal, and the liminoid. Let me briefly try to explain what Mihaly Csikszentmihalyi and my friend John MacAloon mean by "flowing." "Flow denotes the holistic sensation present when we act with total involvement," is "a state in which action follows action according to an internal logic which seems to need no conscious intervention on our part. . . . we experience it as a unified flowing from one moment to the next, in which we feel in control of our actions, and in which there is little distinction between self and environment; between stimulus and response; or between past, present, and future" (Csikszentmihalyi, in press). Some recent research by Callois, Unsworth, Abrahams, and Murphy (and by MacAloon and Csikszentmihalyi) has focused on various forms of play and sport (liminoid metagenres of our society) such as mountaineering, rock-climbing, soccer, hockey, chess, long distance swimming, handball, etc., in which the state of flow can be experienced. MacAloon and Csikszentmihalyi extend their notion of "flow" beyond play to "the creative experience" in art and literature, and to religious experiences, drawing on many scientific and literary sources. They locate six "elements" or "qualities" or "distinctive features" of the "flow experience." These are:

1. *The experience of merging action and awareness:* There is no dualism in "flow"; while an actor may be aware of what he is doing, he cannot be aware that he is aware—if he is, there is a rhythmic behavioral or cognitive break—self-consciousness makes him stumble, and "flow," perceived from the "outside" becomes non-"flow" or anti-"flow." Pleasure gives way to problem, to worry, to anxiety.

2. This merging of action and awareness is made possible by a *centering of attention* on a limited stimulus field. Consciousness must be narrowed, intensified, beamed in on a limited focus of attention. "Past and future must be given up"—only *now* matters. How is this to be done? Here the conditions that normally prevail must be "simplified" by some definition of situational relevance. What is irrelevant must be excluded. Physiological means to simplify experience are drugs (including alcohol) which do not so much "expand" consciousness as limit and intensify awareness. Intensification is the name of the game. In games this is done by formal *rules* and by such *motivational* means as, for example, competitiveness. A game's rules dismiss as irrelevant most of the "noise" which makes up social reality, the mutliform stimuli which impinge on our consciousness. We have to abide by a limited set of norms. Then we are motivated to *do well* by the game's intrinsic structure, often to *do better* than others who subscribe to the same rules. Our minds and our wills are thus disencumbered from irrelevances and sharply focused in certain known directions. *Rewards* for good knowledge and invincible will, when harnessed to tactical technical skill, complete the focusing. But for our authors the flow's the thing, not the rules, motivations, or rewards. This involves "inner resources" too, the "will to participate" (which like all liminoid phenomena goes back to voluntariness; one *opts* to play), the capacity to shift emphases among the structural components of a game or to innovate by using the rules to generate unprecedented performances. But it is the limitation by rules and motive, the centering of attention, which encourages the flow experience.

3. *Loss of ego* is another "flow" attribute. The "self" which is normally the "broker" between one person's actions and another's, simply becomes irrelevant. The actor is immersed in the "flow," he accepts the rules as binding which are also binding on the other actors—no self is needed to "bargain" about what should or should not be done. The rules ensure the reduction of deviance or eccentricity in much of manifest behavior. Reality tends to be "simplified to the point that is understandable, definable, and manageable" (Csikszentmihalyi, in press, p. 11). This holds good, Csikszentmihalyi says, for "religious ritual, artistic performance, games." Self-forgetfulness here does not mean loss of self-

awareness. Kinesthetic and mental awareness is indeed heightened, not reduced, but its full effect comes when flow is recollected later "in tranquility." If flow itself is broken, as we have seen, the special kind of awareness of self intrinsic to it is lost. Again, there is no solipsism, mere autism, about the experience. Flow reaches out to nature and to other men in what Csikszentmihalyi calls "intuitions of unity, solidarity, repletion and acceptance"; all men, even all things, are felt to be one, subjectively, in the flow experience. Much evidence is brought forward to support this; Lévy-Bruhl's "participation mystique" and Suzuki's "nondualistic (Zen) experience" are cited, as are the comments of athletes and sportsmen.

4. A person "in flow" finds himself *"in control of his actions and of the environment."* He may not know this at the time of "flow," but reflecting on it he may realize that his skills were matched to the demands made on him by ritual, art, or sport. This helps him to "build a positive self-concept" (p. 13). Outside "flow," such a subjective sense of control is difficult to attain, due to the multiplicity of stimuli and cultural tasks—especially, I would hold, in industrial societies, with their complex social and technical division of labor. But in the ritualized limits of a game or the writing of a poem, a person may *cope*, if he rises to the occasion with skill and tact. With control, worry goes, and fear. Even, as in rock climbing, when the dangers are real, the moment flow begins and the activity is entered, the flow "delights" outweigh the sense of dangers and problems.

5. "Flow" usually "contains coherent, *noncontradictory demands for action*, and provides *clear, unambiguous feedback* to a person's actions. This is entailed by the limiting of awareness to a restricted field of possibilities. Culture reduces the flow possibility to defined channels—chess, polo, gambling, liturgical action, miniature painting, a yoga exercise, etc. You can "throw yourself" into the cultural design of the game or art, and know whether you have done well or not when you have finished the round of culturally predetermined acts—in the extreme case, if you survive you have performed adequately—in other cases, the public or the critics have an important say, but if you are a real "pro," the final judge is yourself, looking back. Flow differs from everyday in that it contains explicit rules "which make action and the evaluation of action unproblematic" (p. 15). Thus, cheating breaks flow—you have to be a believer, even if this means temporary "willing suspension of unbelief," i.e., choosing (in liminoid fashion) to believe that the rules are "true."

6. Finally "flow" is "autotelic," i.e., *it seems to need no goals or rewards outside itself.* To flow is to be as happy as a human can be—the particular rules or stimuli that triggered the flow, whether chess or a prayer meeting, do not matter. This is important for any study of human behavior, if true, for it suggests that people will culturally manufacture

situations which will release flow, or individually seek it outside their ascribed stations in life if these are "flow-resistant."

Csikszentmihalyi goes on to link "flow theory" with information theory and competence theory—but I am not convinced by these speculations. I think he has superbly pinpointed and ascribed qualities to this experience—which *has* to be dealt with phenomenologically in the first place (though we may be able to get more "objective" later with EEG patterns, changes in metabolic rates, etc.).

I would like to say simply that what I call *communitas* has something of a "flow" quality, but it may arise, and often does arise, spontaneously and unanticipated—it does not need rules to trigger it off. In theological language it is sometimes a matter of "grace" rather than "law." Again, "flow" is experienced within an individual, whereas communitas at its inception is evidently between or among individuals—it is what all of us believe we share and its outputs emerge from dialogue, using both words and nonverbal means of communication, such as understanding smiles, jerks of the head, and so on, between us. "Flow" for me is already in the domain of what I have called "structure"; communitas is always prestructural, even though those who participate in it have been saturated in structure—being human—since they were infants. But "flow," for me, seems to be one of the ways in which "structure" may be transformed or "liquefied" (like the famed martyr's blood) into communitas again. It is one of the techniques whereby people seek the lost "kingdom" or "antikingdom" or direct, unmediated communion with one another, even though severe subscription to rules is the frame in which this communion may possibly be induced (the "mantric" frame, one might say).

In societies before the Industrial Revolution, ritual could always have a "flow" quality for total communities (tribes, moieties, clans, lineages, families, etc.); in post-Industrial societies, when ritual gave way to individualism and rationalism, the flow experience was pushed mainly into the leisure genres of art, sport, games, pastimes, etc. Since work was complex and diversified, its pleasurable, optational equivalent, palliative, or medicine, the domain of leisure genres, also became complex and diversified. However, it was often inversive of the work domain in form if not in function—since the function of many games is to reinforce the mental paradigms we all carry in our heads which motivate us to carry out energetically the tasks our culture defines as belonging to the "work" sphere.

The point here is that ritual (including its liminal phase) in archaic, theocratico-charismatic, patriarchal, and feudal societies (even a little in city-states becoming empires) and certain ancillary institutions such as religious drama provided the main cultural flow-mechanisms and patterns. But in those ages in which the sphere of religious ritual has contracted (as Durkheim puts it), a multiplicity of (theoretically) nonserious, nonearnest genres, such as art and sport (though these may be more serious than the Protestant ethic has defined them to be), have largely taken over the flow-function in culture. Communitas is something else, for it does not have to be induced by rules—it can happen anywhere, often in despite of rules. It is more like the "Witness" in Hindu thought which can only watch and love, but *cannot* act (i.e., cannot "flow" in games terms) without changing its nature.

One final point: I have left out both from communitas and "flow" an essential feature—the *content* of the experience. This is where the analysis of symbols begins—the symbols of chess, of Impressionist art, of Buddhist meditation, of Christian Marian pilgrimage, of scientific research, of formal logic, have different meanings, different semantic contents. Surely, the processes of communitas and flow are imbued with the meanings of the symbols they either generate or are channeled by. Are all "flows" one and do the symbols indicate different kinds and depths of flow?

Reference Notes

1. Sutton-Smith, B. *Games of order and disorder.* Paper presented to the symposium "Forms of Symbolic Inversion," American Anthropological Association, Toronto, December 1972.
2. Abrahams, R., & Bauman, R. *Ranges of festival behavior.* Paper presented to the symposium "Forms of Symbolic Inversion," American Anthropological Association, Toronto, December 1972.

References

BARTHES, R. *Elements of semiology.* London: Jonathan Cape, 1967.

BEAL, S. *Travels of Fah-Hian and Sung-Yun.* London: Susil Gupta, 1964. (Originally published, 1869.)

CSIKSZENTMIHALYI, M. Flowing: A general model of intrinsically rewarding experiences. *Journal of Humanistic Psychology*, in press. (Page references from unpublished manuscript, 1972.)

DANIELOU, A. *Hindu polytheism.* New York: Bollinger Foundation, 1964.

DUMAZEDIER, J. *Le loisir et la ville.* Paris: Editions du Seuil, 1962.

DUMAZEDIER, J. Leisure. In D. Sills (Ed.), *Encyclopedia of the social sciences.* New York: Macmillan and Free Press, 1968.

GRAZIA, S. de *Of time, work, and leisure.* New York: Twentieth Century Fund, 1962.

GURVITCH, G. Mass, community, communion. *Journal of Philosophy*, August 1941, **38**(18), 485-496.

NIKHILANANDA, S. *The Bhagavad Gita*. New York: Ramakrishna-Vivekananda Center, 1969.

NORBECK, E. Man at play. *Play, A Natural History Magazine Supplement*, December 1971, pp. 48-53.

PIAGET, J. *[Play, dreams, and imitation in childhood]* (C. Gattegene & F.A. Hodgson, Trans.). New York: Norton, 1962.

SINGER, M. *When a great tradition modernizes*. New York: Praeger, 1972.

TURNER, V. *Schism and continuity*. Manchester: Manchester University Press, 1957.

TURNER, V. *The forest of symbols*. Ithaca: Cornell University Press, 1967.

TURNER, V. *The ritual process*. Chicago: Aldine, 1969.

TURNER, V. *Dramas, fields, and metaphors*. Ithaca: Cornell University Press, 1974.

VAN GENNEP, A. *[The rites of passage.]* London: Routledge & Kegan Paul, 1960. (Originally published, 1909.)

WATSON, W. Social mobility and social class in industrial communities. In M. Gluckman (Ed.), *Closed systems and open minds*. Edinburgh: Oliver & Boyd, 1965.

Chapter 6
The Second Louis-Schmeling Fight— Sport, Symbol, and Culture

ANTHONY O. EDMONDS

For the professional historian, athletics has long been considered a subject beyond the scope, or perhaps better beneath the contempt, of academic concern.[1] Indeed, sports has usually been relegated to Clio's junk-heap and has been viewed as part of what historian Roland Berthoff (1971) calls "pots and pans" history. Those who have written accounts of athletic heroes have generally consisted of professional sportswriters, or perhaps athletes themselves, composing, with the help of ghost writers, inspirational autobiographies which are usually sold at little tables during Fellowship of Christian Athletes conventions.[2] I would, however, agree with philosopher Paul Weiss (1969), who noted that the study of the ideals and practice of athletes can inform the scholar about some of the basic values of a given society. In fact, an estimated 80 million Americans participate in some form of athletics each year, while far more are spectators at sporting events.

Of all sports, prizefighting has come under the most sustained criti-

From the *Journal of Popular Culture*, 1973, **7**, pp. 42-50. Copyright 1973 by the Journal of Popular Culture. Reprinted with the permission of the editor.

cism. Boxing conjures up the image of sleazy characters hanging around smelly gymnasiums, eagerly seeking fights to fix and boxers to buy. At worst, boxing is a brutal sport, its critics argue, a sport which causes physical harm, brain damage, and often death. But such charges, no matter how valid, should not deter the scholar from examining the sport and its participants. If moral stench be allowed to inhibit scholarship, then no right-minded historian would go near such subjects as crime, perversion, or the fate of 6 million Jews in Europe.

In fact, as writer Budd Schulberg (1972) has pointed out, a boxing champion, particularly one who has captured the public's fancy, can serve as a symbol of the aspirations of his culture. And Heavyweight Champion Joe Louis served just such a function for a great many Americans in the 1930s and early '40s. Moreover, his stunning one-round knockout of Germany's Max Schmeling in 1938, and America's reaction to that victory, reveal several crucial themes in American life of that year.

The story of Joe Louis is one rich in the very stuff of American mythology. Born into a family of poor Alabama sharecroppers in 1914, he moved with his family to Detroit, Michigan, in 1924. He was apparently not attracted to the life of the mind in Detroit; indeed, advised by one of his teachers to "do something with your hands," he went to a manual training school, where he took up both amateur boxing and the violin. His fling at music did not last very long; he tells us, in fact, that he "broke the violin over the head" of a friend who called him a sissie (Louis, 1952). His passion for boxing, however, bloomed. Under the tutelage of a local trainer, the young Negro began to enter Golden Gloves contests. In his first amateur fight, he won a $7.00 gift certificate, and within a few months, he had established himself as a leading amateur. In June, 1934, he became a professional fighter.

Between 1934 and 1938, Joe Louis developed into a national celebrity. Not only did he win all but one of his professional bouts, but in his personal life he seemed, according to observers, to exhibit those qualities which white Americans associated with the "good Negro." Sportswriter Richard Vidmer said of Louis: "He is a God-fearing, Bible-reading, clean-living young man. He is neither a show-off nor a dummy but modest, quiet and unassuming in manner (*New York Herald-Tribune*, 1935). Some evidence suggests that Louis' managers specifically sought to create this image of their fighter. They were quite conscious of the fact that the last prominent black fighter, Heavyweight Champion Jack Johnson, had incurred the wrath of the white community because of his cockiness and his association with white women. John Roxborough, Louis' manager, claimed that he "was going to be careful that Louis is . . . coached to do nothing that would bring discredit to the race he represents in the sports world (*Pittsburgh Post Gazette*, 1935). The one flaw in his spectacular rise to prominence was his loss to German heavyweight Max Schmeling in 1936. Louis went on to become Heavyweight Champion in 1937, but, as he himself put it, " 'If I can't whip Schmeling, I don't deserve to be champion' " (*Nashville Tennessean*, 1938). He was to get his chance in June, 1938.

Before we can fully understand the implications of this second Louis-Schmeling bout, we must briefly examine the international situation in the 1930s and America's attitude towards it. By 1938, the American dream of perpetual peace had apparently been all but shattered. The United States had no desire to enter into the European or Asian imbroglios; the quest for world peace so ardently pursued in the 1920s, however, had reached a dead end. The Italian invasion of Ethiopia in 1935, the German entry into the Rhineland in 1936, the German incorporation of Austria in 1937, and Hitler's rumblings about Czechoslovakia in 1938—all boded ill for the continuation of world peace.

America's reaction to this situation was characteristically ambiguous. Official policy, of course, proclaimed strict neutrality. Even if President Franklin Roosevelt had intended his quarantine speech of 1937 as a trial balloon, he quickly shrank from any commitment to help victims of aggression. Public opinion in these years seems to have followed much the same course. If pollsters are to be believed, a vast majority of Americans fervently hoped to keep the country free of any entanglements which might drag us into war. Historian Brice Harris (1964) has concluded regarding the Italian situation, "Americans agreed almost unanimously that the country should not intervene in the Italo-Ethiopian War (p. 25). A 1937 poll showed that 75% of the population supported the Ludlow Amendment to the Constitution which would have provided for a popular referendum before war could be declared. In fact, as late as June 1940, less than 5% of the population said that the United States should declare war on Germany (Ambrose, 1971; Burns & Dixon, 1970). At the same time, however, Americans seemed to be quite sympathetic towards victims of aggression. Harris (1964, p. 146) noted that "American public opinion condemned Italian aggression against Ethiopia." In that 1940 poll, 40% said that the survival of England was more important than America's staying out of war. On one level, then, Americans wanted to avoid involvement in foreign wars, while concurrently they showed substantial emotional commitment to the victims of Italo-German expansionism (Ambrose, 1971, p. 20; Harris, 1964, p. 146).

In the midst of this ambiguous situation, the second Louis-Schmeling fight took place. Undoubtedly the bout aroused great popular interest. One research organization claimed that 97% of the radios in New York City were turned to the fight (Young, 1968, p. 59). Moreover, many observers apparently saw the bout in symbolic terms: Joe Louis as symbol of American democracy against Max Schmeling, the symbol of German nationalism and racism. Commentators were quick to show connections between Schmeling and the German government. According to the *Boston Evening American*, "The highest officials of the Reich heard the broadcast. Chancellor Hitler . . . listened at his . . . Alpine Chalet, and Marshall Hermann Wilhelm Goering and Propaganda Minister Paul Joseph Goebbels also heard the broadcast (*Boston Evening American*, 1938). After Schmeling had lost, Hitler reportedly telephoned his condolences to Schmeling's wife while Goebbels sent her flowers (*New York Herald-Tribune*, 1938).

Having established that Schmeling was close to the leaders of the Reich, observers sought to tie him to German racial theories. According to boxing historian Wilfrid Diamond (1950, p. 30), Schmeling believed "he was fighting for the Fatherland to prove the superiority of German manhood over decadent Americans." Historian of black athletes, Edward Henderson (1949, p. 39), maintained that "all Aryan Europe was looking to Schmeling as its hero." A reporter writing in the *Lexington (Kentucky) News-Leader* (1938) saw implications beyond the Schmeling bout. "Every American fighter who meets the Germans will have a double task on his hands," claimed this Kentucky writer, "subduing the enemy in the ring as well as suppressing the glowing spirit of the Teuton fighters. There is no denying that to the present generation of German boys, Schmeling is the hero Jack Dempsey was and is to American youth." Even the usually unperturbable Louis was made aware of the racial implications of the bout. "I got that talk again," Louis (1948, p. 133) later recalled,

> about how he was saying around his camp that the Germans were the superrace and he was going to prove it. The sportswriters brought those stories from his camp to mine. Maybe they just meant it to needle me, but I heard it so many times I knew it was true. While I was training, those German Bund storm troopers used to sit around the ring and laugh. They had a camp up that way. When we came into New York on fight night, I was ready for Mr. Schmeling.

When Schmeling lost the bout, it was seen as more than a personal triumph, and revenge, for Joe Louis; it was a defeat for arrogant nationalism and vicious racism. If Hitler was able to use the first Louis-Schmeling fight to prove the racial superiority of Germans over blacks, this bout simply showed how flawed this philosophy was. Noted columnist Bill Corum summed up the opinion of most American correspondents. In an "open letter" to Schmeling, he said,

> You learned Wednesday night, if you did not know before, that not all the so-called kinds of supremacies and "cultures" of which men prate, can withstand an exploding punch. It is only an accident of birth that the

greatest fist fighter in the world today, perhaps the greatest that has lived up to this time, has a brown skin. Only an accident of birth, and surely no man has a right either to be proud of, or disheartened by an accident of birth. (*New York Journal-American*, 1938b)

If the fight saw the symbolic defeat of German racism, it also, according to many observers, witnessed the triumph of American values. Louis was apparently aware of his symbolic role. He said in one prefight interview, "I'm backing up America against Germany so you know I am going to town" (Young, 1968, p. 129). Louis' victory in 2 minutes and 4 seconds of the first round proved to most that he had indeed "gone to town"—for America. Perhaps even more than Louis himself, journalists saw the symbolic nature of his victory. Cartoonists delighted in pointing out that the champion's conquest of the German was a blow for American values. A drawing in the *Baltimore Sun* (1938) portrayed a boxing glove, obviously belonging to Louis, extended in a Nazi salute. The caption read, "Heil! Yo' all—!!!" Another cartoon in the *New York Post* (1938) showed a dejected Hitler with wilted flowers and a swastika forlornly waiting for Schmeling. The *Chicago Daily News* (1938) ran a cartoon picturing an airplane, naturally labeled "The Brown Bomber," dropping its load of explosives on a frustrated Hitler. One columnist went so far as to see the victory as a rare triumph for American diplomacy. "In fact," he wrote,

the Brown Bomber may have done something which the world's diplomats have been unable to accomplish: bring Herr Goebbels, Nazi Minister of Propaganda, to his senses. Goebbels is the man behind the guns in the Aryan superiority campaign. He has been stuffing this dish down the throats of the German people for some time. He has gone to fantastic limits to build up the Aryan as the super-man. Max Schmeling, a gentleman and an able fighter in his own right, has been ballyhooed by Goebbels and his propagandist artists as the embodiment of the super-man. In the minds of the young men of Germany, Goebbels had instilled the belief that Max was unconquerable and his invincibility represented Aryan greatness. But what happens? Louis belts Schmeling out in 2:04 minutes of the first round. In Naziland scheduled celebrations are cancelled, taverns are closed early instead of staying open all night, and gloom envelops the Nazi high command. The Aryan idol, the unconquerable one has been beaten, the bright, shining, shimmering symbol of race glory, has been thumped in the dust. That noise you hear is Goebbels making for the storm cellar.[3]

The nature of the celebrations that followed Louis' victory also illustrate the symbolic content of the fight. Special cause for joy existed in the black community. Louis was already a hero to most Negroes; indeed, in the *Chicago Defender*, a leading black newspaper, more space was devoted to Joe Louis between 1935 and 1941 than to any other Negro (Drake & Cayton, 1970, p. 403). His victory not only avenged his only defeat but also struck a blow against a racial doctrine particularly abhorrent to blacks. The celebration in Harlem had all the trappings of a political convention. According to the *New York Times* (1938), no sooner had the fight ended than "thousands of men, women and children surged out of tenements and stores into the Harlem streets, . . . yelling the plaudits of their hero." One observer claimed that the festivities in Harlem "were marked by political and international implications which the people read into the victory of their idol. Placards denouncing nazism and fascism were everywhere. They proclaimed the knockout a 'victory for democracy' and proof the 'democracies must fight fascism everywhere.' 'Louis wins, Hitler weeps,' one sign said (*Milwaukee Journal*, 1938). Whites apparently shared Negroes' joy at the victory. Louis biographer Wilfrid Diamond (1950, p. 36) maintained that "white folks joined the colored boys in national jubilation, because this was more than an ordinary heavy-weight fight—it was a battle between the Nazi superman Max Schmeling and an American—Joe Louis." A matronly lady from Mississippi vividly recalled the night of the fight. She listened in the lobby of a Vicksburg hotel; when the verdict became clear, she says that "white patrons and colored bellhops hugged each other in joy," providing a brief moment of racial harmony in that benighted state (Edmonds, Note 1). A correspondent for a British paper, the *Manchester Guardian* (1938), accurately gauged the sentiment of many Americans. He wrote, "As an individual Schmeling is obviously popular with most people, but as a German he will have to bear the brunt of Americans' general dislike of many of Germany's recent actions. To them he is a symbol of Nazism."

To be sure, not all Americans saw the fight in these symbolic terms. In fact, some members of the press corps specifically denied any international or racial implications. Writing in *Ring Magazine* in 1937, journalist T.W. McNeil asked that "racial prejudice and international politics" not become involved in the bout. Cartoonist Burris Jenkins claimed that both Americans and Germans had exaggerated the "Nordic supremacy angle." He said that to refuse Schmeling the chance to fight Louis would be just as prejudiced "as for the Nazis to make of this contest any more than just another prizefight" (*New York Journal-American*, 1938a). The most fervent plea for eliminating politics and race came from *New York Sun* columnist Frank Graham. He wrote, "Max is not responsible for the rape of Austria, the persecution of the Jews, or the presence of German spies in this country. He is simply a German prizefighter fighting on foreign soil, and is entitled to an even break. That is all he has ever asked and that is the least he should be" (quoted in the *Manchester Guardian*, 1938).

The comments by Graham and the others who minimized the international implications of the bout suggest that, on one level, the fight reflected the same ambiguity shown in America's attitude toward foreign affairs. Just as the public both opposed German-Italian aggression and sought desperately to keep the country out of the struggle, so were observers of the fight divided in regard to its symbolic meaning. The evidence does indicate, however, that Frank Graham and his like-minded colleagues were voices crying in the wilderness. The overwhelming majority of Americans evidently chose to see the fight in terms of race and politics. Indeed, the interest this bout engendered and the symbolic nature it took on provided a *way out* of the ambiguous feelings Americans had about world affairs. Unable to act positively to stem what was seen as aggression by Germany and her friends, Americans still were emotionally drawn to the victims of this aggression. The Louis-Schmeling bout provided a way for the public to vent its hostilities toward Nazi doctrines and practices. If the United States could not directly intervene in European affairs, it could at least take pleasure in the fact that Louis demolished Schmeling. Indeed, the American public in its support of Louis became as fervently nationalistic as did the German government in its support of Schmeling. Significantly, 4 years later, when America was at war with Germany, an army General introduced Joe Louis to a crowd of soldiers as "the first American to K.O. a Nazi."

Notes

1. An earlier version of this paper was read before a meeting of the Northern Illinois-Wisconsin American Studies Association, May 6, 1972.
2. In the past few years, a new type of sports study has emerged—the athletic exposé. Such works as Jim Bouton, *Ball Four* (1970) and Dave Meggyesy, *Out of Their League* (1971) emphasize the seamier side of athletic life. Bouton, a former major league pitcher, regales the reader with tales of "beaver shooting" among baseball's heroes, while Meggyesy, a former linebacker with the St. Louis football Cardinals, tells a sordid story of drugs, racism, and repression in professional football.
3. Unidentified newspaper clipping, Michigan Historical Collections—Joe Louis Scrapbooks.

Reference Note

1. Edmonds, S.P. Interview, Nashville, Tennessee, June 4, 1971.

References

AMBROSE, S. *Rise to globalism: American foreign policy, 1938-1970.* Baltimore: Penguin Books, 1971.

BALTIMORE Sun, June 24, 1938.

BERTHOFF, R. *An unsettled people: Social order and disorder in American history*. New York: Harper & Row, 1971.

BOSTON Evening American, June 23, 1938.

BOUTON, J. *Ball four*. New York: World Publishing, 1970.

BURNS, R.D., & Dixon, W.A. Foreign policy and the democratic myth: The debate on the Ludlow Amendment. In P. Glad (Ed.), *The dissonance of change, 1929 to the present*. New York: Random, 1970.

CHICAGO Daily News, June 24, 1938.

DIAMOND, W. *How great was Joe Louis*. New York: Paebar, 1950.

DRAKE, S.C., & Cayton, H. *Black Metropolis* (Vol. 2). New York: Harcourt, Brace & World, 1970.

HARRIS, B., Jr. *The United States and the Italo-Ethiopian crisis*. Stanford, CA: Stanford University Press, 1964.

HENDERSON, E.B. *The Negro in sports*. Washington, DC: Associated Publishers, 1949.

LEXINGTON (Kentucky) News-Leader, May 12, 1938.

LOUIS, J. (as told to M. Berger & B. Nagler). My story, Part II. *Life*, November 15, 1948, p. 133.

LOUIS, J. You've got to be hungry. *New York Herald-Tribune Magazine*, May 18, 1952, p. 11.

MANCHESTER Guardian, June 23, 1938.

MEGGYESY, D. *Out of their league*. New York: Warner, 1971.

MILWAUKEE Journal, June 23, 1938.

NASHVILLE Tennessean, June 12, 1938.

NEW York Herald-Tribune, June 30, 1935.

NEW York Herald-Tribune, June 23, 1938.

NEW York Journal-American, May 9, 1938. (a)

NEW York Journal-American, June 24, 1938. (b)

NEW York Post, June 24, 1938.

NEW York Times, June 23, 1938.

PITTSBURGH Post Gazette, June 26, 1935.

RING Magazine, July, 1937, p. 6.

SCHULBERG, B. The Chinese boxes of Muhammed Ali. *Saturday Review*, February 26, 1972.

WEISS, P. *Sport: A philosophic inquiry*. Carbondale: Southern Illinois University Press, 1969.

YOUNG, A.J., Jr. *Joe Louis, symbol*. Unpublished doctoral dissertation, University of Maryland, 1968.

Part 2
Sports and Rituals

Chapter 7
Sport and Ritual:
A Macroscopic Comparison of Form

JANET C. HARRIS

A common theme found in much of the anthropological literature
on games and sports is the notion that these activities frequently
serve as representations of selected aspects of culture, and that these
representations reflect and interpret culture (Arens, 1976; Blanchard,
1974; Cheska, 1978; Edwards, 1973; Geertz, 1972, chapter 1 in this
volume; Guttmann, 1978; Loy, 1978; Montague & Morais, 1976; Real,
1975; Salter, 1974, 1977; Schwartzman, 1978; Stein, 1977, chapter 13 in
this volume; Sutton-Smith, 1977; Tindall, 1975; Turner, 1974, chapter 5
in this volume). Within this overall context of communicative processes
associated with games and sports, the present discussion is focused upon
a consideration of one form of communication—ritual—and the extent
to which sport appears to be ritual-like.

This paper is a modified version of a paper in J.W. Loy (Ed.), *The paradoxes of play: Proceedings of the sixth annual meeting of the Association for the Anthropological Study of
Play*. West Point, NY: Leisure Press, 1982. Copyright 1982 by Leisure Press. Reprinted
with permission.

Several investigators who have discussed communicative dimensions of sport have suggested that spectator sports in the United States are ritual performances (Arens, 1976; Cheska, 1978; Montague & Morais, 1976; Real, 1975; Stein, 1977, chapter 13 in this volume). However, relatively little effort has been expended to examine more closely the nature of sport in relation to the nature of ritual in order to elucidate the characteristics which these phenomena have in common as well as the distinctive attributes of each. Such a systematic analysis is needed in order to evaluate the appropriateness and fruitfulness of examining and interpreting data on the communicative aspects of sport within the context of theoretical frameworks pertaining to ritual. A problem in making such comparisons, of course, is that numerous theoretical conceptualizations of both sport and ritual exist, and this greatly increases the complexity of interrelating the two phenomena.

The present discussion is a comparative analysis of sport and ritual and is limited primarily to an examination of (a) the relatively macroscopic form of ritual and functions associated with that form, and (b) the extent to which relatively highly institutionalized, formally organized sport in the United States exhibits similar form and associated functions. Detailed analyses of verbal and nonverbal communication processes that occur within ritual and sport are not considered here; rather, the concern is with the broad form or structure of ritual within which these more detailed communication processes take place. A consideration of cultural inversions or role reversals occurring in ritual is also omitted from the present discussion because these phenomena deserve detailed analyses which are beyond the scope of the current presentation. Similarly, other important aspects of ritual (e.g., functions beyond those closely associated with macroscopic form, efficacy of ritual processes, and specific content of ritual messages) which should be considered in order to develop a more complete understanding of the phenomenon must be set aside to await future scholarly attention.

The characteristics of ritual emphasized here are drawn primarily from the work of Rappaport (1979), Turner (1964/1967, 1969), Moore and Meyerhoff (1977b), Ortner (1975, 1978), Beattie (1966), and Hunt (1977).Conceptions of sport are influenced primarily by the work of Loy (1968, 1978), Caillois (1958/1961), Montague and Morais (1976), Real (1975), and Sutton-Smith and Roberts (1970), as well as by numerous personal observations of the phenomenon. The following discussion is organized around four frequently suggested characteristics of ritual: performance, formality, fusion of symbol and index, and associations between sacred and secular order. Sport is examined in relation to each of these with regard to ways in which it seems to be similar to as well as different from ritual.

Performance

Ritual is usually characterized as an active performance. Special body movements, body positions, objects, costumes, vocalizations, and/or music are combined to produce a performance that has an "acted out" quality about it, which perhaps is tied to its relatively formal or stereotyped nature. In spite of this staged quality, however, Rappaport (1979) suggests that ritual, as opposed to drama or film, does not tend to be characterized by a quality of make-believe; rather, it is acted out "in earnest" (p. 177). In addition, individuals who are gathered together at a ritual tend to be active participants in the performance rather than passive members of an audience (Rappaport, 1979). One's presence at a ritual performance makes it difficult to disengage from the activity until it is completed. Individuals may, of course, choose not to attend the performance, but as Ortner (1978) states, "once they get in the door . . . the process is powerful enough to engage them and draw them through the transformations of meaning/consciousness that the ritual embodies"(p. 6).

Sport, considered as a performance, appears to be similar to ritual. In spite of conceptualizations of scholars like Caillois (1958/1961) and Huizinga (1944/1955), who attach a make-believe quality to games, formally organized sport in the United States seems to have a rather "earnestly staged" quality associated with it. For example, one has the sense when watching a contest such as the Superbowl that it is "really happening now," that it is not a drama and not make-believe. In fact, when it appears that athletes are acting, there is a temptation to classify the display as something other than sport (Stone, 1971/1973). Barthes (1957/1972) and Stone and Oldenburg (1967), who focus upon the acted out, make-believe, dramatic aspects of professional wrestling contests, offer examples of this. Evidence reveals that ritual participants vary with regard to the nature and extensiveness of their involvement in ritual performances (Beattie, 1966, pp. 67-68; Turnbull, 1961, p. 88), and individuals involved in a sport contest, either as spectators or as athletes, probably vary in a somewhat similar fashion. It can be hypothesized that there are relatively active participants and passive audience members among both the spectators and the athletes, and individuals probably fluctuate considerably in their levels of active participation during the course of a specific contest and from one contest to another.

Formality

Another frequent observation about the nature of ritual is that the performance is relatively formalized, invariant, or stereotyped. Focusing upon this feature, Gluckman and Gluckman (1977, chapter 8 in this volume) conclude that the relatively high level of uncertainty in sport is one of the major reasons why sport should *not* be considered to be ritual. However, others such as Real (1975), Cheska (1978), Arens (1976), and Montague and Morais (1976) find the concept of ritual to be useful for discussions of sport. They emphasize reflective functions of sport within culture and are not sufficiently deterred by the uncertainty connected with sport to eliminate it from the category of ritual.

What are the characteristics of sport which seem to contribute to relatively stable, stereotyped, ritual-like performances? What are the characteristics which seem to contribute to relatively uncertain or variable, nonritual-like performances? The answers to these questions are quite complex and must be interwoven, as this analysis progresses, with additional comparative discussion about the nature of sport and ritual. Here it should be briefly noted that certainty in *ritual* seems to be associated with (a) conventional, idealized normative order that is established and accepted publicly through ritual performance, and (b) higher level order or ultimate sacred postulates that are frequently fused through ritual performances with conventional social order (Hunt, 1977; Moore & Meyerhoff, 1977b; Rappaport, 1979). On the other hand, characteristics of *sport* contributing at least partially to uncertainty within the performance include (a) display of mastery within the idealized social order, (b) display of excellence of performance that may be partially aimed at transcending social order, and (c) chance occurrences that are important features of many contests.

Fusion of Symbol and Index

A third major characteristic of ritual, discussed in considerable detail by Rappaport (1979), is the fusion of messages about (a) the relatively stable, normative social order of culture, and (b) the relatively changeable social and psychobiological conditions or states of the ritual participants. In other words, relatively invariant symbolic and iconic messages (which aid in defining conventional public order) are fused in ritual with relatively variable indexical messages (which convey information about the present and relatively transitory states of the persons and/or objects involved in ritual). Rappaport (1979) supports the notion that a clearer juxtaposition of symbol and index, form and substance, mind and body occurs within ritual than within other communicative frameworks. Furthermore, the fusion of index, icon, and symbol may help to ensure that the intended messages about the idealized social order are communicated clearly and accurately.

An important function of ritual stemming from this fusion, Rappaport (1979) suggests, is the indexical, public display of the participants' current acceptance of the displayed idealized social relations. Performance of the ritual both reinforces the enduring social rules or standards of judgment and at the same time functions as an indexical display of the performers' current acceptance of them. Such display of acceptance can take place outside of ritual, but the formal and indexical nature of ritual may serve to clarify the act of acceptance that is taking place. For example, outside of ritual one could display acceptance of public order by following normative social conventions in daily behavior. Such ordinary usage of social conventions, however, may frequently result in broken rules, and the distinctions between idealized conventions and de facto conventions may become blurred (Rappaport, 1979). Rituals help to establish clearly the nature of the idealized social order and also provide public displays of acceptance of these social conventions.

There are often additional indexical messages in ritual performances concerning other aspects of the current states of the performers. These, of course, vary from performance to performance as the current states of the participants change. Also, they are usually severely limited in number because rituals tend to be relatively invariant. An example of such a message is the substitution of different individuals in prestigious ritual roles based upon shifts in statuses and social relations outside of the ritual performance (Rappaport, 1979).

In similarity to ritual, sport contests appear to be characterized by (a) a fusion of index, icon, and symbol, (b) a public display of the establishment and the acceptance of particular idealized social conventions, and (c) other indexical messages about present states of ritual performers. Elaboration of the specific content of messages concerning the nature of the idealized social order which are communicated through sport performances is beyond the scope of the present discussion. Briefly, however, it is frequently suggested (Arens, 1976; Eitzen & Sage, 1978; Montague & Morais, 1976; Real, 1975; Stein, 1977, chapter 13 in this volume) that sport is a representation of the American success ethic, including notions such as the benefits of competition, survival of the fittest, and the value of hard work in relation to goal achievement.

Although the forms of the messages characteristic of sport seem to be similar to those also found in ritual, a salient distinction seems to exist between the two. Sport seems to consist of a much larger proportion of indexical messages (messages concerning current social and psychobiological states of the performers) than does most ritual. Formally organized sport, considered as a subset of games, appears to share with other games the characteristic of serving as a model of power or mastery (Cheska, 1978; Sutton-Smith & Roberts, 1970). Performance of sport not only establishes idealized social conventions and publicly displays acceptance of them, but in addition it also displays indexically through competition the extent to which the performers can function successfully within the established and accepted idealized order. This display occurs as athletes utilize movement and strategic skills to overcome obstacles in the path toward victory and to create obstacles in the paths of their opponents.

This indexical display of ability to function successfully within the idealized social order contributes to the uncertainty of sport performances. The content of these indexical messages varies from moment to moment and from day to day as the capabilities and health of the athletes change and as different athletes become involved in the performance. Furthermore, the precise manner in which ability to function successfully within the idealized social order is displayed is not invariant; rather, it is relatively uncertain due to the wide range of choices available within the limits of the game. Such choices would be the specific strategic and movement skills used at particular moments. Finally, at times the indexical display of mastery in sport involves cheating or other behavior which is often publicly observable and conveys a disregard of the conventional social order. Depending upon participants' interpretations, such public disregard of normative order may (a) invalidate the performance as a display of ability to function successfully within the idealized social order, or (b) become a means of changing the idealized social order itself.

Both sport and ritual appear to communicate relatively invariant messages about the nature of normative social conventions and the acceptance of those idealized social conventions. Sport seems to differ from ritual, however, in that it additionally displays the ability of the participants to function successfully within the idealized public order that is established. Display of this somewhat uncertain and changeable ability results in a larger proportion of indexical messages in sport which vary with the participants' current social and psychobiological states.

Associations Between Sacred and Secular Order

Opinions continue to differ over whether or not a relatively prominent association with sacred or cosmological order should be included as an essential characteristic of ritual (Moore & Meyerhoff, 1977a). Gluckman and Gluckman (1977, chapter 8 in this volume) assert that in order to classify a formalized performance as ritual, it must be conducted for purposes of influencing supernatural powers. Although Rappaport (1979) admits that rituals vary in extensiveness of reference to conventional social order and to ultimate sacred postulates, he suggests that the social order which is established and accepted through ritual is legitimized, at least in part, by means of its simultaneous association with an unquestionable, intrinsically correct sacred order.

On the other hand, some scholars suggest that the social conventions expressed within formalized performances may be legitimized by association with unquestioned political ideology and/or some other nonsacred source of authority, and they believe that such performances should also be classified as ritual (Moore & Meyerhoff, 1977b). Furthermore, there are numerous indications (d'Aquili, Laughlin, & McManus,1979; Moore & Meyerhoff, 1977b; Ortner, 1975; Rappaport, 1979; Turner, 1964/1967, 1969, 1977) that participants in relatively formalized performances often associate the performance with a somewhat nonspecific sense of cosmological power which may result from strong emotional experiences precipitated by the performance itself. Such experiences, termed "communitas" by Turner (1969), and similar to Maslow's (1964/1970, 1972/1976) concept of "peak experiences" and Csikszentmihalyi's (1975) concept of "flow," appear to be facilitated within ritual performances by the heightened certainty in such settings and by the coordinated coalescence of multiple stimuli and messages. These emotional experiences are, to use Rappaport's (1979) term, "undeniable" (p. 217) and thus seem to have an unquestionable quality about them. Perhaps such experiences work to "deify, sacralize and idealize" (Hunt, 1977, p. 143) the secular order and even partially to shape an ultimate sacred order. As Hunt (1977) concludes:

> Secular and sacred may not be different behaviors but different analytic aspects of the same behaviors. It may even be the case . . . that in all societies . . . the secular order models and shapes the sacred order, and that, in a contiguous systemic feed-back loop, the sacred order models the secular collective behavior. (p. 143)

Thus, it is very difficult to sort out formalized performances which are associated with ultimate cosmological authority from those which are not, and other nonsacred but unquestioned sources of authority may be available at times for the legitimation of the social order expressed through formalized performances. Perhaps it is not analytically fruitful to distinguish between relatively invariant, public performances which appear to be associated with ultimate sacred order and those which do not appear to have such ties.

Sport performances in the United States appear, at least on the surface, to be characterized by relatively little association with sacred postulates or higher cosmological powers. In comparison with the salience of such attachments observed elsewhere, organized sport in the United States appears to be relatively nonsacred. For example, ethnographic data from the Tikopians in the 1920s (Firth, 1930, chapter 10 in this volume) and from the Cherokees in the 1880s (Mooney, 1890, chapter 11 in this volume) suggest that the work of shamans was important during activities that were preparatory for sport and also during the contests themselves. The shamans encouraged cosmological powers to exert favorable influences which would assist their teams to achieve victory. Urban Zulu soccer teams observed in the 1950s in Durban, South Africa (Scotch, 1961, chapter 22 in this volume) employed shamans in important roles to serve similar functions. Other studies indicate that sport contests were sometimes performed in order to encourage supernatural powers to exert favorable influences upon events of major import to the group, such as the weather (Salter, 1977, chapter 9 in this volume), the maintenance of health (Brébeuf, 1897), or the plentifulness of food (Opler, 1944).

In spite of an apparent lack of similar prominent attachments to sacred postulates, the conventional social order which may be, in Rappaport's (1979) terms, "established" and "accepted" partially through sport performances in the United States may receive some legitimation from at least two other sources: (a) strong emotional experiences that often occur during contests, and (b) political ideology. It can be suggested that the competition in sport performances and the numerous other sights, sounds, and social relations (e.g., band music, computerized stadium signs and instant replay devices, play-by-play accounts blaring from portable radios, team colors, and affiliation with a school, community, or nation represented by the athletes) coalesce within the heightened certainty of the limits of the game and frequently seem to produce strong emotional experiences for at least some of the participants. Such experiences, it will be recalled, may partially serve to "deify, sacralize and idealize" (Hunt, 1977, p. 143) the social conventions with which they are associated. In addition, the presence of national flags, national anthems, and political dignitaries may partially serve to legitimize the displayed normative order by attaching it to a dominant, accepted political ideology.

Considering further Hunt's (1977) notion that sacred order and secular order may be related in a "contiguous systemic feed-back loop" (p. 143), it can be suggested that several characteristics of sport may contribute to such feedback processes. The strong and undeniable emotional experiences which frequently occur during sport contests may suggest to participants, as seems to occur in rituals, that there exists a somewhat vaguely defined cosmological power. This process may stem from prior experiences of the participants in which similar emotional states were more explicitly tied to notions of cosmological order. Furthermore, sport performances involve numerous events which happen by chance. Few rituals are characterized by the relatively high frequency of chance occurrences found within most sport contests. If chance occurrences are interpreted by some of the individuals involved, albeit perhaps only very indistinctly, as falling within the control of superhuman powers, then perhaps chance occurrences within sport contests strengthen the concept of the existence of such superordinate powers.

In addition to displaying an ability to function successfully within an idealized social order established by the sport performance, athletes sometimes seem to be striving toward a perfection which is partially defined by the limitations of the game and at the same time has a seemingly ceilingless outer limit. Spectators and athletes marvel at occasional "flashes of excellence" that seem to go beyond previously demonstrated human capabilities. Instant replay systems now make it possible to repeat over and over again these particularly brilliant displays of human functioning. Such striving for perfection or superhumanness seems to assume an ultimate, superordinate image of the nature of the perfection. In striving toward perfection, athletes may provide a demonstration which serves partially to establish the existence of an ultimate cosmological order, but which is also partially structured by the secular order and limitations of the game in which it occurs.

Organized sport in the United States does not appear to be saliently associated with an ultimate, sacred order. The social conventions established through sport performances may be legitimized through associations with alternative sources of authority, however, and there may be several features of sport performances which contribute to more subtle associations, involving mutual feedback processes, between sport and higher cosmological powers. The extent to which sport may be considered to be similar to ritual with regard to associations between secular and sacred order depends upon (a) the extent to which such associations are viewed as essential characteristics of ritual, and (b) the ways in which the associations themselves are defined.

Summary and Conclusions

The theoretical characteristics of ritual utilized in the present analysis are based upon extensive ethnographic research by numerous anthropologists. Using these theoretical dimensions, sport has been examined focusing upon the ways in which it is similar to ritual and ways in which it differs. This analysis suffers from a problem that has plagued almost all theoretical discussions on the nature of organized sport in the United States (Arens, 1976; Cheska, 1978; Ingham & Loy, 1973; Loy, 1968, 1978; Montague & Morais, 1976; Real, 1975). Briefly, the problem is that very few conceptualizations of sport are grounded in ethnographic data. Although the theorists who have examined sport certainly have observed the phenomenon on numerous occasions, there has been little systematic effort put forth to gather data pertaining either to the performances themselves or to interpretations of the performances formulated by the participants.

With regard to the present comparative analysis, this lack of ethnographic data pertaining to sport makes it very difficult to compare and interrelate participants' interpretations of sport and ritual performances. Such participant interpretations could provide valuable information about the viewpoints of members of particular cultures on distinctions and commonalities between the sports and rituals in which they are involved, and these could make important contributions to the broadening of understanding about interrelationships between the two phenomena. For example, a high level of certainty is considered by many scholars to be an important feature of ritual. It was suggested earlier that sport appears to be characterized by somewhat greater uncertainty and variability than is ritual. One of the characteristics of sport to which this variability is frequently attributed is the uncertainty associated with the outcome of the contest. However, Salter (1977, chapter 9 in this volume) provides data which can be used to suggest one instance in which the interpretations attached to sport by the participants may have influenced the extent to which they viewed the uncertainty of the game outcome as a contributor to the overall uncertainty of the performance.

In his discussion of data pertaining to lacrosse played by members of Iroquois tribes as a ritual to bring rain, Salter (1977) indicates that the outcome of this ritual lacrosse game was of no importance to the participants when they viewed the game within the context of the ritual. The most important features of the contest from the participants' ritualistic perspective were the concepts and behaviors that the game displayed which were considered to be important for the encouragement of supernatural assistance in bringing rain. If the outcome of the game was of no significance in this ritual context, an implication here would seem to be that the level of uncertainty connected with the game outcome was also viewed as irrelevant. At the same time, however, the game was a focal point for gambling, and in this context Salter suggests that the outcome was considered to be extremely important. Thus, the same contest, viewed by the participants from the interpretive perspective of gambling, may have been perceived to be highly uncertain, while the outcome of the game and its associated uncertainty may have been completely irrelevant when considered by the participants within the context of the ritual.

Ethnographic data would, of course, be useful for the consideration of other characteristics of sport in addition to the communicative processes involved. However, a theoretical perspective pertaining to such communicative processes, with particular emphasis upon comparisons and contrasts between sport and ritual, is suggested here as a valuable entry point for ethnographic research pertaining to organized sport in the United States. It is important, of course, to maintain theoretical flexibility in such research in light of the knowledge that theoretical modifications and/or major shifts in one's research questions commonly occur in ethnographic investigations.

The similarities between sport and ritual are not clear-cut or simple to delineate. Different theoretical conceptualizations of each phenomenon, as well as different interpretations of the phenomena by the participants, make the areas of distinctiveness and overlap between sport and ritual quite convoluted. Although the comparisons seem to be somewhat relative or conditional, it is suggested here that theoretical analyses should be carried out to examine sport systematically in relation to other aspects of ritual such as content, functions, efficacy, and the details of the processes of verbal and nonverbal communication. Communicative processes associated with sport that may not necessarily be salient characteristics of ritual may also emerge from such analyses, and these should also be elucidated. It is crucial to combine such theoretical analyses with ethnographic research pertaining to sport. The interplay between the two should lead to a greatly broadened understanding of the salience of sport in the United States and the meanings associated with it by the people involved.

References

D'AQUILI, E.G., Laughlin, C.D., & McManus, J. *The spectrum of ritual: A biogenetic structural analysis.* New York: Columbia University Press, 1979.

ARENS, W. Professional football: An American symbol and ritual. In W. Arens & S.P. Montague (Eds.), *The American dimension: Cultural myths and social realities.* Port Washington, NY: Alfred, 1976.

BARTHES, R. The world of wrestling. In *Mythologies* (A. Lavers, trans.). New York: Hill & Wang, 1972. (Originally published, 1957.)

BEATTIE, J. Ritual and social change. *Man,* 1966, **1**, 60-74.

BLANCHARD, K. Basketball and the culture-change process. *Council on Anthropology and Education Quarterly,* 1974, **5**, 8-13.

BRÉBEUF, J. de. Le Jeune's relation, 1636: Chapter IV. In R.G. Thwaites (Ed.), *The Jesuit relations and allied documents, volume X, Hurons: 1636* (J.M. Hunter, trans.). Cleveland: Burrows Brothers, 1897.

CAILLOIS, R. *Man, play, and games.* New York: Macmillan, 1961. (Originally published, 1958.)

CHESKA, A.T. Sports spectacular: The social ritual of power. *Quest,* 1978, **30**, 58-71.

CSIKSZENTMIHALYI, M. *Beyond boredom and anxiety: The experience of play in work and games.* San Francisco: Jossey-Bass, 1975.

EDWARDS, H. *Sociology of sport.* Homewood, IL: Dorsey, 1973.

EITZEN, D.S., & Sage, G.H. *Sociology of American sport.* Dubuque, IA: W.C. Brown, 1978.

FIRTH, R. A dart match in Tikopia: A study in the sociology of primitive sport. *Oceania,* 1930, **1**, 64-96.

GEERTZ, C. Deep play: Notes on the Balinese cockfight. *Daedalus*, 1972, **101**(1), 1-37.

GLUCKMAN, M., & Gluckman, M. On drama, and games and athletic contests. In S.F. Moore & B.G. Meyerhoff (Eds.), *Secular ritual*. Amsterdam: Van Gorcum, 1977.

GUTTMANN, A. *From ritual to record: The nature of modern sports*. New York: Columbia University Press, 1978.

HUIZINGA, J. *Homo ludens: A study of the play-element in culture*. Boston: Beacon, 1955. (Originally published, 1944.)

HUNT, E. Ceremonies of confrontation and submission: The symbolic dimension of Indian-Mexican political interaction. In S.F. Moore & B.G. Meyerhoff (Eds.), *Secular ritual*. Amsterdam: Van Gorcum, 1977.

INGHAM, A.G., & Loy, J.W. The social system of sport: A humanistic perspective. *Quest*, 1973, **19**, 3-23.

LOY, J.W. The nature of sport: A definitional effort. *Quest*, 1968, **10**, 1-15.

LOY, J.W. The cultural system of sport. *Quest*, 1978, **29**, 73-102.

MASLOW, A.H. *Religions, values, and peak-experiences*. New York: Viking, 1970. (Originally published, 1964.)

MASLOW, A.H. *The farther reaches of human nature*. New York: Penguin, 1976. (Originally published, 1972.)

MONTAGUE, S.P., & Morais, R. Football games and rock concerts: The ritual enactment of American success models. In W. Arens & S.P. Montague (Eds.), *The American dimension: Cultural myths and social realities*. Port Washington, NY: Alfred, 1976.

MOONEY, J. The Cherokee ball play. *American Anthropologist*, 1890, **3**, 105-132.

MOORE, S.F., & Meyerhoff, B.G. (Eds.). *Secular ritual*. Amsterdam: Van Gorcum, 1977. (a)

MOORE, S.F., & Meyerhoff, B.G. Introduction — Secular ritural: Forms and meanings. In S.F. Moore & B.G. Meyerhoff (Eds.), *Secular ritual*. Amsterdam: Van Gorcum, 1977. (b)

OPLER, M.E. The Jicarilla Apache ceremonial relay race. *American Anthropologist*, 1944, **46**, 75-97.

ORTNER, S.B. Gods' bodies, Gods' food: A symbolic analysis of a Sherpa ritual. In R. Willis (Ed.), *The interpretation of symbolism*. New York: Wiley, 1975.

ORTNER, S.B. *Sherpas through their rituals*. Cambridge: Cambridge University Press, 1978.

RAPPAPORT, R.A. The obvious aspects of ritual. In *Ecology, meaning, and religion*. Richmond, CA: North Atlantic, 1979.

REAL, M.R. Super bowl: Mythic spectacle. *Journal of Communication*, 1975, **25**, 31-43.

SALTER, M.A. Play: A medium of cultural stability. *Proceedings of the HISPA Seminar*. Vienna: Institute für Leibeserziehung der Universitat Wien, 1974.

SALTER, M.A. Meteorological play-forms of the eastern woodlands. In P. Stevens (Ed.), *Studies in the anthropology of play: Papers in memory of B. Allan Tindall*. West Point, NY: Leisure, 1977.

SCHWARTZMAN, H.B. *Transformations: The anthropology of children's play*. New York: Plenum, 1978.

SCOTCH, N.A. Magic, sorcery, and football among urban Zulu: A case of rein-terpretation under acculturation. *Journal of Conflict Resolution*, 1961, **5**, 70-74.

STEIN, M. Cult and sport: The case of big red. *Mid-American Review of Sociology*, 1977, **2**, 29-42.

STONE, G.P. American sports: Play and display. In J.T. Talamini & C.H. Page (Eds.), *Sport and society: An anthology*. Boston: Little, Brown, 1973. (Originally published, 1971.)

STONE, G.P., & Oldenburg, R.A. Wrestling. In R. Slovenko & J.A. Knight (Eds.), *Motivations in play, games and sports*. Springfield, IL: Charles C. Thomas, 1967.

SUTTON-SMITH, B. Games of order and disorder. *The Association for the Anthropological Study of Play Newsletter*, 1977, **4**(2), 19-26.

SUTTON-SMITH, B., & Roberts, J.M. The cross-cultural and psychological study of games. In G. Luschen (Ed.), *The cross-cultural analysis of sport and games*. Champaign, IL: Stipes, 1970.

TINDALL, B.A. Ethnography and the hidden curriculum in sport. *Behavioral and Social Science Teacher*, 1975, **2**(2), 5-28.

TURNBULL, C.M. *The forest people*. New York: Simon & Schuster, 1961.

TURNER, V. In *The forest of symbols: Aspects of Ndembu ritual*. Ithaca, NY: Cornell University Press, 1967.

TURNER, V. *The ritual process: Structure and anti-structure*. Ithaca, NY: Cornell University Press, 1969.

TURNER, V. Liminal to liminoid, in play, flow, and ritual: An essay in comparative symbology. In E. Norbeck (Ed.), *Rice University Studies: The anthropological study of human play*, 1974, **60**(3), 53-92.

TURNER, V. Variations on a theme of liminality. In S.F. Moore & B.G. Meyerhoff (Eds.), *Secular ritual*. Amsterdam: Van Gorcum, 1977.

Chapter 8
On Drama, and Games and Athletic Contests

MARY GLUCKMAN AND
MAX GLUCKMAN

Drama

Most ceremonies and rituals are spectacles; and among the problems set for this seminar, is the question whether games, athletic contests, sports, and dramas are "secular rituals."[1] After wavering toward thinking they might profitably be so considered, we have decided that they do have similarities with rituals, but have also elements which are so very different, that it is wiser to keep them distinct. Like rituals and secular ceremonies, dramas and even contests may involve powerful moral and ethical themes, but they exhibit these both in different contexts of social relationships and through different mechanisms of action (contrast Turner, 1969, Chapters 4 and 5, where phases in Ndembu rituals, and aspects of the Crusades, of modern communes, and the Woodstock music festival are treated similarly—see below). This statement does not deny that on occasions games or masquerades formed parts of ritual ceremonies; nor does it deny that ceremonies of one kind

From S.F. Moore & B.G. Meyerhoff (Eds.), *Secular Ritual*. Assen/Amsterdam, The Netherlands: van Gorcum, 1977. Copyright 1977 by Mary Gluckman. Reprinted with permission.

or another can be attached to the playing of games, or the staging of dramas. It does deny that all—perhaps most—games and dramas can be so regarded, without putting them out of context and distorting the means by which they exhibit moral values.

Our main argument is well stated in judgments ascribed by Cornelia Otis Skinner in her book on "La belle epoque," the gay 1890s in Paris— *Elegant wits and grand horizontals* (1962, p. 152)[2] to Tristan Bernard, the French dramatist and critic: "The audience always wants to be surprised, but surprised by what they are expecting . . . Write any sort of play as long as the subject amuses you . . . But if you burn Moscow and upset thrones, do so because the little blonde no longer loves her husband on account of the dark young man who lives on the third floor of one of the houses you intend to burn . . . . The principal quality of the successful author is a special gift for handling subjects which are not new, without being stale." In short, the essence of successful drama for Bernard was that the playwright take some well-known theme, possibly a conflict of socially defined moral imperatives, or a conflict between personal drives and moral imperatives, and work it out through the story of specific individuals, battered within a particular social context. The outcome is uncertain: The audience has to be surprised by what it is expecting, and a subject which is not new is handled in a way that is not stale.

This characteristic of the successful drama can be observed strikingly in those dramas which have lasted through many centuries, and which, by their presentation of the dilemmas of the principal characters, have moved audiences in centuries and places very distant from the period and place of their composition. One of us recently (Max Gluckman, 1974a) worked through Sophocles's *Antigone* in order to evaluate the sense of Antigone's soliloquizing defense, after she is sentenced by King Creon to be incarcerated in the cave because she symbolically buried her brother Polyneices in defiance of the orders of Creon. This defense begins by stating that she was impelled by the sacred duty, established by the gods, to perform the last rites for dead kin, instanced by her apostrophizing her dead parents: "When ye died, with mine own hands I washed and dressed you, and poured drink-offerings at your graves; and now [my brother] Polyneices, 'tis for tending thy corpse that I win such recompense as this" (translation by Jebb, 1880/1900, lines 904f). The plea that follows was taken by critics, from Goethe to Jebb, in the 19th century, and even Lesky in the 20th, to be spurious: "And yet I honoured thee, as the wise will deem, rightly. Never, had I been a mother of children, or if a husband had been mouldering in death, would I have taken this task upon me in the city's despite [here she repeats the words in the opening scene of her sister Ismene who refused to aid her]. What law, ye ask, is my warrant for that word? The husband lost, another might have been found, and child from another, to replace the first-born, but, father and mother, hidden in Hades, no brother's life could ever bloom for me again. Such was the law whereby I held thee first in honour; but Creon deemed me guilty of error therein, and of outrage, ah brother mine! And now he leads me thus, a captive in his hands, no bridal bed, no bridal song hath been mine, no joy of marriage, no portion in the nurture of children; but thus forlorn of friends, unhappy one, I go living to the vaults of death."

This passage specifying varying obligations to brother, to husband and to child, is then followed by an appeal again to the gods: "And what law of Heaven have I transgressed? Why, hapless one, should I look to the gods any more—what ally should I invoke, —when by piety I have earned the name of impious? Nay, then, if these things are pleasing to the gods, when I have suffered my doom, I shall come to know my sin; but if the sin is with my judges. I could wish them no fuller measure of evil than they, on their part, mete wrongfully to me."

Nineteenth-century critics, beginning with Goethe in 1827, thought the personal paragraph detracted from the high theme of the conflict between obedience to the gods and disobedience against the king's edict. Goethe, indeed, as quoted by Jebb (1880/1900, p. 259), thought the passage, "ganz schlecht," so absurd as almost to border on the comic. Hence the passage was thought to be a spurious interpolation, not worthy of the master Sophocles, and indeed to be a poor copy from the passage in Herodotus's *Histories*, Book III, in which when Darius has condemned all the family of Intaphrenes to death, the lamentations of Intaphrene's wife moved Darius to grant her the life of one of them, and she chose her brother, not her husband or a child. She explained her choice by argument akin to Antigone's. Later critics (but not Lesky, 1966, p. 282) are now inclined to accept the disputed passage as genuine, since Greek dramas by that stage were seen as dramatic confrontations between the central characters, rather than philosophical debates. In his article Max Gluckman considered how the passage would appear to an African audience, involved in a set of kinship relationships not very different from those we believe to have characterized the Greece of Sophocles's time: some kind of system of agnatic lineages, with conflicts over claims of siblings, parents, spouses, and children crucial in the system.

Antigone was of course performed on the occasion of the great Dionysian rituals in Athens, so it had a ritual setting. Yet it remains a great drama, a tragedy that moves us with its moral dilemmas in a time when the gods involved are for us "fairy-tale" fantastic creatures. And it can move us time and time again, at each new reading or at each viewing. If it had any ritual significance in Sophocles's time, it has long outlived that significance. Modern critics can debate the themes of the play: the *hubris* with which Creon sets himself above the gods, as the *hubris* of a man who does not recognize that there are limits to kingly power, an ever-present problem in political life; the great courage needed, markedly in Antigone's isolation, to defy that power in defense of the right; and so forth; —analyses partly made in the light of other ancient Greek plays and texts, partly in terms of general social and emotional understanding. An anthropologist can even try to introduce another set of conflicts—the pulls between natal kin and spouses, the pulls between filial obedience (for Haemon, Creon's son and Antigone's betrothed) and love for bride-to-be. The themes are found in most societies, and bear, when dramatically presented, frequent repetition. If the dramatist is great, the dilemmas, whether those set in the writing or in later times, are present each time, and there is a kind of emotional hope that the outcome may be different—though it cannot be. This hope, despite the known outcome, is present at each reading or viewing of *Hamlet* and other great tragedies.

It seems probable that the Greek dramas developed out of ritual masquerades of some kind (Aristotle, *Poetics*; Harsh, 1944; Lesky, 1957-58/1966). If so, the great tragedies we know had become liberated from the prescribed forms of ritual. The tragic writers took mostly themes from Greek myths and legends and exploited them in diverse ways: They surprised the audiences with what the latter were expecting, and handled subjects not new without being stale.[3]

What is most significant for our present problem is that the new forms, even when they dealt with old stories, varied the course of events and the outcome, leaving this outcome in some sense uncertain and emphasizing that men and women themselves had choices, even though they still remained subject to the ultimate influence of Fate and the control of the gods. Antigone insisted on defying the king to fulfill her duty to her dead brother and to the gods by burying Polyneices; Ismene, their sister, argued for the path of helpless acquiescence: when Antigone was condemned Ismene took courage to remain faithful to the bond between siblings and wished to die with Antigone, but Antigone rejected her, repeating her own words, because she was first cowardly and rejected that bond as weaker than the king's commands. This is the dramatic working out of the conflicting ties of obedience to king and obedience to sibling loyalty, shown by the adherence of one sister to the latter, and of the failure first of the other sister in that loyalty, and then by the emphatic statement that she can never again be worthy of it (Max Gluckman, 1974a). Dramatic irony, when the audience had foreknowledge from the prologue, often replaced uncertainty of outcome.

Much recent research on the rituals of the tribal peoples has emphasized the extent to which these are marked by the process which one of us (Max Gluckman, 1962) called "ritualization," by which he meant the use of secular relationships and roles in rituals, by acting of them on special occasions, either directly, or by inversion, or in some other symbolical form. That is to say, in such rituals the actors have selected roles in the rituals according to their roles in secular life, and it is believed that by their actions they influence the fertility, fruitfulness, success, prosperity, victoriousness, health, and so forth of the central group, category, or individual of the ritual, through in some way influencing the occult, variously conceived. In that essay, discussing the work of Van Gennep, it was stipulated that the word "ritualization" was thus used specifically to describe the fact that, e.g., father or mother's brother, king and princes and subjects, men or women, old or young, initiates and novices, and so forth, performed actions or recited prayers or spells for a specific congregation constituted by the specificity of day-to-day secular relationships. The word "ritualization" was thus used to define a particular means of operating on, or influencing, occult powers for the good of the congregation as a whole or some of its members. This form of ritual was seen to differ markedly from the rituals of "universalistic" religions, in which adherence to the beliefs was sufficient to give membership in congregations. We stress this operational, stipulated use of the term, defined as a form of ritual distinct from, say, the "ritualism" of the Catholic Church as against the lack of "ritualism" of many Protestant sects. And "ritual" as an embracing category was seen to be part of a whole field of behavior which could by stipulation be called "ceremonial," in that such behavior was marked by high formality and conventionality, perhaps organized into larger units appropriately termed "ceremonies." "Ritual" ceremonialism was stipulated to cover actions which had reference in the view of the actors, to occult powers: Where such beliefs were not present, it was suggested that the word "ceremonious" be used; so that for our present problems, "secular rituals" is a contradiction in those stipulated terms (not, of course, inherently so), and "secular ceremonial" would be a better title. We repeat, what was attempted was an essay at suggesting a series of stipulated terms, defined in relation to one another, in order to further a particular analysis. We have to repeat these suggestions, because in discussions with two other members of the seminar, we found that they had worried over these definitions after reading a comment by Leach (1968, Vol. 13, p. 521) that the terminology was not useful, since words were only concepts and could only be defined operationally. Leach had not taken it into account that the series of definitions were in fact advanced with reference to a specific problem, as he insists (correctly) definitions should be advanced. And this series of definitions does seem to be particularly relevant here.

For it seems that while it is clear that the dithyrambic hymns to Dionysus were ritual, the ancient Greek tragedies that have survived for us were not ritual. It was not believed that with their enactment of major conflicts in the society's social organization, they in themselves influenced the course of events within specific congregations, even if their performance, in the ritual setting, honored the god. We consider that similar conclusions can be drawn about the burlesque satyr-plays, and about the comedies. The tragedies were not prescribed in their course of action or in their outcomes; and in fancy at least, and as perceived by the audience, the protagonists had choices which would allow them to alter the course of events. As some classical scholars maintain, when Oedipus, to evade the Fate ordained by the oracle, fled from what he believed to be his parental home at Corinth, he should still have avoided killing, in anger, an older man, and then marrying a woman so much older than himself. In Sophocles's *Antigone*, Antigone had some choice: She could have harkened to Ismene and obeyed the king, and been spared since she failed in duty to her brother under *force majeure*. But Creon above all could have changed his course of action: Once he committed the impiety of refusing burial to the rebel Polyneices, he could have altered his action when warned of that impiety, rather than insisting that the dead man should not be buried even if the eagles of Zeus carried the remnants of the corpse to the throne of the most high.[4] Again, when Ismene reminded him that the condemned Antigone was betrothed to his son, he could have recognized the attachment of betrothed to each other, not said contemptuously, "Nay, there are other fields for him to plough" (Jebb translation, line 569). Finally, he resisted Haemon's own plea that one man cannot lay down unjust law and insist on its being obeyed. This finally provoked Haemon, mourning over Antigone's corpse, to attack his father, come too late to rescue her, and then, in horror at his potential "parricide," kill himself.

This play like other ancient Greek tragedies, was cast to show the working out through the lives of individuals of conflicts in relationship inherent in the society (individual king vs. the duties of kingship; the pull of sibling loyalties as against the edicts of the king; the strength of sexual and personal attachment of betrothed against absolute obedience to father; the strength of the tie between spouses and potential spouses in a culture where that tie was not always dominant), conflicts all cast against a religious background in which men and women were warned against the uncertainty of Fate and the danger of *hubris*, of setting oneself up to assume that good fortune would continue and that one was favored of the gods. And the most fruitful form of interpreting ritualization has been to see it as the acting of the conflicts which lie deep in the structure of society itself, in the independent, discrepant, inconsistent, principles on which social relationships are built (dating most clearly from Fortes & Evans-Pritchard, 1940, pp. 16f). But though they have this common element of representing the acting of these deep social conflicts, drama and ritualization are very different in their mechanisms.

Turner has pointed out (1968, pp. 135-150) that ritualizations in ceremony involve and organize certain persons, relationships, groups, or categories, but leave other persons, relationships, groups, and categories unorganized. He argued that those elements that are not organized penetrate, so to speak, into the interstices of the ritual, and may raise trouble there. Thus in his example, initiation rituals organize the categories of men and women, and of initiates and uninitiated, but not villages and their headmen: Hence competition between villages and headmen for high status in the rituals may cause difficulties. In this competition the outcome is uncertain and there is choice over strategies; but clearly, he implies, the course and the observable outcome of the ritual is prescribed and predetermined. And we would argue that it is characteristic of ritual as such, that theoretically at least, its main activities are always known in advance, and conformity to rule and tradition is important. The ritual moves to its prescribed ending: The outcome, in the sense whether it will be successful in achieving its "ostensible purpose" (Radcliffe-Brown, 1952) of securing fertility, etc., is of course uncertain—occult, hidden, not known by the senses till some future events demonstrate whether or not this success has been achieved.

The point of Max Gluckman's stipulated definitions set out above, is that they give us the term "ceremonial" to cover all highly conventionalized symbolic forms of action or speech which define social status, relationships, roles, etc., but enable us to distinguish two categories. We can describe as "ceremonious" those actions and words which do not involve beliefs in occult power, and as "ritual" those which do involve such beliefs and which frequently also exhibit conflicts deep in the social structure, conflicts that are portrayed in many rituals, above all in "ritualization" of social roles. Leach does not like this, *ab initio*, because in his *The Political Systems of Highland Burma* (1954, pp. 10-11, but cf. 16) he asserted that ritual was no more than a symbolic expression of status. But great ceremonies, in the common sense use of the word, such as May-day parades of Labor, or military marches past like the British "Trooping of the Colours," or parades on the anniversary of the October Revolution in the USSR, or the ceremonial movement of Barotse king between flood-and-dry-season capitals, and so forth, exhibit clearly enough status and social and political relationships, in a way very different from, say, the great first-fruits rites of the Swazi nation. In the former there is parade, with signs of strength exhibitions of ruling status, and so forth. In the Swazi ceremony, what are employed are not signs but symbols (for distinction see Turner, 1964a). These symbols both ramify their significance in the unconscious psyches of the participants, and refer to underlying conflicts and struggles within the nation—manifested, for example, in the national songs of hatred of subjects against the ruling king, insults to him, and so forth, expressions of disloyalty and resentment which are nevertheless believed to strengthen the king as well as the nation by occult or mystical means (Kuper, 1945, chapter 13;

Gluckman, 1954/1963). It seems sensible to reserve the word "ritual," and its subcategory in this case of "ritualization," to describe these ceremonies as against the "ceremoniousness" of "Trooping of the Colors," etc., because in the instances here defined as "ritual" we are dealing with activity which depends for its social effects on mechanisms which evoke emotion not directly by signs of unity and status, operating patently on emotion and mind, but indirectly in a complex process of "sublimation." Thereby (in Turner's 1964a formulation) psychical energy is evoked by a set of symbolical physiological referents and transposed to strengthen social and moral values which are simultaneously exhibited in the symbols. There is a belief in occult power; and in very fact the process of transfiguration of emotion is occult, operating to a large extent outside the consciousness of the psyche. And it is important to note here that such a restriction on the use of the word "ritual" was adopted by the great ethologist Tinbergen. He stressed that, for example, some of the behavior of herring-gulls could be understood as displacement leading to "compromise" formations. Thus, what he calls the complex signaling "rituals" involved when a male and female meet for the first time, and are caught between hostility as strangers and attraction as potential mates, involve a compromise from initial hostility. In the nonhuman world, it has been thought sensible to see a distinction between signaling a single mood, and symbolizing a compromise from duality of mood, when moods are in conflict: A fortiori such a distinction must be made when we deal with the more complex activities of human beings in social relationship. Van Gennep and Durkheim, Simmel and von Wiese, and other of our great predecessors, were struck by the shift in the modes of dealing with the series of conflicts that arise from clashes of particular with general interests (Fortes & Evans-Pritchard, 1940, pp. 16f.) and with the conflicts of mood and emotion begotten by the human predicament, as we compare ancient and tribal societies with societies based on more advanced technologies. This shift, involves increasingly less of the "ritualization" in our terminology that marks the ceremonies of the former set of societies, with their small-scale view of the universe in which what happens in social relationships is inextricably intertwined with what happens in the physical environment and the relations of occult powers (Max Gluckman, 1965, chapter 5). Increasingly ceremonies involving statements of social status (cf. Leach, 1954, pp. 10-11) are made with only (in some modern societies) initial prayer to God, but no "ritualization" of social relationships and roles themselves. In these ceremonies, even if in some humility before God is expressed, social conflicts are not enacted: The emphasis is patently and observably on social strength, unity, etc., which are assumed to exist. There is no suggestion that harmony and unity exist despite the open, indeed the exaggerated, difference of role and relationships with all their conflicts (as summarized in Max Gluckman, 1955, chapter 5; 1962); and this kind of ritualization of roles, it has been argued, can no longer be used when the conflicts involved are such that they threaten revolutionary as against rebellious change (see Max Gluckman, 1954/1963; and reconsideration in Max Gluckman, 1965, pp. 260-263).

We have started with ancient Greek drama which was performed on ritual occasions, in order to emphasize that here were crucial differences between the dithyrambic hymns to Dionysus and the tragedies performed to honor him—until there developed a saying in ancient Greece in 494 B.C. "nothing to do with Dionysus," arising from the paradoxical absence of his story from the forms intended to do him honor (Lucas, 1969, p. 630). In ritual, actions and words were more stereotyped, set in advance; the actors' roles were prescribed; the outcome was predetermined (i.e., the outcome of the ritual, not of its appeal). In the drama, actions and words were increasingly less stereotyped; the actors had choices set for them; and the outcome in theory (even if by the device of dramatic irony) was uncertain. In the greater dramas, the actors were individuals with specific characters, flawed in some way, acting in terms of their fit and lack of fit to their prototypical social roles: In ritualization, actors played their social roles independently of their characters. If this distinction is clear even in ancient Greek drama, and becoming more manifest from the time of Aeschylus through that of Sophocles to Euripides, the distinction must be accepted as even more marked in later drama, even among the classical Romans, and certainly in drama from the Middle Ages on. The medieval mystery and miracle plays were indeed religious, and it is significant that the nonritual morality plays were a later development.

We point the difference in another way. The medieval mystery and miracle plays, like the recitations, songs, and prayers on the Jewish Passover night, exhibit events that were and are performed out of time, even if they were and are believed to have occurred in time. Each reenactment renews a covenant with God between performers and audience established at a point in history. In an occult sense, the long-past event is symbolically occurring in the performance. This indeed is the essence of tribal rituals, whether these be the Swazi first-fruits rites (Kuper, 1945, chapter 13), or some initiation ritual, or say the fertility rituals of the Australian Aborigines which at the same time reenact and act the doings of the Wawn-Being (on this general point see Max Gluckman, 1965, pp. 268-278). When an ancient myth is reenacted in a drama, there is no idea that the events are in any way occurring then and there, with the actors becoming the heroes and heroines of that distant event, and the audience participating in that event itself. The drama is a presentation, not a representation as ritual is. And this may be true of the present-day passion play at Oberammergau—though some may feel it is a genuine enactment of the story of Christ. Yet since ritualizing ceremonies so often involve the statement—often the exaggerated statement—of standardized conflicts in order to transpose emotional energy from the physiological pole to the ideological pole of social value (see above, and Turner, 1964), and dramas also enact, through the events affecting legendary or historical or fictional individuals, the conflicts that are current in social life, both types of action achieve some similar effects: the catharsis which Aristotle described in his analysis of tragedy, a catharsis in which the excitement evoked is purged through pity and terror. But again there is a difference. In ritual, and particularly in ritualization, the ultimate emphasis is that harmony among people can be achieved despite the conflicts and that social institutions and values are in fact harmonious—ultimate statements that are belied to some extent by the ritualization itself. Ritual can do this since each ritual selects to some extent from the gamut of moods, of cooperative links and of conflicts. Ritual is acted out of time. In what we classify as great drama, the problems are left unsolved, since drama is set in a specific time for a particular set of individuals. The values emphasized are uncertainty, not certainty, of human fate; the difficulties of decision; the pulls of irreconcilable duties and obligations. In lesser drama, the situation is simpler: Goodies win and baddies lose. What is socially valuable triumphs. This is why George Orwell in his *Inside the Whale* (1940, pp. 80-128) urged that the radicals should produce penny horribles and comics in which anarchists and revolutionaries and strikers, and not the police, were the heroes and heroines, the good, triumphing over the wicked, so that the "ritualistic" lesson might be conveyed dramatically.

We argue, in short, that though the emotional effects, and the exciting and purging of emotion, in ritual and in drama show an overlap, that the final effect is not the same and that the means by which that effect is achieved is not the same. Hence, while some overlap has to be handled in analysis, we consider it would be wiser not to bring drama under the rubric of "secular rituals."

We have thus far written of tragedies. Comedies and clowning take a somewhat different course. It does seem that where clowning is allowed in ritual settings among tribal peoples, it gives more rein to innovation: The clowns are allowed to invent new jokes and pranks, even if their general form be stereotyped. We noted this when watching the masquerades of *makishi* masked dancers (all men) of Mbunda, Cokwe, and Lubale immigrants to Barotseland (see Max Gluckman, 1949, 1974b). Each of the masked dancers is in a complicated way, into which we need not enter here, an "ancestral-spirit," with some of the varying characters linked with spirits. Some of the *makishi* are connected with circumcision lodges: They are what Baumann and others have called "ritual" (see Max Gluckman, 1974b). Their performances in the dances staged are very stereotyped. Other *makishi*, without specific roles in the circumcision ritual, also perform stereotyped dances with the women as chorus. And they are all silent, they do not speak. But there are a number of the *makishi* which put on highly inventive performances. One represents a young woman, and "she" may do acrobatics on a pole held on the shoulders of two men; very skilled dancers playing "her" do tricks on ropes tied between two poles stuck in the ground, up to (in our experience) 30 feet high. The best of the performers in this character do clown, making up jokes, indulging in antics, bringing members of the audience into the dance. We have seen three other *makishi* characters behave thus, all comics: an old man, an old woman, and a young man with an enormous straw penis which he kicks off his thighs toward the women while making sexual jokes. Obscene and other jokes and actions are also in the repertory of the oldsters. In these roles dancing is reduced, clowning and joking are the mode. We have been told that there is a similar difference between the clowns and the serious characters in Hopi dances. There was a similar difference in the comedies of ancient Greece, with great license allowed the comic writers, who as we all know developed different themes from the tragedians. Attic comedy developed, according to Aristotle, later than tragedy, into satirical and abusive themes, out of the spoken or shouted improvisations of the leaders, with phallic songs, still heard in his time. But where contemporary historical plays were never popular (only two are known from the 5th centruy B.C.—Harsh 1944, p. 6), comedy dealt with contemporary themes. But the effect of comedy, like that of drama (even where comedy appears in ritual contexts) is quite different from the effect of ritual. Ritual is performed for the benefit of the community, a benefit achieved through its postulated effect on unseen forces, not through its direct effect on the audience.

Games and Athletic Contests

The argument that drama has to be distinguished from ritual because the actors have a series of choices open to them and the outcome is uncertain, applies *a fortiori* to games and athletic contests. In some contexts, games have been connected with ritual occasions, as notably with the original Olympic Games in classical Greece. But though they were held to honor the gods, and during their course each 4 years the Greek city-states involved were supposed to observe a truce in their hostilities, the contests were not of themselves ritual. Contestants sought the blessing of their own gods on their endeavors—which might set the gods themselves in competition. And a winner might in thanks make offerings to a god or a goddess, and even raise a statue to god or goddess; delighted fellow citizens were more likely to raise a statue to their triumphant winner. Cheating, it was believed, might be followed by divine punishment. But the ritual took place in the inauguration and ending of the Games, it was not inherent in the contests themselves. Similarly, in the modern Games, which we have witnessed in 1972 and have seen on other occasions on television, there is great ceremoniousness at each inauguration including the taking of the oath by selected competitors on behalf of all their fellows; there is a ceremonious presentation of medals to winners, seconds, and thirds; there is a somewhat uncontrolled ceremonious closure. But breach of the oath is not believed to bring occult punishment; and the highly militaristic ceremoniousness with which the Nazis surrounded the 1936 Games in Berlin, as against the deliberately civilian and peaceable ceremoniousness which the Germans stressed at Munich in 1972, show how variable the ceremonial may be. Nor was there any feeling that the massacre by Arabs of Israeli athletes was a blasphemy, as a similar breach of truce at the ancient Greek Games would have been regarded. At all modern Games, the American contingent even refuses to dip their flag to the presiding Head of State as other contingents do, because of an alleged offense to their flag at the Games in London in 1908. Nor is there any belief that bias on the part of the judges is a "ritual" offense.

We consider that the same observations apply to other situations where games were said to be "ritual" or "religious." In this light, we came to the conclusion, after reading some general accounts in this form of the ancient Mayan ball-court game, that it could not be in itself religious, as was assumed because stelae show sacrifices of players, but must be at best a form of divination. While we are writing this paper, in a lecture at Yale, Professor Richard E. Adams of the University of Texas stated that the ballgame was a form of divination: A question was asked of the Gods, and one side represented the answer "yes," the other the answer "no": and the outcome was settled by whichever side won. (We have not had time to check the source of this conclusion, which was not known to at least two distinguished Meso-American archaeologists we consulted.) But the form of divination described by Adams is in clear parallel with the way Azande put questions to their oracles (Evans-Pritchard, 1937). Adams did not suggest that the sacrifice of the losers influenced in occult manner events to change their course; and presumably if the losers were sacrificed, this may only have occurred when they represented the desired, auspicious answer.

Again, it has been said that some North American Indian games were ritual, but this does not emerge from the following account taken from Culin's book, or elsewhere there. The contestants may use magic to seek success, and the presiding elders ask for a peaceable game, with none hurt and fair play observed, but there is no suggestion that unfair play or assault or attempts to damage an opponent bring occult retribution, or that the course of the game or its outcome influence in occult manner the course of outside events (see Culin, 1907). For example, Culin (pp. 564f.) cites accounts from Long in 1791 and Carver in 1796 of games of racket or *le jeu de crosse* among the Chippewa. At that time, the games even took place between different bands, and though they were played with "so much vehemence" that players were wounded and bones broken, good humor prevailed and there were no disputes between the parties. The "rules of the game" apparently provided an ethos which kept the games within bounds.

By 1890, according to the accounts cited by Culin from Hoffman and Mooney, stakes in the game had risen among Indians living on reservations: Hoffman said of the Chippewa in Minnesota "severe injuries occurred only when playing for high stakes or when ill-feeling existed between some of the players." This change in ethos may have resulted from penning the Indians on reservations or from the increase of stakes made possible by a relative wealth in new types of goods. Certainly Mooney's [see chapter 11 in this volume] account of a game, also in 1890, between two groups of East Cherokee in North Carolina stresses the roughness of the game, with everything short of murder allowable: Men now sometimes went into the game with the purpose of disabling each other, and even rolled fighting on the ground. These fracas occurred despite an address by an old man who told them that the Sun was looking down upon them, urged them to acquit themselves in the games as their fathers had done before them, but above all to keep their tempers, so that none might say they became angry or quarrelled, and that after it was over each one might return "in peace along the white trail to rest in his white house." (Mooney notes that "white in these formulas is symbolic of peace and happiness and all good things," much as Turner, 1964a and 1966, spoke of "whiteness" among the Ndembu: I would incline to agree with Kuper [1971] that our "bright" is the better English translation.)

This breaking out of violence, despite the ethos of the game and the initial supplication, as well as the fact that players can make choices and the outcome is uncertain, also distinguish most games from ritual. Except when prescribed and limited license, within bounds, is allowed, violence at a ritual may destroy its efficacy. We have cited Turner as reporting the entry of competition and struggle of categories, groups, and persons not controlled by ritual prescription, into the interstices of rituals he observed among the Ndembu. But it is also inappropriate, but not blasphemous, for competition and struggle to break the rules of games. It is unfair and unsporting—not "fairplay" in an English phrase seemingly not found indigenously in, e.g., French and German—for Olympic athletes to use drugs, even those not proscribed by rules. But they do. It is not destructive of the efficacy of the rules.

It is always possible that deep divisions within the social field from which participants enter into competitive contest may break out into violence that is rooted in relationships outside the contest itself. There are many instances of this, some of which Max Gluckman (1973) discussed in a lecture on "Sport to Conflict" delivered to a plenary session of the Congress for the Scientific Study of Sport held in connection with the Olympic Games of 1972. These instances range from the soccer game between San Salvador and Nicaragua in the World Cup which led to actual war, to battles on the field between teams and supporters of each team in the "hick leagues" of Cheshire and Mid-Wales in the United Kingdom. Even out of such amorphous groups as the supporters of rival Manchester soccer teams, City and United, there emerge gangs to battle thus. The battle is exacerbated when allegiance to the teams is associated with religious differences as were allegiances to Glascow Celtics and Glasgow Rangers, or with racial differences, as when the blacks on Minnesota University's basketball team attacked the whites on Ohio State's team (see *Sports Illustrated*, Chicago, February 7, 1972:18f., and Max Gluckman, 1973). Here we are dealing with processes involving deep social conflicts in a quite different context from the expression of social conflicts in ritualization. Games can only be kept going where there is a strong controlling organization, with secular authority, able to expel players and even teams from competition and thus to enforce the rules administered by neutral umpires it appoints.

Yet the rules, and the ethos of games, may contain moral rules as ritual does, and these, together with admiration of a rival's dexterity, may influence participants and spectators as a ritual does. We have space to cite only one example: the admiration which the black Jesse Owens' powerful jumping and running evoked in a German crowd, many of whom must have been Nazis, despite the Nazi press's contempt for blacks and its description of him and fellow blacks as "American auxiliaries"; and above all, the assistance given by his German opponent, Lutz Lang, in the long jump, to Owens in measuring his run to enable him to win. From this sprang a friendship by correspondence which continued until the War in which Lutz was killed, a friendship which Owens continued with Lang's widow and son. C.L.R. James's autobiography, *Beyond a Boundary* (1870), shows brilliantly how in Jamaica the ethos of fair play and play for the team was one of the inconsistent moralities developed in West Indians. Though games and rituals may both *express* moral rules, only ritual affects the fate of the participants through its further effects on mystical powers.

As a final illustration of the difference between rituals and games, we refer to an analysis made by Max Gluckman, which has been published in *The Listener* (February 1959). In a memorial broadcast for the Manchester United football team destroyed in an aircrash in 1957, he exam-

ined how a team that was easily winning the English Championship became unable to win at home, where winning is "statistically" much
easier. Precisely the same thing happened in this last season, 1973-74, to
Leeds United who at one time were leading by 11 points; and it has happened in previous seasons to other teams which were far ahead. In the
phrasing of sports journalists, they lost confidence. What does this
mean? Gluckman had observed that his team's play had become out-
standingly good, indeed brilliant, but eventually the team's supporters
began to treat it as ordinary. (As a Scottish Heart of Midlothian player,
when that team was in a similar position, said: "Man, we were superhuman, and the crowd thought it was ordinary.") Therefore, instead of
applauding the good play, the crowd began to concentrate on inevitable
mistakes or apparent mistakes, and to jeer at and boo the players for
these. This shook the confidence of some: They became more careful,
could no longer "do it simple, do it quick" (which a Scots International
gave as the formula for success), hesitated against fast and skillful opponents—and were lost. The cycle became vicious. Only the dropping of
international players and their replacement by reserves, who were
cheered for what they did right, forgiven for what they did wrong, broke
the vicious circle and enabled the team to win. This tremulous loss of
confidence, caused partly by the very supporters of the team, the immediate and only immediate importance of what went on, is a far cry
from the emotional excitement and sublimation, and confidence in
ultimate mystical effect, that so often marks ritual.

Conclusion

We have here argued that despite the importance of rules which control
actions into what might be called formal and conventional patterns, and
despite the fact that games embody moral principles, it would be missing
essential differences to bring them under the rubric of "ritual." This
emerges even more strongly than the same conclusion has emerged from
our analysis of the differences between drama and ritual; but there the
same cautionary note is necessary. We came to this conclusion on
reading Turner's *The Ritual Process: Structure and Anti-Structure*
(1969). This book has made such a widespread impression and its ideas
have been taken up by so many young anthropologists that we feel
justified in pointing out our doubts, however briefly. Most of the first
part of the analysis, that which deals with Ndembu ritual, we admire
greatly, as our references to his seminal ideas show. But the second part
seems to us to be full of inappropriate categorization. The liminal
period, and the rites associated with it, are, as Van Gennep stressed, a
most important element in all movements in space, in time, and in social

status. But the extent to which during this period ordinary rules of enjoined behavior are suspended sometimes for all, but most commonly for some, of the actors, to give a fellow-feeling which he describes as *communitas*, can only be significant, as his analysis shows, within an established structure which is inserted again afterwards, and which indeed is asserted during the liminal period itself, by inversion. Ordinary activities of producing, preparing, eating food; of herding stock where there is stock; of restraining breaches from the allowable license—these and more continue outside the ritual arena. This kind of ritual liminal period, and therefore of any temporary casting off of roles, must be analyzed as different from such large-scale social and political movements as the Crusades, which various people joined for various motives, often with only some standard expressed adherence to the religious aims of the wars. And that in turn is very different from the temporary agglomeration of young people at a festival like the one at Woodstock, an agglomeration in which all temporarily, as they knew, came to feel a sense of unity with one another—a sense of unity very different from what the British called "the spirit of Dunkirk." And these are again different from the sense of unity—often fictitious if hard-desired—of small communes in modern America, communes supported, like Woodstock, often by the affluence of a highly developed economy and political system. Similarity of emotion, or even a few beliefs, does not make for similarity of social action and structure—or anti-structure. Turner himself (1957) has emphasized the importance of differences in social context and of social mechanism in discussing the situations in which Ndembu resort to judicial investigation and to divination, with ritual or accusations of witchcraft, in his study of what he called "social dramas" (see also Marwick, 1965; Gluckman, 1965, chapters 4 and 5). If the social contexts, processes, and mechanisms involved are different, then we surely need a more differentiated vocabulary to handle those differences. If there are also similarities despite those differences, then the differentiation of vocabulary should be within a hierarchical series of connected terms (see Max Gluckman, 1965, pp. 198f., for discussion of similar problem in analyzing "law"). To call all formality and ceremonial "ritual" is to blur the distinction between formal activities that address and move the spirit world (which I call "ritual") and formal activities that do not. To lump together what has been analytically segregated is justified only if reclassification illuminates. I neither see that much is gained from aggregating all occasions when men have a sense of brotherhood under one rubric, nor that analytic refinement is achieved by enlarging the heretofore limited category "ritual" to include everything that could be considered collective formality.

Notes

1. Professor Gluckman died before this paper could be revised for publication; hence the editors have made a few minor changes which he did not see. The final version is essentially his, and such changes as have been made were added for clarification only.
2. Thanks to Elizabeth Colson who gave us this book to read. This essay was written at the Yale Law School, where we had suggestive discussions with Professor Stanton Wheeler and Mr. Craig Calhoun.
3. Since we have cited Sophocles's *Antigone*, it is relevant to state that in Euripides's lost version of *Antigone*, Haemon was married to Antigone, not betrothed to her. So with each playwright the stories of Oedipus, and other traditional myths, were varied in their emphasis to alter the dramatic development and sometimes even the outcome. In Harsh's (1944) words, variations in the legends and playwright's liberties encouraged vagueness and uncertainty, and therefore suspense. There was a steady and even consistent development away from stereotyped masquerades in ritual dances, though these continued in a sense in the dithyrambic hymns to Dionysus, sung and danced by competing choruses of 50 drawn from the 10 tribes of the Athenian citizenry. Social change, as we know well, may proceed by multiplication rather than by elimination and substitution. These hymns survived in the setting of the ritual occasion, with tragedies and comedies, and satyr-plays, the latter written by the tragic writers. In these last some heroic legend was treated in burlesqued manner, the chorus consisting of satyrs, being represented in human form with animal attributes, often a horse's tail. The hand of the past was also stamped upon the tragedies: The actors remained masked, as in the ritual sets of the past. Aeschylus brought a second actor to vary the former dialogue between one actor and the chorus. He presented human actions in relation to the purposes of the gods, rather than giving dramatic structure through portrayal of character. The drama came from an accumulation of tension because of the emotional force of the long lyric passages and the exciting richness of metaphor. Sophocles reduced the importance of the chorus and introduced a third actor; and where Aeschylus tried to make intelligible the workings of the gods to man, Sophocles more readily accepted the gods as there, and aimed to exhibit the values of life as lived within a traditional moral framework. Some human suffering was due to wickedness of human beings themselves, but not all. Euripides, though only 10 years younger than Sophocles, wrote in a vastly different time, when traditional beliefs and the very gods were being questioned. He strained and twisted the mythic materials on which he had still to draw to incorporate in his dramas contemporary problems (Harsh, 1944; Lucas, 1969).
4. In the course of this development, the gods themselves appeared less and less frequently, though they continued often to speak through the mouths of seers, as with Tiresias in Sophocles's *Antigone* told.

References

CULIN, S. Games of North American Indians. In *24th Annual Report of the Bureau of American Ethnology*. Washington: Government Printing Office, 1907.

EVANS-PRITCHARD, E.E. *Witchcraft, oracles and magic among the Azande*. Oxford: Clarendon Press, 1937.

FORTES, M., & Evans-Pritchard, E.E. Introduction. In M. Fortes & E.E. Evans-Pritchard (Eds.), *African political systems*. London: Oxford University Press for the International African Institute, 1940.

GLUCKMAN, M. The role of the sexes in the circumcision ceremonies of the Wiko of Barotseland. In M. Fortes (Ed.), *Social structure: Essays presented to A.R. Radcliffe-Brown*. Oxford: Clarendon Press, 1949.

GLUCKMAN, M. *Custom and conflict in Africa*. Oxford: Blackwell, 1955.

GLUCKMAN, M. Football players and the crowd. *The Listener*, February 1959.

GLUCKMAN, M. Les rites de passage. In M. Gluckman (Ed.), *Essays on the ritual of social relations*. Manchester: Manchester University Press, 1962.

GLUCKMAN, M. Rituals of rebellion in South East Africa. In M. Gluckman, *Order and rebellion in tribal Africa*. Manchester: Manchester University Press, 1963. (Originally published, 1954.)

GLUCKMAN, M. *Politics, law and ritual in tribal society*. Oxford: Blackwell, 1965.

GLUCKMAN, M. Sport and conflict. In O. Grupe, D. Kurz, & J.M. Teipel (Eds.), *Sport in the modern world—chances and problems; Scientific Congress, Munich, 1972*. Berlin: Springer-Verlag, 1973.

GLUCKMAN, M. Spouse, child, parent or sibling? Who should be saved? (The disputed passage in Sophocles' *Antigone*.) In B. Chapman & A. Potter (Eds.), *Essays presented to W.J.M. Mackenzie*. Manchester: Manchester University Press, 1974. (a)

GLUCKMAN, M. Makishi masked dancers of Barotseland. In *In Memoriam Jorges Dias*, 1974. (b)

HARSH, P.W. *A handbook of classical drama*. Stanford, CA: Stanford University Press, 1944.

JAMES, C.L.R. *Beyond a boundary*. London: Farber & Farber, 1870.

JEBB, R. *Sophocles: The plays and fragments (with critical notes, commentary, and translation into English prose)* (3rd ed.). Cambridge: Cambridge University Press, 1900. (Originally published, 1880.)

KUPER, H. *An African aristocracy: Rank among the Swazi of the Protectorate*. London: Oxford University for the International African Institute, 1945.

KUPER, H. Color, categories and colonialism: The Swazi case. In V.W. Turner

(Ed.), *Profiles of change: The impact of colonialism on Africa.* Cambridge: Cambridge University Press, 1971.

LEACH, E.R. *The political systems of highland Burma, a study of Kachin social structure.* London: Athlone Press, 1954.

LEACH, E.R. Ritual. In D. Sills (Ed.), *International Encyclopedia of the Social Sciences* (Vol. 13). New York: Macmillan and the Free Press, 1968.

LESKY, A. *[A history of Greek literature]* (J. Wilis & C. de Heer, trans.). London: Methuen, 1966. (Originally published 1957/58.)

LUCAS, D.W. Greek drama. In *Encyclopedia Britannica* (Vol. 7), 1969.

MARWICK, M.G. *The social context of sorcery.* Manchester: Manchester University Press, 1965.

ORWELL, G. *Inside the whale, and other essays.* London: Gollancz, 1940.

RADCLIFFE-BROWN, A.R. *Structure and function in primitive society: Essays and addresses.* London: Cohen & West, 1952.

SKINNER, C.O. *Elegant wits and grand horizontals.* Boston: Houghton Mifflin, 1962.

SPORTS Illustrated, February 7, 1972, p. 18f.

TURNER, V.W. *Schism and continuity in an African society.* Manchester: Manchester University Press, 1957.

TURNER, V.W. Symbols in Ndembu ritual. In M. Gluckman (Ed.), *Closed systems and open minds: The limits of naivete in social anthropology.* Chicago: Aldine, 1964. (a)

TURNER, V.W. Color classification in Ndembu ritual. In M. Banton (Ed.), *Anthropological approaches to the study of religion.* ASA monograph no. 3. London: Tavistock, 1966.

TURNER, V.W. Mukanda: The politics of a non-political ritual. In M. Swartz (Ed.), *Local level politics.* Chicago: Aldine, 1968.

TURNER, V.W. *The ritual process: Structure and anti-structure.* Chicago: Aldine, 1969.

Chapter 9
Meteorological Play-Forms
of the Eastern Woodlands

MICHAEL A. SALTER

T his study, historical in nature, focuses on the agrarian-based peoples of North America's Eastern Woodlands.[1] The purpose of the paper is to investigate the relationships that existed between certain games and one aspect of the metaphysical environment—that associated with climatic change.

The natives of this area faced numerous hardships in the course of their day-to-day living. Some, such as sickness and war, could to a limited extent be contained or avoided. Adverse conditions, however, were beyond their direct control. In an aboriginal setting the very survival of an agrarian group was, to a large extent, directly related to the vagaries of the weather. During the summer, frosts and periods of excessive heat or drought always posed a threat to the crops, the products of which even when successful were barely sufficient to sustain a community through the ensuing harsh winter months. Blizzards not only

From P. Stevens (Ed.), *Studies in the anthropology of play: Papers in memory of B. Allan Tindall*, 1977. (Proceedings from the Second Annual Meeting of the Association for the Anthropological Study of Play.) Copyright 1977 by Leisure Press. Reprinted with permission.

made living unpleasant but, particularly among the more northern tribes, effectively prevented them from foraging for the supplies necessary to supplement their ever meager and always dwindling food reserves.

While it is to be suspected that some individuals, notably the shamans, possessed a certain level of meteorological understanding, the average native attributed the behavior of the elements to the actions of specific supernatural entities within their respective pantheons. Therefore, it is understandable that as the Indian possessed no direct means of climatic control, he would endeavor to obtain his objectives indirectly by appealing to and appeasing these metaphysical beings. This resulted in a complex of rituals revolving around celestial bodies and elements of the weather.

In most cases the entities involved were believed to be, like their worshippers, extremely fond of games. Indeed, some of them were thought to have acquired their eminent position as a result of, or during the course of a game. A Caddoan myth serves to illustrate: It speaks of two brothers who began to play the hoop and pole game. After several days of competition the younger brother failed to hit the wheel with his missile, whereupon it continued to roll beyond the designated play-area. Following a series of hair-raising adventures, the brothers succeeded in spearing the wheel and ultimately ascended to the sky-world as the spirits, Thunder and Lightning (Dorsey, 1905, pp. 31-36). As associations of this nature are by no means rare within Indian mythology, it is not surprising to find that some play-forms possessed climatic overtones and served as focal points around which certain meteorological ceremonies revolved.

The peoples of the Six Nations[2] used lacrosse as a means of influencing the elements. They played the game as part of their Thunder Ceremony in order to bring about those climatic conditions necessary to facilitate the growth of their crops. They scheduled the Thunder Ceremony whenever precipitation was required and rarely more than once a year. The most favorable condition for staging the ceremony occurred when the sound of thunder could be heard in the west (Tooker, 1970, p. 34)!

The ceremony was scheduled and conducted by the males to implore the Thunderers—seven old men with vast supernatural powers—to bring rain, to control the winds and to continue their warfare against pestilential creatures, both natural and preternatural. The Iroquois referred to the Seven Thunderers as their "Grandfathers" and viewed them as benevolent agents of the Great Spirit. It was believed that in addition to protecting mankind from evil, they were obligated to use the winds and rain to cleanse the earth. For these services, thanksgiving prayers were offered during the Midwinter Festival. However, unlike the Midwinter Festival, the Thunder Ceremony was directed primarily toward the Seven Thunderers.[3]

The ceremony consisted of a tobacco invocation, a dance and a game of lacrosse. As "lacrosse is the game which supernaturals play in the thunderhead, the lightning bolt their ball" (Eyman, 1964, p. 19), the game was considered the principal rite of the Thunder Ceremony. The speaker appointed to direct the proceedings began by offering prayers and tobacco to the Great Spirit and to the Seven Thunderers. The occasion and the import of the game was next explained to the players who were instructed to be in good spirits while playing, to play fairly, and to avoid causing unnecessary injury. Naturally malicious sentiments were considered out of place in a game contested for the supernatural.

The athletes, who had undergone a period of fasting prior to the contest, were administered an emetic "to clean them out" just before taking the field. Practices such as these were believed to "purify" the individual and accompanied the majority of those rituals directed toward the more prominent members in their pantheon.

The game was contested by seven old men and a like number of young men selected from opposing moieties. Thus the contest was viewed as being played between the Seven Thunderers and their children. It was characterized by few rules, little violence, and considerable emphasis on skill and speed. Although seven goals were required to win, the outcome was of no significance, at least in terms of the ritual. The ceremonial importance of the game lay in its symbolic representation of the "conflict between life and death, good and evil, hope and despair," as well as the eternal "warfare between the thunderers and their enemies, the under-earth deities" (Speck & General, 1949, p. 117). That these dichotomies were reflected in the teams is reinforced by Eyman's (1964, p. 18) observation that the seven older players personified the seven thunder gods—and presumably "life," "good," and "hope."

In another sense the outcome was important, as gambling was commonly associated with the game. Certainly those natives with material items at stake must have displayed more than a passing interest in the result. Although betting was not considered a part of the rite, it "was never reprobated by their religious teachers, but on the contrary rather encouraged" (Morgan, 1954, pp. 281-282). Thus it was not viewed as sacrilegious and hence did not interfere with the ceremony's raison d'etre. Indeed, it was quasi-religious in nature insofar as the wagers increased the potency of the rite. It was believed that the more competitive the game the more acceptable it would be to the supernatural. What better way to foster competition than to encourage gambling on the part of the spectators and participants?

It is of interest to note that the number seven, a number sacred to the Iroquois and already mentioned in relation to the number of players on each team and the number of goals required to conclude the game, occurs again in conjunction with the playing field. The field itself varied in length and possessed no side boundaries. At each end of the playing area two posts were set into the ground, seven paces apart. These posts were said to "reach the sky." The distance between the posts and the concept of their height symbolized respectively, the seven deities to whom the game was dedicated, and a physical link between them and those involved in the ritual.

Following the game, the players entered the longhouse singing and dancing, to be joined by any male spectator who so desired. The ceremony was concluded inside with additional dancing, prayers of thanksgiving, and the distribution of tobacco and corn mush[4] to the players. That the Iroquois obviously had faith in the ceremony's ability to bring about a desired weather change is apparent from the emphatic statement of a native informant: "as soon as the lacrosse game is over, rain comes, even if there have been no previous signs of a rainstorm" (Shimony, 1961, p. 164).

Lacrosse was similarly used by other peoples for purposes of environmental control. We have record of the Huron, for example, playing the game on the advice of a shaman, in an attempt to avert adverse weather conditions. Le Mercier (1898, p. 47) recalls that during May of 1637, just prior to the planting season, the inhabitants of several villages "tired themselves to death [on the playing field, in the belief that] . . . the weather depended only upon a game of crosse." Like many of the games employed for mortuary, fertility, and medicinal purposes (for further information on these games see Salter [1972, 1973, 1974]), the spirit in which this activity was contested was undoubtedly of greater importance in terms of the ritual than was the actual outcome.

Despite the fact that the temperature dropped and some 6 inches of snow fell several days after this particular contest, the natives remained firm in their conviction that lacrosse was an effective agent of climatic control. This faith indicates that the game had undoubtedly been used for similar purposes in the past and would be so employed again when the need arose. Although the shaman's reputation obviously suffered on this occasion, native belief in the ritual points to a considerable degree of past success on the part of the Huron medicine-men in predicting short-range weather conditions.

Another Iroquois ceremony deserves consideration at this point. This ritual, dedicated to the two major celestial bodies—the moon and the sun[5]—served as an occasion during which the people were able to express gratitude for the warmth emanating from the sun and at the same time to request favorable growing conditions and fine weather for their crops. As such, it was more closely related to certain supplicatory/thanksgiving rites than it was to weather control and will not be fully developed here. What is of interest, however, is that while some tribes such as the Cayuga and the Onondaga scheduled and celebrated the ceremony in the spring by itself, others had absorbed elements of the ritual into their Thunder Ceremony.

One such group was the Seneca who, during times of drought, conducted a rite in honor of the Sun and the Seven Thunderers. This ceremony commenced with a tobacco invocation to the Sun and a plea from the shaman requesting "our old brother, the Sun" (Fenton, 1936, p. 8) not to burn the crops. These preliminaries were followed by a game of hoop and pole (Tooker, 1970, p. 34). The game was contested by two teams made up of players from opposing moieties. It seems likely that as the sun and the moon were believed to compete against each other in the game, and as the moon was also considered responsible for the success of the crops, the teams probably represented these two entities. Thus, on this occasion, the game of hoop and pole may be viewed as a symbolic contest between the two. Certainly, as the moon and sun were believed to derive pleasure from watching the game, it was played in their honor and constituted part of an overall attempt to promote more favorable weather conditions. Although a description of the game as it was played in conjunction with the Seneca Thunder Ceremony is unavailable, it is known that the "Sun" was permitted to roll the hoop first—a roll that had to travel toward the west.[6] If the symbolic association is correct, then it is understandable why victory was considered unimportant, for defeat of the "Moon" by the "Sun" or vice versa, could conceivably jeopardize the ritual. Following the contest, a second tobacco invocation was made, this time to the Thunderers. The ceremony concluded indoors with dancing and a series of individual supplications directed toward the Thunderers and the Sun.

One important element appears to be absent from the Seneca Thunder Ceremony; that element being a rite to produce rain—unless, of course, the postgame invocation and prayers were considered sufficient. Shimony (1961, p. 163), however, appears to supply the answer when she notes that the Seneca, like the other Iroquoian tribes, always played lacrosse as part of this ritual. Unfortunately, she does not elaborate, nor does she mention the game of hoop and pole. It is questionable, therefore, whether both lacrosse and hoop and pole were contested as part of the one ceremony or in fact constituted the major rites of two separate, but related, ceremonies.

The Arkansas or Quapaw, linguistically related to the tribes of the Huron and Iroquois Confederacies, were split into two major tribal divisions. One division—"the Earth people"—was responsible for the physical well-being of the tribe, while the responsibilities of the other section—"the Sky people"—lay primarily with the supernatural welfare of the populace. Cooperation between the two groups was thus believed to be essential if the society were to survive physically and spiritually.

One of these cooperative ventures revolved around a game somewhat resembling shinny. This game was originally contested between two teams of young men chosen respectively from "the Earth people" and "the Sky people." As in the Seneca hoop and pole game, the players were considered to represent the principal entities involved in the ritual—in this case, the earth and the sky. The contest was formally opened by a representative of the Wind clan—a subdivision of "the Earth people." Even when played socially, the honor of commencing the game was bestowed on any member of this group present. In the ritualistic version of the game, a large circle-enclosed-cross was scratched in center-field. The ball, having been placed in the center, was first rolled toward the north along the line drawn to the edge of the circle, and then back on the same line to the center. This procedure was repeated along the eastern arm of the cross, the southern arm and finally along the western arm, until the ball again rested in the center of the circle. The individual entrusted with this task next tossed the ball into the air and struck it, to begin the more vigorous part of the rite.

The game was said to have had cosmic significance in reference to the winds and the earth; "the initial movement of the ball [around the cross] referred to the winds, the bringers of life" (Fletcher & La Flesche, 1911, p. 198), the mid-field circle symbolized the earth. Whether the ritual was also an attempt to promote rain is unclear, although the relationship between wind and rain was an extremely close one within the cosmological framework of many Eastern Woodland tribes. (The Thunderers of the Iroquois, for example, were believed to control both these elements.) The north-south orientation of the field seems to indicate that the sun did not occupy a significant place in the rite. In any event, there is no doubt that the ceremony was used as an attempt to influence the weather.

Shinny was played on social occasions although only by the males; men and boys competing separately. The ritualistic version was exclusively an adult-male game. While large wagers were common when the men played socially, it is not certain that this was the case on other occasions. If gambling were associated with the ceremonial game, then there may have been considerable emphasis on victory. It is more likely, however, that in the same way as the Iroquois were able to separate the materialistic and spiritualistic aspects of their ceremonial lacrosse matches, so too were they separated in this game. On the basis of the tribes previously discussed, it seems probable that in terms of the ritual, these people also placed greater emphasis on the spirit in which shinny was contested than they did on the eventual outcome.

Two other Arkansas pastimes deserve brief mention. It has been observed that whip-tops were only played with during the winter months. The climatic association is interesting, although whether it resulted from seasonal taboos, as was the case with the ring and pin, and stick games of the Delaware, or the simple fact that ice served as an ideal base upon which to spin these toys, is questionable. The second activity is in many ways remarkably similar to contemporary Halloween practices. Masked boys circulated throughout the community issuing a "trick or treat" ultimatum to selected elders. Although Fletcher and La Flesche (1911, p. 370) refer to this as a "sport," it seems to be ritualistic in character, particularly as the practice only occurred "in the spring, after the thunder had sounded. . . ."The fact, too, that lightning and thunder were symbolized both in the apparel and behavior of the youngsters, seems to support this. Whatever ceremonial connections there may have been are lost; however, the amusement does appear to have had climatic overtones.

Before proceeding, it should be emphasized that the societies previously referred to—the Huron, Iroquois, Caddo, and Arkansas—were all linguistically related. On the other hand, the tribal group to be discussed below was a member of a different linguistic phylum, a fact that bears remembering when considering the underlying rationale and believed outcomes of these climatic rites.

On the basis of existing evidence, only two Delaware games appear to have had climatic associations. One of these was a pastime that closely resembled the Caucasian game of pick-up sticks. A player dropped some 65 grass straws onto a blanket and, using a hooked quill, attempted to remove as many as possible from the cluster without disturbing the others. Each separated straw contributed, according to its individual value, to the contestant's point-total. The game was terminated when one of the players had achieved the total previously agreed upon. The game of "scattering straws" was played by men and women, either together or separately, and usually involved gambling (Speck, 1937, pp. 104-106). Like this game, the game of ring and pin was also an adult indoor gambling game. The principal item employed consisted of a number of hollow animal bones attached by a piece of string to a sharpened stick or bone. The object of the game was to swing the bones through the air and impale as many as possible on the stick. As in the game of straws, the contest concluded when a predetermined point-total had been reached by one of the competitors (Brinton, 1890, p. 186).

The interesting thing about these two games is that both could only be played during the winter months and participation in them was restricted to those individuals who had been born during that season (Flannery, 1939, p. 88). It was commonly thought that a breach of these conditions would bring about bad luck, assumedly in the form of sickness. However, the climatic association went further than this as the Delaware believed that blizzard conditions would automatically follow the playing of each game. Despite this belief, these games continued to be played. The question as to why the Delaware participated in activities that were thought to create unpleasant conditions is perplexing. However, if one adopts the belief that there is only so much inclement weather that one can be subjected to in an agricultural year, this practice then becomes understandable; for by playing these games during the winter months, the chances of adverse weather occurring during spring (planting season) and summer (growing season) may be decreased. In any event, it would appear that the games were vestiges of earlier rituals conducted in honor of those believed to control the elements. The resultant storms were thus regarded as the means by which these entities acknowledged the ceremony and the ensuing harsh weather was viewed more as a spiritual blessing than as an undesirable event.

Thus, the games of the Delaware differed in several respects from those of the other tribes viewed in this paper. In the first place, the Huron, Iroquois, and Arkansas employed vigorous team games in a standardized ceremonial setting, as devices to influence or control the weather.[7] The Delaware games, on the other hand, individualistic and sedentary in nature, do not appear at the time of their recording to have been conducted as part of a standard ritual. Further, while the games of the other cultures were used to produce positive results by averting inclement weather and/or by promoting favorable climatic conditions, the Delaware believed that the playing of certain games would inevitably result in adverse weather. These differences have a direct linguistic relationship. This would seem to suggest that although cultural artifacts may transgress linguistic boundaries basically unchanged,[8] the ideologies associated with the artifacts, particularly if they relate to the metaphysical, may not diffuse as readily.

In summary, it is apparent that the survival of any agrarian-based society is largely dependent upon the whims of the elements. This was certainly the case with the basically sedentary peoples of eastern North American who relied solely on their summer harvest and the available local game to tide them over the winter months. As extended periods of heat and drought, snap frosts, violent storms, and the like, could rapidly decimate the economic base of a tribe, it is little wonder that the natives did all in their power to prevent such disasters.

Knowing the elements to be beyond the control of mere mortals, these Indians sought to exert some degree of influence through a variety of rituals directed toward the supernatural. Among the Iroquois, Huron, and Arkansas, games frequently served as the principal rites in these ceremonies. Some, like the bowl game, were employed in conjunction with major annual ceremonies such as the Midwinter Festival (Blau, 1967, pp. 35-36). While possessing climatic overtones, they were, however, more in the nature of thanksgiving rites than agents of change. Any effects stemming from these rituals were of the long-term variety. On the other hand, the play-forms previously discussed, when contested under certain conditions, were all believed capable of promoting rapid environmental change. The accompanying table and figure attempt to

Table 1

Meteorological Play-Forms of the Eastern Woodlands

Society	Game	Contestant	Season Played	Spirit(s) Involved	Result of Contest	Remarks
Huron	Lacrosse	Men v men (Intervillage)	Spring	?	Harsh weather averted	
Iroquois	1. Lacrosse	1. Men v men (Intermoiety)	1. Summer -drought	1. Thunderers Great Spirit	1a. Rain b. Favourable winds	1. Gambling. Pre-game preparation
	2. Hoop and Pole	2. Men v men (Intermoiety)	2. Summer -drought and extreme temperatures	2. Sun, Moon Thunderers	2a. Cooler weather b. Rain?	
Arkansas	1. Shinny	1. Men v men (Intermoiety)	1. Summer	1. Winds	1a. Favourable winds b. Rain?	1. Gambling. Pre-game preparation
	2. Whip-tops	2. Boys v boys	2. Winter	2. ?	2. ?	
Caddo	Hoop and Pole	Men v men	Summer	Thunder and Lightning	Rain?	
Delaware	1. Straw Game	1. Men and Women	1. Winter	1. Winter Spirit	1. Blizzard conditions	1. Gambling
	2. Ring and Pin Game	2. Men and Women	2. Winter	2. Winter Spirit	2. Blizzard conditions	2. Gambling

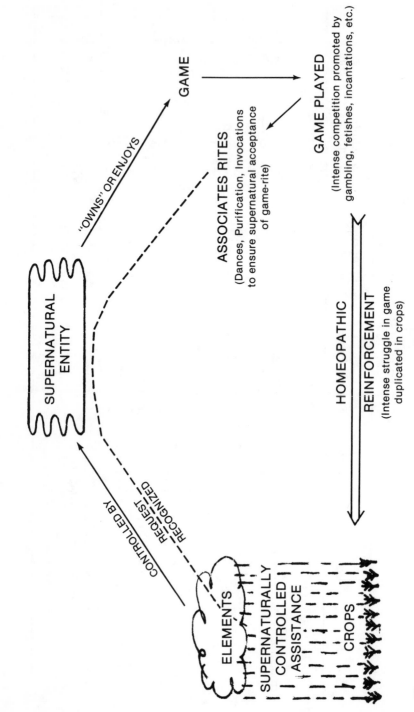

Figure 1

outline, in a diagramatic fashion, the interrelationships among these games, the supernatural, and climatic change. Thus, such activities as hoop and pole, lacrosse, and shinny were played on a needs basis in honor of the thunder, the lightning, the moon, the sun and/or the wind, on the assumption that positive weather changes would result. Failure of these changes to materialize was attributed to incorrect ritualistic procedure and could be rectified by conducting the ceremony again. Other activities, such as the ring and pin and straw games of the Delaware, and possibly the whip-top contests of the Arkansas, were associated with the negative weather conditions. More specifically, these six games were believed: (a) to promote rain; (b) to temper the winds; (c) to avert inclement weather; (d) to terminate periods of excessive heat, and/or (e) to result in adverse weather. Native faith in this cause-effect relationship suggests a considerable degree of meteorological knowledge and predictive skill on the part of the shamans—knowledge that was essential if the expected change were to eventuate and the shamans retain their authority and status within the community.

Notes

1. The Eastern Woodlands extend from slightly north of the St. Lawrence River to the Gulf of Mexico, and from the Atlantic Ocean to just west of the Ohio River in the north and the Mississippi River in the south. They include part of Ontario and Quebec, all New York, southern New England, the middle Atlantic states, and the southern states as far west as Louisiana. When the Europeans first entered the region it housed more than 120 different tribal groups. Although they spoke a variety of languages and dialects, they all fell into one of five linguistic families—families that were affiliated with either the Macro-Siouan or Macro-Algonquian Phyla. This study focuses on 10 of these groups belonging to the Iroquoian, Caddoan, and Siouan Families of the Macro-Siouan Phylum and the Algonquian Family of the Macro-Algonquian Phylum.
2. The Six Nations or the League of the Iroquois, hereafter referred to as the "Iroquois," consisted of the following tribes: Cayuga, Mohawk, Oneida, Seneca, Tuscarora, and Onondaga.
3. The Midwinter Festival was the highlight of the Iroquoian ceremonial calendar. Held in late January or early February, its rites of personal well-being, supplication, and thanksgiving were directed toward the entire agricultural and cosmic hierarchy of the Iroquois.
4. The corn mush appears to symbolize the seventh Thunderer, who as an earthling, was crushed by the other six Thunderers in a corn mortar in order to change his shape and thus facilitate his ascendancy into the spirit world. The Cayuga referred to the game, when played on this occasion as "beating the mush."
5. In point of fact, the Moon Ceremony and the Sun Ceremony were two

separate and distinct rituals; however, as their aims were similar, most Iroquoian tribes conducted them in conjunction with each other.

6. An east-west orientation was common to most activities that involved the sun.
7. An exception here was the whip-top contests of the Arkansas. It is possible that beliefs and taboos, similar to those held by the Delaware, may also have been associated with this activity.
8. Generally speaking, the playforms of the Macro-Algonquian peoples, as represented by the Delaware, are remarkably similar to those found within such Macro-Siouan societies as the Huron, Iroquois, Caddo, and Arkansas.

References

BLAU, H. Notes on the Onondaga Bowl Game. In *Iroquois culture, history and prehistory; proceedings of the 1965 Conference on Iroquois Research*. Albany: The State University of New York, 1967.

BRINTON, D.G. *Essays of an Americanist*. Philadelphia: Porter & Coates, 1890.

DORSEY, G.A. *Traditions of the Caddo*. Washington: Carnegie Institution, 1905.

EYMAN, F. Lacrosse and the Cayuga Thunder Rite. *Expedition 6*, (Summer) 1964, No. 4, pp. 14-19.

FENTON, W.N. An outline of Seneca ceremonies at Cold Spring Longhouse. *Yale University Publications in Anthropology* (No. 9). New Haven: Yale University, 1936.

FLANNERY, R. An analysis of coastal Algonquian culture. *Anthropological Series* (No. 7). Washington: The Catholic University of America, 1939.

FLETCHER, A.C., & La Flesche, F. The Omaha tribe. *Twenty-Seventh Annual Report of the Bureau of American Ethnology to the Secretary of the Smithsonian Institution, 1905-1906*. Washington: Government Printing Office, 1911.

LE MERCIER, F.J. Le Jeunes relation, 1637. In R.G. Thwaites (Ed.), *The Jesuit relations and allied documents 14*. Cleveland: Burrows Brothers, 1898.

MORGAN, L.H. *League of the Ho-De-No Sau-Nee or Iroquois 1*. New Haven: Human Relations Area Files, 1954.

SALTER, M.A. Mortuary games of the eastern culture area. *Proceedings of the Second Canadian Symposium on the History of Sport and Physical Education*. Ottawa: Department of National Health and Welfare, 1972.

SALTER, M.A. Medicinal game-rites of the Iroquoian linguistic family. *Proceedings of the North American Society for Sport History*. University Park: Pennsylvania State University, 1973.

SALTER, M.A. An analysis of the role of games in the fertility rituals of the native North American. *Anthropos: International Review of Ethnology and Linguistics*, 1974, **69**(3-4), 494-504.

SHIMONY, A.A. Conservatism among the Iroquois at the Six Nations Reserve. *Yale University Publications in Anthropology*, No. 65. New Haven: Yale University, 1961.

SPECK, F.G. Oklahoma Delaware ceremonies, feasts and dances. In *Memoirs of the American Philosophical Society, 7*. Philadelphia: The American Philosophical Society, 1937.

SPECK, F.G., & General, A. *Midwinter rites of the Cayuga Long House*. Philadelphia: University of Pennsylvania Press, 1949.

TOOKER, E. *The Iroquois Ceremonial of Midwinter*. Syracuse: Syracuse University Press, 1970.

Chapter 10

A Dart Match in Tikopia:[1]
A Study in the Sociology
of Primitive Sport

RAYMOND FIRTH

C ompetitive dart throwing was a popular sport in old Polynesia. The records which have been preserved of the Maori *teka*, the Samoan *tika* and the *ta-tika* of Niue, as well as the *tiŋga* of Fiji,[2] show that despite variation in details they represented a similar type of pastime, one which appears to have·drawn the interest of the whole community after the manner of our modern football or cricket. The following account describes the game as played with enthusiasm at the present day by the people of Tikopia, a society of which the culture has remained comparatively untouched by the disintegrating influence of the white man.

The island of Tikopia, lying between the Banks and the Santa Cruz groups, about 120 miles south-east of Vanikoro, is a small isolated crater peak, very fertile, measuring about 3 miles long by 2 wide, and inhabited by over 1,200 people. They are Polynesians, with all the usual pleasant traits of their race. A good-tempered folk, fond of laughter and not

From *Oceania*, 1930, **1**(1), 64-96. Copyright 1930 by Oceania Publications. Reprinted with permission.

without wit, they are endowed with much curiosity and sufficient intelligence to make conversation diverting.

When a dart match is in progress the scene is gay and animated. Crowds of spectators of all ages assemble, from the naked toddler gazing wide-eyed at the unaccustomed sight, to the grey-haired veteran, sagely discussing the fine points of the game. Women and girls, who also attend, are almost as keenly interested as the men. The erect carriage of these people, their light-brown, smooth, well-molded limbs, their easy bearing and freedom of movement give a very pleasing impression, the interest of which is heightened by the flowing manes of hair of the young men, their peculiar pride, which is often rendered golden from the liberal use of lime. Flowers or bunches of scented leaves in the ears, aromatic necklets, and shell arm-rings give a festive air to the proceedings, since it is the common practice, if one is not in mourning, to don ornaments for the occasion. The primary function of the sport of dart throwing is that of public diversion. But as will be shown later, it is very closely connected with the social organization and religious belief of the people, and in this way illustrates certain aspects of Polynesian sociology.

The Tikopian form of the game is played on a long narrow stretch of ground, carefully denuded of vegetation, dug out and leveled, rather like an over-developed cricket pitch, but hemmed in by sloping banks on either side, backed by a green wall of shrubs and trees (see Figure 1 and Plate 2). The *marae*, as this is called, measures about 130 yards in length by 6 or 7 in total width, and at each end is a throwing base *(turaŋa)* of soft sand, from which the players hurl their darts. Immediately behind this again is a slight dip in the ground, while on the grass-grown space in rear the players seat themselves in a rough semi-circle to await their turn to throw (see Plate 1).

The Dart and Its Projection

The *tika* or dart is at first sight a curiously unwieldy object. The head *(fue tika)* is about 5 inches long, and reminds one in shape of a thin spinning-top, being circular in cross section and curving gently from base

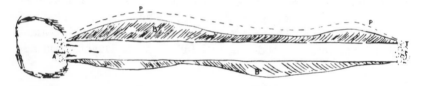

Figure 1—Marae Tika—Dart pitch [length about 130 yards]. P = Path; A = Mua Tika; T = Throwing Base; B = Sloping Banks.

Plate 1 — A dart match in Tikopia: A group of youths with darts, awaiting their turn to throw.

Plate 2 – A dart match in Tikopia: A. Hurling the Dart. B. The "Follow-through." The player has thrown himself off his balance giving full force to his cast.

to point. It is made of *toa (Casuarina)* wood, hard and close-grained, and is polished so smooth with coral stone *(puŋa)* as to give it the appearance of having been turned on a lathe. The object is thus to cause it to slide easily over the ground on being thrown. At the base of the head is a small dowel-like projection, a tang three-quarters of an inch in length, which is fitted into the socket of a reed shaft (see Figure 2). The latter *(te kaso)* varies in length, but usually measures about 3 feet. The *tika* is an awkward implement for the novice to handle, as its balance lies decidedly towards the head, and it is impossible to make a good cast with it in the ordinary way by poising it in the hand. The method is to set the butt end of the reed shaft against the tip of the forefinger, grip the sides of the shaft with the thumb and middle finger, and support it by slightly elevating the head of the dart or by resting it on the other hand. Carrying it thus the player takes a short run to the throwing-base and drawing back his arm hurls the dart with all his force. Thus projected it flies through the air for upwards of 50 yards, but is soon drawn down by the weight at the point. As it strikes the ground, however, its career is not stopped, for the heavy, smoothly polished head, guided but not impeded by the light shaft, which sways to and fro behind it like a rudder, skims along the surface of the *marae* for another 70 or 80 yards, to come to rest near the throwing base at the other end. A low trajectory is essential to a good cast, which may measure up to 150 yards, or even more in exceptional cases.

The pressure on the finger is fairly severe at the moment of projection. As a guard, and still more, to hold the dart firm and so give it greater impetus, the player fits to his finger the *fakatoŋa*, a little ring of cocout fibre *(puru)*, well whipped, with a quaint ornamental whisker left on one side. For its reception the shaft is notched at the butt like that of an arrow. When a player's turn comes to throw he slips the ring on to his forefinger, which it fits closely, and a small cord attached to it is wound round the finger and made fast.

Organization of the Game

The essential principle of the game is the competition of two sides, each comprising a dozen to 20 players. The composition of these sides is of some interest since it is largely determined by tradition, having its origin, according to the Tikopians, in mythological antiquity, dating from the

Figure 2—Dart and projection ring.

time when men were gods and gods were men. The game is sometimes described indeed as "*te tika—takaro o ŋa atua*," "the dart—sport of the gods." On this account a certain degree of *tapu* (sacredness) belongs to it, especially on ceremonial occasions, when all the chiefs and men of rank are present and strive against one another, through the medium of their young relatives, who act as their throwers, for supremacy and honor in the game. On such ceremonial days the gods are in attendance to influence the fortunes of their people. For this reason, combined with its supernatural origins, the dart-throwing is believed to promote the growth of crops, and in particular to cause the *mei* (bread-fruit) to set or "run," though the association between them is not very clearly defined. At times, indeed, a match is instituted for this express purpose, the object being to *sakiri manu ki te fenua*, to seek efficacy for the land—that is, in the direction of increasing the food supply.[3] On such an occasion it is said "*te marae ka tika tapu*," "the pitch will be 'darted' sacred."

As regards the disposition of the sides, one is termed *ŋa Tamaroa* (the Bachelors), the other *ŋa Pure* (the Married Men). These labels are purely figurative; they carry no differentiation on the lines which their literal meaning conveys; some married men make their throws on the side of the "Bachelors," while young unmarried men are to be found equally on the side of the *Pure*. Actually the former comprise the men of the clan *(kainaŋa)* of Tafua, with a few additions from families in other clans, while their opponents come primarily from the ranks of the family of Raropuka, with the clan Kafika to which it belongs, but include also the members of clan Fangarere and the majority of clan Taumako.[4] In point of material to draw upon the *Pure* are perhaps in a better position than the *Tamaroa*, inasmuch as they have three of the four chiefs on their list, and a more numerous personnel. Deference to tradition, however, prevents any ideas arising as to the unfairness of this division, and on the whole the sides appear to be very evenly matched in point of skill. Moreover, it is through the individual brilliance of its members and not through their average skill that a side holds its own. Superficially, the division of the sides rests on the chance allotment of clans and families. In reality, however, it resolves itself largely along the lines of the traditional opposition of the two districts of the island, Faea and Ravenga. The extra families who take part contrary to their clan affiliations have some special over-riding local or ancestral tie of association with the other party. Niumano and Fatumaru, for instance, are enlisted on the side of Tafua clan and the "Bachelors" since their lands adjoin in Uta, an ancient residential area of the people, and in the turbulent old days this was a strong bond of unity. Hence these families are to be found playing against their own chief of Taumako. Other *paito* (family groups) on this side, who play against their own clans are Nga Fiti, sa Torokinga, sa Farekofe and Paito i Asanga.

The *tika* is of interest from the fact that unlike other games in Tikopia its organization is of a rigid character. The personnel of the two sides may vary from one match to another, men attending to play at some and being absent from others, but a man remains always a member of the same side. And, as has been pointed out, this is determined for him, not by his own personal choice, but by his membership through birth of a certain kinship group. Even his clan affiliation here is not the primary factor, but his *paito* (family) alone. In the old "Marae lasi" or "Great Marae" near the village of Matautu, now abandoned for the newer ground at Ratia, the two ends *(potu)* were named "Vokisa" and "Rangitisa," the former being the base for the *Pure*, the latter for the *Tamaroa*. This allocation is rooted not in the merely superficial organization of the game, but in religious and mythological ideas of fundamental interest to the natives.

Method of Scoring: Kasa, Rari, Tuku Té Kai

The method of scoring is rather difficult for a novice to grasp, especially while a game is in progress. The immediate object of every player is to send his dart ahead of all the others, the only position in which it has much chance of scoring. The dart which leads the rest when one side has concluded its throw is termed the *mua tika*, the dart in front, and the other side endeavors to conquer it. If they succeed then it is said to be "eaten" by their darts; if not then it "eats" theirs. "*Sise kaina, kai*" (Not eaten, eats) is the rule. One dart catches another and disposes of it (eats it) if its head comes up level with any part of its rival, even the butt of the shaft. There is no scoring on the part of individual players, but the leading dart scores one point for its side. If the darts next in order belong to the same side, then they increase the score accordingly, counting one for each. "*E kai rua*," "*E kai toru*," "Eat two," "Eat three," it is said, or whatever the number. This count is stopped by the leading dart of the other side; thus if the two longest throws on the pitch are those of the *Tamaroa*, and all others are "eaten" by the best effort of the *Pure*, which, however, has not been able to cope with the leading pair of its opponents, then the *Tamaroa* will score two. All other darts of either side which have come to rest behind this pair do not count. (The inferior side in the throw does not score.)

Thus if darts 2, 3, and 4 [in Figure 3] are the foremost *tika* of the *Tamaroa*, and 1 the best throw of the *Pure*, then 1 "eats" 2, since it has come level with a portion of the shaft, and 3 and 4 remain to score for the *Tamaroa*. But if 1 and 2 are both darts of the *Pure* and 3 and 4 were thrown by the *Tamaroa*, then both these latter are "eaten" by 2, and neither side has any score. The general principle is that only the dart unbeaten by its opponents scores for its side. All others are neglected.

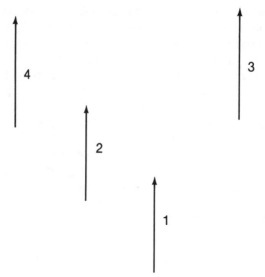

Figure 3—Method of scoring.

The score of the winning side goes on round after round, so long as it does not receive a check. If once, however, their opponents gain the lead, if by a superior throw the latter are enabled to score at the end of a round then all the previous gains of the first side are wiped out, and the opponents begin to accumulate points in their turn. They now go on victoriously until they are mastered by a long throw from the first party and so their score too is barred *(monotia)*, and the others begin again from zero.

On some days one side is clearly superior or in a winning mood, and proceeds without a halt to a sweeping victory, untouched by the most desperate efforts of their opponents to retrieve the position. At other times the sides are very evenly matched, and neither is able to make a score of any size before its lead is torn away.

The initial score of the day is the focus of the greatest interest. It is termed *te kai poŋipoŋi*, "the morning win." If one side keeps on accumulating points without a single check from the moment of starting, until it reaches the total of 10, then a *rari* is said to have been reached. This first count of 10 in the morning is termed the *kasā*, and is regarded as a definite mark of the superiority of the winners. "*Tatou ku kasā*," "We have been *kasā*," the losers say, and feel much ashamed. For one single unbeaten throw on their part would have dissipated the lead of their opponents, and no *kasā* could then have been obtained that day. After this first stage of the *kasā* has been passed without hindrance then the *kai* of each succeeding round score for the winners one point each indifferently, no matter how many unbeaten darts may lie. Such scoring is termed the *tuku te kai* (literally, 'leave remaining win'). Thus if they should have two darts unbeaten in the next round this counts one point for them; they have one *tuku te kai*. Should they have two or three winning darts in the succeeding round they gain another point; they have two *tuku te kai*. Another dart next time gives them a further point; *"Ku toru ko tuku te kai"*; they have three, and so on. It is the fact of each win, and not the actual number of darts unbeaten which now scores for them each time. Finally, perhaps, ten *tuku te kai* have been accumulated over and above the *kasā* of the initial 10 points.

It is the custom after such an event for the winners to go off to their orchards and pluck a large number of green coconuts, which are brought back and distributed among the losers. Both sides then sit down to drink, eat, and refresh themselves. Here it is a case of "the winner pays"—an inversion of the well-known rule which has a very definite social object. For after such a downright beating the losers are filled with great shame. Their weakness has been made apparent before the eyes of a large crowd, and by nightfall the full details of the match will have been carried through all the villages of the island. Such people will say, *"Tatou ku tikaia fakapariki,"* "We have been out-darted terribly." It is recognized on every hand that the situation is unpleasant. *"Te kasā e pariki, e faia take kau tika ku rava."* "The *kasa* is bad, because the other dart side are many" (i.e., their score is large). Like all Polynesians the Tikopian is very keenly sensitive to public opinion and fears nothing so much as ridicule, while he is apt to feel resentment toward those who have exposed him to its shafts. Hence the provision of coconuts as refreshment by the winners and the fraternization which this involves is of distinct socal utility. It helps to restore the equilibrium of the losers, to take the keen edge off their bitter emotions, to prevent their defeat from rankling, and to give them time to assume a natural manner in social intercourse. This is explicit in the view of the custom held by the natives themselves. Its function is summed up by them in the vivid phrase *fakamatamata laui*, of which the nearest rendering, almost literal in fact, is in the idea of 'recovery of face' so dear to the Oriental. The connection between expression of countenance and strength of emotion is indicated, with the implication that control of the one means command of the other. A further reference to the mental attitude of the players as determined by the social configuration of the game will be given later in this article.

Native opinion is not altogether unanimous on the method of scoring. Most people follow that described above, but some men hold that the older and more correct system is to designate as the *kasā* only the complete total of the initial *rari* and the *tuku te kai* together. Apart from the difference in terminology, the procedure is much the same, since in this case, it is said, coconuts would be plucked for the losers immediately on the attainment of the *kasā*. Still another system of scoring was outlined by an elderly man, a former expert, who maintained that in the *kai poŋipoŋi* first came the *kasā*, then a *rari*, then a second *kasā*, then another *rari*, and finally the *tuku te kai* before the absolute *coup de grâce* was held to have been administered. This extended mode of scoring is not followed nowadays.

A complete victory by one side is not often obtained. More commonly, during one round or another the temporarily losing side succeeds at last in making an effort and blocking the score of its opponents. The *kasā* or *tuku te kai* is then abandoned, and all succeeding points count only towards *rari*, or units of 10, a more prosaic affair. A further convention, however, must be indicated here. Suppose one side, despite its failure to gain the *kasā*, is nevertheless definitely the stronger, and continues to win steadily without a further break. They gain the first *rari*, 10 points, and then proceed to score for a second *rari*. For this, however, by custom they have to secure only nine points. For the third *rari* they have to get only eight, for the fourth seven only are counted as a *rari*, and so on, until to win the 10th *rari* a single point suffices, and this concludes the match. In ordinary terminology a *rari* signifies a "unit of 10," but this device of diminishing progressively the number of points required each time means that the 10 *rari*, of a nominal value of 100, represent the attainment of only 55 points in the game. This rather ingenious mode of scoring is adopted since the evident overwhelming superiority of the one side renders it unnecessary and even wearisome to prolong the match unduly. Of course a winning throw by the other side can upset the position at any moment and place both again at zero.

More often than not this is the fortune of the game, and one party no sooner attains a *rari* than it is checked by the other, and sometimes neither is able to secure more than a few points before being passed. The sides are then said to "block each other up" *(femonokaki)*. People who have not attended the match are always eager to hear the result and ask after the news as soon as they have an opportunity. *"Se rari ne tau?"* "A 10 was counted?" *"O siei! nokofemonokaki fuere."* "Oh no! kept on barring each other only." Such is a frequent form of question and answer in the stock phraseology.

Jargon of the Game

The *tika* in fact has a jargon of its own, words which in addition to their normal general meaning have acquired a special significance in this context, and which therefore are difficult to translate except in descriptive terms of the game itself. *Kasā*, used as substantive or verb, is an instance already discussed, as also *kai*. Another expression, *tafi se kai* means to effect a win with a dart, where it is difficult to relate *tafi* to its ordinary meaning of "to follow" or "to adopt." If one *tika* approaches close to another, but does not actually lap and so secure a *kai*, it is said, "*e tautari fuere*," "it merely follows." A dart which has attained a good position is said to have *toto laui* (fallen well), while if it meets with no success it is said to *to pariki* (fall badly), or *pāpā pariki* (smack badly), the latter especially if it buries its nose in the ground instead of shooting along the *marae*. When a dart by reason of a high trajectory strikes the ground at too steep an angle and topples over with its shaft lying up the pitch, it is said, "*ku tupau*" (it has drooped). An expert at the game is described as *te vave*, "the swift one," or *te mavero*; a poor player as *te laŋo*, "the slow one." A person who from clumsiness continually makes awkward, bad casts is called *te ŋeŋe*, a term of opprobrium for ghosts and other supernatural beings, and of which a fair translation would be "the uncouth devil!" To throw the dart hard is described by the terms *fakamafa* or *mero*, while a swift cast is likened to a lightning flash (*so ki foi kamo*). As a rule the experts, men who are relied upon to uphold the reputation of their side, throw toward the end of the round, where their cast will be most decisive. The last man of the opening side is termed *tautari tika* (follow dart). Immediately at his heels comes the first thrower of the opposition. He is said to *tau muri fakatoŋa*, lie on the butt of the shaft. Thus spectators often ask "*Muri fakatoŋa ku tau pe siei?*" meaning "Has the other side begun yet?"

Progress of a Match

The general principles of the game and its terminology, together with the somewhat peculiar method of scoring in vogue, have now been described, so that we may proceed to follow out in more detail the typical sequence of events in a match. An occasion on which the full ritual is performed is naturally of the greatest interest, though unfortunately such a scene is not to be witnessed in all its pageantry nowadays, the introduction of Christianity to the Tafua clan having robbed the game of many of the religious features formerly practiced on sacred occasions. Apart from these, however, it is still carried on with great enthusiasm, and it is only a few years since the more esoteric details were abandoned. For completeness our account will include these latter.

Preliminary Events

The *tika*, like most Tikopian pastimes except dancing, is pursued only spasmodically, so that from time to time the *marae* becomes overgrown

with weeds. When it has been decided to play a game then the first procedure is to go and clear the ground, a work in which the initiative is
taken by the eldest son of the Ariki Tafua, who by ancient privilege is
recognized as being in control of the *marae* and the sport. He accordingly
makes known a time, and the young men assemble, and root up all the
weeds and remove dead leaves and rubbish. A day or two is then allowed
to elapse for the surface to settle down. Meanwhile the actual day of the
match is fixed and the news soon spreads through all the villages. The interest is keen. In every house the darts are taken down from where they
have been thrust in between the layers of thatch in the roof, their reed
shafts are examined, the heads polished up, and new projection rings are
made. The younger boys become fired with excitement, and practice
hurling their darts on the stretches of sand along the sea front, while even
small children fit *Conus* shells to sago leaf ribs and *tika* after the fashion
of their elders.[5]

The grown-ups do not practice at all, unless the occasion is one of
sacerdotal importance. In this case on the evening before the match some
of the *vave*, the experts, go to the *marae* and try out their *tika*. They hurl
them and mark the condition of the shafts. Those which are good are
taken out and laid aside for use on the morrow. Those which are weak
are thrown away, as such a shaft is liable to break at the moment of projection and cause the *tika* to fall ignominiously like a wounded bird a few
yards from the throwing stand. After this testing of shafts is finished the
loose sand of the *turaŋa* is carefully smoothed over so that no footmarks
are visible to mar the perfection of the *marae* for the opening rites of the
morning. This is a rule of esoteric importance.

Meanwhile preparations are being made in the household of each chief
(ariki) and each elder *(pure)* to secure success on the morrow by supernatural as well as by purely physical means.

Ceremonies to Obtain Victory

Since the occasion is one of some sacredness *(tapu)* the ritual of the *kava*
is performed to invoke the aid of the *atua* (deities) of each clan or family
group concerned. *Roi* is prepared, a special kind of food which is placed
in the oven in the evening, left there all night, and taken out hot for the
ceremonies of the next morning. When this is made ready before nightfall, one of the workmen comes to the chief or elder, who is seated in his
house, and says, "The oven has been covered," i.e., the food is cooking
within. "Where are the crowd who have gone to fit reed shafts?" asks
the latter, referring to the experts mentioned above. Soon they return,
each to the head of his own family, and lashing on the approved reeds,
hand him the darts.

A pile of bark cloth, termed the *maro*, is taken up by the *pure* (the following remarks apply equally well to chief and elder alike), unfolded, and laid as an offering to his deities with the formula:

"Kotou ŋa atua!
Feturaki se kai mo tatou
Ke tafi i te poŋipoŋi ka marama nei."
"You the gods!
Set up together a win for us
To gain in the morning which will be light here."

The *pure* then pours coconut oil on his hands, takes up the premier dart *(mua tika)*, and rubs its head all over so that it is thoroughly anointed. As he does so he appeals to his deities again:

"Ia! Tafuri ki tou mua tika
Ki se kai mou ke tafia i te poŋipoŋi nei
Fakaseke i tou tua ki se kai mou."
"There! Turn to your foremost dart
To a win for you to be gained on this morning
Make it slide on your back for a win for you."

This formula is repeated only in the case of the *mua tika*, the principal implement of each man of rank, regarded as being under the direct control of his gods in the sport, and so endowed with an efficacy all its own. This is not to be confused with the *mua tika* in the course of the game, the dart which happens to be in the lead in any particular round, and which may or may not be one of the sacred darts. There is a connection between them, of couse, in that it is these latter, hurled by experts, which are expected to carry off the principal honors. The sacred *mua tika* are part of the religious paraphernalia of each *ariki* and *pure*, and receive special attention. Two of them indeed have names, that of the Ariki Taumako being called "Ngau," while that of the Ariki Kafika, the principal chief of the island, is known as "Matangi aso." These special darts are not brought out for ordinary matches, and a great deal of respect is shown them.

The formula just quoted is that of the *pure* of Raropuka family, one of the most important in the game. In it he requests his deity to cause the dart to slide on his back up the *marae*, and so pass all the others. The deity referred to is the one commonly known as "Te Atua i Raropuka," whose embodiment is the black lizard *(moko)* so familiar in Tikopian houses. The idea is that in this reptilian character, though invisible, the god will bear the dart along on his back and so lend it not wings, but feet to outstrip its rivals.

The other *tika* of the household are anointed also, and they are all stood up together against the wall for the night—hence the phrase "set up together a win for us" recited in the opening formula. Care is taken to see that they are set straight, and not disturbed by human agency. In the morning the *pure* comes to examine them. If he finds that they are lying down, with their heads up to the thatch of the wall, he laughs in delight, for he knows that his *mua tika* will secure a win that day. The gods, it is believed, have made casts with them in the night, in token of their coming cooperation in the sport.

In the morning the darts are given a second rubbing with oil, with a repetition of the formula to increase their chances of success. The oven is then uncovered, soon after sunrise, and the *kava* ceremony is made. Each *ariki* and *pure* does the same in his own house, the essential feature being the invocation of his *atua* in terms similar to those already given, to procure for him a winning throw that day.

To secure further against the possibility of failure in the human element, the players, each dignitary smears the throwing arm of the man who is going to cast his *mua tika* with coconut oil, and in addition ties around his neck a circlet of twisted *dracaena* leaf. Both of these acts are performed to the recitation of a formula:

"Mama tou kapakau
Ke tafi ko se kai ma tau atua
I te poŋipoŋi nei."
"Light be your arm
To gain a win for our deity
On this morning."

Such are common rites of sacralization for a man who has to carry out some task of religious import; their fundamental object is to secure his personal welfare and the success of his mission. In this case the specific purpose, as indicated in the formula, is to give suppleness and vigor to the thrower's arm.

After this the players and spectators begin to assemble at the *marae*. The chiefs and their elders do not take part in the actual sport, but they sit at the ends of the ground and watch the game with the keenest interest, more especially as regards the fate of their respective *mua tika*.

Opening of the Match

The match opens in a very formal manner. The four chiefs are seated at the end called "Rangitisa," the Ariki Tafua on one side of the pitch, the other three *ariki*, his opponents, on the other. A *kava* rite is first performed by the Ariki Tafua to call the attention of the gods in general to the game and appeal for their influence to bring welfare to the land and its people as the result. When this is concluded the game is opened with due formality.

First a man of the Kafika clan rises, goes over to where the *mua tika* has been laid in a piece of bark cloth at the head of the mat whereon his *ariki* is seated—the position of honor. He crouches down, takes the dart, and backs away respectfully as custom demands, then rises to his feet and begins to walk down the length of the *marae*, holding the dart almost upright so that it leans against his shoulder, and looking neither to right nor left. When he has gone a few yards a man of the Taumako clan rises in his turn, takes the *mua tika* of his *ariki* in similar fashion, and follows. When he, too, has reached his distance a man of Fangarere clan rises and follows suit, and the three march in single file down the center of the *marae* to the "Vokisa" end. Arrived, they go to one side and sit down, each binding the *fakatoŋa* ring on his finger. They are the leading representatives of the side of the *Pure*.[6] The man of Tafua whose function it is to open the *marae* on behalf of the *Tamaroa* rises last, goes to the seating-mat of his chief, takes the *mua tika* and walks down the *marae*, putting the *fakatoŋa* on his finger as he goes. At the far end of the pitch he wheels round, takes a short run and hurls the dart. This, the opening throw, is known as "*te ruakivero o Marae*," or "*te matakivero o Marae*." For this the *mua tika* is not thrown hard *(sise fakamafa)*, but is cast gently and with as correct aim as possible that it may glide truly down the center of the *marae*. This is an important precaution, because the other darts of the side, it is believed, will follow the direction of their leader, the *mua tika*; if it diverges one way or another, they will do the same. By reason of the mode of throwing this tendency for the *tika* to fly off to one side of the pitch is a very real one; hence the care taken to establish a good precedent, which may exercise a sympathetic influence. Following the initial cast of the man from Tafua come the throwers of the *mua tika* of Niumano and Fatumaru, both of Taumako clan, and next in order those from Fusi, Sao, Korokoro and Notau respectively, all *pure* families of Tafua. Then follow the ordinary players of the remainder of the side of the *Tamaroa*. When they have completed their throw it is the turn of the *Pure*, their opponents, and now all look anxiously to see if a *kai* will be registered and who, if anyone, can surpass the darts of the first side.

The Appeal to the Deities

The chiefs and their elders, who are usually men of years and dignified, have put their *mua tika* in charge of younger relatives who are fitted by their skill to uphold worthily the reputation of their group. Meanwhile each man of rank sits with bent head, waiting for the turn of his dart to come, not daring to look up, "praying hard" as one might say, murmuring formulae to his ancestors and other deities to vouchsafe to him a win. The natives themselves are quite fond of dilating on the anxiety and suspense of the moment.

"Kotou ŋa atua
Turaki fakamaroi i te poŋipoŋi nei
Ki se kai motou ke tafi
Na kae fakaturu matou"

mutters the old man.

"You the deities
Stand firm on this morning
For a win for you to be gained
Lest we bow our heads."

The psychological implications of this are of interest. In the recital the *pure* makes a double appeal to his *atua* to cause his dart to be successful for their own sakes—a tactful reference—and also to save him from having to sit with lowered head from shame. If such an elder, sitting listening anxiously, hears shouts of *"Ku kai, ku kai,"* which proclaim his success, then he lifts his head, and with a whoop of *"Iefu!"* the *forua*, gives vent to his pleasure. "Lift his head, yell, has looked at the land, has lightened his body," is the graphic description of this moment given by one of them.

The sign that a dart has passed all the others is given from the far end of the *marae* by waving of branches and reed shafts up and down. From this "flagging" the spectators and the thrower know that the dart has "eaten," and shouts respond.

But if no cries greet his ears, then the chief or the elder sits with head downcast in confusion at the failure of his *mua tika*. It is not that he is merely vexed at his lack of success in the game; his keener emotion of shame arises from the fact that his pride in his family has not been sustained, and his deities have shown that they lack power or energy to assist him. He has been "let down" by both men and gods, and in the sight of all the people. He may sit there and brave out the situation, or rise and go to his house in shame. Or else he may bend down and in a whisper remonstrate with his deities.

"Kaia! totou kava e fai atu nei
Se tafuri ki ei!

Sise aŋa ki te kava
Kae aŋa kotou na ki a uruao?"
"Look here! your kava which is made here
Why not turn to it!
You don't look at the kava,
But you there are facing to the woods?"

The touch of sarcasm in the last phrase is meant to bring home to the erring *atua* their responsibilities, which they are apparently either shirking or dreamily failing to realize. Are they, instead of attending to the ritual, gazing away over the landscape? This is one of the rare formulae in which any reproof is offered to the supernatural beings who in Tikopian belief rule in absolute fashion the destinies of men. But one can quite see how in the irritation of the moment a little sharper note than usual tends to creep into the normally respectful appeal!

A point of interest is that the initial throwing of the *marae*, early in the day, is the time when the *atua* are believed to exert their influence on behalf of their protégés. "The time of the gods is in the morning only, but arrived at midday, it is finished," say the natives. It is only for the first few rounds that they take control, and deity strives against deity, as man against man, for mastery. This view is quite explicable. It is in the early hours of the game, especially in the opening rounds, when interest is fresh and expectation at its highest pitch, as the result of the long preparations, that human belief, hope, and anxiety bring the supernatural to their aid. But toward midday, when arms are tiring and nerves are jaded, when the first enthusiasm has lost its edge and the relative strength of the sides is clearly seen, there is every basis for thinking that the gods have retired from the scene. Thus it is said, "The man who whoops in the early morning for a win of his dart, that is a weighty matter; but by the time the sun stands up above, when someone yells—Oh! there's nothing in it."

Some elders are not given to modesty on the score of their success in these significant early stages of the game. Thus the *pure* of Raropuka, for instance, said "Our family here does not fall behind; initial cast, win"—a rather typical statement. This confidence, which is often justified in the case of the most prominent family groups, as the one mentioned, is based partly on the acknowledged skill of the *vave* among their members but more so, as is clear from the data given, on their belief in the power of the *atua* enlisted by the *ariki* or *pure* to assist him. Each *mua tika* has its own *atua*, generally one of the principal deities of the chief or elder whose dart it is. The supernatural being who controls the destinies of the *mua tika* of sa Tafua is "Tinirau," who inhabits for the occasion the throwing stand of "Rangitisa," at the south end of the *marae*. "Varo," a son of "Tinirau," is the *atua* of "Matangi aso" the *mua tika* of sa Kafika. He went from Tafua, i.e., *ŋa Tamaroa*, to be the deity of *ŋa Pure*, so the story goes. Sa Taumako and sa Fangarere have as respective gods for their *tika* "Te Atua i te tai" (Pusiuraura) embodied in the grey eel of the reef, who is in charge of the dart "Ngau," and "Te Atua i te ava" (Tupuafiti) embodied in another banded eel. The various elders appeal mostly to Semoana, a sea deity, under a variety of names. A notable exception is the *pure* of Raropuka, who invokes his principal *atua*—"Te Amafakaro" being his name for this particular function—and is rather scornful of his colleagues for "all pulling at the same deity, pulled by one, pulled by another." Under these conflicting appeals how can the *atua* possibly assist them all to victory? More chance of success, the old sage argues, in having a deity to oneself! Two other *pure*, of Torokinga and Ratia families, address their formulae to Feke, god of the sun, whose more mundane embodiment is the octopus.

To these *atua*, in addition to appeals for the success of their own darts, the competing chiefs and elders proffer request that the chances of the *tika* of their opponents may be spoiled. Thus to his deity, whose dwelling for the occasion is in the throwing stand at "Vokisa," the north end of the *marae*, the *pure* of Raropuka says:

"Seua e a ke Te Amafakaro E!
Pi ke ki se kai mou."
"Be glanced aside by you, Te Amafakaro!
Block it for a win for yourself."

The god is requested to divert the darts of the opposition and retard them that his own may lie secure ahead and win. Moreover, if a youth of this family comes as a novice (*tama fou*—new son) to throw in the *marae*, the *pure* does his best to assist him to gain the much coveted leading position. He addresses the *atua*:

"Te Amafakaro E!
Pi se kai mou ki tau tama fou."
"Te Amafakaro E!
Block a win for you, for your new son."

The form of expression is somewhat condensed; it implies, of course, that it is the darts of the opponents which are to be hindered.

Technique and Procedure

The actual procedure of the game is carried through with great smoothness and ease. This is due to the familiarity of the players with the conditions, but is also assisted by the care and oversight exercised by each "chief of the dart group." Of these there are two, termed *ariki te kau tika*, and their functions are essentially those of captains of the sides. The office is one of standard privilege, the same man retaining it year after year until through age or disability he retires from the game. None but an expert, of course, will hold the position. It tends to run in certain families of rank, though not actually vested in them by tradition. The appointment is made by selection at the instance of the chiefs and men of authority on the side, though in the absence of the real captain a substitute may be chosen by the players to act as their leader for the day. The *ariki* of the side is responsible for the order in which his men throw; this he signifies to them by a word or look as they all sit awaiting their turn. It is he also who must judge the fortunes of the game, and at a critical moment select as thrower a man who may be able to retrieve a bad position or to restore the shattered confidence of the side. Usually the poor players make their cast first, while the experts bring up the rear. If, however, the foremost dart of his opponents has lain unbeaten for several rounds, and they have again made a series of good casts, the captain may reverse the procedure. He says quietly to a *vave* "*Tau tou muri fakatoŋa*," an order to him to lead off in the attempt to surpass their adversaries. The man binds on his throwing ring without a word, rises and hurls his dart. If he should be unsuccessful the captain orders another player to follow, and so on, until the foremost dart of the opposition has been beaten, or the *vave* of his side are exhausted. A superior throw made at the opportune moment can have great effect on the side, where so much depends on the confidence of the players.

When a side has been well beaten in the preceding match, and excitement is keen, the *ariki* of the *kau tika* gives the command, "Not a man may stand up; we shall throw touching the ground only" *(Siei se taŋata ke tu i ruŋa; tatou ka tika po kere fuere)*. This means that to lend greater impetus to his cast every man must throw the whole weight of his body behind it, so that after projecting the dart he loses his balance and is forced to put his hands to the ground to save himself, or may even fall right over. (See Plates 2 and 3.)

The course of the match is a regular one. The opening throw is made as described above, and the rest of the players make their casts in turn. All who have not yet thrown in the round squat in a semi-circle in rear of the throwing stand, and behind them again are the spectators; if a chief or man of rank is present a lane is left through the crowd for him to see down the length of the *marae*, and observe the progress of the game. Women are nearly as numerous as men, though they take no active part.

As the turn of each player comes he fits the throwing ring on to his finger and makes it fast, then rises to his feet. Holding the *tika* across his body, the butt in his right hand, with its end pressed hard against the tip

Plate 3—A dart match in Tikopia: The end of the throw. The dart is speeding along the pitch while the player rises from the ground.

of his fore-finger, and supporting the head with his left, he advances with a graceful swaying motion—the *oriori*—looking straight in front of him, his face serious, with a rather self-conscious air. Then he quickens his pace and covers the last few yards in a sudden sprint, the muscles of his calves standing out noticeably with the effort. At the same time he releases his left hand and swings the *tika* round, poising it in the air and drawing back his right arm to the full as he does so. Reaching the throwing stand, with his eyes firmly fixed on his goal, he checks for an instant and hurls the dart forward in a round-arm movement, with all his strength and no little grace. The arm is not bent at the elbow at the moment of projection, but swung from the shoulder, while at the same time an added impetus is given by twisting the body away and down to the left as the shaft leaves the finger. An energetic player will always throw himself off his balance by the effort, and at the completion of the cast be on his hands and knees or even prone on the ground. The motion imparted to the dart is partly tangential, which means that any mistiming in release causes it to fly to one side of the pitch or even hurtle off into the bushes. Inaccurate release seems to be delayed rather than anticipatory, i.e., most of the wide throws tend to go off to the left. As will be realized, a slight variation in the angle of projection is not difficult in such a method, and makes a considerable difference to the result at the end of a hundred yards or so. Minor variations are corrected to some extent by the slightly hollow formation of the *marae*, with its sloping banks on either side. This is not sufficient, however, to affect materially the course of the dart. The *marae* again, is not a perfect pitch, and a skilled player can assist his throw by taking advantage of a hard patch of ground on one side.

There are many points in the technique of throwing which have to be mastered by one who wishes to be considered an expert. It should not be said of his dart, for instance, "*e meme*" (it sleeps). This means that the *tika* on leaving the hand flies straight through the air horizontally. Such a throw is not good, since the head gradually sinks down and on striking digs into the earth and is slowed up. A high throw again is almost certain to meet with failure, since the steepness of the descending arc makes it almost inevitable that the head will check on striking and not slide freely along. The ideal is for the hand at the instant of actual release to give a slight downward jerk thus depressing the shaft and elevating the head of the dart so that it flies along at first at an angle to the horizontal plane. Gradually the head, with its greater weight, lowers again to the level of the shaft, the dart flattens out, and in that position strikes the ground and glides away with minimum loss of momentum. Of such a throw it is said "*Ku toto laui.*" (It has fallen well.) The above remarks indicate the native theory of casting the dart. They reveal an empirical knowledge of some at least of the elementary principles of dynamics—and the presence of an intelligent capacity to apply these to problems of social interest.

Accidents to the dart are not uncommon. A weak shaft snaps as it leaves the finger, and the *tika* falls miserably, or a poor lashing gives way at the moment of impact with the ground, and the head rolls free. Mishaps of this type, however, are soon remedied as the hard-wood head does not suffer, except from contact with a rare stone, and spare shafts are easily obtainable. In the Marae lasi there is a definite obstacle in the course, a large rock some 4 feet across the top, projecting a few inches above the ground on the seaward side. It lies near the spot where the darts pitch after their flight, and is a constant source of annoyance since the head of any *tika* which lands on it is almost certain to be ruined. Efforts have been made at various times to dig down and remove it, but its base appears to be very large. Report is therefore that its roots "go down to the gods," and are immovable. The boulder is called "Matariki," the same name as is applied to the Pleiades, and it is thought that there may be some vague connection between them. Beyond the fact that both are female and therefore apparently not too well disposed to men, little seems to be known on this point.

Each man after making his throw springs to his feet, takes a look down the *marae* to see how his dart has gone, and then walks off down the path which runs through the bushes along the side to the far end. On the way he picks up his *tika*, if it has fallen far behind or flown off into the undergrowth, and joins his companions to await the next throw. If as sometimes happens, a dart comes to rest with its shaft lying athwart the pitch, there is a shout of *"Foi kaso!"* (A reed!) from players and spectators, and someone near hastens to lay it straight or remove it.

The round of casts is made from alternate ends of the *marae*, and is so arranged that each side throws last from its own base. Thus if the opening throw is made from the north end, the base of the *Pure*, the *Tamaroa* lead off and the *Pure* follow. All then go to the other end of the ground—the earlier throwers are already seated there—and this time the *Pure* begin and the *Tamaroa* follow. Each side thus throws twice in succession, first concluding the round at its own end, then opening the next round at its opponents' end. Moreover, if to-day the *Tamaroa* have made the opening throw, then the next day the *Pure* will lead off the match—from their opponents' end, of course—and so preserve a strict rotation. In the order of players no such definiteness is observed, as this depends largely upon the decision of the *ariki* of the side. The sacred *mua tika* with which the match is opened is nearly always borne by the same man; the privilege of carrying it may even pass from father to son.

When the throw of one side is complete the darts of the other begin to glide up. The principle is to keep the field as clear as possible for succeeding players. All darts of the following side therefore which fail to achieve a win are at once removed, together with all darts of the first side which they have passed. Only the unbeaten darts of the first side remain. But once their *mua tika*, their leading dart, is passed all are removed except this, which is left as an index to the progress of their opponents. Any darts of the latter which pass it or equal it score; all others are taken off at once. Usually the darts which have been successful are allowed to remain till the end of the round; sometimes, however, they are taken off the pitch after having been notified to the man who has been detailed to keep the score. Even if a *tika* of the following side does no more than lap the reed shaft of the *mua tika* of the opposition it is a *kai* and is counted. The *mua tika* is beaten.

A single diagram will illustrate the course of the game [see Figure 4].

Numbers 1, 2, 3, and 4 are the leading darts of the *Tamaroa*, their others having fallen behind. Number 5, the opening dart of the *Pure* comes up, and is removed, together with 3 and 4, which it has beaten. Number 6 comes up and is removed, together with 2. Numbers 7 and 8 come to rest and are taken away. Thus as the position lies, the *Tamaroa* hold the lead and will count one point to their score, whereas the *Pure* have not secured a *kai* at all. But when 9 comes up later, followed by 10, then 1 is doubly beaten, though it is still left in place till the end of the round to enable any later throws of the *Pure* to be judged. If none reach it, then the *Pure* have scored two.

Usages of Marae

Apart from the ordinary rules of the game which comprise its basic organization, there are a number of customs or usages approved by tradition. Some of these have already been described, others are given below.

In the ordinary way a player gives no sign if his dart makes a winning throw; there is no visible appearance of the pleasure which it is known he feels. If his cast has been made with a brand new dart, however, he is entitled to celebrate his success with a whoop or *forua* of *"Iefu!"* as the result is flagged from the other end. *"Tika fou,"* "New dart," say people to one another in explanation. If a winning cast is made by a novice on his first day at the adult game in the *marae*, then also a *forua* is given, the yell of the *tama fou*.

The normal good throw averages about 140 yards, depending to some extent on the condition of the *marae*—"the state of the wicket," so to speak. It is recognized that when the pitch has been cleaned after lying idle for some time that it takes about half a day for the surface to settle and harden and be played into good throwing order. A long throw will run down into the hollow behind the far base. Of such a dart it is said *"Ku to ki muri,"* "Has fallen behind." An exceptionally good throw may exceed this, and the dart emerging out of the hollow again may come to rest in rear. Such a long cast is rare and is greeted by shrieks of *"Iefu! Iefu!"* from the spectators, who crowd in to gaze with astonishment at the dart as it lies there. In this case a stone is planted to mark the spot and so leave a record for future generations with the distance accurately preserved. Such a dart is said to *sora*, to hide; it goes so far as

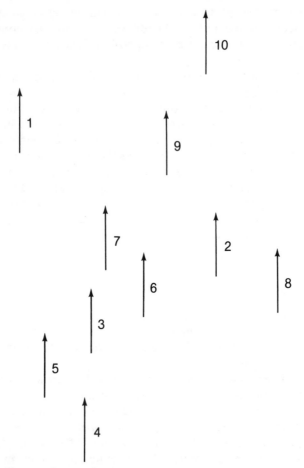

Figure 4—Course of a round.

almost to escape observation! Great interest is taken in the feats of noted *vave*, and incidents of their prowess are related for years afterwards.

Thus Pa Fonga-muna, tall, broad-chested, with sloping shoulders, was renowned from his youth as a thrower of exceptional powers. At an early date he established his reputation by a long cast which allowed him to plant a stone beyond the far throwing base at Marae lasi. Not content with this, from time to time he kept shifting the stone further and further away as he made longer and longer throws. Another *vave* was Pa Veterei, now dead, a man of really exceptional strength, who from the accounts of credible eye-witnesses could twist bar iron in his hands and snap an ordinary chain. One day Pa Fonga-muna was *tautari tika*, last player on one side, and made a phenomenally long cast which caused the crowd to give a shout, and rush in to see. Pa Veterei was sitting among his own *kau tika* when a man near him said, "Go and lie on the butt of his shaft" (i.e., Lead off for your side). He did so, and to the amazement of the crowd, who were still admiring the former throw, he made one as far. The stones of the two *vave* now stand side by side.

A *vave* of old, Pa Mataioa, grandfather of the present man of that name, is credited with special powers. If his dart did not run true but veered off to the bushes at the side, he tapped the ground with his finger and out it sprang again to glide onwards in a straight line! *"E fai e ŋa atua ma tea,"* said my informant reflectively. "It is done by the gods, perhaps!" This is the man whose record stone is ahead of all the rest at the "Vokisa" end of the Marae.

Mua tika of families and clans are treated with some respect. If the thrower of "Matangi aso" the ceremonial dart of sa Kafika scores with his initial cast he continues to throw first in order for his side for a number of rounds. But if after a cast or two the *tika* "falls badly," and has no success then he retires into the body of the side and lets another player take his place. I have heard a young man rebuked by an elder relative who used himself to bear the *mua tika* for disregarding this custom.

"The *mua tika* of sa Taumako is bad," it is said. This dart called "Ngau" makes a man's shoulder ache unless he puts it down after the first two or three throws, and takes up another less ceremonial implement. Then no such unpleasantness ever occurs. *"E tapu; te atua e fakatino ki ei,"* "Is sacred; the god embodies himself in it," is the reason given for this—that is, the eel god mentioned earlier. The dart has a further peculiarity of more value: "On the Marae lasi when the *tika* of the *Tamaroa* has hidden, has run behind, the *mua tika* of sa Taumako goes steadily, goes on, and finally overtakes it."

Another custom of the *marae* is of an economic character. When an exceptional throw is made by a man and he excels all the rest on that day, it is his duty to prepare food in the next day or two and to present it to the other members of the side. The obligation is a considerable one since as much as three or four bowls of pudding and a corresponding number of baskets of cooked taro and breadfruit are required. If a man is a noted *vave*, and always in the lead, the burden on his resources is distinctly heavy. In the case of Pa Fonga-muna mentioned above, this was so onerous that he often used to throw lightly to avoid having to make the customary feast. This man has now ceased to attend the *tika* on account of having been sneered at by the Ariki Kafika on one occasion for the manner in which he had decorated himself. Ordinarily the players are ornamented *(rakei)* with circlets of flowers and aromatic leaves, and bangles of shell. If the match is a sacred one, however, no ornaments may be worn except by the *vave*, who are allowed to have flowers or tassels *(sei)* in their ears. His appearance on this occasion seems to have been quite legitimate, but Tikopians are very quick to take offense. The chief thought fit to be sarcastic and the man resented the affront to his dignity.

The signal for the conclusion of a match is generally given about mid-day, and is made at the instance of either party. It has already been mentioned that each side throws last from its own end. If now one side coming down to the end of its opponents to commence a round sees a man of that group walk up to the throwing base and launch a dart then they know that the match has ceased. "*Te tika kua tuku,*" "The dart game has been laid down." All the players immediately begin to disperse when this traditional signal is given.

Some Emotional Aspects of the Game

The general interest taken in the sport of dart throwing, and the complexity of regulation and ceremony surrounding it are associated with an emotional situation of considerable intensity. An analysis of the principal elements involved can be based on the concrete evidence afforded by the appearance and actions of the players, their comments on the states of feeling experienced at various moments in the game, and also the ideas crystallized in more permanent form in the favorite Tikopian medium of expression, the dance-song. Such data have a sociological value as illustrating the intimate relation between individual emotional attitudes and group interests.

The observer attending a dart match for the first time is struck by the intentness of the players on their game and the curious absence of much of the babel of talk and laughter which usually accompanies any activity where a number of people is present. The spectators are vivacious enough, but the players are quiet. A man rising to throw his dart wears a distinctly serious, even strained, expression. This is due to his intense consciousness of himself as a single figure set over against the assembled crowd. As explicit statement indicates, he knows that he is the cynosure of all eyes, and that the next few moments will earn for him applause—or silence. There is no other form of activity in the community where for a short space of time he is so definitely alone under full public observation, with the inevitable testing of his own powers as the upshot. Success means harmony with the interests of his side; failure means a lack of harmonious adjustment. Little wonder that the player is often nervous as he advances to make his cast, that he is elated if he scores, or depressed if his dart falls short. It is interesting to note how the behavior of the spectators accommodates itself to the situation. An exceptionally good throw is greeted with applause, but usually no demonstration follows a poor throw. Where from the nature of these people laughter and jesting at the expense of those who fail might be expected, silence alone is found, or at most a faint murmur of commiseration. This is due not so much to sympathy with the unsuccessful player as to tacit recognition of the fact that the shame of failure is great, and that any aggravation of it may lead to serious consequences, even suicide. Reference has already been made to the plucking of coconuts by the winners after a crushing victory in order to smooth the feelings of the losers.

This feeling of shame is a very real thing—at least among the good players. Thus it is said *"Te kau tika ka tikaia e take kau tika, na vave e poi, sise laui; matea tona fakama, e faia ko ia sise makeke."* "The dart side shall be out-thrown by another dart side, its expert who goes is not good (is not happy in mind); very great is his shame, because he was not strong." This simple statement is quoted for the light it throws incidentally on the sense of responsibility which the expert has for the fortunes of his side, as well as for the intensity of his feelings after defeat. (In the native speech the emphasis on the words *sise laui, matea,* and *fakama,* all terms of great significance to a Tikopian, give a strength to the statement which it is difficult to convey in translation.) The physical signs of such inner disturbance are well known to the natives. It is noted that with some people the face becomes suffused with blood. *"Ku toto fuere ona mata"*; others lose their temper and show signs of anger *(fai toa)*. Others still after a poor exhibition slink off into the bushes and do not appear again at the match that day. It may be observed also that a similar metaphor is in vogue among the Tikopians as among ourselves to express the desire of a person ashamed to disappear from public view. *"Matea na fakama—feurufi ki tekuŋa kere,"* is said of such an one. "Very great is his shame—dive into the ground" (i.e., he wishes he could disappear in this fashion). In conversation natives elaborate these points with much vigor of expression.

Failure to achieve a win is sometimes felt so keenly as to lead to tragic consequences. The recent suicide of the eldest son of the heir to the chieftainship of Tafua is traced to this immediate cause. The lad attended the match as a novice and failed to score. Being of an excitable temperament, he burned with disgrace and that same night, after dancing furiously for some hours, put off secretly in a small canoe in a raging storm. He was not seen again, and the tragedy has cast a gloom over his family.

Songs of the Tika

In Tikopia the composition of a dance song is one of the common modes of giving expression to an emotional idea which a person wishes to make public—whether it be in praise of oneself or friend, in vituperation of a thief or a rejected mistress, or merely exultation in some particular phase of living. Where emotion occurs in songs it is to some extent conventionalized, if only for the reason that these have to submit to a traditional artistic form. But in spite of limitations they do manage to give a very fair indication of the feelings which actuate the composer—or rather librettist, as he really is. In the case of the dart thrower the songs reveal the actuality of his personal problem conceived in relation to the position of his side and of that impendent larger group, the community as a whole.

Examples are numerous, but a few will be sufficient for illustration.

The first is an ancient song commemorating the anxiety of a player—of rather indifferent caliber, it would seem—after he has made his throw.

Tafito: *"Taku tika kua ifo i a turaŋa*
Ku aua e ŋa mavero
Ka arofa koau se forua.

Safe: *E pote pote ko te manava*
A mata o te fenua
Ku katoa ki te Marae."[7]

Translation:
"My dart has sped down from the throwing stands
It has been caught up by the experts
I shall be sorry and not shout.

Throbbing, throbbing is the heart
Eyes of the land
Are all assembled at the Pitch."

The term *pote* is a synonym for the more usual *pore*, which describes the pulsing of the heart—in this case as the thrower, the momentary center of attraction, waits to see if he has managed to score. The phrase "eyes of the land" is a vivid metaphor to indicate the crowd of onlookers. In comment on this song, which is well known, it was remarked rather needlessly "The man does not want his dart to be 'eaten.' "

Another song of very rhythmic qualities relates a tale of shattered hopes.

Tafito: *"E kou rotu ki te katoaŋa*
Tika o taŋata
Rere toutasi.

Kupu: *E tu oke ou kau oriori*
Ka vero ki te roto Marae
Ka talevaleva koau fakaturu.

Safe: *Fakateka u-e!*
Fakateka i a turaŋa
Se ne forua."

Translation:

"O! I am keen on the assembly
Of dart-throwing people
Each running singly.

I stand up to sway the dart
That will be thrown along the middle of the Pitch
It spins in circles, I lower my head.

Cast myself down O!
Cast myself on the throwing-grounds
And no one shouted."

This is intended to accompany a dance of the *ta marie*, the "gentle beat" type, and was composed by Pa Tavi, father of the present elder of that name. As usual in songs, much meaning is condensed into a single phrase. In explanation of the words *rere toutasi*, "running singly,"—it was pointed out by natives that each man carries his own responsibility as he advances to throw; he is alone, can have no help and is observed by all eyes. The burden of the lament is that despite the enthusiasm of the thrower and all his good intentions to make an accurate cast, despite his energetic efforts to give his dart impetus by hurling himself to the ground, it flies poorly with a twirling motion of the shaft. As a result there is no applause from the crowd to signify a win, and the thrower has to hang his head in confusion.

Of even more gloomy tenor is a brief song of the *ŋore* type composed by Pa Rangi furi, eldest son of the Ariki Tafua and father of the boy who was lost at sea:

Tafito: *"Ku kasā kita ku raria mai*
Taku poipoi fua rei i taku tafau.

Safe: *E fora e fora i a turaŋa*
O te kai aŋafuru."

Translation:

"I have been beaten by the *kasā* and the *rari*
My wandering naked on my walks.

Are spread, are spread on the throwing-stands
The tenfold wins.

A long commentary would be necessary to do justice to this composition, but the general significance can briefly be made clear. It commemorates in fact an actual defeat suffered by the composer, and suggests that his own efforts to score were no more effective than an empty-handed stroll across the Marae would have been. The "tenfold wins" mentioned are of course those of his opponents, who have seemed to have covered the throwing-base with darts in their facility for scoring.

From one point of view the frankness of the composer in exposing his inferiority might be laid directly at the door of relief for pent-up emotion. It seems to be true indeed that song-making does provide the Tikopian with an outlet for that type of passion over which he might otherwise be inclined to brood. The song represents a concrete achievement, the conversion of feelings and impulses into words, which in itself offers a form of relief. But the element of spontaneity is always restricted and enchanneled by the traditional verse-form and the requirements of rhythm—for the essential purpose of the song is to act as a dance-chorus. Moreover, the whole machinery of society which regulates every thought and act of the individual allows him only conditioned modes of expression. The diction of these and similar songs is surprisingly free and unfettered, but it records elements of personal emotion which have become somewhat formalized and reduced to order in their passage through the social mechanism.

A brighter tone is given in a song attributed to Pu Mataioa, the great expert, who as may be remembered used somewhat unorthodox methods to attain his supremacy:

Tafito: *"Taku tika ku maua ruŋa*
Fenaifo papa foi uru toa
Ku feŋaromaki vare i roto Marae.

Kupu: *"E auo ko te tika*
Ka saro moi i a kaso
Rioriokino mai i a potu e rua."

Translation:

"My dart is superior
Comes down, strikes the ground with its wooden head
Then is lost to the eye (in its swift flight) in the middle
of the Pitch.

Surpassing is the dart!
Will be flagged hither with reed-stems
Waving here from both ends."

The ring of confidence and success in this song needs no comment.

As a final example of these compositions bearing on the *tika* that of Pu Torokinga, a former expert of renown *(te vave tu o te marae)* may be considered. The song originated in the circumstance that he, as a skilled player of the *Tamaroa*, had been allotted the *mua tika* of sa Tafua to throw in a match. At the opening ceremony and again in the next round he cast the dart, and each time without success; it fell with a circling motion of the shaft. Folk then began to laugh at the idea of giving the *mua tika* to be handled by such a blunderer. Much mortified at this the *vave* rejected the *mua tika* and took up his own dart, with which in a single throw he redeemed his reputation and blocked the progress of the opposition. In comment on the first part of this incident he composed the following song:

Tafito: *"Takutaku ko toku raveravea i te roki*
          Takutaku ko toku raveravea i te tika ne moe i Uta.

Kupu: *Se ne tuku kau sara ki oku tupua*
          Taku moe ne kau ono ki oi.

Safe: *Rerefaki ke vero ki ruŋo*
          Ku to talevaleva
          Kau fakaturu ifo
          I o kata ŋa mavero."

Translation:

> "Ashamed for my being gazed on in the west
> Ashamed for my being gazed on through the dart that
>   slept in Uta.
>
> Why not have left me to keep in touch with my own
>   deities
> My sleep that I looked after?
>
> Run to hurl it above
> Has fallen with twirling shaft
> I bow down
> Amid the laughter of the experts."

The "dart that slept in Uta" is the *mua tika* of Tafua which, in accordance with the ceremonies already described, had been left overnight in the sacred house of the chief. "My sleep" refers to his own dart, which he had treated and looked after in similar fashion in order to obtain success with it. Hence his desire to keep in touch with his own deities on whom he could rely, through the medium of his own dart, and his complaint when he had to take the *mua tika* of Tafua. "The west" means the "Marae lasi" in Faea, on that side of the island, where the incident took place. The final stanza, in which translation as usual has been compressed to follow the text, describes the result when he attempted to make a cast with the intractable dart, and the ridicule of the spectators.

General Observations

This analysis of the songs and general emotional background of the *tika* has been given because without a knowledge of this aspect it is difficult for anyone unacquainted with the game to understand the interest it possesses for the native and the importance attached to winning and losing. Certainly the thrill of the sport itself, the impulse to self-assertion, the desire to beat an opponent with whom the rivalry is traditional, play a strong part, but the secret of the intensity lies in sensitiveness to public opinion. This then, with its implication of shame through the public exposure of defeat, becomes a factor of sociological and not merely psychological interest.

From these songs and other data it can be realized how the game of *tika* comes to pass beyond the bounds of simple play for exercise and relaxation, and to attain considerable importance in the general economic and religious life, in addition to its reactions on the social organization of the community and on the personality of its component members.

The relation of the player to his side is significant. The side is a permanent institution with a name and a definite place in the social organization, a traditional opponent and a variety of local, historical, and mythological associations which give it further stability. It is the basic feature of the match; it persists generation after generation while the individual members drop out and are replaced. The score, the focus of interest, is kept for the side alone, and no total is made of the winning throws of any single player. Energy of throwing and obedience to the instructions of the captain are expected; it is the recognized duty of a man to 'play for his side,' though there is not much explicit reference to the fact. Yet, naturally enough, while the results of the match to the side are followed with the greatest keenness, the popular interest and enthusiasm are displayed most intensely in regard to the feats of individual players. And the player himself though he throws for the advantage of his side, and is genuinely concerned for its success, is most conscious of his own personal performance and for it feels the greatest intensity of emotion. In particular the condensation of feeling in the songs composed about the game reveals this essentially personal element. The identity of interest between the individual player and his side is not complete, since success of the one does not necessarily connote that of the other. Nevertheless they are so closely related that harmonious adjustment is easily obtained. In the case of the community as a whole the permanent rivalry of the two sides is a constant factor of discordance, but its effects are as constantly overborne by more important social ties.

Sport, as an integral feature in the life of many primitive peoples, offers a number of problems for investigation. Some of these are concerned with questions of organization, of the nature of the factors which differentiate a vague play activity from a regularly established game with clearly defined procedure, hemmed in on every side by rules of strong sanction. Other problems are those of incentive, of the extent to which the impulses to recreation, bodily exercise, and relaxation are involved with other characteristics of a different order, as pride, shame, curiosity, sympathy, loyalty, associated with a more complex set of emotional reactions. An inquiry of a more physiological pattern, though shot with threads of social interest, considers the differential skill and energy displayed by those engaged in the pastime and the extent to which this becomes a matter of recognized concern to the community. The relation of primitive sport to other aspects of the social life, its unique cultural value on the one hand, and its inter-reaction with economic, aesthetic, and religious affairs on the other, presents a field of research which merits even more attention than it has already received.

This brief account of the dart game of Tikopia may at least indicate the reality of these problems, and the human interest to be found in the study of them.

Notes

1. The data which form the basis of this article are taken from the results of my expedition to Tikopia 1928-29, made under the auspices of the Australian National Research Council, to whom my acknowledgments are made elsewhere in this number. For the accompanying sketches I am indebted to my brother, Mr. Cedric Firth.
2. A game of similar type, known variously as *cheda*, or *phyeda*, or *phyelida* in some villages, and *sika* in others, is played among the Angami Nagas and on the plains of Assam (Hutton, 1929).
3. This word *manu* is the equivalent of the widely-known Oceanic *mana*, which latter term is also used in Tikopia, as an alternative, though less frequently. The Tikopian use of this concept appears to lack that more mystical significance apparently found elsewhere. In this community it represents the concrete idea of success or efficacy in definite situations as the cure of sickness or the production of crops or fish.
4. For a short account of these clans see Firth (1930).
5. At one period of my stay a thriving trade was established between the young boys of Matautu and those of Rofaea, the former obtaining *Conus* shells from the latter in exchange for empty tins, begged from my house.
6. The term *pure* means literally "married man," and is also used as the name for one of the sides in the dart game. As such it should be distinguished from its homonym meaning an Elder or Councillor of a chief. The latter has also the forms *matapure*, and *pure matua*. (Cf. Tongan *matabule*.)
7. Songs in Tikopia follow a definite verse form. The opening stanza is termed *tafito*, a word applied to the base of the trunk of a tree, and more generally to

the beginning, or origin of anything. The final stanza is called *safe*, the name also of the fruit stalk of the banana. Any intermediate stanza, there being usually only one, is termed the *kupu i roto*, the "words in the middle."

References

FIRTH, R. Report on research in Tikopia. *Oceania*, 1930, **1**(1), 105-117.

HUTTON, J.H. *Man*, September 1929, No. 112.

Chapter 11
The Cherokee Ball Play

JAMES MOONEY

T he Indian game of the ball play is common to all the tribes from Maine to California, and from the sunlit waters of the Gulf of Mexico to the frozen shores of Hudson bay. When or where the Indian first obtained the game it is not our province to inquire, but we may safely assume that the brown-skinned savage shaped the pliant hickory staff with his knife and flint and twisted the net of bear sinew ages before visions of a western world began to float through the brain of the Italian dreamer.

In its general features, Indian ball play was the same all over the country, with this important exception, that among the northern and western tribes the player used but one ball stick, while in the Gulf States each contestant carried two and caught the ball between them. In California men and women played together, while among most of the more warlike tribes to the eastward it was pre-eminently a manly game, and it was

---

From the *American Anthropologist*, April 1890, 3(2), 105-132. Copyright 1890 by the American Anthropological Association. Reprinted with permission.

believed to insure defeat to a party if a woman even so much as touched a ball stick.

The game has a history, even though that history be fragmentary, like all that goes to make up the sum of our knowledge of the aboriginal race. The French, whose light-hearted gaiety and ready adaptability so endeared them to the hearts of their wild allies, were quick to take up the Indian ball game as a relief from the dreary monotony of long weeks in the garrison or lonely days in the forest. It became a favorite pastime, and still survives among the creoles of Louisiana under the name of *Raquette*, while in the more invigorating atmosphere of the north it assumed a new life, and, with the cruder features eliminated, became the famous Canadian national game of *La Crosse*. It was by means of a cleverly devised stratagem of a ball play that the savage warriors of Pontiac were enabled to surprise and capture the English garrison of old Fort Mackinaw in 1763. Two years before the Ojibwa chief had sent the ominous message: "Englishmen, although you have conquered the French, you have not yet conquered us"; but the warning was unheeded. The vengeance of the savage may sleep, but never dies. On the fourth of June, 1763, the birthday of King George of England, the warriors of two great tribes assembled in front of the fort, ostensibly to play a game in honor of the occasion and to decide the tribal championship. The commandant himself came out to encourage his favorites and bet on the result, while the soldiers leaned against the palisades and the squaws sat about in groups, all intently watching every movement of the play. Suddenly there comes a crisis in the game. One athletic young fellow with a powerful stroke sends the ball high in air, and as it descends in a graceful curve it rolls along the ground to the gate of the fort, followed by 400 yelling savages. But look! As they run each painted warrior snatches from his squaw the hatchet which she had concealed under her blanket, and the next moment it is buried in the brain of the nearest soldier. The English, taken completely by surprise, are cut down without resistance. In a few minutes all is over, and a solitary trader, looking out from the garret where he had been hidden by a friendly squaw, sees the ground covered with the bodies of his slaughtered countrymen, while with yells of savage victory their butchers are drinking the blood scooped up in the hollow of their joined hands.

Let us turn from this dark picture to more recent times. In the late war 300 of the East Cherokee entered the Confederate service, and in the summer of 1863 — just a century after the fatal day of Mackinaw — a detachment of them was left to guard the bridge over the Holston River, at Strawberry Plains, in Tennessee. But an Indian never takes kindly to anything in the nature of garrison duty, and time hung heavy on their hands. At last, in a moment of inspiration, one man proposed that they make some ball sticks and have a game. The suggestion was received with hearty favor, and soon all hands were at work putting up the poles, shaping the hickory sticks, and twisting the bark for the netting. The preliminary ceremonies were dispensed with for once, the players stripped, and the game began, while the rest of the Indians looked on with eager interest. Whether Wolf Town or the Big Cove would have won that game will never be known, for in the middle of it an advanced detachment of the "Yankees" slipped in, burned the bridge, and were moving forward, when the Cherokee, losing all interest in the game, broke for cover and left the Federals in possession of the ground.

In 1834, before the removal of the Cherokee to the west, a great game was played near the present site of Jasper, Georgia, between the settlements of Hickory Log and Coosawattee, in which there were 18 players on a side, and the chiefs of the rival settlements wagered $1,000 apiece on the result.

There is a tradition among the few old traders still living in upper Georgia, to the effect that a large tract in this part of the state was won by the Cherokee from the Creeks in a ball play. There are no Cherokee now living in Georgia to substantiate the story, but I am inclined to put some faith in it from the fact that Coosawattee, although the name of a Cherokee settlement, signifies "the old country of the Creeks." The numerous localities in the Southern States bearing the name of "Ball Flat," "Ball Ground," and "Ball Play" bear witness to the fondness of the Indian for the play. To the red warrior it was indeed a royal game, worthy to be played on the king's day, with the empire of the northwest for the stake.

As speed and suppleness of limb and a considerable degree of muscular strength are prime requisites in the game, the players are always selected from among the most athletic young men, and to be known as an expert player was a distinction hardly less coveted than fame as a warrior. To bring the game to its highest perfection, the best players voluntarily subjected themselves to a regular course of training and conjuring; so that in time they came to be regarded as professionals who might be counted on to take part in every contest, exactly like the professional ball player among the whites. To farther incite them to strain every nerve for victory, two settlements, or sometimes two rival tribes, were always pitted against each other, and guns, blankets, horses — everything the Indian had or valued — were staked upon the result. The prayers and ceremonies of the shamans, the speeches of the old men, and the songs of the dancers were all alike calculated to stimulate to the highest pitch the courage and endurance of the contestants.

It is a matter of surprise that so little has been said of this game by travelers and other observers of Indian life. Powers, in his great work upon the California tribes, dismisses it in a brief paragraph; the notices in Schoolcraft's six bulky volumes altogether make hardly two pages, while even the artist Catlin, who spent years with the wild tribes, has but little to say of the game itself, although his spirited ball pictures go far to make amends for the deficiency. All these writers, however, appear to have confined their attention almost entirely to the play alone, noticing the ball-play dance only briefly, if at all, and seeming to be completely unaware of the secret ceremonies and incantations—the fasting, bathing, and other mystic rites—which for days and weeks precede the play and attend every step of the game; so that it may be said without exaggeration that a full exposition of the Indian ball play would furnish material for a fair sized volume. During several field seasons spent with the East Cherokee in North Carolina, the author devoted much attention to the study of the mythology and ceremonial of this game, which will now be described as it exists today among these Indians. For illustration, the last game witnessed on the reservation, in September, 1889, will be selected.

According to a Cherokee myth, the animals once challenged the birds to a great ball play. The wager was accepted, the preliminaries were arranged, and at last the contestants assembled at the appointed spot—the animals on the ground, while the birds took position in the tree-tops to await the throwing up of the ball. On the side of the animals were the bear, whose ponderous weight bore down all opposition; the deer, who excelled all others in running; and the terrapin, who was invulnerable to the stoutest blows. On the side of the birds were the eagle, the hawk, and the great *Tlániwă*—all noted for their swiftness and power of flight. While the latter were pruning their feathers and watching every motion of their adversaries below they noticed two small creatures, hardly larger than mice, climbing up the tree on which was perched the leader of the birds. Finally they reached the top and humbly asked the captain to be allowed to join in the game. The captain looked at them a moment and, seeing that they were four-footed, asked them why they did not go to the animals where they properly belonged. The little things explained that they had done so, but had been laughed at and rejected on account of their diminutive size. On hearing their story the bird captain was disposed to take pity on them, but there was one serious difficulty in the way—how could they join the birds when they had no wings? The eagle, the hawk, and the rest now crowded around, and after some discussion it was decided to try and make wings for the little fellows. But how to do it! All at once, by a happy inspiration, one bethought himself of the drum which was to be used in the dance. The head was made of ground-hog leather, and perhaps a corner could be cut off and utilized for wings. No sooner suggested than done. Two pieces of leather taken from the drumhead were cut into shape and attached to the legs of one of the small animals, and thus originated *Tlameha*, the bat. The ball was now tossed up, and the bat was told to catch it, and his expertness in dodging and circling about, keeping the ball constantly in motion and never allowing it to fall to the ground, soon convinced the birds that they had gained a most valuable ally.

They next turned their attention to the other little creature, and now behold a worse difficulty! All their leather had been used in making the wings for the bat, and there was no time to send for more. In this dilemma it was suggested that perhaps wings might be made by stretching out the skin of the animal itself. So two large birds seized him from opposite sides with their strong bills, and by tugging and pulling at his fur for several minutes succeeded in stretching the skin between the fore and hind feet until at last the thing was done and there was *Tewa*, the flying squirrel. Then the bird captain, to try him, threw up the ball, when the flying squirrel, with a graceful bound, sprang off the limb and, catching it in his teeth, carried it through the air to another tree-top a hundred feet away.

When all was ready the game began, but at the very outset the flying squirrel caught the ball and carried it up a tree, then threw it to the birds, who kept it in the air for some time, when it dropped; but just before it reached the ground the bat seized it, and by his dodging and doubling kept it out of the way of even the swiftest of the animals until he finally threw it in at the goal, and thus won the victory for the birds. Because of their assistance on this occasion, the ball player invokes the aid of the bat and the flying squirrel and ties a small piece of the bat's wing to his ball stick or fastens it to the frame on which the sticks are hung during the dance.

The game, which of course has different names among the various tribes, is called *anetsâ* by the Cherokee. The ball season begins about the middle of summer and lasts until the weather is too cold to permit exposure of the naked body, for the players are always stripped for the game. The favorite time is in the fall, after the corn has ripened, for then the Indian has abundant leisure, and at this season a game takes place somewhere on the reservation at least every other week, while several parties are always in training. The training consists chiefly of regular athletic practice, the players of one side coming together with their ball sticks at some convenient spot of level bottom land, where they strip to the waist, divide into parties, and run, tumble, and toss the ball until the sun goes down. The Indian boys take to this sport as naturally as our youngsters take to playing soldier, and frequently in my evening walks I have come upon a group of little fellows from 8 to 12 years old, all stripped like professionals, running, yelling, and tumbling over each other in their scramble for the ball, while their ball sticks clattered together at a great rate—altogether as noisy and happy a crowd of children as can be found anywhere in the world.

In addition to the athletic training, which begins 2 or 3 weeks before the regular game, each player is put under a strict *gaktûnta*, or tabu, during the same period. He must not eat the flesh of a rabbit (of which the Indians generally are very fond) because the rabbit is a timid animal, easily alarmed and liable to lose its wits when pursued by the hunter. Hence the ball player must abstain from it, lest he too should become disconcerted and lose courage in the game. He must also avoid the meat of the frog (another item on the Indian bill of fare) because the frog's bones are brittle and easily broken, and a player who should partake of the animal would expect to be crippled in the first inning. For a similar reason he abstains from eating the young of any bird or animal, and from touching an infant. He must not eat the fish called the hog-sucker, because it is sluggish in its movements. He must not eat the herb called *atûnka* or Lamb's Quarter *(Chenopodium album)*, which the Indians use for greens, because its stalk is easily broken. Hot food and salt are also forbidden, as in the medical gaktûnta. The tabu always lasts for 7 days preceding the game, but in most cases is enforced for 28 days—i.e., 4 × 7—four and seven being sacred numbers. Above all, he must not touch a woman and the player who should violate this regulation would expose himself to the summary vengeance of his fellows. This last tabu continues also for 7 days after the game. As before stated, if a woman even so much as touches a ball stick on the eve of a game it is thereby rendered unfit for use. As the white man's law is now paramount, extreme measures are seldom resorted to, but in former days the punishment for an infraction of this regulation was severe, and in some tribes the penalty was death. Should a player's wife be with child, he is not allowed to take part in the game under any circumstances, as he is then believed to be heavy and sluggish in his movements, having lost just so much of his strength as has gone to the child. At frequent intervals during the training period the shaman takes the players to water and performs his mystic rites, as will be explained further on. They are also "scratched" on their naked bodies, as at the final game, but now the scratching is done in a haphazard fashion with a piece of bamboo brier having stout thorns which leave broad gashes on the backs of the victims.

When a player fears a particular contestant on the other side, as is frequently the case, his own shaman performs a special incantation, intended to compass the defeat and even the disabling or death of his rival. As the contending sides always belong to different settlements, each party makes all these preliminary arrangements without the knowledge of the other, and under the guidance of its own shamans, several of whom are employed on a side in every hotly contested game. Thus the ball play becomes as well a contest between rival shamans. Among primitive peoples the shaman is in truth all-powerful, and even so simple a matter as the ball game is not left to the free enjoyment of the people, but is so interwoven with priestly rites and influence that the shaman becomes the most important actor in the play.

Before introducing the ball dance it is in place here to describe the principal implements of the game, the ball and ball stick. The ball now used is an ordinary leather-covered ball, but in former days it was made of deer hair and covered with deer skin. In California the ball is of wood. The ball sticks vary considerably among different tribes. As before stated, the Cherokee player uses a pair, catching the ball between them and throwing it in the same way. The stick is something less than 3 feet in length and in its general appearance closely resembles a tennis racket, or a long wooden spoon, the bowl of which is a loose network of thongs of twisted squirrel skin or strings of Indian hemp. The frame is made of a slender hickory stick, bent upon itself and so trimmed and fashioned that the handle seems to be one solid round piece, when in fact it is double. The other southern tribes generally used sticks of the same pattern. Among the Sioux and Ojibwa of the north the player uses a single stick bent around at the end so as to form a hoop, in which a loose netting is fixed. The ball is caught up in this hoop and held there in running by waving the stick from side to side in a peculiarly dextrous manner. In the St. Lawrence region and Canada, the home of *La Crosse*, the stick is about 4½ feet long, and is bent over at the end like a shepherd's crook, with the netting extending half way down its length. The Passamaquoddy Indians of Maine use a stick with a strong, closely woven netting, which enables the stick to be used for batting. The sticks are ornamented with designs cut or burnt into the wood, and are sometimes further adorned with paint and feathers.

On the night preceding the game each party holds the ball-play dance in its own settlement. On the reservation the dance is always held on Friday night, so that the game may take place on Saturday afternoon, in order to give the players and spectators an opportunity to sleep off the effects on Sunday. It may be remarked here in parenthesis that the Cherokee word for Sunday signifies "when everybody does nothing all day long," showing that they fully appreciate its superior advantages as a day of rest. The dance must be held close to the river, to enable the players to "go to water" during the night, but the exact spot selected is always a matter of uncertainty, up to the last moment, excepting with a chosen few. If this were not the case a spy from the other settlement might endeavor to insure the defeat of the party by strewing along their trail a soup made of the hamstrings of rabbits, which would have the effect of rendering the players timorous and easily confused.

The dance begins soon after dark on the night preceding the game and lasts until daybreak, and from the time they eat supper before the dance until after the game, on the following afternoon, no food passes the lips of the players. On the occasion in question the young men of Yellow Hill were to contend against those of Raven Town, about 10 miles further up the river, and as the latter place was a large settlement, noted for its

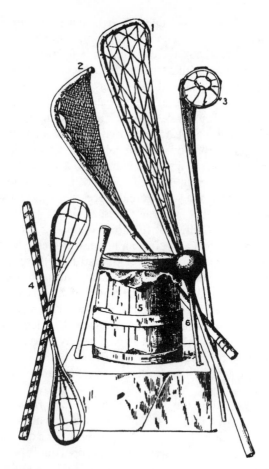

Figure 1—Instruments of the game. 1. Iroquois; 2. Passamaquoddy; 3. Ojibwa; 4. Cherokee; 5. Drum; 6. Rattle.

adherence to the old traditions, a spirited game was expected. My headquarters were at Yellow Hill, and as the principal shaman of that party was my chief informant and lived in the same house with me, he kept me well posted in regard to all the preparations. Through his influence I was enabled to get a number of good photographic views pertaining to the game, as well as to observe all the shamanistic ceremonies, which he himself explained, together with the secret prayers recited during their performance. On a former occasion I attempted to take views of the game, but was prevented by the shamans, on the ground that such a proceeding would destroy the efficacy of their incantations.

Each party holds a dance in its own settlement, the game itself taking place about midway between. The Yellow Hill men were to have their

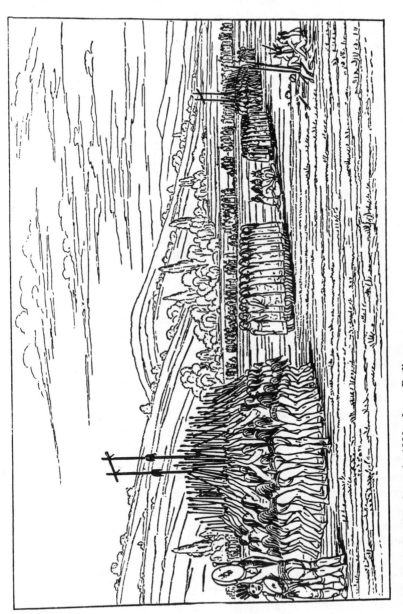

Choctaw ball-play dance in 1832—from Catlin.

dance up the river, about half a mile from my house. We started about 9 o'clock in the evening — for there was no need to hurry — and before long began to meet groups of dark figures by twos and threes going in the same direction or sitting by the roadside awaiting some lagging companions. It was too dark to distinguish faces, but familiar voices revealed the identity of the speakers, and among them were a number who had come from distances of 6 or 8 miles. As we drew nearer, the measured beat of the Indian drum fell upon the ear, and soon we saw the figures of the dancers outlined against the firelight, while the soft voices of the women as they sang the chorus of the ball songs mingled their plaintive cadences with the shouts of the men.

The spot selected for the dance was a narrow strip of gravelly bottom, where the mountain came close down to the water's edge. The tract was only a few acres in extent and was covered with large trees, their tops bound together by a network of wild grape-vines which hung down on all sides in graceful festoons. From the road the ground sloped abruptly down to this bottom, while almost overhead the mountain was dimly outlined through the night fog, and close at hand one of the rapids, so frequent in these mountain streams, disturbed the stillness of the night with its never-ceasing roar.

Several fires were burning and in the fitful blaze the trees sent out long shadows to melt into the surrounding darkness, while just within the circle of light, leaning against the trees or stretched out upon the ground, were the Indians, the women with their motionless figures muffled up in white sheets seeming like ghosts returned to earth, and the babies, whose mothers were in the dance, laid away under the bushes to sleep, with only a shawl between them and the cold ground. Around the larger fire were the dancers, the men stripped as for the game, with their ball-sticks in their hands and the firelight playing upon their naked bodies. It was a weird, wild picture, not easily effaced from the memory.

The ball-play dance is participated in by both sexes, but differs considerably from any other of the dances of the tribe, being a dual affair throughout. The dancers are the players of the morrow, with seven women, representing the seven Cherokee clans. The men dance in a circle around the fire, chanting responses to the sound of a rattle carried by another performer, who circles around on the outside, while the women stand in line a few feet away and dance to and fro, now advancing a few steps toward the men, then wheeling and dancing away from them, but all the while keeping time to the sound of the drum and chanting the refrain to the ball songs sung by the drummer, who is seated on the ground on the side farthest from the fire. The rattle is a gourd fitted with a handle and filled with small pebbles, while the drum resembles a small keg with a head of ground-hog leather. The drum is partly filled with water, the head being also moistened to improve the tone, and is beaten with a single stick. Men and women dance separately throughout, the music, the evolutions, and the songs being entirely distinct, but all combining to produce an harmonious whole. The women are relieved at intervals by others who take their places, but the men dance in the same narrow circle the whole night long, excepting during the frequent halts for the purpose of going to water.

At one side of the fire are set up two forked poles, supporting a third laid horizontally, upon which the ball sticks are crossed in pairs until the dance begins. As already mentioned, small pieces from the wing of the bat are sometimes tied to these poles, and also to the rattle used in the dance, to insure success in the contest. The skins of several bats and swift-darting insectivorous birds were formerly wrapped up in a piece of deerskin, together with the cloth and beads used in the conjuring ceremonies later on, and hung from the frame during the dance. On finally dressing for the game at the ball ground the players took the feathers from these skins to fasten in their hair or upon their ball sticks to insure swiftness and accuracy in their movements. Sometimes also hairs from the whiskers of the bat are twisted into the netting of the ball sticks. The players are all stripped and painted, with feathers in their hair, just as they appear in the game. When all is ready an attendant takes down the ball sticks from the frame, throwing them over his arm in the same fashion, and, walking around the circle, gives to each man his own. Then the rattler, taking his instrument in his hand, begins to trot around on the outside of the circle, uttering a sharp *Hí!* to which the players respond with a quick *Hi-hí!* while slowly moving around the circle with their ball sticks held tightly in front of their breasts. Then, with a quicker movement, the song changes to *Ehú!* and the response to *Hăhí!* — *Ehú! Hăhí! Ehú! Hăhí!* Then, with a prolonged shake of the rattle, it changes again to *Ahiyé!* the dancers responding with the same word *Ahiyé!* but in a higher key; the movements become more lively and the chorus louder, till at a given signal with the rattle the players clap their ball sticks together, and facing around, go through the motions of picking up and tossing an imaginary ball. Finally with a grand rush they dance up close to the women, and the first part of the performance ends with a loud prolonged *Hu-ŭ!* from the whole crowd.

In the meantime the women have taken position in a line a few feet away, with their backs turned to the men, while in front of them the drummer is seated on the ground, but with his back turned toward them and the rest of the dancers. After a few preliminary taps on the drum he begins a slow, measured beat and strikes up one of the dance refrains, which the women take up in chorus. This is repeated a number of times until all are in harmony with the tune, when he begins to improvise, choosing words which will harmonize with the measure of the chorus and at the same time be appropriate to the subject of the dance. As this requires a ready wit in addition to ability as a singer, the selection of a drummer is a matter of considerable importance, and that functionary is held in corresponding estimation. He sings of the game on the morrow, of the fine things to be won by the men of his party, of the joy with which they will be received by their friends on their return from the field, and of the disappointment and defeat of their rivals. Throughout it all the women keep up the same minor refrain, like an instrumental accompaniment to vocal music. As Cherokee songs are always in the minor key, they have a plaintive effect, even when the sentiment is cheerful or even boisterous, and are calculated to excite the mirth of one who understands the language. This impression is heightened by the appearance of the dancers themselves, for the women shuffle solemnly back and forth all night long without ever a smile upon their faces, while the occasional laughter of the men seems half subdued, with none of the hearty ringing tones of the white man or the negro. The monotonous repetition, too, is something intolerable to any one but an Indian, the same words, to the same tune, being sometimes sung over and over again for a half hour or more. Although the singer improvises as he proceeds, many of the expressions have now become stereotyped and are used at almost every ball-play dance. The song here given is a good type of the class.

Through the kind assistance of Prof. John P. Sousa, director of the Marine band, I am enabled to give also the musical notation.

The words have no fixed order of arrangement and the song may be repeated indefinitely. *Higanuyahi* is the refrain sung by the women and has no meaning. The vowels have the Latin sound and *u* is the French nasal *un*:

FIRST SONG.

Hi′ganu′ya,	hi′ganu′yahi′
Hi′ganu′ya	hi′ganu′yahi′
Sâ′kwĭli-te′ga	tsĭ′tûkata′sûni′ !
As′taliti′ski	tsĭ′tûkata′sûni′ !

As'taliti'ski	tsa'kwakilû'testi !
U'watu'hi	tsĭ'tûkata'sûni' !
Tĭ'kanane'hi	a'kwakilû'tati' !
Uwa'tutsû'hi	tsĭ'tûkata'sûni' !
Uwa'tutsû'hi	tsa'kwakilû'testi' !
I'geski'yu	tsa'kwakilû'testi' !
Tĭ'kanane'hi	tsĭ'tûkata'sûni' !—Hu-ŭ !

Which may be freely rendered :

What a fine horse I shall win !
I shall win a pacer !
I shall be riding a pacer !
I'm going to win a pretty one !
A stallion for me to ride !
What a pretty one I shall win !
What a pretty one I shall ride !
How proud I'll feel when riding him !
I'm going to win a stallion !—Hu-ŭ !

But *sic transit gloria!*—in these degenerate days the pacer is more likely to be represented by a cheap jack-knife. Another very pretty refrain is:

SECOND SONG.

Yo'wida'nuwe'   Yo'widanu'-da'nuwe'.

At a certain stage of the dance a man, specially selected for the purpose, leaves the group of spectators around the fire and retires a short distance into the darkness in the direction of the rival settlement. Then, standing with his face still turned in the same direction, he raises his hand to his mouth and utters four yells, the last prolonged into a peculiar quaver. He is answered by the players with a chorus of yells—or rather yelps, for the Indian yell resembles nothing else so much as the bark of a puppy. Then he comes running back until he passes the circle of dancers, when he halts and shouts out a single word, which may be translated, "They are already beaten!" Another chorus of yells greets this announcement. This man is called the *Talala*, or "woodpecker," on account of his peculiar yell, which is considered to resemble the sound made by a woodpecker tapping on a dead tree trunk. According to the orthodox Cherokee belief, this yell is heard by the rival players in the other settlement — who, it will be remembered, are having a ball dance of their own at the same time — and so terrifies them that they lose all heart for the game. The fact that both sides alike have a *Talala* in no way interferes with the theory.

At frequent intervals during the night all the players, accompanied by the shaman and his assistant, leave the dance and go down to a retired spot at the river's bank, where they perform the mystic rite known as "going to water," hereafter to be described. While the players are performing this ceremony the women, with the drummer, continue the dance and chorus. The dance is kept up without intermission, and almost without change, until daybreak. At the final dance green pine tops are thrown upon the fire, so as to produce a thick smoke, which envelops the dancers. Some mystic properties are ascribed to this pine smoke, but what they are I have not yet learned, although the ceremony seems to be intended as an exorcism, the same thing being done at other dances when there has recently been a death in the settlement.

At sunrise the players, dressed now in their ordinary clothes, but carrying their ball sticks in their hands, start for the ball ground, accompanied by the shamans and their assistants. The place selected for the game, being always about midway between the two rival settlements, was in this case several miles above the dance ground and on the opposite side of the river. On the march each party makes four several halts, when each player again "goes to water" separately with the shaman. This occupies considerable time, so that it is usually after noon before the two parties meet on the ball ground. While the shaman is busy with his mysteries in the laurel bushes down by the water's edge, the other players, sitting by the side of the trail, spend the time twisting extra strings for their ball sticks, adjusting their feather ornaments and discussing the coming game. In former times the player during these halts was not allowed to sit upon a log, a stone, or anything but the ground itself; neither was it permissible to lean against anything excepting the back of another player, on penalty of defeat in the game, with the additional risk of being bitten by a rattlesnake. This rule is now disregarded, and it is doubtful if any but the older men are aware that it ever existed.

On coming up from the water after the fourth halt the principal shaman assembles the players around him and delivers an animated harangue, exhorting them to do their utmost in the coming contest, telling them that they will undoubtedly be victorious as the omens are all favorable, picturing to their delighted vision the stakes to be won and the ovation awaiting them from their friends after the game, and finally assuring them in the mystic terms of the formulas that their adversaries will be driven through the four gaps into the gloomy shadows of the Darkening Land, where they will perish forever from remembrance. The address, delivered in rapid, jerky tones like the speech of an auctioneer, has a very inspiriting effect upon the hearers and is frequently interrupted by a burst of exultant yells from the players. At the end, with another chorus of yells, they again take up the march.

On arriving in sight of the ball ground the *Talala* again comes to the front and announces their approach with four loud yells, ending with a long quaver, as on the previous night at the dance. The players respond with another yell, and then turn off to a convenient sheltered place by the river to make the final preparations.

The shaman then marks off a small space upon the ground to represent the ball field, and, taking in his hand a small bundle of sharpened stakes about a foot in length, addresses each man in turn, telling him the position which he is to occupy in the field at the tossing up of the ball after the first inning, and driving down a stake to represent each player until he has a diagram of the whole field spread out upon the ground.

The players then strip for the ordeal of scratching. This painful operation is performed by an assistant, in this case by an old man named Standing Water. The instrument of torture is called a *kanuga* and resembles a short comb with seven teeth, seven being also a sacred number with the Cherokees. The teeth are made of sharpened splinters from the leg bone of a turkey and are fixed in a frame made from the shaft of a turkey quill, in such a manner that by a slight pressure of the thumb they can be pushed out to the length of a small tack. Why the bone and feather of the turkey should be selected I have not yet learned, but there is undoubtedly an Indian reason for the choice.

The players having stripped, the operator begins by seizing the arm of a player with one hand while holding the *kanuga* in the other, and plunges the teeth into the flesh at the shoulder, bringing the instrument down with a steady pressure to the elbow, leaving seven white lines which become red a moment later, as the blood starts to the surface. He now plunges the *kanuga* in again at another place near the shoulder, and again brings it down to the elbow. Again and again the operation is repeated until the victim's arm is scratched in 28 lines above the elbow. It will be noticed that 28 is a combination of four and seven, the two sacred numbers of the Cherokees. The operator then makes the same number of scratches in the same manner on the arm below the elbow. Next the other arm is treated in the same way; then each leg, both above and below the knee, and finally an X is scratched across the breast of the sufferer, the upper ends are joined by another stroke from shoulder to shoulder, and a similar pattern is scratched upon his back. By this time the blood is trickling in little streams from nearly 300 gashes. None of the scratches are deep, but they are unquestionably very painful, as all agree who have undergone the operation. Nevertheless the young men endure the ordeal willingly and almost cheerfully, regarding it as a necessary part of the ritual to secure success in the game. In order to secure a picture of one young fellow under the operation I stood with my camera so near that I could distinctly hear the teeth tear through the flesh at every scratch with a rasping sound that sent a shudder through me, yet he never flinched, although several times he shivered with cold, as the chill autumn wind blew upon his naked body. This scratching is common in Cherokee medical practice, and is variously performed with a brier, a rattlesnake's tooth, a flint, or even a piece of broken glass. It was noted by Adair as early as 1775. To cause the blood to flow more freely the young men sometimes scrape it off with chips as it oozes out. The shaman then gives to each player a small piece of root, to which he has imparted magic properties by the recital of certain secret formulas. Various roots are used, according to the whim of the shaman, their virtue depending entirely upon the ceremony of consecration. The men chew these roots and spit out the juice over their limbs and bodies, rubbing it well into the scratches, then going down to the water plunge in and wash off the blood, after which they come out and dress themselves for the game.

The modern Cherokee ball costume consists simply of a pair of short trunks ornamented with various patterns in red or blue cloth, and a feather charm worn upon the head. Formerly the breechcloth alone was worn, as is still the case in some instances, and the strings with which it was tied were purposely made weak, so that if seized by an opponent in the scuffle the strings would break, leaving the owner to escape with the loss of his sole article of raiment. This calls to mind a similar custom among the ancient Greek athletes, the recollection of which has been preserved in the etymology of the word *gymnast*. The ornament worn in the hair is made up of an eagle's feathers, to give keenness of sight; a deer tail, to give swiftness; and a snake's rattle, to render the wearer terrible to his adversaries. If an eagle's feathers cannot be procured, those of a hawk or any other swift bird of prey are used. In running, the snake rattle is made to furnish a very good imitation of the sound made by the rattlesnake when about to strike. The player also marks his body in various patterns with paint or charcoal. The charcoal is taken from the dance fire, and whenever possible is procured by burning the wood of a tree which has been struck by lightning, such wood being regarded as peculiarly sacred and endowed with mysterious properties. According to one formula, the player makes a cross over his heart and a spot upon each shoulder, using pulverized charcoal procured from the shaman and made by burning together the wood of a honey-locust tree and of a tree which has been struck by lightning, *but not killed*. The charcoal is pulverized and put, together with a red and a black bead, into an empty cocoon from which one end has been cut off. This paint preparation makes the player swift like the lightning and invulnerable as the tree that defies the thunderbolt, and renders his flesh as hard and firm to the touch as the wood of the honey-locust. Among the Choctaws, according to Catlin, a

Choctaw ball player in 1832—from Catlin.

tail of horse hair was also worn, so as to stream out behind as the player ran. Just before dressing, the players rub their bodies with grease or the chewed bark of the slippery elm or the sassafras, until their skin is slippery as that of the proverbial eel.

A number of precautionary measures are also frequently resorted to by the more prudent players while training in order to make assurance doubly sure. They bathe their limbs with a decoction of the *Tephrosia Virginiana* or Catgut in order to render their muscles tough like the roots of that plant. They bathe themselves with a decoction of the small rush *(Juncus tenuis)* which grows by the roadside, because its stalks are always erect and will not lie flat upon the ground, however much they may be stamped and trodden upon. In the same way they bathe with a decoction of the wild crabapple or the ironwood, because the trunks of these trees, even when thrown down, are supported and kept up from the ground by their spreading tops. To make themselves more supple they whip themselves with the tough stalks of the *Wằ takû* or Stargrass or with switches made from the bark of a hickory sapling which has grown up from under a log that has fallen across it, the bark being taken from the bend thus produced in the sapling. After the first scratching the player renders himself an object of terror to his opponents by eating a portion of a rattlesnake which has been killed and cooked by the shaman. He rubs himself with an eel skin to make himself slippery like the eel, and rubs each limb down once with the fore and hind leg of a turtle because the legs of that animal are remarkably stout. He applies to the shaman to conjure a dangerous opponent, so that he may be unable to see the ball in its flight, or may dislocate a wrist or break a leg. Sometimes the shaman draws upon the ground an armless figure of his rival, with a hole where his heart should be. Into this hole he drops two black beads, covers them with earth and stamps upon them, and thus the dreaded rival is doomed, unless (and this is always the saving clause) his own shaman has taken precautions against such a result, or the one in whose behalf the charm is made has rendered the incantation unavailing by a violation of some one of the interminable rules of the gaktunta.

The players having dressed are now ready to "go to water" for the last time, for which purpose the shaman selects a bend of the river where he can look toward the east while facing up-stream. This ceremony of going to water is the most sacred and impressive in the whole Cherokee ritual, and must always be performed fasting, and in most cases also is preceded by an all-night vigil. It is used in connection with prayers to obtain a long life, to destroy an enemy, to win the love of a woman, to secure success in the hunt and the ball play, and for recovery from a dangerous illness, but is performed only as a final resort or when the occasion is one of special importance. The general ceremonial and the principal formulas are nearly the same in all cases. I have collected a number of the formulas used on these various occasions, but it is impossible within the limits of this paper to give more than a general idea of their nature.

The men stand side by side looking down upon the water, with their ball sticks clasped upon their breasts, while the shaman stands just behind them, and an assistant kneeling at his side spreads out upon the ground the cloth upon which are placed the sacred beads. These beads are of two colors, red and black, each kind resting upon a cloth of the same color, and corresponding in number to the number of players. The red beads represent the players for whom the shaman performs the ceremony, while the black beads stand for their opponents, red being symbolic of power and triumph, while black is emblematic of death and misfortune. All being ready, the assistant hands to the shaman a red bead, which he takes between the thumb and finger of his right hand; and then a black bead, which he takes in the same manner in his left hand. Then, holding his hands outstretched, with his eyes intently fixed upon the beads, the shaman prays on behalf of his client to *Yû wĭ Gûnahi'ta*, the "Long Man," the sacred name for the river:

"O Long Man, I come to the edge of your body. You are mighty and most powerful. You bear up great logs and toss them about where the foam is white. Nothing can resist you. Grant me such strength in the contest that my enemy may be of no weight in my hands—that I may be able to toss him into the air or dash him to the earth." In a similar strain he prays to the Red Bat in the Sun Land to make him expert in dodging; to the Red Deer to make him fleet of foot; to the great Red Hawk to render him keen of sight; and to the Red Rattlesnake to render him terrible to all who oppose him.

Then in the same low tone and broken accents in which all the formulas are recited the shaman declares that his client (mentioning his name and clan) has now ascended to the first heaven. As he continues praying he declares that he has now reached the second heaven (and here he slightly raises his hands); soon he ascends to the third heaven, and the hands of the shaman are raised still higher; then in the same way he ascends to the fourth, the fifth, and the sixth heaven; and finally, as he raises his trembling hands aloft, he declares that the spirit of the man has now risen to the seventh heaven, where his feet are resting upon the Red Seats, from which they shall never be displaced.

Turning now to his client, the shaman, in a low voice, asks him the name of his most dreaded rival on the opposite side. The reply is given in a whisper, and the shaman, holding his hands outstretched as before, calls down the most withering curses upon the head of the doomed victim, mentioning him likewise by name and clan. He prays to the Black Fog to cover him so that he may be unable to see his way; to the Black Rattlesnake to envelop him in its slimy folds; and at last to the Black Spider to let down his black thread from above, wrap it about the soul of the victim and drag it from his body along the black trail to the Darkening Land in the west, there to bury it in the black coffin under the black clay, never to reappear. At the final imprecation he stoops and, making a hole in the soft earth with his finger (symbolic of stabbing the doomed man to the heart), drops the black bead into it and covers it from sight with a vicious stamp of his foot; then with a simultaneous movement each man dips his ball sticks into the water, and bringing them up, touches them to his lips; then stooping again he dips up the water in his hand and laves his head and breast.

Below is given a translation of one of these formulas, from the collection of original Cherokee manuscripts obtained by the writer. The formulistic name for the player signifies "admirer or lover of the ball play." The shaman directs his attention alternately to his clients and their opponents, looking by turns at the red or the black bead as he prays. He raises his friends to the seventh heaven and invokes in their behalf the aid of the bat and a number of birds, which, according to the Cherokee belief, are so keen of sight and so swift upon the wing as never to fail to seize their intended prey. The opposing players, on the other hand, are put under the earth and rendered like the terrapin, the turtle, the mole, and the bear—all slow and clumsy of movement. Blue is the color symbolic of defeat, red is typical of success, and white signifies joy and happiness. The exultant whoop or shout of the players is believed to bear them on to victory, as trees are carried along by the resistless force of a torrent:

"THIS IS TO TAKE THEM TO WATER FOR THE BALL PLAY."

"Sgĕ! Now, where the white thread has been let down, quickly we are about to inquire into the fate of the lovers of the ball play."

They are of *such* a descent. They are called *so and so*. (As they march) they are shaking the road which shall never be joyful. The miserable terrapin has fastened himself upon them as they go about. They are doomed to failure. They have become entirely blue.

But now my lovers of the ball play have their roads lying down in this direction. The Red Bat has come and become one with them. There, in the first heaven, are the pleasing stakes. There, in the second heaven, are the pleasing stakes. The Peewee has come and joined them. Their ball sticks shall be borne along by the immortal whoop, never to fail them in the contest.

But as for the lovers of the ball play on the other side, the common turtle has fastened himself to them as they go about. There, under the earth, they are doomed to failure.

There, in the third heaven, are the pleasing stakes. The Red Tla'niwă has come and made himself one of them, never to be defeated. There, in the fourth heaven, are the pleasing stakes. The Crested Flycatcher has come and joined them, that they may never be defeated. There, in the fifth heaven, are the pleasing stakes. The Martin has come and joined them, that they may never be defeated.

The other lovers of the ball play—the Blue Mole has become one with them, that they may never feel triumphant. They are doomed to failure.

There, in the sixth heaven, the Chimney Swift has become one with them, that they may never be defeated. There are the pleasing stakes. There, in the seventh heaven, the Dragonfly has become one of them, that they may never be defeated. There are the pleasing stakes.

As for the other lover of the ball play, the Bear has come and fastened himself to them, that they may never be triumphant. He has caused the stakes to slip out of their hands and their share has dwindled to nothing. Their fate is forecast.

Sgĕ! Now let me know that the twelve (runs) are mine, O White Dragonfly. Let me know that their share is mine—that the stakes are mine. Now he [the rival player] is compelled to let go his hold upon the stakes. They [the shaman's clients] are become exultant and gratified. Yû!"

This ceremony ended, the players form in line, headed by the shaman, and march in single file to the ball ground, where they find awaiting them a crowd of spectators—men, women, and children—sometimes to the number of several hundred, for the Indians always turn out to the ball play, no matter how great the distance, from old Big Witch, stooping under the weight of nearly a hundred years, down to babies slung at their mothers' backs. The ball ground is a level field by the river side, surrounded by the high timber-covered mountains. At either end are the goals, each consisting of a pair of upright poles, between which the ball must be driven to make a run, the side which first makes 12 home runs being declared the winner of the game and the stakes. The ball is furnished by the challengers, who sometimes try to select one so small that it will fall through the netting of the ball sticks of their adversaries; but as the others are on the lookout for this, the trick usually fails of its purpose. After the ball is once set in motion it must be picked up only with the ball sticks, although after having picked up the ball with the sticks the player frequently takes it in his hand and, throwing away the sticks, runs with it until intercepted by one of the other party, when he throws it, if he can, to one of his friends further on. Should a player pick up the ball with his hand, as sometimes happens in the scramble, there at once arises all over the field a chorus of *Uwâ'yi Gûtï! Uwâ'yi Gûtï!* "With the hand! With the hand!"—equivalent to our own "Foul! Foul!" and that inning is declared a draw.

While our men are awaiting the arrival of the other party their friends crowd around them, and the women throw across their outstretched ball sticks the pieces of calico, the small squares of sheeting used as shawls, and the bright red handkerchiefs so dear to the heart of the Cherokee, which they intend to stake upon the game. It may be as well to state that these handkerchiefs take the place of hats, bonnets, and scarfs, the women throwing them over their heads in shawl fashion and the men twisting them like turbans about their hair, while both sexes alike fasten them about their throats or use them as bags for carrying small packages. Knives, trinkets, and sometimes small coins are also wagered. But these Cherokee today are poor indeed. Hardly a man among them owns a horse and never again will a chief bet a thousand dollars upon his favorites, as was done in Georgia in 1834. Today, however, as then, they will risk all they have.

Now a series of yells announces the near approach of the men from Raven Town, and in a few minutes they come filing out from the bushes—stripped, scratched, and decorated like the others, carrying their ball sticks in their hands and headed by a shaman. The two parties come together in the center of the ground, and for a short time the scene resembles an auction, as men and women move about, holding up the articles they propose to wager on the game and bidding for stakes to be matched against them. The betting being ended, the opposing players draw up in two lines facing each other, each man with his ball sticks laid together upon the ground in front of him, with the heads pointing toward the man facing him. This is for the purpose of matching the players so as to get the same number on each side; and should it be found that a player has no antagonist to face him, he must drop out of the game. Such a result frequently happens, as both parties strive to keep their arrangements secret up to the last moment. There is no fixed number on a side, the common quota being from 9 to 12. Catlin, indeed, speaking of the Choctaws, says that "it is no uncommon occurrence for six or eight hundred or a thousand of these young men to engage in a game of ball, with five or six times that number of spectators;" but this was just after the removal, while the entire nation was yet camped upon the prairie in the Indian Territory. It would have been utterly impossible for the shamans to prepare a thousand players, or even one-fourth of that number, in the regular way, and in Catlin's spirited description of the game the ceremonial part is chiefly conspicuous by its absence. The greatest number that I ever heard of among the old Cherokee was 22 on a side. There is another secret formula to be recited by the initiated at this juncture, and addressed to the "Red Yahulu" or hickory, for the purpose of destroying the efficiency of his enemy's ball sticks.

During the whole time that the game is in progress the shaman, concealed in the bushes by the water side, is busy with his prayers and incantations for the success of his clients and the defeat of their rivals. Through his assistant, who acts as messenger, he is kept advised of the movements of the players by seven men, known as counselors, appointed to watch the game for that purpose. These seven counselors also have a general oversight of the conjuring and other proceedings at the ball-play dance. Every little incident is regarded as an omen, and the shaman governs himself accordingly.

An old man now advances with the ball, and standing at one end of the lines, delivers a final address to the players, telling them that *Uné'lanû'hĭ*, "the Apportioner" — the sun — is looking down upon them, urging them to acquit themselves in the game as their fathers have done before them; but above all to keep their tempers, so that none may have it to say that they got angry or quarreled, and that after it is over each one may return in peace along the white trail to rest in his white house. White in these formulas is symbolic of peace and happiness and all good things. He concludes with a loud *"Ha! Taldu-gwŭ!"* "Now for the twelve!" and throws the ball into the air.

Instantly 20 pairs of ball sticks clatter together in the air, as their owners spring to catch the ball in its descent. In the scramble it usually happens that the ball falls to the ground, when it is picked up by one more active than the rest. Frequently, however, a man will succeed in catching it between his ball sticks as it falls, and, disengaging himself from the rest, starts to run with it to the goal; but before he has gone a dozen yards they are upon him, and the whole crowd goes down together, rolling and tumbling over each other in the dust, straining and tugging for possession of the ball, until one of the players manages to extricate himself from the struggling heap and starts off with the ball. At once the others spring to their feet and, throwing away their ball sticks, rush to intercept him or to prevent his capture, their black hair streaming out behind and their naked bodies glistening in the sun as they run. The scene is constantly changing. Now the players are all together at the lower end of the field, when suddenly, with a powerful throw, a player sends the ball high over the heads of the spectators and into the bushes beyond. Before there is time to realize it, here they come with a grand sweep and a burst of short, sharp Cherokee exclamations, charging right into the crowd, knocking men and women to right and left and stumbling over dogs and babies in their frantic efforts to get at the ball.

It is a very exciting game as well as a very rough one, and in its general features is a combination of base ball, football, and the old-fashioned shinny. Almost everything short of murder is allowable in the game, and both parties sometimes go into the contest with the deliberate purpose of crippling or otherwise disabling the best players on the opposing side. Serious accidents are common. In the last game which I witnessed one man was seized around the waist by a powerfully built adversary, raised up in the air and hurled down upon the ground with such force as to break his collar-bone. His friends pulled him out to one side and the game went on. Sometimes two men lie struggling on the ground, clutching at each other's throats, long after the ball has been carried to the other end of the field, until the "drivers," armed with long, stout switches, come running up and belabor both over their bare shoulders until they are forced to break their hold. It is also the duty of these drivers to gather the ball sticks thrown away in the excitement and restore them to their owners at the beginning of the next inning.

When the ball has been carried through the goal, the players come back to the center and take position in accordance with the previous instructions of their shamans. The two captains stand facing each other and the ball is then thrown up by the captain of the side which won the last inning. Then the struggle begins again, and so the game goes on until one party scores 12 runs and is declared the victor and the winner of the stakes.

As soon as the game is over, usually about sundown, the winning players immediately go to water again with their shamans and perform another ceremony for the purpose of turning aside the revengeful incantations of their defeated rivals. They then dress, and the crowd of hungry players, who have eaten nothing since they started for the dance the night before, make a combined attack on the provisions which the women now produce from the shawls and baskets. It should be mentioned that, to assuage thirst during the game, the players are allowed to drink a sour preparation made from green grapes and wild crabapples.

Although the contestants on both sides are picked men and strive to win, straining every muscle to the utmost, the impression left upon my mind after witnessing a number of games is that the same number of athletic young white men would have infused more robust energy into the play — that is, provided they could stand upon their feet after all the preliminary fasting, bleeding, and loss of sleep. Before separating, the defeated party usually challenges the victors to a second contest, and in a few days preparations are actively under way for another game.

Chapter 12
Ceremony, Rites, and Economy in the Student System of an American High School

JACQUETTA HILL BURNETT

Recently, John L. Fischer (1965, p. 284) described as "common sense" the view that the progress of civilization leads to the reduced importance of ritual. If one changes "progress of civilization" to "urbanization," Fisher's description seems to understate the professional respectability of the proponents of this position. Only 5 years ago, Max Gluckman expressed the view that "modern urban life" is correlated with the disappearance of the ritualization of social relations. Gluckman (1962) said:

> I consider that rituals of the kind investigated by Van Gennep are "incompatible" with the structure of modern urban life. (pp. 36-37)

He goes on to say, with respect to helping people of the secular urbanized world in their transitions from one status to another:

> I do not believe that it [i.e., help] can come from the tribal type of *rites de*

From *Human Organization*, Spring 1969, **28**(1), 1-10. Copyright 1969 by the Society for Applied Anthropology. Reprinted with permission.

passage in which social relationships are ritualized to assist persons at what are defined as crises. (pp. 36-37)

On the basis of nearly a year's field work in a small midwestern high school in 1960-61, I wish here not only to present a description of one aspect of the culture of an American secondary school, but also to question on empirical grounds the extinction of ritual as an effective, functional device in urbanized societies.[1] In fact, the empirical extension of the concepts "ceremony" and "ritual" was critical to the analysis of the calendar of events of the high school, although the clearly nonsupernatural character of the symbolism associated with the student's public events placed those data in a rather awkward relationship to the conceptual schema usually employed to analyze ritual and ceremony. By most of the traditional anthropological canons for using "ritual" and "ceremony," many of the most dramatic and behaviorally significant events of the student system would have to be relegated to the analytic insignificance of the general category, "custom." Yet is it not legitimate conceptually to view certain student activities as ceremonies and rituals?

The Conceptual Rationale

When focusing upon the action dimensions of these high school events, I found practices that readily fit Nadel's (1954) action criterion for ritual: "any type of behavior may thus be said to turn into 'ritual' when it is stylized or formalized, and made repetitive in that form" (p. 99). Moreover, following on careful attention to modes, order, and frequencies of interaction, I found I could readily distinguish "rites of intensification" and "rites of passage" in these events, in accord with the Chapple and Coon (1942) criteria. Indeed, Van Gennep's (1909/1960) original schema of separation, transition, and incorporation as phases of rites of passage also was helpful analytically when applied to certain parts of the data.

The quandary over the conceptual status of the data is most marked in the consideration of the associated belief system. When one pursues the course, so eloquently and persuasively recommended by Geertz (1958, pp. 449-512), of concentrating on the symbolic system, one often interviews students in vain for anything more elaborate than "we do it because it's fun" or "we do it because it was done that way last year." This minimal development of myth and belief might cast doubt on the ritual status of the associated events were it not for Kluckhohn's (1958, pp. 135-151) demonstration that, although ritual often is associated with elaborate mythical development, this need not always be the case. More recently, Lévi-Strauss (1963), in his penetrating essay on the totemic illusion, argues that because nonsentient norms, or customs, determine the sentiments of the individuals in whatever society, the individual can rarely assign cause to his conformity, other than to say that "things have always been like this, and he does what people before him did" (p. 70). Feeble elaboration of rationale, then, need not exclude the associated action systems or events from the field of ritual phenomena.

Recently, Jack Goody (1961), Robin Horton (1960), and S.H. Posinsky (1962) have made relevant reexaminations of the issue of the conceptual relationships among religion, magic, ceremony, ritual, belief, and action. In particular, Jack Goody's clarification of the definitional problem of religion and ritual seems to justify the conceptual decision to view certain student activities as ritual events. He uses the insight that much magico-religious behavior is nonrational, rather than irrational.

Goody's general purpose is to advance the development of a cross-culturally useful data language, and to advance the concern of anthropological science with the study of conditions under which similar entities recur in different populations. When Goody analyzes magic, religion, science, ceremony, and ritual with respect to one another and with respect to rationality of belief, he is concerned with developing a more powerful etic orientation, or observer's data language and frame of reference (p. 160). One of the key problems of an adequate emic, or actor's, frame of thought is to develop a system that is sufficiently isomorphic to all emic systems of the world to allow the objective transformation of the latter into the former, and at the same time have an etic system of thought that is sufficiently powerful and discriminating to bring observed phenomena into theoretically significant relationship to other phenomena.

Goody's purpose is particularly salutary with respect to the analytic dilemma of what to do with student behaviors that in action dimension look like ritualistic and ceremonial behavior, but under the more current canons of analysis of ritual and ceremony would not be included there. Goody devotes patient attention to a range of western theorists' positions—Durkheim, Malinowski, Frazer, Radcliffe-Brown, Parsons, and even others—on the definitions of magic and religion and rational and irrational distinctions in magical and religious phenomena. He finds that our understanding of magic and religious behavior has been confounded by the assumption that certain distinctions are universal to the actor-oriented—or to the emic—standpoint, when as a matter of fact, the distinction is a vestige of our own folk taxonomy intruding upon the observer's frame of reference. He goes to careful lengths to show that such category systems as sacred/profane, natural/supernatural, rational/irrational are not universals to the actor's views within all cultural systems, but are observer frames of reference. Not only have the actor and the observer frames of reference in other cultures been confused with our own emic perspective, or folk taxonomy, with a resultant retarding of the development of cross-cultural theory and an intersubjective data language of religion and ritual with respect to other cultures; it also seems to have inhibited our ability to relate that theory to new emergences in western culture.

In agreement with Radcliffe-Brown, Goody holds that ceremonial has to do with "collective action required by custom." It is an elaborate conventional form of expression of feeling, not confined, however, to religious occasions. It is public in nature and consists of ritual acts. He says

> ceremonial may . . . be used to refer to those collective actions required by custom, performed on occasions of change in social life. Thus a ceremonial consists of a specific sequence of ritual acts, performed in public. (Goody, 1961, p. 159)

Goody notes that *ritual* often has wider reference than magico-religious behavior. The fundamental criterion of ritual is the idea of formality of procedure or action that either *is not* directed toward a pragmatic end, or *if so* directed, will fail to achieve the intended aim. Goody notes with approval that Nadel views ritual inclusively to apply to any type of excessively formal action. Religious ritual, however, under which Nadel also includes magic, covers only those excessively formal acts where the means/end relationship is deemed inadequate by empirical standards. Goody suggests, however, that incongruous rigidity in itself is also to some extent empirically inadequate. He suggests that Pareto's view that much magico-religious behavior is *nonrational*, rather than irrational, can be used to conceptualize ritual behavior in which the means/end relationship is deemed inadequate merely because of its incongruous rigidity.

For Goody, then, ritual is not simply equated with religious action, but is a more general category of action. If ritual activities are addressed to some mystical or supernatural power, they *are* religious activities. Some religious acts may be irrational, as is the case of many forms of sacrifice and prayer, because they have a pragmatic end which the procedures fail to achieve, or achieve for other reasons than the actors suppose. Religious acts may be nonrational, as in many public celebrations. But in both types, the activities are addressed to some mystical or supernatural power. Magical action falls within the general category of ritual, but is essentially irrational in any particular case since it has a pragmatic end which its procedures fail to achieve or achieve for reasons other than the patient, or possibly the practitioner, supposes.

There is ritual which is neither religious, because it does not assume the existence of spiritual beings, nor magic, because it is not aimed at some empirical end. Goody emphasizes that the absence of explicit empirical ends for nonmagico-religious ritual does not preclude its having recognized purpose within the actor's frame of reference, as well as having some "latent" purpose or function from the observer's standpoint.

The nonmagico-religious category of ritual may include such things as civil marriage ceremonies, rituals of birth and death in secular households or societies, and the rituals of family living described by Bossard and Boll (1950), as well as rituals of liquidation as described by Leites and Beraut (1954), and other similar types of formalized interpersonal behavior. I include here also the rituals connected with high school football and basketball homecoming, graduation, junior and senior proms, freshmen initiations, senior trips, and sundry other ceremonial events in the student systems of American high schools. Usually these ritual acts are nonmagico-religious and are nonrational rather than irrational. By accepting the conceptual advances of Kluckhohn, Goody, and others, the public events of the student system fall safely and logically within the perimeter of the concepts of ritual, rite, and ceremony.

Turning now to the culture of the American high school, what are these ceremonial events like? How do they fit with the other aspects of the institutional context to form that set of people, relations, and events which I have called the student subsystem?

Ritual and Ceremonial in an American High School

The ceremonies and rites of the American high school which I studied were a regular part of extracurricular or student activities. Beyond the formal organization of work and the ubiquitous informal network of clique relationships, there were associational sets (or student clubs) of three general types that sponsored, planned, and carried out the annual calendar of activities. The most dominant type was formed out of the age-grade statuses in the high school. The second type grew out of the subject matter and work of formal courses in the regular curriculum, though the activities of these associations often seemed far removed from that subject matter. Finally, there was a type formed out of participation in interschool sports competition—a type with only one member, the Varsity Club.

Although teachers participated in these associations and activities as advisors and counselors and stressed their importance in teaching students a "sense of responsibility" (i.e., independence of initiative and decision-making), participation by the teachers was a matter of tradition and expectation, not of contract. The fact that they, as a body, could have withdrawn from participation, emphasized the semiformal character of this extracurricular sector of the institution.

Although the activities and events of the system were patterned into an annual cycle, for each age-grade or year-class status there was a 4-year cycle of changing relationships to the annual cycle of student activities. From freshman initiation through sophomore, junior, and senior years, each year-class group experienced increasing opportunities for mobility in the student prestige hierarchy, increasing access as a group to commercial enterprises of the system, increasing financial affluence of the class-group, increasing political power and responsibility for important ceremonial events, and increasing opportunity to engage in student self-regulation of the subsystem.

The temporal aspect of the student system is diagrammed in Figure 1, in which I have tried to summarize the system's time cycles and phases of activities. Moving around the circle clockwise, one band notes the rites of passage, with freshman initiation occurring in September and a cluster of ceremonies in May marking separation of the senior class from the high school system. One group enters in the fall and is incorporated into the student subsystem, and an older group departs during the spring. The next inner band notes the annual cycle of rites of intensification. At several points it is related to the sports seasons and to the traditional seasonal calendar in the center circle. The black bars in the circle, A-G, show the various significant ceremonies that mark a change in the character of interaction, in the configuration of relationships, and in the nature of activity.

An Illustration of Student Ritual

Here we will first consider in some detail one of the ceremonies, the pep rally, to illustrate the criteria and data used in analysis of these ceremonial events. The pep rallies involved full assemblage of the high school body to "work up school spirit," as the explanation usually went, just before an extramural sports event. The pep rally for football season struck me as somewhat more elaborate than the ones preceding basketball. No pep rallies preceded track meets, an incongruity that will be explained later. The rite was a regular, recurrent part of student life and very much a mainstay of the student system.

Chapple and Coon's (1942) theory of ritual is very much concerned with crisis in systems and with interaction of participants as the basic component structure. To understand the systemic significance of ritual, one must take note of who interacts with whom and of the regular habitual order, duration, and temporal distribution of their actions with respect to one another. Human social systems are continuously faced with crisis in their need to change the characteristic modes of interaction to carry out the instrumental requirements of a living system, and to meet shifts in their internal aspects as well as in the external environment. Disturbances, or required changes, in interaction relationships result in

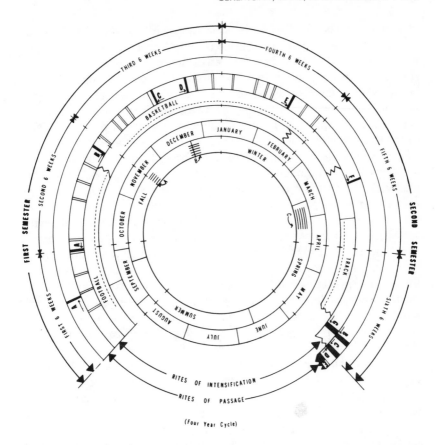

(Four Year Cycle)

Rites of Intensification

A. Homecoming
B. Football Banquet
C. Christmas Dance
D. New Year's Eve Party
E. Sweetheart Dance
F. Athletes Banquet
G. Honors Day
□. Pep Rallies

Rites of Passage

A. Freshman Initiation
B. Baccalaureate
C. Graduation
D. Alumni Banquet
E. Senior Trip

School Holidays

A. Thanksgiving
B. Christmas
C. Easter

Figure 1—Time cycles and phases of activities.

crisis and adjustment of the individual or of a group to the new arrangement and frequency of interaction.

Adjustment to change or to crisis may be secured either through associational interaction or through ritual. Associations hold a very special place in the Chapple and Coon (1942) theory of institutional equilibrium, but the main points here are that crisis is an everyday reality in social systems and that both associational interaction and ritual interaction can be used to restore effective interactive equilibrium. Rites of passage are used at some points of crisis in the individual life cycle and rites of intensification are used to restore the interactive balance for a group when some change of conditions or disturbance affects all or a part of the members of a system. Through the rituals of the ceremony, rites of passage provide the individual with practice in new orders and distribution of interaction entailed in a change in his status in the system. The ritual in the ceremony of rites of intensification provides group members with a dramatic presentation of habitual relationships associated with the activities of the system. Shifts in required activities bring about crisis through demanding changes in the interaction needed to carry out the activities. A rite of intensification is one functional device for carrying off the shifts in habitual relationships. Pep rallies, then, are ritual means of quickly carrying the students through a transition in interaction from work activity and the everyday relations of daily school life to the characteristically different relationships of extramural athletic events, when students relate to large numbers of members of the community and relate to one another in somewhat different ways.

The course of the events during football season can illustrate the characteristic order and interrelationship of aspects of ceremonial events. Football games were held on Friday evenings around 8:00 p.m. out-of-doors under floodlights. (Basketball games were also held in the evenings, but on Tuesday as well as Friday in a large new gymnasium in a new section of the school building.) During football season, the order of events of the day ran its familiar course until a special bell rang 10 minutes earlier than the usual dismissal bell. At this signal, the entire high school population, including teachers, assembled in the old gymnasium. When all were assembled, the school principal called the group to order and made a few announcements. Then the cheerleaders, as a group, trotted before the audience, and in well-practiced formation initiated cheers to the students and led them in highly synchronized cheers, first for the team, then for the coaches. They retired and one or two of the varsity players (always either seniors or juniors in class standing) stood before the group and gave a pep talk on the coming game. The talks always ended on a note of determination to strive to win. The player was greeted with a cheer; his talk was sometimes interrupted with cheers and always closed with a cheer from students. Next, the head coach or assistant coach gave a pep talk always concerned with the reputation of this week's opponent and the good features and improvements in the home team. The coach's talk always closed with a statement of his confidence in the players and their determination to play hard and to play to win. Finally, he usually alluded to the helpfulness toward victory of the spirit and support of the rest of the students. Then, the cheerleaders led the entire student body in more cheers and, as the dismissal bell rang, the students filed out, cheering as they went.

As the girls and boys dispersed to walk home or ride home in bus or car, there was an unusual degree of segregation of boys and girls. The occupants of cars were particularly noticeable for their sexual homogeneity. According to training rules, the players reported to me, the boys on the team were to go straight home to rest and prepare themselves for the game. Those boys were not to engage in interaction with girls from the time they departed from school until after the game. As the boys usually put it, "You aren't supposed to be seen with girls."

The male/female segregation actually began during the pep rally. In the old gymnasium, there were bleachers running the length of the south side of the gym; they were separated into an east and a west side by the entrance and steps leading down into the gymnasium. During pep rallies, the students always sat on the west side of the bleachers; the teachers, except for coaches, always sat on the east side; the coaches sat with their players. The students further segregated themselves: The players sat toward the west end of the west bleachers near the playing floor of the gymnasium; the boys who weren't on the team sat at the back of the west bleachers from the center aisle to the west wall. The girls sat toward the front of the west bleachers nearest the aisle and well separated from the players. The cheerleaders, all girls, sat on the lowest bleachers adjoining the gymnasium floor directly in front of the other girls. The students were further organized spatially through the tendency of students to cluster near one another in clique groups.

During the evening event in the course of the game, the social relations and orders of action that were prominent in the pep rally occurred repeatedly. For example, players were segregated from other students, particularly from girls; cheerleaders initiated and synchronized cheers during the course of the game; and students were not subject to their usual relationship to teachers and other adults. And those who acted as vendors of drink and food had a different type of relationship with adults.

After home games, a student dance, called a soc hop, was usually held in the gymnasium with music provided on phonograph records. At this event players and females once more interacted with one another. The dances were called "soc hops" because they were held on the sleek, waxed perfection of the basketball court that must not be marred or scratched with ordinary shoes, thus requiring that students remove their shoes and dance in stocking feet.

The mode of activity and interactive relationships characteristic of evening events like this were markedly different from the mode of activity and interaction that characterized the school workday. Clearly, the ritual of the pep rally ceremony could be said to help with the quick transition by organizing, dramatizing, and actively illustrating the change in interaction and relationship.

Other Student Ceremonials

The football banquet marked the end of football season. The banquet—for football players, their coaches, and the school principal and superintendent—was a boisterous, rowdy, stag affair that signaled a change in the characteristic mode of interaction among players. Relationships with other students, among community members, and between players and spectators did not change enough from football to basketball seasons to require ritual dramatization for student body and community. The rite, therefore, involved only the players and the coaches, who were deeply affected by the cessation of certain modes of relationship and interaction.

The Christmas dance and New Year's Eve dance related to the culture-wide temporal event of the Christmas season. They marked the beginning and close, respectively, of a long recess from schoolwork and from regular modes of interaction among students. The Sweetheart Dance anticipated the end of "soc-hop season," the Friday evening dances that followed home games.

The athletes' banquet, in contrast to the football banquet, was sponsored by parents and attended by parents as well as students and players. It posed an interesting challenge to the view that rites of intensification mark changes in group social relations. One asks why did it occur before, rather than after, track season? The explanation lies in the fact that track meets were held in the afternoon immediately after school rather than later in the evening. Despite several winning track seasons, few students attended, only a handful of adults attended, no money-earning enterprises were operated, and no cheerleaders or other means were used to organize spectator response. Most heads of households drove to nearby cities to their work and, consequently, did not arrive in time for events beginning around half past three in the afternoon. Track meets after school just didn't fit the community time schedule. The significant change in interaction for the community occurred with the cessation of basketball games, which were evening games they could attend. It is this which was marked by a rite of intensification—the community-sponsored athletes' banquet.

Homecoming, which occurred in the fall just a few weeks after the school year began, was an event that brought together students, former students, and the community in general, and that gave expression to every significant relationship in the student subsystem—because successful execution of the ceremony *demanded* the operation of all these relationships. The political dominance of the seniors was reflected in the fact that they were entirely in charge of planning, organizing, and supervising Homecoming. From the building of parade floats, through the ritual beginning of Homecoming with a bonfire and snake dance on Thursday, a parade in town on Friday afternoon, the half-time activities at the football game Friday evening, the decoration of the gymnasium, sponsorship of the Homecoming Dance, to the ritual climax of the Homecoming ceremony with the crowning of the King and Queen of Homecoming, seniors were in charge. But they relied on the cooperation of all the student organizations in the school. By the time the first preparations for Homecoming began in late September, positions in the various associations had been assigned personnel, from presidents to minor standing committees. Homecoming activities were handled within the permanent associations through both special and standing committees. But the structures were not activated and put into motion until Homecoming and its preparation, colored by intensity of feeling, deadline rush, and anxiety for success, touched the whole system with a sense of crisis and the need to mobilize. The organizational system then moved into forward gear as the senior class offered a monetary prize for the best float. The year-class, age-graded associations were the liveliest competitors in that contest. In addition, whether or not they organized to build floats, *all* associations carried out elections to nominate a king and queen candidate—although seniors always won the final crowns. The student council had exercised its function as a control for allocating money-earning enterprises. The community at several points assumed its role of interested, responsive spectator to the knowledge, performances, and products of the high school students.

Details might be added, but it seems clear that Homecoming was a system-wide rite of intensification. The usual role positions of the associations were filled; certain organizations had begun to operate; year-class groups were poised to behave in a new status in relationship to the total system. But without a very dramatic challenge it might have required a long time for the complex interdependencies and synchronization of activity and positional duties to work in smooth, orderly fashion. All these new characteristics of interaction amount to a crisis of the system that is resolved through carrying out a complex event in the form of ritualized, traditional patterns of action and interdependencies. In accordance with Chapple and Coon's (1942) view of what a rite of intensification does, everyone gets practice in the patterns of action and interaction that will be characteristic of associational work throughout the rest of the year.

Ritual, Ceremony, and the Student Economic System

Turning finally to the manner in which the entire ceremonial system was supported by and related to the student economic system, one must consider a special rite of passage: the senior trip. The senior trip was the main objective in the money-earning activities of each year-class. Every year, after going through several ceremonial events that dramatized the separation of the seniors from the high school system, the senior class departed on a 3- or 4-day trip. Accompanied only by the class sponsor, bus driver, and their respective spouses, the seniors rode to a resort in the Missouri Ozarks where other senior classes from other high schools also gathered for 3 or 4 days of "gay abandon." This was the final event of the school year and the final student activity of the seniors' high school career. It showed the characteristic isolation that Van Gennep (1960) found associated often with the transition or marginal phase in his tripartite schema.

Though the beliefs associated with most of these ceremonial events mentioned above were skimpy to nonexistent, there was a rather more elaborate development of myth in connection with the senior trip. These myths, told more often by boys than girls, centered on tales of curfew violation, smoking, drinking, and sex. Ex-seniors emphatically declared to me that there was much fiction and little fact in these stories. Perhaps each group found that the outside world of "peerdom"—members of which they met at the resort—was little more marked by drunken busts, nocturnal merrymaking, and sexual abandon than their own world. But I think, although I cannot prove, that the myths were perpetuated by young post-high school males of the community.

The senior trip was the keystone of the student economy and the integrating goal of the student system. That this economic goal took priority over all other goals was reflected in the student council's policy of allocating the best and the greatest number of money-making enterprises to the seniors and juniors, in that order. I would not argue that economic motive was the only propelling force of the system. For example, yearning for prestige among their peers and within their immediate social milieu surely impelled students to expend thought, time, and energy in student activities. Yet the economic goal of financing special events of the year welded atomistic desires into group effort. Each student association had a main annual event around which to muster the efforts and economic enterprise of its members. However, the main event around which each year-class association organized its economic activities was the senior trip which was quadrennial rather than annual. By providing motive and direction over a 4-year cycle rather than an annual cycle, the senior trip provided the focus for an intergenerational tradition which upperclassmen could transmit to lowerclassmen, thus forming a pattern of enculturation for the student system as a whole.

The most common means of earning money was through selling food, and sometimes services. Except where long tradition had given another association a particularly lucrative resource, class associations, especially seniors, were granted the more profitable enterprises.

The frequent coincidence of entertainment activities and relationships with commercial activities and relationships was a salient characteristic of the system. The most successful entertainment events from the commercial point of view were the athletic events, for the needs of the crowd during the games were fulfilled by the goods sold by student associations. School spirit and school pride notwithstanding, the better the team the bigger the crowd; the bigger the crowd the more popcorn, candy, hot dogs, soda pop, and coffee sold. Thus, a good team, along with star athletes, not only carried responsibility for the reputation of the school *vis-à-vis* other schools; it was an economic asset to the student system.

There were other ways of making money from persons outside the student body than selling refreshments, but most of these required an assemblage of persons from the community. A group could earn money through admissions to dances, but the size of the crowd was critical. The sponsoring group hired an orchestra and a certain minimum attendance was required before the initial investment could be recovered and a profit made. Scheduling the dance after an athletic event was one of the best means of assuring at least this minimum profitable attendance. In light of this relationship it does not seem entirely unwarranted to suggest that between the athletic events and the student systems there was a kind of ecological connection.

Without the participation of adults and community members as spectators, these events would have gradually disappeared from the calendar of events. Through student activities, adults and parents were involved in socialization into that special style we have come to call "independence training." The adult was spectator to the performance, learning, success or failure of the young. Much of this learning was from peers, but it was then tested against the positive or negative response of adults as spectators. The adults in the community, through their interest in local high school athletics and other entertainment events, ultimately influenced and affected the value system of the students in the school—not in a one-to-one, adult-to-young relationship, but through a complex network of influence.

Conclusion

At the empirical level, this study challenges the position that rites and ceremonies of "status change" necessarily disappear with the rise of secular urban institutions. The analysis is based on the premise that many current arguments for the disappearance of such rites and ceremonies resemble in certain respects earlier arguments for definitions of totemism that totally divorce primitive institutions from those of modernity.[2] The act of assuming their disappearance places an intellectual blindfold upon the investigation of this aspect of behavior in modern institutions. The cultural patterns and practices of various types of school environments provide a context in modern society where both proponents and opponents of the disappearance of rites of transition can test their ideas empirically in the interest of resolving the problem.

Some may argue that the rural setting of the high school studied here is a survival from the past and that data from this community are not relevant to the modern urban world. Actually, this type of rural community is a necessary part of the urban scene. The mechanized, market-oriented, commercialized agriculture and the salient presence of commuting by nonfarmers to nearby urban centers for employment declare this community's membership in the broad urban scene and the relevance of this study to urban society. This is the agricultural sector of an urbanized society.

The town and school are admittedly small and highly homogeneous. These facts may limit the extension of any generalization from this setting. We know, however, that elaborate ceremonial cycles characterize secondary schools across the United States, although the interrelationships among ceremonial cycle, the academic work system, clique structure, immediate community, and association structure may vary greatly with the heterogeneity and size of the high school population. But this study does raise the question of what part ritual plays in the multichartered, multigrouped institutions that educate, socialize, and enculturate young people into modern megalopolises.

Notes

1. I spent 9 months as a participant observer in an American high school of 110 students, 7 teachers, and a teaching principal. Although I presented myself as a researcher, the students and faculty soon interpreted my activities and assigned me the role of guidance counselor. Throughout the 9-month school term, I observed the students during free periods of the day and during school-sponsored and school-related afternoon and evening activities. I gathered data on the relation between academic work and the student system by observing students in the study halls and in and between classes for several hundred hours. Interviews of an extemporaneous kind, semi-structured interviews, structured interviews, and several questionnaires based on structured interviews rounded out the data collection techniques.

2. Lévi-Strauss (1963) eloquently demonstrates how the conceptions of totemism in primitive society have been used to dissociate the thought processes and practices of modern western tradition from the taint of commonality with primitive peoples of the world. With respect to a related set of concepts, Mur-

ray and Rosalie Wax (1963, pp. 495-518) show that much the same kind of "protectionist" thinking has dominated the problem of distinguishing among magic, science, and religion.

References

BOSSARD, J.H.S., & Boll, E.S. *Ritual in family living*. Philadelphia: University of Pennsylvania Press, 1950.

CHAPPLE, E., & Coon, C.S. *Principles of anthropology*. New York: Henry Holt Company, 1942.

FISCHER, J.L. Psychology and anthropology. In B.S. Siegel (Ed.), *Biennial review of anthropology*. Stanford: Stanford University Press, 1965.

GEERTZ, C. Religion as a cultural system. In W.A. Lessa & E.Z. Vogt (Eds.), *Reader in comparative religion*. New York: Harper & Row, 1958.

GLUCKMAN, Max. Les rites de passage. In M. Gluckman (Ed.), *Essays on the ritual of social relations*. Manchester, England: Manchester University Press, 1962.

GOODY, J. Religion and ritual: The definitional problem. *The British Journal of Sociology*, 1961, **12**, 142-164.

HORTON, R. A definition of religion and its uses. *The Journal of the Royal Anthropological Institute*, 1960, **90**, 201-226.

KLUCKHOHN, C. Myths and ritual: A general theory. In W.A. Lessa & E.Z. Vogt (Eds.), *Reader in comparative religion*. New York: Harper & Row, 1958.

LEITES, N., & Bernaut, E. *Ritual of liquidation*. Glencoe, IL: Free Press, 1954.

LÉVI-STRAUSS, C. *Totemism*. Boston: Beacon Press, 1963.

NADEL, S.F. *Nupe religion*. London: Routledge & Paul, 1954.

POSINSKY, S.H. Ritual, neurotic and social. *American Imago*, 1962, **19**, 375-390.

VAN GENNEP, A. *[The rites of passage]* (M.B. Vizedom & G.L. Caffee, trans.). Chicago: University of Chicago Press, 1960. (Originally published, 1909.)

WAX, M., & Wax, R. The notion of magic. *Current Anthropology*, 1963, **4**, 495-518.

Chapter 13
Cult and Sport: The Case of Big Red

MICHAEL STEIN

T hough it is certainly conceivable that there are countless persons for whom the name Nebraska elicits absolutely no associations, it is more doubtful that anyone who has heard of the state is not aware of "Big Red" football: the only game in town. It is an activity of sufficient impact to have attracted the attention of television (a special), magazines *(Sports Illustrated, National Geographic)*, and has been noted by "legitimate" authors (e.g., James Michener). It is also felt to be worthy of attention by sociologists. The theoretical frame of this paper revolves around the concept of cult. That is, the "complex of gesture, word and symbolic vehicle which is the central role of this phenomenon. . ." (O'Dea, 1966, p. 39). Further, the cultic act "is a social or congregational act in which the group re-enacts its relationship to sacred objects . . . and in so doing reinforces its own values" (O'Dea, 1966, p. 40).

As Klapp (1964) has suggested, cults may take on a variety of interests and forms including that of recreation. Certainly, sports in general, foot-

From *Mid-American Review of Sociology*, 1977, 2(2), 29-42. Copyright 1977 by Mid-American Review of Sociology. Reprinted with permission.

ball in particular, and University of Nebraska football specifically, can rest comfortably under the rubric of a "recreational" cult. It is hoped, however, that this paper will be suggestive of more than mere recreation.[1] Of course, *tradition* seems endemic to college football, and though this in itself lends credence to the notion of a recreational cult, it paradoxically has "establishment" connotations which would seem to imply some category other than cult. It is here asserted that tradition sets the stage— provides the backdrop of scenery, as it were—on which this "little world" is enacted. "The transcending power of drama works even when the drama itself is part of the [larger] social structure. . ." (Klapp, 1964, p. 254).

There is, then, an element of drama, a theatrical flair, that is part of this tradition which begins to suggest something more going on than "just a game." Specifically, it is felt that *fan*atism coupled with unique "local" rituals lend Nebraska football a (possibly latent) "centering function" (Klapp, 1964), suggestive of a cult. As such, there is an assumption concerning a "civil" or secular religion, and consequently, the metaphor of religion is given some consideration in another part of this paper. The use of metaphors in sport suggests it represents more than a mere contest. By employing a religious metaphor we are suggesting that sport (like religion) may be a source of identity and belonging (i.e., a sense of community), transcendence, and catharsis.

Before turning to "Big Red" football in particular, however, it would do well to briefly consider spectator sports generally in our culture, as this is the context from which the phenomenon arose.

> There is no lack of evidence, in all kinds of odd places, of the overwhelming importance of sports in American life. In many American newspapers the sports page constitutes the largest specialized daily section. One-tenth of *The World Almanac* is devoted to sports. In both newspapers and the Almanac, the sports sections are greater in volume than the sections about politics, business, entertainment, or science. (Beisser, 1967, p. 2)

In addition to the presentation of sport via the printed word, it is further "validated" by omnipresent television coverage and, of course, massive live audiences. It should be emphasized that the "goodness," "badness," or danger of this consumption of sport is not the concern of this paper.[2] Instead, it is wished only to acknowledge the rather impressive mark of sports on culture, and, incidentally, the ironic reticence of sociology to more fully examine the area.

Such an examination offers advantages as a result of sport's permeation of our society. "Sport often provides a means of uncovering major social value themes (which) in turn channelize behavior" (Snyder, 1974, p. 359). In addition, sport is also "interrelated with social institutions, values, and social change; indeed via sport we may traverse much of the social landscape" (Snyder, 1974, p. 359). As Ball and Loy (1975) have noted, "sport is an especially useful substantive area within which to do sociological analysis" (p. 40). Such analysis could easily be quantitative in nature given sports' meticulous and easily accessible records and statistics. For the purpose of this paper, however, concern is given to the symbolism and imagery of sport in an attempt to grasp the meaning it has for its adherents. For as Stone notes, man "imbues his play with meanings and affect, arranges it, stylizes it" (Stone, 1955, p. 84). It is thus maintained that we bring meaning to sport and it, in turn, gives its fans something more than the mere contest.

It was suggested in the introduction that sport possesses a dramaturgical quality, and as a consequence it is appropriate to consider the metaphors of sport. By doing so, one may begin to understand the motivation of the fan. Perhaps the most apparent metaphor for sports in general, and football in particular, is that of the military. "Many games and athletic contests have a function similar to the military, and in more or less evident form exhibit something of war's relentless insistence on victory"[3] (Weiss, 1969, p. 32). This has been made abundantly clear in some of the imagery employed by our two most recent Presidents. "In some ways football more than any other sport in America seems to evoke local pride, patriotism, love and 'fight for the team' " (Miller & Russell, 1971, p. 57). Terms such as "blitz" and "in the trenches," and "the bomb" are common to both football and the military.

Besides the military, many see football as a microcosm of our own society. "Football is a modern invention that metaphors the modern business world—specialization, division of labor and efficiency" (Snyder, 1974, p. 360). If this is the case, fans' "worship" of football may represent the worship of society, a thought that strongly suggests football as a modern variant of the totem. Durkheim (1954), in his classic study of religion, asserted that the worship of God (through the totem) was a worship of society. Through the rites of the cult "society reaffirmed itself in a symbolic acting-out of its attitudes, which by strengthening the commonly-held attitudes, strengthened society itself" (O'Dea, 1966, p. 12). For Durkheim, then, "before all, rites are means by which the social group reaffirms itself periodically" (Durkheim, 1954, p. 387).

This brief discussion of Durkheim nicely serves as an introduction to the last and most germane metaphor to be considered in this paper: religion.

Many previous functions once carried out by the church were, of course, usurped by the creation of other autonomous institutions. The separation of church and state is the most obvious example. With less influence in matters of state, education, and the family, religion's province is firmly entrenched in "spiritual" concerns. This ultimately is taken to mean those issues that revolve around order, meaning, and purpose in one's life. An important corollary of this is that the religious experience offers transcendence, a rising above the more mundane prosaic features of "everyday life," i.e., the profane in Durkheim's analysis. As a consequence, religion is filled with rituals that are at once transcendent and offer the worshipper a sense of belonging. Through industrialization and rationalization our society has become much more secular in orientation, yet the need for ritual has not diminished but rather has been displaced in secular activity (see O'Dea, 1966).

> The evolution of man has demonstrated a constant and prevailing need for ritual . . . .
> . . . With the reduction of ritual in religion, it is not surprising man turns to other "rites" to again see some form of quasi-order to his life. For many, sport fulfills this function. (Slusher, 1967, p. 130)

It is therefore suggested that for some followers of the "home team," sport takes on the quality of a secular religion. There exist some intriguing parallels. "Both sport and religion employ intricate rituals which attempt to place events in a traditional and orderly view" (Slusher, 1967, p. 121). To place events in an orderly view is to give one a sense of meaning. "Sport, as religion, is a form of symbolic representation of meaningful realities" (Slusher, 1967, p. 129). It is through these symbols and rituals that sport is transformed into something much more than the contest itself.

If the metaphor of religion and sport holds, one would then expect the functions of each to be somewhat similar. At various times religion has served to offer continuity in life, an institutionalized agency for catharsis, a transcendent experience giving followers an escape from the mundane, and to foster a sense of belonging, of community. With the secularization of religion these functions are sought elsewhere, many times with a cultic flair.

It has been noted elsewhere that sport is digested (directly and indirectly) with ferocity by its fans. A partial explanation may lie in the fact that sport, as a "little world," offers its followers an island of continuity amidst a sea of chaos.

> We suspect, for example, that the sports pages in the daily newspaper are important for many consumers primarily because they provide some confirmation that there is a continuity in the events and affairs of the larger society. (Stone, 1955, p. 89)

An additional attraction for the fan is the opportunity to "blow off steam" in a setting that is appropriate for such behavior. "Another function sport has often been said to perform for its consumers is the legitimate outlet it provides for cathartic-expressive behavior and for the pent-up frustrations which would otherwise lead to serious violence"[4] (Kando, 1975, p. 234).

Closely aligned with this cathartic function is that of transcendence. It was elsewhere noted that sports may be approached dramaturgically. "A central fact about all drama, as opposed to daily life, is that the role one gets is not part of his regular routine and structure" (Klapp, 1964, p. 254). The "big game" then represents a brief hiatus from the ordinary mundane routine of the "everyday world," a movement, as it were, from the profane. Thus, the *event* of the game is approached, by many, with the intensity that a revival has for others. The fan "performs his weekly tasks in perfunctory manner, but when it comes time for sports he comes alive and is transformed by his enthusiasm" (Beisser, 1967, p. 226). The "houses" of this transformation, the gathering place for worshippers, are great, grey, concrete and steel cathedrals. Stadiums "are little more than shrines for spiritual activity. They allow man to escape the boredom of everyday life and reach out to a larger existence" (Slusher, 1967, p. 127).

Perhaps the most poignant attraction sport-as-religion has for its followers is the sense of "belonging" and "community" it elicits.[5] "The fan in relationship to his team is like the member of a family or tribe. He can share intense feelings in victory or defeat" (Beisser, 1967, p. 129). Viewed thusly, sport coupled with such variables as a winning tradition, lack of "competition" from other sources, and a vociferous following, can offer a sense of *identity* and belonging.[6] In short, "sport has become a function of communal involvement" (Slusher, 1967, p. 136). In terms of Football at the University of Nebraska, this communal involvement extends over the entire state and at times beyond.

Go Big Red: The Case of Nebraska's Civil Religion

For an initial appreciation of the extent to which University of Nebraska football "Cornhuskers" offer their followers an identity, one need only consider the number of faithful. Beginning with the 1967 season, Nebraska has played before 87 consecutive sellout crowds. This record streak will continue as the entire 1977 home season is again sold out. Even with continual stadium expansion from 1964 through 1972, which raised the seating capacity to 73,000 plus, demand has always exceeded supply. Last year, the mere *suggestion* of an additional 8,000 seats resulted in over 20,000 ticket requests in less than a month.

At the university, an extraordinarily high proportion of students (roughly 90%) buy season tickets, which in some instances are sold to the highest bidder (read: "more faithful"). During their first general registration, graduate students, as a matter of course, are checked for full-time status, "so you can be eligible for football tickets."[7] As if these numbers were not impressive in themselves, they become extraordinary when considered in relation to the state's small, and in most places, sparse, population. On a football Saturday, Memorial Stadium is not only by far the third largest "city" in the state, but the third largest county as well. This devotion on the part of the fans begins to suggest "Big Red" as a source of identification, and it is important to note that this is not exclusive to the more populous eastern quarter of Nebraska. Fans stream into Lincoln from all areas of the state, including the western panhandle, a pilgrimage of over 900 miles roundtrip for some faithful. Indeed, this sense of identification stretches beyond the borders of Nebraska. Former in-state fans now living in such places as California and Texas make an annual voyage to attend at least one home game. In addition, many followers trek to "away" games in large enough numbers at times to constitute half the crowd (the 1975 Kansas State game for example). The 1976 Hawaii game (a travel agent's dream) sent 20,000 fans to Honolulu.

As previously mentioned, many thousands wishing to attend Nebraska games cannot do so, owing to the large demand for tickets. Yet these people may share vicariously in this seasonal celebration: Highlights of all Husker games can be watched on "The Tom Osborne Show" each Sunday night, and radio coverage is massive. The broadcast network carrying Nebraska games consists of 54 stations located in all areas of the state. It is difficult to be in a public place during a game and not be in earshot of a radio broadcast. For those wishing to attend the game in person, listen to the broadcast *and* keep their hands free and ears warm, "earmuff" radios may be purchased.

Likewise, newspaper coverage is impressive. The Lincoln papers begin daily features of Nebraska football news in mid-August with their annual football review. From this point to the start of the season, the front page of the sports section will daily feature a story on some aspects of Nebraska football fortunes (i.e., returning stars, new players, coaches, etc.). Once the season begins in September, coverage becomes even more expansive, of course, including scouting reports ("Know the Foe" appears each Thursday), and Nebraska depth charts. The Sunday paper quite naturally devotes several pages to the preceding game. This generally includes two pages consisting entirely of photographs of key plays, interviews with both winning and losing coaches and players, and various commentaries on the game. Though this coverage decreases markedly after bowl games have been completed, one may still find occasional stories throughout the year. This would include notes on former Huskers now playing in the professional ranks, and speculations on the previous or forthcoming season. In addition, rather extensive coverage is given to the annual intersquad scrimmage played in the Spring. This event, incidentally, generally draws over 10,000 fans.

The favorite gathering place of the faithful, of course, is Memorial Stadium, looming large on the campus of the University of Nebraska. We have suggested that for the football fan the stadium may be likened to a house of worship. This cathedral metaphor received strong support on December 11, 1976, when a Husker football player was married in the south end-zone of Memorial Stadium. A news photo of the story fairly dominated the front page of "The Lincoln Sunday Journal and Star."

In addition to a large and faithful congregation, "tithings" are offered which (along with a continual packed house) assist in keeping Nebraska football, and consequently the entire athletic program, "in the black" without the aid of tax dollars. These donations are given by various auxiliary organizations and include the "Extra-Point" and "Touch-Down" clubs. Members' contributions range from 1 to 1,000 dollars a year. The "Wheel Club" consists of auto dealers who supply coaching and scouting staffs with cars. Members of the "Beef Club" supply training tables with Nebraska-raised steak.

With such a large number of followers (be it in person or via radio), Nebraska football serves a (cultic) "centering function" in that it is a common ground of interest and passion for the state: It offers a source of pride and sense of identity.

The reason football has taken on this identity function for Nebraskans is a source for speculation. From 1962 to 1972 the "Cornhuskers" were coached by Bob Devaney (currently athletic director and deity) who established a winning tradition. From the time of his arrival, Nebraska has been a consistent "top ten" finisher, including consecutive national championships in 1970 and 1971. The 1971 team was voted "team of the century" by sports scribes. This winning tradition, coupled with a total lack of competition from other university level or professional teams, and a dearth of scenic wonders, undoubtedly helps fuel the mystique.

The impact of this seasonal rite can be further assessed by other sources. Artifacts celebrating Big Red football are ubiquitous. They range from humble matchbook covers to oil paintings. Phone booths around campus and the adjacent downtown Lincoln are topped with a powerful-looking, rosy-cheeked, straw-hatted Cornhusker. Many stores offer a variety of Cornhusker glasswear and assorted knick-knacks. For those more thoroughly smitten, a toilet paper dispenser with radio pretuned to the Nebraska game is reported by Michener (1976, p. 221).

Nearly all the artifacts (those listed above are only intended to suggest a range) share a common quality: redness. Red is the color of "true believers" and can be seen everywhere, most conspicuously in the attire of the faithful. Entire ensembles are unveiled with the arrival of fall fashions. One may simply wear a red scarf or jewelry, or abandon all restraint and purchase a complete wardrobe, including shoes, socks, pants, shirts, sweater, coat, and hat. Perhaps the quintessence of the Big Red follower was described by author James Michener. As reported, a couple lived in a house in which "everything on the ground floor, including carpets, furniture, wall paper, decorations, and a three-wall bulletin board dominating the living room was shattering red, including [the couple], two attractive people in their mid-forties who during the football season dress only in red" (Michener, 1976, p. 219). For the true afficionado, there is an additional artifact which takes on the quality of a religious relic. Local businessmen have purchased the old astroturf and are selling the historic carpet in small, Nebraska-shaped pieces.

Customs of coverage and clothing aside, one may further gauge the impact of Nebraska football by the "suspension of ordinary rules" during home games. Indeed, because a sell-out is assured, many teams stand to gain more financially by traveling to Lincoln each time they play the Cornhuskers. As a consequence, Nebraska nearly always plays more games at home during a season than on the road. 1975, for instance, found Nebraska playing the first five games, and seven out of eleven regular season games, at home. The 1977 season finds six of the first seven games at Memorial Stadium.

As so many people do attend the games, "ordinary" parking rules are suspended in favor of those reflecting the amount of financial commitment. University lots near the stadium, normally allowing only cars with a proper parking sticker, are cleared the night before a game, to make space for "special" ticket holders. One lot, directly behind the stadium, is reserved for campers and larger recreation vehicles, many of which have traveled hundreds of miles. On returning home, those taking the Interstate are warned during the game that certain "normal" access routes are closed to interstate traffic. In fact, Big Red even indirectly influences governmental agencies, as the following front-page article in the Lincoln Journal of July 28, 1977 suggests:

By The Associated Press: Nothing, absolutely nothing, is allowed to get in the way of Big Red football.

The Nebraska Roads Dept. has vowed to halt any construction projects on Interstate 80 that might delay Big Red football traffic en route from Omaha to Lincoln.

Don Cook, district construction engineer, said Wednesday that five bridges near Lincoln on I-80 and 180 leading to Memorial Stadium are being resurfaced this summer.

If they're not finished by Sept. 10, the date of Nebraska's first home game, the construction companies will have to pack up and leave.

Cook said *all construction contracts in the Lincoln area carry a stipulation that they must be completed by the first Big Red game.*

"If the construction isn't done, the company has to quit, clean everything up and finish it next year," he said.

From what has been completed so far, Cook figures all construction should be finished by the first week in September.

There is no choice.

The onslaught of many fans begins on a Friday afternoon immediately preceding the Saturday game. It thus takes on the quality of an event, spilling into activities prior to and following the game itself. Motel rooms in Lincoln are filled on football weekends, and are the scene of countless celebrations. This indicates another loosening (if not suspension) of ordinary rules, as the consumption of alcohol is seen by many as an appropriate pregame and postgame ritual. The author personally rode to one game in a city-owned "mini bus" rented by a private club. The bus was packed far beyond its legal capacity. Countless six-packs of beer were sold and consumed en route to the stadium.

The central focus of the event, of course, is the game itself, and a football Saturday finds Lincoln streaming with fans resplendent in red, winding their way to the stadium. If one of the many ads requesting tickets has been left unanswered, the fan may still purchase a ticket from scalpers who line the periphery of the stadium. Informal norms have established the distance from the stadium scalpers may stand. The mode of advertising (other than ads) consists of holding the tickets or fingers in the air. The price asked depends on the importance of the game and/or the devotion of the fan. Though subfreezing temperatures may keep some at home, the stadium is always filled and blazing in red by game time.

The game itself must simply be experienced to be believed. Certain rituals occur during the game that serve not only to identify the faithful, but also "localize" the cultic flair of college football. Dressing in red is the most conspicuous of such behavior. Then, too, one could add the "ritual of red balloons," in which thousands of these spheres are released by the faithful upon the first Nebraska score. For many this is followed by the "ceremony of oranges," in which the fruit is hurled onto the field after each score, symbolically indicating the faithful's desire to see the Cornhuskers in the postseason Orange Bowl. At times (including last season) these "magic rites" fail, and Nebraska finds itself playing bowl games of lesser prestige.

Regardless of the season's outcome, however, there is "always next year," and starting in January the faithful await eagerly the annual Spring game in April and the August "football review" in the Lincoln papers. These two events (and the anticipation of them) serve to titilate and remind the faithful that Nebraska football *remains* the only game in town.

Notes

1. This is not to imply that "mere" recreation is not a worthy endeavor for sociologists. The author acknowledges the importance of recreation in social life (especially with the increase of leisure time).
2. Vanderzwaag (1972) considers a phenomenological approach, suggesting "not to regard experience with suspicion, but to accept it as a valid and meaningful aspect of being or existing in the world" (p. 220).
3. This insistence on victory is particularly acute for Nebraska football, whose fans have been somewhat jaded by recent (1970 and 1971) national championships, and a decade of being in the final "top ten." Losing has become tantamount to "sacrilege."
4. In terms of institutionalized religion, festivals such as Mardi Gras once served the same purpose.
5. Any reader interested in the forms "community" has taken in impersonal society is directed to Ralph Keyes' *We the Lonely People*, a wise and perceptive introduction to the topic.
6. Variables such as "big time" football and a winning tradition may be crucial in differentiating Nebraska (cultic) football from other schools (e.g., South Dakota).
7. Based on the author's personal experience.

References

BALL, D.W., & Loy, J.W. *Sport and social order.* Reading, MA: Addison-Wesley, 1975.

BEISSER, A.R. *The madness in sports.* New York: Meridith, 1967.

DURKHEIM, E. *[The elementary forms of religious life]* (J.W. Swain, trans.). Glencoe, IL: The Free Press, 1954.

KANDO, T.M. *Leisure and popular culture in transition.* St. Louis: C.V. Mosby, 1975.

KENYON, G.S. *Sociology of sport.* Chicago: The Athletic Institute, 1968.

KLAPP, O.E. *Public dramas and public man.* Chicago: Aldine, 1964.

MICHENER, J.A. *Sports in America.* New York: Random House, 1976.

MILLER, D.M., & Russell, K.R.E. *Sport: A contemporary view.* Philadelphia: Lea & Febiger, 1971.

O'DEA, T.F. *The sociology of religion.* Engelwood Cliffs, NJ: Prentice Hall, 1966.

SLUSHER, H.S. *Man, sport and existence: A critical analysis.* Philadelphia: Lea & Febiger, 1967.

SNYDER, E.E. Kickoff. *Journal of Popular Culture*, 1974, **8**(2), 359-360.

STONE, G. Play and display. *Chicago Review*, Fall 1955.

VANDERZWAAG, H.J. *Toward. a philosophy of sport*. Reading, MA: Addison-Wesley, 1972.

WEISS, P. *Sport: A philosophic inquiry*. Carbondale: Southern Illinois University Press, 1969.

Part 3
Play and
Interpretations

Chapter 14
A Theory of Play and Fantasy[1, 2]

GREGORY BATESON[3]

his research was planned and started with an hypothesis to guide
our investigations, the task of the investigators being to collect
relevant observational data and, in the process, to amplify and modify
the hypothesis.

The hypothesis will here be described as it has grown in our thinking.

Earlier fundamental work of Whitehead and Russell (1910-13), Wittgenstein (1922), Carnap (1937), Whorf (1940), etc., as well as my own attempt (Ruesch & Bateson, 1951) to use this earlier thinking as an
epistemological base for psychiatric theory, led to a series of generalizations:

1. That human verbal communication can operate and always does

From *Approaches to the Study of Human Personality*, pp. 39-51 [Psychiatric Research
Reports, 1955, No. 2]. Copyright 1955 by the American Psychiatric Association. Reprinted
with permission.

The complete title to this article is "A Theory of Play and Fantasy: A Report on Theoretical
Aspects of the Project for Study of the Role of the Paradoxes of Abstraction in Communication."

operate at many contrasting levels of abstraction. These range in two directions from the seemingly simple denotative level ("The cat is on the mat"). One range or set of these more abstract levels includes those explicit or implicit messages where the subject of discourse is the language. We will call these meta-linguistic (for example, "The verbal sound 'cat' stands for any member of such and such class of objects," or "The word, 'cat,' has no fur and cannot scratch"). The other set of levels of abstraction we will call meta-communicative (e.g., "My telling you where to find the cat was friendly," or "This is play"). In these, the subject of discourse is the relationship between the speakers.

It will be noted that the vast majority of both meta-linguistic and meta-communicative messages remain implicit; and also that, especially in the psychiatric interview, there occurs a further class of implicit messages about how meta-communicative messages of friendship and hostility are to be interpreted.

2. If we speculate about the evolution of communication, it is evident that a very important stage in this evolution occurs when the organism gradually ceases to respond quite "automatically" to the mood-signs of another and becomes able to recognize the sign as a signal: that is, to recognize that the other individual's and its own signals are only signals, which can be trusted, distrusted, falsified, denied, amplified, corrected, and so forth.

Clearly this realization that signals are signals is by no means complete even among the human species. We all too often respond automatically to newspaper headlines as though these stimuli were direct object-indications of events in our environment instead of signals concocted and transmitted by creatures as complexly motivated as ourselves. The non-human mammal is automatically excited by the sexual odor of another; and rightly so, inasmuch as the secretion of that sign is an "involuntary" mood-sign: i.e., an outwardly perceptible event which is a part of the physiological process which we have called a mood. In the human species a more complex state of affairs begins to be the rule. Deodorants mask the involuntary olfactory signs, and in their place the cosmetic industry provides the individual with perfumes which are not involuntary signs but voluntary signals, recognizable as such. Many a man has been thrown off balance by a whiff of perfume, and if we are to believe the advertisers, it seems that these signals, voluntarily worn, have sometimes an automatic and autosuggestive effect even upon the voluntary wearer.

Be that as it may, this brief digression will serve to illustrate a stage of evolution—the drama precipitated when organisms having eaten of the fruit of the Tree of Knowledge, discover that their signals are signals. Not only the characteristically human invention of language can then follow, but also all the complexities of empathy, identification, projection, and so on. And with these comes the possibility of communicating at the multiplicity of levels of abstraction mentioned above.

3. The first definite step in the formulation of the hypothesis guiding this research occurred in January, 1952, when I went to the Fleishhacker Zoo in San Francisco to look for behavioral criteria which would indicate whether any given organism is or is not able to recognize that the signs emitted by itself and other members of the species are signals. In theory, I had thought out what such criteria might look like—that the occurrence of meta-communicative signs (or signals) in the stream of interaction between the animals would indicate that the animals have at least some awareness (conscious or unconscious) that the signs about which they meta-communicate are signals.

I knew, of course, that there was no likelihood of finding denotative messages among nonhuman mammals, but I was still not aware that the animal data would require an almost total revision of my thinking. What I encountered at the zoo was a phenomenon well known to everybody: I saw two young monkeys *playing*, i.e., engaged in an interactive sequence of which the unit actions or signals were similar to but not the same as those of combat. It was evident, even to the human observer, that the sequence as a whole was not combat, and evident to the human observer that to the participant monkeys this was "not combat."

Now, this phenomenon, play, could only occur if the participant organisms were capable of some degree of meta-communication, i.e., of exchanging signals which would carry the message "this is play."

4. The next step was the examination of the message "this is play," and the realization that this message contains those elements which necessarily generate a paradox of the Russellian or Epimenides type—a negative statement containing an implicit negative meta-statement. Expanded, the statement "this is play" looks something like this: "These actions in which we now engage do not denote what those actions *for which they stand* would denote."

We now ask about the italicized words, *"for which they stand."* We say the word "cat" stands for any member of a certain class. That is, the phrase "stands for" is a near synonym of "denotes." If we now substitute "which they denote" for the words "for which they stand" in the expanded definition of play, the result is: "These actions, in which we now engage, do not denote what would be denoted by those actions which these actions denote." The playful nip denotes the bite, but it does not denote what would be denoted by the bite.

According to the Theory of Logical Types such a message is of course inadmissable, because the word "denote" is being used in two degrees of abstraction, and these two uses are treated as synonymous. But all that we learn from such a criticism is that it would be bad natural history to expect the mental processes and communicative habits of mammals to conform to the logician's ideal. Indeed, if human thought and communication always conformed to the ideal, Russell would not—in fact could not—have formulated the ideal.

5. A related problem in the evolution of communication concerns the origin of what Korzybski (1941) has called the map-territory relation: the fact that a message, of whatever kind, does not consist of those objects which it denotes ("the word 'cat' cannot scratch us"). Rather, language bears to the objects which it denotes a relationship comparable to that which a map bears to a territory. Denotative communication as it occurs at the human level is only possible *after* the evolution of a complex set of meta-linguistic (but not verbalized)[4] rules which govern how words and sentences shall be related to objects and events. It is therefore appropriate to look for the evolution of such meta-linguistic and/or meta-communicative rules at a prehuman and preverbal level.

It appears from what is said above that play is a phenomenon in which the actions of "play" are related to, or denote, other actions of "not play." We therefore meet in play with an instance of signals standing for other events, and it appears, therefore, that the evolution of play may have been an important step in the evolution of communication.

6. *Threat* is another phenomenon which resembles play in that actions denote, but are different from, other actions. The clenched fist of threat is different from the punch, but it refers to a possible future (but at present nonexistent) punch. And threat also is commonly recognizable among nonhuman mammals. Indeed it has lately been argued that a great part of what appears to be combat among members of a single species is rather to be regarded as threat (Lorenz, 1952; Tinbergen, 1953).

7. Histrionic behavior and deceit are other examples of the primitive occurrence of map-territory differentiation. And there is evidence that dramatization occurs among birds: A jackdaw may imitate her own mood-signs (Lorenz, 1952), and deceit has been observed among howler monkeys (Carpenter, 1934).

8. We might expect threat, play, and histrionics to be three independent phenomena all contributing to the evolution of the discrimination between map and territory. But it seems that this would be wrong, at least so far as mammalian communication is concerned. Very brief analysis of childhood behavior shows that such combinations as histrionic play, bluff, playful threat, teasing play in response to threat, histrionic threat, and so on form together a single total complex of phenomena. And such adult phenomena as gambling and playing with risk have their roots in the combination of threat and play. It is evident also that not only threat but the reciprocal of threat—the behavior of the threatened individual—are a part of this complex. It is probable that not only histrionics but also spectatorship should be included within this field. It is also appropriate to mention self-pity.

9. A further extension of this thinking leads us to include ritual within this general field in which the discrimination is drawn, but not completely, between denotative action and that which is to be denoted. Anthropological studies of peace-making ceremonies, to cite only one example, support this conclusion.

In the Andaman Islands, peace is concluded after each side has been given ceremonial freedom to strike the other. This example, however, also illustrates the labile nature of the frame "this is play," or "this is ritual." The discrimination between map and territory is always liable to break down, and the ritual blows of peace-making are always liable to be mistaken for the "real" blows of combat. In this event, the peace-making ceremony becomes a battle (Radcliffe-Brown, 1922).

10. But this leads us to recognition of a more complex form of play; the game which is constructed not upon the premise "this is play" but rather around the question "is this play?" And this type of interaction also has its ritual forms, e.g., in the hazing of initiation.

11. Paradox is doubly present in the signals which are exchanged within the context of play, fantasy, threat, etc. Not only does the playful nip not denote what would be denoted by the bite for which it stands, but, in addition, the bite itself is fictional. Not only do the playing animals not quite mean what they are saying but, also, they are usually communicating about something which does not exist. At the human level, this leads to a vast variety of complications and inversions in the fields of play, fantasy, and art. Conjurers and painters of the *trompe l'oeil* school concentrate upon acquiring a virtuosity whose only reward is reached after the viewer detects that he has been deceived and is forced to smile or marvel at the skill of the deceiver. Hollywood film makers spend millions of dollars to increase the realism of a shadow. Other artists, perhaps more realistically, insist that art be nonrepresentational; and poker players achieve a strange addictive realism by equating the chips for which they play with dollars. They still insist, however, that the loser accept his loss as part of the game.

Finally, in the dim region where art, magic, and religion meet and overlap, human beings have evolved the "metaphor that is meant," the flag which men will die to save, and the sacrament that is felt to be more than "an outward and visible sign, given unto us." Here we can recognize an attempt to deny the difference between map and territory, and to get back to the absolute innocence of communication by means of pure mood-signs.

12. We face then two peculiarities of play: (a) that the messages or signals exchanged in play are in a certain sense untrue or not meant; and (b) that that which is denoted by these signals is nonexistent. These two peculiarities sometimes combine strangely to reverse a conclusion reached above. It was stated (4) that the playful nip denotes the bite, but

does not denote that which would be denoted by the bite. But there are other instances where an opposite phenomenon occurs. A man experiences the full intensity of subjective terror when a spear is flung at him out of the 3D screen or when he falls headlong from some peak created in his own mind in the intensity of nightmare. At the moment of terror there was no questioning of "reality," but still there was no spear in the movie house and no cliff in the bedroom. The images did not denote that which they seemed to denote, but these same images did really evoke that terror which would have been evoked by a real spear or a real precipice. By a similar trick of self-contradiction the film makers of Hollywood are free to offer to a puritanical public a vast range of pseudo-sexual fantasy which otherwise would not be tolerated. In "David and Bathsheba," Bathsheba can be a Troilistic link between David and Uriah. And in "Hans Christian Andersen," the hero starts out accompanied by a boy. He tries to get a woman, but when he is defeated in this attempt, he returns to the boy. In all of this, there is, of course, no homosexuality, but the choice of these symbolisms is associated in these fantasies with certain characteristic ideas, e.g., about the hopelessness of the heterosexual masculine position when faced with certain sorts of women or with certain sorts of male authority. In sum, the pseudo-homosexuality of the fantasy does not stand for any real homosexuality, but does stand for and express attitudes which might accompany a real homosexuality or feed its etiological roots. The symbols do not denote homosexuality, but do denote ideas for which homosexuality is an appropriate symbol. Evidently it is necessary to re-examine the precise semantic validity of the interpretations which the psychiatrist offers to a patient, and, as preliminary to this analysis, it will be necessary to examine the nature of the frame in which these interpretations are offered.

13. What has previously been said about play can be used as an introductory example for the discussion of frames and contexts. In sum, it is our hypothesis that the message "this is play" establishes a paradoxical frame comparable to Epimenides' paradox. This frame may be diagrammed thus:

> All statements within this
> frame are untrue.
>
> I love you.
>
> I hate you.

The first statement within this frame is a self-contradictory proposition about itself. If this first statement is true, then it must be false. If it be false, then it must be true. But this first statement carries with it all the other statements in the frame. So, if the first statement be true, then all the others must be false; and, *vice versa*, if the first statement be untrue then all the others must be true.

14. The logically minded will notice a *non sequitur*. It could be urged that even if the first statement is false, there remains a logical possibility that some of the other statements in the frame are untrue. It is, however, a characteristic of unconscious or "primary process" thinking that the thinker is unable to discriminate between "some" and "all," and unable to discriminate between "not all" and "none." It seems that the achievement of these discriminations is performed by higher or more conscious mental processes which serve in the nonpsychotic individual to correct the black-and-white thinking of the lower levels. We assume, and this seems to be an orthodox assumption, that primary process is continually operating, and that the psychological validity of the paradoxical play frame depends upon this part of the mind.

15. But, conversely, while it is necessary to invoke the primary process as an explanatory principle in order to delete the notion of "some" from between "all" and "none," this does not mean that play is simply a primary process phenomenon. The discrimination between "play" and "nonplay," like the discrimination between fantasy and nonfantasy, is certainly a function of secondary process, or "ego." Within the dream the dreamer is usually unaware that he is dreaming, and within "play" he must often be reminded that "this is play."

Similarly, within dream or fantasy the dreamer does not operate with the concept "untrue." He operates with all sorts of statements but with a curious inability to achieve meta-statements. He cannot, unless close to waking, dream a statement referring to (i.e., framing) his dream.

It therefore follows that the play frame as here used as an explanatory principle implies a special combination of primary and secondary processes. This, however, is related to what was said earlier, when it was argued that play marks a step forward in the evolution of communication—the crucial step in the discovery of map-territory relations. In primary process, map and territory are equated; in secondary process, they can be discriminated. In play, they are both equated and discriminated.

16. Another logical anomaly in this system must be mentioned: that the relationship between two propositions which is commonly described by the word "premise" has become intransitive. In general, all asymmetrical relationships are transitive. The relationship "greater than" is typical in this respect; it is conventional to argue that if A is greater than B, and B is greater than C, then A is greater than C. But in psychological processes the transitivity of asymmetrical relations is not observed. The proposition P may be a premise for Q; Q may be a premise for R; and R may be a premise for P. Specifically, in the system which we are con-

sidering, the circle is still more contracted. The message "All statements within this frame are untrue" is itself to be taken as a premise in evaluating its own truth or untruth. (Cf. The intransitivity of psychological preference discussed by McCulloch [1945] and paradigm for all paradoxes of this general type, Russell's [Whitehead & Russell, 1910-13] "class of classes which are not members of themselves." Here Russell demonstrates that paradox is generated by treating the relationship, "is a member of," as an intransitive.) With this caveat, that the "premise" relation in psychology is likely to be intransitive, we shall use the word "premise" to denote a dependency of one idea or message upon another comparable to the dependency of one proposition upon another which is referred to in logic by saying that the proposition P is a premise for Q.

17. All this, however, leaves unclear what is meant by "frame" and the related notion of "context." To clarify these, it is necessary to insist first that these are psychological concepts. We use two sorts of analogy to discuss these notions: the physical analogy of the picture frame and the more abstract, but still not psychological, analogy of the mathematical set. In set theory the mathematicians have developed axioms and theorems to discuss with rigor the logical implications of membership in overlapping categories or "sets." The relationships between sets are commonly illustrated by diagrams in which the items or members of a larger universe are represented by dots, and the smaller sets are delimited by imaginary lines enclosing the members of each set. Such diagrams then illustrate a topological approach to the logic of classification. The first step in defining a psychological frame might be to say that it is (or delimits) a class or set of messages (or meaningful actions). The play of two individuals on a certain occasion would then be defined as the set of all messages exchanged by them within a limited period of time and modified by the paradoxical premise system which we have described. In a set-theoretical diagram these messages might be represented by dots, and the "set" enclosed by a line which would separate these from other dots representing nonplay messages. The mathematical analogy breaks down, however, because the psychological frame is not satisfactorily represented by an imaginary line. We assume that the psychological frame has some degree of real existence. In many instances, the frame is consciously recognized and even represented in vocabulary ("play," "movie," "interview," "job," "language," etc.). In other cases, there may be no explicit verbal reference to the frame, and the subject may have no consciousness of it. The analyst, however, finds that his own thinking is simplified if he uses the notion of an unconscious frame as an explanatory principle; usually he goes further than this and infers its existence in the subject's unconscious.

But while the analogy of the mathematical set is perhaps over abstract, the analogy of the picture frame is excessively concrete. The psychological concept which we are trying to define is neither physical nor logical. Rather, the actual physical frame is, we believe, added by human beings to physical pictures because these human beings operate more easily in a universe in which some of their psychological characteristics are externalized. It is these characteristics which we are trying to discuss, using the externalization as an illustrative device.

18. The common functions and uses of psychological frames may now be listed and illustrated by reference to the analogies whose limitations have been indicated in the previous paragraph:

a. Psychological frames are exclusive, i.e., by including certain messages (or meaningful actions) within a frame, certain other messages are excluded.

b. Psychological frames are inclusive, i.e., by excluding certain messages certain others are included. From the point of view of set theory these two functions are synonymous, but from the point of view of psychology it is necessary to list them separately. The frame around a picture, if we consider this frame as a message intended to order or organize the perception of the viewer, says "Attend to what is within and do not attend to what is outside." Figure and ground, as these terms are used by Gestalt psychologists, are not symmetrically related as are the set and nonset of set theory. Perception of the ground must be positively inhibited and perception of the figure (in this case the picture) must be positively enhanced.

c. Psychological frames are related to what we have called "premises." The picture frame tells the viewer that he is not to use the same sort of thinking in interpreting the picture that he might use in interpreting the wallpaper outside the frame. Or, in terms of the analogy from set-theory, the messages enclosed within the imaginary line are defined as members of a class by virtue of their sharing common premises or mutual relevance. The frame itself thus becomes a part of the premise system. Either, as in the case of the play frame, the frame is involved in the evaluation of the messages which it contains, or the frame merely assists the mind in understanding the contained messages by reminding the thinker that these messages are mutually relevant and the messages outside the frame may be ignored.

d. In the sense of the previous paragraph, a frame is meta-communicative. Any message, which either explicitly or implicitly defines a frame, *ipso facto* gives the receiver instructions or aid in his attempt to understand the messages included within the frame.

e. The converse of (d) is also true. Every meta-communicative or meta-linguistic message defines, either explicitly or implicitly, the set of messages about which it communicates, i.e., every meta-communicative message is or defines a psychological frame. This, for example, is very evident in regard to such small meta-communicative signals as punctuation marks in a printed message, but applies equally to such complex meta-communicative messages as the psychiatrist's definition of his own curative role in terms of which his contributions to the whole mass of messages in psychotherapy are to be understood.

f. The relation between psychological frame and perceptual géstalt needs to be considered, and here the analogy of the picture frame is useful. In a painting by Rouault or Blake, the human figures and other objects represented are outlined. "Wise men see outlines and therefore they draw them." But outside these lines, which delimit the perceptual gestalt or "figure," there is a background or "ground" which in turn is limited by the picture frame. Similarly, in set theoretical diagrams, the larger universe within which the smaller sets are drawn is itself enclosed in a frame. This double framing is, we believe, not merely a matter of "frames within frames" but an indication that mental processes resemble logic in *needing* an outer frame to delimit the ground against which the figures are to be perceived. This need is often unsatisfied, as when we see a piece of sculpture in a junk shop window, but this is uncomfortable. We suggest that the need for this outer limit to the ground is related to a preference for avoiding the paradoxes of abstraction. When a logical class or set of items is defined—for example, the class of match boxes—it is necessary to delimit the set of items which are to be excluded, in this case, all those things which are not match boxes. But the items to be included in the background set must be of the same degree of abstraction, i.e., of the same "logical type" as those within the set itself. Specifically, if paradox is to be avoided, the "class of match boxes" and the "class of nonmatch boxes" (even though both these items are clearly not match boxes) must not be regarded as members of the class of nonmatch boxes. No class can be a member of itself. The picture frame then, because it delimits a background, is here regarded as an external representation of a very special and important type of psychological frame—namely a frame whose function is to delimit a logical type. This, in fact, is what was indicated above when it was said that the picture frame is an instruction to the viewer that he should not extend the premises which obtain between the figures within the picture to the wall paper behind it.

But, it is precisely this sort of frame that precipitates paradox. The rule for avoiding paradoxes insists that the items outside any enclosing line be of the same logical type as those within, but the picture frame, as analyzed above, is a line dividing items of one logical type from those of another. In passing, it is interesting to note that Russell's rule cannot be stated without breaking the rule. Russell insists that all items of inappropriate logical type be excluded (i.e., by an imaginary line) from the background of any class, i.e., he insists upon the drawing of an imaginary line of precisely the sort which he prohibits.

19. This whole matter of frames and paradoxes may be illustrated in terms of animal behavior, where three types of message may be recognized or deduced: (a) Messages of the sort which we here call mood-signs; (b) messages which simulate mood-signs (in play, threat, histrionics, etc.); and (c) messages which enable the receiver to discriminate between mood-signs and those other signs which resemble them. The message "This is play" is of this third type. It tells the receiver that certain nips and other meaningful actions are not messages of the first type.

The message "This is play" thus sets a frame of the sort which is likely to precipitate paradox: it is an attempt to discriminate between, or to draw a line between, categories of different logical types.

20. This discussion of play and psychological frames establishes a type of triadic constellation (or system of relationships) between messages. One instance of this constellation is analyzed in paragraph 19, but it is evident that constellations of this sort occur not only at the nonhuman level but also in the much more complex communication of human beings. A fantasy or myth may simulate a denotative narrative, and, to discriminate between these types of discourse, people use messages of the frame-setting type, and so on.

21. In conclusion, we arrive at the complex task of applying this theoretical approach to the particular phenomena of psychotherapy. Here the lines of our thinking may most briefly be summarized by presenting and partially answering these questions:

a. Is there any indication that certain forms of psychopathology are specifically characterized by abnormalities in the patient's handling of frames and paradoxes?

b. Is there any indication that the techniques of psychotherapy necessarily depend upon the manipulation of frames and paradoxes?

c. Is it possible to describe the process of a given psychotherapy in terms of the inter-action between the patient's abnormal use of frames and the therapist's manipulation of them?

22. In reply to the first question, it seems that the "word salad" of schizophrenia can be described in terms of the patient's failure to recognize the metaphoric nature of his fantasies. In what should be triadic constellations of messages, the frame-setting message (e.g., the phrase "as if") is omitted, and the metaphor or fantasy is narrated and acted upon in a manner which would be appropriate if the fantasy were a message of the more direct kind. The absence of meta-communicative framing which was noted in the case of dreams (15) is characteristic of the waking communications of the schizophrenic. With the loss of the ability to set meta-communicative frames, there is also a loss of ability to achieve the more primary or primitive message. The metaphor is treated directly as a message of the more primary type. (This matter is discussed at greater length in a paper by Jay Haley, Note 1.)

23. The dependence of psychotherapy upon the manipulation of frames follows from the fact that therapy is an attempt to change the patient's meta-communicative habits. Before therapy, the patient thinks and operates in terms of a certain set of rules for the making and understanding of messages. After successful therapy, he operates in terms of a different set of such rules. (Rules of this sort are in general, unverbalized and unconscious both before and after.) It follows that, in the process of therapy, there must have been communication at a level *meta* to these rules. There must have been communication about a *change* in rules.

But such a communication about change could not conceivably occur in messages of the type permitted by the patient's meta-communicative rules as they existed either before or after therapy.

It was suggested above that the paradoxes of play are characteristic of an evolutionary step. Here we suggest that similar paradoxes are a necessary ingredient in that process of change which we call psychotherapy.

The resemblance between the process of therapy and the phenomenon of play is, in fact, profound. Both occur within a delimited psychological frame, a spatial and temporal bounding of a set of interactive messages. In both play and therapy, the messages have a special and peculiar relationship to a more concrete or basic reality. Just as the pseudo-combat of play is not real combat, so also the pseudo-love and pseudo-hate of therapy are not real love and hate. The "transfer" is discriminated from real love and hate by signals invoking the psychological frame; and indeed it is this frame which permits the transfer to reach its full intensity and to be discussed between patient and therapist.

The formal characteristics of the therapeutic process may be illustrated by building up a model in stages. Imagine first two players who engage in a game of canasta according to a standard set of rules. So long as these rules govern and are unquestioned by both players, the game is unchanging, i.e., no therapeutic change will occur. (Indeed many attempts at psychotherapy fail for this reason.) We may imagine, however, that at a certain moment the two canasta players cease to play canasta and start a discussion of the rules. Their discouse is now of a different logical type from that of their play. At the end of this discussion, we can imagine that they return to playing but with modified rules.

This sequence of events is, however, still an imperfect model of therapeutic interaction, though it illustrates our contention that therapy necessarily involves a combination of discrepant logical types of discourse. Our imaginary players avoided paradox by separating their discussion of the rules from their play, and it is precisely this separation that is impossible in psychotherapy. As we see it, the process of psychotherapy is a framed interaction between two persons, in which the rules are implicit but subject to change. Such change can only be proposed by experimental action, but every such experimental action, in which a proposal to change the rules is implicit, is itself a part of the on-going game. It is this combination of logical types within the single meaningful act that gives to therapy the character not of a rigid game like canasta but, instead, that of an evolving system of interaction. The play of kittens or otters has this character.

24. In regard to the specific relationship between the way in which the patient handles frames and the way in which therapist manipulates them, very little can at present be said. It is however suggestive to observe that the psychological frame of therapy is an analogue of the frame-setting message which the schizophrenic is unable to achieve. To talk in "word salad" within the psychological frame of therapy is, in a sense, not pathological. Indeed the neurotic is specifically encouraged to do precisely this, narrating his dreams and free associations so that patient and therapist may achieve an understanding of this material. By the process of interpretation, the neurotic is driven to insert an "as if" clause into the productions of his primary process thinking, which productions he had previously deprecated or repressed. He must learn that fantasy contains truth.

For the schizophrenic the problem is somewhat different. His error is in treating the metaphors of primary process with the full intensity of literal truth. Through the discovery of what these metaphors stand for he must discover that they are only metaphors.

25. From the point of view of the project, however, psychotherapy constitutes only one of the many fields which we are attempting to investigate. Our central thesis may be summed up as a statement of the necessity of the paradoxes of abstraction. It is not merely bad natural history to suggest that people might or should obey the theory of Logical Types in their communications; their failure to do this is not due to mere carelessness or ignorance. Rather, we believe that the paradoxes of abstraction must make their appearance in all communication more complex than that of mood-signals, and that without these paradoxes the evolution of communication would be at an end. Life would then be an endless interchange of stylized messages, a game with rigid rules, unrelieved by change or humor.

Notes

1. Transmitted to APA Regional Research Conference by Jay Haley, Veterans Administration, Palo Alto, California, in *A.P.A. Research Reports, II*, 1955.
2. This paper was completed in February 1954 as part of the project mentioned in the subtitle. The project was financed by the Rockefeller Foundation. Since then work has continued upon the same theoretical base but focused specifically upon the problems of schizophrenia. This development of the work is now financed by the Josiah Macy, Jr., Foundation.

3. At the time of this writing, ethnologist, Veterans Administration, Palo Alto, California.
4. The verbalization of these meta-linguistic rules is a much later achievement which can only occur after the evolution of a non-verbalized meta-meta-linguistics.

References

CARNAP, R. *The logical syntax of language*. New York: Harcourt Brace, 1937.

CARPENTER, C.R. A field study of the behavior and social relations of howling monkeys. *Comparative Psychology Monographs*, 1934, **10**, 1-168.

KORZYBSKI, A. *Science and sanity*. New York: Science Press, 1941.

LORENZ, K.Z. *King Solomon's ring*. New York: Crowell, 1952.

MCCULLOCH, W.S. A heterarchy of values, etc. *Bulletin of Mathematical Biophysics*, 1945, **7**, 89-93.

RADCLIFFE-BROWN, A.R. *The Andaman Islanders*. Cambridge: Cambridge University Press, 1922.

RUESCH, J., & Bateson, G. *Communication: The social matrix of psychiatry*. New York: Norton, 1951.

TINBERGEN, N. *Social behavior in animals with special reference to vertebrates*. London: Methuen, 1953.

WHITEHEAD, A.N., & Russell, B. *Principia mathematica* (3 vols.). Cambridge: Cambridge University Press, 1910-1913.

WHORF, B.L. Science and linguistics. *Technology Review*, 1940, **44**, 229-248.

WITTGENSTEIN, L. *Tractatus logico-philosophicus*. London: Harcourt Brace, 1922.

Chapter 15
Passages, Margins, and Poverty: Religious Symbols of Communitas

VICTOR TURNER

Introduction

The Constitution on the Sacred Liturgy *(Sacrosanctum Concilium)* promulgated at the Second Vatican Council on December 4, 1963, by Pope Paul VI, has been enthusiastically hailed by many Catholics as a revision which has deracinated "useless forms and repetitions" (to cite a recurrent stricture) and enabled the faithful to use their native tongues in worship, thus transforming them from observers into participants. *Worship* magazine has asked me to comment on the current problem of ritual and liturgy in the church, in the perspective of the past 8 years. I do this with some hesitation, since I am an anthropologist, not a liturgiologist, and even within my own profession have never laid claim to be an "applied" anthropologist. I have attended many performances of ritual in Central and East African rural societies, written books and articles on

Introduction and Part 1 from *Worship*, September 1972, **46**(7), 390-412. Part 2 from *Worship*, October 1972, **46**(8), 482-494. Copyright 1972 by The Liturgical Press. Reprinted with permission.

my observations, and, in general, made the field of "primitive" ritual my focus of specialization. In my private capacity I am a Catholic and have participated in many "ceremonies of the Roman Rite" both before and after Vatican II. Whether my comments as a cultural scientist with experience of the simpler societies are pertinent to the massive changes occurring in a major historical religion I cannot judge, but it might be useful to make the attempt.

As my article indicates, I distinguish between human life as a series and structure of status incumbencies and as a series of intervals or *limina* of passage between social experiences in this domain of getting and spending prestige and material resources. Some of these intervals are "sacred," and may be termed "anti-structural" in the social sense, for they represent a stripping and leveling of men before the transcendental. In liminal sacredness many of the relationships, values, norms, etc., which prevail in the domain of pragmatic structure are reversed, expunged, suspended, reinterpreted, or replaced by a wholly other set. But what is *socially* "anti-structural" is often protected and enclosed by complex *cultural* structures.

Liturgical forms are among these, and they have a decisively inverse character to those prevalent in the social structural domain. One of the ways in which they reverse secular structures is in their "archaic" quality. It is a mistake to think that the archaic is the fossilized or surpassed. The archaic can be as contemporary as nuclear physics. In ritual it is a metaphor for anti-structure. We must recognize "minuses" and "zeroes" in the calculus of cultural symbolism as well as the "pluses." Positivism and rationalism have reduced ritual and its symbolism to scarcely more than the reflection or expression of aspects of social structure, direct or "veiled" or "projected." The liminal, and the ritual which guards it, are proofs of the existence of powers antithetical to those generating and maintaining "profane" structures of all types, proofs that man does not live by bread alone.

If ritual is not to be merely a reflection of secular social life, if its function is partly to protect and partly to express truths which make men free from the exigencies of their status incumbencies, free to contemplate and pray as well as to speculate and invent, then its repertoire of liturgical actions should not be limited to a direct reflection of the contemporary scene. Its true modernity should be mediated through forms, some of which, at least, should be inherited. Inherited forms will not be "dead" forms if they have themselves been the product of "free" religious or esthetic creativeness, in brief, of liminality and communitas (between man and God as well as between man and man). Archaic patterns of actions and objects which arose in the past from the free space within liminality can become protective of future free spaces. The archaic is not the obsolete.

In Central Africa I have listened to songs and prayer formulae in "dead languages" (archaic Lunda, no longer spoken) at the initiation rites of the Ndembu and Lunda, and observed persons thoroughly immersed in the modern world of the "money economy" taking a wholehearted part in ritual actions "hallowed by antiquity." I do not believe such actions are hallowed merely because they are old but because they are metaphors for something most precious to all "modernities," to every living, viable society. They represent the chalice in which truth is conveyed, the symbolic inversion of the utilitarian, of the currently fashionable, and indeed, of the ensemble of institutionalized status-roles which composes the social structure. In other words, always and everywhere ritual *ought* to have a pervasive archaic, repetitive, formal quality if it is to be a vehicle for values and experiences which transcend those of status-striving, money-grubbing, and self-serving. At the purely human level its archaisms and formalisms respond to deep collective needs. Liminality is the "unconscious" of cultural man; it is where the "species life" opens into the individual "surface" life.

For these reasons many have begun to feel that some liturgical changes experimentally introduced since 1963 into the Catholic Church have an incongruous, "inappropriate" character. This should not surprise us, since some ritual "reforms" are based on supposedly "scientific" theories of society which do not respond accurately to the human condition. The Constitution on the Sacred Liturgy was clearly influenced by structural-functionalism, which holds that ritual structure reflects social structure—hence should change *in response* to social structural changes—and that the "social function" of ritual is to reanimate periodically the "sentiments" on which a given social formation depends for its successful running. It was also influenced by behaviorism with its assumption that the faithful can be "conditioned" by "reinforcement" to accept what Establishment theoreticians of liturgy regard as being sociologically appropriate and hence "good" for them. Both structural-functionalism and behaviorism are obsolete formulations since they depend upon the metaphor or model of society as a closely integrated system, like an organism or a machine, rather than upon regarding it as a *process* with some systematic characteristics, a process that moves necessarily through creative moments of anti-structure as well as through long periods of structural regularity. I believe that one cause of the large-scale withdrawal of many Catholics from the institutional life of the church—who still think of themselves as Christians (and sorrow as widows do for the death of someone beloved)—is the comprehensive transformation of ritual forms under the influence of theoreticians drawn from the positivist and materialist camps. There is a failure to understand the masses of believers, their need for repetition and archaism. There is a failure also to appreciate prayer and the inner life. But there is really no contradiction between liturgical archaism and religious creativity: They are two sides of the one liminal coin. Both must be affirmed, for the Philistines are upon us!

Part 1

This article is concerned with the study of a modality of social interrelatedness which I have called communitas in my book *The Ritual Process* (1969), borrowing the term, though not its denotation, from Paul Goodman, and which I oppose to the concept of social structure. Communitas is a fact of everyone's experience, yet it has almost never been regarded as a reputable or coherent object of study by social scientists. It is, however, central to religion, literature, drama, and art, and its traces may be found deeply engraven in law, ethics, kinship, and even economics. It becomes visible in tribal rites of passage, in millenarian movements, in monasteries, in the counterculture, and on countless informal occasions. Later I shall try to spell out a little more explicitly what I mean by "communitas" and by "structure."

Something should be said about the kind of cultural phenomena that started me on this quest for communitas. Three aspects of culture seemed to me to be exceptionally well endowed with ritual symbols and beliefs of a nonsocial structural type. These may be described, respectively, as "liminality," "outsiderhood," and "structural inferiority."

"Liminality" is a term borrowed from Arnold van Gennep's (1908, 1960) formulation of *rites de passage*, "transition rites," which accompany every change of state or social position, or certain points in age. These are marked by three phases: separation, margin (or *limen*, the Latin for threshold, signifying the great importance of real or symbolic thresholds at this middle period of the rites though *cunicular*, "being in a tunnel," would better hit off the quality of this phase in many cases, its "hidden" nature, its sometimes mysterious darkness), and reaggregation.

The first phase, separation, comprises symbolic behavior signifying the detachment of the individual or the group from either an earlier fixed point in the social structure or from an established set of cultural conditions (a "state"). During the intervening liminal period, the second phase, the state of the ritual subject (the "passenger," or "liminar") becomes ambiguous; neither here nor there, betwixt-and-between all fixed points of classification, he passes through a symbolic domain that has few or none of the attributes of his past or coming state.

In the third phase the passage is consummated and the ritual subject, the neophyte or initiand re-enters the social structure, often but not always at a higher status level. (For court martials and excommunication ceremonies create and represent descents, not elevations. There is ritual degradation as well as elevation. Excommunication rituals were performed in the *narthex* or porch of a church, not in the nave or main body, from which the excommunicated was being expelled symbolically.) But in liminality, the symbolism almost everywhere indicates that the initiand (*initiare*, "to begin"), novice (*novus*, "new," "fresh"), or neophyte (*neos-phytos*, "newly-grown") is structurally if not physically "invisible" in terms of his culture's standard definitions and classifications. He has been divested of the outward attributes of structural position, set aside from the main arenas of social life in a seclusion lodge or camp, and reduced to an equality with his fellow initiands regardless of their preritual status. I would argue that it is in liminality that communitas emerges, if not as a spontaneous expression of sociability, at least in a cultural and normative form, stressing equality and comradeship as norms rather than generating spontaneous and existential communitas, though of course spontaneous communitas may and does arise in most cases of protracted initiation ritual.

As well as the betwixt-and-between state of liminality there is the state of "outsiderhood," referring to the condition of being either permanently and by ascription set outside the structural arrangements of a given social system, or being situationally or temporarily set apart, or voluntarily setting oneself apart from the behavior of status-occupying, role-playing members of that system. Such outsiders would include, in various cultures, shamans, diviners, mediums, priests, those in monastic seclusion, hippies, hoboes, and gypsies. They should be distinguished from "marginals," who are simultaneously members (by ascription, optation, self-definition, or achievement) of two or more groups whose social definitions and cultural norms are distinct from, and often even opposed to, one another (see Stonequist [1937], Thomas, and Znaniecki [Znaniecki & Thomas, 1918]). These would include migrant foreigner, second-generation Americans, persons of mixed ethnic origin, parvenus (upwardly mobile marginals), the déclassés (downwardly mobile marginals), migrants from country to city, and women in a changed nontraditional role. What is interesting about such marginals is that they often look to their group of origin, the so-called "inferior" groups, for communitas, and to the more prestigious group in which they mainly live and in which they aspire to higher status as their structural "reference-group."

Sometimes they become radical critics of structure from the perspective of communitas, sometimes they tend to deny the affectually "warmer" and more egalitarian bond of communitas. Usually they are highly conscious and self-conscious people and may produce from their ranks a disproportionately high proportion of writers, artists, and philosophers. David Riesman's (1954, p. 154) concept of "secret" marginality where there are people who subjectively fail to feel the identities expected of them seems to overinflate the concept. Marginals like liminars are also betwixt-and-between, but unlike ritual liminars they have no cultural assurance of a final stable resolution of their ambiguity. Ritual liminars are often moving symbolically to a higher status and their being stripped of status temporarily is a "ritual," an "as-if," or "make-believe" stripping dictated by cultural requirements.

The third major aspect of culture that is of concern to the student of religion and symbolism is "structural inferiority." This again may be an absolute or a relative, a permanent or a transient matter. Especially in caste or class systems of social stratification we have the problem of the lowest status, of the outcast, the unskilled worker, the *harijan*, and the poor. A rich mythology has grown around the poor, as also has the pastoral genre of literature (according to W. Empson); and in religion and art, the peasant, the beggar, the *harijan*, Gandhi's "children of God," the "despised and rejected" in general, have often been assigned the symbolic function of representing humanity as such, without status qualifications or characteristics. Here the lowest represents the human total, the extreme case most fittingly portrays the whole.

In many tribal or preliterate societies, with little in the way of stratification along class lines, structural inferiority often emerges as a value-bearer whenever structural strength is dichotomously opposed to structural weakness. For example, many African societies have been formed by the conquest of indigenous peoples by incomers who were militarily more powerful. The invaders control high political office, such as the kingship, provincial governorships, and headmanships. On the other hand, the indigenous people, through their leaders, frequently are held to have a mystical power over the fertility of the earth and of all upon it. These autochthonous people have religious power, the "power of the weak" as against the jural-political "power of the strong" and represent the undivided land itself as against the political system with its internal segmentation and hierarchies of authority. Here the model of an undifferentiated whole whose units are total human beings is posited against that of a differentiated system, whose units are status and roles, and where the person is segmentalized into positions in a structure. One is oddly reminded of those Gnostic notions of an extraterrestrial "fall" in which an originally undivided "Human Form Divine" became divided into conflicting functions, each incompletely human and dominated by a single propensity, "intellect," "desire," "craftsmanship," etc., no longer in orderly harmonious balance with the others.

A similar contrast may be found, in societies based primarily on kinship, between the "hard" legal line of descent, patrilineal or matrilineal, through which authority, property and social placement pass, and the "soft," "affectional" side of the family through the parent of so-called "complementary filiation" (mother's side in patrilineal systems, father's side in matrilineal systems). This "side," as distinct from the legal "line," is often attributed with mystical power over a person's total welfare. Thus in many patrilineal societies, the mother's brother has powers of cursing or blessing his sister's child, but no legal power. In others, the mother's kin may act as a sanctuary against paternal harshness. A man is, in any case, more clearly an *individual* in relation to his kin of complementary filiation or of what Meyer Fortes (1949) calls the "submerged side of descent," than he is to his lineal kin, for whom he is importantly a "bundle of jural rights and obligations."

In this article I am going to examine several aspects of the relationship between liminality, outsiderhood, and structural inferiority, and to show in the course of it something of the dialectical relationship over time, between communitas and structure. But if we are going to say that a process such as ritualization tends to occur frequently in the interstices or on the edges of something, we have to be fairly clear about what that "something" is. What *is* "social structure"? The term "structure" is, of course, commonly employed in all analytical sciences, and even in geology, which is mainly taxonomic or descriptive. It evokes architectural images, of houses awaiting inhabitants, or bridges with struts and piles; or it may invoke the bureaucratic image of desks with pigeon holes—each hole being a status, and some being more important than others.

Now, the social sciences, like biology, are partly analytical and partly descriptive; the result is that there is wide variation in the meaning of "structure" in the work of anthropologists and sociologists. Some regard "structure" as primarily a description of repeated patterns of action, i.e., of an observable uniformity of action or operation, in brief, of something "out there," capable of being empirically observed and, hopefully, measured.

This viewpoint, represented most prominently in anthropology by the work of Radcliffe-Brown and his British followers, has been severely criticized by Claude Lévi-Strauss (1958/1963), who holds that "social structures" are "entities independent of men's consciousness of them (although they in fact govern men's existence)" (p. 121). All that can be directly observed in societies, he says, is "a series of expressions, each partial and incomplete, of the same underlying *structure*, which they reproduce in several copies without ever completely exhausting its realities." He taxes Radcliffe-Brown for his "ignorance of hidden realities" *(sic)* and for believing that structure is of the order of empirical observation when in fact it is beyond it.

But it is not with Lévi-Strauss's concept of "social" structure, really cognitive structure, that I wish to begin this analysis. Nor shall I invoke here the concept of structure as "statistical categories." Again, I shall not for the purposes of this article regard "structural" as what Leach has called "the statistical outcome" of multiple individual choices. Sartre's view of structure as "a complex dialectic of freedom and inertia," where "the formation and maintenance of each group is contingent on the free engagement of each individual in its joint activities" (Rosen, 1971, p. 281) is closer to my own theoretical position, though it is not what I mean by "structure" in this argument. What I intend to convey by "social structure" here—and what is implicitly regarded as the frame of social order in most societies—is not a system of unconscious categories, but, quite simply, in Robert Merton's terms "the patterned arrangements of role-sets, status-sets, and status-sequences" consciously recognized and regularly operative in a given society. These are closely bound up with legal and political norms and sanctions. By "role-sets" Merton designates "the actions and relationships that flow from a social status"; "status-sets" refers to the probable congruence of various positions occupied by an individual; and "status-sequences" means the probable succession of positions occupied by an individual through time.

Thus, for me, liminality represents the mid-point of transition in a status-sequence between two positions, outsiderhood refers to actions and relationships which do not flow from a recognized social status but originate outside it, while lowermost status refers to the lowest rung in a system of social stratification in which unequal rewards are accorded to functionally differentiated positions. A "class system," for example, would be a system of this type.

Nevertheless, Lévi-Strauss's concept of "unconscious social structure" as a structure of relationships between the elements of myth and ritual must enter into our reckoning when we consider liminal ritual phenomena. Here I must pause to consider once more the difference between structure and communitas. Implicitly or explicitly, in societies at all levels of complexity, a contrast is posited between the notion of society as a differentiated, segmented system of structural positions (which may or may not be arranged in a hierarchy), and society as a homogeneous, undifferentiated *whole*.

The first model approximates to the preliminary picture I have presented of "social structure." Here the units are statuses and roles, not material human individuals. The individual is segmentalized into roles which he plays. Here the unit is what Radcliffe-Brown has called the *persona*, the role-mask, not the unique individual. The second model, communitas, often appears as a union of free and equal comrades in an Eden or millennium. Myths vouch for the existence of past communitas and prophesy its coming in the fullness of time. *Societas*, or "society," as we all experience it, is a process involving both social structure and communitas, separately and united in varying proportions.

But even where there is no such myth or prediction, rituals may be performed in which egalitarian and cooperative behavior is characteristic, and in which secular distinctions of rank, office, and status are temporarily in abeyance or regarded as irrelevant. On these ritual occasions, anthropologists who have previously, from repeated observations of behavior and interviews with informants in nonritual situations, built up a model of the socio-economic structure, cannot fail to note how persons deeply divided from one another in the secular or nonreligious, nevertheless in certain ritual situations cooperate closely to ensure what is believed to be the maintenance of a cosmic order which transcends the contradictions and conflicts inherent in the mundane social system. Here we have an unstated model of communitas, an operational model.

Practically all rituals of any length and complexity represent a passage from one domain of structure to another. In this regard they may be said to possess "temporal structure" and to be dominated by the notion of time. But in passing from structure to structure many rituals pass through communitas. Communitas is almost always thought of or portrayed by actors as a timeless condition, an eternal now, as "a moment in and out of time," or as a state to which the structural view of time is not applicable. Such is frequently the character of at least parts of the seclusion periods found in many protracted initiation rites.

Such is the character, too, I have been finding, of pilgrimage journeys in several religions. In ritual seclusion for example, one day repeats another for many weeks. The novices in tribal initiations waken and rest at fixed hours, often at sunrise and sunset, as in the monastic life in Christianity and Buddhism. They receive instruction in tribal lore, or in singing and dancing from the same elders or adepts at the same time. At other set times they may hunt or perform routine tasks under the eyes of the elders. Every day is, in a sense, the same day, writ large or repeated. Then again, seclusion and liminality may contain what Eliade calls "a time of marvels." Masked figures, representing gods, ancestors, or chthonic powers may appear to the novices or neophytes in grotesque, monstrous, or beautiful forms. Often, but not always, myths are recited explaining the origin, attributes, and behavior of these strange and sacred habitants of liminality. Again, sacred objects may be shown to the novices. These may be quite simple in form like the bone, top, ball, tambourine, apples, mirror, fan, and woolly fleece displayed in the Lesser Eleusinian Mysteries of Athens. Such *sacra*, individually or in various combinations, may be the foci of hermeneutics or religious interpretations, sometimes in the form of myths, sometimes of gnomic utterances hardly less enigmatic than the visible symbols they purport to explain.

Such symbols, visual and auditory, operate culturally as mnemonics, or as communications engineers would no doubt have it, as "storage bins" of information, not about pragmatic techniques, but about cosmologies, values, and cultural axioms, whereby a society's "deep knowledge" is transmitted from one generation to another. Such a device, in the setting of "a place that is not a place, and a time that is not a time" (as the Welsh folklorist and sociologist Alwyn Rees once described for me the context of Celtic Bardic utterance), is all the more necessary in cultures without writing, where the whole cultural deposit has to be transmitted either through speech or by repeated observation of standardized behavioral patterns and artifacts. And I am beginning to wonder whether it is not the structuring of functionless elements in myth and ritual patterns which preserves such elements through centuries until they find a socioeconomic milieu in which they may become functional again—as the Cruzob replicated pre-Columbian Maya Social organization in Quintana Roo during the War of the Castas in 19th century Yucatan, described by Nelson Reed (1964) in his exciting book *The Caste War of Yucatan*.

Major liminal situations are occasions on which, so to speak, a society takes cognizance of itself, or rather where, in an interval between their incumbency of specific fixed positions, members of that society may obtain an approximation, however limited, to a global view of man's place in the cosmos and his relations with other classes of visible entities.

Also, importantly, in myth and ritual an individual undergoing passage may learn the total pattern of social relations involved in his transition and how it changes. He may, therefore, learn about social structure in communitas. This view need not depend heavily on explicit teaching, on verbal explanations. In many societies it seems to be enough that neophytes learn to become aware of the multiple relationships existing between the *sacra* and other aspects of their culture, or learn from the positioning of sacred symbols in a structure of relationship (above, below; on the left, on the right; inside, outside), or from their prominent attributes (sex, color, texture, density, temperature, etc.), how critical aspects of cosmos and society are interrelated, and the hierarchy of such modes of interlinkage. The neophytes may learn what Lévi-Strauss calls the "sensory codes" underlying the details of myth and ritual and the homologues between events and objects described in different codes—visual, auditory, and tactile. The medium here "*is* the message," and the medium is nonverbal, though often meticulously "structured."

It can be seen from all this that there is a certain inadequacy in the contrast I have just made between the concepts of structure and communitas. For clearly the liminal situation of communitas is heavily invested with a "structure" of a kind. But this structure is *not* a social structure in the Radcliffe-Brownian sense but a structure of symbols and ideas; if you like, an "instructional" structure. Within it, it is not too difficult to detect a Lévi-Straussian structure, a way of inscribing in the mentalities of neophytes generative rules, codes, and media whereby they can manipulate the symbols of speech and culture to confer some degree of intelligibility on an "experience" that "perpetually outstrips the possibilities of linguistic (and other cultural) expression." Within this, it is not too difficult to detect what Lévi-Strauss would call "a concrete logic," and behind this, again, a fundamental structure of human mentality or even of the human brain itself. In order to implant this instructional structure firmly in the minds of neophytes it seems necessary that they should be stripped of "structural" attributes in the social, legalistic, or political sense of the term.

Simpler societies seem to feel that only a person temporarily without status, property, rank, or office, is fit to receive the tribal *gnosis* or occult wisdom which is in effect knowledge of what the tribes people regard as the deep structure of culture and indeed of the universe. The content of such "knowledge" is, of course, dependent on the degree of scientific and technological development; but, so Lévi-Strauss argues, the "savage" *mental* structure, which can be disengaged from the palpable integument of what often seem to us bizzare modes of symbolic representation, is identical with our own mental structure. We share with primitive men, he holds, the same mental habits of thinking in terms of binary discriminations or oppositions; like them, too, we have rules, including "deep structural" rules, governing the combination, segregation, mediation, and transformation of ideas and relations.

Now men who are heavily involved in jural-political overt and conscious structure are *not* free to meditate and speculate on the combinations and oppositions of thought; they are themselves too crucially involved in the combinations and oppositions of social and political structure and stratification. They are in the heat of the battle, in the "arena," competing for office, participating in feuds, factions, and coalitions. This involvement entails such affects as anxiety, aggression, envy, fear, exultation, etc., an emotional flooding which does not encourage either rational or wise reflection. But in ritual liminality they are placed, so to speak, outside the total system and its conflicts; transiently, they become men apart—and it is surprising how often the term "sacred" may be translated as "set apart" or "on one side" in various societies. If getting a living and struggling to get it, in and despite of a social structure, be called "bread," then man does not live "by bread alone." Life as a series and structure of status-incumbencies inhibits the full utilization of human capacities, or as Karl Marx would have said, in a singularly Augustinian fashion, "the powers that slumber within man." I am thinking of Augustine's *rationes seminales*, "seminal reasons," implanted in the created universe at the beginning, and left to work themselves out over historical time. Both Augustine and Marx favored organic metaphors for social movement, seen in terms of "development" and "growth." Thus, for Marx, a new social order "grows" in the "womb" of the old and is "delivered" by the midwife "force."

Preliterate societies, out of the need for mere survival, provide little scope for leisure. So that it is only by ritual *fiat*, acting through the

legitimate authority vested in those who operate the ritual cycle, that opportunities can be created to put men and women outside their everyday
structural positions in family, lineage, clan, and chieftainship. In such
situations as the liminal periods of major *rites de passage* the passengers
and crew are free, under ritual exigency, to contemplate for a while the
mysteries that confront all men, the difficulties that peculiarly beset their
own society, their personal problems, and the ways in which their own
wisest predecessors have sought to order, explain, explain away, cloak,
or mask these mysteries and difficulties. In liminality resides the germ
not only of religious *askesis*, discipline, and mysticism, but also of
philosophy and pure science. Indeed, such Greek philosophers as Plato
and Pythagoras are known to have had links with the Mystery cults.

I would like to make it clear at this point that I am here referring not to
such spontaneous behavioral expressions of communitas as the kind of
good fellowship one finds in many secular marginal and transitional
social situations, e.g., an English pub, a "good" party as distinct from a
"stiff" party, the "eight-seventeen [a.m.] club" on a suburban com-
muters' train, a group of passengers at play on an ocean voyage, or, to
speak more seriously, at some religious meetings, a "sit-in," "love-in,"
"be-in," or more dramatically, the Woodstock or Isle of Wight "Nations." My focus here is rather on *cultural*—and hence *institutionalized*—expressions of communitas, communitas as seen from the perspective of structure, or as incorporated into it as a potentially dangerous but
nevertheless vitalizing moment, domain, or enclave.

Communitas is, existentially speaking and in its origins, purely spontaneous and self-generating.[1] The "wind" of existential communitas
"bloweth where it listeth." It is essentially opposed to structure, as
"anti-matter" is hypothetically opposed to matter. Thus, even when
communitas becomes "normative" its religious expressions become
closely hedged about by rules and interdictions—which act like the lead
container of a dangerous radioactive isotope. Yet exposure to or immersion in communitas seems to be an indispensable human social require-
ment. People have a real need to doff the masks, cloaks, apparel, and in-
signia of status from time to time even if only to don the liberating masks
of liminal masquerade. But they do this freely. And here I would like to
point out the bond that exists between communitas, liminality, and
lowermost status.

It is often believed that the lowest castes and classes in stratified
societies exhibit the greatest immediacy and involuntariness of behavior.
This may or may not be empirically true but it is at any rate a persistent
belief held perhaps most firmly by the occupants of positions in the middle rungs of structure on whom structural pressures to conformity are
greatest, and who secretly envy even while they openly reprobate the
behavior of those groups and classes less normatively inhibited, whether

highest or lowest on the status ladder. Those who would maximize communitas often begin by minimizing or even eliminating the outward marks of rank as, for example, Tolstoy and Gandhi tried to do in their own persons. In other words, they approximate in dress and behavior the condition of "the poor." These signs of indigence include the wearing of plain or cheap apparel or the assumption of the peasant's smock or workers' overalls. Some would go even further and try to express the "natural" as opposed to "cultural" character of communitas, even though natural is here, of course, a cultural definition, by allowing their hair and nails to grow and their skin to remain unwashed, as in the case of certain Christian saints and Hindu and Moslem holy men. But since man is inveterately a "cultural" animal, as I have just said, "nature" here itself becomes a cultural symbol for what is essentially a human social need—the need to be fully together with one's fellows and not segregated from them in structural cells. A "natural" or "simple" mode of dress, or even undress in some cases, signalizes that one wishes to approximate to the basically or merely human, as against the structurally specific by way of status or class.

A random assortment of such aspirants to pure communitas would include: the mendicant friars of the Middle Ages, especially those of the early Franciscan and Carmelite Orders, for example, whose members by their constitutions were forbidden to possess property, not merely personally, but even in common, and therefore had to subsist by begging and were hardly better clothed than beggars; some modern Catholic saints, like St. Benedict Labré, the Palmer (d. 1783), who was reputed to be always covered with vermin as he traveled ceaselessly and silently around the pilgrimage shrines of Europe. Similar qualities of poverty and mendicancy are sought by Hindu, Moslem, and Sikh holy men of India and the Middle East, some of whom even dispense with clothing altogether. In America today we have the counter-culture people, who like holy men of the East wear long hair and beards and dress in a variety of ways ranging from the clothes of the urban poor to the attire of underprivileged rural and ethnic groups, such as Amerindians and Mexicans. So critical were some hippie men not long ago of the principles underlying the structure "out" of which they have "opted" that they even rejected in their dress the dominant American stress on virility and successful aggressiveness in a competitive business milieu by wearing beads, bangles and earrings, just as "flower power," 2 or 3 years ago, was opposed to military strength and business aggressiveness. In this they share common ground with the Virasaiva saints of medieval South India. My colleague Professor A.K. Ramanujan (1973) has recently translated from the Kannada language some poems known as *vacanas* which, in their protest against traditional structural dichotomies in orthodox Hinduism, reject the differences between man and woman as superficial.

There is no doubt that from the perspective of incumbents of positions of command or maintenance in "structure," communitas—even when it becomes normative—represents a real danger. Indeed, for all those who spend much of their lives in structural role-playing, including even political leaders, it also represents a temptation. Who doesn't really want to shuck off that old armor plating? This situation was dramatically exemplified in the early history of the Franciscan Order. So many rushed to join St. Francis's followers that recruitment to the secular clergy fell off sharply, and the Italian bishops complained that they could not maintain ecclesiastical discipline when their dioceses were overrun by what they considered to be a "mendicant rabble." In the last quarter of the 13th century Pope Nicholas III decreed that the Order modify its rule with regard to the abandonment of all property. In this way a "communitarian" threat to the jural structure of the church was turned to her advantage, for the doctrine of poverty has left a permanent impress on Catholicism acting as a constant check on the growth of Roman legalism, with its heavy involvement in political and economic structures.

Liminality, then, often draws on poverty for its repertoire of symbols, particularly for its symbols of social relationship. Similarly, as we have seen, the voluntary outsiders of our own society, particularly today's voluntary rural communards, also draw upon the symbolic vocabulary of poverty and indigence. Both the mendicant orders and today's counterculture have affinities with another social phenomenon which has recently aroused great interest among anthropologists and historians. I refer to that range of religious movements, scattered throughout history and of wide geographical provenience, which have variously been described as "enthusiastic," "heretical," "millenarian," "revitalistic," "nativistic," "messianic" and "separatist"—to cite but a few of the terms by which they have been called by theologians, historians, and social scientists.

I shall not enter into the problem of providing an adequate taxonomy of such movements, but will content myself with mentioning a few of their recurrent attributes which seem closely similar to those of (1) ritual liminality in tribal societies, (2) religious mendicancy, and (3) the "counterculture." In the first place, it is common for members of these movements either to give up what property they have or to hold all their property in common. Instances have been recorded of the destruction of all property by the members of religious movements at the command of their prophetic leaders. The rationale here, I believe, is that in most societies differences in property correspond to major differences of status or else in simpler stateless societies relate to the segmentation of corporate groups. To "liquidate" property is to erase the lines of structural cleavage that in ordinary life prevent men from entering into communitas.

Similarly, the institution of marriage, source of the family, a basic cell of social structure in many cultures, also comes under attack in many religious movements. Some seek to replace it by what Lewis Morgan would have called "primitive promiscuity" or by various forms of "group marriage." Sometimes this is held to demonstrate the triumph of love over jealousy. In other movements, on the contrary, celibacy becomes the rule and the relationship between the sexes becomes a massive extension of the sibling bond. Thus some religious movements are similar to religious orders in abstaining from sexual activity, while others resemble some groups of hippies in breaking down sexual exclusiveness.

Both attitudes toward sexuality are aimed at homogenizing the group by liquidating its structural divisions. In tribal societies too, there is abundant ethnographic evidence to testify that an interdiction is laid on sexual relations during the liminal period in major *rites de passage*. Sometimes, too, episodes of sexual license may follow periods of sexual abstinence in such ceremonies, in other words, *both* antithetical modes of representing the destruction of monogamous marriage are utilized.[2]

If I may digress here for a moment, I would like to say that it seems to make more sense of the facts if we regard "sexuality" not so much as the "primordial source" of sociality and sociality as "neutralized libido" but as the expression, in its various modalities, either of communitas or structure. Sexuality, as a biological drive, is culturally and hence symbolically manipulated to express one or the other of these major dimensions of sociality. It thus becomes a means to social ends, quite as much as an end to which social means are contrived. Whereas structure emphasizes, and even exaggerates, the biological differences between the sexes, in matters of dress, decoration, and behavior, communitas tends to diminish these differences.

Thus in many tribal initiations where both sexes appear as neophytes, men and women, boys and girls, are often dressed alike and behave similarly in the liminal situation. Afterwards, custom segregates them and stresses sexual differences as they are restored to the structural order. In religious movements, at some of the critical rites of incorporation, such as baptism by immersion, male and female neophytes or catechumens may wear the same type of robe—a robe which often deliberately conceals sexual differences, as it does among one of the offshoots from the Bwiti cult of Gabon described by James Fernandez. It is still today a commonplace of conversation in situations dominated by structural (or "middle class") values to hear such comments on hippies as, "How can one tell whether it's a boy or a girl? They all have long hair and dress alike."

Nevertheless, similarity in appearance between males and females does not necessarily mean the disappearance of sexual attraction between them. There is no evidence to suggest that members of the alternate culture are less sexually active than their "squarer" fellows. But sexuality, sometimes perhaps in the "polymorphously perverse" forms recommended by Norman Brown, and extolled by Allen Ginsberg, seems to be here regarded by them rather as a way of enhancing the inclusiveness of communitas, as a means to wide-range mutual understanding. Such a means is positively opposed to asserting the exclusive character of certain structural bonds, such as marriage or unilineality.

The many traits that such "enthusiastic" and chiliastic religious movements share with the liminal situation in traditional ritual systems suggest that these movements too have a liminal quality. But their liminality is not, as it were, institutionalized and preordained. Rather it should be viewed as spontaneously generated in a situation of radical structural change, what Parsons, following Weber, calls the "prophetic break," when seemingly fundamental social principles lose their former efficacy, their capacity to operate as axioms for social behavior, and new modes of social organization emerge, at first to transect and, later, to replace traditional ones. Religion and ritual, it is well known, often sustain the legitimacy of social and political systems, or provide the symbols on which that legitimacy is most vitally expressed, so that when the legitimacy of cardinal social relations is impugned, the ritual symbolic system too which has come to reinforce such relations ceases to convince. It is in this limbo of structure that religious movements, led by charismatic prophets, powerfully reassert the values of communitas, often in extreme and antinomian forms.

This primal impetus, however, soon attains its apogee and loses its impetus; as Weber says, "*charisma* becomes routinized," and the spontaneous forms of communitas are converted into institutionalized structure, or become routinized, often as ritual. What the prophet and his followers actually did becomes a behavioral model to be represented in stereotyped and selected liturgical form. This ritual structure has two important aspects. On the one hand, the historical deeds of the prophet and his closest companions become a sacred history, impregnated with the mythical elements so typical of liminality, that becomes increasingly resistant to criticism and revision and consolidates into a "structure" in the Lévi-Straussian sense: Binary oppositions are set up and stressed between crucial events, individuals, groups, types of conduct, periods of time, etc. On the other hand, both the deeds of the founder and his visions and messages achieve crystallization in the symbolic objects and activities of cyclical and repetitive rituals. Indeed, it may well be that even in tribal religions, where there is no written religious history, the cyclical rites that seem so closely in their stability and repetitiveness to resemble natural phenomena, such as the seasonal round and the life cycles of birds and animals, may well have originated in times of social crisis, whether man-made or due to natural catastrophes, in the novel and idiosyncratic visions and deeds of inspired shamans or prophets.

Freud's notion of "repetition compulsion," whatever may be its causes, fairly well describes the process whereby the inspirational forms generated in some experiences of communitas get repeated in symbolic mimesis and become the routinized forms of structure. The outcomes of "vision" become the models or patterns of repetitive social behavior. The word or act that appeared to heal or amend personal or social disorder comes to be accorded intrinsic power in isolation from its original context and is formally repeated in ritual and incantatory utterance. A creative deed becomes an ethical or ritual paradigm.

Let me give a simple illustration from my own field experience. Among the Ndembu of Zambia, I have been able to allocate approximate dates to the introduction of certain rites to the hunting and curative cult systems which, although they now share many of the properties of the more traditional rites, nevertheless betray their origins in some disturbed phase of Ndembu history. Here external threat seemed to intensify the sentiment of Ndembu unity. For example, the *Wuyang'a* gun hunters' cult and the *Chihamba* curative cult, in their prayers and symbolism, refer unmistakably to the traumatic impact of the 19th century slave trade on the harassed and fleeing Ndembu; while the quite recently introduced *Tukuka* cult, marked by hysterical trembling and a concept of possession by alien, notably European spirits, stands in marked contrast to the almost Apollonian dignity and restraint of many of the traditional ritual performances. These rituals, however, despite their differences, present the Ndembu as a communitas of interdependent sufferers.

It is not only among the Ndembu but also in the history of most of the great religions that we see crisis disclosing communitas, and the manifest form of such communitas subsequently reinforcing an old structure or replacing it by a new one. Various reform movements within the Catholic Church, the Protestant Reformation itself, not to mention the innumerable Evangelical and Revivalistic movements within the whole Christian world, attest to this. In Islam, Sufism and the Sanusi reform movements among the Bedouin and Berbers exemplify but two among many. The many attempts in Indian Hinduism to liquidate the caste structure, from Buddhism, through Jainism and Lingayatism and the Virasaiva saints to Gandhism—not to mention such syncretic Hindu-Islamic religions as Sikhism—are further examples.

I mention this correlation between crisis, communitas, and the genesis of religions mainly because it is too often held by sociologists and anthropologists that "the social" is at all times identical with the "social-structural," that man is nothing but a "structural" animal, and consequently a *homo hierarchicus*. Thus the breakdown of a social system can only result in *anomie*, *angst*, and the fragmentation of society into a mass of anxious and disoriented individuals, prone, as Durkheim (1961) would have said, to pathologically high rates of suicide. For if such a society is unstructured it is nothing. It is less often seen that the dissolution of structural relationships may sometimes give communitas a positive opportunity.

One recent historical example of this is the "miracle of Dunkirk," when from the destruction of the formal organization of the Allied armies in 1940 an informal organization arose, deriving from the liberated spirit of communitas. The rescue of small groups of soldiers by the crews of small boats gave rise to a spirit of resistance generally known as "the spirit of Dunkirk." The general careers of guerrilla bands as against formally regulated and hierarchical armies in the recent history of China, Bolivia, Cuba, and Vietnam may be further examples. I am not suggesting that there is no *anomie*, no *angst*, no alienation (to mention three currently popular "A's") in such situations of drastic structural change—one must not be surprised or indignant that in any social field contrary social processes may be simultaneously at work. But I am suggesting that there are socially positive forces at work here too. Structure's breakdown may be communitas' gain.

Durkheim (1912/1961), whose work has been so influential, both in England and France, is often so difficult to understand precisely because at different times he uses the term "society" to represent a set of jural and religious maxims and norms on the one hand, coercing and constraining the individual and, on the other, "an actual living and animating force" closely approximating to what we are here calling communitas. Yet it is not a complete approximation, for Durkheim conceives of this force as "anonymous and impersonal" and as passing through the generations, whereas we see communitas rather as a relationship between persons, an *I-Thou* relationship in Buber's terms or a *We*, the very essence of which is its immediacy and spontaneity. It is structure that is transmitted by rote and repetition; though under favorable circumstances some structural form generated long ago, from a moment of communitas, may be almost miraculously liquified into a living form of communitas again. This is what revitalistic or revivalistic religious movements, as against radical or transformist ones, aim to do: to restore the social bond of their communicants to the pristine vigor of that religion in its days of generative crisis and ecstasy. For example, as Ramanujan (Note 1) writes, "like European Protestants, the Virasaivas returned to what they felt was the original inspiration of the ancient traditions no different from true and present experience" (p. 17).

Perhaps this, too, underlies the notion of "permanent revolution." It was certainly present in the "Evénements of Mai-Juin 1968" in Paris when the students adopted symbols of unity and communitas from earlier French revolutions. Just as during the Paris Commune of 1871, the communards identified themselves with the revolutionaries of 1789, even to the point of adopting the revolutionary calendar for the commune's magazines, the 1968 events identified themselves as a kind of reenactment of the Paris Commune. Even the barricades erected there had little instrumental value, but were a symbol of continuity with the grandeur of the 1871 uprising. When a social system acquires a certain stability as in most of the societies until recently studied by anthropologists, there tends to develop in the temporal relationship between structure and communitas a process to which it is hard to deny the epithet "dialectical." The life-cycles of individuals and groups exhibit alternating exposure to these major modes of human intercourse. Individuals proceed from lower to higher statuses through interim periods of liminality, where they are stripped of all secular status, though they may possess a religious status. But this status is the antithesis of status in the "structural" domain. Here the high are obliged to accept the stigmata of the lowly, and even to endure patiently the taunts of those who will become their inferiors, as in the installation rites of many African chiefs and headmen.

Since liminality represents what Erving Goffman would call "a leveling and stripping" of structural status, an important component of the liminal situation is, as we saw earlier, an enhanced stress on "nature" at the expense of culture. Not only does it represent a situation of instruction—with a degree of objectivity hardly found in structural situations where status differences have to be "explained away" or merely accepted—but it is also replete with symbols quite explicitly relating to biological processes, human and nonhuman, and to other aspects of the natural order. In a sense, when man ceases to be the master and becomes the equal or fellow of man, he also ceases to be the master and becomes the equal or fellow of nonhuman beings.

It is culture that fabricates structural distinctions; it is culture too that eradicates these distinctions in liminality, but in so doing culture is forced, as it were, to use the idiom of "nature" to replace its fictions by natural facts, even if these "facts" themselves only possess what reality they have in a framework of cultural concepts. Thus it is in liminality, and also in those phases of ritual that abut on liminality, that one finds profuse symbolic reference to beasts, birds, and vegetation. Animal masks, bird plumage, grass fibers, garments of leaves swathe and enshroud the human neophytes and priests. Thus, symbolically, their structural life is snuffed out by animality and nature, even as it is being regenerated by these very same forces. One dies *into* nature to be reborn *from* it. Structural custom, once broken, reveals two human traits. One is liberated *intellect*, whose liminal product is myth and protophilosophical speculation; the other is *bodily energy*, represented by animal disguises and gestures. The two may then be recombined in various ways.

One classical prototype of this revealed duality is the centaur Cheiron, dwelling in his mountain cavern which epitomizes outsiderhood and liminality. There he instructed and even initiated the adolescent sons of Achaean kings and princes who would later occupy leading positions in the social and political structure of Hellas. Human wisdom and animal force meet in this liminal figure, who is both horse and man. As is well known, theranthropic figures combining animal with human characteristics, abound in liminal situations; similarly, human beings imitate the behavior of different species of animals. Even angels in the Iranian, Judaeo-Christian, and Islamic traditions may perhaps be regarded in this way—as ornith-anthropic figures, bird-humans, messengers betwixt-and-between Absolute and Relative reality.

Yet it would be unwise, and in fact incorrect, to segregate structure too radically from communitas. And I stress this most vigorously for both modes are human. For each level and domain of structure there is a mode of communitas, and there are cultural links established between them in most stable, ongoing, socio-cultural systems. Usually, in the seclusion or liminal phases of *rites de passage*, at least some of the symbols, even of the *sacra* displayed, have reference to principles of social structure. For example, among the Nyakyusa of Tanzania, who are patrilineal, an important symbolic medicine in all *rites de passage* is a reddish fluid, rather endearingly called *ikipiki*, which represents the principle of patrilineal descent. Terence Turner (Note 2) distinguishes between two aspects of the "structure" of the myth: "the internal structure of logical relations of opposition and mediation between the discrete symbolic elements of the myth (the aspect of structure upon which Lévi-Strauss prefers to concentrate), and the relation between the myth as a whole and the social situation to which it refers."

This continuous thread of "structure" through ritualized communitas in liminality is, to my mind, highly characteristic of long-established and stable cultural systems, in which, as it were, communitas has been thoroughly domesticated, even "corralled" as among the Elks and Kiwanis in the United States. "Raw" or "wild" communitas is, more typically, a phenomenon of major social change, or, it may be, sometimes a mode of reaction against too rigid a structuring of human life in status and role-playing activities—as some of the hippies claim their revolt to be against what they call "American middle-class values," against the organization men, or against the tacit regimentation imposed on many levels and domains of society by the dominance of a "military-industrial" complex with its complicated repertoire of covert social controls.

Part 2

To my mind it is the analysis of culture into factors and their free recombination in any and every possible pattern, however weird, that is most characteristic of liminality, rather than the establishment of "implicit syntax-like rules" or the development of an "internal structure of logical relations of opposition and mediation." The limitation of possible combinations of factors by convention would indicate to me the growing intrusion of structure into this potentially free and experimental region of culture.

Here a remark of Sartre (1969, pp. 57-59) seems apposite: "I [agree] that social facts have their own structure and laws that dominate individuals, but I see in this the reply of *worked matter* to the *agents* who work it. *Structures are created by activity which has no structure*, but suffers its *results as structure*." I see liminality as a phase in social life in which this confrontation between "activity which has no structure" and its "structured results" produces in men their highest pitch of self-consciousness. Syntax and logic are *problematic* and not axiomatic features of liminality. We have to *see* if they *are there*—empirically. And if we find them we have to consider well their relation to activities that have as yet no structure, no logic, only potentialities for them. In long-established cultural systems I would expect to find the growth of a symbolic and iconographic syntax and logic; in changing or newly established systems I would expect to find in liminal situations daring and innovation both in the modes of relating symbolic and mythic elements and in the choice of elements to be related. There might also be the introduction of new elements, and their various combination with old ones, as in religious syncretisms.

The same formulation would apply to such other expressions of liminality as Western literature and art. Sometimes art expresses or replicates institutionalized structure to legitimate or criticize; but often it combines the factors of culture—as in cubism and abstract art—in novel and unprecedented ways. The unusual, the paradoxical, the illogical, even the perverse, stimulate thought and pose problems, "cleanse the Doors of Perception." This is especially likely to be the case when art is presented in preliterate societies in an instructional situation like initiation. Thus the portrayal of monsters, and of "unnatural" situations in terms of cultural definitions, like the incestuous ties connecting the gods in the myths of some religions, may have a pedagogical function in forcing those who have taken their culture for granted to rethink what they have hitherto taken to be its axioms and givens. For each society requires of its mature members not only adherence to rules and patterns, but at least a certain level of scepticism and initiative. Initiation is to rouse initiative at least as much as to produce conformity to custom. Accepted schemata and paradigms must be broken if initiates are to cope with novelty and danger. They have to learn how to generate viable schemata under environmental challenge. Something similar may be found in European literature, e.g., in the writings of Rabelais and Gênet. Such mastery over phenomena taken for granted by the uninstructed may well be thought to give enhanced "power" during the later incumbency of a new and higher status.

But the frequency with which such unnatural—or rather anti-cultural or anti-structural—events as incest, cannabalism, murder of close kin, mating with animals are portrayed in myth and liminal ritual surely has more than a pedagogical function. It is more too than a mere cognitive means of coding relationships between ritual elements, of assigning to them pluses or minuses or indicating transformations as Lévi-Strauss would assert. Here, I think, we must return to our earlier point about certain aspects of nature asserting themselves in liminal situations. For human nature as well as culture has its unconscious regularities, though these regularities may be precisely such as have to be denied expression if human beings are to go about their business of getting a living and maintaining social control as they do so. Much that the depth psychologists insist has been "repressed into the unconscious" tends to appear, either in veiled form or, sometimes, perfectly explicitly, in liminal ritual and its connected myths.

In many mythologies, the gods slay or unman their fathers, mate with their mothers and sisters, copulate with mortals in the form of animals and birds—while in rites that act these out, their human representatives imitate in symbol, or sometimes even literally, these immortal amoralities. In rituals, especially in the seclusion rites of initiations into manhood, womanhood, or into tribal associations and secret societies, there may be episodes of real or symbolic cannibalism, in which men eat the flesh of the recent dead or of captives, or else eat the symbolic flesh of deities spoken of as their "fathers," "brothers," or "mothers." Here there are regularities and repetitions indeed, yet they are not those of law and custom but of unconscious cravings which stand opposed to the norms on which social bonding secularly depends, opposed to the rules of exogamy and the prohibition of incest, to rules enjoining respect for the bodily person of others, to veneration of elders, and to definitions that class men differently from animals. Here again I would revert to my characterization, in several previous articles, of certain key symbols and central symbolic actions as "semantically bipolar." That is, they are "culturally intended" to arouse a gross quantity of affect, even of illicit affect, only to attach this quantum of affect, divested of moral quality, and in a later phase of a great ritual, to licit and legitimate goals and values. The consequence is a restoration of moral quality but this time positive instead of negative. Perhaps Freud and Jung, in their different ways, have much to contribute to the understanding of these nonlogical, nonrational (but not irrational) aspects of liminal situations.

What seems to emerge from this brief glance at some of the cultural apparatus of liminal rituals, symbols and myths is that all these phenomena exhibit great depth and complexity, and emphatically do not lend themselves to attempts to reduce them to the terms of practitioners of a single discipline or subdiscipline, such as the various and opposed schools of psychology, emotionalist and intellectualist, the various schools of sociologistic reductionism from the followers of Radcliffe-Brown to those of Lévi-Strauss, or philosophers and theologians who may tend to neglect the contextual involvement of these phenomena with the social structure, history, economy, and ecology of the specific groups in which they ocur. What we do not want is a Manichean separation of what is purely intellectual or "spiritual" in such pivotal religious phenomena from what is material and specific. Nor should we separate, in considering the liminal symbol, "*something* which offers itself to experience" from "*someone* who actually does experience it." Here I would say that if the cultural form of communitas, as found in liminality, can correspond with an actual experience of communitas, the symbols there presented may be experienced more deeply than in any other context, if the ritual subject has what theologians would call the "proper dispositions."

Here what Dr. Vereno (Note 3) has called "the essentially relational or predicative *esse*" of the symbol is most fully exemplified—a relation which he calls a "gnostic" one. Men "know" less or more as a function of the quality of their relationship with other men. Gnosis, "deep knowledge," is highly characteristic of liminality, certainly in many parts of Africa, as Germaine Dieterlen has shown for the Dogon and Audrey Richards for the Bemba, where it is believed that the esoteric knowledge communicated in symbols in the girl's puberty rites changes the inmost being of the neophyte. It is not merely that new knowledge is imparted, but new power is absorbed, power obtained through the weakness of liminality which will become active in postliminal life when the neophyte's social status has been redefined in the aggregation rites. Among the Bemba a woman has been "grown" from a girl through the importation of gnosis in a communitas of women.

To recapitulate the argument so far: In a situation which is temporally liminal and spatially marginal the neophytes or "passengers" in a protracted *rite de passage* are stripped of status and authority—in other words removed from a social structure which is ultimately maintained and sanctioned by power and force—and further leveled to a homogeneous social state through discipline and ordeal. Their secular powerlessness may however be compensated by a sacred power, the "power of the weak" derived on the one hand from resurgent nature and on the other from the reception of sacred knowledge. Much of what has been bound by social structure is liberated, notably the sense of comradeship and communion, in brief, of communitas; on the other hand, much of what has been dispersed over many domains of culture and social structure is now bound or "cathected" in the complex semantic systems of pivotal, multivocal symbols and myths which achieve great conjunctive power and possess what Erik Erikson, following Otto, would call "numinosity." It is as if social relations have been emptied of their legal-political "structural" character and this structural character, though not its specific structure, has been imparted to the relations between symbols, ideas, and values rather than between social *personae* and statuses. In this no-place and no-time that resists classification itself, the major classifications and categories of the culture emerge within the integuments of myth, symbol, and ritual.

In everyday life people in tribal societies have little time to devote to protophilosophical or theological speculation. But in protracted liminal periods, through which everyone must pass, they become, as it were, a privileged class. They are largely supported by the labor of others, though often exposed by way of compensation to annealing hardships, with abundant opportunity to learn and speculate about what the tribe considers its "ultimate things." Here we have a fruitful alienation of the total individual from the partial *persona* which must result in the development, at least in principle or potentiality if not always in practice, of a total rather than a partial perspective on the life of society. After his immersion in the depths of liminality, very frequently symbolized in ritual and myth as a grave that is also a womb, after this profound experience of humiliation and humility, a man who at the end of the ritual becomes the incumbent of a senior political status or even merely of a higher position in some particularistic segment of the social structure, can surely never again be quite so parochial, so particularistic, in his social loyalties. This can be seen in many tribal societies which practice protracted circumcision rites: the initiands are drawn from diverse tribal segments; when the rites are completed they form an association with mutual rights and obligations which may last until death and which cuts right across cleavages on the basis of ascribed and achieved status.

It would seem that where there is little or no structural provision for liminality, the social need for escape from or abandonment of structural commitments seeks cultural expression in ways that are not explicitly "religious," though they may become heavily "ritualized." Quite often this retreat from social structure may appear to take an individualistic form, as in the case of so many postrenaissance artists, writers, and philosophers. But if one looks closely at their productions, one often sees in them at least a plea for communitas. The artist is not really alone, nor does he write, paint, or compose for "posterity," but for living communitas. Of course, like the initiand in tribal society, the novelistic hero has to be reinducted into the structural domain, but for the "twice-born" (or "converted") the *sting* of that domain—its ambitions, envies and power struggles—has been removed. He is like Kierkegaard's "knight of faith" who, having confronted the structured and quantitative crowd as "the qualitative individual," now moves from antithesis to synthesis and, though remaining outwardly indistinguishable from others in this order of social structure, is henceforth inwardly free from its despotic authority and an autonomous source of creative behavior. This acceptance or "forgiveness" (to use William Blake's term) of "structure" in a movement of return from a liminal situation is a process that recurs again and again in Western literature, and, indeed, in the actual lives of many writers, artists, and political folk heroes from Dante and Lenin to Nehru and the African political exiles who became leaders. It represents a "secularization" of what seems to have been originally a religious process.

But there is now a tendency among many people, especially those under 30, but now spreading, to try to create a communitas and a style of life that is permanently contained within liminality. Their motto is Timothy Leary's "Tune in, turn on and drop out." Instead of "the liminal" being a *passage* it is coming to be regarded as a *state*, although only time will tell. Some seem to think of communes as initiation lodges rather than permanent homes. Of course, this conversion of liminality, in modified form, into a way of life, has also been true of the monastic and mendicant orders, for example, in Christianity and Buddhism; but the religious state has been clearly defined as an exceptional condition reserved for those who aspire after perfection, except in Thailand where all young men spend a year as monks. The religious life is not for everyone, but only for those "elected by grace." Even so we have seen how dangerous primitive Franciscan communitas was held to be by the structured church.

The Western urbanized hippies share with many historical "enthusiastic" sects a desire to generalize and perpetuate their liminal and outsider condition. One of my graduate students in a seminar at Cornell gave me some Haight-Ashbury[3] literature, produced during the brief heyday of the "Hashbury" culture. I would like to quote some passages from a journal called *The Oracle* which used to be published "approximately bi-monthly" in San Francisco, where it was described as the hippies' "house journal." I quote from volume I, number 6 which appeared in February 1967, and has subsequently been spoken of as "a vintage number." Most of the features which we have ascribed to the liminal phases of *rites de passage* and to the early stages of religious movements reappear in this literature with startling clarity. We have seen that in liminality social structure disappears or is simplified and generalized while the cultural apparatus often becomes structurally complex.

We find on the very first printed page of this copy of *The Oracle* a series of statements about "rock" (described as "the first 'head' music we've had since the end of the baroque"). Rock is clearly a cultural expression and instrumentality of that style of communitas which has arisen as the antithesis of the "square," "organization man" type of bureaucratic social structure of mid-20th century America. I will now quote freely (but exactly) from this page, on which it seems that the term "rock" sometimes represents a form of music and sometimes a modality of communitas. The author of "Notes for the New Geology" (geology—the study of rock!) is enunciating "some principles." These include:

"That rock principles are not limited to music, and that much of the shape of the future can be seen in its aspirations today (these being namely total freedom, total experience, total love, peace and mutual affection)" [note: the emphasis on totality or "totalism" rather than partial perspectives and on the *"prophetic"* character of this liminal manifestation];

"That rock is a way of life, international and verging in this decade on universal; and can't be stopped, retarded, put down, muted, modified or successfully controlled by typeheads, whose arguments don't apply and whose machinations don't mesh because they can't perceive (dig) what rock really is and does" [note: the stress on the pan-human yet immediate quality of this "new" social relationship and its cultural product, both called "rock"];

"That rock is a *tribal* phenomenon [sic], immune to definition and other typographical operations, and constitutes what might be called a twentieth century magic" [note: "typeheads," as against acid heads, "define" and "stereo*type*"—but of course *truly* "tribal" phenomena are really highly involved with classifications as Lévi-Strauss and the "thought structuralists" have shown];

"That rock is a vital agent in breaking down absolute and arbitrary distinctions" [note: the expression of communitas' power of dissolving structural divisions];

"That group participation, total experience and complete involvement are rock's minimal desiderata and those as well of a world that has too many people" [note: the stress on the need for face-to-face relationships, in which communitas best flourishes];

"That rock is creating the social rituals of the future" [note: the stress on the *creative* role of certain social situations in which new definitions and models for behavior are constructed];

"That rock presents an aesthetic of discovery" [note: the experimental quality of liminality is here recognized];

"That rock is evolving Sturgeonesque *homo gestalt* configurations."

So much for the social characteristics of this "rock communitas."

Perhaps I should explain that "typographic" for this author designates that kind of analytical thinking that presupposes a corpse, as against "vital agencies" of discovery, that "typeheads" are sterile and authoritarian "labelers," and that "Sturgeonesque" refers not to the Russian fish, but to an American author of science fiction who wrote a novel, popular some years ago among the hippies, about a group of people who constituted a human *gestalt*, "the next stage in human evolution," when the individual is replaced by the cluster as the crucial human unit. These people "bleshed" together, just as Heinlein's cult group in *Stranger in a Strange Land* "grocked" together. Incidentally students of symbolism and myth should take note of science fiction, for this genre provides many examples of just such a juggling of the factors of culture, in new and often bizarre combinations and settings, as we postulated earlier might be a feature of liminality in initiations and mystery religions. Here we are dealing with "an esthetic of discovery," a mythology of the future, an "omega" mythology, as appropriate for a society undergoing rapid and unceasing change as a mythology of the past or an "alpha" mythology is appropriate for a stable and relatively repetitive and cyclical social order.

The structure-dissolving quality of liminality is clearly present, for "rock . . . breaks down absolute and arbitrary distinctions." I have written elsewhere (1969) that communitas is, in principle, universal and boundless, as against structure which is specific and bounded. Here we find rock described as "international and . . . universal." But now let us look at what *The Oracle's* "geologist" says about rock as a cultural manifestation rather than a mode of social relationship:

"Rock is a legitimate *avant-garde* art form with deep roots in the music of the past (especially the baroque and before), great vitality and vast potential for growth and development, adaptation, experiment, etc.;

"Rock shares most of its formal/structural principles with baroque music . . . and it and baroque can be judged by the same broad standards (the governing principles being those of mosaic structure of tonal and textural contrast: tactility, collage)."

Here again we see the contrast between the unstructured communitas (or in the words of the author "the groups themselves far more intimately interrelated and integrated than any comparable ensemble in the past") and its highly elaborate cultural product and medium which, like the myths analysed by Lévi-Strauss and Leach, has a logical framework of "formal/structural principles."

The pedigree of "rock" communitas is, of course, much longer than our author supposed. There was no doubt a palaeolithic "rock"! And anthropologists the world over have participated in tribal "scenes," not dissimilar to the rock "scene," in the seclusion lodges of initiation or in the rhythmical dances, with improvised singing, of many kinds of ritual in many kinds of societies. Our author speaks, too, of "synesthesia," the union of visual, auditory, tactile, spatial, visceral, and other modes of perception under the influence of various stimuli such as music, dancing, and drugs. This "involvement of the whole sensorium" is found in tribal ritual and in the services of many modern religious movements. Arthur Rimbaud, one of the folk heroes of the counter-culture, would have approved of this as *un dérèglement ordonné de tous les sens*, "a systematic derangement of all the senses." And just as Rimbaud wrote about the vowel sounds having distinctive colors, so our author talks about "sensory counterpoint—the senses registering contradictory stimuli and the brain having fun trying to integrate them . . . imagine *tasting* G-minor . . . the incredible synesthesia!"

One could point out the detailed resemblances between liminal phenomena of all kinds. But I will conclude by calling attention to the way that certain cultural attributes of ascribed inferior status acquire a communitas significance as attributes of liminal situations or liminal personae. This stress on the symbolism of weakness and poverty is not confined to the counter-culture. Here, of course, I am not talking about the actual social behavior of persons of structurally inferior caste, class, or rank. Such behavior may be as much or as little dependent upon social-structural considerations as the behavior of their status superiors. What I have in mind is the symbolic value of the "poor man" or *harijan* of religion, literature, and political philosophy. In religion, the holy man who makes himself to all appearances poorer than the meanest beggar may, and in fact often does, come from a wealthy or aristocratic, or at least highly educated stratum of the social structure. St. Francis, for example, was the son of a rich merchant; Gautama was a prince. In literature, we find the values of communitas represented by such types as Tolstoy's peasants and by such characters as Dostoevski's prostitute Sonia, Tchekov's poor Jewish fiddler Rothschild (the irony of that name!), by Mark Twain's black slave Jim and youthful vagrant Huckleberry Finn of whom jointly Lionel Trilling (1953, pp. 110ff) has said that they form "a primitive community of saints . . . because they do not have an ounce of pride between them," and the Fool in Shakespeare's *King Lear*. In political philosophy we have the images of Rousseau's Noble Savage, Marx's proletariat, and Gandhi's Untouchables, whom he called *harijans* or "the children of God."

Each of these thinkers, however, had different structural recipes and different formulae for relating communitas to structure. Now liminal poverty must not be confused with real poverty, although the liminally poor may become actually poor. But liminal poverty, whether it is a process or a state, is both an expression and instrumentality of communitas. Communitas is what people really seek by *voluntary* poverty. And because communitas is such a basic, even primordial mode of human interlinkage, depending as it does neither on conventions nor sanctions, it is often religiously equated with love, both the love of man and the love of God. The principle is simple: Cease to have and you are; if you "are" in the relationship of communitas to others who "are," then you "love one another." In the honesty of "being," people naturally relate to or "dig" one another. The difficulty experienced by these Edenic prescriptions in a post-Edenic world is that men have to organize structurally in order to exist materially at all, and the more complex the technology of living becomes, the more finely cut and finely intermeshed does its social division of labor become, and the more time-consuming and absorbing become society's occupational and organizational statuses and roles.

One great temptation in this milieu is to subordinate communitas totally to structure so that the principle of order will never be subverted. The opposite temptation is to opt out of structure altogether. The basic and perennial human social problem is to discover what is the right relation between these modalities at a specific time and place. Since communitas has a strong affectual component, it appeals more directly to people; but since structure is the arena in which they pursue their material interests, communitas, perhaps even more importantly than sex, tends to get repressed into the unconscious, there to become either a source of individual pathological symptoms, or to be released in violent cultural forms in periods of social crisis. People can go crazy because of communitas-repression; sometimes people become obsessively structural as a defense mechanism against their urgent need of communitas.

The major religions have always taken account of this bipolarity, and have tried to maintain these social dimensions in balanced relationship. But the countless sects and schismatic movements in the history of religions have almost always asserted the values of communitas against those of structure, and claimed that the major religions from which they have seceded have become totally structured and secularized, "mere empty forms." Significantly such separatist movements have almost invariably adopted a cultural style dominated by the cultural idiom of indigence, poverty. In their first impetus, such movements often strip their members of the outward show of wealth or status, adopt a simple form of speech and to a considerable extent strip their religious practices of ritualism and visual symbolism. Organizationally, they often abolish priestly hierarchies, and substitute for them either prophetic charismatic leadership or democratic methods of representation. If such movements attract great numbers and persist for many years, they often find it necessary to compromise with structure once again, both liturgical and organizational.

The great historical religions have, in the course of time, learned how to incorporate enclaves of communitas within their institutionalized structures—just as tribal religions do with their *rites de passage*—and to oxygenate, so to speak, the mystical body by making provision for those ardent souls who wish to live in communitas and poverty all their lives. Just as in a ritual of any complexity there are phases of separation from and reaggregation to the domain of social structure (phases which themselves contain many structural features, including symbols which reflect or express structural principles) and a liminal phase representing an interim of communitas with its own rich and elaborate symbolism, so does a great religion or church contain many organizational and liturgical sectors which overlap with and interpenetrate the secular social structure but maintain in a central position a sanctuary of unqualified communitas, of that poverty which is said to be "the poetry of religion" and of which St. Francis, Angelus Silesius, the Sufist poets, Rumi and Al-Ghazali, and the Virasaiva poet Basavanna were melodious troubadours and jongleurs.

Now I would like to bring my argument round full circle and state that from the standpoint of structural man, he who is in communitas is an exile or a stranger, someone who, by his very existence, calls into question the whole normative order. That is why when we consider cultural institutions we have to look in the interstices, niches, intervals and on the peripheries of the social structure to find even a grudging cultural recognition of this primordial human modality of relationship. On the other hand, in times of drastic and sustained social change, it is communitas which often appears to be central and structure which constitutes the "square" or "straight" periphery.

If one may dare to venture a personal evaluation of such matters, one might say that much of the misery of the world has been due to the "principled" activities of fanatics of both persuasions. On the one hand, one finds a structural and ultimately bureaucratic *"übermensch"* who would like to array the whole world of lesser men in terms of hierarchy and regimentation in a "New Order," and on the other the puritanical levelers who would abolish all idiosyncratic differences between man and man (even necessary organizational differences for the sake of the food quest), and set up an ethical tyranny that would allow scant scope for compassion and forgiveness. "One Law for the Lion and the Ox is Oppression," said Blake with reference to such ethical tyranny. Yet since both social modalities are indispensable for human social continuity, neither can exist for long without the other. Indeed, if structure is maximized to full rigidity, it invites the nemesis of either violent revolution or uncreative apathy, while if communitas is maximized, it becomes in a short while its own dark shadow, totalitarianism, from the need to suppress and repress in its members all tendencies to develop structural independences and interdependences.

Moreover, communitas, which is in principle boundless and universal, has been in historical practice limited to particular geographical regions and specific aspects of social life. Thus the varied expressions of communitas such as monasteries, convents, "socialist bastions," semireligious communities and brotherhoods, nudist colonies, communes in the modern counter-cultures, initiation camps, have often found it necessary to surround themselves with real as well as symbolic walls—a species of what structural sociologists would call "boundary maintaining mechanisms." When large scale communities are involved, these tend to take the form of military and police organizations, open and secret. Thus to keep out "structure," "structure" has to be constantly maintained and reinforced. When the great principles regard one another as antagonists, each "becomes what it beholds." What seems to be needed, to quote William Blake again, is to "destroy the negation" and thus "redeem the contraries," i.e., as we said before, discover what is the *right relationship* between structure and communitas at a given time and place—in history and geography—to give to each its due.

To sum up: A major stumbling block in the development of sociological and anthropological theory has been the almost total identification of the social with the social-structural. Even "informal" relations are considered "structural." Many of them are, of course, but not all, and these include the most relevant ones; it *is* possible to distinguish the deep from the shallow here. This has created enormous difficulties with regard to many problems, such as social change, the sociology of religion and role theory, to name but a few. It has also led to the view that all that is not social structural is "psychological"—whatever this may mean. It has also led to the positing of a false dichotomy between the individual as subject, and society as object. What seems to be the case is that the social has a "free" or "unbound" as well as a "bonded" or "bound" dimension, the dimension of communitas in which men confront one another not as role players but as "human totals," integral beings who recognizably share the same humanity.

Once this has been recognized, it will be possible for the social sciences to examine more fruitfully than hitherto such cultural phenomena as art, religion, literature, philosophy, and even many aspects of law, politics, and economic behavior which have hitherto eluded the structuralist conceptual net. Such domains are rich with reference to communitas. The vain task of trying to find out in what precise way certain symbols found in the ritual, poetry, or iconography of a given society "reflect" or "express" its social or political structure can then be abandoned. Symbols may well reflect not structure, but anti-structure, and not only "reflect" it but contribute to *creating* it. Instead, we can regard these phenomena in terms of the *relationship between* structure and communitas, to be found in such "relational" situations as passages between structural states, the interstices of structural relations, and in the powers of the weak.

Notes

1. Here I would contrast "existential" with "normative" communitas.
2. Though clearly the organizational outcomes of celibacy versus orgy must be very different as must the attitude of the guardians of orthodox structure to movements of these rival types!
3. This district in San Francisco was the main center of "hippiedom" in 1966 and 1967. Its name gave rise to such posters and grafitti as: "Haight is love."

Reference Notes

1. Ramanujan, A.K. *Structure and anti-structure: The Virasaiva example.* Paper for the Seminar on Aspects of Religion in South Asia at the School of Oriental and African Studies, University of London.
2. Turner, T. *The fire of the Jaguar: Myth and social organization among the Northern Kayapo of central Brazil.* Paper given at the Conference on Myth and Ritual, Dartmouth College, August 1967.
3. Vereno, M. (University of Salzburg) Comment made at the Conference on Myth and Ritual, Dartmouth College, August 1967.

References

DURKHEIM, E. *[The elementary forms of the religious life]* (J.S. Swain, trans.). New York: Collier, 1961. (Originally published, 1912.)

FORTES, M. *The web of kinship among the Tallensi.* London: Oxford University Press, 1949.

LÉVI-STRAUSS, C. On manipulated sociological models. *Bijdragen tot de Taal, Land en Volkenkunde,* 1960, **116**(1), 45-54.

LÉVI-STRAUSS, C. [Structural anthropology] (C. Jacobson, Trans.). New York: Basic Books, 1963. (Originally published, 1958.)

THE ORACLE (San Francisco), February 1967, **1**(6).

RAMANUJAN, A.K. *Speaking of Siva.* Baltimore: Penguin Books, 1973.

REED, N. *The caste war in Yucatan.* Stanford: Stanford University Press, 1964.

RIESMAN, D. *Individualism reconsidered and other essays.* Glencoe, IL: The Free Press, 1954.

ROSEN, L. Language, history, and the logic of inquiry in Lévi-Strauss and Sartre. *History and Theory,* 1971, **10**(3), 269-294.

SARTRE, J.P. *Search for a method.* New York: Knopf, 1963.

SARTRE, J.P. Itinerary of a thought. *New Left Review,* 1969, **58**, 57-59.

STONEQUIST, E.V. *The marginal man.* New York: Scribner, 1937.

TRILLING, L. *The liberal imagination*. New York: Anchor Books, 1953.

TURNER, V. *The ritual process*. Chicago: Aldine, 1969.

VAN GENNEP, A. *Les rites de passage*. Paris: E. Nourry, 1908.

VAN GENNEP, A. *[The rites of passage]* (M.B. Vizedom & G.L. Caffee, trans.). Chicago: University of Chicago Press, 1960.

ZNANIECKI, F., & Thomas, W.I. *The Polish peasant in Europe and America*. Boston: Badger, 1918.

Chapter 16
Deep Play and the Flow Experience in Rock Climbing

JOHN MACALOON AND
MIHALY CSIKSZENTMIHALYI

Because it involves physical danger and no discernible external re-wards, rock climbing is an outstanding example of a particular class of flow activities. Furthermore, the artificial, sheltered universe of climbing can assume a reality of its own more meaningful to the actor than the reality of everyday life. In this sense, the analysis of rock climb-ing shows how flow activities can serve as models for societal transfor-mation and provide experiences that motivate people to implement change.

The presence of risk places rock climbing squarely in what Jeremy Bentham, the 18th-century British philosopher, called "deep play." He used that phrase with misgivings, to describe "play in which the stakes are so high that it is, from his [Bentham's] utilitarian standpoint, irra-tional for men to engage in it at all" (Geertz, 1973, p. 432; see chapter 1 in this volume). And certainly, if one thinks in terms of economic utility and the support of existing cultural values, deep play is useless, if not

From M. Csikszentmihalyi, *Beyond Boredom and Anxiety*. San Francisco: Jossey-Bass, 1977. Copyright 1977 by Jossey-Bass. Reprinted with permission.

subversive. But that is exactly why it interests a student of human nature. Why are people attracted to an activity that offers no "rational" rewards? That is the question we shall try to answer with the help of the flow model. The second issue, concerning the effects that playful activities may have on "real" life, has been often mentioned in the past but with very few concrete examples. This study of rock climbers may help to redress the lack of empirical information on the topic, for rock climbing is a form of deep play in the sense of involving an extreme wager which acts as a vehicle for the deeper personal and cultural interests of the participants who risk it.

Climbing and Climbers

Rock climbing is an autonomous sport which developed out of the older and more general activity of mountaineering. The separation began roughly half a century ago, when in the 1920s some mountain climbers in the Alps perfected the use of equipment and techniques to make *direttissima* (most direct rather than roundabout) ascents of mountain faces previously thought to be unassailable. The two sports still overlap, but there is now a clearly established group of "technical climbers," interested not in reaching summits but in climbing the sheerest faces, as opposed to traditional climbers (Csikszentmihalyi, 1969).

Climbers consider their sport one of the purest forms of human activity, partly because achievement in it is a private experience rather than a public event. Feats of rock climbing are impervious to inclusion in the Guinness *Book of Records*: neither speed nor height nor any other measurable dimension is meaningful to assess performance. Only the initiated can appreciate the blend of objective difficulty and the artistry of the climber; however, climbing is usually done without an audience, and no one but the climber himself knows what he has accomplished and how well. Rock climbing is the exact antithesis of the American preoccupation with spectator sports.

Advances in technology and physical conditioning, together with the conquest of all the major summits, have led to the pursuit of ever more challenging rock walls, regardless of their location. More and better climbers regularly queue up at local climbing areas or jet about the world seeking new challenges. But the basic nature of the activity as a form of deep play has not changed. As far back as 1854, Thomas Murray confidently noted in his *Handbook for Travellers in Switzerland* that mountaineers suffer "of a diseased mind" (quoted in Lukan, 1968, p. 43). Contemporary opinions of rock climbers are not too different. We have undertaken to question what there is in the activity itself which leads men to engage in it despite its "irrationality." Historical and literary references are employed where helpful, but the bulk of the material comes from the climbers we interviewed.

Informants

Thirty rock climber/mountaineers were personally interviewed, by researchers who themselves are rock climbers, in Boulder, Colorado; Chicago, Illinois; and Devil's Lake, Wisconsin. Informants were selected to provide a range of experience, involvement, and skill. The mean age of the group was 28, with a range from 19 to 53. Five were female; twenty-five were male. The educational level ranged from high school equivalency to PhD, with most at or near the BA level. Place of birth, father's occupation and income, and personal financial status varied widely.

Mean length of experience was 5 years of technical rock climbing and 8 years of general mountaineering, with the range in each case being from 1 to 36 years. In the summer, most of those interviewed climb once every two weeks, though some get out as often as four times a week and others as infrequently as once a month. During the winter, the activity level is approximately halved for most of the sample. Mean investment in rock-climbing gear—rope and hardware—approximated $138 at 1972 prices. Five climbers owned no equipment of their own; two had equipment worth more than $400.

A word on the international rating system is necessary, since this system permits a fairly accurate absolute and comparative estimate of the climbers' skills. In the last two decades a system of numerical ratings has been devised to describe the strenuousness of individual climbs. The rating expresses the most arduous move or series of moves to be encountered, taking into account such factors as type of move; degree of strength and gymnastics required; size and number of holds; and shape, inclination, friability, and exposure of the rock. The rating is established by the climber who makes the first ascent, although it may later be revised by a more recognized expert or by subsequent alteration of the rock itself. This rating system seems very subjective and mysterious, especially to the beginner; in practice, however, it is remarkably objective and consistent.

Serious rock climbs are termed "fifth-class" climbs, further broken down into a decimal range from 5.0 to 5.11. Climbs which are made "free"—that is, via the natural footholds and handholds provided by the rock alone—are rated by this system. An additional numerical value, from A-1 to A-6, describes direct-aid or "high-tension" climbs, in which artificial holds are created with the help of equipment designed for this purpose. The climbers interviewed in the course of this study ranged in ability from 5.3 to 5.11/A-6, from moderate skill to the limit of human potential, as it is currently estimated. Mean ratings indicate a slight skew toward the upper reaches of the spectrum (5.8/A-2).

On fifth-class climbs, climbers must be protected by ropes anchored to the rock by lashes, pitons, or chockstones. Such climbs generally involve two or more individuals and proceed in inchworm fashion. The first climber up the pitch, the "leader," is belayed from below and places his own protective anchors when he reaches a convenient perch. The skill ratings just mentioned for the climbers in the sample are for "following." Because a leader's fall is likely to involve more serious consequences than a follower's, separate ratings are kept for leading, according to the same numerical schema. The mean grade of rock led by the informants is 5.5/A-1, representing a more even distribution. Two climbers had led at the 5.11/A-6 level, while five had not led at all.

In addition to the quantitative skill ratings, attention was paid to the qualitative reputation of the individuals from the standpoint of the climbing population. Three of our respondents are quite well known to the American climbing community. Each has international experience and first ascents to his credit, and is known as a local hero in his home climbing area. Two others have made important first ascents, and one other has made a name for himself locally. The remaining 24 are not publicly distinguished.

Throughout the interview the accent was placed on obtaining the climber's own interpretation of his involvement in the activity. A common set of directed questions was asked of all informants, but the individual was allowed, even encouraged, to commandeer the interview vehicle to his own purpose. Many of the individuals whom we approached were initially reluctant to be interviewed. For the two most renowned climbers, this skepticism reflected past experience with journalists and psychologists; for others, with friends and family. Still others were generally (and understandably) leery of exposing the deeper layers of their personalities and social relationships. These misapprehensions (discussed freely and fully after they had been overcome in the interview process) reflected the desire to protect the integrity of the deep-play sphere from the perennially reductive glosses of the outsider.

Characteristics of Flow Experience

From the viewpoint of the outsider who uses the utilitarian calculus of normal life, climbing is indeed an irrational activity which needs to be explained by reducing it to a subtle form of mental derangement. But the previous results of this study have alerted us to the fact that certain forms of experiences are their own reward. We know that climbers, when they describe what they do, note "exploring a strange place" as the closest experience to climbing, followed by "designing or discovering something new," "being with a good friend," and "solving a mathematical problem" (Table 1). We also know that the intrinsic rewards of climbing are

Table 1
Ranking of Similarity of Experience Items Within Each Autotelic Activity (Based on Mean Rank Scores)

Factors	Rock Climbers N = 30	Composers N = 22	Dancers N = 27	Male Chess N = 30	Female Chess N = 22	Basketball N = 40
1. Friendship and Relaxation						
Making love	6.0	6.5	4.5	16.5	17.5	14.0
Being with good friend	3.0	9.0	4.5	9.0	14.5	8.0
Watching a good movie	15.5	5.0	9.0	12.0	17.5	6.0
Listening to good music	6.0	3.0	2.0	10.0	12.5	3.0
Reading an enjoyable book	8.0	8.0	6.5	5.0	12.5	15.5
2. Risk and Chance						
Swimming too far out on a dare	13.0	13.5	15.0	14.0	7.0	17.5
Exposing yourself to radiation to prove your theory	17.0	10.0	12.0	12.0	10.0	9.5
Driving too fast	10.0	16.5	12.0	12.0	10.0	6.0
Taking drugs	10.0	13.5	15.0	15.0	14.5	9.5
Playing a slot machine	18.0	18.0	15.0	18.0	16.0	17.5
Entering a burning house to save a child	13.0	11.0	12.0	16.5	10.0	4.0
3. Problem Solving						
Solving a mathematical problem	4.0	2.0	9.0	1.5	2.0	12.0
Assembling equipment	13.0	6.5	17.0	7.5	7.0	15.5
Exploring a strange place	1.0	4.0	3.0	4.0	4.0	12.0
Playing poker	15.5	13.5	18.0	6.0	5.0	12.0
4. Competition						
Running a race	6.0	16.5	9.0	7.5	7.0	2.0
Playing a competitive sport	10.0	13.5	6.5	1.5	3.0	1.0
5. Creative						
Designing or discovering something new	2.0	1.0	1.0	3.0	1.0	6.0

the ones rated highest by the respondents. But how exactly does the activity provide this creative, enjoyable experience? To answer this question, we turn to an analysis of the structural components of rock climbing and the associated experiences they stimulate, within the framework of the flow model.

Opportunities for Action

Rock climbing provides an unlimited range of action challenges—both "horizontally," in the sense of progression from easy to difficult, and "vertically," in that, like chess, it permits the actor to be involved in the activity on a variety of dimensions. By Dember's (1960) definition, climbing offers "high complexity values" with "graduated pacers." A 5.5 climber may select the increased challenges of a 5.7 route, or he may choose to decrease the demands with a 5.3 climb: "It depends on the mood I'm in. There are days when you're not up to perfection, when you want to mellow out on some easy rock; others when you're quite willing to maim yourself for all time."

To a large degree one can choose in advance the level of challenge that best suits one's level of skills. Moreover, within each class of climbs, variability is potentially infinite; no two climbs are ever exactly alike: "The rock changes with a kind of psychological ecology. Depending on that ecology, which is to say where your head is, the 5.4 move you did yesterday might be a 5.10 ass-buster today." Differences in the kinds of moves required, texture of the rock length of the route, quality of protection, and so on, render the hundreds of available climbs at, for instance, the 5.7 level into thousands of novel and interesting action opportunities. In addition, less predictable factors—weather, conditioning, mood, partner's performance, equipment failure—can always provide unexpected challenges.

The climber may also recomplexify a familiar route by adding new goals to the obvious central one of safely and successfully completing the climb. He may lead others to their limits; or he may change the demands upon himself by focusing on aesthetic criteria, such as the elimination of wasted motion or the reduction of reliance upon equipment; or he may increase the danger by eliminating equipment altogether on a solo climb. As one climber puts it, "When you run into something you've either done before or experienced the equivalent to, . . . you're going to be concentrating more on form than achievement. When you get up to 5.9, you get more into the achievement side of things. You just want to live through the son of a bitch. 5.4 is achievement, but in the form sense. It's achievement of as close to perfect balance, perfect gracefulness as you can get."

By a variety of such measures, the individual in effect "changes the rules" and alters the evaluative criteria. Climbers may return time and again to the same route and find it freshly interesting. Whether one chooses progression to higher objective ratings, or increased aesthetic and emotional achievement at a set skill level, climbing offers perpetual novelty: "Obviously you're not going to reach any perfection in climbing because your mind is always one step ahead. . . . You can always think of one step more perfect than you can do. Each time you move up, your present flow is imperfect. . . . It's an endless moving up."

Good flow activities, like chess and rock climbing, offer a wide range of "flow channels" at various levels of skill and commitment. As in all forms of deep play, control over the choice of challenge levels—the calculation of the "odds," so to speak—is extremely important. At the same time, a degree of uncertainty is always implicit and necessary to the process: "The uncertainty factor is the flow factor. Uncertainty is the existence of a flow, whereas certainty is static, is dead, is not flowing. . . . You can't have a certain flow any more than an uncertain staticness. They cancel each other out."

Centering of Attention on Limited Stimulus Field

In contrast to normative everyday life, the action of rock climbing is narrow, simplified, and internally coherent. From all the actions an individual might undertake, sensations he might process, thoughts he might entertain, the parameters of the activity define a narrow subset as relevant—a man climbing a rock. The remainder of the human repertoire is rendered irrelevant and irritant and is screened out from this simplified, manageable stimulus field. The physical and mental requirements involved in staying on the rock act as a screen for the stimuli of ordinary life—a screen maintained by an intense and focused concentration. Our informants universally recognize this effect, as these sample comments indicate.

> When I start on a climb, it's as if my memory input had been cut off. All I can remember is the last thirty seconds, and all I can think ahead is the next five minutes. . . . With tremendous concentration the normal world is forgotten.

> When you're [climbing] you're not aware of other problematic life situations. It becomes a world unto its own, significant only to itself. It's a concentration thing. Once you're into the situation, it's incredibly real, and you're very much in charge of it. It becomes your total world.

> It's a centering thing, being absolutely in the here and now, in the present. It's the most important part of climbing.

> You're moving in harmony with something else, you're a part of it. It's one of the few sorts of activities in which you don't feel you have all sorts of different kinds of conflicting demands on you.

One thing you're after is the one-pointedness of mind.

You're into an entirely different universe that the usual daily things don't really affect that much.

An expert and sensitive climber, Doug Robinson, in an article entitled "The Climber as Visionary," refers to this limited stimulus field as "the sensory desert of the climb." "To climb with concentration," he writes, "is to shut out the world, which, when it reappears, will be as a fresh experience, strange and wonderful in its newness" (Robinson, 1969, pp. 7-8). As in any "desert," there is less to look at, but what there is is seen more intensely.

How do climbers maintain this intense concentration? First of all, climbing problems attract the individual's interest, pique his curiosity, and titillate his desire for a decision: "One of the nicest things about climbing is figuring out the potentials of any one position. Each has an infinite number of balance potentials, and figuring out the best moves from among all those potentials, both moving from the position you're in and what the next move is going to be from the position you will be in, is really wild!" Some compare this intrinsic interest to problem solving in mathematics or engineering: "The satisfaction of working out a problem . . . like a math problem. You keep trying till you find a solution. It seems like there's always a solution." Others relate it to artistic creativity: "It's almost like an art, putting different combinations of moves together in order to get to the top"; "It's an aesthetic dance"; "It's a physical poem on the rock." This is the aspect of the activity which prompted the climbers to rate "designing or discovering something new" and "solving a mathematical problem" as experiences similar to their own.

But in rock climbing, as in most forms of deep play, a heightened concentration and enforcement of attention boundaries is achieved through the addition of risk to the intellectually engaging aspects of the activity. Whatever subsequent meanings the informants attach to physical danger in rock climbing, it functions principally as a compelling motivation to attend to the immediate situation. Any lapse of concentration, any opening of the postern gate to the concerns of ordinary life, is always potentially disastrous: "Mind wandering is dangerous. The more competent you get, the less your mind wanders." "If you're thinking about your old lady, you're not thinking about where your hand's going. You'll be back with your old lady soon enough, but right now you've got to put your hand in a place were it's going to stay. . . . Death's always on the mat with you."

Feelings of Competence and Control

In his attitude toward deep play, as we have seen, the outsider systematically misestimates the role played by the "irrational" counters of the activity, either by mistaking them for an end rather than a means or by assuming the player's obsession with them. As Geertz (1973) has shown for the Balinese cockfight, money is not *all that* paramount in the minds of the bettors. Similarly, in rock climbing, physical danger, while a very real and structurally crucial aspect of the activity, stands neither as an end in itself nor as a dominant preoccupation of the climbers. Only one respondent claimed that he climbs "for cheap thrills," and his statement was extremely qualified. No one else gave any indication of pursuing danger for its own sake. "Danger" as one put it, "is not a kick." Rather, danger is accepted and utilized as a part of the gestalt of climbing, in which feelings of control and competence predominate over voluntary risk in the figure-and-ground relationship. Indeed, when asked directly whether they consider climbing dangerous, 21 of the 30 informants responded negatively. Sample comments include these:

> No I don't think it's too dangerous, if you take a little precaution and use your head.

> No more dangerous than driving a car. You just can't let it affect you.

> No, emphatically. I did snow skiing since childhood; it's twice as dangerous. Climbing is only dangerous if you climb in a dangerous way.

> Very rarely, once in a while I do something insane but most of the time I'm safety conscious.

> No, I don't consider it dangerous. . . . I'm belayed and I'm sure of the people I go with, mainly because I trained them myself.

> You get so absorbed in the climb that you no longer think about danger.

> No, I consider it as dangerous as driving a car.

> The sport itself is safe, safer than driving a car.

> Most of it isn't dangerous, not more dangerous than walking in Hyde Park.

> The press and popular media overemphasize the danger. They generalize from the carelessness of irresponsible climbers. People see climbers as risqué, danger-loving daredevils—all misconceptions.

> Climbing may be less dangerous than walking down the street, because I haven't got control over the latter; there are more variables that can't be calculated.

> The degree of danger is in a way determined by you.

> Not really. The most things happen out of ignorance; the better climber you are, the more you can judge what's ahead.

> I like being up and looking down. When I look down, I look at the view, not the danger; I know I'm protected from that.

> No, I don't consider it that dangerous. The variables are subject to evaluation.

The intriguing recurrence of the statement that rock climbing is less dangerous than everyday activities, such as driving a car or walking down a street, is a point to which we shall later return. For the moment it is sufficient to note the objective correlates of the feelings of control: experience, training, precaution, anticipation, protection, judgment, responsibility, evaluation. All these qualities unite into the "discipline" of mind and body in climbing and allow the degree of danger to be managed by the individual. Most informants would concur with the climber who summarized it this way: "There's risk, to be sure, but it's a highly calculated risk, much more so than driving a car. You relate the risk involved to your own experience and that suggests the number and kinds of precautions you must take. If you do, you'll feel in control. Beyond that, there is always the unknown which simply is there and nothing can be done about it, so you can't worry about it." "Control," said another, "is just a feeling, but it's a very accurate feeling. That's what climbing depends on, how accurate that analysis is."

Unambiguous and Immediate Feedback

Along with its function as a device for centering and intensifying attention, physical danger provides the clear and immediate feedback requisite of a good flow activity. Eleven informants imagined that it is possible ideally for a good climber to always feel in control; 19 did not. But in the actual experience of all informants, control feelings are not always present. In figure-and-ground relations, control feelings sometimes give way to anxiety feelings. The climber knows he is "doing well" if he feels in control of his actions, whereas the arousal of fear signals immediately that he is "doing poorly" and must make adjustments. In the course of the average climb, this feedback loop, regulated by differential control/fear signals of varying intensity, is continuously operating. In those rare moments when the climber enters the deep-flow channel, control feelings intensify and stabilize to the point of presumption.

Merging of Action and Awareness: Transcendence of Ego Boundaries

If the ego is taken as that construct we learn to interpose between self and environment (Freud, 1927; Mead, 1934), as a broker for competing demands and an arbiter of ambiguities, we may begin to grasp the origins of that "egolessness" reported by our informants. When the actor's attention is highly focused in a limited stimulus field which provides noncontradictory demands for action appropriate to the actor's resources, with clear and immediate feedback in the form of control feelings, a state may be reached in which the ego has, so to speak, nothing to do, and awareness of it fades. The extremely processual nature of climbing—the continuous alternation between balance and movement, homeostasis and change, from position to position—is nicely expressed in one informant's statement: "It's self-catalyzing. . . . The moves . . . create each other. The move you're planning to do is also the genesis of the move you're going to do after you've done that one. It's an indefinite interrelationship, a kind of crystalline hookup."

This fluid process of movement-balance-perception-decision-movement-balance . . . forms the internal dynamic of climbing. One might visualize it as a strip of movie film. Each synchronic slice of the action (balance, decision, movement, and so on) is like a frame of that film. When the action is too easy or too difficult, the film stutters and the actor is very aware of the black borders of each frame, the negotiation of the ego construct. But when the difficulty is just right, action follows action in a fluid series, and the actor has no need to adopt an outside perspective from which to consciously intervene. Awareness of the individual frames disappears in the unbroken flow of the whole. "Your moves," as one respondent noted, "become one move." Action merges with awareness. The actor is immersed in the flow of his movement. The flow experience emerges as the psychological correlate of this kinesthetic-cognitive process.

Dennis Eberl (1969, p. 13), recounting a trying Matterhorn ascent, expresses this point clearly: "Just as we reached the base of a small icefield, the clouds enveloped us. I resigned myself to the fight and even began to hope that our struggle would be a classic one. What followed was one of *those rare moments of almost orgiastic unity as I forgot myself and became lost in action.* . . . At the top of the icefield I placed a rock piton, and as I reached to clip in, I was surrounded by a blue flash as a two-foot spark jumped from the rock to my hand. Unhurt, I traversed away from the rock and then downclimbed the ice. When I reached Gray, the *moment of unity between my thoughts and actions* was already over" (emphasis added).

But one need not turn to accounts of heroic success or retreat to find validation of this aspect of the flow experience in climbing. Our informants' statements are replete with it.

> You don't feel like you're doing something as a conscious being; you're adapting to the rock and becoming part of it.

> You feel more alive; internal and external don't get confused. The task at hand is so rich in its complexity and pull [that] your intensity as a conscious subject is diminished; a more subtle loss of self than mere forgetfulness.

It's a pleasant feeling of total involvement. You become like a robot . . . no, more like an animal . . . getting lost in kinesthetic sensation . . . a panther powering up the rock.

When things are going poorly, you start thinking about yourself. When things go well, you do things automatically without thinking. You pick the right holds, equipment, and it is right.

You're so involved in what you're doing [that] you aren't thinking about yourself as separate from the immediate activity. You're no longer a participant observer, only a participant. You're moving in harmony with something else you're part of.

When you first start climbing, you're very aware of capabilities. But after a while you just do it without reflecting on it at the time.

When you're climbing, you have to devote yourself totally to the climb; you fuse your thinking with the rock. It's the ultimate in participation sports, participation endeavors.

It's the Zen feeling, like meditation or concentration. One thing you're after is the one-pointedness of mind. You can get your ego mixed up with climbing in all sorts of ways and it isn't necessarily enlightening. But when things become automatic, it's like an egoless thing, in a way. Somehow the right thing is done without you ever thinking about it or doing anything at all. . . . It just happens. And yet you're more concentrated.

If you can imagine yourself becoming as clear as when you focus a pair of binoculars, everything's blurred and then the scene becomes clear, as you focus them. If you focus yourself in the same way, until all of you is clear, you don't think about how you're going to do it, you just do it.

The right decisions are made, but not rationally. Your mind is shut down and your body just goes. It's one of the extremes of human experience.

Strongly correlated with the merging of action and awareness is an altered time sense, a distortion in the congruence of chronological and psychological time. The climber who finds himself in a fearful predicament may feel time speeded up and may consistently misestimate the duration of his strain. Similarly, in periods of boredom, when time drags along, the subject often overestimates its passage. In both cases, self-consciousness or ego awareness is accented. In the flow experience, however, where ego awareness is decreased, the climber loses track of time altogether. Later he may even feel that for the duration of his flowing he was lifted out of time entirely, disattached from internal and external clocks. The temporal aspect of the deep-flow experience is characteristically reported with such oxymorons as "an eternal moment." In Robinson's words (1969, p. 6): "It is said to be only a moment, yet by virtue of total absorption he is lost in it, and the winds of eternity blow through it."

Transcendent Aspects of Deep-Flow Experience

Thus far we have stressed the narrow, contracted nature of the activity frame of rock climbing, its irrelevance to the concerns of normative life, its literal and figurative "away-from-it-all" qualities, the internal focusing of attention and merging of action and awareness on a severely restricted field of action and cognition. But within this intense contraction, indeed on account of it, there occurs a grand expansion, an opening out to the basic concerns of the human condition, a blossoming invisible to the flatland observer but real and compelling in the minds of the climbers. As one informant said about the pursuit of the useless in this human "miniature": "That one thing [climbing] is a complexity as great as the whole."

Before discussing these extraordinary aspects of the climbers' deepest experiences, for which adjectives such as *transcendent, religious, visionary*, or *ecstatic* are traditionally employed, we must make two important qualifications.

The first is that by no means all of the climbers in our sample reported these deep-flow experiences; only 9 out of 30 consistently did. Others apparently had brushed with them at one time or another but either paid them little attention or even denounced them as mystical tommyrot.

I just don't feel that. I can't say much about its importance because it doesn't affect me.

I don't feel it really. I'm always conscious of the decisions I make on rock.

Bullshit. Of course, you're very self-conscious. At least many people are. I am.

God only knows [what such people are talking about]. Sounds mighty strange because in climbing you're most aware of yourself. I think somebody must be trying to be spectacular. Sounds like Greek to me.

I don't think it's important to me, I don't think that's why I climb. My main reason for climbing is the physical exercise. Well, I suppose it would be a different experience without it [the feeling of egolessness]; it's part of the total experience.

We find ourselves faced with the same phenomenon which afflicted Maslow (1964) in his work on "peak experiences" and led him to divide the human population into "peakers" and "nonpeakers." While this radical bisection might be premature, it is important to search out the reasons for the difference. At the present stage of our work it is not yet possible to say anything systematic about why some people report deep-flow experiences, value them absolutely, and pursue them with vigor, while others do not. However, the climbers themselves offer some hints.

One climber who does have deep-flow experiences suggests the inhibiting effects of ego intrusions: "You can get your ego mixed up with climbing in all sorts of ways, and it isn't necessarily enlightening." Another climber, who does not have deep-flow experiences but wishes she did, explains why she does not: "I'm too into competition with myself to feel that. I haven't done it long enough and am not in good enough shape."

To slip into the flow channel at all, then, an individual must attain certain levels of experience, skill, and conditioning appropriate to the challenges before him. Some simply have not climbed enough, with the right companions, or under the right circumstance to have happened upon the experience or to be able to preselect situations in which it is likely to occur. Then again, various personality and sociocultural factors may interpose themselves between the individual and the flow experience through a process of selective attention. "Getting one's ego mixed up with climbing" may involve overemphasis on one of its structural features, such as competition with self and others. The transformation of conscious attention requisite to the flow experience may thus be inhibited.

The second point is that our informants' accounts of deep-flow experiences are translations of great emotions made after the fact—"emotion recollected in tranquility," as the poet would have it. As with any report of religious, creative, or visionary experiences, more is left behind than crosses the border of speech. Geertz (1973, p. 449) writes, "What the cockfight says it says in a vocabulary of sentiment." So too with rock climbing. While language is the only instrument we have to communicate these emotions and to discover their meaning, the emotions themselves are valued for their own sake as significant messages. Rock climbing, like the cockfight, is finally in this sense a form of art, though one which produces events and not objects. George Mallory, in "The Mountaineer as Artist," speaks to this point: "Artists . . . are not distinguished by the power of expressing emotion but by the power of feeling that emotional experience out of which Art is made. . . . Mountaineers are all artistic . . . because *they cultivate emotional experience for its own sake*" (quoted in Robinson, 1969, p. 4; emphasis added).

As we have seen, the merging of action and awareness which typifies the flow state does not allow for the intrusion of an outside perspective with such worries as "How am I doing?" or "Why am I doing this?" or even "What is happening to me?" In the moments of flow the individual does not even consciously acknowledge that he is flowing, much less elaborate and comment on the experience and its meaning. Realization, translation, and elaboration take place when the action has ceased: briefly at a belay stance, when the summit is finally reached, or after the climber is back on level ground. The processual structure of rock climbing not only produces great emotions but also offers regular opportunities to elaborate and solidify the experiences through reflection. Robinson (1969, pp. 7-8) describes this aspect of the activity very clearly:

> The concentration is not continuous. It is often intermittent and sporadic, sometimes cyclic and rhythmic. After facing the successive few square feet of rock for a while, the end of the rope is reached and it is time to belay. The belay time is a break in the concentration, a gap, a small chance to relax.The climber changes from an aggressive and productive stance to a passive and receptive one, from doer to observer, and in fact from artist to visionary. The climbing day goes on through the climb-belay-climb-belay cycle by a regular series of concentrations and relaxations. . . . When the limbs go to the rock and muscles contract, then the will contracts also. And at the belay stance, tied in to a scrub oak, the muscles relax; and the will also, which has been concentrating on moves, expands and takes in the world again, and the world is bright and new. It is freshly created, for it really had ceased to exist. . . . We notice that as the cycle of intense contractions takes over, and as this cycle becomes the daily routine, even consumes the daily routine, the relaxations on belay yield more frequent and intense visionary experiences. . . . The summit, capping off the cycling and giving final release from the tension of contractions, should offer the climber some of his most intense moments.

Most climbers, at one time or another, experience aspects of the entwined formal and affective features of the flow experience on a lowered level of intensity. The deep-flow or visionary experience is by all accounts rarer: "It is a state that one flows in and out of, gaining it through directed effort or spontaneously in a gratuitous moment. . . . It is at its own whim momentary or lingering suspended in the air, suspending time in its turn, forever momentarily eternal, as, stepping out on the last rappel you turn and behold the rich green wonder of the forest" (Robinson, 1969, p. 9).

One may say quite properly that the structured behavioral and thought processes involved in climbing point to and manipulate richer referents in the wider realm of cultural interest. But it would be a mistake to assume that climbers ordinarily are concerned with, or even aware of, the symbolic nature of their enterprise. However many symbolic relations are coalesced and condensed by the activity, in the deep-flow experience a sense of participation and immediacy, rather than condensation and displacement, is the key feature. The deep-flow experience is, as one informant said, "particle, wave, and source at the same time." The objects of perception in the sensory desert of climbing are transformed in this way into what Blake called the "minute particulars." The universe is not merely symbolized in the "grains of sand." The microcosm does not simply *stand for* the macrocosm; it *is* the macrocosm, fully experienced and assented to.

> With the more receptive senses we now appreciated everything around us. Each individual crystal in the granite stood out in bold relief. The varied

shapes of the clouds never ceased to attract our attention. For the first time, we noticed tiny bugs that were all over the walls, so tiny that they were barely noticeable. While belaying, I stared at one for fifteen minutes, watching him move and admiring his brilliant red color.

How could one ever be bored with so many good things to see and feel! This *unity with our joyous surroundings*, this *ultra-penetrating perception*, gave us a feeling that we had not had for years (Yvon Chouinard on El Capitan; quoted in Robinson, 1969, p. 6; emphasis added).

With the intense seeing, the *vision* induced by the activity, comes the transformation of material objects and the generalized "oceanic feeling of the supreme sufficiency of the present," "oceanic feelings of clarity, distance, union and oneness" (Robinson, 1969, pp. 6, 8).

After one prolonged climb in bad weather without food, I had this experience of having always climbed, always will. Once on top I felt as if I could open my arms and merge with the whole surroundings. I felt part of the greater whole—oneness.

It's a physical transcendence, adapting to an unchangeable reality. You merge with it rather than change it.

You could get so immersed in the rock, in the moves, the proper position of the body, that you'd lose consciousness of your identity and melt into the rock and the others you're climbing with.

I would begin to look at it in religious terms. Certain natural settings represent some intensity or eternity. You can lose yourself in that. It's linked to the idea of creation, intense wonder, and realization.

Your mind is more likely to be integrated with your body and you with the rocks and mountains themselves. . . . I like them so much. I feel really high in a way, grateful that I'm up there and not just drudging along in life below.

The only religious feelings I ever have stem from the mountains. I feel that the mountains make one aware of spiritual matters. . . . I'm fortunate because I can appreciate these places where you can appreciate nature, the minisculeness of man and his aspirations, which can elevate one. Spiritually, religiously I can see in many ways the same thing.

Climbing is unbelievably solo, [yet] the flow is a multitude of one. Climbing is dreamlike. When you're climbing, you're dealing with your subconscious as well as conscious mind. . . . You're climbing yourself as much as the rock. . . . If you're flowing with something, it's totally still. . . . There's no possibility of judging from the inside of a car whether the car is moving or the freeway. So you're not quite sure whether you are moving or the rock is, for the same reason, being inside yourself as you usually are. So it becomes very still. . . . Lack of self-awareness is totally self-aware to me. If the whole is self-awareness, you can have a lack of self-awareness because there's nothing else there.

Like all numinous experiences, deep flow "elevates and humiliates simultaneously" (Jung, 1963, p. 154). At once critical and synergic, these experiences provide new modes of evaluation and acceptance. The normative order, until now carefully screened out from the deep-play sphere, is made subject to new interpretation and criticism.

Metasocial Commentary: Antistructure and Protostructure

The Dutch historian Huizinga first elaborated the paradox that play forms are "good for nothing" in terms of existing economic, biological, or psychological needs, but are "good for everything" because they serve as experiments for new ways of living. "For many years," he wrote, "the conviction has grown upon me that civilization [*Cultuur*] arises and unfolds in and as play" (Huizinga, [1939] 1950, p. i). He went on to suggest that the main patterns of human society—arts, religions, science, law, government—had their historical origins in playful activities; after proving themselves enjoyable and viable, these activities then became accepted and institutionalized to give structure to "real" life. From this evolutionary point of view, deep play and other complex flow activities are like laboratories in which new patterns of experience are tested. Although this analogy misses the fact that the "testing" is enjoyable in itself, it may have more truth in it than one would ordinarily expect.

Recently the anthropologist Victor Turner (1969, Note 1) has looked at certain symbolic and ritual activities which are "antistructural" in the sense of breaking down utilitarian norms and status roles, but are in a deeper sense "protostructural" because they suggest ways of reformulating the normative order that gives pattern to everyday life. The connection between the rituals studied by Turner and the protostructural potential of games has been noted by Sutton-Smith (1973).

A classic example of the relationship between the world of play and the world of the normative order is Geertz's recent description of cockfighting in Bali. The Balinese spend a great deal of time and money training and wagering on roosters, and social status is briefly gained or lost depending on how one handles the game. Yet, Geertz concludes, the Balinese cockfight is finally useless in terms of economic utility or status concerns; the deep play provides, above all, a *metasocial commentary*. "Its function, if you want to call it that, is interpretive—it is a Balinese reading of Balinese experience, a story they tell about themselves" (Geertz, 1973, p. 448; also see chapter 1 in this volume).

How can an autotelic activity like rock climbing provide a base from which one can perceive culture more clearly? And are the interpretations of society thus obtained protostructural as well as antistructural; in other words, do they point toward new structures or simply ignore or countermand the existing ones? Does rock climbing produce metasocial commentary? These questions are addressed in a single text of one informant's deep-flow experience:

> You see who the hell you really are. It's important to learn about yourself, to open doors into the self. The mountains are the greatest place in the twentieth century to get this knowledge. . . . [There's] no place that more draws the best from human beings . . . [than] a mountaineering situation. Nobody hassles you to put your mind and body under tremendous stress to get to the top, there's nobody there to hassle you, force you, judge you. . . . Your comrades are there, but you all feel the same way anyway, you're all in it together. Who can you trust more in the twentieth century than these people? People after the same self-discipline as yourself, following the deeper commitment. The façades come rolling off. A bond like that with other people is in itself an ecstasy.
>
> . . . The investment is bigger. It's exhilarating to come closer and closer to self-discipline. You make your body go and everything hurts; then you look back in awe of the self, at what you've done, it just blows your mind. It leads to ecstasy, to self-fulfillment. If you win these battles enough, that battle against yourself, at least for a moment, it becomes easier to win the battles in the world. Sometimes I think it's my only survival in the space age; without that I wouldn't last a week out here. It gives you courage you can't draw in the city. . . .
>
> Too many stimuli in the world, it's a smog, a quagmire. Up there the clouds lift . . . the façades are all gone. Down here people live a sheltered reality, a false security arranged by extracurricular thoughts. The self-consciousness of society is like a mask. We are born to wear it. . . . Up there you have the greatest chance of finding your potential for any form of learning. Up there the false masks, costumes, personae that the world puts on you—false self-consciousness, false self-awareness—fall away. People miscommunicate all the time . . . find it impossible to break through the fog of façades, begin to lose their identity. In civilization man doesn't live reality. One never thinks about the universe and man's place in it . . . you think about cars, schools, parties.
>
> There is great potential when man is on the mountain. People are always searching, through booze, drugs, whatever. The closest man can come to it is through nature. Mountaineering builds up body and mind while learning about the deepest chasms of man. Up there you see man's true place in nature, you feel one with nature.
>
> The mountains and nature bombard the mind with the question of what man is meant to be doing. The fact that one's mind freaks out in civilizations shows how unhealthy and abnormal they can be. We are the animals that have been most fucked up in the last thousand years. Up there you know you're right, down here you think you're right. How could so many things come from nature if we did not belong there. . . ? We consume natural resources at a rate greater than at any time in history. Once resources are gone, that's it. The Indians have a simple life. They will survive. They live as nature teaches and know so much about the environment and

world . . . a religious knowing. They know far better who they are . . . they are who they are. I want most of all to learn something deep about the animal man; then I can get my ticket and check out. I just have a better chance to find it in the mountains.

Although our informants differ somewhat in their choice of issues and values, and in their degree of concern with them, they reinforce the points made in this extended statement. Taken together, our climbers' statements clearly offer a metasocial commentary along the lines suggested by Geertz. The recurrent themes of this critique are summarized in Table 2. The listing could, of course, be expanded, but it includes the most consensual topics discussed by our informants. Several of these items may be found to overlap with the Balinese example or with other deep players if fieldwork focusing on cross-cultural descriptions of flow experience was available. Other items in Table 2 are perhaps more tied to our own society and peculiar level of culture.

Both the Balinese and the rock climbers' "tales" are antistructural in Turner's sense because they involve the experience and portrayal of values, themes, and relations which are underplayed, repressed, or ignored in "real" life. According to Geertz, the Balinese find true but unsettling what they see of themselves in the cockfight. For the rock climbers, on the contrary, the alternative vision induced by climbing is intensely critical of the normative order. As one informant stated, "The self-consciousness of society is like a mask. . . . We are born to wear it." When society is "unmasked" in climbing, he much prefers its novel visage.

The cockfight, in Geertz's view, displays the social order in a new light, and the matter seems to end there. Comparing the cockfight to another genre in which metasocial commentary regularly appears, Geertz (1973, p. 443) writes: "Poetry makes nothing happen, Auden says in his elegy of Yeats. 'It survives in the valley of its saying . . . a way of happening, a mouth.' The cockfight too, in a colloquial sense, makes nothing happen." What about the climbers who must reenter the realm of facades, social and chemical smog, and worries about money and spouses, jobs and school? Do real changes take place as a result of their climbing experiences?

The climber-poet Guido Rey in *Peaks and Precipices* (1914, quoted in Knight, 1970, p. 44) answered the question in a pessimistic vein: "If climbers remained as good and as pure in the plains as they were in their ideal moments on the summit, other men, seeing them return, would believe them to be a troop of angels descended from heaven. But climbers, when they go home, become once more prey to their weaknesses, resume their bad habits, and write their articles for alpine journals." But for our informants, notably those who have deep-flow experiences, climbing

Table 2

Deep-Flow Experience in Rock Climbing[1]

Normative life	Rock-climbing experience
Informational noise: distraction and confusion of attention	One-pointedness of mind
Nebulosity of limits, demands, motivations, decisions, feedbacks	Clarity and manageability of limits, demands, decisions, feedbacks
Severing of action and awareness	Merging of action and awareness
Hidden, unpredictable dangers; unmanageable fears	Obvious danger subject to evaluation and control
Anxiety, worry, confusion	Happiness, health, vision
Slavery to the clock; life lived in spurts	Time out of time: timelessness
Carrot-and-stick preoccupation with exotelic, extrinsic material and social reward; orientation toward ends	Process orientation; concern for autotelic, intrinsic rewards; conquest of the useless
Dualism of mind and body	Integration of mind and body
Lack of self-understanding; false self-consciousness; war between the selves	Understanding of the true self, self-integration
Miscommunication with others; masks, statuses, and roles in an inegalitarian order; false independence or misplaced dependency	Direct and immediate communication with others in an egalitarian order; true and welcomed dependency on others
Confusion about man's place in nature or the universe; isolation from the natural order; destruction of the earth	Sense of man's place in the universe; oneness with nature; congruence of psychological and environmental ecology
Superficiality of concerns; thinness of meaning in the flatland	Dimension of depth "up there"; encounter with ultimate concerns

does make things happen. They would, it might be said, send out Shelley as their champion against Auden, for they consciously attempt to use the discoveries generated by their "physical poems on the rock" as legislative protostructures for the redesign of daily life.

For some of our respondents, climbing itself forms the center of any new road map of life. They may, as two of our informants have done, exchange lucrative positions for carpentry jobs in the mountains, so that they can climb every day. One of these subjects explains: "I would have made a great deal of money in corporate life, but I realized one day that I wasn't enjoying it. I wasn't having the kind of experiences that make life rewarding. I saw that my priorities were mixed up, spending most of my hours in the office. . . . The years were slipping by. I enjoy being a carpenter. I live where it's quiet and beautiful, and I climb most every night. I figure that my own relaxation and availability will mean more to my family than the material things I can no longer give them." Other informants also have cross-cut traditional financial, educational, and status pathways to stay close to climbing. For some of these, climbing has become "a bloody drug," generally because it is the only activity in which they regularly have the experiences they have come to prize most highly.

Most, however, believe that the proper course lies not in the intensification of activity within this one narrowed field but in the *internalization* of the properties and characteristics of the structure that produced these experiences. The experiences can then be *generalized* to whatever other situations the individual is forced into or chooses to enter. Some climbers report that they use climbing as a paradigm to which they refer situations from other realms of life for clarity and decision. Others recognize that their goal is to learn to flow in any given situation they find themselves in. Any number of citations could be offered here to show the conscious transfer of formal and affective components from climbing into ordinary life. It seems that the deeper the flow experiences reported by the individuals, the greater effort they put forth in this protostructural cause. It cannot be contested that rock climbing has altered the lives of many individuals; at the same time, no one would suggest that the course of American culture has been seriously affected by the small band of visionaries climbing has produced. However, when we understand the importance of flow experiences in the lives of people in a wide range of activities—particularly those activities classed as "work," where flow experiences might be least expected—we may find ourselves in possession of a new set of analytical tools with which to approach a class of phenomena too often overlooked. An important new set of questions and insights, perhaps even programs for change, could result.

Conclusions

Like any flow activity, rock climbing has structural elements which produce in the actor a set of intrinsically enjoyable experiences. In chess the structure involves the actor through intellectual competition; in climb-ing, danger draws the actor into physical and mental concentration. In each case, the person discovers a state of being which is rare in normative life. For a climber this state of being includes a heightened sense of physical achievement, a feeling of harmony with the environment, trust in climbing companions, and clarity of purpose. These experiences are in some ways different from what one gets from chess or from other flow activities. Yet what is common to all experiences is the total involvement of body and mind with a feasible task which validates the competence, indeed the very existence, of the actor. It is this that makes the activity worthwhile, despite the absence of utilitarian rewards.

A person who has attained this state of being inevitably compares it with the experiences of normative life. The comparison affords a relativizing perspective on the culture in which one is usually immersed. Deep flow is an ecstatic experience, in the sense that ecstasy means "standing out from" the ordinary. Whether this comparative glimpse will be liberating, and result in personal or social change, depends on many internal and external factors. But it seems appropriate to consider the heightened mental state of flow a prerequisite for the development of new cultural forms.

The practical consequences of what one can learn about intrinsic re-wards from rock climbers are suggestive but difficult to apply to concrete social change. Our interest in this topic has been both antistructural and protostructural. We are aware of the amount of worry and boredom that people experience in schools, factories, and their own homes. We are concerned about the meaninglessness and alienation in daily activities, and hence the constant efforts we make to get extrinsic rewards which will serve as symbolic counters to compensate for the barrenness of ex-perience. It is for this reason that we have turned to flow activities, to learn from them the mechanisms by which ordinary life could be made more enjoyable.

The most general conclusion to be drawn from this analysis is that to make tasks more enjoyable to a significant proportion of the population, there should be a variety of graduated activities available, covering the range of native and acquired skills. In his novel *Island*, Aldous Huxley made rock climbing mandatory for all the adolescents of that happy uto-pian society. But since the same challenges are unlikely to produce flow in people of very different skills, prescribing rock climbing to all is no solution to the problem of alienation. By the same token, our com-pulsory and uniform educational system is a sure guarantee that many, perhaps a majority in each generation, will spend their youth in mean-ingless unrewarding tasks. To provide intrinsic rewards, an activity must be finely calibrated to a person's skills—including his physical, intellec-tual, emotional, and social abilities. Such a personalized concern for each individual is antithetical to the structure of mass society with its rigidly bureaucratic forms of production, education, and administration.

If nothing else, the study of flow has produced some concepts and methods for working more purposefully toward institutions that provide growth and enjoyment. Besides the utilitarian calculus of productivity and material gains, we can set up a criterion of personal satisfaction. Once we succeed in defining flow operationally, we may be able to use it as a benchmark of societal progress, complementing the one-sided indicators of material achievement currently in use.

Note

1. In the original article, this is Table 5 rather than Table 1. (Editor's Note.)

Reference Note

1. Turner, V. *Liminality, play, flow, and ritual: Optational and obligatory forms and genres.* Paper presented at the Burg Wartenstein Symposium, No. 64, 1974.

References

CSIKSZENTMIHALYI, M. The Americanization of rock climbing. *University of Chicago Magazine*, 1969, **61**(6), 20-27.

DEMBER, W.N. *The psychology of perception.* New York: Holt, 1960.

EBERL, D. Matterhorn. *Ascent*, 1969, **9**, 11-15.

FREUD, S. *The ego and the id.* London: Allen & Unwin, 1927.

GEERTZ, C. *The interpretation of culture.* New York: Basic Books, 1973.

HUIZINGA, J. *Homo ludens.* Boston: Beacon Press, 1950. (Originally published, 1944.)

JUNG, C.G. *Memories, dreams, reflections.* New York: Vintage, 1963.

KNIGHT, M. *Return to the Alps.* New York: Friends of the Earth, 1970.

LUKAN, K. Climbers in the Alps. In K. Lukan (Ed.), *Alps and Alpinism.* New York: Coward-McCann, 1968.

MASLOW, A.H. *Religions, values, and peak-experiences.* Columbus, OH: Ohio State University Press, 1964.

MEAD, G.H. *Mind, self, and society.* Chicago: University of Chicago Press, 1934.

ROBINSON, D. The climber as visionary. *Ascent*, 1969, **9**, 4-10.

SUTTON-SMITH, B. *The folkgames of children*. Houston: University of Texas Press, 1973.

TURNER, V. *The ritual process*. Chicago: Aldine, 1969.

Part 4
Socialization and Enculturation Through Play, Games, and Sports

Chapter 17
Socializing Play:
Functional Analysis

HELEN B. SCHWARTZMAN

"Kitty, dear, let's pretend ——." And here I wish I could tell you half the things Alice used to say, beginning with her favourite phrase "Let's pretend." She had had quite a long argument with her sister only the day before—all because Alice had begun with "Let's pretend we're kings and queens"; and her sister, who liked being very exact, had argued that they couldn't because there were only two of them, and Alice had been reduced to say "Well, *you* can be one of them, then, and I'll be all the rest."

Lewis Carroll, *Through the Looking Glass, and What Alice Found There*

Beginning in the early 1920s a number of anthropologists began to indicate their disenchantment with the atheoretical approach of the historical particularists and diffusionists. Two of the most prominent critics in this regard were A.R. Radcliffe-Brown, a British anthropologist trained at Cambridge, and Bronislaw Malinowski, a Pole who studied

From H.B. Schwartzman, *Transformations: The anthropology of children's play*. New York: Plenum, 1978. Copyright 1978 by Plenum Publishing Corporation. Reprinted with permission.

anthropology at the London School of Economics. Together these two men were responsible for formulating what was to become known as the functional approach in anthropology.

A.R. Radcliffe-Brown and Bronislaw Malinowski

In reacting to what they considered to be the overly inductive approach of many of their predecessors, Radcliffe-Brown and Malinowski argued "that anthropology should be a science, that it should not be history," and that, to be a science, it must be deductive and begin to search for generalizations or laws of social behavior (Langness, 1974, pp. 74, 82). In arguing against the trait-list approach of the historical particularists, they presented the idea that cultures or social systems must be studied as wholes, not as separate and disconnected traits or parts. Society, in their view, could be conceptualized as a biological organism; however, Radcliffe-Brown and Malinowski were attracted to this analogy for very different reasons than the early evolutionists, who used it to formulate stages of cultural growth. In contrast, functionalists (see particularly Radcliffe-Brown, 1952/1968, pp. 188-204) used the organismic metaphor as a way to describe the stability and consistency, as opposed to change and development, of social systems as cultures. In this way Radcliffe-Brown and Malinowski suggested that the parts or *structures* of any whole (e.g., an organism or a culture) had to *function* for the "maintenance," "unity," "harmony," "consistency," or "solidarity" of the whole. The goal of functional analysis was, therefore, to explain how it is that structural systems maintain *sameness*.

In formulating and accepting the basic premises of functionalism, Radcliffe-Brown and Malinowski presented two quite different orientations to the actual practice of functional analysis. Radcliffe-Brown's approach is generally referred to as *structural-functionalism* and is characterized by the study of social structures as sets of relationships that can be discovered "between acts of diverse individuals" and *not* within the "mind" or in the "acts of behavior of one and the same individual" (Radcliffe-Brown, 1957, pp. 45-46). Radcliffe-Brown believed that this latter focus was the province of the psychologist, not the anthropologist.

The approach of Malinowski, however, was quite the opposite of his contemporary's, particularly in regard to his emphasis on the combined study of psychological, biological, and social needs. Malinowski emphasized, in his "pure functionalism" (now sometimes called *psychological functionalism*), that culture was the instrument through which man's needs were met. According to Malinowski, individuals had seven "basic needs": reproduction, bodily comforts, safety, relaxation, movement, growth, and health (1944/1960, p. 91). These needs were satisfied by various cultural responses (e.g., marriage and family systems were direct responses to the reproductive need). Malinowski differed most strongly with Radcliffe-Brown in his insistence that these were individual, not group, needs, therefore bringing in the taboo topic of individual psychology.

Functionalists and Play

Faced with the spontaneous, seemingly useless, and often deviant nature of play, functionalists might well despair. However, one of the earliest interpretations of play is Groos's (1898, 1901) *practice theory*, which in essence is a functional explanation of this activity. It was Groos's suggestion that play allowed "animals" and "man" to practice or rehearse the daily activities of their present (not past) life. This view of play as practice or rehearsal for adult activities has since become one of the most commonly accepted explanations available in the literature (Loizos, 1967/1969, p. 236).

An early application of functional analysis to the topic of children's play is available in George Herbert Mead's classic study *Mind, Self and Society* (1934). In this work, Mead paid particular attention to the development of language, play, and games in children. Play and game activities are clearly differentiated here as they are thought to have distinct functions in relation to the development of the child's sense of self. According to Mead, "ordinary play" (e.g., playing Indians) allows the child to imagine himself in various social roles and, by so doing, to "build up" his own character. In order to play games, however, the child must be able "to take the attitude of everyone else involved" and to see that "these different roles must have a definite relationship to each other" (p. 151). For example, in the game of baseball, the child must know his own role in the game (e.g., as a catcher) and must also be able to take the role of others (e.g., the pitcher) by being willing to risk his own identity for the sake of the "generalized other" (e.g., the team). In Mead's view, once the child is able to take the attitude of the other, he/she is on the way to "becoming an organic member of society" (p. 159).

The most common expression of this approach in the anthropological literature appears in descriptions of play as imitative or preparatory activity and, therefore, functional as an enculturative mechanism. Malinowski illustrated this perspective by contending that play should be studied in terms of its educational value and in relation to its "function as preparation for economic skills" (1944/1960, p. 107). He also suggested that peer play groups perform a socializing function in meeting the "growth needs" of individuals:

The foundations of all synthetic knowledge, the first elements, that is, of the scientific outlook, the appreciation of custom, authority, and ethics, are received within the family. Later on, the growing child enters the group of his playmates, where, once more, he is dulled towards conformity, obedience to custom and etiquette. (1944/1960, pp. 107-108)

Adopting this perspective, the seemingly nonpurposeful actions of children's play, particularly their make-believe or sociodramatic play, are transformed into activities functional for the maintenance (i.e., "unity," "harmony," "consistency," and "solidarity") and perpetuation of the social order.

Radcliffe-Brown paid little attention to the play of children in his studies, and there are almost no reports of this activity in his ethnographies. As he was adamant about the fact that the study of individual psychological processes was not an appropriate topic for anthropological analysis, this neglect is perhaps understandable. Radcliffe-Brown (1952/1968) did, however, develop an interest in at least one adult play form: the joking relationship. He believed that this activity functioned to channel, ritualize, and, therefore, neutralize hostile feelings in social systems. And this is now a standard explanation for the function of adult "expressive" behavior in culture.[1]

Functional explanations of children's play most commonly employ the play-as-imitation/preparation metaphor. Malinowski used this perspective in both his theoretical and his ethnographic works, but he was certainly not unique in this regard. The assumption that children's play is always based on imitation of adult activities and, therefore, either implicitly or explicitly functional as a socializing activity is far and away the most common anthropological interpretation of this behavior (see Schwartzman & Barbera, 1976). Turnbull's description of the play of Mbuti Pygmy children is quite typical:

Like children everywhere, Pygmy children love to imitate their adult idols . . . at an early age boys and girls are "playing house" or "playing hunting." . . . And one day they find that the games they have been playing are not games any longer, but the real thing for they have become adults. (1961, p. 129)

Edel's (1957) description of children's play for the Chiga of western Uganda also expresses this theme:

Playing with a small gourd, a child learns to balance it on his head, and is applauded when he goes to the watering place with the other children and brings it back with little water in it. As he learns, he carries an increasing load, and gradually the play activity turns into a general contribution to the household water supply. (pp. 176-177)

And Kenyatta illustrated this emphasis on imitation and preparation in his discussion of Kikuyu children's play. He stated that

> children do most things in imitation of their elders and illustrate in a striking way the theory that play is anticipatory of adult life. Their games are, in fact, nothing more or less than a rehearsal prior to the performance of the activities which are the serious business of all members of the Gikuyu tribe. (1939, p. 101)

These descriptions portray the major themes evident in functional discussions. Children's play is simple imitation, therefore, because it is "simple" and because it is "mere imitation," it can be quickly dismissed with a few short descriptions. Play "works" because it serves an obvious socialization function for society. The possibility that these activities were not as simple nor as imitative as they appeared to be was, for the most part, not considered by these researchers.

Functionalism reigned between the 1930s and the 1950s in anthropology, and during these years, the study of children's play advanced little beyond statements such as those appearing in the above quotations. It is probably true that Radcliffe-Brown's antipsychological stance contributed to this neglect, along with the fact that most young anthropology students at this time were attracted to the structural functionalism of Radcliffe-Brown and not to the psychological functionalism of Malinowski (see Langness, 1974, p. 79). Functionalists examined only "serious" social structures (e.g., kinship and political systems) and, for the most part, neglected the study of play and games. Even with the recent resurgence of interest in the "psychological" topic of socialization evidenced by British social anthropologists (e.g., Mayer, 1970), there is little indication that the study of play is considered an important research field by these authors. In Mayer's (1970) collection of papers, there is only brief mention of play and games in the article written by P. and I. Mayer (pp. 159-189), discussing the youth organization of the Red Xhosa, and a specific consideration by Loudan (pp. 203-332) of teasing and ridicule as socialization techniques utilized on the island of Tristan da Cunha.

One important exception to this history of neglect is presented by one of Radcliffe-Brown's most famous students: Meyer Fortes. Fortes's study of "Social and Psychological Aspects of Education in Taleland" (1938) includes one of the most significant and insightful investigations of children's play available in the ethnographic literature. This article also includes one of the few early critiques of the play-as-imitation metaphor utilized by most ethnographers at this time. Play, according to Fortes, "is the paramount educational exercise of Tale children" (p. 44). *It is never, however, simple and mechanical reproduction of adult activities:*

In his play the child rehearses his interests, skills, and obligations, and makes experiments in social living without having to pay the penalty for mistakes. Hence there is already a phase of play in the evolution of any schema preceding its full emergence into practical life. Play, therefore, is often mimetic in content and expresses the child's identifications. But the Tale child's play mimesis is never simple and mechanical reproduction; it is always imaginative construction based on the themes of adult life and of the life of older children. He or she adapts natural objects and other materials, often with great ingenuity, which never occur in the adult activities copied, and rearranges adult functions to fit the specific logical and affective configuration of play. (pp. 58-59)

In this paper, Fortes also specifically recognized the need for anthropologists and others to rethink their view of imitative learning:

Writers on primitive education have often attributed an almost mystical significance to "imitation" as the principle method by which a child learns. The Tallensi themselves declare that children learn by "looking and doing," but neither "imitation" nor the formula used by the Tallensi help us to understand the actually observable process. Tale children do not automatically copy the actions of older children or adults with whom they happen to be without rhyme or reason and merely for the sake of "imitation." (p. 54)

In describing a typical play situation (pp. 59-61) for the Tallensi children of Ghana, Fortes illustrated the complex nature of this activity and the way that "recreational and imaginative play are interwoven with practical activities," as well as the moment-to-moment changes in a child's interests in specific types of play. The episode that he described lasted for 30 minutes and involved four children: Gɔmna (male, 7 years), his half-sister Zɔŋ (female, 6 years), his friend Zoo (male, 7 years), and Tɔŋ (male, 10 years). The event began with the first three children scaring birds from their parents' grain fields. Soon Gɔmna located three locusts and described them to Zɔŋ and Zoo by saying, "These are our cows, let's build a yard for them." Immediately the children began to build a yard out of pieces of decayed bark, with Gɔmna giving orders while all three maintained a running verbal commentary about their activities. Tɔŋ helped Gɔmna build and roof the yard, and then Gɔmna pushed the "cows" in and declared, "We must build a gateway." Two large pebbles were found and set up as gateposts, and then an argument ensued about how they should stand. At this point, the structure collapsed, and Tɔŋ began to build it again. Meanwhile Zɔŋ found a pair of stones and a potsherd and began "grinding grain." Suddenly Gɔmna and Zoo ran after birds to scare them and then returned to the "cattle yard" discussing wrestling. Tɔŋ was called away, and Zɔŋ finished her "grinding" and brought "flour" to the two boys, saying, "Let's sacrifice to our shrine." Gɔmna said, "Let Zoo do it," but Zoo said that Gɔmna was senior to him, and they then began to argue about who, in fact, was senior. Eventually Gɔmna declared, "I'm the senior." Zɔŋ put down her "flour" and forgot about it, and then Zoo challenged Gɔmna's assertion. However, Gɔmna reacted by saying that he had to be senior because he could throw Zoo in wrestling, which Zoo denied. Soon the two boys were wrestling with one another, and Gɔmna managed to throw Zoo, but they both stood up and were still friends. At this point, Gɔmna climbed up on a baobab branch, followed by Zoo, who said, "Let's swing." They swung for a few minutes, and then Gɔmna remembered the "cows." He accused Zɔŋ of having taken them, but she denied this, at which point he challenged her to "swear" to this. She agreed to do so, and he took a pinch of sand in his left hand and put his right thumb on it. Zɔŋ licked her thumb and pressed down with it on Gɔmna's thumbnail. He stood still for a minute and then quickly withdrew his thumb. (Fortes stated that this is a children's play ordeal.) Gɔmna examined Zɔŋ's thumb and found sand adhering, and he said, "There you are"; and he then rapped her on the head with a crooked finger. The "cows" were forgotten again, and they began to ask Fortes questions. After this, Gɔmna, who had been looking at Fortes's shoes, said, "Let's make shoes"; and he took a few pieces of bark (formerly used for the cattle yard) and proceeded to make shoes. He and Zɔŋ found some grass and string and tried to tie the pieces of bark onto the soles of their feet. Gɔmna now noticed his "cows" and began to move them about. He said, "I'm going to let them copulate," and he tried to put one locust on top of the other. Suddenly he looked up and noticed birds in the field and cried to Zɔŋ, "Scare the birds!" All three children ran after the birds into the grain field and spent the next 5 minutes shouting at the birds and throwing handfuls of gravel at them.

Along with presenting this unique and lengthy description of Tallensi children's play, Fortes also offered a detailed discussion of the developmental phases of these children's play behavior. Here he described the play of boys and girls at various ages, concurrent with a discussion of the children's expected economic duties and activities (a chart that summarizes these play phases appears at the conclusion of this article [in original article only]). For example, Tallensi boys between the ages of 3 and 6 initially have no economic duties to perform; however, as they get older (e.g., 5-6), they begin to assist in pegging-out goats and in scaring birds from newly sown fields and from crops (as Gɔmna, Zɔŋ, Zoo, and Tɔŋ did). The play of boys of this age consists at first of "motor and exploratory play"; later they use "mimetic toys" (e.g., bows and drums) in "egocentric" play; and then they begin to engage in social and imaginative play at "cattle" and "house-building" activities, often playing with older children of either sex (p. 72).

Another relatively early critique of the simple imitation view of play appears in Otto Raum's well-known study of *Chaga Childhood* (1940). Raum, whose father spent 40 years working with the Chaga as a missionary, was born and raised in Tanzania and developed an intimate knowledge of this group, which he reported both skillfully and sensitively as an educator and a scholar. In *Chaga Childhood*, Raum presented an extensive account of this group's socialization patterns and included a lengthy discussion and description of children's games, in which the "representative" (as opposed to strictly "imitative") quality of these activities is stressed. In this regard, Raum suggested the following:

> The essential feature of "imitative" play is . . . make-believe, the tendency of the child to construct an imaginary adult society from the scraps he is allowed to know about it . . . In the majority of cases, the themes of "imitative" play are not immediately suggested by events in adult life at all. Rather, the choice of subject and its development are a result of the child's independent and spontaneous action. (p. 256)

Furthermore, Raum argued that so-called childish imitativeness is directed not so much "to making the copy exact, but towards caricaturing the pattern" (p. 257). This interest in caricature is revealed, Raum suggested, when one looks closely at the selection process used by children in their presumably "imitative" representations. In these events, the process "tends more and more to stress aspects which make adults appear to be ridiculous" (p. 257).

This view of play as caricature or as satire is discussed in more detail in a later section of this chapter; however, Raum presented an amusing series of examples of Chaga children "imitating" (but actually caricaturing) "the white man" and his institutions, which are described briefly here. A popular play theme for Chaga children is said to be "school and teacher," where the teacher's obsession (to the Chaga) with time is symbolized by placing "a great clock of sand in front of the make-believe school" (p. 258). Likewise, the emphasis on memorization and recitation of literature is parodied by children reading from "books" of vegetable leaves in the monotonous tone of the teacher. The sermons of missionaries are also satirized by exaggerating the linguistic mistakes and mannerisms of the minister, which are said to cause "uproarious applause" from the "congregation." Baptism ceremonies are also favorite events for caricature, as the "minister" is able to sprinkle

> his converts with water according to their deserts, while in the choice of names he selects characteristic ones, such as "Lover-of-Food," "Stupid," "Dwarf," and "Bully." (p. 258)

Raum delineated three different types of play activities: the playful exercise of sensory and motor activities (see pp. 140-146); representative play (see pp. 250-264); and competitive games (see pp. 264-272). Raum also discussed the "culture" or social system of play groups, emphasizing how these groups develop leaders (pp. 273-274, 277-278); allocate resources (pp. 275-277); expel "cheaters" (see his discussion of children's ordeals, pp. 278-279); create secret languages ("speech perversions," pp. 280-282); and invent new games and/or "toy" objects (pp. 283-284). Raum specifically emphasized the ingenious nature of many of these inventions. He cited examples of Chaga children's inventions of "bicycles," "carts," "cars," and a particularly creative "machine gun." This was produced by making 12 shallow cuts into the midrib of a banana leaf. These "tongues" would be cocked, "and when the hand passed over them they fell back, each producing a report" (pp. 284 ff.).

Recent attempts to explore the idea that play functions both to socialize and to enculturate children have been made by Langsley (1967), Eifermann (1970), Salter (Note 1), and Lancy (1974, 1976, Note 2, Note 3).[2]

Socializing Play: The Kibbutz

Rivka Eifermann (1970) used information collected in her large-scale quantitative study of Israeli children's play to investigate whether the life of the kibbutzim, with its stress on cooperation, the achievement of common aims, and egalitarianism, is expressed in kibbutz children's games. In formulating this study, she devised a classification scheme of collected games based on guidelines related to (1) competitiveness; (2) grouping in the game; and (3) symmetrical or nonsymmetrical relationship of players. On the basis of this classification, eight categories of games are considered in the study: (1) single-party games (e.g., "feet canon," in which "two players who face each other skip in different styles, but in rhythm, aiming to reach in harmony a predetermined number of skips"); (2) symmetrical single-party games (e.g., "head ball," in which "a ball is kept from falling to the ground by the cooperative efforts of all players who bounce it off their heads for as long as they can"); (3) singletons (e.g., "Dutch rope," in which "two players stretch an elastic band between their legs, while others jump within it; failure of a jumper leads to an exchange of places with one of the holders"); (4) singletons, with (roughly) interchangeable roles (e.g., variants of hopscotch, chess); (5) singletons versus many (two or more) singletons (e.g., simple tag, hide-and-seek); (6) singletons with overprivileged and/or underprivileged singleton(s) (e.g., jump rope "with a leader who calls out the jumping rhymes and participates in the jumping herself"); (7) two groups (e.g., soccer, basketball); and (8) two intrasymmetrical groups (e.g., cops and robbers, tug-of-war) (pp. 580-581).

Eifermann formulated two major hypotheses utilizing this classification scheme for this study: (1) "Since kibbutz children are raised in the spirit of cooperation with the other members of the kibbutz, their games tend to be of less competitive types"; and (2) "Since kibbutz children are raised in the spirit of egalitarianism—one child, one vote in their societies—their games tend to be of the more symmetrical types" (p. 581). On the basis of the first hypothesis, it was expected that more kibbutz than nonkibbutz players would participate in (1) single-party games and (2) two-group games. Furthermore, it was expected that fewer kibbutz than nonkibbutz players would participate in singleton games. On the basis of the second hypothesis, it was expected that more kibbutz than nonkibbutz players would participate in (1) symmetrical single-party games; (2) singleton games with interchangeable roles; and (3) games of two intrasymmetrical groups. And it was also expected that fewer kibbutz than nonkibbutz players would participate in (1) singleton games with overprivileged and/or underprivileged singleton and (2) one singleton versus many (two or more) singletons.

For this study, Eifermann selected four different schools from her larger sample: two moshav and two kibbutz. She pointed out that the moshav is a family-based cooperative settlement "in which economic equality is maintained only to a degree," whereas complete equality is maintained in the kibbutz. Also, in the kibbutz, the family is neither an economic nor the central educational unit (p. 582). All schools were located in rural areas.

On the basis of her comparative analysis of material on these four schools, it was found that five of the eight predictions from Hypotheses 1 and 2 were confirmed, and two predictions (those regarding single-party games) were disconfirmed. Most significantly, it was discovered that single-party games were scarcely played by kibbutz children. However, group games, which call for cooperation toward the achievement of a common aim within a competitive framework, were found to be more popular among kibbutz children than among moshav children. She related this finding to Spiro's (1958/1965) observation that while kibbutz grammar-school pupils are opposed to personal competition, they are indeed competitive about group activities and also the fact that some practices in the kibbutz educational policy encourage "cooperation within competition" (p. 585). It was also found that kibbutz children insist, more readily than moshav children, that in singleton games there should be as few overprivileged or underprivileged participants as possible (p. 386). She argued that this is a way to preserve egalitarianism.

Eifermann suggested that the results of this research appear to support theories of play that view it as a preparatory or practical activity (as kibbutz children prefer games that are cooperative and egalitarian). In contrast, she stated that this study does not support the idea that children's games are "expressive of a hidden revolt against adult values, or as measures taken to reduce conflicts created by adults' attempts to impose their values on them" (p. 586).

Socializing Play: The Australian Aborigine

Michael Salter (Note 1) has also recently explored the idea "that play serves as a major vehicle of enculturation" (p. 3). In this study, he examined the games played by a number of central Queensland aboriginal groups, and he specifically described how these indigenous play forms both *reflect* and *reinforce* cultural subsystems such as *the economic system* (e.g., tree climbing, underwater endurance, play with miniature canoes); *the normative order* (e.g., mock marriage, pretend families, play with dolls); *the political system* (e.g., mud-ball fights, stick dueling, hide-and-seek); and *the world view* (e.g., evil "spirits," string figures, singing).[3] He also discussed a category of games that do not seem to be directly related to the maintenance of the traditional culture (e.g., top spinning, mud sliding, skipping). Salter pointed out that play was *a* (if not *the*) form of learning for the aboriginal child, and he suggested that given the cooperative, egalitarian nature of these societies, it would be expected that their play forms would be of a cooperative and not a competitive nature (p. 18). This expectation is confirmed, Salter reported, by the fact that most games in these societies "are group, as opposed to team oriented, play forms"; and there is also a general lack of emphasis on victory (p. 18). This study, therefore, coincides with Eifermann's investigation of kibbutz children's games.

Socializing Play: The Kpelle

David Lancy (Note 2) has recently noted that the idea that play functions to enculturate and/or socialize children is frequently expressed in the ethnographic literature but has rarely been tested. In order to explore its validity, he has used a variety of techniques (e.g., participant observation, interviews, and experiments) in studies of African (Liberia—Kpelle) and, more recently, American children (1974, 1976, Note 2, Note 3).

In his studies of Kpelle children's play (1974, 1976, Note 2, Note 3), two strategies were used. First information was collected on linguistic distinctions made in this society between work *(tii)* and play *(pele)* activities. On the basis of these data, an attempt was made to move *backwards* "from adult work to children's play, interviewing informants and speculating on possible play antecedents of adult skills" (Note 2, p. 4). In conjunction with this effort, Lancy also started from play and moved *forwards*, analyzing play forms for evidence of skills, etc., to be used later in adult life. Lancy presented a great deal of information on all types of children's and adults' play activities in Kpelle society (see particularly 1974), and, taken as a whole, these accounts represent one of the few detailed collections and analyses of children's play behavior in a non-Western society available in the literature. One of the few comparable studies is Centner's (1962) description of Luba, Sanga, and Yeke children's play, which is discussed in chapter 7 [in *Transformations*].

Lancy's study, however, is most significant for his attempt to examine explicitly whether or not play serves a socialization function in Kpelle society and to relate play behavior to work activities in this culture. He specifically made these associations in his discussions of "make-believe" blacksmith play, hunting play, the *bambé* game (a model of the adult secret society), warrior play, and new occupations incorporated into children's play (e.g., driver, soldier, and rubber tapper).

The most important description of relations between play and work and play as socialization is Lancy's discussion of "talking matter." "Talking matter" is a type of "court appearance" that virtually all Kpelle adults, and many adolescents, engage in at some time as defendant, plaintiff, witness, elder, or judge. However, this legal process is loosely structured and does not depend on a codified set of laws:

> This means that the degree of success that an individual achieves in his/her "court appearance" is heavily dependent on their verbal fluency, memory of past events, and ability to use one or several of the "speech events" (self-evident, staged-anger, penitent, and expository). One's wealth, prestige in the community, marriage and family relations, even one's place of residence may hinge on how well an actor can "perform" in the public drama of the court. (Note 2, p. 17)

Lancy illustrated how a variety of children's play activities serve to develop the verbal and acting skills necessary to engage successfully in "talking matter." For example, in telling *mini-pele* stories, boys are frequently challenged in jest about the meaning and validity of what they are saying, causing frequent interruptions in the teller's narrative. Similar interruptions are reported to occur frequently in "talking matter," and the speaker (just as the player) must develop the ability of "verbal agility in the face of a hostile audience" (p. 18). *Pole-yee* stories (telling long stories, of which the content is generally known by the audience) require that the narrator hold an audience's attention for a long time. In order to do this, events are dramatized in a variety of ways through gestures, changes of speech tone, facial expressions, and so on. All of these skills are useful to the participant in "talking matter" because it is to his benefit to hold the attention of the court. *Sia-polo* (riddles) are also appropriate play models for "talking matter," where evidence is presented and cannot be referred to again and also where one's rationale for his/her position must be defended (p. 19). Finally, the *kolong* game (a verbal memory game involving the memorization of proverbs) also provides practice for serving as "elder" in "talking matter." Elders use jokes and proverbs either to lower the esteem of a speaker in the eyes of the audience in the "court apperance" or, in the specific case of proverbs, to justify an action (similar to the manner in which legal precedents are cited in the West). Lancy suggested that

> children learn the syntax of proverbs and jokes in their play, but learning the semantics and meaning of jokes and proverbs comes only through exposure to, and participation in, adult-play and "talking matter." (p. 19)

A number of other associations between children's play behavior and adult work activities are presented (including a variety of field experiments conducted by the investigator). In concluding his 1975 paper, Lancy (Note 2) summarized the examples presented in his study of how play "trains" children for four major cultural subsystems: (1) social relations (e.g., sex-role behavior, patterns of deference); (2) language (e.g., vocabulary, speech-making skills); (3) technology (e.g., tool use and practice); and (4) ideology (e.g., reticence, ambition, cleverness). The results of this study indicate, according to Lancy, that

> the evidence for the learning of adult roles, patterns of thought, and values in play, while not impressive, is at least encouraging to a theory of play in enculturation. (p. 13)

Play and Sex Roles

A current interest of anthropologists, sociologists, and psychologists is the study of sex roles. Anthropologists are particularly concerned with examining how cultures transform the obvious biological differences between men and women into social systems that are almost universally characterized by some degree of male dominance and, therefore, sex-role asymmetry (see Rosaldo & Lamphere, 1974, p. 3). Accumulating evidence collected in a number of different societies suggests that there are sex differences in the behavior of children (e.g., Barry, Bacon, & Child, 1957; Ember, 1973; Whiting & Edwards, 1973). Boys are reported to behave in a more aggressive, assertive, and self-reliant fashion than girls, while girls are said to be more nurturant, obedient, and sensitive to others than boys (but see Mead, 1935/1963). The existence and possible universality of these differences does not, however, mean that these are innate, biologically determined characteristics. A number of researchers have suggested that there are features present in *all* cultures that are responsible for the production of these differences (e.g., the sexual division of labor and differential sex-role socialization [Maccoby, 1959] and, more specifically, differential task assignment for boys and girls [Ember, 1973; Whiting & Edwards, 1973][4]; the universal symbolic association of women with "nature," an association that all cultures devalue [Ortner, 1974]).

Children's play has been investigated as both an indicator of children's gender identity and also as a vehicle for the learning and practicing of culturally appropriate sex roles. Psychologists have concentrated on investigations of the former topic, using a variety of "toy preference" or "doll-play" tests that presumably indicate the child's sexual identification (e.g., boys choose "feminine" toys such as dolls—see Garvey's 1977 discussion of these investigations).

Studies of sex differences exhibited in children's "play configurations" have also been made (e.g., Erikson, 1941, 1951). In this investigation, a group of 11-year-old children were asked to construct a scene for a "movie" using a variety of toys (e.g., dolls, cars, animals, blocks) and a small stage that was set up on a table. After the child had constructed his/her scene, the investigator asked for an explanation of what it was about. These scenes were interpreted in a variety of ways in conjunction with Erikson's psychosexual theory of development, which has been discussed in chapter 4 [in *Transformations*]. The most interesting sex-typed features of these constructions relate to the children's differential preference, use, and arrangement of toys in the "movie" scene. Here boys were found consistently to "erect structures, buildings and towers, or to build streets," while girls viewed the play table as "the interior of a house" and proceeded to arrange furniture and place people inside the "house" (p. 136). Boys concentrated on height of structure and the downfall or "ruins" of these structures, with a related emphasis on motion and its arrest.

The "high-low" concern of boys is interpreted, not surprisingly, as "a doubt in, or a fear for, one's masculinity" (p. 137). The "enclosure" or "open-closed" configurations of girls are viewed as a reflection of concern over the feminine role, or as "over sensitiveness and selfcenteredness" (p. 137). Both types of configurations are explained as unconscious reflections of biological sex differences because they are said to parallel the morphology of the sex organs (e.g., the "*external* organs of the male," which are "erectible and intrusive," and the "*internal* organs of the female with vestibular *access* leading to *statically expectant* ova," pp. 139, 142).

The psychologists' preoccupation with "toy tests" probably reflects the object orientation of Western adults as much as it does the sex-role identification of their children. Observational studies of what children *actually do* in free play and game activities are more likely to provide investigators with useful information on sex differences. Fortunately, there are a number of interesting studies of this type focusing on children's sociodramatic or role play and games. These studies also tend to view play as both a shaper and an indicator of sex differences. Sutton-Smith and Savasta (Note 5) have recently reviewed a number of these studies covering the age period of 5-12, and they suggested that these investigations indicate the following:

> for males games may be an exercise in power tactics but . . . for females they generally are not. . . . The games preferred by boys show a greater emphasis on bodily strength and bodily contact, the use of larger spaces, for success achieved through active interference in the other play activities, for well-defined outcomes in which winners and losers are clearly labelled, for games permitting personal initiative, for a continuous flow of activity, for motor activity involving the whole body, for players acting simultaneously or in concert. Any type of sport could be taken to exemplify these dimensions. Girls for their part show a greater interest in games where turns are taken in ordered sequence, where there is choral activity, song and rhyme, verbalism, where rhythm is involved, where the stages in play are multiple but well-defined, where competition is indirect, where there is a multiplicity of rules dictating every move, where only parts of the body are involved and where there is much solitary practice, where there is competition between individuals rather than groups. The games of hopscotch, jump rope and jackstones are good examples. (pp. 2-3)

A recent investigation of sex differences in children's games has been reported by Lever (1974, Note 6). In this research, a group of American, white, middle-class, fifth-grade children was investigated (using observations and also reported game preferences) to determine: (1) if there are any sex differences in their game patterns and preference, and (2) if involvement in particular games affects the performance of adult roles. Most specifically, an attempt was made to test whether boys' games are more "complex" (in the way that complexity is defined in formal organizations) than girls' games. It is argued that, if this is so, then it can be proposed that boys' games better prepare them "for successful performance in a wide range of work settings in modern complex societies" (Note 6, p. 3). The dimensions of game complexity outlined and analyzed here are role differentiation, interdependence between players, size of play group, degree of competition and explicitness of goals, number and specificity of rules, and degree of team formation. On the basis of her research, Lever reported that there are indeed sex differences displayed in the games played by children and that, with respect to each of the six dimensions described above, "boys' activities were often more complex" (Note 6, p. 12).

In another study of sex-typed behavior exhibited in children's spontaneous play on school playgrounds in Austin, Texas, Robinson (1978) reported specifically on "self-structured chase games." Differences in boys' and girls' (7- and 8-year-olds) styles of play in these games reflect again the differences that have been generally noted regarding the behavior of boys and girls; that is, the boys' chase style is aggressive and physical, while the girls' style is passive and teasing. Robinson also discussed the "chaotic and disorderly" style of chase games that involve both boys and girls (these games are frequently initiated by girls). She suggested that these games allow the girls to abandon the restrictive conventions of traditionally "nice" and appropriately "feminine" games, such as hopscotch and jump rope, and to experiment with a form of aggression (although performed in a "feminine" style). Robinson proposed that these games may also allow girls "to experiment with disorder and the challenges of a changing society," which is particularly appropriate in a cultural context where women's roles are currently in flux (p. 17).

In order to investigate whether sex differences are exhibited in the play of younger (3- to 4-year-olds) American children, Sutton-Smith and Savasta (Note 5) initiated a videotape study of a group of 17 children attending a university nursery school. It was expected that because of the professional nature of the parent group, there would be a reduction in marked sex differences in the children's play activities. This was indeed found to be true. However, for the observational category "social testing" (i.e., the child asserts something about him/herself), it was found that boys engaged in significantly more episodes of this type of play than girls. By breaking this category into four subcategories, each with three modes (physical, verbal, or strategic techniques)—(1) supplication, (2) inclusion-exclusion, (3) attacks, and (4) authority or dominance—it was found that the difference between boys' and girls' engagement in "social testing" was produced by the boys' larger amounts of attack. However, this difference was not just isolated to physical attack; it was also evidenced in verbal and strategic attacks. Therefore the boys did not just engage in more frequent physical and aggressive attacks but also in more frequent verbal and strategic attacks and concern with defining their place within a group. It is suggested that what is evidenced here is perhaps an early stage in the exploration of power phenomena, such as dominance hierarchies. The girls in this study engaged more frequently in inclusion-exclusion "social testing" (e.g., controlling others by promising inclusion; threatening exclusion; physically through smiling, giving gifts, etc.). The authors suggested that these inclusion-exclusion tactics, because they are generally applied to smaller groups than boys, may be "power tactics relevant to the nuclear or intimate group, whereas boys' tactics are more relevant to the larger gang type group" (p. 11). Finally, it is suggested that, if, indeed, there are sex differences in the learning of power or testing tactics at this age, the next step for researchers is to discover how it is that sexes learn these differences from their mothers and fathers at such an early age.

These findings are also supported by a recent study by Grief (1976), similarly conducted with American, white, middle-class, preschool-aged children. Children in this study were reported to engage frequently in sex-role play in free play situations, with older (4½-5½) children exhibiting more use of sex roles than younger (3½-4½) ones. Grief also reported instances of role reversals, where a dominant girl attempted to adopt a male role, much to the distress and protest of the defined male "mother." This is interpreted as evidence of the general view that male roles have more status (p. 390).

In attempting to sort out the problem of early sex-role learning, a topic of great importance as suggested by Sutton-Smith and Savasta, an interesting study of sex differences exhibited in the play of infants is useful to consider. Goldberg and Lewis (1969) have investigated the play behavior of a sample of American infants (13 months) with their mothers in a standardized free play situation. In these settings, "striking" sex differences were observed (e.g., girls were extremely reluctant to leave their mother's lap; in response to a barrier placed between infant and mother, girls stood still and cried or motioned for help, whereas boys attempted to get around the barrier; girls sat quietly and played with toys, while boys responded more actively, standing up and banging the toys around). On the basis of earlier observations of these mothers' interactions with their infants at 6 months, it was found that mothers behaved very differently toward girls and boys, which, the authors suggested, reinforced sex-typed behavior at a very early age.

In all of these studies, and also in most ethnographies that contain information on children, it is reported that children engage in culturally defined sex-appropriate behavior and sex-appropriate roles in their play activities. This is not surprising because the first activities and roles that children encounter are always culturally defined caretaker roles and activities, and these are generally sex-typed. It is important to emphasize here, however, that most investigators have *not* studied children's play *with* sex roles but rather how sex roles *play* children. This follows from the play-as-imitation/preparation/socialization perspective adopted by most functional analysts, who seek to examine how children are "dulled towards conformity" (in the words of Malinowski, 1944/1960, pp. 107-108) by the socialization pressure of play. A view of play as caricature (see Raum, 1940) or satire would lead researchers to investigate the various ways in which children's behavior exaggerates and parodies the behavior of adults, and, particularly, of mothers and fathers. These would truly be studies of play *with* sex roles. This point will be returned to in a later section of this chapter.

Games and Power Roles

Power roles and sex roles are frequently inseparable; however, there are a number of studies available in which types of role and status positions within specific games are investigated and then relationships between these roles and the larger social context are drawn. In one study, by Gump and Sutton-Smith (1955), an attempt is made to classify rule games on the basis of the kinds of status positions that they contain (e.g., leader-follower, attacker-defender, taunter-taunted) and the controls over the allocation of such positions (e.g., leader chosen by popularity, leader chosen by chance, leader chosen by defeat or triumph). After classifying a variety of games in this way, the authors proceeded to analyze the status positions and allocation of power in "it" games (e.g., tag, king of the mountain) with the idea that such roles offer players the opportunity to gain experience and/or practice in handling such positions. In other related studies, Sutton-Smith (Sutton-Smith, 1966; Sutton-Smith, Roberts, & Rosenberg, 1964) examined associations between sibling relationships and role involvement in play. In one study (1964), a role-reversal phenomenon is noted in which it is found that firstborn children who occupy a dominant/leader role in sibling relations within the family often act in nondominant/follower roles in peer play situations.

More general studies of games as models of power are available in Roberts, Arth, and Bush (1959); Roberts and Sutton-Smith (e.g., 1962, 1966); Roberts, Sutton-Smith, and Kendon (1963); and Sutton-Smith and Roberts (e.g., 1964, 1967, 1970). As these studies are discussed in more detail in chapter 7 [in *Transformations*], they are only briefly described here. The basic argument of the investigators in this research is that three different types of games found in various societies of the world (i.e., games of physical skill, games of chance, and games of strategy) are systematically related to both psychogenic (child training) and sociogenic (economics, politics, etc.) cultural variables. Examples of these relationships are illustrated by the fact that games of physical skill are found in cultures where physical abilities are essential to survival; games of chance appear most frequently in cultures where divinatory procedures are important in decision making; and games of strategy exist in cultures where class stratification and warfare are institutionalized. In cultures where all three types of games appear, there tends to be more emphasis on achievement. These findings led the investigators

> to view these competitive games as models of the larger cultural processes and, in a sense, as a preparation for the use of the type of power relevant to life in the larger culture. (Sutton-Smith & Savasta, Note 5, p. 1)

In looking at variations in these types of games in American society, it was found that males more frequently played physical skill games, whereas females were more likely to play strategic and chance games. And it was also found that strategy games were more often preferred by individuals of higher social status, whereas chance games were preferred by persons of lower social status.

Imitation, Imagination, and Culture

A recent interest of students of children's play is the study of relationships between play behavior and culture. In these investigations, it is assumed that play serves a socializing function for society and that certain types of cultures encourage the development and elaboration of certain types of play forms. The studies of Roberts, Arth, and Bush (1959) and Roberts and Sutton-Smith (1962) described above illustrate this approach, particularly in relation to the association of particular types of competitive games with particular types of cultures.

More recently, studies of the relationship between children's imaginative play and culture have been made. Smilansky's (1968) investigation of children's sociodramatic play in Israel is probably the most well known. In this work, Smilansky's adoption of the play-as-imitation/socialization perspective is evidenced in her view that make-believe play *aids* imitation as it is "a technique by which the child's limitations can be overcome and by which a richer reproduction of adult life is made possible" (p. 7). Sociodramatic play is said to be characterized by six play elements: (1) imitative role play; (2) make-believe in regard to objects; (3) make-believe in regard to actions and situations; (4) persistence; (5) interaction (two or more players); and (6) verbal communication (Smilansky, 1971, pp. 41-42). On the basis of this research, Smilansky suggested that certain groups of children have less facility for imaginative role play than others. In her study, children of North African and Middle Eastern parents (referred to here as "disadvantaged preschool children") are said to engage in this type of play with much less frequency and with less ability than children of European parents.[5] (Children of Kurdish Jews who have recently immigrated to Israel are also reported to exhibit a paucity of imaginative play; see Feitelson, 1954, 1959.)

Smilansky suggested that this research and also more recent studies of the play of "culturally disadvantaged" children in Ohio and Chicago indicate that "without some degree of positive intervention by parents and/or teachers, these children will lack the requirements essential to develop sociodramatic play" (1971, p. 39; also see 1968). If this type of play does not develop, children may be retarded in the development of skills and behavior patterns that are "necessary for successful integration into the school situation or full cooperation in the 'school game' '' (p. 42). Sociodramatic play is said to develop three aspects of children that are essential to this "school game": (1) creativity; (2) intellectual growth (and particularly the "power" of abstraction); and (3) social skills. Therefore, because of the importance of sociodramatic play to children's development, Smilansky believes that adults, as parents and teachers, must actively intervene in order to improve or "raise significantly" the "low performance in play" that certain children exhibit (p. 45). A variety of intervention techniques are described (e.g., adult modeling of sociodramatic play techniques), and Smilansky reported that in both the Israeli (1968) and the American (1971) studies, these interventions improved the children's ability to engage in this form of play behavior.

In a study of Russian nursery-school children, El'Konin (1971) reported that these children engage *only* in imitative play activities. It is suggested here that what look like imaginative, spontaneous play productions on the part of children are often, in fact, direct copies of adult behavior. According to El'Konin, it is possible to discover the adult source of a child's pretense if the investigator knows the history of these transformations. For example, he cited an instance in one school in which a stick was called a "thermometer" by a child in a play situation simply because a teacher had suggested this transformation to the child some time earlier.

Sutton-Smith used Smilansky's and El'Konin's research, as well as the earlier study of Roberts, Arth, and Bush, to argue for the existence of "The Two Cultures of Games" (1972; also see Herron & Sutton-Smith, 1971, pp. 218-219). In "ascriptive game cultures," children are said to engage in imitative and nonimaginative play activities that are hierarchically organized, where one child bosses all the others and is often quite aggressive. Central-person games and, later, games of physical skill are most commonly played in these cultures. The types of societies associated with "ascriptive" games, however, are not clearly described except insofar as they are said to be characterized by (1) extended families; (2) leaders' domination by the use of arbitrary power; and (3) the lack of a clear separation of children and adults (p. 299). Children in "achievement games cultures" are said to play imaginatively and in a more egalitarian style. Likewise, there is less physical aggression and less emphasis on ritualized and formalistic games (e.g., singing games). Western (i.e., Western middle-class) societies are said to be typical of "achievement game cultures." In these cultures children are segregated from the rest of society, and nuclear families predominate (pp. 303-309).

More recent experimental studies (e.g., Feitelson, 1972; Feitelson & Ross, 1973; Freyberg, 1973; see also Singer, 1973; J. Singer & D. Singer, 1976) report both cultural and class differences in the quantity and quality of children's imaginative play behavior. For example, Freyberg (1973) stated that a group of 80 "urban disadvantaged" American kindergarten children, who were the subjects of her study, exhibited very little imaginative play (using a rating scale described in Singer, 1973) in free play settings prior to the introduction of a training program. Before this intervention occurred, "there was very little role-playing or elaboration of themes; seldom was a pretend situation concerned with themes not in the child's direct experience" (p. 151). However, following a series of training sessions,

> there was more and qualitatively different imaginative play. There was much more organization in the pretend situations, which often involved themes not part of the daily life of the child. (p. 151)

Feitelson and Ross (1973) also reported similar results in a study of white, lower-middle-class kindergarten children living in the Boston area. These children were found to exhibit "surprisingly low levels of thematic play" prior to participation in a series of play-tutoring sessions (which stressed adult modeling of thematic play), which led to a "significant increase" in their thematic play (p. 218). Feitelson and Ross argued that this research (in conjunction with the studies of Smilansky and Feitelson in Israel and El'Konin in the Soviet Union) indicates that thematic play must be learned by some form of modeling, and that, if this does not occur, then this play does not develop naturally or spontaneously in all children. The investigators appear to assume, however, that "high levels" of imaginative or thematic play are found among middle- and upper-middle-class children (where presumably such modeling occurs). Unfortunately, we do not know that this is the case from their study because the investigators did not use their assessment techniques to rate a group of middle- or upper-middle-class children (comparisons of this sort were made by Smilansky, and Freyberg's study is somewhat comparable to Pulaski's 1973 investigation of American upper-middle-class children's imaginative use of toys, because similar rating scales were used).

Feitelson and Ross also cited "accumulating ethnographic evidence" in support of the view that children in "rural communities" do not engage in thematic play because this activity is not modeled for them by adults or because sufficient "play props" and play spaces are not available (pp. 204-206). Aside from Feitelson's research on the children of Kurdish Jews who have recently immigrated to Israel (1954, 1959), the authors also cited the studies of Ammar (1954) on Egyptian village children and LeVine and LeVine (1963) on Gusii children in Kenya. In this regard, it is interesting to note that Ammar devoted one entire chapter (pp. 144-160) to a description of Silwa children's play and games. Although he reported that these children (particularly boys) play mostly competitive games, engaging only infrequently in constructive or imaginative play (which he considered transformations of *objects*), he stated that a popular play situation for girls is the representation of adult female occupations and ceremonies. As he described this play, it would certainly seem to fit most investigators' definitions of sociodramatic or thematic play. According to Ammar, this play involves

> making straw figures, bedecked in bits of cloth as men and women and children, and with the help of stones, building a house. All the details of an event or ritual are played out in a make-believe way. Thus marriage, circumcision, cooking, and social meetings are all imitated. (p. 154)

The LeVines' study is discussed in more detail in chapter 7 [in *Transformations*]; however, one variable contributing to these children's reported lack of thematic play appears to be the geographic distance between households, which makes it difficult for groups of children to form. In this case, instead of a scarcity of space, there appears to be too much space.

The most important thing to emphasize here, however, is that "accumulating ethnographic evidence" does *not* support the idea that rural or non-Western children do not engage in thematic play activities. Considering the fact that most ethnographers have not systematically studied this behavior (Ammar stated that he made "no detailed observations of play situations," 1954, p. 159), the reports of children's ingenuity in constructing thematic play events that do appear in the literature (e.g., Centner, 1962; DuBois, 1944; Fortes, 1938; Maretzki & Maretzki, 1963; Nydegger & Nydegger, 1963; Raum, 1940; Roth, 1902; Lancy, Note 2) suggest that this is, in fact, a well-developed play form in many non-Western cultures.

As Sutton-Smith particularly used the work of Smilansky to support his "two cultures" view (and Freyberg, Feitelson and Ross, and Singer also utilized her research to support their arguments), it is important to consider again Eifermann's recent studies of children's play in Israel (1971a, 1971b). In this study, she challenged Smilansky's findings by suggesting that the form of play (i.e., sociodramatic/imaginative) that Smilansky reported to be lacking in her sample of "disadvantaged" children appeared at a later age (i.e., at age 6-8 rather than 3-6) for a comparable group of children in Eifermann's own study. And she stated that her analysis indicates that at this later age, "culturally deprived" children not only develop the ability to engage in symbolic/thematic play but also "engage in such play at a significantly higher rate than do their 'advantaged' peers" (1971b, p. 290).

There are other problems as well with these research studies that propose that children from certain cultures or classes are "imaginatively disadvantaged." In many of these investigations, associations between imaginative (or thematic or sociodramatic) play and particular cognitive and social skills are made. These associations are reflected in hypotheses that suggest that children who receive training in imaginative play (1) will also improve their scores on standard creativity tests (e.g., CATB tests for exploratory and innovative behavior; the Torrence "Thinking Creatively with Pictures" test) (Feitelson & Ross, 1973; also see Lieberman, 1977); (2) display a "higher degree of concentration," "more positive affect," and also "more tolerance and consideration" than children who do not receive training (Freyberg, 1973; Smilansky, 1968, 1971); (3) exhibit more verbal communication (i.e., longer and more complete sentences) after training sessions (Smilansky, 1968); (4) exhibit increased attention span and also improved "waiting behavior" (Singer, 1973; Singer & Singer, 1976); or (5) improve problem-solving abilities, specifically the ability to think abstractly (e.g., Smilansky, 1968).

These associations may be very valid, but they encourage researchers to neglect the investigation of alternate expressions of imagination or creativity, which lower-class children may display. Instead, these children are found to be *deficient* in the style of play associated with middle- and upper-middle-class children, which is then taken to indicate (or at least suggest) deficiency in the cognitive, verbal, and social skills said to be associated with this form of play and these children. In order to correct this deficit (which may actually be an artifact of the investigators' theories and/or the testing context), researchers then proceed to train children to play in a "middle-class" manner, which is then said to produce improved scores in the display of cognitive, verbal, and social skills.

Since middle-class children are, on the whole, more successful at playing the "school game" (in Smilansky's terms) than lower-class children, it may be that teaching them to engage in a middle-class form of play will improve their performance in school. Unfortunately, however, this view leads investigators not only to assume that lower-class children are deficient in the style of play in which middle-class children excel, but also to assume that these children are generally deficient in imaginative abilities and related cognitive, verbal, and social skills.

This is both an inaccurate and a dangerous assumption for researchers to make. For example, studies (e.g., Labov, 1972; Reissman, 1964) of lower-class children's expressive and imaginative use of language in role play and other situations *outside* of the school or the experimental context indicate that in these situations these children are highly creative, are more verbal, and display a variety of social and survival skills. This research also points to the importance of considering situational factors in the analysis and rating of children's play behavior (e.g., the "disadvantaged" children in Smilansky's study may have been fearful of the new and strange school that they were attending; neither Smilansky, Feitelson and Ross, nor Freyberg conducted observations of play outside of the school context; and, in the case of Feitelson and Ross, observations were not even conducted in the child's school, but instead in a strange and possibly frightening "Mobile Laboratory," where children were observed "one at a time" instead of in an "interaction" situation with other players, which Smilansky defined as an essential component of sociodramatic play). Freyberg has recognized these problems by suggesting the following:

> Lower-class children should perhaps be observed away from school, in which authority figures may be inhibitory. Use of para-professionals from the community may be essential in determining whether differences in verbal and cognitive style mask abilities among lower-class children when observed by middle-class persons. (1973, p. 136)

These studies, however, are also problematic in a way that I believe most investigators have not realized. These problems are best expressed in Labov's (1972) excellent critique of the verbal and cultural deprivation theories of Bernstein (1966) and Deutsch (1967) and the pragmatic programs formulated by individuals such as Bereiter and Engelmann (e.g., 1966) to correct such deprivations. In his analysis of the Black English Vernacular (BEV), Labov suggested that the view that black children in ghetto areas receive little verbal stimulation, hear very few well-formed sentences, cannot speak complete sentences, do not know the names of common objects, cannot form concepts or think logically, and are generally impoverished in their means of verbal expression "has no basis in social reality" (p. 201). Instead, his study demonstrates that, in fact, these children do receive a great deal of verbal stimulation, hear more well-formed sentences than middle-class children, have the same basic vocabulary, possess the same capacity for conceptual learning, and use the same logic as anyone who learns to speak and understand English (p. 201). Labov also demonstrated how the situational factors of schoolrooms and testing contexts influence the verbal productions of urban black children (see pp. 205-213; also see Dickie & Bagur, 1972).

Labov presented a particularly interesting analysis of what he believes to be the faulty reasoning of the verbal-deprivation theorists. The six statements, or logical steps, that Labov outlined are strikingly similar to the reasoning of what may be called the play-deprivation or play-training researchers. Therefore, following each step described by Labov (1972, pp. 229-230), I will present my view of these researchers' use of this logic:

1. "The lower-class child's verbal response to a formal and threatening situation is used to demonstrate his lack of verbal capacity or verbal deficit." (The lower-class child's play response to a formal and threatening situation is used to demonstrate his lack of imaginative capacities or his play deficit.)

2. "This verbal deficit is declared to be a major cause of the lower-class child's poor performance in school." (It is suggested that this play deficit is a cause of the lower-class child's poor performance in school.)

3. "Since middle-class children do better in school, middle-class speech habits are seen to be necessary for learning." (Since middle-class children do better in school, middle-class play habits are seen to be necessary for learning.)

4. "Class and ethnic differences in grammatical form are equated with differences in the capacity for logical analysis." (Class and ethnic differences in expressions of imagination are equated with differences in the capacity for logical analysis, verbal communication, and social skills.)

5. "Teaching the child to mimic certain formal speech patterns used by middle-class teachers is seen as teaching him to think logically." (Teaching the child to mimic certain play patterns displayed by middle-class children, and adult play tutors, is seen as helping him to develop imaginative skills and to improve his cognitive, verbal, and social functioning.)

6. "Children who learn these formal speech patterns are then said to be thinking logically and it is predicted that they will do much better in reading and arithmetic in the years to follow." (Children who learn these play patterns are then said to have improved their imaginative, cognitive, verbal, and social skills, and it is suggested that they will do better in school in the years to follow.)

Even if this logic can be shown to be faulty, is it necessarily harmful to teach children new ways to play? Labov asked a similar question in his study in regard to the effect of verbal training programs on children, and he suggested that on the surface, such programs are not harmful. However, he argued that these programs may actually prove to be very damaging to children in the long run because of the problem of *labeling* (e.g., teachers who hear children speaking BEV will constantly label them as illogical or nonconceptual thinkers) and also because when these programs fail to improve scholastic performance (which he feels is inevitable), they will be used to support the belief in the genetic inferiority of blacks (as an example, he cited Jensen's use of these studies in his controversial 1969 paper in the *Harvard Educational Review*).

It does not necessarily follow that the play-deprivation or play-training research discussed above will be used in the same manner. However, as this is a new field, it is not too soon to ask questions about the implications of this research, particularly when there appear to be striking correspondences between the arguments of these investigators and those of the verbal- or cultural-deprivation school. In both instances, the deficiencies of children are thought to be related to personal deficiencies residing *in* the child or *in* his home or neighborhood environment.

Adopting this view, programs (such as Head Start or play-tutoring sessions) are designed in Labov's terms, "to repair the child, rather than the school," and to the extent that they are based on this "inverted logic," they are "bound to fail" (1972, p. 232). Feitelson and Ross illustrated this view of the child's personal inadequacy in the following statement:

> Our study showed that some present day preschool pupils are unequipped to show initiative in the use of equipment, and in engaging on their own in those kinds of behavior deemed especially conducive to their future development. . . .
> Marion Blank, the Deutsches, Bereiter and Engelmann and others have demonstrated succinctly that improved performance can only be achieved by way of well planned tutoring sequences which rely on active participation by the child. (1973, p. 221)

Instead of assuming that some form of play deprivation exists and then proceeding to formulate training or facilitation programs, it would be much more valuable at this time for researchers to move out of the school or laboratory context to investigate whether or not they may have created (by the use of inappropriate theories and/or methods) the idea of play deprivation. In formulating these studies, researchers may discover that children are often critical observers of the adult world who have as much to say about adult behavior as adults who are researchers have to say about theirs.

Play: Socialization, Satirization, or Innovation?

Anthropologists have frequently commented on specific forms of symbolic inversion found in various societies of the world. The Cheyenne *massaum*, or contrary, ceremony; the *incwala*, or kingship, ceremony of the Swazi; and the Ndembu twin ritual, *wubwang'u*, are all rites of reversal and examples of play in religious dress (Norbeck, 1971, pp. 51-52). These institutionalized play forms sanction insults and derision of authority figures, social status inversions, parody, satire, lampooning, and clowning (see Norbeck, 1971; also Turner, 1974).

Sutton-Smith has recently undertaken the study of symbolic reversals and inversions apparent within the structure of certain plays and games of children (1974, Note 7). He called these the "games of order and disorder" and suggested that examples may be found in both Western and non-Western societies. Examples of such games for Western children are: ring-around-the-rosy, poor pussy, and Queen of Sheba. In the Trobriand Islands, similar games are played by children. For example, Malinowski described a game where all the players hold hands like a long string and wind around each other until they are a tight ball, and then they run out until it breaks, at which point everyone falls down or apart (Sutton-Smith, Note 7, p. 24).

Sutton-Smith stated that these types of games are significant because they suggest that play and games are not always socializing or social-ordering activities, as they may, in fact, seek to challenge and reverse the social order. This is so because these games often model the social system "only to destroy it" (e.g., everyone acts in concert and then collapses) (1974, p. 12). These games also often mock conventional power roles and frequently provide unconventional access to such roles (e.g., everyone gets a turn).

Four different types of order-disorder games were described by Sutton-Smith, and these categories were arranged to reflect "a series of structures of succeeding complexity" (Note 7, p. 10). The first level (presumably the least complex) is made up of games in which "everyone acts at the same time either diffusely or more or less in parallel, and the outcome may occur to one or all. The outcome is usually a motor collapse" (e.g., ring-around-the-rosy or the Trobriand game mentioned above) (p. 10). The second level consists of games in which "there is role differentiation to the extent that one or more players have a central role in bringing about the collapse" (e.g., I see a ghost) (p. 11).[6] In games of the third level, "actions are coordinated in turns through a cumulating series of actions and there is a common outcome" (e.g., consequences) (p. 12). Finally, fourth-level games are said to be those in which "the actions of the players are coordinated as in a dramatic plot toward the downfall of some central person" (e.g., Queen of Sheba) (p. 13). Younger children are said to engage in play at the first two levels, while older children play at levels 3 and 4.

In analyzing these games, Sutton-Smith was particularly concerned with examining the innovative quality of these activities. A view of play as an integrative mechanism or socializing force for society is a perspective focusing on only one aspect of the character of play and games. The novelty that these forms give rise to may ultimately be their most significant "function." Sutton-Smith suggested this in the following quote:

> If play is the learning of variability, a position for which we now have increasing experimental evidence, then we can perhaps say also that all these forms of inversion involve experimentation with variable repertoires. All involve the development of flexible competencies in role taking and the development of variable repertoires with respect to these roles. . . . In this view the anti-structural phenomena [the games of order and disorder] not only make the system tolerable as it exists, they keep its members in a more flexible state with respect to that system, and, therefore, with respect to possible change. Each system has different structural and anti-structural functions. The normative structure represents the working equilibrium, the anti-structure represents the latent system of potential alternatives from

which novelty will arise when contingencies in the normative system require it.[7] We might more correctly call this second system the *proto-structural* system because it is the precursor of innovative normative forms. It is the source of new culture. (1972, p. 20)

However, the innovative quality of play texts is also dependent on the ideology of the larger culture or context in which such activities exist. Therefore,

in a closed work ethic society there is no scope for the novelty and facetiousness to which play gives rise. In an open society this novelty is a source of potential adaptation, albeit an over-productive source being no guarantee of preparation, as Groos thought, but at least of the promise of being ready.

In this interpretation . . . play, games and sports both mirror and provide potential novelty for the larger society. In this interpretation also, social scientists, including anthropologists, have been mainly concerned with what I would like to consider the *integrative* functions of play in society. They have been concerned . . . with normative socializing. The more static, the more relevant, the type of play theorizing is. What an increasingly open society like ours needs, however, is to consider the innovative functions of playing and to try to account for ways in which novelties introduced into the text ultimately transfer back to the society at large. (1974, p. 15)

While play may encourage "experimentation with variable repertoires" and can be a "source of new culture," it is also frequently an arena for comment and criticism on the "old" culture, the status quo. Satire and parody, caricature and burlesque are all examples of play forms that *invert* and may also seek to *subvert* (see Turner, 1974, p. 72) the existing social system. Sutton-Smith has recognized (but does not emphasize) the fact that certain children's play and games may mock, make fun of, and, in a sense, challenge the status quo. For children, the social order is most obviously symbolized by adult figures, who represent the existing power and authority structure of society (i.e., the "older" culture) as parents, teachers, police, and so forth.

A number of researchers have remarked on the antiauthoritarian themes evident in many children's games. For example, Abrahams reported that, in the content of English-speaking children's jump-rope rhymes, "a strong antitaboo and antiauthoritarian tone is assumed" (1969, p. xxiv). He went on to suggest that this theme is

evident in the numerous taunts and parodies throughout this volume and in the attachment to clown figures . . . that is, to adult figures that children can at the same time both identify with and make fun of. Parents, when they appear, are portrayed more often than not as ridiculous, more to be laughed at than feared, and the same could be said of other authority figures such as policemen, doctors, judges, even movie stars. (p. xxiv)

Iona and Peter Opie also noted similar forms of parody and satire of adults—as well as adult-taught hymns, carols, and nursery rhymes—in their collection of the language and lore of English schoolchildren (1959). They suggested that these sorts of satirical rhymes are often created and recited "just for the fun of versification, and perhaps because, in the crude images evoked, adults are made to look undignified" (pp. 18-19).

As already mentioned, the butt of many of these jokes and parodies is the adult *as parent*:

> Mother made a seedy cake.
> Gave us all the belly ache;
> Father bought a pint of beer,
> Gave us all the diarrhoea. (I. & P. Opie [1959, p. 19])

> You're mad, you're barmy,
> Your mother's in the army,
> She wears black britches,
> With pink and white stitches. (Sutton-Smith [1959, p. 133])

As teacher:

> God made the bees,
> The bees make honey;
> We do the work,
> The teacher gets the money. (I. & P. Opie [1959, p. 361])

As law official:

> No wonder, no wonder, the coppers are so fat,
> They go around the market and eat up all the fat,
> And what they can't eat they put in their 'at.
> No wonder, no wonder, the coppers are so fat. (I. & P Opie [1959, p. 370])

> Order in the court,
> The judge is eating beans.
> His wife is in the bathtub,
> Counting submarines. (Evans [1955, p. 16])

And as political figure:

> Roosevelt in the White House,
> Waiting to be elected;
> Dewey in the garbage can,
> Waiting to be collected. (Withers [1947, p. 218])

Adult-taught prayers, hymns, and rhymes are also the subject of satire and parody, as well as historical commentary. For example, *the Christmas carol*:

No ale, no beer, no stout, sold out,
Born is the king with his shirt hanging out. (I. & P. Opie [1959, p. 88])

Hark the herald angels sing,
Mrs. Simpson's pinched our king. (I. & P. Opie [1959, p. 6])

Or the nursery rhyme:

Mary had a little lamb,
She also had a bear;
I've often seen her little lamb,
But I've never seen her bear. (I. & P. Opie [1959, p. 90])

In these examples, satire, parody, and implied criticism are found in the content of the rhyme or song. However, ridicule and challenge may also be evident (as Sutton-Smith, 1974, Note 7, has suggested) in the structure of the game itself. In the example of ring-around-the-rosy, the harmony of the social order is modeled and then mocked as everyone falls down and collapses. Similarly, conventional power roles, which are generally asymmetrical with unequal provision for access to leadership, are reversed as everyone (no matter who he/she is) gets a turn.

Satire may also be apparent in games in which the content looks imitative—and therefore functional for socialization—while the enactment of the game (i.e., the way it is played) is mocking and farcical. The following interpretation of the game "Mother, May I?" appears in Dolhinow and Bishop's (1970) recent article, which stresses the importance of play in the development of motor skills and social relationships in primates (particularly nonhuman primates). In their interpretation of this game, the use of a play-as-socialization perspective is clearly illustrated:

Just as the nonhuman primates learn and practice the appropriate "rules" of adult behavior in the play group, so does the human child. He is actively discouraged from developing a second set of standards for conduct. The American game, Mother, May I, is an example of this principle, in which we find a sequence of a mother-child interaction.
MOTHER: Susie, you may take two baby steps.
SUSIE: Mother, May I?
MOTHER: Yes, you may, or, no you may not. You may take three umbrella steps.
SUSIE: Mother, May I?

There is no element of strategy or chance in this game; the "mother" is in strict control, and a "child" is penalized for a breach of etiquette (i.e., not asking, "Mother, May I?"). (pp. 188-189)·

However, if American children are watched actually playing this game, the socialization perspective, as articulated above, may not be so immediately apparent. Sutton-Smith (personal communication) states that the enactment of such a game may suggest not rigid control and perfect socialization but a burlesque of social etiquette and rules, as when the "child" inches forward while "mother" is not looking and everyone conceals this transgression while laughing and giggling. In short, when the game is played, we cannot necessarily assume that "mother" is always in control of her "children," as they may sometimes (or often) act to make her look foolish and ridiculous.

The children of the !Kung Bushmen of Southwest Africa also play a number of caricature games. Lorna Marshall presented a detailed description of play and games in Bushmen society in her most recent account (*The !Kung of Nyae Nyae*, 1976) of this now vanished way of life. In chapters entitled "Play and Games" (pp. 313-362) and "Music for Pleasure" (pp. 363-381), Marshall surveyed the various forms of recreation engaged in by both adults and children. Here she described the play of very young children (e.g., "imitation" plays, vocabulary and counting games), boys' play (e.g., tree climbing, sand patterns, cartwheels, somersaults and hopping, string figures, and toy inventions) and games (e.g., war games, tug-of-war, stick throwing), and girls' play (e.g., sand patterns, hopping, riding games, string figures, dolls) and games (e.g., ball games that involve singing, dancing, and clapping—see Figure 11 [Figure 1 in this chapter]; jump-rope; a type of London Bridge; dances). Marshall also discussed the !Kung children's ingenuity in manufacturing foreign objects (e.g., a toy gun made out of a reed; "autos" made from tubers and bulbs modeled after the Marshalls' jeeps and accompanied by motor sounds imitated by the boys, who specialized "in the roar of low gear pulling out of heavy sand," p. 342). A number of short movies of Bushmen play and games are available that depict tug-of-war, playing with toy assagais, baobab (a large tree) play, the lion game, playing with scorpions, and song games. These films are discussed in more detail in chapter 12 [in *Transformations*].

Marshall stated that !Kung children play "all their waking hours," either free play or structured games and that adults also engage in a variety of play and game activities (p. 313).[8] However, the !Kung do not play competitive team games (except tug-of-war),[9] and the idea of winners and losers is not emphasized as this is a culture that stresses the importance of group and not individual performance. On the other hand, conflict, satire, and mimicry (of animals, other !Kung, and also the prac-

Figure 1—!Kung Bushmen girls' ball game (L. Marshall, 1976, p. 323).

tices of other societies[10]) are evidenced in a variety of Bushmen play activities. Marshall described a series of "dramatic games" (pp. 356-362) that can be viewed as expressions of conflict in the form of playful satires of three of the "basic polarities" of !Kung life: parents-children, herders-hunters, and humans-animals.

One of these games is called "frogs," and it can best be described as a reverse "Mother, May I?" because, instead of stressing obedience (although in conjunction with covert transgressions), the game emphasizes disobedience to the parental figure, which results in chaos and pandemonium (perhaps this is the game's "moral"). The game is played by girls and boys (between the ages of 8 and 12) and sometimes women. All players begin by sitting in a circle, and one player is chosen to be "mother of all" while the others become her "children." First, "mother" taps each of her children on the ankle with a stick, and they lay back, pretending to fall asleep. The mother then pulls some hairs from her head and places them on an imaginary fire in the center of the circle. These hairs represent "frogs," which the mother has gathered for food. After the frogs have "cooked" on the fire, the mother calls to the children, and they all stand up in the circle. She goes to each child and taps him/her on the chest with a twig and asks him/her to fetch her mortar and pestle so that she can finish the preparation of the frogs. Each child turns away, refusing to perform this task while mother feigns annoyance and finally leaves to retrieve her mortar and pestle.

While mother is away, the children steal the frogs and run off to various hiding places. When she returns, she pretends to be very angry and starts looking for her disobedient children. When she finds one, she strikes him/her on the head with her forefinger. This action "breaks the head" so that the child's "brains run out," and she then pretends to drink the "brains." The final part of the game frequently ends in chaos and pandemonium as the children try to dart away from mother's grasp. Soon everyone is chasing everyone else, shrieking and laughing and whacking each other on the head. The other "dramatic games" described by Marshall are "ostrich," "cattle," and "python."

Children may also act as critics and satirists of adult speech. For example, Mary Ellen Goodman, in her book *The Culture of Childhood* (1970), provided a brief example of two American 4-year-old boys caricaturing the greeting behavior and intonation patterns of two adult women. The burlesque is evident as the boys, in repeating the set phrases and exaggerating the word intonation, are reported to be laughing and "convulsed by their own wit":

Jack: It's *lovely* to see you!
Danny: I'm *so* happy to see you!
Jack: How *are* you? How have you been?
Danny: Sorry I have to go so quick. (p. 138)

Kornei Chukovsky, the Russian children's poet, presented an analysis of the thought processes and imagination of children as reflected in their language in his book *From Two to Five* (1963). Although this study is not intended to be a scientific investigation of Russian children's verbal play, it is one of the few detailed descriptions of this activity available for any group of children [other examples will be discussed in chapter 9 (in *Transformations*.)] Chukovsky attempted to illustrate the "linguistic genius" of a young child in his/her word inventions, which are created "in accordance with the norms made known to him through adult speech," as when a bald man is described "as having a barefoot head" or a mint candy is said to "make a draft in one's mouth" (pp. 2, 9).

Chukovsky believes that "the basis for all linguistic aptitude attributed to the child . . . is imitation. . . . However, he does not copy adults as simply (and docilely) as it seems to the casual observer" (p. 9). In a special section entitled "Children as 'Critics' of Adult Speech," Chukovsky presented evidence designed "to show that in the process of assimilating his native spoken language the child, from the early age of two, introduces a critical evaluation, analysis, and control" (p. 9). As examples, he cited a number of instances of the child's sometimes mocking and often "strict and even disparaging criticism of the way adults use certain words and expressions" (p. 11).

> "I'm dying to hear that concert!"
> "Then why don't you die?" a child would ask sarcastically. (p. 11)

> After a long separation, a mother said to her little girl: "How thin you've become, Nadiusha. All that's left of you is one little nose."
> "Well Mommie, did I have more than one nose before you left?" (p. 12)

> An exasperated mother said to her son: "Some day you'll lose your head, so help me God!"
> "I'll never lose *my* head," was the reassuring reply, "I'll find it and pick it up. (p. 13)

> A visitor asked about five-year-old Seriozha's baby sister, "Does your little Irishka go to sleep with the roosters?"
> "No, she doesn't go to bed with the roosters. They scratch! She sleeps in her cradle." (p. 13)

It is possible that implicit in the imitation/socialization interpretations of children's play, which consistently disregard the critical and satirical qualities of these activities, is the child-centered view of many Western and also non-Western adults. That is, if adults as parents are expected to direct a large portion of their time and energy toward children (i.e., to raise or rear them), then perhaps it is necessary to believe that children reciprocate by directing all of their time in play toward adults (i.e., by imitating them). At least, at one level, it may be that interpretations of play as imitation are actually manifestations of, and rationalizations for, these common-sense (i.e., adult) beliefs (see Mackay, 1974).

In searching for ways to understand and evaluate social roles, and particularly sex roles, it may be useful to consider the role and structural inversions and satirical content characteristic of many children's games. Perhaps in certain of their play and game activities children have been questioning and/or mocking culturally stereotyped sex roles all along, and as adults we thought (or hoped) they were just being socialized.[11]

In searching for ways to understand and evaluate the role of anthropologists in the societies that they study, it may be useful to turn back to the description of Yoruba children "playing anthropologist," which appears in chapter 1 [in *Transformations*]. Is this an example of children "merely imitating" in play the anthropologist at work, or is there possibly an element of playful satire and parody apparent? If this play incident is viewed from the latter perspective, it is possible to learn something new not only about the child at play but also about the anthropologist at work.

Summary

In the 1920s and 1930s a new approach to the study of culture was advocated by anthropologists who had grown tired of the overly inductive methods and atheoretical approach of the diffusionists and particularists. A.R. Radcliffe-Brown and Bronislaw Malinowski were the two major spokesmen for this new movement, which came to be known as *functionalism*. Although they differed greatly in regard to their particular orientation to functional analysis, they agreed on one basic premise: "that the parts of any whole, whether a social system or a culture, had to function for the maintenance of that whole" (Langness, 1974, p. 82).

During the reign of functionalism, anthropologists pursued the study of the "serious" social systems of kinship, religion, politics, and economics. Because of the popularity of Radcliffe-Brown's structural-functionalism and his deemphasis on psychological studies, the study of childhood socialization, and in particular children's play behavior, was neglected. Except for analyses of adult joking relationships in various societies (e.g., Radcliffe-Brown, 1952/1968) and Fortes' (1938) excellent discussion of Tallensi children's play behavior, detailed considerations of play phenomena were generally avoided by the functionalist.

Investigations of children's play that were conducted by researchers at this time—whether they were anthropologists, sociologists, or psychologists—gave emphasis to the imitative character of this activity. In these instances, children were depicted as imitating the activities (generally economic) of adults in their play behavior. The function of this imitative/mimetic play was to provide children with an opportunity to learn and practice culturally appropriate adult roles. These studies are important because, by stressing play's value as a socialization mechanism, they were able to challenge traditional views of play as a frivolous and useless activity. In this way, play itself became socialized and legitimated as proper and respectable behavior.[12] Unfortunately, in describing children's play as imitation of and/or preparation for adult activities, investigators examined only the social *contexts* (i.e., social functions) of play, to the exclusion of analyses of specific play *texts*.

Over the years, a number of researchers have indicated their dissatisfaction with a view of play that emphasizes only its imitative character and socializing function (e.g., Fortes, Raum, Chukovsky, Sutton-Smith, Schwartzman). Recently, studies of children's play and games that stress the innovative and satirical qualities of game and play structure content, and enactment have been made (e.g., Sutton-Smith, 1974; Note 7). This research concentrates on studies of Western children's play, but it is also necessary to investigate the extent and kind of "games of order and

disorder" in non-Western societies. These investigations are also important to initiate in order to question the validity of the "two cultures of
games" notion. At present, because detailed material on this topic is
scarce, cultural and class differences in children's play behavior are often
interpreted as evidence of deficiency rather than variation in play styles.
As anthropologists know from their studies of other topics, such views
generally last only as long as there is a deficiency of rich ethnographic
material.

All of these recent studies challenge and criticize the prevailing
theoretical order of the times (which is still functional analysis for play
researchers), just as they claim that certain children's games challenge
and parody the existing sociocultural order of adult society. This
research also reflects current critiques of the structural-functional approach in anthropology (see Jarvie, 1969) and emphasizes this theory's
inability to deal with social change, deviance, or novelty in a cultural
system and its implicit and explicit acceptance and perpetuation of the
status quo.

Notes

1. The idea that children's play serves an expressive and cathartic function for
   individuals and society was developed much more thoroughly by psychoanalytic and psychological researchers. The effect of this view on anthropological
   studies is discussed in chapter 7 [of *Transformations: The Anthropology of
   Children's Play*].
2. The terms *socialization* and *enculturation* have been variously defined. For
   example, Margaret Mead defined *socialization* "as the set of species wide requirements and exactions made on human beings by human societies" and
   enculturation as "the process of learning a culture in all its uniqueness and
   particularity" (1963, p. 187). It is, however, extremely difficult to consider
   these two processes separately in discussing a topic such as play, and so I have
   chosen to use the term *socialization* to refer to both processes.
3. Cheska (Note 4) has recently presented a similar analysis of North American
   Indian games as "strategies of social maintenance." Here the relationship of
   games to the social processes of sex role differentiation, group identity,
   decision-making models, and symbolic identification is examined.
4. Whiting and Edwards (1973) reported that in societies where boys are required to take care of infants and perform other domestic chores, there are
   fewer sex differences between boys and girls. Ember's (1973) study of the effect of feminine task assignment on the social behavior of Luo (a Nilotic people living in southwestern Kenya) boys supports this finding. However,
   Draper (1975) reported that sex differences observed in the behavior of !Kung
   Bushmen children "are not attributable, at least not in any obvious way, to
   differential socialization" (p. 605).
5. Samples of play texts for both the so-called disadvantaged and advantaged
   children are presented in an appendix to the 1968 report.

6. An equivalent from Mota Banks Island, Melanesia, was cited by Sutton-Smith (p. 11) from Lansley's (1968) studies. The game is played in the following manner. Two lines face each other and chant about a magic wand. In order to get the wand, a player must make faces and twist his body or distort his voice. If he makes the rest of the group laugh, he becomes the possessor of the wand and someone else must try to get it.

7. In these remarks, Sutton-Smith invoked and expanded on the notions of structure and antistructure articulated by Victor Turner in *The Ritual Process* (1969). Turner has recently expanded on these ideas in an essay attempting to delineate differences between liminal phenomena ("ergic-ludic" rituals characteristic of tribal and early agrarian societies) and liminoid phenomena ("anergic-ludic" games and actions and literature characteristic of societies shaped by the Industrial Revolution) entitled "Liminal to Liminoid in Play, Flow, and Ritual: An Essay in Comparative Symbology" (1974) [chapter 5 in this volume].

8. In fact, according to Draper (1975), the "nomadic !Kung are a remarkably leisured society. Men and women work on the average only about three days per week in the food quest" (p. 609). This finding challenges the conventional assumption that significant amounts of leisure time are only found in industrialized societies.

9. An ancient tale of the !Kung describes how the fate of the Bushmen was decided by a tug-of-war (see Marshall, 1976, pp. 336-337).

10. The movie *The Lion Game* shows the !Kung's clever satire of Bantu hunting practices. The !Kung do not hunt lions.

11. Another way to explain (and again "adulterate") these games would be to say that they provide children with the opportunity to practice "role distance," in Goffman's (1961) terms.

12. For an expanded critique of the play-as-socialization perspective, see Sutton-Smith's new book, *The Dialectics of Play* (1976, also see 1977).

Reference Notes

1. Salter, M.A. *Play: A medium of cultural stability*. Paper presented at the International Seminar on the History of Physical Education and Sport, Vienna, April 17-20, 1974.

2. Lancy, D.F. *The role of games in the enculturation of children*. Paper presented at the 74th annual meeting of the American Anthropological Association, San Francisco, December 2-6, 1975.

3. Lancy, D.F. *Socio-dramatic play and the acquisition of occupational roles*. Paper presented at the second annual meeting of The Association for the Anthropological Study of Play, Atlanta, March 31-April 3, 1976.

4. Cheska, A. *Native American games as strategies of societal maintenance*. Paper presented at the joint meeting of the American Ethnological Society and The Association for the Anthropological Study of Play, San Diego, April 1977.

5. Sutton-Smith, B., & Savasta, M. *Sex differences in play and power*. Paper presented at the annual meeting of the Eastern Psychological Association,

April 1972. (Reprinted in Sutton-Smith, *The dialectics of play*. Schorndoff, West Germany: Verlag Hoffman, 1976.)

6. Lever, J. *Sex-role socialization and social structure: The place of complexity in children's games*. Paper presented at the annual meeting of the Pacific Sociological Association, Victoria, BC, 1975.

7. Sutton-Smith, B. *Games of order and disorder*. Paper presented at the annual meeting of the American Anthropological Association, Toronto, Canada, December 1972. (Reprinted in B. Sutton-Smith, *The dialectics of play*. Schorndoff, West Germany: Verlag Hoffman, 1976.)

References

ABRAHAMS, R.D. (Ed.). *Jump-rope rhymes: A dictionary*. Austin: University of Texas Press, 1969.

AMMAR, H. *Growing up in an Egyptian village*. London: Routledge & Kegan Paul, 1954.

BARRY, H.A., III, Bacon, M.K., & Child, I.L. A cross-cultural survey of some sex differences in socialization. *Journal of Abnormal and Social Psychology*, 1957, **55**, 327-332.

BEREITER, C., & Engelmann, S. *Teaching disadvantaged children in the preschool*. Englewood Cliffs, NJ: Prentice-Hall, 1966.

BERNSTEIN, B. Elaborated and restricted codes: Their social origins and some consequences. In J. Gumperz & D. Hymes (Eds.), *The ethnography of communication*. Special publication, *American Anthropologist 1966*, **66**, Part 2.

CENTNER, T. *L'enfant africain et ses jeux*. Elisabethville: CEPSI, 1962.

CHUKOVSKY, K. [From two to five] (M. Morton, Ed. & trans.). Berkeley: University of California Press, 1963.

DEUTSCH, M., et al. *The disadvantaged child*. New York: Basic Books, 1967.

DICKIE, J., & Bagur, J.S. Considerations for the study of language in young low-income minority group children. *Merrill-Palmer Quarterly of Behavior and Development*, 1972, **18**, 25-38.

DOLHINOW, P.J., & Bishop, N. The development of motor skills and social relationships among primates through play. In J.P. Hill (Ed.), *Minnesota Symposia on Child Psychology* (Vol. 4). Minneapolis: University of Minnesota Press, 1970.

DRAPER, P. Cultural pressure on sex differences. *American Ethnologist*, 1975, **2**, 602-616.

DUBOIS, C. *The people of Alor*. Minneapolis: University of Minnesota Press, 1944.

EDEL, M.M. *The Chiga of Western Uganda*. New York: Oxford University International African Institute Press, 1957.

EIFERMANN, R. Cooperation and egalitarianism in kibbutz children's games. *Human Relations*, 1970, **23**, 579-587.

EIFERMANN, R. *Determinants of children's game styles*. Jerusalem: Israel Academy of Sciences and Humanities, 1971. (a)

EIFERMANN, R. Social play in childhood. In R. Herron & B. Sutton-Smith (Eds.), *Child's play*. New York: John Wiley, 1971. (b)

EL'KONIN, D. Symbolics and its functions in the play of children. In R. Herron & B. Sutton-Smith (Eds.), *Child's play*. New York: John Wiley, 1971.

EMBER, C.R. Feminine task assignment and the social behavior of boys. *Ethos*, 1973, **1**, 424-439.

ERIKSON, E.H. Further exploration in play construction: Three spatial variables in their relation to sex and anxiety. *Psychological Bulletin*, 1941, **38**, 748.

ERIKSON, E.H. Sex differences in play configurations of pre-adolescents. *American Journal of Ortho-Psychiatry*, 1951, **21**, 667-692. (Reprinted in R. Herron & B. Sutton-Smith [Eds.], *Child's play*. New York: John Wiley, 1971.)

EVANS, P. *Jump rope rhymes*. San Francisco: The Porpoise Bookshop, 1955.

FEITELSON, D. Patterns of early education in the Kurdish community. *Megamot*, 1954, **5**, 95-109.

FEITELSON, D. Some aspects of the social life of Kurdish Jews. *Jewish Journal of Sociology*, 1959, **1**, 201-216.

FEITELSON, D. Developing imaginative play in preschool children as a possible approach to fostering creativity. *Early Child Development Care*, 1972, **1**, 181-195.

FEITELSON, D., & Ross, G.S. The neglected factor—play. *Human Development*, 1973, **16**, 202-223.

FORTES, M. Social and psychological aspects of education in Taleland. *Africa*, 1938, **11**(4), Supplement. (Reprinted in J. Middleton [Ed.], *From child to adult*. Garden City, NY: Natural History Press, 1970.)

FREYBERG, J. Increasing the imaginative play of urban disadvantaged kindergarten children through systematic training. In J.L. Singer (Ed.), *The child's world of make-believe*. New York: Academic Press, 1973.

GARVEY, C. *Play*. Cambridge: Harvard University Press, 1977.

GOFFMAN, E. *Encounters*. Indianapolis: Bobbs-Merrill, 1961.

GOLDBERG, S., & Lewis, M. Play behavior in the year-old infant: Early sex differences. *Child Development*, 1969, **40**, 21-31.

GOODMAN, M.E. *The culture of childhood*. New York: Teachers College Press, 1970.

GRIEF, E.B. Sex role playing in pre-school children. In J.S. Bruner, A. Jolly, &

K. Sylva (Eds.), *Play: Its role in development and evolution*. New York: Basic Books, 1976.

GROOS, K. *The play of animals*. London: Chapman & Hall, 1898.

GROOS, K. *The play of man*. New York: Appleton, 1901.

GUMP, P.V., & Sutton-Smith, B. The "it" role in children's games. *The Group*, 1955, **17**, 3-8.

HERRON, R.E., & Sutton-Smith, B. (Eds.). *Child's play*. New York: John Wiley, 1971.

JARVIE, I. *The revolution in anthropology*. New York: Humanities Press, 1969.

JENSEN, A. How much can we boost IQ and scholastic achievement? *Harvard Educational Review*, 1969, **39**, 1-123.

KENYATTA, J. *Facing Mount Kenya*. London: Secker & Warburg, 1939.

LABOV, W. *Language in the inner city: Studies in the Black English vernacular*. Philadelphia: University of Pennsylvania Press, 1972.

LANCY, D.F. *Work, play, and learning in a Kpelle town*. Unpublished doctoral dissertation, University of Pittsburgh, 1974.

LANCY, D.F. The play behavior of Kpelle children during rapid cultural change. In D.F. Lancy & B. Allan Tindall (Eds.), *The anthropological study of play: Problems and prospects*. Cornwall, NY: Leisure Press, 1976.

LANGNESS, L.L. *The study of culture*. San Francisco: Chandler & Sharp, 1974.

LANSLEY, K. *A collection and classification of the traditional Melanesian play activities with a supplementary bibliography*. Unpublished master's thesis, University of Alberta, 1968.

LEVER, J. *Games children play: Sex differences and the development of role skills*. Unpublished doctoral dissertation, Yale University, 1974.

LEVINE, R., & LeVine, B. Nyansongo: A Gusii community in Kenya. In B. Whiting (Ed.), *Six cultures: Studies of child rearing*. New York: John Wiley, 1963.

LIEBERMAN, J.N. *Playfulness: Its relationship to imagination and creativity*. New York: Academic Press, 1977.

LOIZOS, C. Play behavior in higher primates: A review. In D. Morris (Ed.), *Primate ethology*. Garden City, NY: Doubleday Press, 1969. (Originally published, 1967.)

MACCOBY, E.E. Role-taking in childhood and its consequences for social learning. *Child Development*, 1959, **30**, 239-252.

MACKAY, R. Conceptions of children and models of socialization. In R. Turner (Ed.), *Ethnomethodology*. Harmondsworth, England: Penguin, 1974.

MALINOWSKI, B. *A scientific theory of culture*. New York: Oxford University Press, 1960. (Originally published, 1944.)

MARETZKI, T., & Maretzki, H. Taira: An Okinawan village. In B. Whiting (Ed.), *Six cultures: Studies of child rearing.* New York: John Wiley, 1963.

MARSHALL, L. *The !Kung of Nyae Nyae.* Cambridge: Harvard University Press, 1976.

MAYER, P. (Ed.). *Socialization: The approach from social anthropology.* A.S.A. Monograph #8. London: Tavistock, 1970.

MEAD, G.H. *Mind, self and society.* Chicago: University of Chicago Press, 1934.

MEAD, M. An investigation of the thought of primitive children with special reference to animism. *Journal of the Royal Anthropological Institute,* 1932, **62,** 173-190. (Reprinted in R. Hunt [Ed.], *Personalities and cultures.* Garden City, NY: Natural History Press, 1967.)

MEAD, M. *Sex and temperament.* New York: Dell, 1963. (Originally published, 1935.)

MEAD, M. Socialization and enculturation. *Current Anthropology,* 1963, **4,** 184-188.

NORBECK, E. Man at play. *Natural History* (Special Supplement on Play), December 1971, pp. 48-53.

NYDEGGER, W., & Nydegger, C. Tarong: An Ilocos barrio in the Philippines. In B. Whiting (Ed.), *Six cultures: Studies of child rearing.* New York: John Wiley, 1963.

OPIE, I., & Opie, P. *The lore and language of school children.* Oxford: Oxford University Press, 1959.

ORTNER, S.B. Is female to male as nature is to culture. In M.Z. Rosaldo & L. Lamphere (Eds.), *Woman, culture and society.* Stanford: Stanford University Press, 1974.

PULASKI, M.A. Toys and imaginative play. In J.L. Singer (Ed.), *The child's world of make-believe.* New York: Academic Press, 1973.

RADCLIFFE-BROWN, A.R. *A natural science of society.* Glencoe, IL: Free Press, 1957.

RADCLIFFE-BROWN, A.R. *Structure and function in primitive society.* New York: Free Press, 1968. (Originally published, 1952.)

RAUM, O. *Chaga childhood.* London: Oxford University Press, 1940.

RIESSMAN, F. The overlooked positives of disadvantaged groups. *Journal of Negro Education,* 1964, **33,** 225-231.

ROBERTS, J.M., Arth, M.J., & Bush, R.R. Games in culture. *American Anthropologist,* 1959, **61,** 597-605.

ROBERTS, J.M., & Sutton-Smith, B. Child training and game involvement. *Ethnology,* 1962, **2,** 166-185.

ROBERTS, J.M., & Sutton-Smith, B. Cross-cultural correlates of games of chance. *Behavior Science Notes,* 1966, **1,** 131-144.

ROBERTS, J.M., Sutton-Smith, B., & Kendon, A. Strategy in games and folk tales. *Journal of Social Psychology*, 1963, **61**, 185-199.

ROBINSON, C. Sex-typed behavior in children's spontaneous play. *The Association for the Anthropological Study of Play Newsletter*, 1978, **4**, 14-17.

ROSALDO, M.Z., & Lamphere, L. (Eds.). *Woman, culture and society*. Stanford: Stanford University Press, 1974.

ROTH, W.E. Games, sports, and amusements. *North Queensland Ethnography*, 1902, Bulletin No. 4.

SCHWARTZMAN, H.B., & Barbera, L. Children's play in Africa and South America: A review of the ethnographic literature. In D.F. Lancy & B.A. Tindall (Eds.), *The anthropological study of play: Problems and prospects*. Cornwall, NY: Leisure Press, 1976.

SINGER, J.L. *The child's world of make-believe: Experimental studies of imaginative play*. New York: Academic Press, 1973.

SINGER, J.L., & Singer, D. Imaginative play and pretending in early childhood: Some experimental approaches. In A. Davids (Ed.), *Child personality and psychopathology* (Vol. 3). New York: John Wiley, 1976.

SMILANSKY, S. *The effects of sociodramatic play on disadvantaged preschool children*. New York: John Wiley, 1968.

SMILANSKY, S. Can adults facilitate play in children? Theoretical and practical considerations. In *Play: The child strives toward self-realization*. Washington, DC: National Association for the Education of Young Children, 1971.

SPIRO, M.E. *Children of the kibbutz*. New York: Schocken, 1965. (Originally published, 1958.)

SUTTON-SMITH, B. *The games of New Zealand children*. Berkeley: University of California Press, 1959. (Reprinted in B. Sutton-Smith, *The folkgames of children*. Austin: University of Texas Press, 1972.)

SUTTON-SMITH, B. Role replication and reversal in play. *Merrill-Palmer Quarterly of Behavior and Development*, 1966, **12**, 285-298. (Reprinted in B. Sutton-Smith, *The folkgames of children*. Austin: University of Texas Press, 1972.)

SUTTON-SMITH, B. The two cultures of games. In B. Sutton-Smith, *The folkgames of children*. Austin: University of Texas Press, 1972.

SUTTON-SMITH, B. Toward an anthropology of play. *The Association for the Anthropological Study of Play Newsletter*, 1974, **1**, 8-15. (Reprinted in B. Sutton-Smith, *The dialectics of play*. Schorndoff, West Germany: Verlag Hoffman, 1976.)

SUTTON-SMITH, B. *The dialectics of play*. Schorndoff, West Germany: Verlag Hoffman, 1976.

SUTTON-SMITH, B. Play, games and sports: Socialization or innovation? In P. Stevens (Ed.), *Studies in the anthropology of play: Papers in memory of B. Allan Tindall*. Cornwall, NY: Leisure Press, 1977.

SUTTON-SMITH, B., & Roberts, J.M. Rubrics of competitive behavior. *Journal of Genetic Psychology*, 1964, **105**, 13-37.

SUTTON-SMITH, B., & Roberts, J.M. Studies in an elementary game of strategy. *Genetic Psychology Monographs*, 1967, **75**, 3-42.

SUTTON-SMITH, B., & Roberts, J.M. The cross-cultural and psychological study of games. In G. Lüschen (Ed.), *The cross-cultural analysis of games.* Champaign, IL: Stipes, 1970.

SUTTON-SMITH, B., Roberts, J.M., & Rosenberg, B.G. Sibling association and role involvement. *Merrill-Palmer Quarterly*, 1964, **10**, 25-38.

TURNBULL, C. *The forest people.* New York: Simon & Schuster, 1961.

TURNER, V. *The ritual process: Structure and anti-structure.* Chicago: Aldine, 1969.

TURNER, V. Liminal to liminoid in play, flow, and ritual: An essay in comparative symbology. In E. Norbeck (Ed.), The Anthropological study of human play. *Rice University Studies*, 1974, **60**, 53-92.

WHITING, B.B., & Edwards, C.P. A cross-cultural analysis of sex differences in the behavior of children aged 3-11. *Journal of Social Psychology*, 1973, **91**, 171-188.

WITHERS, C. Current events in New York City children's folklore. *New York Folklore Quarterly*, 1947, **3**, 213-222.

Chapter 18

Play, Games, and Sport: Developmental Implications for Young People

JAY J. COAKLEY

T he participation of youngsters in organized sport programs has increased dramatically over the past two decades. Until recently, few people questioned this trend; it was usually assumed that participation in sport was wholesome and conducive to normal child development (especially for males). But during the past few years, organized sports have elicited considerable criticism. They have been accused of being overly competitive, work-oriented, funless programs causing participants to become anxiety-ridden failures or cynical sport specialists. The proponents of the programs have consistently responded with equally extreme statements about the positive consequences of participation.

Project Description and Methodology

This paper attempts to provide information for those interested in starting to untangle the complex developmental implications of a young per-

From *Journal of Sport Behavior*, 1980, 3(3), 99-118. Copyright 1980 by the United States Sports Academy. Reprinted with permission.

son's involvement in various types of physical activities. In searching for an answer for those who ask if parents should encourage their sons and daughters to become involved in organized sports, my students and I observed and talked to hundreds of youngsters (under 14 years old) about their personal experiences in physical activities.[1] However, we did not limit our attention to the participants in organized programs. We made observations and conducted informal interviews in a variety of settings in which physical activity and movement were prevalent.

Our major concern was to discover if the types of experiences, and the subjective meanings assigned to those experiences varied with the characteristics of the contexts in which they emerged. After a few attempts to make observations and talk to children involved in physical activities, it was discovered that there were numerous varieties of participation contexts and that it would be difficult to look at samples of each of them. For example, participation in an organized *team* sport program may occur in regular scheduled games, practice games, tournament games, all-star games, scrimmage games, practices with the coach present, practices without the coach, practices in which drills are run, and those in which sides are selected and competitive games played, and so on. There was a similar variety of participation settings for those involved in organized *individual* sport programs such as tennis, track and field, figure skating, gymnastics, etc. Variations were also noted in the numerous informal activity settings unrelated to organized sport programs.

Our solution was to limit the initial investigation to a few well-defined, distinguishable physical activity settings. Since most of the literature on this general topic ultimately distinguishes between play, games, and sport, we decided to focus on three specific contexts:

1. Spontaneous play (i.e., participant initiated, vigorous or relatively complex physical activities in which action is not governed by pre-established rules).

2. Informal games (i.e., participant controlled, competitive physical activities governed at least partially by pre-established rules related to expectations for collective and individual behavior).

3. Organized team sport events (i.e., regular season, scheduled games between two official teams in a formally established league).

As would be expected, we had no difficulty locating and observing organized team sport events. In fact, nearly 100 undergraduate sociology students observed at least one game each and talked with a minimum of two of the participants involved in each game (one from each team). The different organized sports included in the observations were football, boys' soccer, girls' soccer, hockey, boys' baseball, and girls' softball.[2]

Unlike organized sport, neither informal games nor spontaneous play necessarily involve any vigorous or complex physical activity or movement. Because of this, it took some time and ingenuity to track down the occurrence of informal games but eventually most of the student-observers were successful in making at least one observation. The games most frequently observed occurred on elementary school playgrounds during recess periods. Others were observed in popular gathering places in residential areas, especially in small neighborhood parks, vacant lots and large private yards.

Spontaneous play situations, especially those involving physical activity, are difficult to observe. The students quickly learned that by their very nature, spontaneous activities of any type tend to defy prediction. Some of the more patient students were able to view clearcut cases of spontaneous play on school playgrounds and in preschool and child-care facilities. Others were able to observe a neighbor's or their own children playing in or around their homes. An additional methodological problem interfering with the completion of observations of spontaneous play was that the presence of observer, even a relatively unobtrusive one, often tended to stifle the continuation of the activity by many of the older participants, especially when they were involved in solitary play.

Because of the exploratory nature of our project, observational categories were general and the recording of specific events was largely determined by the individual observers. Listed below are the categories which guided observations and in which information was recorded:[3]

- amount of time devoted to initiating the activity
- key factors in sustaining action
- formulation and application of rules
- the nature of interpersonal relationships (support, disagreement, hostility, assistance)
- displays of satisfaction or disappointment
- status hierarchy
- incidence of deviance
- locus of decision-making and social control
- tension management (solution of arguments)
- reasons for breakdowns in or completion of action
- total action time

Although observer biases undoubtedly influenced the recording of information (in spite of our in-class training discussions), it is likely that they served primarily to emphasize the positive aspects of the activities in each of the three settings. The reason for this is that the students tended to devote the largest proportion of their observational time to the activity setting they most preferred.

In all, 252 observations were recorded and included in the analysis (121 organized team sport events, 84 informal games, and 47 cases of spontaneous play). Unfortunately, thère was no precise record of the characteristics of the young people observed and interviewed. However, feedback from the student-observers permits some general statements to be made. Participants were predominantly white with no more than 10% being black or chicano.[4] Socioeconomic status was difficult to determine but it was generally concluded that participants came from lower-middle to upper-middle income families. Boys tended to outnumber girls in each of the activity contexts by a ratio of 2-1. The age range of participants in organized sport programs and informal games was 6-13 years old, with the majority being 10-12 years old. In spontaneous play, the age range was about 3-12 years old. Observed cases of spontaneous play among children over 8 years old were rare and they were likely to be discontinued when the observer was noticed, even when the observer was a parent or an older brother or sister of one of the participants.

The verbal data from the participants were collected primarily as a source of clarification for what was recorded during the observations. They were the "insiders' explanations" of things such as rules, emotional displays, decision-making procedures, responses to deviance, types of sanctions used, etc. Because questions were related to the specific event, these data varied greatly within and between each of the three types of activity contexts. However, there was an attempt to obtain some comparable data by asking two relatively standard questions to each of the participants with whom there was a conversation. The students could alter the wording of the questions to fit the specific setting but the focus was always on (a) what the participant enjoyed most about the activity (i.e., the thing making it the most fun) and (b) what the biggest source of problems was in the activity (i.e., the thing most likely to keep the activity from being fun).

Findings

The initial data analysis was done by hand in an attempt to capture all of the descriptive material recorded by the observers.[5] The goal was to construct separate models for each of the activity contexts and to assess the models in terms of their implications for socialization and development. The analysis clearly demonstrated that the structure and dynamics of the activities and the patterns of participant experiences varied considerably according to the contexts in which they occurred. Table 1 summarizes these variations along 10 major dimensions.[6] Although the information in the table should not be surprising to anyone familiar with the literature on play and games, it does provide a basis for comparing the experience

Table 1

Dimensions of Experience in Spontaneous Play, Informal Competitive Games, and Organized Team Sport Events

Dimensions of Experience	Spontaneous Play	Informal Games	Organized Team Sport Event
I. Basis of Action	A search for mastery, a use of imagination, and a coincidental meshing of personal interests and/or role playing activities	Prior experiences and existing social relationships coupled with the interpersonal and decision-making abilities of group members	Predesigned system of roles, adult leadership, and the collective role learning abilities of team members
II. Norms Governing Actions	Emergent and created to meet personal standards, interest, and/or to simulate imagined role relationships	Carried over from past experience with changes and qualifications based on individual needs and maintenance of uncertainty	Highly formalized and specific, serving both organizational needs and formal team goals
III. System of Social Control	Internally generated and dependent on individual role playing and role taking interests and abilities	Generally internal and dependent on the collective vested interests in the game at hand	Partially internal but heavily maintained by formal standards enforced by external agents and dependent on the compliance of players
IV. Types of Sanctions Used	Self-imposed on a token basis or informally administered when a scene is disrupted	Informal and primarily used to minimize threats to the maintenance of action, personal involvement, and uncertainty	Both informal and formal and used for the preservation of values as well as order

Table 1 (Cont.)

V. Basis of Group Integration	Generally coincidental and dependent on a continual commitment to and overlap of the roles played by each of the individuals involved	Generally based on the strength of personal relationships combined with a process of social exchange between group members	Based on a combination of collective satisfaction and an awareness of and compliance with a formal set of norms and role expectations
VI. Meanings Attached to Actions and Events	Emergent, nebulus, and vary with each individual's conception of what is or should be going on	Personal, situational, and related to the intensity of action and the social implications of the experience	Often serious, assuming relevance beyond the game itself, and frequently related to instrumental concerns
VII. Nature of Status Structure	Intrinsic and vary with each individual's personal experience	Primarily intrinsic and dependent on each individual's assessment of personal involvement and success	Both intrinsic and extrinsic; related to the experience itself, the quality of performance and/or game outcomes
VIII. Basis of Status Structure	Combination of age, individual creative abilities, and arbitrary situational distinctions	Age combined with interpersonal and physical abilities	Physical abilities, contributions to team success, and conformity to the coach's expectations
IX. Extent of Individual Freedom	Limited only by self-imposed restrictions with involvement voluntary at all times	Variable with restrictions related to individual physical skills and prior status within the group	Variable but restricted to the range of behavior accepted within the rules and expectations of the coach
X. Amount of Structural Stability	Variable and depends on the time span over which collective involvement can be maintained	Relatively high and grounded in prior group experiences and the anticipation of future games	Very high and grounded in the endorsement of adults and the formal goals of the team

differences between spontaneous play, informal games, and organized sport programs. A further explanation of these contexts is necessary to discuss the possible developmental implications of each.

A. Spontaneous Play

Observations of 47 cases of spontaneous play along with the usable verbal data from the participants indicated that the action in play is clearly based on the expressive feelings of the participants.[7] For example, a 9-year-old girl, when asked what made her play activity the most fun, responded by saying that "it's what I feel like doing." In spontaneous play, the expressive feelings of those involved are embodied in the frequently heavy use of imagination. But underlying the feelings and the imagination there was often an indication of a search for self-mastery, i.e., an attempt to create a situation or to perform an action up to some *personal* standard of satisfaction.

Because of its heavy basis in personal interest and in the use of imagination, spontaneous play only rarely involved the interaction of more than three or four individuals. Sharing an imaginary scene or locating others with identical personal interests was apparently difficult. Sometimes it was possible to "instill" interests in one or two others but the recruiting of more than a couple of playmates was unlikely. Part of the reason for this was that most of the play situations were not complex enough to demand the simultaneous involvement of more than 2-4 *real* people.

Furthermore, over 30% ($N = 16$) of the spontaneous play activities involved a solitary participant.[8] The interaction in the observed play situations was generally not so much a product of role taking (i.e., putting yourself in the positions of each of the others) as it was a coincidental meshing of two or more individual lines of role playing or role modeling behaviors. However, there were two relatively common exceptions to this. One occurred in cases in which an individual participant was clearly dominant in the relationships involved and tried to effectively control the actions of the others. The second exception occurred when one participant had a strong commitment to maintaining the action while the other(s) wanted to withdraw. In both of these cases, there was a necessity for anticipating the abilities and interests of the other participants so that the desired scene or action could be created and/or maintained. Related to these two exceptions, interview responses to the question on the biggest problem in the activity indicated that the major obstacle to having fun in play was the absence of others wanting to play, i.e., to do the same thing "I" want to do. In many cases, what this meant was that the nonoccurrence or the cessation of the activity itself was the major problem.

Since spontaneous play has a focus on expressive action and is based on personal interest, social control is likely to be internal. The observers noted that as long as interest remained high and role playing abilities met minimum requirements, social control in any external overt form was absent. Sanctions were rare and when play action was in progress they were used cautiously to avoid turning off fellow participants to the point where they might withdraw. Only when the action was viewed as impossible to initiate or when it was already approaching an end were sanctions administered with an intent to damage the feelings of others. In a few cases, sanctions were self-imposed and took the form of token verbal reprimands for something done wrong (e.g.: "Am I ever dumb!" "Why did 'you' do that?").

Meanings attached to play experiences could not usually be inferred by observers nor were they easily articulated by participants. The activities were ends-in-themselves. Even when self-mastery was being sought, success seemed to be imminent because evaluative standards were defined by each participant for himself/herself; if failure was experienced, it seemed easy for players to alter expectations so that it would not be likely the next time.

Status structures in play groups were informal and usually based on a combination of age and creative abilities. The oldest and/or the most clever in maintaining captivating play action was the most likely to initiate decisions although consensus was required before they would be followed. Observers noted that a couple of creative players and an interesting activity could maintain spontaneous play for hours. However, the range of action times for play situations was very wide with some lasting only minutes. The length of action time depended solely on the extent to which continued personal and/or collective involvement could be maintained.

B. Informal Games

The observation of 84 cases of informal games and the associated verbal data indicated the primary focus in such activities was on the initiation and maintenance of a combination of action, personal involvement, a close contest, and the reaffirmation of friendships. In the majority of games observed, the number of participants was relatively small, ranging from 2-12. However, there were 31 cases of games on school playgrounds during recess periods in which the number of participants exceeded 12, but when the number went beyond 20, other games were usually started to handle the "extras." The participants generally knew one another quite well and had played the same or similar games on previous occasions. It was probably because of this that the games were preceded by little "organization time." In most cases, teams were quickly constructed on the basis of two considerations: (1) skill differences and (2) friendship patterns. Only occasionally was there a process of systematically choosing players one by one.

The games and game rules were usually based on popular game models but contained many modifications to maximize action and involvement and to preserve stimulating competition (i.e., a chance to win for both teams). However, there were frequent cases in which friendship patterns were given a higher priority in team construction than a desire for stimulating competition. For the most part, the modification of game models and traditional rules served to heighten and sustain an uninterrupted flow of action. For example, free throws were often eliminated in all forms of basketball games, throw-ins were minimized in soccer games, yardage penalties eliminated in football, pitcher's mound distance altered in all types of softball and baseball games so that hitting was always likely. Similar rule structures were observed in varieties of kickball, team 4-square, 4-square, 2-square, 1-wall handball, street hockey, "ultimate frisbee," tennis, volleyball, and other games for which there are no common names. Further documentation for the emphasis on action was the extremely high scores in all but a few of the games.

The personal involvement of each of the players was promoted by sometimes complex sets of rule qualifications and handicap systems. The more highly skilled players were often prevented from dominating the game action by being given restrictive handicaps; the less skilled players were given advantages. Furthermore, these latter players seemed to be given implicit permission to use special rules in their own favor. In cases of doubt about what actually happened or should have happened in a game, they were most likely to use "do over" and "interference" calls so that they could either get another chance or lower the implications of their lower skill levels for game outcomes. This seemed to save them some personal embarrassment and allow their integrity as "contributing team members" to be preserved. Preventing the overuse of special rules was not usually necessary but when it was, it was done informally through jests or verbal barbs.

The emphasis on personal involvement was embodied in rules like "no called strikes" in baseball, the rule allowing everyone to be eligible to receive a pass in football, and other rules allowing the "little kids to have a chance." In fact, the question which asked participants what it was that made the game the most fun elicited answers such as "getting chances" to hit, catch, run with the ball, kick it, score, serve it often, etc.

Individual and collective commitment to action and personal involvement provided the basis for social control during the game. Sanctions were informal and were employed to discourage interruptions of the action or the destruction of involvement for individual participants. Joking around and cases of deviance were not absent from informal games but they were only defined as problems to be coped with when they jeopardized the flow of action. Observers noted that any number of different performance styles such as batting left-handed, throwing around-the-back passes, running unplanned pass patterns, moving out of position, etc., were all accepted in the games as long as action was not destroyed. In line with this, players with the highest amounts of skill were allowed the greatest amount of freedom to play "as the spirit moved them." At the same time, such freedom seemed to give the older and high-ability participants a means through which their interest could be sustained.

The verbal data indicated that the meanings attached to game action and events were personal and had direct connection with the nature of the action in the game, the sharing of action with friends, or the personal performance displays occurring at various times during the action. Rewards were primarily intrinsic but they were occasionally tied into achievement-related self-assessments of involvement and success. Visible extrinsic rewards were limited to immediate feedback from peers.

The status structure among players in the informal games was usually important because it determined the extent to which individuals would participate in decision-making processes during the game. Generally, the older players or those with the best physical skills were accorded the highest status but there were cases observed in which individuals who were adept at handling interpersonal relationships were heavily involved in decision-making processes, especially when arguments occurred.

Surprisingly to most of the observers, arguments were not very frequent. Over 50% ($N = 44$) of the games observed did not have an argument lasting long enough to slow down the normal flow of action in the game. In the remaining games, arguments occurred but they were solved in all but about 9% ($N = 8$) of the total cases. Players had apparently played together often enough so that maintaining the game to some logical end point was not a problem. Interestingly, the single major factor interrupting a game before it reached its logical end point was the intervention of an adult who informed one or more of the players that it was time to quit.

C. Organized Team Sport Events

The observations of 121 regular season games in organized programs coupled with clarifying verbal data from over 242 participants indicated that the structure and the meaning of the experiences in such games were unique when compared to the other two activity settings. Participants in the organized games remained interested in action and personal involvement but they were more serious and more likely to couch their interests in a concern with individual and team efficiency and the outcomes of games. According to the observers, the most apparent aspect of the games was that both action and involvement were under adult control and the behavior of the players was strictly patterned by specialized rules and roles. This was brought out in the verbal data when the players readily identified themselves by the positions they played and seemed to take pride in being a defensive this or an offensive that, or a center forward, or left winger or catcher, etc. This was even characteristic among players who did not get in the games for more than a short period of time. The importance of positions was further emphasized by adults, both coaches and spectators, who frequently encouraged players to "stay in position" (especially common in soccer, hockey, and occasionally in girls' softball).

The actual play of the game was governed by time schedules, the weather, and the setting of the sun. Individual playing time for the participants generally varied according to skill levels. Most often it was the smaller, visibly timid, and less skilled children who sat on the sidelines. Although everyone usually got into the game for at least a short period of time, those whose action time was low often maintained only a token interest in the game, and while on the sidelines, seemed to be generally bored with the whole situation or interested in things unrelated to the game. Those whose skill level was high were most likely to exhibit strong game interest and express visible disappointment at being taken out of the action. When they were taken out, they stayed close to the coach and waited or asked to be put back into the game.

An additional consequence of adult control and high degree of organization was the visible absence of arguments and overt displays of hostility between *the players*. The few cases in which arguments did occur were between members of the same team and the cause was generally a player's inability to stay in position, play it efficiently, or carry out a preplanned pattern of game strategy. Adult control and the degree of organization also seemed to have an effect on the visible display of affection and friendship during the play of the game. The exceptions to this were observed during halftime breaks and the half of the inning during which a team came to bat in baseball and softball. However, the nature of interpersonal relationships seemed to have little relevance for what happened in the game itself.

The major manifest function of game rules seemed to be the standardization of competition and the control of player behavior. The impact of the rules on the extent of action and involvement was most apt to take the form of an interruption but there were few visible indications from the players that they resented this fact. The only displays of being annoyed occurred when the delay was related to a penalty call against their team. Rule enforcement was always in the hands of adults and the applications of rules were based on universalistic criteria, i.e., there were no visible exceptions made taking into consideration individual abilities or characteristics.

The compliance of participants was extremely high and deviance resulted most often from a player not knowing or forgetting what to do rather than from a desire to gain an unfair advantage. On the playing field, the observed cases of deviance were generally accompanied by formal sanctions regardless of whether they had an effect on game action or on the success of the team. Off the field, norms varied from team to team. When deviance occurred, it usually took the form of "joking around" or exhibiting a blatant lack of interest in the game or the team. Responses to these behaviors were also varied. Sometimes sanctions were nonverbal and other times they took the form of requests to stop or actual commands to do something else. In all, the game rules and team rules were used to not only control behavior; they were also used to apparently preserve the system of organization in the game and the values underlying the authority of referees and coaches.

The observations and the verbal data indicated that the players were generally serious but that excessive concerns about personal performance standards and game outcomes were not characteristic. Interestingly, such concerns were most likely to be visibly manifested by the highly skilled players and among members of the most successful teams. In other words, the outward emphasis on performance and victory was highest for those who performed best and won most frequently. Among the majority of others, participation was described in terms of intrinsic rewards. Similarly, the disappointment associated with a specific game (or an entire season of team membership) was usually related to personal opportunities to play in games. Of course, a desire to play more is not always just related to intrinsic rewards. Playing for the better part of a game or making a starting team may be a channel for gaining many extrinsic rewards from peers, parents, and others. Lastly, players were almost always able to provide an exact statement of their team record and what that meant in the league standings.

The formal status structure on the organized teams seemed to be ultimately dependent on the coach's assessment of relative physical abilities and the potential for contributing to team success. It was also observed that the better players were sometimes given more responsibility on the team and more latitude in determining what they would do during the game. In general, it was physical skill and coach acknowledgment that was at the basis of the status and the individual autonomy of the players.

Summary and Conclusions

Although the data collected in the pilot project do not provide a definite answer to the question of whether a person should encourage his/her children to play organized sports, they do point out that there are major differences between organized sports and other settings in which physical activity occurs. If the activity occurs in spontaneous play it will tend to be characterized by a high degree of expression and individual freedom and involve the use of imagination and creative skills and efforts focused on extending one's personal range of self-mastery. Informal competitive games, on the other hand, are characterized by strong concern for action and personal involvement and depend heavily on the interpersonal and decision-making abilities and the organizational skills of the participants. Finally, organized team sports events are characterized by adult control and formally organized interaction with personal involvement (a central concern of most participants) closely related to individual physical skills and the abilities to learn the roles through which skills are displayed.

Unfortunately, the data do not deal directly with developmental factors but they strongly suggest that the developmental implications of involvement in organized sport programs are considerably different than what they might be in play and informal games. Most importantly, the organized sport experience consists of individual and collective responses of children to a relatively serious, adult-controlled, formally established system of rules and relationships. In light of the literature on the developmental benefits of play and informal games, this is an important point to consider. The research on play and games has consistently emphasized the significant development implications of participant control as well as the absence of factors which increase the "reality consequences" (i.e., the psychological risks associated with evaluative feedback from influential others) of the young person's involvement in the activity.

The importance of participant control was recognized by Piaget (1951) when he pointed out that the value of play lies in the opportunities it affords a child to alter reality so that it corresponds with his/her unique conceptions of the world. Similarly, Erikson (1963) emphasized individual experimentation, exploration, and the creation of "model situations" as the means through which a child learns to cope with experience and master reality. Recent discussions of play and individual development have merely supported and re-emphasized these points made by Piaget and Erikson (see Ciuciu, 1974; Devereux, 1976; Ellis, 1973; Kleiber, 1976; Peller, 1971; Polgar, 1976; Stone, 1965; Suttie & Shearer, 1976; Wade, 1976; Watson, 1976, 1977). Although research has not been able to pinpoint precisely how the development process occurs through play and games it does suggest that if an activity setting does not allow for the manipulation and control of the environment by those involved, it is unlikely to provide anything beyond a relatively restricted learning experience. According to Brian Sutton-Smith, any activity setting not subject to participant control generally involves behavior based on an "objective accommodation" to a given set of conditions rather than a "subjective assimilation" of those conditions for the purpose of using them to meet personal objectives. In other words, spontaneous play and informal games characteristically involve a subjective internalization of the elements of the activity setting, while organized sport characteristically involves a response conforming to expectations which are grounded in a system or organization and adult leadership. The former experience would seem to contribute to the development of an ability to create, organize, and change while the latter would seem to contribute to the development of obedience, conformity to authority, and an ability to meet expectations in highly structured settings. These are very similar to conclusions made by Sutton-Smith (1975) and Sage (1978) in their respective discussions of play and organized sport. Sutton-Smith points out that the learning which occurs in play is most useful when the future is characterized by uncertainty and when there is a need for a person to be flexible and maintain "a wide repertoire of potential responses up his sleeve" (1975, p. 214). However, according to Sutton-Smith, the play experience has little to offer "if the pressures of adaptation require a very clear cut response" (1975, p. 214). Related to this latter point, Sage has recently argued that the organized sport experience "is substantially influential in producing . . . the bureaucratic personality" (1978, p. 12).

In the project, the absence of arguments and even the potential for arguments in organized sport would seem to be strongly related to these inferred developmental consequences of participant control. Because play and informal games generate issues and conflict situations that threaten their existence, participants gain experiences in not only anticipating and preventing arguments but they also have the opportunity to deal with differences and disagreements in a setting in which they themselves must directly face the consequences of their solutions. They learn that their solutions are necessary for the continuation of the activity and that they cannot base those solutions on coercion without creating severe negative side effects jeopardizing the long and short-term future of the activity. In organized sport programs, arguments about judgments or the appropriateness of rules and procedures do not occur between players because of the universalistic applications and interpretations of norms by referees and coaches. Therefore, the experience in play and informal games emphasizes interpersonal skills (negotiations and compromise), while the experience in organized sport emphasizes a knowledge and dependence on strict rules and the acceptance of the decisions of others in positions of legitimate authority. This seems to be very consistent with the conclusions made by Sutton-Smith (1975) and Sage (1978).

In addition to participant control, another important element of play and informal games is that they afford children opportunities to create, experiment with, and alter their involvement in physical activities without the threat of high reality consequences. For example, Kleiber points out that a "game situation with its separateness from reality and limiting boundaries allows for self-expression and experimentation in a safe context with peers who are making judgments only in that context" (1976, p. 69). Of course, neither organized sport programs nor adult supervision inevitably increase the reality consequences of involvement to a point where they stifle creativity, self-expression, and experimentation, but according to observations in our project, they have a tendency to do so. With a general participant awareness of factors such as team records, the relative amounts of playing times in games, and both formal and informal evaluative feedback from adults who favorably respond to technique and performance, a participant is quite likely to limit his/her range of expression and experimentation to maximize immediate and visible success experiences.[9] Thus, organized programs would seem to emphasize the utility of cautious, achievement-oriented, "professional" attitudes among participants (see also Maloney & Petrie, 1972; Petrie, 1971; Webb, 1969; Mantel & Vander Velden, Note 1).

The way many of the participants in the organized programs responded to questions about team practices, one of the components of this "professional attitude" may be a strong tendency to distinguish between the *process* of achieving a goal and actual achievement. Practices were often viewed as the *means* to preparing oneself and the team for meeting expectations in games. It would seem that as the reality consequences of participation increased there would be associated increases in the development of priorities in which a product orientation would exist at the expense of a process orientation. In other words, the formal games are fun, the practices are generally not; the achievement rests in the actual meeting of a challenge rather than in preparing for it. In the cases of play and informal competitive games, the goal orientation of the participants was unlikely to lead to a distinction between process and product; achievement rested primarily in maintaining the activity, i.e., the process of involvement. Evaluative standards were relative to that process rather than being based on external sources. This seemed to give the participants a wide range of opportunities to express themselves and to experiment with personal styles and techniques; reality consequences were low.

The developmental implications of differences in the level of reality consequences are vague at best. The higher reality consequences in organized sport may ultimately emphasize the development of a strong product orientation coupled with a dependence on external sources of evaluative feedback for advice and evaluation, and the tendency to value caution and specialization as the most appropriate methods of achieving success. The lower reality consequences of informal games and especially spontaneous play may ultimately emphasize the development of a strong process orientation coupled with a reliance on self-evaluation and the tendency to value and utilize diversified and general abilities in coping with reality.

Before concluding, it should be pointed out that this discussion on developmental implications must be carefully interpreted. For example, levels of adult control and reality consequences may vary in organized programs. Furthermore, individual experiences in such programs are likely to vary greatly; general patterns do exist but individual consequences depend on a variety of factors, including program structure, parental and peer influence and length of involvement. General patterns exist in spontaneous play and informal games but there will be experience differences from situation to situation depending on the nature of interpersonal relationships, the prior experiences of participants, and the organizational characteristics of the activities themselves (such as the number of participants, complexity of rules, the diversity of roles, etc.).

Fortunately, the experiences of many young people are not usually limited to only one of these activity settings. If the experiences in each do, in fact, lead to different developmental consequences, then it may be that the most beneficial involvement pattern would consist of participation in all of the settings. This possibility raises important questions regarding the relationships between play, games, and sport. It may be that they are different enough activities that their developmental consequences will not always be complementary and that extended participation in one will eventually preclude involvement in one or both of the other settings.[10] This latter prospect has led Devereux (1976) to discuss the growth of organized sport and the associated "impoverishment" of play and informal games among young people. Janet Lever (1978) has recently made the case that for young girls to confine themselves to simple, undifferentiated play and noncompetitive games may make it difficult later to become successfully involved in more highly structured, complex activities.

In general, it seems that if play and informal games have something positive to offer, increased efforts should be made to encourage and precipitate them whenever possible (without destroying participant control or increasing reality consequences). If organized sports provide developmental benefits, administrators and coaches should become more sensitive to why many children refrain from or discontinue participation. Programs should be altered so that wider participation is encouraged. It seems that the trend over the last 30 years has been to emphasize organized programs and heavily supervised game playing and to generally ignore the promotion of play and informal games. It may be that the media and our tendency to organize has begun to not only destroy an ability to create and sustain on-the-spot activities but also the desire to do so because such activities lack the formal requirements that have come to be defined as necessary for a sport event to occur. Therefore, if a uniform is not worn, if official equipment and facilities are unavailable, if the activity itself does not meet formal specifications, and if no referee is present, it is not worth doing—even if there were some young people around with the abilities to get the activity started.

Notes

1. This project was initially designed as a learning experience for the students in three different sections of an undergraduate sociology of sport course.
2. The observations were made over a 12-month period of time since the students were not all in the same class. There were three different classes spanning three successive semesters (including an 8-week summer session).
3. This list is by no means inclusive of all the dimensions of experience which might be observed in physical activity settings. The "final" set of categories we used in this set of observations was arrived at through a process shaped by pragmatic considerations along with an interest in the major components of social organization.

   Sociologists generally agree that the components of social organization include norms, roles, methods of social control, and a status hierarchy (see DeFleur, D'Antonio, and DeFleur, 1971, pp. 38-47). Furthermore, the dynamics of any ongoing social system are at least partially shaped by collective efforts to meet four functional imperatives: (1) pattern-maintenance and tension management, (2) integration, (3) goal attainment, and (4) adaptation (see Parsons [1966, p. 7]). These factors—the major components of social organization and the functional imperatives—served as the basis for the development of the categories.

   The additional categories related to time (organizing time and total action time) were included in the list because they could be measured with reasonable accuracy and because they were found to be negatively associated with the amount of external organization control in the group activities of children by Polgar (1976).

   The categories focusing on "the nature of interpersonal relationships" and "displays of satisfaction or disappointment" were included primarily to obtain some measure of the extent to which participants displayed expressive or instrumental behaviors.

   The final consideration was that the categories should sensitize the observers to a wide range of the experience dimensions characterizing the physical activities of children. This, of course, creates some significant methodological shortcomings in the project. The students were not all expert observers nor were the observational categories defined precisely enough or limited enough in scope to guarantee a highly reliable set of data. The categories were intended to serve as catalysts for awareness rather than an unalterable list of experience dimensions on which specific precoded observations could be made; in reality, no single observer could handle the systematic recording of data for each of the 11 categories.

4. Only in 5 cases in informal games was there an indication that race or ethnicity was a factor in the composition of teams. In each of those cases, it seemed as if race and/or ethnicity served as a basis for social ties which then became the basis for team selection procedures.

5. In addition to summarizing the recorded data, analysis was completed in three sessions with the three different groups of student-observers so that they could provide direct feedback in the final interpretation of their own observations. This occurred in small group settings (10-12 students) during which questions were raised and discussed. The outcome of these sessions took the form of the material in Table 1.

6. These 10 dimensions are directly related to the 13 categories which guided the student's observations. The dimensions focus primarily on the major social components of group activity.

7. The observed cases of spontaneous play involved a variety of physical actions including throwing, rolling, kicking, or hitting some kind of object; riding bikes or skateboards; playing on park equipment; dancing; skiing; tubing (on snow); diving or swimming; ice skating; doing gymnastics; among others.

8. These cases were included in the final analysis only if there was the "presence" of an imaginary other person during the activity.

9. Most of the observers reported that beyond the actual control exercised by adults, the mere presence of adults seemed to change the atmosphere surrounding the activity. This has also been noted by Brower (1978), Underwood (1978), and Yablonsky and Brower (1979).

10. The relationship between organized programs and informal games may be quite complex. Our observations indicated that activities and game models were often influenced by events receiving media coverage and the types of organized sports in which youth involvement is relatively high. It may be that the media and organized programs provide the knowledge of game models and initial incentives to try the games informally but there may also be a severe limiting of activity and game diversity in this process.

Reference Note

1. Mantel, R.C., & Vander Velden, L. *The relationship between the professionalization of attitude toward play of pre-adolescent boys and participation in organized sport.* Paper presented at Third International Symposium on the Sociology of Sport, Waterloo, Ontario, 1971.

References

BROWER, J.J. Little League baseballism: Adult dominance in a child's game. In R. Martens (Ed.), *Joy and sadness in children's sports.* Champaign, IL: Human Kinetics, 1978.

CIUCIU, G. The socialization process of children by means of extemporized and organized games. *International Review of Sport Sociology*, 1974, 9(1), 7-18.

DEFLEUR, M., D'Antonio, W.V., & DeFleur, L. *Sociology: Man in society.* Glenview, IL: Scott, Foresman & Company, 1971.

DEVEREUX, E.C. Backyard versus Little League baseball: The impoverishment of children's games. In D.M. Landers (Ed.), *Social problems in athletics.* Urbana: University of Illinois, 1976.

ELLIS, M.J. *Why people play.* Englewood Cliffs, NJ: Prentice-Hall, 1973.

ERICKSON, E.H. *Childhood and society.* New York: W.W. Norton, 1963.

KLEIBER, D. Playing to learn. *Quest,* 1976, **26,** 68-74.

LEVER, J. Sex differences in the complexity of children's play. *American Sociological Review,* 1978, **43**(4), 471-483.

MALONEY, T.L., & Petrie, B. Professionalization of attitude toward play among Canadian school pupils as a function of sex, grade, and athletic participation. *Journal of Leisure Research,* 1972, **4,** 184-195.

PARSONS, T. *Societies.* Englewood Cliffs, NJ: Prentice-Hall, 1966.

PELLER, L.E. Models of children's play. In R.E. Herron & B. Sutton-Smith (Eds.), *Child's play.* New York: John Wiley, 1971.

PETRIE, B. Achievement orientations in adolescent attitudes toward play. *International Review of Sport Sociology,* 1971, **6,** 89-101.

PIAGET, J. *Play, dreams and imitation in childhood.* London: Routledge & Kegan Paul, 1951.

POLGAR, S.K. The social context of games: Or when is play not play? *Sociology of Education,* 1976, **49,** 265-272.

SAGE, G. American values and sport: Formation of a bureaucratic personality. *Journal of Physical Education and Recreation,* 1978, **49**(8), 42-44.

STONE, A. The play of little children. *Quest,* 1965, **4,** 23-31.

SUTTIE, S.J., & Shearer, H.L. Play behavior: From concepts to the play environment. *Quest,* 1976, **26,** 96-101.

SUTTON-SMITH, B. The useless made useful: Play as variability training. *School Review,* 1975, **83,** 197-214.

UNDERWOOD, J. Taking the fun out of a game. In R. Martens (Ed.), *Joy and sadness in children's sports.* Champaign, IL: Human Kinetics, 1978.

WADE, M.G. Method and analysis in the study of children's play behavior. *Quest,* 1976, **26,** 17-25.

WATSON, G.G. Reward systems in children's games: The attraction of game interaction in Little League baseball. *Review of Sport and Leisure,* 1976, **1,** 93-117.

WATSON, G.G. Games, socialization and parental values: Social class differences in parental evaluation of Little League baseball. *International Review of Sport Sociology,* 1977, **12**(1), 17-47.

WEBB, H. Professionalization of attitudes toward play among adolescents. In

G.S. Kenyon (Ed.), *Aspects of contemporary sport sociology*. North Palm Beach, FL: The Athletic Institute, 1969:

YABLONSKI, L., & Brower, J.J. *The Little League game*. New York: Times Books, 1979.

Part 5
Acculturation, Cultural Pluralism, Games and Sports

Chapter 19
Play and Inter-ethnic Communication[1]

CLAIRE R. FARRER

his paper is a report of an on-going research project. I would like to acknowledge the financial support of the Whitney M. Young, Jr. Memorial Foundation and the courtesy of Mr. Wendell Chino, President, Mescalero Apache Tribal Council, for allowing me to live and work among his people.

This paper makes two points: first—free play is a valuable, though largely neglected, tool for anthropologists, folklorists, and educators; second—research cooperation between social scientists and the people we study is becoming essential in the contemporary situation.

I am currently living and working on the Mescalero Apache Indian Reservation in southcentral New Mexico. This reservation was closed to

This article is a short version of the author's dissertation, "Play and Inter-ethnic Communication: A Practical Ethnography of the Mescalero Apache," University of Texas, Austin, 1977, and originally appeared in D.F. Laney & B.A. Tindall (Eds.), *The anthropological study of play: Problems and prospects.* (Proceedings of the first annual meeting of the Association for the Anthropological Study of Play.) Cornwall, NY: Leisure Press, 1976. Copyright 1976 by Claire Farrer. Reprinted with permission.

research workers for close to 20 years prior to my being allowed to work there beginning in 1974. Over a year's negotiation preceded permission being granted me to do my work. It is *still* closed without special Tribal permission. Ours is a business agreement: I am allowed to do the research which will form my PhD dissertation in anthropology and folklore in return for services I can provide which the Tribe needs. Specifically, I write graded reading materials, based upon Apache traditions and lifestyle, for first through sixth grade pupils in the reservation school. Additionally, as the situation has developed, I serve as an educational consultant for the Tribe. Our agreement further stipulates that I will not publish nor publicize information about the Mescalero people without first submitting the data to the Tribal Council for approval—and this paper has been through the Council. Should any royalties accrue, they will be divided equally between the Tribe and me. Further, my project is an applied one which, if the results are consistent with the report I'm giving today, will provide additional benefit to the people through increasing the communication between non-Indian teachers and Indian children. This is not to say there are no theoretical applications—quite the contrary, as will become obvious.

The point to which I am alluding is that we who study living populations as anthropologists—or as behavioral scientists in general—have entered a new era which finds those people we study taking a more active part in our research, from the design through to the result stages. This, I believe, is particularly true in the American Southwest where there is a new consciousness of both ethnic identity and power, as well as pride, among Native Americans and Spanish-speaking groups. While it necessitates changes in our basic orientation, I personally believe the new liaison produces data which are more reliable. At the same time, the liaison vastly increases rapport. My work is a case in point.

Since September 1974 I have been developing a technique that utilizes the free play of young children as a tool to improve communication between teachers and children from other than mainstream American backgrounds. For the purpose of my study, young children are those between the ages of 3 and 9 years. The inter-ethnic component is between non-Indian teachers and Native American children, specifically Mescalero Apache children. While I have data from other ethnic groups, these will not be considered because of time limits.

The guiding hypothesis of the study is that the free play activities of young children replicate the communication system they have been taught by their parents and, therefore:

1. Observation of free play activities will yield insights into values and how children have been taught to learn allowing,

2. Classroom teachers to re-structure teaching techniques and, if necessary, the physical environment of the classroom to take advantage

of the pre-existing, culture-specific communication patterns and, thereby,

3. More effectively communicate with children in their charge.

The investigation of the hypothesis and its corollary propositions required what I've called an ethnography of a playground. One segment of that ethnography, a game of tag, I'll discuss here.

First, however, let me remind you of standard, mainstream American tag games. When predominantly Anglo-American children play tag there is an initial period of negotiating who will be "it." The game proceeds in lines with the rectangular or square playground being utilized in a grid pattern of horizontal, vertical, and diagonal avenues. Rules are negotiated too. I often hear, "That's no fair!", or, "Janie's cheating!", or "You can't *do* that!". Tag, for mainstream American children, involves one's own personal space in which the child is encapsulated—even when several are involved in running from the "it" individual, each runs by him/herself. Touching another, other than in a tag move, is deemed an impediment to rapid progress. Tag is usually played with one's friends and is often an indicator of who likes whom.

Tag play at Mescalero, in contrast, is initiated in one of two ways: either children run from the building yelling "Not it!" and proceed to the tag area or they spontaneously break into a tag game as the result of one child tagging another on the jungle gym. The tag area for Mescalero Apache children is the jungle gym. I've not seen tag played on the ground. There are chasing games and "games" where one child will run up to another to hit, kick, or offer verbal abuse for a past wrong, real or imagined, but these are not tag games. However the game is initiated, a group of children—as few as three or as many as eight—will begin circling the jungle gym by moving left hand and foot to the left, then sliding the right hand and foot to the left to a position by the left ones which, in turn, move again. In other words, they stand on the lowest level of the jungle gym with their hands holding onto the next higher or second higher bar, depending upon their size. From this position they race around and around. Movement is to the left, clockwise. Oftentimes the children's bodies touch as they race around. However, a tag occurs only when the "it" person touches another's head (the preferred tag spot), shoulder, arm or leg in a deliberate movement. Bodies may be in continuous contact, but a tag is effected only when a child removes his/her hand from the bar and touches a particular place on another child.

At all times verbal interaction is minimal, even when the game isn't being played by the rules. For instance, occasionally a child will circle to the right, causing momentary confusion. Perhaps the counter-clockwise circling will last for one complete tag round, but not often. Usually counter-clockwise movement—or going through the bars of the jungle gym in a linear fashion—forces the game to disintegrate or causes it to stop momentarily so it can begin again "properly." When a child does go through rather than around, or when an "it" child moves around counter-clockwise, there is no verbal correction. The others either allow the aberrant movement or stop the game. There is, however, much giggling and laughter while the game is in progress—little, if any, verbal interaction but much vocalization.

How the game is played obviously differs from standard Anglo-American tag. It is a round game, not a linear one. Bodies may touch during play. There is no calling out of corrections or amendments to rules during play. It is recognizable as tag, but still it is very different. Each of these differences is predicated on an aspect of standard, adult, Mescalero behavior. The children are replicating, or acting out, basic tenets of the culture. They stress in their play the importance of contact, circularity, and learning by observation. They are making statements about standard communication patterns: when it is appropriate to speak and when to remain silent; to whom one speaks; and in what manner; and whether "speech" is verbal or nonverbal. Thus, play is metacommunication.

Circularity is of paramount importance for the Mescalero Apache and this is readily evident in the play of children. It could be argued that playing on a jungle gym changes the form of the game. It's difficult, even for an agile child, to move through the bars of a jungle gym quickly in a linear fashion. It's much easier to go around and around on a jungle gym. However, I maintain the jungle gym was *chosen* as the accepted arena for tag precisely because it lends itself to a circular game. Circles are important to the Mescalero Apache people. Their traditional homes, whether tipi or brush arbor, were circular. Dance patterns are circular and, incidentally, move clockwise. Tribal decisions are made by consensus; each speaks until no one has more to say. The circle pattern is egalitarian as is the society. No one is the obvious leader in a circle. And unless you see the beginning of the game or an actual tag, no one is obviously "it" in Mescalero tag.

In standard Anglo-American tag, a touch is a tag. In Mescalero style tag, bodies may touch throughout the game. Indeed, the children usually group themselves so that their bodies *must* touch. A tag, then, has to be a specific movement of a hand to one of the few specific places I've already ennumerated. Touching is likewise common to adult Mescalero Apache people. When friends are speaking, they frequently stand side by side with arms touching. During meetings, pow-wows, or church services one's personal space is only what one is physically occupying. There are no bubbles of encapsulated space which one claims as one's own. If it is crowded, people sit with bodies touching at hips, arms, and shoulders: comfortable for the Mescalero but too intimate for Anglos. When chairs were set up for the choir last Christmas for the annual pageant, they were placed much closer than normal in Anglo situations and much closer than they need have been, since space was no problem. Choir members' shoulders often touched. When the women dance, there is just enough space between them so one's foot won't kick another's; but shoulders often touch during side-by-side dances. To be close to another is to be involved in the event. Touching in tag identifies the participants in the game and excludes others who may be on the jungle gym at the same time but not part of the tag game.

In Mescalero style tag mistakes are not called out; rules are not negotiated. Similarly, Mescalero Apache parents rarely correct their children in public. Children are expected to behave properly by observing and copying their older siblings, cousins, and parents. When a child misbehaves, he is ignored, if the infraction is slight. If the infraction is more serious, he is physically restrained or removed from the scene. When a child goes through the jungle gym linearly or moves counter-clockwise, the group will often go along for a short period of time or the game will stop. All this occurs without verbal interaction. But children simply won't play with those who don't play properly. The deviant is effectively, and nonverbally, removed from play. Children are again replicating in play what they observe in the larger society. And again play may be seen as metacommunication.

The participants in any one tag game are usually cousins. (And let me add parenthetically that cousinship among Mescalero is reckoned well beyond the fourth degree.) Relatives play together much more often than nonrelatives. Frequently teams of relatives will join each other for a game, though. During a person's lifetime the family of orientation will join together on important occasions; this family is of vital importance to an individual. When a girl has her puberty feast, for instance, her mother, mother's sisters, mother's sisters' daughters, mother's mother, and mother's mother's sisters will all be helping with the food. When a child needs a babysitter, the sitter will probably be an aunt, uncle, cousin, or grandparent. When a man kills an animal, he divides the meat among his family of procreation as well as among his sisters' families and the household of his parents. Relatives are the ones to turn to in time of need or celebration. And you play tag with your relatives first and others second, if you are a Mescalero Apache child.

By now I assume I've convinced you that this game of tag is indeed metacommunication. Let's look at it as a miniature communication system. Four areas of interest are immediately apparent:

1. Relatives play together;
2. Verbal interaction is minimal with teaching and correction by example and learning by observation;
3. Physical closeness is desirable;
4. Circularity is important while linearity is merely tolerated.

If space allowed, I'd like to relate each of these four items to cultural values as expressed in mythology, the politeness-decorum system, dance, social organization, etc. However, instead I'll be extremely practical and relate these items to an on-the-ground problem: the failures of communication between non-Indian teachers and Mescalero Apache children.

The implications of these four areas for non-Indian teachers working with bicultural Mescalero Apache children are enormous. Relatives do work and play together. In the classroom I have seen two little girls constantly chatter to each other even when they have been placed as far apart as is physically possible. Their teacher is at a loss "to get them to be quiet and work independently." These girls are cousins and are trying to help one another as they've seen their mothers do and as they will be expected to do throughout their lives. This work and play dependence upon relatives should be taken into consideration by non-Indian teachers. It is blatant in play as well as in the larger society.

Minimal verbal interaction characterizes both play and the larger society. When a child causes a fuss in public, the child is ignored or removed from the scene, as I've already mentioned. Children play and arbitrate disputes nonverbally just as they are nonverbally taught rules of behavior in public. When a child attempts to circle counter-clockwise, the game usually disintegrates. Teachers would be more effective if they, too, relied less on verbal instruction and instead tried to find ways of teaching by example so the children could learn by observation as they are used to doing. Discipline would be more meaningful if teachers would correct privately and remove the offending child from the group. As it is, teachers lose face by public correction and they lose the respect of the children as well.

Physical closeness has a positive value for Mescalero Apache people. Closeness implies security and serves to identify co-participants in events, thus serving a phatic end much as some of our verbal chatter, like "you know," does. Perhaps the Mescalero Apache children should be allowed to practically sit on each other's laps, if they so choose, since to a Mescalero person closeness is security whether in a game, church, pow-wow, pick-up truck, or the home. Closeness could be security in school too. Utilization of the phatic channel differs for Mescalero and Anglo-Americans; non-Indian teachers should be made aware of this.

The Mescalero Apache world-view structures reality into circles and circular patterns, whether in meetings, housing, dance, or cosmology. Mescalero Apache children prefer round patterned games. Teachers could easily allow children to sit in circles or clusters rather than in lines and rows. Thus the classroom could more closely conform to the Mescalero view of reality, rather than to the Anglo-American one predicated on lines and grids.

The implications for anthropologists and folklorists are numerous.

I've combined theoretical constructs from anthropology and linguistics and applied them to a folkloristic form. I've done this in order to facilitate inter-ethnic communication in an area where such communication is most desirable and least achieved, that is, between Anglo-American teachers (or those teachers trained on the Anglo-American model) and bicultural children. My model of play as metacommunication obviously is indebted to linguistic theory and particularly to the work of Bateson (1972, pp. 9-26, 177-193) and Jakobson (1960, pp. 350-377). The statements made during play about culture-specific communication patterns reflect both deep and surface structures apparent in everyday Mescalero Apache verbal interactions. The model also relies upon anthropological theory, especially kinesics and proxemics (Hall, 1959, 1966). Just as friends stand close to one another when they are co-participants in a communicative event, so children place themselves close to each other in play. Movement was seen to follow dance movement; further, children exhibit in play the same stereotyped body movements evident in ritual dancing.

We are also in a position to benefit from the new liason and working partnership between ourselves and our informants. For instance, I *know* what I've just told you is true as concerns Mescalero values and their evidence in play. I can justify my statements on an etic level. But also I am convinced my statements are valid on an emic level, since my work is open to the people I'm studying and they, in turn, keep me from making data errors. The problems of bicultural education are of interest not only to professional anthropologists, sociologists, linguists, and educators but also are of vital importance and interest to the parents of the bicultural child. An open, exchanging relationship works to the benefit of us, those we study, and, more importantly, to the children.

I had a social anthropology professor who used to repeat this bit of doggerel:

Tell me where is structure found:
In the head or on the ground? (Selby, Note 1)

Of course, the answer is both. And the play of young children is one of the easier ways of moving from one level of organization to the other. By making that move, much more than structure is elucidated.

Note

1. This paper has been seen and approved by members of the Mescalero Apache Tribal Council.

Reference Note

1. Selby, H.A. *Introduction to social anthropology*. Graduate seminar, University of Texas, Austin, Fall 1971.

References

BATESON, G. *Steps to an ecology of mind*. New York: Ballentine Books, 1972.

HALL, E.T. *The silent language*. New York: Doubleday, 1959.

HALL, E.T. *The hidden dimension*. New York: Doubleday, 1966.

JAKOBSON, R. Closing statement: Linguistics and poetics. In T.A. Sebeok (Ed.), *Style in language*. Cambridge, MA: MIT Press, 1960.

Chapter 20
Children's Games as Mechanisms for Easing Ethnic Interaction in Ethnically Heterogeneous Communities: A Nigerian Case

FRANK A. SALAMONE

Discussion of Theory

P roperly speaking, consideration of children's games belongs to the broader category of play. In that category there is a wide range of human activity too long studied in isolation: jokes, relations of privileged familiarity, riddles, puns, sporting events, etc. Some areas now considered part of play were at best until recently only peripheral or esoteric interests of the anthropologist. For whatever reason, this regrettable neglect now seems to be at an end. A number of recent articles (Bateson, 1955; Handleman & Kapferer, 1972; Miller, 1973; and others) attest to the lively interest in the subject among anthropologists.

This paper focuses on one theoretical issue: the relationship between children's games and what Goffman (1959) has termed the front and back stage areas of social interaction. In particular, it looks at children's games as mechanisms for socialization and in that respect offers some

From *Anthropos*, 1979, **74**, 202-210. Copyright 1979 by Anthropos-Institut. Reprinted with permission.

methodological suggestions regarding the study of cultural imprinting of patterns. Games clearly reflect underlying cultural patterns and prepare children, including adolescents, for proper interaction in the "real" world beyond games. Thus, there may be games common to members of all ethnic groups in a heterogeneous area while at the same time there may be games reserved for members of a given ethnic group. The sharing of common cognitive patterns found in games known and played by all facilitates ethnic interaction while the reservation of certain games "for members only" emphasizes ethnic uniqueness. In brief, both ethnic cooperation and separateness are needed in interaction fields where ethnicity forms the primary basis of intergroup interaction. Therefore, mechanisms for preserving and transcending ethnic identity are vital to the efficient functioning of the system. Among these mechanisms are children's games which control the area of play reality and thus clearly manipulate appropriate variables in order to convey certain underlying patterns for interaction to the participants. These variables include rules, players, occasion, duration, location, and nature of the game. A careful study of children's games promises significant theoretical and method-ological rewards for anthropology.

The Interethnic Nature of Yauri Division, North-Western State, Nigeria

I have described the ethnic heterogeneity of Yauri in a number of places (most comprehensively in Salamone, 1974a). Yauri Division is located about 5° East Longitude and 11° North Latitude. Its area is 1,306 square miles and population about 100,000. There are four groups indigenous to Yauri: the Shangawa, Gungawa, Dukawa, and Kamberi. The politically dominant Hausa are not considered by Yauri's peoples to be indigenous to the area. Traditionally they have incorporated members from politi-cally subordinate groups, most notably the Gungawa and Shangawa. The Hausa of Yauri, unlike those in many other areas of Northern Nigeria, do not have a ruling stratum of Hausa-Fulani. While there are Cattle Fulani present, there are few, if any, Town Fulani in Yauri. In ad-dition, there are members from other ethnic groups present, Yoruba, Igbo, Itsekiri, Edo, Nupe, and a scattered few others. The five major groups, however, have been in Yauri together for at least 500 years. Thus, they have worked out clearcut patterns of interactions which are reflected in a vast number of ways through various traditional activities. This paper, then, focuses on children's games as one means for facilitat-ing ethnic interaction through preparing children both to rehearse as well as to observe a number of adult roles in a number of different contexts.

Thus games played in a number of different contexts are described. These contexts are: games played primarily within one's ethnic group, games played only by members of one sex, games played by both sexes but not in a male-female context, and games played interethnically.

The relative frequency of these games is an index of kinds of social interaction. In fact, who plays with whom is a sign of relative status and mutual regard. Indeed, it is a matter of some significance to note the ethnic membership of those who initiate games with members of ethnic groups different from their own. For example, it is common to see Hausa children initiate games with Gungawa children but not vice-versa.

These play patterns are modeled on and mirror adult relationships. Therefore, either Dukawa or Kamberi children may freely initiate games with one another. However, rarely, if ever, do they play with Hausa or Shangawa children. In fact, this play-avoidance relationship holds true even if Hausa, Gungawa, or Shangawa children are near Dukawa or Kamberi parties. Certainly the frequency, occasion, and composition of children's interaction groups mirrors relationships found in the world of adults. (Cf. Brewster, 1954, for comparative data from other areas of Nigeria.) This issue will be discussed in the conclusion. At this point I wish to describe a few of the more common games played in Yauri.

Among the more popular girls' games is one called in Hausa, *sunana bojo ne* "My name is Bojo" [see Figure 1]. I shall first describe the standard game and then a variation of it. The standard game is usually played when the moon is bright. The average age of the players is about 10. Occasionally, an unmarried adolescent girl may play, but if she does it is only for a brief period and in a spirit of extreme hilarity. The eligible number of players is limited only by the number of prepubescent girls present when the game is begun. The usual number of players is between 10 and 15. These players form a half circle, with each girl taking a turn at being in the middle, the largest girl is first and so on to the smallest.

The girls sing and dance, moving in a clockwise direction. Their hands are joined as they circle the girl in the middle, who claps her hands and does a spirited dance. She serves as a song leader, with the girls improvis-

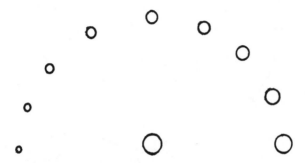

Figure 1—Circle for "My name is Bojo."

ing replies to her verses. Frequently she turns her back to the circle. Finally, without warning, she will throw herself backward into it, leaving her feet with great force. She has complete confidence that her age-mates will catch her before she reaches the ground.

This game is known in the above form throughout Yauri. At Shabanda, among the Gungawa, I witnessed an interesting variation.[1] The following description refers to the game and variation I witnessed on July 19, 1972.

The game began in the moonlight as a response to my request to see some dancing. As part of the dancing and games, the young girls began to play "My name is Bojo." As a courtesy they sang in Hausa and not in their own language, Reshe. After half an hour or so of adhering to the standard game, the girls almost imperceptively transformed it into a variant called "Three boys" [see Figure 2]. One of the three boys wished to make love with them, a constant theme of "My name is Bojo." The pace of "Three boys" was even faster than that of the former game, while the dancing, and accompanying drumming were even more rhythmically complex. The bridge between the two games consisted of a call and response pattern in which anti-male insult followed anti-male insult in alternating ingenious verses. The girls formed a complete circle for "Three boys" and enacted the storyline in fulsome acrobatic detail.

"My name is Bojo" is universal throughout Yauri. However, "Three boys" seems to be primarily a Gungawa game. The fact that Gungawa

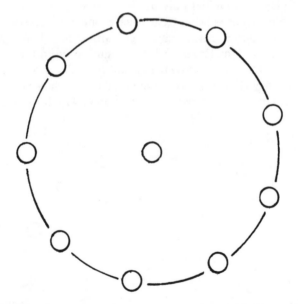

Figure 2—Circle for "Three boys."

will allow non-Gungawa to play it with them seems a rather significant point since it so clearly reinforces major themes of Gungawa life. Perhaps, because most of the ruling Hausa in Yauri have Gungawa ancestors (Salamone, 1974a) it is not surprising that many Gungawa themes are compatible with those of Yauri's Hausa.

The games described above provide means for crosscutting kinship ties and establishing networks useful in later life. None of the groups indigenous to Yauri have, in fact, very deep or extensive kinship organizations. Each provides a great deal of individual choice in the use and manipulation of kin ties. The Kamberi, for example, have septs, cognatic groups notable for the leeway they provide for individual adaptation. Furthermore, there are no groups with lineage organizations in Yauri. Each group, however, strongly stresses the principle of seniority, increasing the probability that age-groups will play a significant role in structuring interpersonal relationships.

The games do, in fact, emphasize the solidarity of age-groups. They provide a means for reestablishing confidence, so necessary to the smooth functioning of face-to-face societies. The absolutely complete abandon with which even the largest girl tosses herself into the arms of even the smallest demonstrates rather concretely the depth of that trust. It is rather significant that such confidence on occasion transcends ethnic ties. These interethnic situations of confidence mirror the "real" world, the world beyond that structured by play. Thus, Dukawa and Hausa may play together quite freely when events bring them together. Rarely, however, if at all, do Hausa and Gungawa invite Dukawa and Kamberi to join them in playing traditional games. On the other hand, Dukawa and Kamberi need no invitation to join in one another's games.

The traditional girls' games described above express and reinforce proper behavior. In brief, they express the need for girls to stick together and to present a united front against young men. "Three boys" goes beyond that theme and clearly expresses the theme of ambivalent male-female relationships common to the Gungawa and Hausa of Yauri, but not to the Dukawa or Kamberi. Hausa and Gungawa are much more likely to be in a co-wife relationship than are women of any other two groups. Not surprisingly, therefore, they are more apt to play traditional games together as girls than are girls from other groups. Although Hausa men sometimes marry Kamberi women, they do so primarily because they are reputed to be different from Hausa or Gungawa women. Kamberi women have a reputation for being "gentle" and "faithful." Therefore, it is relatively rare to see Kamberi girls playing traditional games with members of other ethnic groups.

A brief description of one other game common to girls in Yauri helps illustrate some further points. "Balibaligun" is a dance game. For it the girls hire a drummer to accompany them. They form a complete circle around two girls who stand shoulder to shoulder without touching. These two girls dance while the girls in the circle improvise verses to the drum's rhythms. The girls in the circle do not dance. There is no special order in which girls enter the center of the circle. Any two girls may start at the center.

Each pair of girls displays remarkable dexterity in its dance. Each girl improvises steps and through nonverbal cues signals her partner to move in tandem with her. Any failure in communication would lead to one girl's tripping the other. This rarely, if ever, happens, so in tune with each other are the girls in each pair. Thus, intricate movements to either side cause no missed steps, for the girls seemingly think and act as one, a pattern necessary to successful interaction in adult life. The presence of female bond friendship is quite prevalent in Yauri among all of its ethnic groups. It is quite clearly displayed in this game. The game can be played at any time of day and is not confined, as are most traditional games, to late at night.

The traditional girls' games are a means for establishing social control through reinforcing proper behavior in a group setting. Thus, the call and response pattern helps establish, as well as reflect, the importance of cooperative effort (cf. Lomax, 1968). It rewards innovation but within recognized contexts. It is a means for shoring up friendship within a common work group while stressing a need for reliance on a wide circle of friends. These friends literally uphold one another in games. The exclusion of men from the group is reflected in the play activity of older men (and women) who exclude members of the opposite sex from their recreation and, at times, jokingly chase them away. The possibility of these games being interethnic opens the way for future study of the cross-cutting role-identity of "women" vs. "men" in Yauri, for just as there are traditional games open to all girls in Yauri and closed to boys, there are games open to all boys that exclude girls.

Perhaps the most common traditional boys' games shared cross-ethnically in Yauri are ring toss, the snail shell game *(alkwato),* and *zulli.* These games have a number of underlying patterns in common, which emerge from even the briefest descriptions.

Ring toss is a game common to all ethnic groups in Yauri. Ideally, it is played by five people. The participants form a circle, and play moves counterclockwise. Each player tosses a rubber ring at a bottle or other necked object. The game continues until the last player scores a ringer. There is a good deal of joking accompanying the game and the last one to score is ragged rather unmercifully.

The snail shell game *(alkwato)* and *zulli* were played in much the same way in 1972 as they were when Harris (1930) described them. Thus, I shall quote his descriptions of the games.

Alkwato (Snail Shell). — This game is played by five or six boys. A small heap of sand is made and flattened on top. One boy spins the shell, and while it is spinning hits it to one side. If it comes point upwards the first spinner stays in until the next has spun. If, in the next spin, it falls over, the first goes out (the first being Sarki). The third then spins, and if successful stays in till the fourth spin is seen. If the fourth spin is unsuccessful, the third goes out, and so on until one is left in, whose shell does not come up. This boy puts his hand, palm downwards, on the pile of sand, and each of the others in turn hits it hard three times with his fist (Harris, 1930, pp. 318-319).

Zulli. — Each boy has ground-nuts in a small gourd. A small hole, about 5 inches deep, is dug, and round this hole each boy makes a small heap leading to the hole. Each boy sits round the hole (the game is usually played by three to five boys) and the first boy to play puts two nuts *(yan gidda)* in the hole. The next boy puts two nuts on his heap, and they roll into the hole and so on round the circle. The boy whose nut or nuts rest on the *yan gidda* originally put in the hole becomes Sarki, and sits out for the next round. The game goes on until each boy's nuts have rested on the *yan gidda*, and each boy is given a title in decreasing seniority from the first. The first out being called Sarki, the next is called Dan Galadima, the next Ubandawaki, and so on (p. 318).

There are other traditional boys' games but the basic underlying patterns of those that can be shared interethnically resemble the three described above. Each is played by a small group (three to five). Each allots prestige in decreasing order. *Zulli* explicitly assigns each boy a rank from Sarki (emir) downward. Goodnatured teasing accompanies each effort. The teasing can get quite uncomfortable at times, but open aggression rarely breaks out. When it does, the command of older boys to cease fighting is instantly obeyed, further emphasizing both the importance of ranking and the principle of age seniority. The most usual expression for both teasing and correcting is *ba hankali*. Literally, the phrase means careless. However, its connotations are a bit more complex. It can mean "senseless," "stupid," "hasty," "useless," or even, at rare times, "crazy." It generally refers to incautious, unthinking action, the antithesis of both Hausa and Gungawa ideals. While these three games, and other similar ones, are played by members of all Yauri's ethnic groups, they are primarily Hausa and Gungawa games and emphasize the predominance of these two groups in Yauri's interethnic relations.

The ambivalence that Yauri's Hausa and Gungawa men and women feel for one another is clearly shown in games, played by boys and girls jointly, a number of which Harris (1930, pp. 317-318) describes. These games range from tug of war to guessing games in which the loser is beaten until refuge is found with the leader. Once again patterns of behavior appropriate to adult life are reflected in children's games. The consonance of Hausa and Gungawa values is again illustrated by their sharing of the same games.

The study of children's games as a means of viewing adult themes enables one to note areas of change as well as those of persistence in interethnic relationships. Peshkin (1972) notes that in developing countries, schools are often primary causes of social and cultural discontinuity. Thus, it is logical to study schools to attempt to discover discernible patterns of change. For present purposes, that means looking at the kinds of games schoolchildren play, under what conditions they are played, and who plays them.

In general, while traditional games are still popular, modern games are replacing them. Thus, while *zulli*, for example, is played during the breakfast break in the school yard, football (soccer) is much preferred if time and circumstances allow. Every student, teacher, and headmaster I interviewed expressed a desire for equipment for more modern games. All nine schools in Yauri in 1972 had facilities for soccer. A few had table tennis and badminton equipment. All schools want these as well as basketball equipment. Whenever possible girls as well as boys play all the above games.

Interestingly, no boxing or wrestling is performed in Yauri's schools. These sports are ethnically differentiating ones. School sports, on the other hand, endeavor to promote interethnic cooperation. When Wali school, for example, competes against Waje, Hausa students will cheer on a Dukawa team member against Hausa. Skill, not ethnicity, becomes a means for achievement. While, of course, ethnic factors do not always disappear, they frequently are submerged in a broader identity, that of the school. The modern sports gaining popularity in the schools are team sports in which cooperation is needed to succeed. While individual stars do emerge, they are as likely to be from politically subordinate ethnic groups as not. Furthermore, in contrast to traditional games, the best players do not get to leave the game early and sit back to watch the others. Rather, as in traditional girls' games, all players stay in the game until it ends, the success of the groups depending on the success of each of its members. This cooperation is a reflection of the ideal which Nigeria seeks to attain: viz., a united Nigeria in which members of individual ethnic groups cooperate as members of a larger group identity, Nigerians. Perhaps, such an interpretation places too heavy a burden on games, but these games do serve in Yauri to promote an identification that extends beyond a given ethnic identity and do facilitate interethnic cooperation.

Games Unique to Individual Ethnic Groups

Although a number of games, or at least aspects of them, are often restricted to members of particular ethnic groups, wrestling and boxing serve as ethnic boundary markers par excellence in Yauri. Elsewhere (Salamone, 1974c) I have discussed the use of wrestling as an ethnic boundary marker in Yauri. Here, I wish only briefly to emphasize the fact that games are used to separate groups in Yauri as well as to integrate them. Wrestling and boxing reserve large backstage areas for group members. So clearly is that fact understood in Yauri that: style of wrestling is ethnically determined, boxing is reserved only for Muslims, changes in wrestling style or the abandonment of wrestling signal particular kinds of ethnic change. Each non-Hausa ethnic group has its own unique style of wrestling. Members from one group will not, even jokingly, wrestle people from other groups. In explanation, they state that the rules of the match will determine the winner. ("If we wrestle Dukawa-style, a Dukawa will win. If Gungawa-style, a Gungawa will win. So, why wrestle?") In short, nothing will be proved, except the obvious; viz., that ethnic groups are different, and each excels at what it does within the limits of its rules. Thus, wrestling marks a number of splits: Muslim/pagan, Hausa/non-Hausa, Gungawa/non-Gungawa, Dukawa/non-Dukawa, Shangawa/non-Shangawa, and Kamberi/non-Kamberi.

Not surprisingly, in activities associated with wrestling and boxing a number of major ethnically differentiating themes are observable. In brief, the clear association of wrestling with ethnic preservation is a major reason that Gungawa who have become Hausa take care to separate themselves and their children from any sort of participation in wrestling activities. At wrestling events forbidden drinking of *giya* and *barukatu*, indigenous alcoholic beverages, takes place. Religious ceremonies occur. Courtship is carried on. These and other activities serve to emphasize group solidarity, but the new Hausa who were formerly members of other ethnic groups cannot take part in rituals of solidarity for a group they have left and still validate membership in the newly entered group. Quite rightly a new Hausa who attends wrestling matches is suspect. What is true of wrestling for all groups in Yauri is that it complements those elements of ethnic groups that each perceives to be essential to its self-definition.

Boxing is generally a functional equivalent to wrestling. Like wrestling it takes place in the open. Unlike wrestling it is not tied to the harvest season. Hausa in Yauri are not farmers. Ideally, they are engaged in urban employment (government service, trade, craftwork, etc.). Boxing usually takes place during a Muslim festival. Thus, it is associated with religion just as is wrestling. The rules are quite simple. There are three rounds. No gloves are worn. Shrunken leather, however, may be worn over the knuckles. The length of the rounds seems to vary. Generally, the audience influences the referee regarding duration. There can be no victory by decision. The first man knocked off his feet is the loser. Both boxing and wrestling are fraught with supernatural dangers. Wrestling is so only in intervillage matches. Furthermore, while these matches are filled with danger they do promote solidarity among team members. Boxing is not a team sport. The boxer is on his own. While the wrestler is on his own during a match, he is part of a village team. The boxer is not. His solitariness contrasts strongly with ideal Hausa behavior, and the supernatural danger he is in is a warning to others of the dangers attached to solitary activities. The wrestler is warned of the dangers inherent in dealing with people of other villages, even if they are part of his own ethnic group. Boxing and wrestling, then, both serve to preserve ethnic identities. Both emphasize key areas of within-group interaction while instructing members in proper rules for behavior. In brief, they serve as key backstage areas of life. In order to effect an ethnic identity change, a person must leave one such backstage area and penetrate another.

Conclusions

Children's games are primary means for socialization. Through them, carefully chosen and structured bits of reality are presented to participants. The games clearly reflect patterns present in adult life. These patterns are both cognitive and behavioral. In other words, the games teach patterns of thought (conceptions of reality) and the interactional results, or consequences, of these patterns. The rules of the games are, on examination, rules for life. The incidences and occasions of interethnic interaction or its lack are reflected in children's games. The lessons of the games are indeed preparation for life, or more aptly, life itself.

Changes in interethnic patterns are evident in a study of modern games. However, it seems likely that a statistical study of traditional games would also clearly measure patterns of change. Certainly measures of the frequency of interethnic participation, occasion, duration, number of players, popularity, rules, type of game, etc., could be obtained. Whether obtained from a study of modern or traditional games, it is clear that games reflect changes in society.

Note

1. Shabanda is an unresettled Gungawa area. Its people were not forced to abandon it when Kainji Dam was being built. Thus, the Gungawa there are still in their "normal" ecological habitat. Shabanda is a peninsula, with a population of about 500 people, administratively part of the village of Gebbi. There are about 50 Muslims and 60 Gungawa Christians in the population.

References

BATESON, G. A theory of play and fantasy. *Psychiatric Research Reports 2*, 1955, 39-51.

BREWSTER, P.G. Some Nigerian games with their parallels and analogues. *Journal de la Société des Africanistes*, 1954, **24**, 25-48.

GOFFMAN, E. *Presentation of self in everyday life*. New York: Anchor Books, 1959.

HANDELMAN, D., & Kapferer, B. Forms of joking activity: A comparative approach. *American Anthropologist*, 1972, **74**, 484-517.

HARRIS, P.G. Notes on Yauri (Sokoto Province), Nigeria. *Journal of the Royal Anthropological Institute*, 1930, **60**, 283-334.

HUIZINGA, J. *Homo ludens: A study of the play element in culture*. Boston: Beacon Press, 1955. (Originally published, 1944.)

LOMAX, A. *Folk song and culture*. Washington, DC: American Association for the Advancement of Science, 1968.

MILLER, S. Ends, means, and galumphing: Some leitmotifs of play. *American Anthropologist*, 1973, **75**, 87-98.

PESHKIN, A. *Kanuri schoolchildren*. New York: Holt, Rinehart & Winston, 1972.

PLAY. *Natural History Magazine*, 1971, pp. 46-76. (Special Supplement)

SALAMONE, F.A. From Bungawa to Hausa or "I'd rather switch than fight." *Afrika und Übersee*, 1974, **57**, 273-296. (a)

SALAMONE, F.A. *Gods and goods in Africa*. New Haven: HRAFLEX, 1974. (b)

SALAMONE, F.A. Gungawa wrestling as an ethnic boundary marker. *Afrika und Übersee*, 1974, **57**, 193-201. (c)

Chapter 21
Basketball and the Culture-change Process: The Rimrock Navajo Case[1]

KENDALL BLANCHARD

Every fall the Rimrock area of New Mexico is besieged with its annual epidemic of basketball fever.[2] Despite the fact that the sport is a relatively recent form of entertainment for the region's 1,300 Navajos, they are as captured by the craze as their 300 Anglo neighbors. Navajo youngsters will hitchhike 15 miles into Rimrock on Saturday to play for a few hours, high school boys will endure the boredom of the classroom for the pleasure of the afternoon on the court, and adults will travel as far as 30 miles on weekday evenings to sit and watch a hastily organized contest between two sandlot teams.

The People's impassioned involvement in the sport is the subject of this article, specifically, the description of basketball and its role in the changing Rimrock Navajo community.

The sociology and philosophy of sport treat athletic contests (e.g., basketball, football, baseball) as integral parts of their generating social contexts (Maheu, 1964, p. 111; Tunis, 1958, p. vii), instruments of

From *Council on Anthropology and Education Quarterly*, 1974, **5**(4), 8-13. Copyright 1974 by the Council of Anthropology and Education. Reprinted with permission.

cultural education (Dumazedier, 1964, p. 214), applied art (Friedenberg, 1967, p. vii), tools of civilization (Huizinga, 1970, p. 352); and make frequent reference to their range of functions within society itself (Frederickson, 1969). Also, several recent articles (Krawczyk, 1973; Miller & Russell, 1971, p. 352) treat sporting events as "factors of acculturation."

From a lay perspective, the Mormon element in Rimrock, which comprises about 95% of the town's Anglo population, views recreation in general and basketball in particular as having necessary spiritual dimensions (O'Dea, 1957, p. 146). The Saints further assume that the Lamanites (*Book of Mormon* for Native Americans), by their participation in athletic events, undergo a vital process of religious education in addition to learning to play the game (O'Dea, 1953, p. 101). Basketball is also seen as a significant preliminary adjustment to the world of White Mormondom as one is taught the importance of aggression and winning, the value of team effort and sportsmanship, and the spiritual significance of a healthy body and general wholesomeness (Albert, 1967, p. 274). For these reasons, the game is an important phase of LDS mission activities.

In opposition to the popular or folkview, I am arguing that basketball is not a significant culture change factor in the Rimrock Navajo situation. In the first place, despite their obvious fascination and obsession with the game, the Navajos, spectators and players alike, are not internalizing the meaning intended by the local Mormons who have taught them the fundamentals of the sport. By pragmatically picking-and-choosing only the vital prerequisites of the game, Navajo hoopsters are circumventing value conflicts. Basketball is simply a new vehicle for the expression of traditional play needs. This hypothesis is reinforced by the suggestion that physical games (see Roberts, Arth, & Bush, 1959, p. 597) are less culture specific than other forms of play and more adaptable to new social environments.

Basketball has been a popular sport among the Anglo Mormons in Rimrock since the 1920s, but did not become a significant element in the lives of the Navajos until the late 40s. By this time, many of The People in the area had been away to government boarding schools, mission schools, or on the Mormon placement program, and had developed an appreciation for the game. After 1951, when the Navajos were allowed to attend Rimrock High School, the game became an increasingly important facet of their lives, especially as the boys were playing and starring for the local high school. By the early 50s most of the traditional games such as cat's cradle, stick dice, hoop and pole, and the moccasin game had disappeared (Kluckhohn, 1967, p. 289), and basketball was one of several replacements.

By the late 1960s, during the appropriate season, basketball was included in the normal daily activities of most Rimrock Navajos. Grade school children played at recess and after school, while the high schoolers were exposed to the game in physical education classes, afternoons, and in connection with the formal athletic program. Those young adults not in school organized to play in the evenings at the high school against other Indian teams from on and around the Reservation. During the 1970-71 season, for example, they formed two men's and one women's teams, and on every night that the local gymnasium was not being used they scheduled at least one game. On those evenings the bleachers would often be filled to capacity with Navajo spectators who had driven in from the surrounding areas and had paid the 25 cents admission.

During the 1970-71 season in Rimrock the most exciting events were the games involving the two men's teams, the Warriors and the Onions. Dressed in their uniforms of blue-and-white and red-and-white, respectively, they would play visiting teams from Zuni, Gallup, Laguna, Crownpoint, Tohatchi, Window Rock, and areas as far away as Winslow, Arizona. On several weekends there were tournaments, but often the evening's program was limited to a contest between the two Rimrock quintets.

The two teams were composed of a total of 22 Navajos and one Anglo. The ages ranged from 16 to 37, and most were high school graduates who lived and worked in the Rimrock area. All had extensive experience with basketball, some having played for a year or two in college.

The characteristic style of these two Rimrock men's teams I have isolated and defined as Navajo basketball behavior. It is this general pattern that I am comparing with that of a similar group of Anglo Mormon men in Rimrock who organize a basketball team every year and compete in a nearby city league and in occasional tournaments in the area (see Table 1).

Table 1
Rimrock Basketball Behavior
(Anglo Mormon versus Navajo)

Attribute Category	Anglo	Navajo
General goals	Recreational, morally educative, purposeful, fun but serious; emphasis on winning	Pleasurable, aesthetic, light; importance of having fun
Style of play	More deliberate strategy, passing, and emphasis on teamwork	Free-lance, run-and-shoot; more dribbling and fast-break individualism

Table 1 (Cont.)

Strategy	Ball played off center; more deliberate picks and screens; working for inside shots	Ball played on periphery and shot from strong side; inside shots only on fast break
Practice	Some scrimmage, but emphasis on fundamentals and strategy	Some work on fundamentals, but only in context of scrimmage
Rule infractions	More body contact, passing violations, infractions under the boards, and deliberate fouls	More dribbling violations and infractions away from the boards and in backcourt
Ideal player	Team player with many assists and consistent scoring	Individualistic player with scoring ability and razzle-dazzle style
Concept of relative player size	Tall: above 6'3" Ave.: 5'11" to 6'3" Short: below 5'10"	Tall: above 5'11" Ave.: 5'6" to 5'11" Short: below 5'6"
Authority	Definite order of command and regular pattern of substitution	Vaguely defined authority roles with frequent substitution confusion
Reaction to pressure	Deliberate strategy	Flurry of increased speed and offensive display with limited deliberation
Team play	More concern for team as unit; superior skill as most significant factor in on-court decision-making	Less concern for team as unit; kinship as the most significant factor in on-court decision-making, with some regard for superior skill
Attitude toward officials	Greater tendency toward direct, physical confrontation with occasional violence	Only indirect objection without physical confrontation or threat of violence

Such comparison reveals many obvious distinctions. In the first place, the Navajo teams tend to play a dramatically different type of basketball than their Anglo counterparts. Strategically, they are much less deliberate and pattern-oriented, opting for a more wide-open, run-and-shoot brand of ball that places a premium on individual speed and maneuverability at the expense of teamwork.

On defense, the Indian teams tend to be less aggressive than the Anglos, choosing man-to-man as opposed to zone techniques.

With reference to the rules, the Navajos are less concerned with the "proper" administration of principles. In other words, "bad calls" are not as trauma-stimulating as among Anglo teams in the area. In the area of rule infractions, the most notable distinction is the fewer number of contact fouls committed by the Navajos.

One means of raising team morale and effectiveness that has long been associated with basketball in the United States has been the use of "chatter." Players talk encouragingly to each other on the one hand and attempt to intimidate their opponents on the other. Navajo teams are much slower to engage in on-court banter and outward physical demonstration than are their Anglo neighbors.

Another unique characteristic of Navajo basketball behavior is its informal organization. Unlike the Anglo situation where authority (e.g., manager, captain, coach) is clearly defined, Navajo groups are usually vague in the assignment of decision-making roles and in their response to these roles. As a result, confusion is a frequent state of affairs during substitution and at critical points during the game. In most cases, when a player is assigned a position of responsibility and required to make decisions regarding strategy he is hesitant to act with forcefulness. Instead, he will generally attempt to achieve some consensus, suggesting and advising rather than commanding.

The Indian teams in Rimrock view kinship as the most significant factor in on-court decision-making, as opposed to individual skill or team unity, the primary values expressed by their Anglo counterparts (see Figure 1). In other words, a Navajo will, in a situation involving several alternatives, usually make a decision to include another team member in a particular play on the basis of degree of relationship. This has been observed by high school coaches in the area, and as a result they argue that fielding a group composed of three Navajos and two non-Navajos is tantamount to playing a three-man team, the Indian faction automatically excluding the others in the play-making process unless absolutely unavoidable.

Generally, Navajos in Rimrock use the English term "basketball" when talking about the game. They also employ their second language when referring to items or events that are significant only in a basketball context (e.g., zone defense, double dribble, foul shot). In some cases,

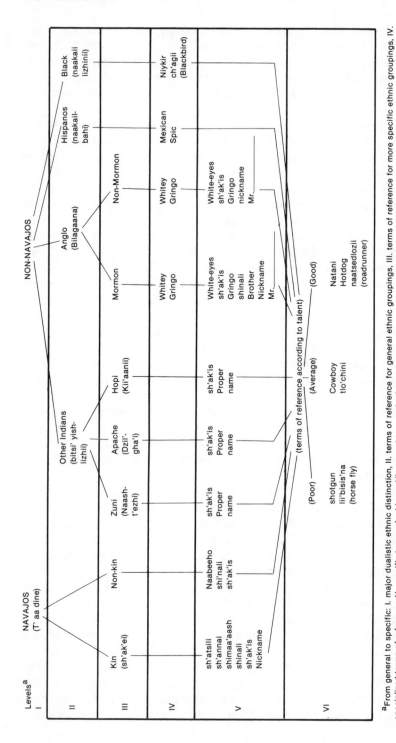

Figure 1—Taxonomic categorization of basketball players among the Rimrock Navajos.

[a]From general to specific: I. major dualistic ethnic distinction, II. terms of reference for general ethnic groupings, III. terms of reference for more specific ethnic groupings, IV. specialized terms of reference, V. specific terms of address, VI. general terms of reference according to individual basketball ability.

there are simply no Navajo equivalents for certain words associated with the sport, nor for descriptive nicknames borrowed from Whites (see Figure 1). However, most on-court communication is in Navajo.

Perhaps the most significant differential between the so-called basketball behavior of the Rimrock Navajo and their White neighbors is to be seen in the area of purpose or meaning. The Mormon group sees the sport as primarily a serious, though recreational, contest within which one receives a moral and spiritual education as well as a lesson in the realities of Western economic survival. On the other hand, the Navajos see the event as purely a pleasurable pastime and put a greater emphasis on having a good time than winning.

Even from the most nonscholarly perspective, Navajo basketball must be seen as a different game. Behaviorally, it is less aggressive, structured, outwardly enthusiastic, and morally educative; while at the same time it is more individualistic, kin-oriented, and pure good times than that of the town's Anglo Mormon population.

This observation is reinforced by the behavior of Navajo spectators who appear to enjoy the continuing play of the game more and get involved in the final outcome possibilities less than do the Mormons. Persistent losing by an Indian team has only minimal effect on fan attitudes, while the prestige of individual players does not appear to depend on the success of the rest of the squad. In the 1970-71 season, the Warriors in Rimrock had a much poorer won-lost record than the Onions, but consistently drew larger crowds. One of the reasons was that the former had a broader network of kin ties among area basketball fans, and another was simply that they were more entertaining. Deliberate clowning, repeated comical floor mistakes, and the involvement because of relatedness completely outweighed winning among the factors underlying spectator enthusiasm.

Anglo Mormon interest tends to be directly correlatable with victories and defeats. By their own admission, Rimrock Whites find little pleasure in supporting a team that loses repeatedly, and in most cases do so only out of a sense of duty.

Many of the differentials between the Navajo and Anglo game of basketball in Rimrock can be explained by reference to physical factors. For example, on an average the Navajo men are smaller than area Whites, but at the same time more fleet of foot. Therefore, it is no surprise that the former put a greater emphasis on speed and maneuverability than on height.

On the other hand, many of the unique elements of Navajo basketball behavior have to be explained in terms of traditional cultural characteristics. The catalytic function of kinship in personal encounter (Aberle, 1961, p. 99), the vagaries of authority role definition (Lamphere, 1970, p. 44), the attempt to avoid inequitable accumulations of personal power, the legitimation of recreational activities from an amoral, pure-play perspective (Kluckhohn, 1967, p. 289), and the tendency toward less demonstrative emotional behavior, are all important.

There are also certain characteristics of Navajo basketball that can be understood only in reference to the nature of physically combative sports in general. One such case is The People's disregard of normal respect relationships on the court. Mother's brothers, sister's husbands, and elder brothers become simply other members of a team as the finer points of genealogical reality are forgotten in the excitement of the contest.

There are still elements of Rimrock Navajo basketball that remain in-explicable. The individualism manifested by talented players in the game setting is not consistent with the oft-observed tendency for the children of The People to avoid disproportionate individual excellence in the classroom (Leighton & Kluckhohn, 1948). Superior skill and flash (i.e., pizazz) on the court are unquestioned values among Rimrock Navajos, and those so excelling (e.g., high scorers, fancy dribblers and ball handlers) receive vast amounts of respect and acclaim within the Indian as well as the White communities. This value is directly evident in the language the Navajos use to refer to good ball players (see Figure 1). The term "hot dog," for example, has a positive connotation when they use it, but a "hot dogger" from an Anglo perspective is a grandstander who threatens team unity.

Still, as Fox (1961 [chapter 24 in this volume]) has noted in connection with the introduction of baseball into Pueblo society, even though some athletic activities demand behavioral styles that are not only novel, but directly contradictory to existing patterns of interaction, tradition is not necessarily violated. Functional adjustments can be made. This appears to be the case in Rimrock. The Navajos have taken the mandatory requi-sites of the game (i.e., the equipment and essential rules; see Figure 2) and have developed a type of basketball that is conveniently consistent with traditional values and styles of play.

This notion is reinforced by the observation that physical games are the most cross-culturally flexible types of play behavior, and thus the most adaptable. Roberts et al. (1959, p. 598) have defined games in three categories: those involving (1) physical skill, (2) strategy, and (3) chance. They argue that the first is the least complex of the three in terms of total attributes and also suggest that such games occur more regularly in the ethnographic record than do the others (88% of the cases investigated as opposed to 38% for the other two).

The idea that basketball is of only limited acculturative significance among The People in Rimrock is given additional credibility when the Navajo approach to novelty in general is considered. The group has long had a reputation for being soundly pragmatic in decision-making (Ladd, 1957, p. 204) and consistently rational in dealing with new cultural alter-

I. EQUIPMENT	Court			
	Goals			
	Ball			
	Backboards			
	Nets			

II. PHYSIOLOGY	Physical attributes	size		
		speed		
		coordination		
		endurance		
		strength		
	Skills	shooting		
		dribbling		
		passing		
		jumping		
		rebounding		
		defensing		

III. RULES	Limits	Equipment	court size	
			ball size	
			ball shape	
			boundaries	
			foul lines	
			jump circles	
			time zones	
			goal size	
			goal height	
		Process	Time limits	back-court
				3-second
				zone
				time outs
				periods
			Areal limits	back-court
				out-of-
				bounds
			Contact limits	fouls
			Technique limits	ball-handling

Figure 2—Basketball behavior: General componential definition (attributes in order of increasing flexibility).

Figure 2, continued.

	Process	Enforcement		
IV. PROCESS	Technique	shooting dribbling passing rebounding defensing		
	Strategy	Patterns	Specific	offense defense
		Style	General	offense defense
V. VALUES	Purpose	Immediate	desired outcome	
		Ultimate	meaning	

natives (Adair & Vogt, 1949, p. 559). Again, Vogt (1955, p. 836) has observed that the Navajos attending the annual Laguna Fiesta in the early 1950s viewed their participation in the event in a uniquely Navajo way, even though this contrasted dramatically with the perspective of the other groups (e.g., Eastern Pueblo, Acomites, Spanish-Americans, Zunis, Anglos) involved in the same general activities.

From the other side of the picture, no one has yet demonstrated in any convincing way that exposure to basketball does any more than teach one to play basketball. Educative-acculturative functions appear at best incidental.

It is concluded that basketball, in light of its inherent flexibility and the way that the Navajos deal with novelty in general and this sport in particular, is of little culture-change significance. The Rimrock Navajos have simply borrowed a new form of play and molded its essentials to fit ongoing needs and values. In this sense, basketball is providing recreational and entertainment opportunities for members of the Navajo community without forcefully subjecting them to the Wall Street ethic of White America.

Notes

1. Data for this paper were collected in the 15 months between June 1970 and September 1971, as well as the summer months of 1972 and 1973. During this time I played on several Navajo basketball teams, coached one Navajo

women's team, and spent many hours talking to Navajo friends about basketball.

2. The name Rimrock is a pseudonym.

References

ABERLE, D. Navajo. In D.M. Schneider & K. Gough (Eds.), *Matrilineal kinship*. Berkeley: University of California Press, 1961.

ADAIR, J., & Vogt, E.Z. Navajo and Zuni veterans: A study in contrasting modes of culture change. *American Anthropologist*, 1949, **51**, 547.

ALBERT, E. Introduction to Kluckhohn's "Expressive activities." In E.Z. Vogt & E. Albert (Eds.), *People of Rimrock*. Cambridge: Harvard University Press, 1967.

BROWN, E. An ethnological theory of play. In G. Sage (Ed.), *Sport and American society*. Reading, MA: Addison-Wesley, 1970.

DUMAZEDIER, J. The point of view of a social scientist. In E. Jokl & E. Simon (Eds.), *International research in sport and physical education*. Springfield, IL: C.C. Thomas, 1964.

FOX, J.R. Pueblo baseball: A new use for old witchcraft. *Journal of American Folklore*, 1961, **74**, 9.

FREDERICKSON, F.S. Sports and the cultures of man. In J.W. Loy & G.S. Kenyon (Eds.), *Sport, culture and society*. New York: Macmillan, 1969.

FRIEDENBERG, E.Z. Forward. In H.S. Slusher, *Man, sport, and existence: A critical analysis*. Philadelphia: Lea & Febiger, 1967.

HUIZINGA, J. Play and contest as civilizing functions. In G. Sage (Ed.), *Sport and American society*. Reading, MA: Addison-Wesley, 1970.

KLUCKHOHN, C. Expressive activities. In E.Z. Vogt & E. Albert (Eds.), *People of Rimrock*. Cambridge: Harvard University Press, 1967.

KRAWCZYK, Z. Sport as a factor of acculturation. *International Review of Sport Sociology*, 1973, **8**(2), 63-75.

LADD, J. *The structure of a moral code*. Cambridge: Harvard University Press, 1957.

LAMPHERE, L. Ceremonial cooperations and networks: A re-analysis of the Navajo outfit. *Man*, 1970, **5**, 39.

LEIGHTON, D., & Kluckhohn, C. *Children of the people*. Harvard University Press, 1948.

MAHEU, R. Sport and culture. In E. Jokl & E. Simon (Eds.), *International research in sport and physical education*. Springfield, IL: C.C. Thomas, 1964.

MILLER, D.M., & Russell, K.R.E. *Sport: A contemporary view*. Philadelphia: Lea & Febiger, 1971.

MILLER, S. Ends, means, and galumphing: Some leitmotifs of play. *American Anthropologist*, 1973, **75**, 87-98.

O'DEA, T.F. *Mormon values: The significance of a religious outlook for social action*. Unpublished doctoral dissertation, Harvard University, 1953.

O'DEA, T.F. *The Mormons*. Chicago: University of Chicago Press, 1957.

ROBERTS, J.M., Arth, M.J., & Bush, R. Games in culture. *American Anthropologist*, 1959, **61**, 597-605.

TUNIS, J.R. *The American way in sport*. New York: Duell, Sloan & Pearce, 1958.

VOGT, E.Z. A study of the southwestern fiesta system as exemplified by the Laguna Fiesta. *American Anthropologist*, 1955, **57**, 820.

Chapter 22
Magic, Sorcery, and Football Among Urban Zulu: A Case of Reinterpretation Under Acculturation[1]

N.A. SCOTCH

In discussing beliefs in witchcraft in Africa, Gluckman (1955) points out that native beliefs in witchcraft not only persist in the face of continuing acculturation but often expand and change to meet the exigencies of new life situations. In fact, the impact of science, and particularly the impact of modern medicine, on previously nonliterate Africans actually inhibits their traditional beliefs and practices much less than might be expected; and although it would be incorrect to assert that Africans have rejected modern medicine — rejected, say modern germ theories of disease — the fact remains that they sustain the basic structure of their traditional beliefs in spite of elemental contradictions between those beliefs and scientific explanations.

But how can opposing explanations of cause and effect be held simultaneously? According to Gluckman, concepts of science and witchcraft fulfill different functions: Science explains *how* a given process occurs, as in the course of a disease, for example, whereas witchcraft explains

From the *Journal of Conflict Resolution*, March 1961, **5**(1), 70-74. Copyright 1961 by Sage Publications, Inc. Reprinted with permission.

why the process occurs at all, or why one man and not another contracts the disease. From the African point of view, modern medicine is extremely limited in explaining total situations. It may contribute dependable probabilities, as when it predicts that 10 of a tribal population will die of tuberculosis, or when it prognosticates a specific disease in the individual; but it fails to explain, from the African perspective, why one particular child among 10 sharing the same conditions contracts tuberculosis whereas the remaining nine do not, and it is this last explanation that witchcraft continues to provide with assurance for modern Africans. As Gluckman (1955, p. 101) observes: "The difficulty of destroying beliefs in witchcraft is that they form a system which can absorb and explain many failures and apparently contradictory evidence."

This functional aspect of witchcraft may explain, to a very great extent, its persistence in the belief system of Africans, its expansion and peculiar adaptability to industrialized Euroamerican modes of life. As Gluckman (1955) points out:

> African life nowadays is changing rapidly, and witchcraft accusations now involve circumstances arising from Africa's absorption in Western economy and polity. Conflicts between old and new social principles produce new animosities, which are not controlled by custom, and these open the way to new forms of accusation. Charges, previously excluded, as by a Zulu against his father, are now made. The system of witchcraft beliefs, originally tied to certain social relations, can be adapted to new situations of conflict — to competition for jobs in towns, to the rising standard of living, made possible by new goods, which breaches the previous egalitarianism, and so forth. (p. 101)

One example of such innovation in the application of magic and sorcery — terms which I prefer to witchcraft — to cultural change and urban living came to my attention during my recent research among the Zulu in South Africa. It illustrates not only how the changing pattern of magic is related to the changing way of life, but it does the reverse as well, and shows how innovations can only be built on previous cultural patterns. In Durban the Africans show a great enthusiasm for soccer, or, to use the local term, football. Much of the limited leisure of the native male population is devoted to watching, discussing, and participating in this game, and organized football leagues resembling, in their hierarchies of skill, our own major and minor leagues in baseball, engage in complex rivalries no less extreme, bitter, and unremitting than in Chicago or Cleveland. This exemplifies the "new situations of conflict" to which Gluckman refers. Interpersonal and intergroup hostility and aggression are much greater in an urban setting than in the more traditional rural Zulu community. Unnaturally crowded conditions and competition for scarce employment opportunities lead to more frequent accusations of sorcery in the city. Football, it may be hypothesized, serves a dual function in this context: First, it is one of the few opportunities open to the Zulu for release from the anxiety and tensions of anomic urban life; and more specifically, it allows the expression of the increased aggression and hostility that arises in the city between Africans, within the framework of a modern, acceptable form.

It is common knowledge, and not surprising, that in an effort to produce winning teams each of these football teams employs an *inyanga*, or Zulu doctor, who serves the dual purpose of strengthening his own team by magic and ritual, and of forestalling the sorcery directed at his team by rival *inyangas*. Although no *inyanga* with whom I talked would admit that he employed sorcery against opposing teams, each was convinced that this was the practice of rival *inyangas*. Actually magic in Durban football is so widespread that although in searching for players there exists at least a minimal recognition of individual talent, few players known to be the object of *umtagathi*, or sorcerers, would be considered by a team regardless of their ability; moreover, success or failure of a team is invariably attributed to the skills of the *inyangas*, as well as to the natural talent of the players. However, when a team consistently loses it is the *inyanga* who is replaced, not the players. When, on the other hand, an individual player is suspected of being the object of sorcery he may be dropped from the team for fear that the spell might generalize to include the teammates of the unfortunate victim.

That football holds a place of extreme importance to the African community is demonstrated in several ways. Players of considerable talent are much sought after and part of the work of the trainer is to scout other teams and to attempt to entice skilled players of opposing teams into joining his own. In fact, although ostensibly this is an amateur sport, players of promise are frequently paid a salary from the treasury of the team as a means of keeping them. If a skilled player has had difficulty in finding employment, it is incumbent on all members of the team to find suitable and well-paying employment for the star. So involved are the efforts of teammates to keep them happy that star players are known to pass from club to club for the "best deal."

Because of this, and for other reasons as well, strict discipline is maintained on the team. The trainer—or what we would call coach—is in a position of supreme authority. All the normal rules of status and interpersonal relationships which have long traditions and history may be discarded in the interests of winning games. Thus, it is even possible for a trainer to strike a man older than himself—perhaps considerably older— if the trainer feels he is not doing his share. This, of course, is a gross transgression against important Zulu norms regarding seniority and status.

The supernatural is enlisted in every possible way to aid in the production of a successful football team. Thus, ritual and ceremony are used on a number of occasions, connected with football, and serve the functions of sanctioning and supporting the efforts of a team. Before the season even opens, the team slaughters a goat "to open the doors to luck" and the season's end is marked by another slaughter.

Much of the ritual is propitiative as in the example of the slaughter cited above, but most ceremonies combine propitiation with positive attempts to combat sorcery. The following is an account, related by an educated Zulu health educator of the ritual conducted by *inyangas* on the night preceding a match:

> All the football teams have their own *inyanga* who doctors them all for each match. The night before a match they must "camp" together around a fire. They all sleep there together, they must stay naked and they are given *umuthi* and other medicines by the *inyanga*. Incisions are made on their knees, elbows, and joints. In the morning they are made to vomit. They must all go together on the same bus to the match, and they must enter the playing grounds together. Almost every team I know has an *inyanga* and does this—it is necessary to win. Even though players are Christians and have lived in towns for a long time, they do it, and believe in it.

Another informant gave as the reasons for this practice of camping-out the following account:

> The purpose is to avoid liquor, sexual intercourse, mixing with enemy players who might bewitch them, and mixing with other persons who might affect them with ill-luck.

The camping group is composed of the starting team and reserves, plus administrative members of the club, loyal and enthusiastic supporters, and the *inyanga*. The morning after the camping the whole group moves to the playing grounds together. A certain procedure is followed: The group keeps a very tight formation with every man touching the man in front of, behind, and beside him, the pace is very slow and stylized and the group may be likened to a millipede—one organism with a million legs. Even when the group has to take a bus from one part of town to another where the football field is, they still make every effort to maintain their formation. The players themselves are placed right in the center of the group in order that they might be protected. Moving out onto the actual playing field with their stylized trotting step, the group acts very hostile to outsiders for fear that intruders will attempt to bewitch the players or in some way to weaken the "umuthi" or the medicine of the *inyanga*.

Now, when we compare the description of the ritual magic involved in "camping-out" with accounts by Bryant (1949, p. 501) and Krige (1936, p. 272) of doctoring of Zulu warriors in the time of Shaka during the early 1800s, we perceive many elements of unmistakable similarity: the circle around the fire; the medicines to endow strength and courage; the medicines on the weapons (currently, on football jerseys and shoes) to increase their potency (currently, to make them slippery); and the purificatory emetic which, in Shaka's time, was taken on the morning of the battle, and nowadays on the morning before the football match.

Further, the formation followed in reaching the playing field derives, without doubt, from historical military formations. The avoidance of sex on the eve of battles can also be traced back to earlier customs connected with warfare. These are but a few examples of the basic similarities of the ritual and ceremony used currently by football teams and formerly by army regiments.

There is an interesting parallel to be found to the above example of cultural syncretism. Sundkler (1948), in describing Zulu leadership patterns in separatist churches, has shown that the traditional roles of chief and medical specialist are carried over into the modern Christian church in much the same way as these roles are found in modern football teams.

Returning to the point made earlier—why does a belief in magic in football exist at all? As Gluckman (1955) says, because such a belief explains the inexplicable. Why does one football team win consistently and another lose? Certainly the winning team will have players who are more talented—but why, in the first place, do these teams manage to gather more talented players, and, in the second place, why are these players more talented, where does their skill come from? Why is it that the talented players avoid sorcery? These are the questions with which magic deals.

That beliefs in magic help to explain the inexplicable is illustrated by the following account:

> We health educators started a team and did very well. We made a point of not using an *inyanga*. We advertised the fact that we did not use one. We even invited a few outsiders on to our team so that they would see that we used no witchcraft, and we hoped that they would tell others about this. Well, we won a lot of games—and do you know what the people said? They said that because we work with European doctors we were given injections to make us strong so that we could win. We could not convince them otherwise.

By this account a number of things are made clear. Modern medicine is viewed as essentially similar to the magic of the Zulu doctor, except in this case it is the magic of the European. Formerly, Zulu avoided European doctors (except in the case of trauma) in the belief that they could only help or cure Europeans. Today, they accept the fact that an African can be helped in many cases by modern Western medicine. Nonetheless, it is still believed that there are some diseases—which they refer to as

Bantu diseases—which cannot be helped by the European. Such diseases as *umfufuyana, chayiza,* and *spoiliyana,* which are essentially psychosomatic, hysterical-type personality disorders, are rarely taken to the European doctor.

On the other hand, the injections used by European doctors are viewed as being entirely magical, and Zulu who come to the European doctor for help of any kind always insist on a *jovo*—an injection—as part of any treatment. No distinction is drawn between the *jovo* of the white jacketed European doctor or the roots or herbs of the *inyanga* clad in skins. Thus, when we view the football team we clearly see how the winning of matches is almost always explained by references to magic. In usual cases it is magic of the *inyanga*, while in unusual cases, like that of the health educator team, the magic of the European doctors.

Retention by urban Zulu of magical beliefs and practices also throws some light on the persistence of conflict patterns in a changing culture. The use of sorcery practices and warfare rituals within the framework of the game of soccer introduced by Europeans illustrates the adaptation of old methods of expressing hostility to the new and highly frustrating urban situation.

Note

1. I wish to thank M.J. Herskovits, A. Vilakazi, R. LeVine, and W. Elmendorf for having read and made valuable suggestions regarding this paper. The responsibility for this final version is, of course, completely my own. I also wish to thank the National Institutes of Health, the Program of African Studies at Northwestern University, Washington State University, and the Russell Sage Foundation for the financial support that made possible the field work and analysis of data on which this paper is based. This is a revised version of a paper read at the 1959 meetings of the American Anthropological Association.

References

BRYANT, A.T. *The Zulu people.* Pietermaritzburg: Shuter & Schooter, 1949.

GLUCKMAN, M. *Custom and conflict in Africa.* Oxford: Blackwell, 1955.

KRIGE, E.J. *The social system of the Zulus.* London: Longmans, 1936.

SUNDKLER, B. *Bantu prophets in South Africa.* London: Lutterworth, 1948.

Chapter 23
From Javanese to Dani:
The Translation of a Game[1]

KARL G. HEIDER

Introduction

This paper deals with the interrelationship between play and the rest of culture. It is an account of what happened to a game which was introduced into the culture of the Grand Valley Dani, a group of New Guinea highland Papuans who live in the Indonesian province of Irian Jaya. The game came from Java, and was part of a concerted program of culture change being carried out by the Indonesian government. The goal of the program was to change the Dani into proper Indonesians. The introduction of the game was not a success. Although the Dani children avidly adopted the game, they also adapted it. Instead of the game transforming the Dani into Javanese, the Dani translated the game into Dani.

We begin with the assumption that play is a basic part of culture. The

From P. Stevens, Jr. (Ed.), *Studies in the anthropology of play: Papers in memory of B. Allan Tindall.* (Proceedings from the second annual meeting of the Association for the Anthropological Study of Play.) West Point, NY: Leisure, 1977. Copyright 1977 by Leisure Press. Reprinted with permission.

trivial implication of this for anthropology is that therefore play, and games in particular, should be recorded, described, and catalogued. So we have countless publications on cat's cradles and the like. Too often these are merely descriptive lists, giving no idea of the circumstances and cultural context of the game.

But there is also a nontrivial implication: that games can be studied holistically, as functional elements in a sociocultural system. Cross-cultural studies show that the different sorts of cultures and the different sorts of games are not randomly associated, but rather, some sorts of games tend to be associated with some sorts of cultures. If, then, games co-vary with other cultural traits, we are led to the important question of Why?, and What is the process of this co-variance?

John Roberts and his associates have done much work along these lines. With Sutton-Smith, he has written about the "conflict-enculturation" hypothesis (Roberts & Sutton-Smith, 1962). From their work comes the suggestion that childhood conflicts lead to games and other "expressive models" which result in the assuaging of that conflict.

What they show, in fact, is that cultures tend to display 1) certain kinds of culture-specific conflicts (or problems or frustrations) and 2) certain types of games. They assume that the conflicts result from peculiarities of the specific sociocultural system, and that in some way or another the people in that system will choose or develop means to ameliorate the conflict. And they call these means "expressive models."

Underlying all this is a dynamic assumption, an assumption of process, or selection, or problem-solving devices on the part of the culture. Roberts and his colleagues do not explore this, for their studies are concerned with showing that there is a general pattern. And in fact, they state quite explicitly that "although the importance of acculturation in the study of games was recognized, recently introduced games were excluded from consideration" (Roberts & Sutton-Smith, 1962, p. 169).

But the very valuable work of Roberts and his colleagues points the way to the next step, which is the investigation of the dynamics of the process. We can move beyond the static model of culture, and use a dynamic model to deal with the idea that as problems arise, solutions are worked out.

The simplest of these dynamic models would be a kind of cafeteria-line concept: When cultures are faced with a wide range of possibilities, they choose to adopt those traits (in this case, games) which fit their needs. A variation of this model would see culture as changing, and in the course of this change, accepting or rejecting games according to the changing needs of the culture. For examples of such studies, there is Sutton-Smith's paper on Maori games (1951) and Kuschel's (1975) account of games on Bellona, a Polynesian outlier in the Solomon Islands.

I call these simple models because although they may allow for changes in the culture as a whole, they tend to treat the games themselves as immutable static traits to be ingested or expelled from the culture.

In the Dani case which I shall describe here, it was the culture which remained virtually constant, and the game which was plastic. It is clear that the model should be complex, allowing for the possibility that both culture and game can change, presumably in the direction of greater mutual consistency. The value of this model is to focus attention to the change in the game as well as the culture. A good example of this is a paper in which Maccoby and his colleagues describe the relationship between "Games and Social Character in a Mexican Village" (1964). This is the account of a cultural experiment—they introduced a new sort of game, apparently in the attempt to help children of the village alter their social character. (They were particularly concerned with the submissive attitude towards authority which they saw expressed in games as well as in the culture as a whole.) This attempt at culture change failed. The children quickly distorted the game to conform with other games and even then seem to have stopped playing it after the experimenter withdrew.

The Dani

The Grand Valley Dani are a Papuan culture living in the central highlands of West New Guinea (now the Indonesian province of Irian Jaya). They are best known through Robert Gardner's film, *Dead Birds* (1963). My own research began in association with Gardner, and I have made four trips to the Dani, staying for a total of about 2½ years between 1961 and 1970.

In many respects the Grand Valley Dani are a typical New Guinea Highland Papuan culture: They practice sweet potato horticulture and raise pigs; until the mid 1960s they used mainly stone axes and adzes, and warfare with bows and arrows and spears was endemic. (For a general ethnography, see Heider, 1970). On the other hand, they are particularly unusual in having a general pattern of low psychic energy, manifested as little interest in sexuality, intellectualty, and peak experiences of all sorts, a pattern which I have described elsewhere (Heider, 1976, Note 1). But here the main feature of interest is the nature of Dani play.

Roberts and his colleagues have made a useful definition of games which specifies one part of the total realm of play: they define games as

recreational activity characterized by
1) organized play
2) competition
3) two or more sides
4) criteria for determining the winner, and
5) agreed-upon rules. (Roberts, Arth, & Bush, 1959, p. 597)

They point out that play is pan-cultural and that nearly all societies know games of some sort. "Games are found in most tribal and national cultures, but in some interesting cultures they are either absent or very restricted in kind and number" (Roberts & Sutton-Smith, 1962, p. 167).

The Dani are one of those interesting cultures which have no games. Previously, in describing Dani play, I had remarked that "there is almost complete lack of competition in play" and "there are no games in which score is kept or in which there is even a winner" (1970, p. 193).

In terms of crucial criteria of the Roberts definition, the Dani lacked games.

Then, about 1969, a true game was introduced to the Dani, and in 1970 I frequently saw it played. (Also, I made two 20-minute videotape records of it, and one of which I have had printed out on 16 mm film for purposes of close analysis.[2])

But according to our definition of games, what I saw was play and no longer a true game. It was the feeble shadow of a formerly robust Asian game which the Dani children had already managed to strip of most of its game attributes.

I call the game Flip-The-Stick. (I could discover no Dani name for it in 1970.) It is fairly simple, although at first glance it does seem complex. There are two sides, a batter and one or two outfielders. The batter stands at the goal (a small depression in the ground, made by rotating a heel in the soft earth) and uses a 2-foot long reed bat to flip or hit a short reed stick toward the outfield. The outfielder catches the stick or, if he has missed it, picks it up and throws it back, trying to do something which will allow him to take over as a batter. The batter tries to stay at bat, racking up points. There are three different ways to hit and score, which the batter goes through in turn and, if not put out, begins again. (The next section describes the game in detail.)

That is the way the game should be played, and the way it is played elsewhere. The game is known from Pakistan to Korea (according to various people from South and East Asia who have seen the Dani film and recognized the game) and east into the Pacific as far as the Gilberts, (according to Kuschel's Bellonese informants, who said that their version "originally came from the Gilbert Islands" [1975, p. 55]).

Apparently the game was introduced to the Dani schoolchildren as a recess game by one or more Javanese schoolteachers. But I have no data on what took place at the moment of introduction. (It is clear from the Maccoby et al. [1964] account of introducing a game to a Mexican village how important such data are.) At any rate, I did not see it played by Dani in 1968 or between 1961 and 1963. So it is possible to say with fair confidence that the game was introduced about 1969 by Indonesian (and probably Javanese) schoolteachers, that the Dani children took it up and transformed it, and that in 1970 it was being played spontaneously by

Dani boys and girls both at school (during recess) and at home.[3]

Unfortunately, I have no first-hand account of the details of the Asian form of the game. But I make certain assumptions about that form based on comments by Asians who have seen the Dani film and drawn by logical inference from the structure of the game as played by the Dani. For example, when the batter measures out a distance with the bat and shouts out Indonesian number words (otherwise the game is carried on in the Dani language) I conclude that in Java this was to reckon the score.

The Rules of the Game: A Formal Description

The goal of this paper is to examine the changes which the Dani made on a Javanese game, and to describe how, in important ways, the game was made Dani. But here, in this section, I shall describe the basic rules or procedure of the game which can be discovered from watching the Dani children play it. This formal description of the game is more elegant than the behavioral description on which this paper is based, and of course, much more elegant than the complex activity which I observed and filmed in the Grand Valley. Although the formal description is in some respects and for some purposes adequate, it is obviously a stripped-down account, and it totally neglects those behavioral aspects of the game which figure in this analysis. (And, incidentally, it is quite different from what Sutton-Smith [1959] calls "formal analysis.") Now, if we had comparable conventional formal descriptions of the game from Java and elsewhere (and it is certainly a major defect of this study that we do not), I assume that they would be very similar to what I shall present below. The methodological implications of this are important: These formal descriptions would not identify the various important differences in the way the game is played, and so would not allow the sort of cultural analysis which I attempt here.

The formal description, then, of an unnamed game observed and recorded on videotape among the Grand Valley Dani of Irian Jaya, Indonesia in 1970, is as follows:

Players

One batter; one or two (rarely more) fielders; played by boys and girls, ages about 6 to 14, usually with children of their own sex.

Equipment

One reed, about 1 cm in diameter, and about a meter long ("the bat"); one shorter reed, about 10 cm long ("the stick").

Place

A reasonably level field extending out at least 10 or 15 meters from the goal; a shallow depression ("the goal") a few centimeters deep, dug out by rotating a heel in the earth; there are no boundaries—the goal is the only ground mark.

Rules

The game proceeds through each of three variations and then begins again until a fielder is able to replace the batter. In each variation, the batter sends the stick to the outfield; the fielder tries to catch it in the air and if successful, becomes the batter.

Variation 1

The Hit. The short stick rests across the goal depression, perpendicular to the batter-fielder axis. The batter puts the end of the bat under the stick and flips it out toward the outfield.

The Return. If the outfielder fails to catch the stick, he picks it up and throws it at the bat, which the batter either holds upright in the goal, or lays across the goal (these alternatives are apparently in free variation). If the fielder hits the bat with the stick, he takes over as batter; if not, they proceed to—

Variation 2

The Hit. The batter holds the stick upright in the goal with one hand and, wielding the bat in the other, hits the stick toward the outfield.

The Return. If the outfielder fails to catch the stick, he picks it up and throws it as close to the goal as possible. The batter now defending the goal with his bat, tries to hit the stick away.

From wherever the stick lands, whether hit away by the batter or not, the batter measures out the distance to the goal in bat lengths, shouting out the numbers as he goes. If the distance is less than one bat length, they exchange positions; if not, they proceed to—

Variation 3

The Hit. The stick now rests with one end protruding out over the goal depression. The batter hits that end with his bat to send the stick spinning up into the air, and then hits the air-borne stick toward the outfield.

If he succeeds in both, and if the stick is not caught in the air by the outfielder, the batter measures the distance from the stick to the goal, again in bat lengths shouting out numbers. If the distance is more than one bat length, they proceed to **Variation 1** and so forth.

The Translation

The basic assumption of this paper has been that play is a part of culture, consistent with the rest. Without taking the assumption of consistency to a ridiculous extreme, it does make sense that a game which was totally inconsistent with a culture would have a hard time. If it did not actually alter the culture, it would be rejected or itself altered.

The game came to the Dani as part of a whole program of schooling introduced by the Indonesian government, which is intended to educate—that is, to transform—the Dani children. We have some evidence that in its early years, at least, the program was not at all successful. The schoolrooms were in the hands of the teachers, who could maintain the appearance, at least, of Indonesian structure. On the other hand, this game, Flip-The-Stick, is a much more sensitive test to what really was happening. It had been turned over to the children, with no external controls or corrective forces, and they had a free hand to make it Dani.

The game is still recognizable, but in terms of several major aspects it has undergone change. In each of these aspects the game was brought closer to other Dani play forms and to Dani culture in general.

Competition

An important criterion in the definition of games quoted above is "competition."

In Dani life as a whole there is strikingly little competition. An obvious place to look for competition would be in the maneuvering for various statuses, or ranks, in a society. But Dani Society is quite egalitarian. There are leaders, of course, but they are Big Men who lead by consensus, rather than Chiefs who rule by virtue of coercive authority. And, although there are some differences in wealth, these differences are not displayed. Houses, attire, and even the sizes of pig herds are not overt signs of importance (cf. Heider, 1970, p. 88).

Also, the Dani engage in little competitive confrontation in their interpersonal relations within the group.

The Javanese game, on the other hand, is quite competitive, with two sides, with scores tallied and a winner determined. The Dani version of the game does retain the two sides. And one might say that when one player replaces the other at bat, a winner of sorts has been determined. But the idea of counting an overall score and ending up with the winner of the game has been lost. The play is relaxed and noncompetitive.

Quantification

Dani culture has little concern with quantification (Heider, 1970, p. 170). The scorekeeping, which is so essential to the form of the original game, has been dropped from the Dani version. And that scorekeeping was, of course, not merely competition, but it was quantified competition, and so it was inconsistent with Dani culture on two counts.

Interestingly enough, the Dani children retain a vestige of scorekeeping in their version of the game. Although when playing they speak their own language, at the appropriate moments they do shout out Indonesian number words (there are no Dani number words beyond three or four). However, these number words are not being used for counting and, indeed, are not always spoken in the same order.

Casualness

The Dani children show a remarkable degree of casualness in the playing of the game. Several games go on simultaneously in overlapping spaces with only the slightest signs of defense of space. Sometimes a single player will be an outfielder for two games at once. There clearly are rules as described in the formal account above, but they are not strictly observed. There is a great deal of what I would call fudging or even cheating. For example, outfielders, instead of playing the stick from where it has landed, would usually kick it forward into a more advantageous position. And only rarely, in the most blatant situations, does one child challenge another for breaking a rule.

This casualness, or flexibility, has often been mentioned in accounts of New Guinea Highland societies and the Dani are no exception. Elsewhere I have discussed how difficult it can be to use such terms to characterize an entire culture (1970, pp. 5-7). But on the whole, Dani behavior does often seem to exhibit casualness. And this play, which is so far from the strict insistence on rules and procedures, is a good example.

Discussion

Not only do the Dani lack true games, but certainly as late as 1970 their traditional culture was strong enough to resist games by altering one introduced game into a more compatible form of play. This is a strong conclusion which raises questions about the nature of a society which lacks and even rejects games. But before pursuing this, we should take a look at the definition of "game."

One might hold that the five criteria quoted above are absolute attributes, present or absent, according to which we can say that the Dani are one of the few cultures in the world which lacks games. However, it seems more realistic to treat the boundary which marks games off from the rest of play as a fuzzy one, or rather, a zone of transition, and the criteria as relative, not absolute. Then we can accurately say that when the Dani play Flip-The-Stick, they have tremendously de-emphasized competition, winning, and score keeping, thus moving the game away from that end of the play spectrum in which are found true games.

Elsewhere I have interpreted the general Grand Valley Dani resistance to change in terms of their basic conservatism (Heider, 1975). The game of Flip-The-Stick provides a partial exception to this resistance to change, in the sense that it is one of the few traits which the Dani did accept from the outside; but because of the changes which it underwent, it supports the general principle of Dani conservatism.

The functional approach to the study of games (in contrast to mere description or historical/diffusionist studies) focuses on the ways in which the games fulfill certain basic needs, whether they be practice at skills which are important in the culture ("the psychoanalytic notion that games are exercises in mastery" [Roberts, Arth, & Bush, 1959, p. 604]) or working out of cultural conflicts arising from the socialization process (Roberts & Sutton-Smith, 1962). Since the Dani do not have games to perform these functions, they presumably have other means. Certainly many of the less formal amusements of the children are means of learning and practicing skills (see Heider, 1970, pp. 193-199).

But there is a final, tantalizing suggestion: If, following Roberts and Sutton-Smith's line of thought, we suggest that games function to resolve various sorts of conflicts, and further, if games are in some respects especially good ways of resolving some kinds of conflicts and preparing children for adult life, then might it not be that one would expect to find an absence of games in those cultures with relatively low conflict? This is all very speculative. But elsewhere I have developed the case that the Dani culture is resistant to change in part at least because of its remarkably low level of stress (Heider, 1975) and that there is in general little conflict in Dani society (Heider, Note 1). So the Grand Valley Dani do present a single case of association between low conflict and absence of games. This I present as suggestion, not as conclusion.

Notes

1. This paper is based on fieldwork carried out in Indonesia in 1970 under a grant from the Foundations' Fund for Research in Psychiatry. It was first presented, in somewhat different form, at the Council on Anthropology and Education Symposium held in conjunction with the American Anthropological Association meetings in San Francisco, December 7, 1975. This paper will appear, again in somewhat different form, as a chapter in a forthcoming book on Dani Thought and Personality.

It is particularly appropriate that this paper appears in a volume which honors the memory of Allan Tindall, for the writing of it was done only after months of his gentle insistence and under his strong encouragement.

2. One of the two 20-minute videotapes which I made of this game at Wakawaka in 1970 has been printed out on 16 mm film (black and white, with synchronous sound) through the good offices of Professor Henry Breitrose of the Department of Communication, Stanford University. I have used this film in two ways: 1) to give Introductory Anthropology classes a chance, in 20 minutes, to do some "fieldwork" by studying the film and trying to work out the rules of the game in relation to the behavior which appears on the screen; and 2) to give classes in Nonverbal Behavior a common resource for a wide range of micro-analyses. Despite the relatively poor resolution of the images, fairly fine details can be studied. I hope to be able to make this film available through a distributor in the near future.

3. Interestingly, around the school at Jibika only girls played it; but at the Wakawaka school, an easy hour's walk away, where I made the video-tape records, it was played by both boys and girls.

Reference Note

1. Heider, K.G. *Dani thought and personality*. Unpublished manuscript.

References

GARDNER, R. *Dead birds*. Film Study Center, Peabody Museum, Harvard University (Producer). New York: McGraw-Hill Contemporary Films, 1963. (Film)

HEIDER, K.G. *The Dugum Dani. A Papuan culture in the highlands of West New Guinea*. Chicago: Aldine, 1970.

HEIDER, K.G. Societal intensification and cultural stress as determining factors in the innovation and conservatism of two Dani cultures. *Oceania*, 1975, **46**(1), 53-67.

HEIDER, K.G. Dani sexuality. A low energy system. *Man, N.S. II*, 1976, **2**, 188-201.

KUSCHEL, R. Games on a Polynesian outlier island: A case study of the implications of cultural change. *Journal of the Polynesian Society*, 1975, **84**(1), 25-66.

MACCOBY, M., Modiana, N., & Lander, P. Games and social character in a Mexican village. *Psychiatry*, 1964, **27**, 150-162.

ROBERTS, J.M., Arth, M.J., & Bush, R.R. Games in culture. *American Anthropologist*, 1959, **61**, 597-605.

ROBERTS, J.M., & Sutton-Smith, B. Child training and game involvement. *Ethnology*, 1962, **2**, 166-185.

SUTTON-SMITH, B. The meeting of Maori and European cultures and its effect upon organized games of Maori children. *Journal of the Polynesian Society*, 1951, **60**(2, 3), 93-107.

SUTTON-SMITH, B. A formal analysis of game meaning. *Western Folklore*, 1959, **18**, 13-24.

Chapter 24
Pueblo Baseball:
A New Use for Old Witchcraft

J.R. FOX

The ideals of harmony and cooperation and the outlawing of competition among the Pueblo Indians have become an anthropological commonplace over the last few decades.[1] Benedict's confusion of institutions with personality traits which led her to believe that the Puebloans were "harmonious" people has since been corrected. Such books as *Sun Chief* (Simmons, 1942) have shown vividly the amount of hate, aggression, and suspicion which lies behind the conscious harmony of Pueblo social life. If one could characterize the content of interpersonal relations in the Pueblos with one word, I think "cautious" would be that word. One has to be careful in dealing with others for fear of "what people will say." The power of public opinion in these crowded little communities is the strongest force for social conformity, and manifests itself in the extreme fear of witchcraft accusations. Indeed, the fear of being accused is greater than the fear of actual witchcraft. Informants are vague about the powers and practices of witches and often

From *Journal of American Folklore*, 1961, 74(291), 9-16. Copyright 1961 by the American Folklore Society. Reprinted with permission.

complain that they have forgotten what witches are supposed to do—
"only the old people remember what the *kanatya* do."² But everyone is
agreed that the most terrible thing that one can say of another is "everyone knows he (or she) is a witch." Thus, while the cultural trappings and
elaborations surrounding witch behavior have largely been forgotten, the
motivational basis for this projective system remains strong. It exists, as
it were, in the raw.

Everyone is suspect. The Sun Chief of Oraibi even suspected his own
mother on her deathbed of being a "two-heart." All interpersonal relations are fraught with danger and there are few people one can wholly
trust. In particular women do not trust each other. The Don Juanism of
the males and the relative promiscuity of the women means that no
woman can be really sure that any other is not her husband's lover, or
has not been at some time. A woman can trust her sisters, more or less,
and of course her mother, primarily because it would be difficult for
members of the same household group to carry on affairs under each
other's noses.³ Affines are very much mistrusted and often with good
cause.

What is involved is not so much sexual jealousy as, again, the fear of
"talk." This also is not just fear of gossip. Words have power and are
not to be used lightly. "Bad thoughts" have tremendous repercussions
and are believed to have effects in the real world. Bad words, as the
manifestations of bad thoughts, "poison the air of the Pueblo."⁴ The
real repercussions of accusation and insults are in fact disturbing to
Pueblo peace. In societies based on extended kin groupings one cannot
insult one person at a time. Thus any accusations may lead to a widespread split-up of the village, and this fear of internal dissension provides
strong motivation for not making open accusations, or at least for toning
them down. In the case of a philandering husband caught *in flagrante
delicto*, relatives on both sides will try to patch the matter up or at least
persuade the pair to part quietly and without fuss. In "the old days" a
woman could be rid of her husband fairly easily by ordering him out of
her house. This is becoming more impossible today as men are now more
likely than women to be houseowners. In the Eastern Pueblos the Catholic Church complicates matters by forbidding divorce and remarriage. A
wronged woman will often go to live with her sister or mother, taking her
children, but life becomes hard because she cannot remarry and she risks
priestly censure if she takes another mate.

The frustrations consequent upon these limitations to direct action
cause much bitterness between women, and witchcraft accusations are
more likely to be female affairs than male. In the old days the War Captains, ceremonial police of the Pueblos, would have dealt with the
witches once sufficient proof had been gathered of their activities. Death
or banishment would have been the punishment. Today, however, and

often in the past, nothing would be done about it. "People just got mad and didn't speak to each other or they left the village." Today also the relatively sophisticated Cochiti realize that white people think these beliefs silly, and tend to shrug off or deny them. Some members of the ultra-Catholic progressive faction share the white man's contempt for these beliefs. But beneath this air of careless disbelief and denial there lies the motivational and social basis for the interpersonal fear that has not changed.

Formal Pueblo institutions, then, as a counter to, rather than an acting out of, personality forces, stress harmony and cooperation. People must dance together, work together, play together. They are enjoined to think good harmonious thoughts so as not to spoil the air of the Pueblo. Bad thoughts are as dangerous as bad deeds and conscious effort should be made to eradicate them. Drunkenness is feared, as it lets loose all the aggressive impulses which one must constantly work to damp down. All forms of overt hostility are taboo.

In Cochiti, the intricate criss-crossing of clans, societies, Kivas (dual ceremonial organizations), extended families, church, and other groups helps to ensure that no permanent oppositions and cleavages can occur which would channel hostilities into armed camps. The factional split (conservatives and progressives) came nearest to open war, but the cross-cutting of these divisions by others (particularly extended families) saved the village from complete disintegration. As long as any two groups continue to exchange women in Cochiti, it is difficult for them to remain in hostile opposition. All formal divisions within the village have been divisions of labor and not of enmity or opposition. The cooperation of the two Kivas is essential to the proper performance of public ceremonies and they in no way compete with each other. All medicine societies complement each other's work—there are never two societies for one cure. A careful political balance is struck so that every group is evenly represented on the council. As the village is small, the result is a series of overlapping roles with a consequent impossibility of permanent conflict, despite the fact of continually recurring conflicts.

The old competitive games of the Pueblo followed this principle and were never played between any two formal groups. For races and shinny games the categories of "married" versus "unmarried" were employed, or teams were picked from the young men on a count-out method. There was never a competitive alignment in terms of the existing social groupings and teams were not permanent affairs. Since the advent of baseball in Cochiti, however, and particularly within the last decade, a new and unique situation has arisen. Cochiti now has two baseball teams playing in the same league (Inter-Pueblo Baseball League)[5] and in open competition with each other. The original team, now called the Redskins, was formed many years ago and old photographs testify to the long-standing interest in baseball in the Pueblo. Support comes from all sections of the population including the old medicine men and the ceremonial heads of the Kivas. Baseball is not thought of as alien. Most men now playing grew up in a society which was already enthusiastic about the sport. The present *cacique*, the religious leader of the tribe, was for a long time a pitcher for the second team. On his assuming office the medicine men forbade him to continue, as playing ball was not consonant with the dignity of his office—but he is the sole exception. The original team, first known as the Eagles, was the sole focus of interest for many years, but with the return of servicemen to Cochiti after the Second World War, interest grew and a second team, the Silversmiths, built its own ball park and entered the league in competition with the Redskins. They were immediately successful and won the championship 3 years in succession. Thus a new and potentially dangerous situation occurred—these two teams had to meet each other in the village and fight it out twice a year. The situation was wildly at variance with the whole Pueblo ethos.

What happened was interesting. The first game was played and while all went reasonably well on the field there were fights on the sidelines and these between the *mothers* of the players. As the momentum of the game increased these ladies began to abuse each other, to brawl, and finally to do open battle.The horrified Pueblo council immediately banned all future games between the teams in the Pueblo.

An examination of the original membership in the two teams shows that, because of the voluntary nature of their recruitment, they were a perfect breeding ground for factions. One was not constrained by kinship ties, initiation, or any other automatic factor to join either team, but could choose. The Braves, when they broke away from the Redskins, broke away by family groups, i.e., several families of players left the one and formed the other. Thus the choice was made, not by individuals, but by families. It seems from the statements of informants that there have always been, within living memory, two ill-defined groups of extended families which formed opposing "blocks" on the basis of quarrels now forgotten. Previously these two blocks had never had occasion or excuse to come out in opposition to each other, as there had been no basis for such an oppositional grouping, and the two groups even cut across the conservative-progressive factional boundaries—but in the baseball split there was a unique opportunity for the old latent hostilities to come to the surface. Allegiance to the team is patrilineal as with the Kivas, but the two teams are by no means coterminous with the Kivas. Thus the two teams represent a dual alignment of families for purely competitive purposes. Families which mistrusted or disliked each other could readily line up on opposite sides of the fence and even to uncommitted families the infection spread. The cross-cutting tendency in Pueblo institutions of course works to mitigate this as it did with the factions, but here the essential factor of the exchange of women has not had time to work itself out. What is more, the away games of the teams have increased the chances of young men to meet girls from outside the village and hence increased the number of outmarriages. The wives of these marriages, having no female relatives in Cochiti, tend to become assimilated into the husband's mother's extended family and this increases the gap between the two sides. Out of eight marriages in 1 year, three were to San Juan girls—results of the popular away game at that Pueblo. It is not the young wives, however, but rather the older women who are the "troublemakers." These women who would formerly have had little chance to attack other women they disliked without invoking the frightening subject of witchcraft, now have excuse and opportunity to do battle royal over the bodies of their sons and grandsons. The epithet *cheater* has become a virtual synonym for witch.[6]

The council ban was effective in preventing open war in the village for a time, but it only served to drive the feelings underground. Suspicion and hostility grew until this year (1959), when they broke out again into the open. By this time the antagonism had spread to the players. Previously the teams had made strenuous efforts to be fair and play the game, but the noise from the sidelines had made this difficult. This year the Braves had indulged in a series of rulebreaking episodes which flared into open quarrels. These were accentuated by the fact that after a trial game last year which rumbled but went off without incident, the council had reluctantly decided that the annual games could be played again. Significantly the games were placed at the beginning of the week during which the annual corn dance was to take place, on the feast day of the village saint (St. Bonaventure). Thus they should come at a time when "all hearts are in harmony" and everyone is bending his efforts toward the success of the great communal dance for rain, good harvest, and long life.

The Braves, according to their opponents, had not been in with the spirit of the thing. A Redskin commented, "Rules don't mean nothing to them; they don't care." It seems that the Braves had gone to town with the rule book. They had: 1) played people in the finals who had not played five consecutive games; 2) failed to turn up for games but refused to forfeit the points for them; 3) played men who had previously played for other sides and refused to relinquish them even after threats of suspension; 4) cheated in the games; 5) threatened umpires (unspecified); 6) attempted to maim opponents. A rule which was not in the official book but which, I was told, the Braves and their female supporters broke most often was to influence the course of the game by occult means— witchcraft. Particularly, it seems, they attempted to cause "accidents," to make the ball hit a runner, etc. To any enquiries as to why they hadn't been suspended or denied the replays, I was told, "they get their own way because the other teams are scared of them." San Juan had a good claim to two forfeited games but gave in because "they were scared." The manager of the Braves is a feared man in being the *Kwirena Nawa*, head of the powerful *Kwirena* society, one of the "managing societies" in Pueblo ceremonial. He is also head of the Pumpkin Kiva. Some of the Redskins spoke out against the Braves' conduct at meetings of the league, and in a confused bit of political maneuvering, the Braves were alternately suspended, reinstated, quit the league, and rejoined. By the time of the Cochiti games they were in again but had lost points for two games the league decided they must forfeit.

The Cochiti games, set on Sunday, were to have made up a double-header—the first game in the morning after Mass and the second in the afternoon prior to the Kiva practice for the corn dance. For some reason I was never able to fathom, the Braves failed to show up for the morning game. The Redskins, in an attempt to be friendly and keep things on an even keel, agreed to play the lost game on the following Saturday. Several female relatives of the Redskins muttered that the game should have been claimed; "the men are too soft." But the men were making a conscious if nervous effort to keep things going smoothly. Several men said they would not watch the game: "They'll only fight, those ladies; they'll just yell and shout and upset everybody; people don't forget easily." "They don't care about the game, they just want to fight and upset other people." Sometimes, "they don't speak to each other for a year or more." Other times, "they are just mad in the season, they forget it in the winter." The Redskins' supporters could name only one Braves family which was consistently friendly with any Redskin family. Asked why this antagonism didn't exist between Kivas, they told me, "Why should it? They don't have nothing to fight about." But no one could explain why the antagonism was there in the first place, or rather no one was willing to risk the analysis for fear of reaching conclusions too unpleasant to bear about his beloved village. All the men agreed that it was the fault of "them old ladies. I guess they just like fighting."

The afternoon game was played in a fit of nerves and deliberate efforts were made to keep things calm. To lend weight to the authority of the council, both the Governor and the Lieutenant Governor came and sat together, and the War Captain and his assistant were present, strategically placed between the supporters of the two sides. The men of the village deliberately chose a neutral spot behind the wire and huddled there while the women of the teams stood around their respective dugouts.

The game progressed in a lively fashion and the women gathered force as it went on. The comments, at first mild—"Get him glasses, he can't see," "He can't hit what he can't see; he's blind"—became bitter, personal, and obscene.[7] The men meanwhile made polite comments and factual observations and differences of opinion were glossed over. At one point the comments of the women became so noisy that the Redskins' manager, at his team's request, hurried over to the female supporters and gave them a lecture. This had no noticeable effect. However, the game passed off without any really unruly incident, although the nervousness of the players led to a phenomenal number of errors. Two factors led to a relaxation of tension: There was a neutral umpire (a colored boy from Virginia), and the game was never in doubt. The Redskins went into an early lead and finally won 18 to 8. Everyone left the ball ground quickly and irate old ladies were hustled away by sons and grandsons.

During the following week tension mounted toward the second game. Many people declared they would stay away, while others were equally sure they wouldn't miss it for anything. The latter were usually women. "There's going to be a lot of accidents," I was told by a Redskin mother, " 'cause them Braves is sure mad they lost last Sunday." The corn dance served to lessen the tension somewhat in midweek, and opposing families had to dance together in the communal prayer for harmony and happiness. But by the Saturday morning the tension was high again. The intention to stay away was carried out by many people. Those that came, perhaps lacking the feeling of safety in numbers, stayed mostly in their pick-ups and cars and watched from inside. The Lieutenant Governor, not himself a regular fan, placed himself between the two blocks of women and invited me to join him. Some Redskins had been to the local Spanish-American town of Pena Blanca and returned drunk and excited. Twice in the previous week I had been cautioned to "watch out for their (the Braves') magic."

I did not have long to wait. After the game had been tied up at one-one for four innings and the tension was increasing, the skies suddenly darkened, lightning flashed and thunder rolled, but no rain fell. A huge pre-storm wind swept across the valley and lifted clouds of sand many feet into the air. The field was obliterated and players crouched down to avoid being blinded by the stinging dirt. I took refuge in a Redskin car, where it was pointed out to me that had the other ground been used (the Redskins') this would not have happened as there was less loose dirt there. But the Braves had insisted on using their own inferior ground, "so that they could work more of their magic." How this complete stoppage of play was to the Braves' advantage, I failed to see.

The game should have been halted until the sand cleared but the Braves insisted on continuing to play. So play went on sporadically between sharp bursts of wind, swirling sandstorms, and the crashing of thunder. And still no rain fell. Sun Chief describes how if, instead of rain, at the end of a Katsina dance only a strong wind blew spreading sand, then this showed that those who sent for the Katsinas had bad hearts and had done evil. This feeling was present at the Cochiti game. Thunder, lightning, and storm clouds which bring only the dead dust and no life-giving rain are the worst of portents. One Redskin going out to bat fell on his knees, crossed himself, and muttered a prayer.

Things were complicated by the presence of a non-neutral umpire. He was in fact of the Redskin faction, but was courting the daughter of a prominent Braves family (Q*). The only reason he was made umpire was that he was on leave from the Navy and hence would be returning, taking any bad feelings with him. He gave a faulty-seeming decision which cost the Redskins a base. Immediately insults were flung at him by the Redskin women. Out loud they called, "Some of the Q* dirt has rubbed off on you!" and "She's got you under her skin, that Q* girl." Amongst themselves they used other epithets than girl, and muttered about "influences." Complications were added by the fact that the umpire was the son of the Lieutenant Governor, and no one wished to offend the much liked and respected official. This served in some ways to prevent more trouble.

In between the sandstorms the game continued and the score leveled to two-two at the bottom of the eighth inning. In the final innings the Redskins seemed to go to pieces as the sand lashed their faces, while the Braves hit two runs to win the game four to two. The players ran to shake hands, although some refused—an unheard-of thing in previous games. The male participants by and large tried to keep things calm. The Braves women were screaming with delight at the success of their side, while the Redskin women went away tight-lipped and furious, convinced of dirty work. That dirty work was involved was obvious to these women. The storm, the influenced umpire, the unaccountable reversal of the Redskins (an admittedly superior team under "normal" conditions), all added up—to witchcraft.

In the weeks following the games, tensions remained high, with rival families not speaking. About 3 weeks after, however, an incident occurred which brought the whole thing out again. The Redskins had just lost a game and were returning home disconsolate, when a Braves mother accosted one of them as he entered his house. The burden of her remarks seemed to be that he had lost the game because his love life was sapping his strength. All this was said in the presence of the Redskin's wife, who was furious but mute. The Redskin hurled a few replies and went indoors. The Braves mother had not finished however; she stood on her own roof top and hurled insults across at her neighbor. The Redskin took his whole family to the Governor's house and asked for the council's protection against these onslaughts. That evening a council meeting was called, and in typical Pueblo fashion the combatants were told to shake hands and apologize to each other. An announcement was made to the Pueblo to the effect that this baseball antagonism must cease or the sport would be stopped. This was a desperate measure and a test of the council's authority that may only serve to weaken it, as the council has precious few sanctions left at its disposal. The young people are not at all likely to give up baseball whatever the council may say, and the antagonism is likely to continue. However, as harvest and winter approach and the baseball season draws to a close, hard feelings tend to soften and some wounds to heal. This factor obviously helps to preserve harmony, as there is time during winter to forget the summer's quarrels.

Competitive Western games that have been introduced into primitive societies have usually been substituted for some more violent forms of competition. For example, football in New Guinea replaced intervillage spear fighting. Baseball in the Pueblos is a competitive intrusion into essentially noncompetitive social systems. While competition is between villages, no untoward events occur, as this is in line with tradition, but within villages, it is, as we have seen, potentially destructive. Pueblo institutions act as a counter to aggressive tendencies in the Puebloans and are so constructed as to eliminate and nullify aggressive conflict between people by placing them in automatically determined overlapping role situations. The baseball teams, based on voluntary recruitment and stressing competition, allow for the acting out of aggressive and competitive tendencies. Various steps are taken by the Pueblo to neutralize this effect but the participants seem bewildered in the face of the turn of events. Resort to naked authority in the settlement of interfamilial disputes is a new thing to Cochiti and in a way a confession of weakness in the social system, previously so ingeniously adequate to deal with conflict. It looks for the moment in Cochiti as if the male forces of authority and order may be able to keep the peace for the time being. But the women especially have married the old witch fears to the new sport and thus directed a whole body of deep-rooted motivations into new and pertinent channels. When the tension is high and feelings rise, the old cries of "witch" fly from the women and the suppressed rages are given full vent. It may even prove therapeutic.

Notes

1. The research on which this paper is based was made possible by the Social Science Research Council and the Laboratory of Social Relations, Harvard University. It was carried out largely in the Pueblo of Cochiti, New Mexico (approximate population in 1959: 500, of which 300 were actually resident in the Pueblo).
2. Full descriptions of witch beliefs in Cochiti are to be found in Dumarest (1919) and E.S. Goldfrank (1927).
3. The number of actual matrilocal households is declining in Cochiti, but as Fred Eggan says of the Hopi, "the *conceptual* unity of the household group still remains (1950, p. 30).
4. "Breathing" and "blowing" are two common ritual gestures and there is a

whole system of beliefs concerning the taking in and giving out of power by breathing. Thus the importance of "the air" of the village.
5. The teams are: Cochiti (2), Santa Ana, San Felipe, Santa Clara (2), San Juan, San Ildefonso, Tesuque, Santa Fe Jays (based at the Santa Fe Indian School).
6. There was a chance that the "Little League" team, formed in 1958, would pull the two teams together by drawing on children of both parties. This failed to happen and such was the bickering and dispute over the children's team that this year it was discontinued. No one wanted the responsibility for it, as there was too much fighting between the mothers.
7. "Baseball talk" is all in English. See Fox, 1959.

References

DUMAREST, N. Notes on Cochiti, New Mexico. *Memoirs of the American Anthropological Association*, 1919, **6**(3).

EGGAN, F. *The social organization of the Western Pueblos*. Chicago: University of Chicago Press, 1950.

FOX, J.R. Note on Cochiti linguistics. In C.H. Lange (Ed.), *Cochiti: A New Mexico Pueblo, past and present*. Austin: University of Texas Press, 1959.

GOLDFRANK, E.S. The social and ceremonial organization of Cochiti. *Memoirs of the American Anthropological Association*, 1927, No. 33.

SIMMONS, L.W. (Ed.). *Sun Chief: The autobiography of a Hopi Indian*. New Haven: Yale University Press, 1942.

Epilogue

I n concluding this book, it may be useful to summarize some of the
ideas that we have considered to be particularly important and to
provide a few final observations regarding how the study of play, games,
and sports from a sociocultural perspective may be of value to physical
educators and to others interested in expanding their understanding of
these seemingly pervasive cultural phenomena. A few years ago, the
noted anthropologist Victor Turner introduced a new volume in the
series "Symbol, Myth and Ritual" with the following remarks:

> Too often, disciplines are sealed off, in sterile pedantry, from significant
> intellectual influences. . . .
>
> The present series *[Symbol, Myth and Ritual]* is intended to fill this lacuna.
> It is designed to include not only field monographs and theoretical and
> comparative studies by anthropologists, but also field work by scholars in
> other disciplines, both scientific and humanistic. (Grimes, 1976, pp. 7-8)

This present volume has shared a similar premise. As we stated in the preface, we believe that physical education, a field which has been aptly identified as cross-disciplinary in nature (Henry, 1964, 1979), has benefited and will continue to benefit from a thoughtful utilization of the intellectual insights and achievements of other disciplines. In particular, we believe that in attempting to better understand what play, games, and sports mean to the people who engage in such activities, the field of physical education has neglected the contributions which the anthropological viewpoint might offer. In the introduction we commented upon this fact, offered some historical evidence regarding the dearth of attention which researchers in our field have paid to such questions until quite recently, and argued that the time has come for more scholars—whether their parent discipline is physical education, anthropology, sociology, social psychology, or history—to consider the possible insights which an understanding of play, games, and sports as salient sociocultural phenomena might contribute to informing their own research questions.

We have endeavored to show that although a considerable number of ethnographic research reports and theoretical papers concerned with understanding games and sports as sociocultural phenomena exists, the majority of these are still widely scattered throughout numerous research monographs and journals or are included in books dealing with a broad range of topics. This poses a particular problem for the individual unfamiliar with the literature of the field. Hence, one of the purposes of this volume has been to provide an organized selection from among the available works. The reader who wishes to engage in further study will find many other useful titles referred to in the introductory chapter and in the references that accompany the papers. Additionally, although many works can be found which deal in a more general sense with ethnographic cultural research, symbols, interpretation and meaning, rituals, socialization/enculturation, acculturation, and cultural pluralism, to date relatively few of these have sought to relate such studies directly to play, games, and sports. The introductory chapter was intended to help readers make such applications.

We believe that the sociocultural study of play, games, and sports is, in itself, an extremely interesting, intellectually challenging, and worthwhile undertaking, and it is our hope that more individuals will wish to turn their attention to this subject. We would be encouraged if this book has served as a catalyst for stimulating such interest. We also believe that theoretical insights which might be gleaned from studies such as those appearing in this book may be of value to scholars in numerous areas of research. While another field (e.g., social psychology, sociology) might just as well have been chosen, we have decided to draw upon history for our example, for, as Beattie (1964/1972) has noted, both historians and social anthropologists:

are concerned with the description and understanding of real human societies, and they use whatever methods are available and appropriate to this purpose. . . . Both anthropologists and historians attempt to represent unfamiliar social situations in terms not just of their own cultural categories, but, as far as possible, in terms of the categories of the actors themselves. (p. 25)

Anthropologists have long recognized how useful historical understanding of the culture they are studying can be. Blanchard (1981), for example, opens his account of the seriousness with which contemporary Mississippi Choctaws "define many of their leisure-time activities . . . ," and utilize team sports to maintain traditions and preserve cultural heritage and identity (p. xiii), with a chapter which traces three centuries of Choctaw games and sports. Azoy (1982) perceptively analyzes and contrasts *buzkashi* as a folk game *(tudabarai)* dominated by 1,000 years of Afghan tradition of power and authority, with *buzkashi* as a contemporary form of sport *(qarajai)* which has been created relatively recently by elected government officials in an effort to lend legitimacy to the modern political hierarchy.

Conversely, some historians have begun to turn to anthropology for possible insights which might help them to frame the questions which they ask of the past. Lawrence Stone (1977), for example, points out that the work in symbolic anthropology by scholars like Mary Douglas, Victor Turner, and Clifford Geertz "has begun to have a major impact upon the historical profession, particularly in the development of studies of popular religion . . . symbolic rituals (for example, coronation and funerary ceremonies, public festivities and group displays) or folklore and forms of meanings of popular culture. . ." (pp. 13-14). In introducing *New Directions in American Intellectual History* (1979), John Higham recently pointed to "the increasing affinity intellectual historians have recently felt for the social science [anthropology] that shares most fully their own engagement with community and with culture . . . [and] has in recent years notably enriched our grasp of the meanings expressed in symbol, ritual and language" (p. xvii). Gordon S. Wood, in the same volume, has maintained that,

of all the social sciences anthropology seems to have the greatest kinship with history because it treats the people it studies on their own terms and begins with the assumption that such people do things differently. . . . Borrowing from ethnography, historians have begun examining rituals, iconography, and popular "languages" and signs of past cultures and now are reconstructing mental worlds we scarcely knew existed. (pp. 29-30)

Indeed, some historians who are concerned with better understanding the lives of ordinary people have found insights that anthropologists find particularly useful to be of considerable use in their own studies of "popular" or "mass" culture; others have found such insights useful in re-examining ways in which earlier societies have viewed themselves. (See, for example, Bailey, 1978; Boyer, 1978; Malcolmson, 1973; Park, Note 1). John MacAloon's recently published *This Great Symbol: Pierre de Coubertin and the Origins of the Modern Olympic Games* (1981) is a work which aptly demonstrates how historical studies of sports may be enriched by a judicious use of sociocultural understandings. The author notes in his preface that although his study is a history of the origins of the modern Olympics and a biography of Coubertin, their founder, his "interest in the Games has remained holistic, essentially ethnographic and anthropological . . . [and his] central concern is the creation of the Olympic spectacle. . ." (pp. xi-xiii). An example of this is MacAloon's discussion of the elite Paris International Athletic Congress of 1894, which was arranged by Coubertin to win wide international approval for the idea of reviving the Olympic Games. MacAloon suggests that Coubertin's "understanding of the power of dominant symbols" (p. 170) was an important factor in the success of this Congress. Not only did Coubertin intend that the modern Olympic Games be heavily laden with symbolism, he also stressed the importance and uniqueness of the Games which he sought to revive by specifically planning the 1894 Congress meetings on a lavish scale, complete with poetry, ancient Greek music, sumptious banquets, athletic exhibitions, fireworks, and greetings from well-known politicians.

Important concepts in a society frequently seem to be expressed through the use of symbols that are viewed as special or extraordinary by the people involved. Sports, games, and play seem to be sociocultural phenomena that members of a society often consider to be "set apart" from ordinary life and thus special. In the introduction, we pointed out that these three phenomena seem to differ in some important ways, and these differences may mean that each of the three has somewhat different expressive capabilities. However, to the extent that each phenomenon is considered to be special or extraordinary, each may provide valuable opportunities for people to express important ideas which may help them to understand their own culture.

If, as has been claimed in the introduction to this present volume, the study of sociocultural phenomena is in large measure a search for shared meanings or understandings which people attach to events, then the study of play, games, and sports from a sociocultural standpoint might involve at least two lines of inquiry: (a) investigations of the ways in which members of particular societies—past and present—conceive of these activities; and (b) investigations of the extent to which play, games, and sports provide people with opportunities to develop and express shared understandings of their overall society, the ways in which this occurs, and the major values and social relationships which are highlighted and/or commented upon through participation in these activities. These two paths of investigation are not, of course, unrelated. If this volume has done anything to advance studies in these directions, we are gratified.

Reference Note

1. Park, R.J. *Boys into men—State into nation: Rites of Passage in College Football, 1890-1905.* Paper presented at the Annual Meeting of The Association for the Anthropological Study of Play, London, Ontario, April 1982.

References

AZOY, G.W. *Buzkashi: Game and power in Afghanistan.* Philadelphia: University of Pennsylvania Press, 1982.

BAILEY, P. *Leisure and class in Victorian England: Rational recreation and the contest for control, 1830-1885.* London: Routledge & Kegan Paul, 1978.

BEATTIE, J. *Other cultures: Aims, methods and achievements in social anthropology.* London: Routledge & Kegan Paul, 1972. (Originally published, 1964.)

BLANCHARD, K. *The Mississippi Choctaws at play: The serious side of leisure.* Urbana: University of Illinois Press, 1981.

BOYER, P. *Urban masses and moral order in America: 1820-1920.* Cambridge, MA: Harvard University Press, 1978.

GRIMES, R.L. *Symbol and conquest: Public ritual and drama in Santa Fe, New Mexico.* Ithaca: Cornell University Press, 1976.

HENRY, F.M. Physical education: An academic discipline. *Proceedings of the 67th annual conference of NCPEAM,* January 8-11, 1964, 6-9.

HENRY, F.M. The academic discipline of physical education, *Quest,* 1979, **29,** 13-29.

HIGHAM, J. Introduction. In J. Higham & P.K. Conkin (Eds.), *New directions in American intellectual history.* Baltimore: The Johns Hopkins University Press, 1979.

MALCOLMSON, R.W. *Popular recreations in English society, 1700-1850.* Cambridge: Cambridge University Press, 1973.

MACALOON, J.J. *This great symbol: Pierre de Coubertin and the origins of the modern Olympic Games.* Chicago: University of Chicago Press, 1981.

STONE, L. History and the social sciences in the twentieth century. In C.F. Delzell (Ed.), *The future of history.* Nashville, TN: Vanderbilt University Press, 1977.

WOOD, G.S. Intellectual history and the social sciences. In J. Higham & P.K. Conkin (Eds.), *New directions in American intellectual history*. Baltimore: The Johns Hopkins University Press, 1979.

Index

519